D0875583

Psychological Principles of Marketing and Consumer Behavior

Psychological Principles of Marketing and Consumer Behavior

Steuart Henderson Britt

Lexington Books
D.C. Heath and Company
Lexington, Massachusetts
Toronto

Library of Congress Cataloging in Publication Data

Britt, Steuart Henderson, 1907-
   Psychological principles of marketing and consumer behavior.

   Bibliography: p.
   Includes index.
   1. Marketing—Psychological aspects. 2. Advertising—Psychological aspects. 3. Motivation research (Marketing) 4. Consumers—Psychology.
I. Title.
HF5415.125.B74   1978   658.8'001'9   77-75658
ISBN 0-669-01513-X

Second printing, June 1979.

Published simultaneously in Canada.

Printed in the United States of America.

International Standard Book Number: 0-669-01513-X

Library of Congress Catalog Card Number: 77-75658

Contents

List of Figures   xi

List of Tables   xiii

Introduction   xv

Acknowledgments   xvii

Part I	*A Psychological Approach to Marketing Communication*	1
Chapter 1	**Psychological Principles in Marketing**	3
	Objectives	3
	A New Approach	3
Chapter 2	**Psychological Principles Applied**	9
	Some Problems	9
	Two Major Difficulties	10
	Probability	10
	A Question Answered	12
Part II	*Models and the Psychology of Communication*	13
Chapter 3	**Model Definition and Classification**	15
	Definition	15
	Classifications	15
Chapter 4	**Some Early Models of Communication**	21
	S-O-R Models	21
	Feedback-Control Models	23
	Sociocultural Models	25
Chapter 5	**Models of Marketing**	27
	Models of Advertising and Promoting	27
	Attitude Change	29
	Decision Processes	30
	Four Related Models	33

Chapter 6	**A New Psychological Model of Marketing**	37
	Model Comparisons and Considerations	37
	Basic Propositions	38
	Interpreting the Psychological Model of Communicating	41
	Uniqueness of the Psychological Model	43
Part III	*Exposing*	45
Chapter 7	**Message and Medium Variables**	47
	Background	47
	Variables	47
Chapter 8	**Variables within the Audience**	51
	Background	51
	Variables	51
Chapter 9	**An Overview of Exposing**	57
	Implications	57
	Model of Exposing	57
Part IV	*Attending*	61
Chapter 10	**Message and Medium Variables**	63
	Background	63
	Variables	63
Chapter 11	**Variables within the Audience**	85
	Background	85
	External Variables	85
	Internal Variables	88
Chapter 12	**An Overview of Attending**	99
	Implications	99
	Model of Attending	99
Part V	*Perceiving*	103
Chapter 13	**Message and Medium Variables**	105
	Background	105
	Variables	108

Chapter 14	**Variables within the Audience: Cue Categorizing**	125
	Background	125
	Cue Categorizing	125
Chapter 15	**Variables within the Audience: Symbolic Communicating**	147
	Background	147
	Symbolic Communicating	147
Chapter 16	**Variables within the Audience: Associating**	159
	Background	159
	Associating	159
Chapter 17	**Variables within the Audience: Personality Correlates**	179
	Personality Correlates	179
Chapter 18	**An Overview of Perceiving**	193
	Implications	193
	Model of Perceiving	193
Part VI	*Learning*	199
Chapter 19	**Message and Medium Variables: Cognitive Variables**	201
	Background	201
	Cognitive Variables	204
Chapter 20	**Message and Medium Variables: Affective Variables**	239
	Background	239
	Affective Variables	239
Chapter 21	**Variables within the Audience: Psychological State**	257
	Background	257
	Psychological State	257

Chapter 22	**Variables within the Audience: Self-Generated Processes**	281
	Background	281
	Self-Generated Processes	281
Chapter 23	**Variables within the Audience: Sociocultural Factors**	293
	Background	293
	Sociocultural Factors	293
Chapter 24	**An Overview of Learning**	303
	Implications	303
	Model of Learning	303
Part VII	*Motivating*	309
Chapter 25	**Beliefs, Attitudes, and Opinions**	311
	Motivating and Persuading	311
	Beliefs-Attitudes-Opinions	316
Chapter 26	**Message and Medium Variables: Rational and Nonrational Messages**	325
	Background	325
	Rational Messages	325
	Nonrational Messages	345
Chapter 27	**Message and Medium Variables: Credibility**	359
	Credibility	359
Chapter 28	**Variables within the Audience: Individual Variables**	381
	Background	381
	Individual Variables	381
Chapter 29	**Variables within the Audience: Group Variables**	399
	Group Variables	399

Chapter 30	**An Overview of Motivating**	417
	Implications	417
	Model of Motivating	417
Part VIII	*Persuading*	423
Chapter 31	**Message and Medium Variables**	425
	Background	425
	Message and Medium Variables	426
	Summary	430
Chapter 32	**Variables within the Audience: Dissonance Factors**	431
	Dissonance Factors	431
Chapter 33	**Variables within the Audience: Individual Variables and Group Variables**	455
	Individual Variables	455
	Group Variables	471
Chapter 34	**An Overview of Persuading**	479
	Implications	479
	Model of Persuading	479
	A Final Word	485
	References Cited	487
	Additional References	515
	Index	525
	About the Author	533

List of Figures

3-1	Feedback	19
4-1	Weaver and Shannon Model	22
4-2	Miller Model	22
4-3	Schramm Primary Model	23
4-4	Wiener Model	24
4-5	Solley and Murphy Model	25
4-6	DeFleur Concept	26
5-1	Lavidge and Steiner Model	28
5-2	Marketing Communications Spectrum, Colley Model	29
5-3	Complete Model of Consumer Behavior Showing Purchasing Process and Outcomes	31
5-4	A Simplified Description of the Theory of Buyer Behavior	32
5-5	A Wärneryd and Nowak Model (with Feedback)	34
5-6	Interaction Model of Advertising Communication	35
6-1	The Psychological Model of Communicating	40
9-1	The Exposing Stage of the Psychological Model of Communicating	58
10-1	Examples of Different Typefaces that Emphasize the Quality or Meaning of the Words Used	75
12-1	The Attending Stage of the Psychological Model of Communicating	100
13-1	The Factor of Similarity	113
13-2	The Factor of Uniform Destiny or Common Fate	114
13-3	The Factor of Objective Set	114
13-4	The Factor of Direction	115

13-5	The Factor of Closure	116
13-6	The Factor of the Good Curve or Contour	116
14-1	Rubin Vase/Twins	140
17-1	Douglas, Field, and Tarpey's Four Interlocking Selves	183
18-1	The Perceiving Stage of the Psychological Model of Communicating	194
24-1	The Learning Stage of the Psychological Model of Communicating	304
25-1	Beliefs Forming an Attitude	320
25-2	Beliefs as Members of More than One Attitude System	320
25-3	Attitudes as a Basis of an Opinion	321
25-4	Opinions Based on Beliefs	321
25-5	Beliefs and an Attitude	322
25-6	Changes in Belief	322
25-7	Eventual Changes in Belief	322
30-1	The Motivating Stage of the Psychological Model of Communicating	418
34-1	The Persuading Stage of the Psychological Model of Communicating	480

List of Tables

10-1	Readership and Size of Advertisements	66
10-2	Ten Typefaces Ranked According to Reader Opinions of Relative Legibility	70
17-1	Spranger's Personality Characterization Classifications	180
19-1	Recall Scores as a Function of Degree of Learning	204
19-2	Recall and Position of Commercials	212
19-3	Effects of Various Stimulus-Response Relationships Between First and Second Task on the Amount and Kind of Transfer	224
25-1	Mode of Evaluation Framework	315
25-2	Comparisons of Belief and Opinion as to Consistency	324

Introduction

Ideas won't keep. Something must be done about them.

Alfred North Whitehead

What is this book about?

It demonstrates both in theory and in practice how almost 200 psychological principles of communicating—developed principally from the results of experimental investigations—can be utilized for the benefit of consumers as well as business firms. The 188 psychological principles discussed are theoretically sound, are of practical value, and most of them can be tested experimentally.

My emphasis is on ways in which teachers, students, and practitioners of advertising/marketing can apply psychological findings to consumer behavior, as the consumer is *exposed* to, *attends* to, *perceives, learns* about, is *motivated* by, and is *persuaded* by products, packages, retailing, advertising, selling, public relations, and other promotional phases of marketing.

In addition, this book provides some significant insights for psychologists and other behavioral scientists about the utilization of empirical data from their disciplines in the business world of marketing and advertising. Accordingly, this book will be useful to:

Schools of business (Management)—especially in courses in marketing and organizational behavior

Schools of journalism—especially in courses in advertising

Schools of communication and speech—especially in courses on communication

Departments of psychology—especially in courses in experimental sociology and methodology

Departments of anthropology—especially in courses on culture

Marketing practitioners

Advertising practitioners

In the correct meaning of the adjective *unique*, this book is unique; that is, it is the only book of its kind. It also is a pioneering book, based on my special combination of training and practical experience in both psychology and marketing/advertising.

Some years ago a Swiss business executive, Peter C. Induni, said something to me that stimulated me to write this book. Following my audiovisual presentation in Zürich of examples of outstanding American and European advertising, given for some executives of the Lintas advertising agency and some of their clients, Herr Induni diplomatically suggested to me that it would have been even more useful if I (as he said, with a combination background of psychologist, marketing professor, marketing author and editor, and marketing consultant) had developed and presented a new philosophy of advertising/ marketing.

On the plane back to the United States Peter Induni's words took root. But little did I know that it would require several years for that root to sprout and spread into final form, namely, the present book.

If I could have anticipated the complexity of the task of trying to locate, sort out, read, and analyze the tremendous number of books and articles in the psychological literature that might relate to marketing communicating in the period primarily from 1930 through 1970, I doubt that I ever would have started this lengthy project. What I naively thought could be accomplished on a parttime basis within a couple of years has taken an enormous amount of time over several years.

Why, I have asked myself, did I get into this "business" of trying to write a book along lines that no one else has tried? Why, oh, why? For those of us who are writers, why didn't we learn to do something more simple, such as raising peaches or selling Fuller brushes?

The answer is that at some point in our lives we all got bitten by what I call the Communications Bug. Once in the bloodstream, the bite of this Bug, while not deadly, is in most instances incurable. It creates a metabolism which thirsts for insight and knowledge ... It turns you in upon yourself. ... It makes you impatient with the banal and ordinary, and skeptical about the verity of internal verities. [Anonymous.]

This quotation is not presented to be amusing or facetious. It is my way of indicating that it has been no easy matter to write this book, a serious and important undertaking.

Anyhow, my sincere hope is that this book will be both stimulating and useful to a great many thoughtful people: teachers of marketing and advertising and their students; marketing/advertising practitioners; behavioral scientists, especially psychologists and sociologists; and various specialists in the field of communication.

Acknowledgments

I am grateful for grants-in-aid from the California-Time Petroleum Company, the Foods Division of The Coca-Cola Company, and the Marsteller Foundation.

Sincere thanks go to several Northwestern University students who over the years patiently and painstakingly helped me in reading, absorbing, and analyzing scores of articles and books, and who also wrote materials, checked references, developed marketing examples, verified quotations, and gave me useful criticisms and suggestions.

Eleven former students deserve special recognition:

Marian S. Adams developed materials on some of the basic concepts.

Sabra E. Brock served for an entire year as my special assistant on this project, particularly in the planning stages.

Jean-Michel Cousin constructed the plan and coordinated materials for certain chapters.

Robert E. Donath in the early stages of the book created and developed numerous useful ideas.

Janice Ginsberg (nee Gordon) devoted several weeks to library search and the development of background materials.

Patricia Eastham (nee Haeberle) located new materials and developed several psychological propositions.

Michael F. Heffring aided in the rewriting of the final chapters of the book.

Mark J. Merriman developed most of the marketing examples.

Thomas A. Moore made important contributions, especially to the materials on perceiving and learning.

Joyce Gravlee (nee Roose) while a student almost "lived" the development of this book over a three-year period.

Melanie Morgan (nee Satkowski) assisted in editing and rewriting several chapters.

The following students also contributed significantly to my thinking: Todd S. Abrams, Richard Anderson, Mary Jean Bach, Mark E. Bean, Nancy Dall, Luis V. Dominguez, Mark D. Goldstein, Janice Graham, Jerome M. Juska, Barbara L. Kaplan, Gerald E. Kayser, Nikki Lewy, Roberta E. Kirstein, James L. Lubawski, Mary Ann McGrath, Alan M. Oshima, Nancy Pollens, Stephen F. Phelps, Margaret Roberts, James S. Rubin, Nancy Schierer, Corinne Russell (nee

Schmid), Bruce D. Smith, Madeleine Tolmach, Stuart L. Tomey, Daniel Truman, Nancy L. Tuttle, and Lynn Upshaw.

Finally, my drafting and redrafting, writing and rewriting, until a final manuscript of the book emerged could not have been accomplished without the secretarial assistance of Marion Davis, Darlene E. Nilges, Irene E. Peach, and Gere Masters (nee Wageman).

Part I:
A Psychological Approach
to Marketing Communication

1 Psychological Principles in Marketing

Objectives

Two crucial questions are to be asked and answered in this book:

1. What happens psychologically to a person confronted with a marketing communication—such as an advertisement or a sales message?
2. How can empirical data from psychological experiments and observations be applied in various areas of marketing communication?

My overall objectives are to increase our knowledge of marketing processes and how they work and thus to provide marketers with psychological insights of practical use. Accordingly, an entirely new theoretical framework of marketing communication has been developed. The psychological principles about marketing communication derived therefrom are based on empirical findings; and these principles are presented in each of the main chapters, first, independently of any application to marketing, then, in relation to applicabilities to marketing, and finally, with actual marketing examples.

The result is the creation of 188 psychological principles that are directly applicable to marketing communication. Every one of these propositions is believed to be theoretically sound, primarily based on data from various empirical studies with people, and directly applicable to marketing communication.

In summary, this book represents the development of an intricate but practical inventory of scientific principles from the literature of the behavioral sciences that has been coupled with descriptive models of the behavior of people with respect to various kinds of marketing communications.

A New Approach

The communication aspects of marketing—especially advertising—need an entirely new approach. The usual approach in advertising seems to consist of showing a good many advertisements and rating each according to such nebulous criteria as "interesting graphics," "provocative copy," or "hard to beat."

The need instead is for the development of more objective criteria to complement, qualify, or refute these primarily subjective statements—that is, a

3

need for psychological principles about communication that will provide new insights into advertising creativity and allow measurement advertising effectiveness.

As so astutely pointed out by Charles F. Adams, President of D'Arcy-MacManus & Masius, Inc., advertising agency: "Most people who create advertising and most people who approve it live in a dream world." And he goes on to say,

They labor endlessly on the finer points of each advertisement and each commercial. They fill it with so many facts that it fairly bulges with information. They argue about color tones and semantic nuances. They fret over phraseology. They have conferences on commas. Their search for perfection is commendable—but they are all too often spending their effort and their time on the wrong thing.

They believe that the audience they have purchased to view their advertising is going to give it the same loving attention that they have lavished on it. And they want it to be absolutely perfect for the careful reading or the detailed viewing that it is going to receive from the tremendous numbers to whom it will be presented. [Adams, 1965, p. 3.]

Anything that can be done to develop better understanding of what happens psychologically to an individual at the moment of confrontation with an advertisement, a sales message, or any other marketing communication is significant for future development of more creative and more effective marketing than at present.

To recapitulate, so much of the material on communication fails because of:

Too many subjective criteria that have little or no empirical support.

A lack of sound theoretical frameworks applicable to marketing communication.

Too much time spent on trivia instead of on basic concepts.

In attempting to cope with these faults, my investigation revealed that the most promising areas of study were the specialized literature of psychology and communications research. Accordingly, numerous concepts from these areas of behavioral science are used in all chapters of this book.

Some useful insights into new ways of analyzing marketing and marketing processes are developed. In the field of advertising, for example, let us assume that a certain vehicle of advertising has been distributed; that an individual has been exposed to this vehicle; and that the same individual has been exposed to an advertisement of this vehicle. So far, not enough is known to allow us to describe very accurately any of the following:

1. What happens psychologically to the individual *exposed* to the advertisement of the vehicle?

2. How does he respond psychologically in *attending* to the advertisement?
3. What does the individual *perceive* of the advertisement?
4. What does the individual *learn and remember* of what was intended to be communicated?
5. Was the individual *motivated* by the advertisement?
6. Was the individual *persuaded*?

For these reasons it is very important for us to analyze the psychological processes of

exposing
attending
perceiving
learning (and remembering)
motivating
persuading.

The results of this type of analysis in this book are:

1. An increase in our knowledge of marketing processes and how they work.
2. An understanding of a scientific approach to marketing.
3. Development of a significant "crossover" between psychology and marketing.
4. Understanding of a new theoretical framework of psychological principles of marketing communication, supported by empirical data.
5. Insights as to what specific applications to marketing can be made from psychological principles of communication.
6. Stimulation of increased creativity and effectiveness in marketing.

Several years have been spent in a search of the literature of the behavioral sciences, primarily psychology, for articles and books mainly in the 1930-1970 period dealing with such topics as relevance, repetition, congruity, reminiscence, affective stimuli, and perseveration.

Psychological journals and books on psychology published during the 1970s also were checked for recent experimental data materially affecting the basic psychological principles, but no information has been found that would negate or modify the basic principles as stated. Accordingly, and purposely, the literature cited is for the most part from the period prior to 1970.

From the literature on psychology and communication I developed a series of specific principles or propositions about the variables that affect marketing communications. The major emphasis is on the *communicatee* as the recipient of communications from a *communicator*. My procedure involved five steps:

1. Search, search, search the behavioral science literature.
2. Invent and formulate psychological principles about communication that are based on empirical data.

3. Make each principle as operational as possible.
4. Apply the principles to marketing communication.
5. Relate the principles to each other in a logical framework.

Note that my views as a psychologist are functional. More specifically, my analyses of what happens to an individual mentally when confronted with a marketing communication are functional, and not structural. This means that throughout this book I shall be discussing psychological processes, not things.

This point of view was stated succinctly many decades ago by psychologist James Rowland Angell when he wrote that functional psychology involves "the effort to discern and portray the typical *operations* of consciousness under actual life conditions, as over against the attempt to analyze and describe its elementary and complex *contents*" (Angell, 1907, p. 49). He also made the point that mental activities are "evanescent and fleeting, . . . [which] marks them off in an important way from the relatively permanent elements of anatomy" (Angell, 1907, p. 51).

In this same way, I shall be analyzing mental goings-on, not entities. If we were to begin to think of mental structures or entities instead of mental processes, we would be committing the error of *reification*—acting as if some process or quality actually has concrete reality or existence. That is why I use such words as *perceiving* or *persuading* instead of *perception* and *persuasion*; and in certain instances in which noun forms have been employed, such as *symbolic communication,* what really is meant is *symbolic communicating.*

The purpose of each one of the 188 psychological principles to be discussed in this book is to give an interpretation of one part of the psychological process by which an individual is exposed to a marketing communication, attends to the communication, perceives it, learns (and remembers) it, is motivated by it, or is persuaded by it.

Of course, an individual does not necessarily go through all six processes when confronted with a communication—all, some, or none may occur, depending upon message, medium, and audience variables. Also, although psychological principles are individually identified and explained, it should be remembered that there are definite interactions among the various processes.

For practically every principle to be discussed in this book (1) the principle is stated; (2) supporting empirical data are marshalled, largely from experimental investigations by psychologists; and (3) marketing examples are provided that illustrate the principle.

However, instead of attempting to summarize most of the literature in support of a psychological principle or proposition, I select only a few (sometimes only one or two) studies for discussion—studies that seem to typify the results of other empirical investigations that relate to the particular principle.

As for the marketing examples, even though some of these might seem to "fit" in more than one place—or to put it another way, even though some of the psychological principles might seem to "fit" more than one kind of marketing example—these examples in the field of marketing demonstrate the significance of the psychological principles in the "real" world.

2 Psychological Principles Applied

Some Problems

The need to draw from the behavioral sciences in this study has been demonstrated. However, even though psychology has provided many sound tools for marketing research—and even though it has become somewhat fashionable for people in marketing to talk about models, especially models of advertising—marketers need considerably greater amounts of useful psychological knowledge than they possess at present. Most of what marketers have learned from psychology is highly abstract and likely to elicit such comments as "the ideas are interesting but do not really help me to market my product (or service)."

Many notable advances in psychology have been made through empirical studies of both mass and interpersonal communication. Much of this work has considerable significance for advertising, sales promotion, and other facets of communication in a firm's marketing mix. Unfortunately, though, too little of this psychological knowledge has filtered through to marketing executives. The literature of psychology and related fields is simply too vast to be examined systematically by marketing executives. There are literally dozens of behavioral science periodicals, thousands of books and monographs, and scores of unpublished works that relate to the psychology of communication. Further, severe limitations exist for the marketing practitioner not only in finding but in utilizing special materials from psychology and other behavioral sciences. Studying behavioral science literature on his own, the marketing practitioner is frequently frustrated by conflicting hypotheses and simply gives up in despair. Confusing terminology also can obscure significant factors. One psychologist may speak in terms of consistency maintenance, while another talks about dissonance reduction. One psychologist will emphasize need-serving recall, while another refers to selective retention. This will not seem very helpful to the marketing practitioner.

In addition, the great majority of psychological literature—dealing with such areas as physiological psychology, neuroanatomy, sensory psychology, genetics, animal psychology, psychotherapy, and various aspects of abnormal psychology—is rarely of value to the marketing executive. However, a vast literature on such subjects as learning, thinking, language, personality, and attitudes exists, within which the marketing executive can find nuggets of wisdom. Of special interest are materials from the fields of social psychology and communications research.

9

A major difficulty in bridging these information gaps centers on the fact that behavioral scientists rarely show any interest in problems of advertising, consumer psychology, and other aspects of marketing. Most psychologists are involved in highly specialized studies, but very few in interdisciplinary relationships within areas of business. Professional and scientific interest in advertising and marketing is almost totally lacking among the two largest groups of behavioral scientists—psychologists and sociologists.

Two Major Difficulties

The number of books and articles on psychology and the behavioral sciences for the period 1930-1970—the main period of analysis for this book—is so vast that it would not be possible to encompass all the pertinent materials in one volume.

If sufficient empirical data exist to demonstrate the soundness of a certain psychological principle, there is no need to write about a whole series of additional studies that also demonstrate that psychological principle. Accordingly, for each psychological principle the selection of the most pertinent references has been a real difficulty, not to mention the discussion of these materials. For the present book to be publishable, I had to perform major surgery on my manuscript by cutting out over one-third of the content and of the citations.

Probability

All statements about behavior or communication can be ordered along a continuum from a very high degree of probability to a high degree of probability to a low degree of probability to a very low degree of probability. For example:

Degree of Probability	*Statement*
Very high degree	The next U.S. President will be either a Democrat or a Republican.
High degree	The next U.S. President will be a married man.
Low degree	The next U.S. President will be black.
Very low degree	The next U.S. President will be less than 5 feet tall.

The point is that a statement of a principle about behavior or communication always represents some degree of probability. If there is evidence that a statement is probable, then it must be probable to some degree: very high, high, low, or very low.

What this means, of course, is that evidence of a very high degree of probability about a principle in general implies that the principle has been proved. That is, by inference, the principle represents a very high degree of truth. In this sense, *inference* and *proof* are names for the same series of acts or processes, processes by which statements of principle are believed to be true—that is, have a very high degree of probability.

In their book *Human Behavior: An Inventory of Scientific Findings,* Berelson and Steiner set forth over 1000 principles dealing with the ways in which Homo sapiens behaves (Berelson and Steiner, 1964). Although their principles do not have the precision of an Ohm's law or a Boyle's law or the demonstrability of $I = E/R$, they are statements about human behavior that have a very high degree of probability. Another significant book that sets forth in rigorous terms some basic principles of behavior and their applications is *Behavior Principles* by Ferster, Culbertson, and Boren (1975).

Berelson and Steiner pointed out at the outset of their book that their ambition was "to present as fully and as accurately as possible, what the behavioral sciences now know about the behavior of human beings: what we really know, what we nearly know, what we think we know, what we claim to know" (Berelson and Steiner, 1964, p. 3).

Just as Berelson and Steiner set forth what is known about human behavior, or at least what seems to be known and supported by empirical data, similarly the purpose of this book is to set forth what is known about the psychology of communication—especially as applied to promotional aspects of marketing—or, at least, what seems to be supported by empirical findings.

As for my psychological principles, the discussion of which takes up most of this book, not one is to be considered completely true or completely false. I learned a long time ago in studying with Professor Jerome Michael at the Columbia University School of Law that no proposition (by the way, not even this one) ever is proved to be more than probable to some degree. As previously indicated, this probability may be of four degrees: very high, high, low, or very low; but this does not necessarily imply measurement by numbers (Michael and Adler, 1934). However, for each of the principles set forth here, the probability is at least high, and in most instances it is very high. To put it another way, each of the principles is closer to truth at one end of a scale than to falsehood at the opposite end of the same scale.

Since the words *principle* and *principles* have been used, you might ask: Are there really *principles* of communication? Would it be more accurate to refer to *rules* of communication? Or to *propositions* of communication? However, because of the firmness of the evidence in support of each of these principles, it would be incorrect to refer to them as *statements, rules, propositions,* or *hypotheses.* Such nouns imply greater flexibility than is represented by empirically supported principles—which, as previously mentioned, are in the high to very high categories of probability.

A Question Answered

But a question arises. Every marketing teacher, marketing student, and marketing executive recognizes the very real differences between the results of specific psychological experiments and the applications of these results to specific problems of communication in marketing. In addition, the subjects (people) used in most experiments are not representative or typical of an audience for a marketing communication, the duration of the usual experiment is relatively short as compared with longer periods of communication in the world of marketing, and the experimental situation tends to be artificial as compared with the conditions of daily life.

Therefore, you, as a thoughtful reader, may be asking: How can it be possible to develop acceptable marketing-communication principles based mostly on investigations conducted by psychology professors with relatively small samples of college students in somewhat artificial situations?

The answer is threefold. First, there are almost no other kinds of experimental data available on various aspects of communication. Second, almost all the psychological principles set forth in this book have been deduced not from one but from several different experimental investigations. Finally, although none of the various psychological principles can represent complete certainty, in every instance there is supporting evidence that the principle has a very high, or a high, degree of probability.

Part II:
Models and the Psychology
of Communication

3 Model Definition and Classifications

Definition

Even as the electrical impulses in a telephone cannot communicate the full dimensions of the message, so the methods of interpersonal and mass communications are incomplete. A great number of variables surround the transmission of a message, such as personality factors, the mental sets of the members of the audience, and sociocultural factors. These are never fully duplicated at the reception of the message. It is logical to assume, however, that the more of these variables that are duplicated, the more likely is the success of the communication.

For many years communications theorists have been trying to explain how messages are passed from one individual to another, and they have constructed various models to explain the steps of communicating as they see them.

A model represents a particular construction, using theory designed to serve an instrumental purpose. It is an operating framework that relates the inferences that can be made about any process. A model, by definition, is an artificial device, and is a simplification of the process it portrays. It is an indication of a more accurately determinable state of affairs directed toward greater understanding.

Communicating models do not allow for the fact that communication is an ongoing process that can never be naturally divided. As the biologist must use the artificial process of dissection to analyze the living process, so communication theorists must use models to analyze the process they study. For our purpose, therefore, a *communicating model* may be defined as a set of hypotheses or theories set forth as propositions portraying actual human communication behavior. Diagrams make it easier for the reader to perceive and appreciate the interrelationships among the propositions of the models.

Classifications

Models can be classified to allow greater understanding of their purposes and the techniques used in developing them.

Implicit versus Explicit Models

An interesting classification of models involves the distinction between *implicit* and *explicit models* (Buzzell, 1964, pp. 9-33). Since human perceiving and thought processes are themselves models, it can be argued that every human action must be based on one implicit model or another. In one sense, the process of model building is one of formalizing, or making explicit, the implicit models that already exist in our minds.

Descriptive versus Decision Models

Another distinction is between descriptive models and decision models. Whereas a *descriptive model* purports to describe processes as they are, containing no value judgments about the phenomena depicted, a *decision model* portrays processes as the model-builder believes they should be.

Explicit and Descriptive Models

The psychological models to be developed in this book are both *explicit* and *descriptive*. They are explicit models of what takes place among people as they are confronted with marketing concepts or entities. Each model also is descriptive in the sense that it shows what happens among the members of an audience rather than trying to explain what should happen. An understanding of the processes that audience members go through is an essential step to being able eventually to predict audience behavior. Although prediction is the eventual aim of the psychological models to be presented, accurate description of the behavior of audience members is the present objective.

Black-Box versus Behavioral Models

A *black-box model* acknowledges what goes into the system—the black box—and what comes out, but makes no attempt to describe what happens within the system, or box, to produce a particular output. A *behavioral model* attempts to specify what happens between the time the members of the audience receive the stimuli and when they react. Therefore, the behavioral model attempts to explain what happens inside the black box, while a black-box model ignores it (Buzzell, 1964, pp. 206-226).

One lucid description of the theory of the black box is the following:

Let us imagine that we have a black box in front of us. The box has several buttons and according to how these are pressed, the box moves on its wheels in this direction or that. It is quite a complicated box and repeated pressing of Button 'A' does not produce the same result; what happens will depend on what other buttons have been pressed, or will be pressed, in what order. The problem is to predict the box's movements from various combinations of button-pressing.

There is one general rule: you may not lift the lid off the box to see how the buttons are connected to the wheels; you may only guess the nature of these connections. [Biggs, 1968, pp. 12-13.]

The psychological theory of communicating to be presented here in one sense can be compared to such an idea of a black box. Before any buttons are pressed, the audience member is exposed to a message and attends to it. The audience member's perceiving of the message can be compared to a button being pushed on the box. Then something occurs within the box—the individual learns and remembers. Finally, the individual is motivated and behaves—the box moves.

But as for the psychological models to be developed here, the attempt is not only to describe inputs and outputs but also to understand and specify the inner workings of the system. Hence they are behavioral. An understanding of the system helps the communicator to communicate in ways that are more likely than otherwise to result in behavior by communicatees or audience members that is compatible with the communicator's desired goals.

Mathematical versus Verbal Models

Models can also be classified as mathematical (quantitative) or verbal (qualitative). The essential distinction is that *mathematical models* express the variables and their relationships in mathematical language and, in many cases, make it possible to assign probabilities to the occurrence of certain events. *Verbal models* describe variables and their relationships in prose rather than in mathematical terms.

The psychological models in this book are *verbal*. But hopefully as a better understanding of human behavior is achieved, and as the models become predictive, probabilities may be assigned and at least parts of the models can be expressed in mathematical terms. These models ought eventually to become predictive of what is likely to occur in the situations described and of the propositions of which they are composed. However, before these models can become truly predictive, the following steps must take place:

1. The principles that make up the models will need to be put in *operational terms*; that is, they will have to be stated in such ways as to be subject to testing.
2. These operational principles must then be subjected to *actual tests*; that is, they must be tested so that degrees of probability can be assigned to them in their present form or so that the propositions can be modified and then tested in modified form.
3. The descriptive models that have been tested and modified must then be used for *forecasting*; that is, the extent to which these models enable accurate predictions in realistic situations should be determined.

When these steps have been completed, what were at the outset descriptive models will have been reworked sufficiently to be classified as truly simulation models, that is, representing a total life situation.

Flowcharts

The models to be developed in this book are flowcharts, which are a graphic means of showing chronological and other relationships among various factors and principles in the communicating process. A flowchart makes use of boxes, arrows, and other symbols to represent the relationships among the components of the model. As soon as the meaning of each of the symbols is perceived and understood, the reading or interpreting of a flowchart is easy.

In a particular process or communication, *inputs* enter the system; and as a result of the process, an *output* occurs. By comparing the output to a desired objective, it can be determined whether or not this objective is being reached. If the objective is being reached, the system is doing what it is intended to do; but if the output is different from the desired objective, it becomes necessary to adjust the inputs.

Feedback

The comparison of output with a criterion is defined as *feedback.* The objective of feedback is control. In the control state, system operations are maintained by adjusting for differences between output and criteria. Feedback implies the presence of a subsystem designed to sense output, with the purpose of achieving or maintaining control. Control implies a programmed means of measuring output deviations from what was planned or anticipated. In a flowchart a feedback intervention represents an adjustment on the inputs, which in turn influence the process or system. Figure 3-1 is an illustration of feedback (Optner, 1965, p. 55).

In establishing the various propositions for this book's models, I have emphasized the effects the communicated message has on various aspects of the communicating process, as well as the effects that characteristics of individual audience members—including personality, sociocultural class, past experience, etc.—have on reactions to the communicating process.

The principles are interrelated because they act as partial descriptions of possible actions taken because of communications. Their interrelations help to explain the reactions of the members of an audience. The combination of propositions helps to explain the *whole* behavioral pattern of audience members.

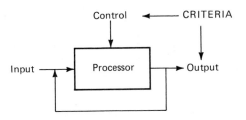

Source: Optner, *Systems Analysis for Business and Industrial Problem Solving* (Englewood Cliffs, N.J.: Prentice-Hall, 1965), p. 55. Reprinted with permission.

Figure 3-1. Feedback.

4 Some Early Models of Communication

The process of communicating has been observed and analyzed by specialists in a variety of disciplines—by psychologists, sociologists, anthropologists, engineers, mathematicians, political scientists, and educators. Thus, over the years, communication models have varied widely in orientation as well as in application. In this chapter a brief historical overview of the three main types of models is presented: S-O-R models, feedback-control models, and sociocultural models.

S-O-R Models

The earliest and most elementary models of communicating were based on the S-O-R formula, in which S stands for the stimulus, O for the organism, and R for the response. The response of an organism to a stimulus is determined not only by the stimulus but also by factors within or affecting the organism that can be classified as heredity, environment, chemical state, emotional state, and activities in progress.

In the 1940s political scientist Harold D. Lasswell added new components to the original concept, which included just the message, the receiver, and his response. Lasswell's model asked (Lasswell, 1948, pp. 37-51):

> Who
> Says What
> To Whom
> With What Effect?

A different type of model came from Weaver and Shannon. They talked about the encoding function of the transmitter and the decoding function of the receiver, using the model shown in figure 4-1 (Weaver and Shannon, 1949, p. 98).

George A. Miller in effect translated the simpler interpersonal models into a more elaborate view (Miller, 1951, p. 76). See the model of his translation in figure 4-2. Most noticeable in Miller's model is the appearance of the "noise" concept, that is, interference, as part of a translation of a two-person communication model into a model of mass communication.

Schramm's model also is of considerable importance because it considers what might be called the *conditions of success* in communicating (Schramm, 1971, both references; originally proposed by Schramm, 1955):

21

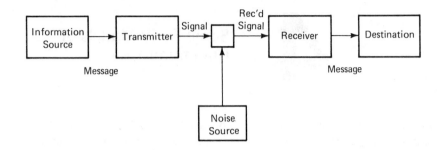

Source: Weaver and Shannon, *The Mathematical Theory of Communication* (Urbana, Ill.: Univ. of Illinois Press, 1949), p. 98. Reprinted with permission.

Figure 4-1. Weaver and Shannon Model.

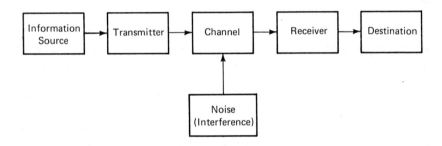

Source: Miller, *Language and Communication* (New York: McGraw-Hill, 1951), p. 76. Reprinted with permission.

Figure 4-2. Miller Model.

1. The message must be designed and delivered to gain the attention of the intended "destination." The destination may be an individual listening, watching, or reading.
2. The message must employ signs that refer to experience common to source and "destination."
3. The message must arouse personality needs in the "destination" and suggest some ways to meet these needs.

According to Schramm, these conditions of success in communicating must be fulfilled if the message is to arouse its intended response. They are fulfilled if the process continues from the source to the destination and elicits the desired response (Schramm, 1971, second reference, pp. 11-12) Schramm's primary model of communication is shown in figure 4-3. The source attempts to encode the message so as to make it easy for the destination to decode it—"to relate it to parts of his experience which are much like those of the source."

Thus the message consists of a collection of objectively measurable signs. It may have to go to another interpretation level in order to bring about a response, or it may be translated into a grammatical response on the dispositional level—the "level of learned integrations (attitudes, values, set, etc.)." The response may be automatic, or it may go through intervening variables to "where meanings are assigned and ideas considered." Final interpretation occurs when decoding terminates and encoding begins. The message then proceeds through intervening variables to the output in a response (Schramm, 1971, second reference, pp. 3-26).

Feedback-Control Models

Feedback in communication processes is portrayed primarily in two senses: first, in an *internal* manner as an automatic means of regulating performance by linking input to output; and second, in an *external* manner as any kind of direct information from an outside source about the effects and/or results of one's behavior (Wolman, 1973, p. 143).

Wiener used a more internal-oriented concept of feedback when he introduced this concept on communication models (Wiener, 1948, pp. 113-136), as shown in figure 4-4.

In this model, the communicator is represented by both the subtractor and the compensator because he restates his message, the output, by adding to it or subtracting from its contents. He makes these changes based upon the feedback take-off from the effector, his intended audience.

Solley and Murphy, in a later attempt to portray the communication process, identified feedback in the individual as being both of an internal and

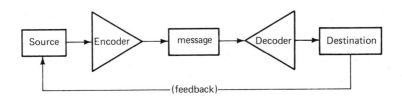

Source: Schramm, "The Nature of Communication Between Humans," in Schramm and Roberts, editors, The Process and Effects of Mass Communication. Urbana, Ill.: University of Illinois Press, 1971), p. 23. Reprinted with permission.

Figure 4-3. Schramm Primary Model.

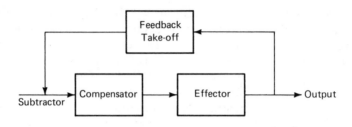

Source: Wiener, *Cybernetics* (Cambridge, Mass.: M.I.T. Press, 1948), p. 132. Reprinted with permission.

Figure 4-4. Wiener Model.

external nature. On the internal level, their model of the perceptual act indicates the feedback concept (Solley and Murphy, 1960, p. 25), as shown in figure 4-5.

Expectancy in their model is the condition of the individual that makes him seek out particular stimuli from the environment. The motives and desires of the individual are influences at this stage of the process. As a simple example, if he is hungry, he will be sensitive to pictures of food. *Attending* involves the "moment before stimulation" and is an observable reaction of the organism. An ear is cocked; an individual takes on a specific posture of stance with reference to the stimuli. *Reception* involves the stimulation of the receptor organs, with all perception limited by physiological stimulation. An individual can see only those colors within a certain range of the spectrum and hear sounds within a certain range of frequencies.

Trial-and-check is very closely related to reception because of the feedback it provides to the system. According to Solley and Murphy, trial-and-check is a short but measurable time lag between reception and final percept. Here sensory input is analyzed and synthesized with regard to past remembering, expectancies, and judgmental "frames of reference." More trial-and-check continues until a system that will integrate the stimuli is formed. For example, on a foggy day it is difficult to see very far ahead while driving. A dark object ahead, which is poorly visible, cannot be immediately identified. A driver is barely aware that something is on the road and consequently makes several trial-and-checks, testing a number of tentative assumptions. He focuses and refocuses his eyes, makes small adjustments of his head and body to get a better reception, and keeps looking until he gets a stable percept.

Percept is the fifth stage in the Solley and Murphy model. It is a "consolidation" of relevant or meaningful stimuli into the perceived situation. If the object that an individual sees is an apple, the individual forms a sociocultural model "picture" of an apple in his mind.

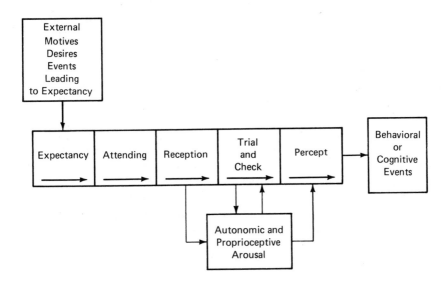

Source: Solley and Murphy, *Development of the Perceptual World* (New York: Basic Books, 1960), p. 25. Reprinted with permission.

Figure 4-5. Solley and Murphy Model.

Sociocultural Models

A different framework of communicating is that of Klapper. As he pointed out, "The fact that persuasive mass communication serves more often as an agent of reinforcement than of conversion seems to be due, at least in part, to the way in which its influence is mediated by certain extra communication factors and conditions" (Klapper, 1960, p. 50). These factors include:

1. Predispositions and the derived processes of selective exposure, selective perception, and selective retention.
2. The group, and the norms of the group to which the audience member belongs.
3. Interpersonal dissemination of communication content.
4. Opinion leadership.
5. The nature of commercial mass media in a free enterprise society.

In another type of communication model developed by DeFleur, the two-step flow of communication of Katz and Lazarsfeld is expanded upon. The two-step flow of communication is based on the idea that the flow of mass communication takes place in, at least, two stages. Katz and Lazarsfeld found that influences stemming from the mass media first reach "opinion leaders," and that opinion leaders, in turn, pass on what they read and hear to those around them (Katz and Lazarsfeld, 1955, pp. 175-177). Utilizing this concept, DeFleur designed the communication system shown in figure 4-6 (DeFleur, 1966, p. 135).

From this very brief survey, it becomes clear that two types of variables occur in the communicating process—those *external* to the members of the audience and those *internal* to each member. The variables that occur *externally,* or outside the individuals in the audience, are measurable by direct means. Examples of external variables are word-of-mouth discussions and point-of-purchase influences. However, the variables of particular interest generally take place *internally,* or within the audience members, although these variables cannot be measured by direct means. Therefore, the nature of these paths of the communicating process must be deduced by inferences from behavior that is observable. The S-O-R, feedback-control, and sociocultural models have been presented quite briefly—in a chronological order—so as to indicate trends in the model-development sequence. This material serves as a background for the discussion of models of marketing in the following chapter.

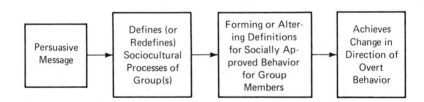

Source: DeFleur, Theories of Mass Communication (New York: McKay, 1966), p. 135.

Figure 4-6. DeFleur Concept.

5 Models of Marketing

In this chapter some of the models that relate directly to the promotion of products and services will be described, as well as models that relate to other aspects of the marketing mix.

Models of Advertising and Promoting

In analyzing and modeling the reaction processes of audience members to an advertisement or promotion it is important to understand the principles that affect consumer behavior. Five of these principles are outlined by Wasson, Sturdivant, and McConaughy as (1) selective exposure, (2) selective appeal, (3) differential intellectual appeal, (4) differential personality response, and (5) group membership effect. Explanations of these principles follow (Wasson, Sturdivant, and McConaughy, 1968, pp. 147-155).

1. *Selective exposure:* People tend to seek out, see, and hear communications congenial to their predispositions—in other words, what they want to see and hear and already believe or feel.

2. *Selective Appeal:* Communications are more effective in gaining attention when they are explicitly addressed to the receiver's specific group or segment than when addressed to the public at large.

3. *The differential intellectual appeal of logic:* The kinds of arguments that are effective depend on the achieved intelligence level of the receiver. Communicatees of high intelligence tend to respond better to appeals relying mainly on impressive logical arguments. They are likely to be less responsive to appeals consisting of unsupported generalities or illogical or irrelevant arguments. Those with a lower intellectual achievement tend to be persuaded by appeals relying less on logic and more on emotions.

4. *Differential personality response:* Different kinds of personalities respond differently to different kinds of appeals. Whereas an aggressive personality tends to respond favorably to a frank, outspoken advertising appeal, a quiet, sensitive personality may react negatively.

5. *Group membership effect:* Resistance to communications that are contrary to the standards of the group will be in proportion to the value attached to group membership by the individual.

In an article by Lavidge and Steiner the purchasing process was described by a series of steps. "Ultimate consumers normally do not switch from disinterested

27

individuals to convinced purchasers in one instantaneous step. Rather, they approach the ultimate purchase through a process or series of steps in which the actual purchase is but the final threshold" (Lavidge and Steiner, October, 1961, pp. 59-62). Their model is shown in figure 5-1.

In 1961, in his book *Defining Advertising Goals for Measured Advertising Results,* Colley discussed the marketing communications spectrum of unawareness, awareness, comprehension, conviction, and action (Colley, 1961, p. 55). His model illustrating these concepts is shown in figure 5-2.

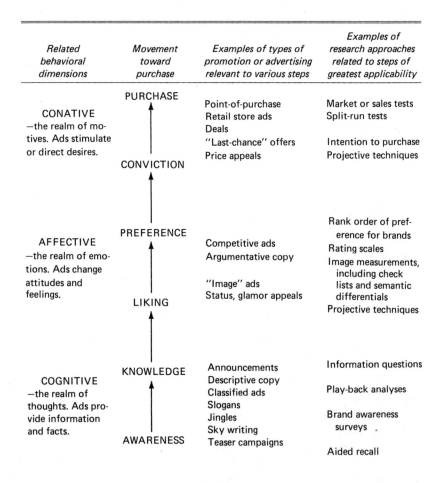

Related behavioral dimensions	Movement toward purchase	Examples of types of promotion or advertising relevant to various steps	Examples of research approaches related to steps of greatest applicability
	PURCHASE ↑		
CONATIVE —the realm of motives. Ads stimulate or direct desires.		Point-of-purchase Retail store ads Deals "Last-chance" offers Price appeals	Market or sales tests Split-run tests Intention to purchase Projective techniques
	CONVICTION ↑		
AFFECTIVE —the realm of emotions. Ads change attitudes and feelings.	PREFERENCE ↑	Competitive ads Argumentative copy "Image" ads Status, glamor appeals	Rank order of preference for brands Rating scales Image measurements, including check lists and semantic differentials Projective techniques
	LIKING ↑		
COGNITIVE —the realm of thoughts. Ads provide information and facts.	KNOWLEDGE ↑ AWARENESS	Announcements Descriptive copy Classified ads Slogans Jingles Sky writing Teaser campaigns	Information questions Play-back analyses Brand awareness surveys Aided recall

Source: Lavidge and Steiner, "A Model for Predictive Measurements of Advertising Effectiveness," *Journal of Marketing* 25 (October 1961): 61. Reprinted by permission.

Figure 5-1. Lavidge and Steiner Model.

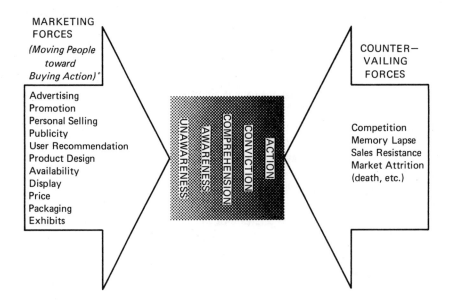

Source: Colley, *Defining Advertising Goals for Measured Advertising Results* (New York: Association of National Advertisers, 1961), p. 55. Reprinted with permission.

Figure 5-2. Marketing Communication Spectrum, Colley Model.

Unawareness is the lowest of the communications spectrum, consisting of people who have never heard of the product or company. *Awareness* is the basic minimum for communication. After awareness is *comprehension.* In this area of knowledge, the consumer possesses some understanding of what the product is, its brand name, package, and so on. *Conviction* is characteristic of the consumer who is confident of the product and its qualities. And finally, *action* describes the consumer whose behavior is directed toward purchase of the product.

Attitude Change

The study of attitudes leads to the discovery of additional stimuli that affect an individual's reactions to various products and advertisements for those products. An individual's attitudes toward a particular product or advertisement for that product is determined at any given time by at least five principal factors (Andreasen, 1965, pp. 1-16):

1. Information and feelings gathered from past want-satisfaction experiences
2. Information gathered in the past but unrelated to the immediate want-satisfying effort

3. Group affiliations (specifically, the individual's perception of the beliefs, norms, and values of "significant others")
4. Attitudes toward related objects
5. The individual's personality

Consequently, attitude change is brought about by:

1. Further or different want-satisfaction experiences
2. Exposure to further or different other information
3. Changes in group affiliation
4. Changes in attitudes toward other "cluster" objects
5. Changes in personality

Thus, when a consumer is unaware of the existence of a product that can be added to his inventory, he naturally possesses no information about it and holds no attitude toward it. However, through either voluntary or involuntary exposure to some primary unit of information, he becomes aware of the product's existence. "This first unit of information, like each one following it, is screened through the individual's perceptual filtration system before coming to have, in a reduced and often distorted form, an effect on each of the three attitude components" (Andreasen, 1965, p. 2). The reception of the information may lead to an attitude change that will result in a decision to acquire the product, an inclination to search for more information, or an acceptance of the status quo.

Decision Processes

In 1968 Engel, Kollat, and Blackwell discussed a slightly different view of the consumer decision process. They explained the decision process as beginning with problem recognition and then proceeding through four other stages:

1. Internal search and alternative evaluation
2. External search and alternative evaluation
3. Purchasing processes
4. Outcomes

They emphasized that although each step may occur, the steps do not necessarily have to be present in every purchase decision. Interactions within and among three areas—the information processing sequence, the control unit interactions, and the environmental influences—determine the final outcome of the consumer decision process. Their model is shown in figure 5-3.

Howard and Sheth developed a special model (figure 5-4) of consumer behavior:

31

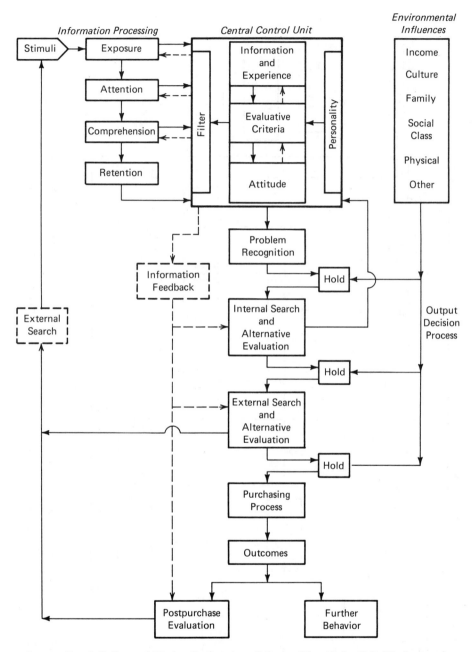

Source: Engel, Kollat, and Blackwell, *Consumer Behavior* (New York: Holt, Rinehart, and Winston, 1968), p. 58. Reprinted with permission.

Figure 5-3. Complete Model of Consumer Behavior Showing Purchasing Processes and Outcomes.

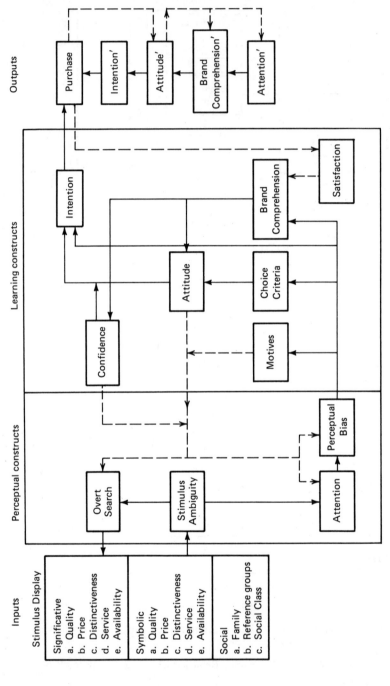

Solid lines indicate flow of information; dashed lines, feedback effects.

Source: Howard and Sheth, *The Theory of Buyer Behavior* (New York: Wiley, 1969), p. 30. Reprinted with permission.

Figure 5-4. Simplified Description of the Theory of Buyer Behavior.

The theory of buyer behavior consists of four sets of abstractions, interchangeably called constructs or variables: (1) input variables, (2) output variables, (3) hypothetical constructs, and (4) exogenous variables. The input and output variables are the least abstract, anchored directly to reality, and operationally well defined. They are called intervening variables. . . .

The hypothetical constructs in the theory are more abstract, only indirectly related to reality, and not operationally defined. . . . They give a description of the buyer's mental state related to a buying decision, and, therefore, map it by identifying, classifying, and labeling various conditions. They encourage speculative theorizing and to that extent serve the generative function.

The exogenous variables describe the contexts in which buying behavior occurs, and they are used for analysis and market segmentation. These contexts are not integral to the decision-making process, but they are powerful influences that the buyer takes into consideration. We isolate them, label them, and show their relations to hypothetical constructs, but do not explain changes in them. [Howard and Sheth, 1969, p. 25.]

Kotler broke down what he calls "the most useful behavioral models for interpreting the transformation of buying influences into purchasing responses" into four categories (Kotler, 1967, pp. 101-109):

1. *Marshallian models* (stressing economic motivations): The theory holds that purchasing decisions are the result of largely rational and conscious economic calculations. The individual buyer seeks to spend his income on those goods which will deliver the most utility (satisfaction) according to his tastes and the relative prices.

2. *Pavlovian models* (stressing learning): Learning is largely an associative process, and a large component of behavior is conditioned in this way.

3. *Freudian models* (stressing psychoanalytic motivations): Individuals try, at first, to get others to gratify their needs through a variety of blatant means, including intimidation and supplication. Continual frustration leads to more subtle mechanisms for gratifying desires.

4. *Veblenian models* (stressing social-psychological factors): Human beings are seen as primarily social animals—conforming to the general forms and norms of the larger culture and to the more specific standards of the subcultures and face-to-face groupings to which life is bound.

This book's model—to be presented in the next chapter—does not fall within any of these categories. For instance, in my models we must consider both the rationality and the nonrationality of the consumer in making a buying decision—the Marshallian model. We must also take into account factors of conditioning—the Pavlovian model; gratifying of desires—the Freudian model; and the effect of other individuals on the buying decision—the Veblenian model.

Four Related Models

Turning to a different interpretation of marketing communication, Swedish scholars Wärneryd and Nowak developed an interesting model with four major components (Wärneryd and Nowak, 1967): the *communicator,* the *message,* the *channel* (which they define as either the medium or the language of the communication), and the *receiver.* See figure 5-5.

At all points in the Wärneryd and Nowak model there exists the possibility of interference by other stimuli—"noise" in the system. For instance, the communicator's aims may be affected by competitive pressures. His choice of channels may be affected by availabilities. The individual's attitude structure is constantly being changed by other stimuli in his environment; and as attitude structure "fluctuates," so does the way in which the message is received.

Bråten put forth a four-stage model that indicates various problems in constructing and delivering a marketing communication (Bråten, 1968):

1. *Exposure:* concerning the degree to which the selected technical and personal channels covered the target categories and the degree of the latter being exposed to the produced signals.
2. *Attention:* concerning the target's selection and recognition of the message forms.
3. *Interpretation:* concerning the target interpreting, recalling, and accepting the message content, and the possible reorganization of their cognitive and noncognitive patterns.
4. *Reaction:* concerning the evocation or fixation of overt target behavior, i.e., trial, purchase, and information actions.

Sandage and Fryburger proposed a verbal model, also based on four broad categories of response:

Exposure. The audience is within range and is capable of seeing and/or hearing the message.

Perception. The audience sees and/or hears the message and relates to prior learning the word/picture/sound symbols making up the message.

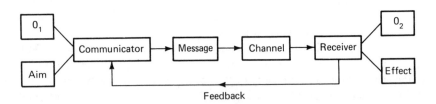

Source: Wärneryd and Nowak, *Mass Communication and Advertising* (Stockholm: Economic Research Institute, 1967), p. 13. Reprinted with permission.

Figure 5-5. A Wärneryd and Nowak Model (with Feedback).

Integration. The audience accepts or rejects the message; believes or disbelieves; remembers or forgets, modifies or retains, relevant attitudes and perceptions.

Action. Members of the audience buy, try, serve, repeat, purchase, advocate, or openly endorse the product advertised. [Sandage and Fryburger, 1971, p. 243.]

Their model illustrating these concepts is shown in figure 5-6.

Schramm views the communicating process as a sharing relationship with an active audience, essentially consisting of information processing organized around a shared orientation to certain signs. His approach to the process of communicating stresses the need for interaction between social and psychological theories. His model is composed of various subsystems that should be treated individually. He starts with the basic information processing system of communicator (A), message (M), and receiver (B).

$$A \longrightarrow M \longrightarrow B$$

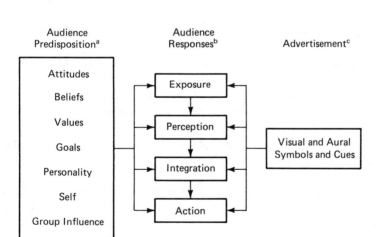

[a] Also called cognitive structure, neural trace patterns, acquired behavioral dispositions.
[b] Perception includes responses referred to as attention, cognition, comprehension, distortion meaning. Integration includes acceptance, rejection, memory; modification or reinforcement of attitudes, beliefs, and perceptions.
[c] A single advertisement or a series of advertisements (a campaign).

Source: Sandage and Fryburger, *Advertising Theory and Practice* (Homewood, Ill.: Irwin, 8th edition 1971), p. 243.

Figure 5-6. Interaction Model of Advertising Communication.

He then modifies this to include B as an *active* participant in the communicating relationship:

$$A \longrightarrow M \longleftrightarrow B$$

The signs (or message) not only act on B, but B acts on the signs. Similarly, Schramm represents successive acts that constitute the interaction process as follows:

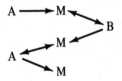

Inherent in this relationship are a myriad of psychological processes that affect reception, perception, interpretation, and distortion (noise and feedback effects).

Schramm also stresses four levels of social relationships:

1. The physical communication situation itself (private versus public, face-to-face versus interposed, etc.)
2. Situational peculiarities, such as content of message, social setting, purpose of individuals involved, and relationships brought into the situation
3. Norms and role patterns of groups involved with the communication process
4. Norms and constraints of society as a whole, such as language used, distance between communicators, and topics discussed

Incorporated within this social framework are the frames of reference of the individuals involved, that is, their storehouse of usable experiences that overlap with one another. The similarity of meaning the participants will perceive depends on the attainment of an area where the experience of two people is sufficiently similar that the same signs can be shared efficiently.

My new psychological model, next to be discussed, differs from earlier models in purpose, design, theoretical framework, and applications. As will be seen, the specific propositions based on the model can be utilized for a more complete understanding of many different phases of marketing.

6

A New Psychological Model of Marketing

Model Comparisons and Considerations

The psychological model to be described in this chapter is different from other models of marketing, and it represents the basic framework for this entire book. My model of the communicating process revolves around individual rather than group behavior. However, it must be remembered that as a psychologist-marketer, I am not defining the term *individual* in the narrow sense of a particular person but instead as referring to members of various audiences. Thus experimental conclusions are based on composite findings about many individuals.

In this psychological model of communicating, six stages are identified: exposing, attending, perceiving, learning (and remembering), motivating, and persuading. Thus it is not enough to say that there is a process of perceiving; this process is an aspect of a broader process or series of processes, all interrelated. This model is an attempt to analyze in detail the variables in each of six stages of the communicating process in order to form basic principles about the complete communicating process.

Several of the models discussed in the previous chapter might be compared to my psychological model and to each other. But the number of differences and similarities among the models would be too great for our purposes here.

However, my model has many similarities to the Wärneryd and Nowak model. The principal differences are:

1. What in my model is called *perceiving*, Wärneryd and Nowak call *interpretation*. The difference is more semantic than conceptual.

2. My model utilizes two categories prior to discussing persuading to explain what happens after perceiving; learning (and remembering); and motivating. Wärneryd and Nowak use only one category: attitudes and action. They refer to *attitude* as a result of the learning process; and they point out that learning describes the process by which attitudes are formed, but do not give learning a separate category, as is done in my model.

3. Wärneryd and Nowak use the construct of *attitude change* to refer to the final category, discussed in my model as persuading. The use of learning (and remembering) and motivating as the categories preceding persuading allows for a discussion of reinforcement of the variables associated with persuading.

Basic Propositions

The basic principles of my model to be presented in later chapters have various types of evidence in their support. These types of evidence can be ranked as follows:

1. Experimental evidence relating directly to some specific phase of communicating
2. Experimental evidence relating to mass communicating in general
3. Experimental evidence relating to small group communicating
4. Expert opinion
5. No evidence to the contrary

Only the likelihood of behavior is indicated in the model, not 100 percent correctness. All that any model can do is to specify the relevant variables and their functional relationships to each other under specific circumstances (Bauer, 1966, p. 35)

Six Stages

A further consideration in understanding this book is the "breakdown" into six stages of the overall reaction processes of an individual to a marketing communication: exposing, attending, perceiving, learning (and remembering), motivating, and persuading. This breakdown makes it easier to understand the communicating process as a whole and the interrelationships that make up that whole. Note that the six key words end in "*ing.*" The word is expos*ing,* not exposure . . . attend*ing,* not attention . . . perceiv*ing,* not perception . . . learn*ing* (and remember*ing*), not memory . . . motivat*ing,* not motivation . . . and persuad*ing,* not persuasion. We are not dealing with things or entities, but with processes or activities.

Moreover, it is understood that for any or all of the six stages of communicating to occur, message distributing or delivering must take place; that is, there must be distributing or delivering of the message before the communicating process itself begins.

It must be understood also that an individual can enter the communicating process at any stage. The implication is *not* that the communicating process actually occurs in six discrete parts. The separation has been made simply for the purpose of organizing the supporting data in each of the six areas of study. Of necessity, considerable overlap occurs among the six stages, and some factors—such as needs and wants—apply to all phases of the process.

The psychological model in each section of this book assumes two types of variables—*message and medium variables,* and *audience variables.* The alternative method of organizing the variables would have been to arrange them in a continuum, running from those which can be completely altered by the communicator to those variables over which he has no control, but such an organization would not have been practical. It is much more useful in terms of the kinds of supporting evidence available to use only the two general types of variables: message and medium variables . . . and audience variables.

At the end of each major part of this book, each of which describes and discusses one of the six stages in the communicating process, a graphic model of that stage of the communicating process is presented. These models are diagrammatic representations of the general psychological model and the specific relationships described. The model presented in this chapter, for example, is a simplification of the general model. It does not include a diagrammatic representation of all principles, but rather just shows the six basic steps in the communicating process (see figure 6-1).

This psychological model, however, does take into account the possibility of an audience member's misunderstanding the communicator's message at some stage of the process. Should this misinterpreting occur, the communicating process will continue, but the audience member's behavior will not likely be that which the communicator desired. The point is that the six processes are interrelated. They have been "dissected out" only for purposes of analysis.

A useful analogy is the dissection of a cadaver in a course in anatomy in a school of medicine. Separately an analysis is made of the muscular system, the nervous system, the skeletal system, the digestive system, and the circulatory system; and yet, all these systems are interrelated and function together physiologically. Likewise, "dissection" of the six psychological processes helps in understanding the overall process of communicating; and yet, the psychological processes are interrelated and function together psychologically.

The model presented in the present chapter—see figure 6-1, *The New Psychological Model of Communicating*—does not include a diagrammatic representation of all principles, but does show the six basic steps in the communicating process.

Feedbacks

All aspects of the communicating process affect each other greatly. The specific models of this book that show relationships among principles in any one step of the communicating process would be much too complicated if *all* feedbacks were illustrated. It must be understood, however, that many feedbacks between and among propositions and external and internal stimuli do exist in all parts of the communicating models.

A little reflection reveals the complications that result from the fact that the flowchart must illustrate a course from the first to the last step without getting "caught up" in an infinite loop. Examples of feedback are the effects of:

Perceiving on subsequent exposing and attending

Order of presentation on perceiving and learning

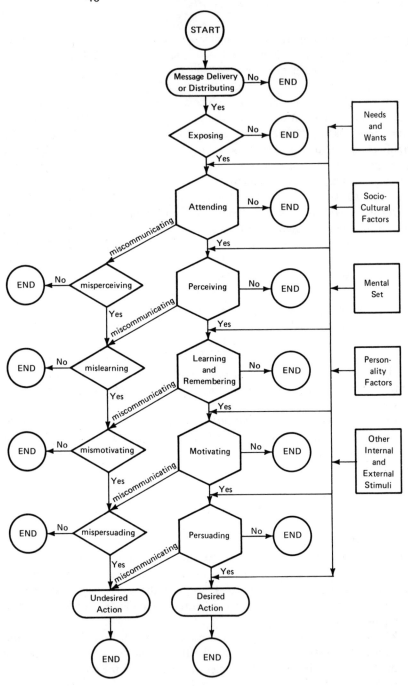

Figure 6-1. The New Psychological Model of Communicating.

Communicator credibility on learning and motivating

Learning and motivating on selective exposing and attending

However, because of the visual complications, feedbacks are *implicit* but are not shown explicitly in the various models to be set forth in this book.

Interpreting the Psychological Model of Communicating

The initial step in the communicating process is, of course, the *distributing* of the message. The communicator must make sure that his message physically is available to those audience members he wishes to reach.

1. *Exposing* occurs when the audience member actually comes in contact with the message. This can happen when an intended communicatee turns on his television set or buys a newspaper or magazine, for example.

2. *Attending* is the process during which the individual becomes actively aware of the message. He receives the physical stimuli that make up the message of the communicator. He is positively attending to the message if he is aware of his reception of the physical stimuli. If he is not attending completely, he will probably misperceive the message, thus leading to the miscommunicating of the intended message.

3. *Perceiving* is the process by which the audience member organizes and interprets stimuli that previously have been only sensory data. At this point he is aware of the message and organizes its parts into some sort of understanding. If he is misperceiving, he is organizing these stimuli into a meaningful (to himself) pattern that is different from the one the communicator desired. If the audience member is not perceiving, no organizing of the sensory material takes place.

4. *Learning (and remembering)* involve bringing together and relating the message to the "framework" of the communicatee. He relates the message to himself and stores the information for possible use. He is positively learning and remembering if he relates the situation described in the message to himself. He is mislearning the communicator's intended message if he understands the situation in the message but sees no relevance in it to his situation. The audience member does not learn what was intended.

5. *Motivating* is the process that takes place in the audience member's mind and leads him toward some action. He is positively motivated if the message causes him to decide to act in the way intended by the communicator. The audience member is negatively motivated if his intended action is different from that desired by the communicator. If motivating has not taken place, no action will follow on the part of the audience member. Motivating involves reinforcement of beliefs, attitudes, and opinions. In other words, motivating is covert behaving (behavior); changes in overt behaving (behavior) are not observable.

6. *Persuading* is the process of acting, functioning, or reacting in various

ways, with actual changes in behaving occurring. *Positive behaving* in the communicating process is behaving in the way the communicator desired. *Undesired behaving* usually involves an unfavorable change in the audience member's desire from that which the communicator wished him to have; the audience member may have been neutral toward it prior to being persuaded by the message. *No behaving* occurs if the audience member experiences no change of beliefs or attitudes.

Here it is important to indicate the psychological differences between the processes of motivating and persuading. Both processes deal with the beliefs and attitudes, and both are concerned with interactions of audience-message-object characteristics, as well as with influencing behavior in a specific direction. The process of *motivating* arouses certain responses in the minds of people by relating the message to their needs and wants. In motivating, the message is related to and is congruent with people's beliefs and attitudes and reinforces these beliefs and attitudes. By comparison, the process of *persuading* tends to change the beliefs and attitudes of people. Persuading goes beyond relating the message to the audience members' beliefs and attitudes in such a way that they will tend to reevaluate their beliefs and attitudes.

Five Sets of Outside Stimuli

The entire communicating process is affected by several kinds of outside stimuli that the communicator cannot control. When planning his message, the communicator needs to be aware of the following five sets of outside stimuli.

1. *Needs and wants* vary not only from individual to individual but also from time to time on the basis of urgency. *Needing* means being able to use something in a situation that has some reasonable chance of arising and *wanting* means recognizing something as a means of meeting a situation that is regarded as both probable and important (Alderson, 1955, p. 2). Wants are derived from needs. A communicator can make his audience members aware of their needs by identifying specific ways in which their wants might be met. These needs then become wants; and from the communicator's standpoint, hopefully the audience members seek ways to fulfill these wants. The communicator hopes that fulfillment will be through the desired behavior implied by his message.

2. *Sociocultural factors* include those traits of an audience member's environment which are common to his particular peer group. These material and behavioral arrangements for a particular group include social customs and beliefs, habits, mores, and taboos. Included also are esthetic aspects of the lifestyle of the group, such as taste in personal conduct, knowledge of heritage, appreciation of art, and a general philosophy of life.

3. *Mental set* of an audience member is his preparatory adjustment or readiness for a particular kind of action or experience. The many aspects of mental set have been defined (Gibson, November, 1941, p. 811) as follows:

1. A prearoused expectation of stimulus objects, qualities, or relations
2. A conceptual schema, not expected, but aroused by the stimulus pattern
3. An expectation of stimulus relationships either prearoused or acquired during repeated stimulation
4. An intention to react by making a specific movement, or not so to react
5. An intention to perform a familiar mental operation
6. A mental operation or method, not intended, but aroused by the problem or learned in the course of problem solving
7. A tendency to complete or finish an activity
8. A tendency to go on performing an activity after the occasion is over

Any and all of these aspects of mental set can pertain to the members of an audience during the communicating process, and the variables can affect the act of communicating in many different ways. For example, they can affect a message by: selecting and accentuating some part of experience; selectively utilizing the residues of experience; regulating the course of action; sustaining activity; or organizing the patterns of experience (Young, 1961, pp. 276-277).

4. *Personality factors* involve various individual traits that are different for each member of an audience. Some of these factors can be isolated and used by the communicator in designing his message to reach a particular type of audience member. Of course, a great number of such factors are "hidden" within an individual and make it difficult to predict how he will be affected by a particular message.

5. *Other internal and external stimuli* are endless in number. The overabundance of distractions and interferences from an audience member's environment complicate the communicator's job. Furthermore, the dynamic nature of these stimuli makes them difficult to pinpoint and for the most part impossible to predict. An audience member may be distracted from concentration on a message because of his individual state of health or his preoccupation with a current thought. For example, the weather or a noise at the time of the communication might distract him.

Taken together, these five sets of outside stimuli act as somewhat unpredictable and complicating variables of which the communicator cannot always be aware, but around which he must try to "style" his message for maximum positive communicating. But consideration of these outside stimuli helps to explain why a well-designed message does not necessarily elicit the desired responses.

Uniqueness of the Psychological Model

To summarize, my new psychological model of communicating is unique in four ways.

1. Its purpose is unique, in the attempt to construct a psychological model of communicating from behavioral science data.

2. Its design is unique, in its components and interrelationships with six specific stages of communicating.
3. Its theoretical framework is unique, in its consideration of each of the six stages as an active, continuing process rather than a passive condition (for example, it uses the concept of attending rather than attention).
4. Finally, its applications are unique, in that the communicating processes have significant relationships to a number of phases of marketing (as will be shown).

**Part III:
Exposing**

7 Message and Medium Variables

Background

This chapter deals with exposing, by far the simplest step in the total process of communication. *Exposing* is the condition that makes a message physically accessible to the audience (Zajonc, 1968, p. 100). Without exposing, no communication could take place.

The first influence on exposing is the physical availability (or distributing) of a message. It is understood that in order for exposing to occur, message distributing must take place so that the potential members of the audience can see or hear it. If this does not occur, the communicating process ends rather abruptly.

The discussion in this chapter will break down the variables involved in exposing into two major areas: *message and medium variables* and *the variables within the audience.* However, the message and medium variables depend to a great extent upon the variables within the audience.

Although the material on exposing is not difficult to understand, its importance should not be minimized. In this part of the book we set up the framework for the entire discussion on the process of communicating: exposing, attending, perceiving, learning, motivating, and persuading.

Considerable similarity exists among the variables involved in this and following chapters. This duplication is necessary in order to break down into discrete parts what essentially is a continuum. Because behavior is a *process*, many interrelations occur; and the repetition of the variables is necessary in order to communicate the complexity of the audience-behavior model.

Variables

From the point of view of the marketer, the choice of the message and the medium to fit his purposes is among the factors of greatest flexibility for him. The *medium* (plural, *media*) for an advertisement is the agent that conveys it to the public. The medium may be entertainment, news communication, or nonadvertising matter carrying or surrounding the message. It also can be one of the forms of communication that are purely advertising, such as fliers or posters. The media are not only television, radio, magazines, and newspapers, but also direct mail, outdoor posters, car cards, point-of-purchase displays, and so on. (Kleppner, 1966, p. 177). The *message* is found in the section of the medium where the communicator presents materials about his products or services. For the advertiser, the message is the commercial or the printed advertisement.

Both the message and the medium choice are extremely important. The message variables are closely concerned with the specific product or service class and the specific intended market segment, while the media variables are more closely concerned with exposing per se.

Both the medium and the message select; that is, the medium selects the overall audience that composes the advertiser's market and holds their attention long enough—ideally—to ensure their exposure to the advertising message. The message then acts as a way of selecting an even more specific audience.

Consider an advertisement in several periodicals. An individual will be exposed effectively to the advertisement if any one of the following conditions obtains:

1. The exposing is the first for the particular individual.
2. The individual is a member of the customer class regarded as the most important target audience of the advertisement.
3. The periodical involved provides the best environment for the advertisement.
4. The individual is actually exposed to the advertisement in that periodical.

Given these standards of effective exposing, the problem, of course, is to maximize effective exposing for the target audience within budget limitations (Asker, 1968).

Compatibility with Possible Current Beliefs and Activities

I.A1 *The members of an audience are more likely to be exposed to a message or medium that is compatible with their beliefs and activities than to a message or medium that is incompatible with such beliefs or activities.*

Several studies indicate that most audiences for mass communications tend to overrepresent individuals already sympathetic with or in agreement with the views of the message. Individuals tend to be exposed disproportionately to communications that support their opinions. This might be called *de facto selectivity* (Freedman and Sears, 1965, p. 89).

A study by Schramm and Carter using political propaganda conveyed the same results. "Voters tend to expose themselves to media in order to reinforce their predispositions and reduce the dissonance resulting from challenge to those predispositions, rather than to see what the other side has to offer" (Schramm and Carter, 1959).

In a study of five Michigan school districts during another election, it was found that individuals who believed that their side of a local bond-issue question would win experienced more exposing to information about the campaign than did individuals who feared their side would be defeated (Greenberg, 1965, p. 153).

The compatibility of the medium to the activities of the audience is important as a basic consideration. A marketer can improve the effectiveness of his message by considering the compatibility factor. A program demanding strict visual attention (such as television) or constant close presence to the sound source (such as radio) may be incompatible with the activities of an audience and therefore subject to fragmentary exposing or, possibly, no exposing at all. The communicator can allow for the compatibility variable if he imagines what individuals do when they use the medium.

Marketing Examples of Compatibility with Possible
Current Beliefs and Activities

One effective use of radio is the timed advertising of dinner foods during the morning: "What will your husband want for supper tonight? How about . . . ?" Communicating to the housewife before she leaves to shop for groceries is clearly to the advertiser's advantage. Later in the day, when the evening meal plan may be already underway and other activities occupy the housewife's time, effective exposing to such a message is far less assured.

Mayor John Lindsay of New York City had one particularly effective television commercial in one of his campaigns for reelection because it appealed to the beliefs of a majority of the voters. In the commercial, Lindsay spoke about what he had been unable to do as mayor while films of problems in the city were shown. This obviously facilitated exposing for those who believed the mayor had not done an effective job. Then the commercial showed films of successful programs while Lindsay spoke of what he had done and the reasons why he wanted to try again. By illustrating both sides of the issue, the commercial was compatible with a large portion of the audience's beliefs.

Freedom from Distractions

I.A2 *Members of an audience are more likely to be exposed to a message or medium if conflicting activities are minimized than if the audience members are distracted from the message or medium.*

Deliberate exposing to a medium is increased if it does not conflict with more valued activities. So magazine and newspaper advertisers must compete for prime placements within the pages, whereas outdoor advertisers must consider the competing stimuli of outdoor surroundings. Radio and television advertisers vie for time slots that are relatively free of the distractions of outside activities.

Marketing Examples of Freedom from Distractions

The Bell Telephone System compensated for distractions by showing its series of commercials on long-distance dialing on television stations on Sundays. Approaching the members of an audience on a relaxed, traditional family day increased the likelihood of their messages being exposed. Thoughts of long-distance relatives were stimulated, reminding audience members that they should take time and "keep in touch" with people they do not see every day.

"Filler" advertisements are frequently stuffed in with the other sections of Sunday newspapers. People usually read the Sunday paper while relaxing. Again, the "fillers" are more likely to gain attention on Sunday than if they were included in workday morning editions.

8 Variables within the Audience

Background

Variables within the audience are those characteristics which vary greatly from individual to individual. Each member of an audience may be described in terms of personality aspects, and these variables most certainly affect the probability of that individual's being exposed to any message.

Internal variables affecting exposing are difficult to define because they are unique to each individual and are not always manifested by behavior. After all, an individual's *personality* is comprised of all his distinguishing qualities taken as a unit. These traits include those aspects of the person's nature which have been developed through social interaction.

Another set of variables for each individual is determined by his actions or overt lifestyle. The *lifestyle* of an individual is determined by his social rank or prestige and his usual patterns of behavior. An urban lawyer is likely to read different magazines, communicate with different types of people, and have different shopping habits than a small-town clothing clerk.

Another set of individual variables has to do with the *cultural framework* of each member of the audience. Social institutions, beliefs, morals, customs, habits, capabilities, knowledge, and artifacts of a particular group in society make up its culture and distinguish its members from the members of other cultures. An individual is placed in a cultural framework through his heritage and also through his environment.

A communicator can hardly change these individual variables, yet must consider them carefully in deciding what target audience to try to reach. In designing a message, the marketer must understand that his audience is composed of individuals with these differences and should seek to reach his audience through their similarities.

Variables

Lifestyle

I.B1 *The more compatible a medium is with audience members' lifestyles or their desired lifestyles, the greater is the probability that they will be exposed to the medium and subsequently to the message, as contrasted with a medium less compatible with their lifestyles.*

Media select their audience, largely because of the type of editorial matter. The more specific a medium is in choosing editorial matter, the greater the probability that individuals with similar lifestyles and interests will expose themselves to the medium and eventually to the message.

Marketing Examples of Lifestyle

Individuals can be grouped into audiences by the type of appeals that will reach them. Magazine readership studies have been conducted with the purpose of characterizing the readers of various magazines as a possible guide to editors. *Better Homes and Gardens* readers, for instance, in a 1956 study of that magazine, characterized themselves as venturesome. In the sense that the magazine specialized in creative suggestions in home improvement, requiring thought and effort on the part of homeowners, this personality characterization seemed appropriate (Politz, 1956).

Consider also the sale of insurance, and the norm of being a good father of one's family by giving them protection. Likewise, advertising for college educations is well exposed to the majority of Americans who believe strongly in providing college educations for their children. Promotion for vacation cruises gains exposure usually for older Americans who can afford long, leisurely vacations.

Cultural Framework

I.B2 *The members of an audience are more likely to be exposed to messages and media that are in agreement with the norms of their cultural framework than to those messages and media which are not.*

It was once believed that opinion leaders, found in every social and economic level of society, received information from the media and then transmitted it to less active members in their society. According to this theory, the great majority of the population often relied upon opinion leaders for exposure to information. This theory has been known as the two-step flow of communication (Katz and Lazarsfeld, 1955, p. 310).

Because of a lack of a standardized definition of an opinion leader, this theory needs revision. While opinion leaders are important at the exposing stage, they may, in fact, be more influential at the evaluation stage. The less active members of society as well as opinion leaders are exposed to and are affected by the mass media. An individual can selectively expose himself to television, radio, or magazines. Rogers found that "the 1960 television debates indicate that personal conversations about the debates the following day reached many individuals who avoided watching the debate broadcasts" (Rogers, 1969, p. 225).

Marketing Examples of Cultural Framework

In the July 1972 issue of *Car and Driver* magazine, an advertisement for a midsize Plymouth Satellite showed the car in the driveway of a typical suburban home, complete with basketball hoop over the garage door. In contrast, an advertisement for the Ford Mustang had a picture of a surfer negotiating a steep wave. Finally, the advertisement for Jaguar XJ6 pictured the car surrounded by the untouched splendor of nature. The messages with the advertisements were: "The family car for fun-loving families" (Plymouth Satellite); "Control, balance, style" (Ford Mustang); and "To a world filled with compromise, we make no contribution" (Jaguar XJ6). The advertisement's copy and pictorial material helped to "sharpen" the portrayal of the distinct lifestyles each automobile symbolized. Thus, with such a diversity of lifestyles represented, a wider audience appeal could be gained.

The following list of commercials that were aired during a sample hour of prime time on a Chicago-area FM rock-music station give an idea of the lifestyle of its young adult audience: (1) a new community of townhouses, (2) a new rock record album, (3) a rock concert, (4) a hair conditioner for girls with long hair, (5) an underground movie, (6) a "unisex" clothing store, (7) a speed reading course, (8) another new rock record album, and (9) a hair conditioner.

The billboards in the New York area for Levy's Bread that proclaimed "You don't have to be Jewish to love Levy's Jewish Rye Bread" appealed not only to Jewish audience members but also to members of several other groups by showing Negroes, Indians, and other minority group members enjoying the product. People with many different cultural frameworks could identify with portrayed users of the product, while exposed to the message.

Ebony is another example of a medium that adapted itself to a particular culture. Blacks are more likely to be exposed to this magazine than is a white audience. Likewise, an audience of Jewish faith is not likely to tune in Sunday morning church broadcasts.

Expected Benefits of the Medium

I.B3 *The more valuable a medium is in satisfying audience members' needs and wants, the more likely that they will be exposed to that medium.*

An individual's preference for one of several media is based upon his own judgment of the value of the various media. His own experiences and his own personality determine what expectations he may have concerning the various media, that is, what he thinks exposing himself to each of the media might do for him. Each type of media is thus assigned a certain value by each individual, according to its suitability for meeting his information and entertainment wants and needs.

Marketing Examples of Expected Benefits of the Medium

An individual's expected benefits often differ between broadcast and print media. People who read newspapers want to keep up with the news in other ways also—by watching a certain news program, by reading one of the news magazines, or by listening to a certain radio news broadcast. Thus the audience comes to depend upon the medium. It becomes satisfying; and, as a result, the audience is more likely to be exposed to its advertising messages than otherwise.

Playboy magazine readers have been the subject of attempted readership characterizations. The *Playboy* reader is more likely than not to be male, morally broad-minded, and at least somewhat concerned about masculinity and sophistication regarding current topics. The expectation that topics of interest to a playboy will be discussed in the magazine increases the likelihood of exposing to such readers.

Many advertisers of home products and family products advertise in *Parents' Magazine* and *Good Housekeeping* because these magazines have built a reputation for recommending only good products to their readers. The consumer's trust then becomes an expected benefit of the medium and is imposed on the products advertised in the magazines, to increase exposing of the advertisers' messages.

Repeated Exposing to the Medium

I.B4 *The more often that audience members are exposed to a medium, the more likely that they will develop positive attitudes toward that medium.*

Zajonc studied the effects of attitudes on exposing and defined *exposure* as "the condition making the stimulus accessible to the individual's perception" (Zajonc, 1968, p. 1). He stated that the ratings of "goodness of meaning," that is, the judgment of the individual that the stimulus of the message is pleasant or favorable, increased significantly with repeated exposing.

Marketing Examples of Repeated Exposing to the Medium

To gain repeated exposing, newspapers often have subscription drives during which free issues of the paper are given to prospective customers to increase their awareness of the publication and to make them accustomed to receiving it.

Popular radio stations gain repeated exposing by holding contests that require viewers to stay tuned to the station in order to win. Such contests serve to increase awareness of the station's programs and to increase loyal listening to the station.

Repeated Exposing and Attending and Perceiving Behavior

I.B4.1 *The more often a message is exposed to audience members, the more likely they will attend to and perceive the product or service advertised.*

MacDonald studied relationships between advertising exposing and purchasing behavior. On the basis of products bought and advertising exposure of 225 London housewives he demonstrated that repeated exposing to a message resulted in the greater likelihood of the purchase of that brand. "In short, not only is increased weight of exposure to a brand more likely to result in a purchase of that brand; increased exposure to the other brands which are also bought are less likely to result in a purchase of that brand" (MacDonald, 1969, p. 153).

Moreover, MacDonald recognized that the further back in time exposing took place, the less it influenced purchase behavior. Although further research must be done on repetition, timing of exposures, and related factors, the effects of frequency are of great importance to the marketer; and such variables will be discussed in later parts of this book in terms of *learning, motivating,* and *persuading.*

Mere number of *exposure opportunities,* that is, the number of times a message is repeated, does not alone determine actual exposing. Another significant factor is the *structure* of the message. The structure of or degree of differentiation within an advertisement is a function of its content. In discussing how much exposing is needed to ensure effective communication, Drugman suggested that "high structure transmits information via focusing and requires few exposures, while low structure permits repeated scanning" (Krugman, 1968, p. 249).

His data suggested that a highly structured or controlled response caused by a highly structured or controlled advertisement, while it may be most communicative or informative, may be least motivating or persuasive. In other words, a highly structured advertisement with much copy, illustrations, and a consistent theme will generate a highly structured response that will match the advertisement in its consistency, which may not be the desired result.

Marketing Examples of Repeated Exposing and Attending and Perceiving Behavior

To get repeated exposing for a new product and to increase desire for it, sample sizes or portions of the product can be distributed through the mail, door-to-door, at conventions, or during in-store demonstrations.

Several Midwestern and Southern tourist attractions and novelty stores have used repeated exposing to increase consumer interest. Their method is to display large billboard advertisements at varying intervals along major highways, announcing the attraction many miles before its location. By the time the motorist has reached the location, he has been exposed to many messages.

9

An Overview of Exposing

Implications

The principles discussed in this early part of the book are intended to show that exposing is *not* automatic. The wise marketer will view these principles not as limiting factors but rather as opportunities for creative thinking.

Model of Exposing

Figure 9-1 is a diagrammatic representation of the interactions of these principles of exposing. The communicating process begins when the medium is distributed to the members of the audience. If the newspaper is not delivered to the individual's door, obviously communication is not going to occur. *Distributing* or delivering, then, is really the initial variable in the communicating process, as shown in the model.

The continuing variables that affect all stages of communicating are the audiences' needs and wants, sociocultural factors, mental set, personality factors, and other internal and external stimuli. The next two influences, which relate to the external message and media variables, are compatibility and freedom from distractions. If the messages and media are compatible with the audience's environment, cognitive set, and current needs and wants, and if they are convenient in the sense that they do not conflict with other activities, then the exposing process will be unimpeded. If not, serious roadblocks will be set up to effective exposing.

Next to be considered are the audience variables. The audience selects messages in coincidence with its lifestyle. Its members seek out certain types of information in order to discriminate between desired and undesired messages. An inherent factor in determining exposing is the audience's cultural framework. Although a message may be properly distributed, social and cultural pressures against this type of message may force the audience to remain unexposed.

Audience members have certain expectations of benefit related to each medium and tend to associate messages with media in qualitative terms. Repeated exposing to a medium will enhance the audience's attitude toward it, and the exposing to that medium will likely continue. Increased exposing to a product or message is also positively related to the acceptance of that product or message, as shown by its effects on attending and perceiving behavior.

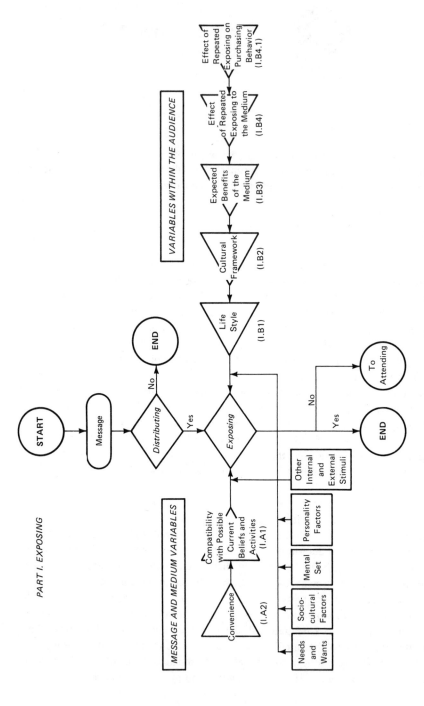

Figure 9-1. The Exposing Stage of the Psychological Model of Communicating.

The preceding constitute the influences that together determine the probability of a particular target audience being exposed to a particular message placed in a medium. If these influences exist in the right "mix," the target audience is more likely to be effectively exposed to the message than otherwise.

Part IV:
Attending

10 Message and Medium Variables

Background

Every day hundreds of messages bombard the members of an audience, but the audience attends to or notices only a relatively small number. What determines which messages an audience will notice? An understanding of the process of attending is necessary to answer this question.

Attending is the skimming and selecting process that precedes the actual perceiving of a message. It is the mental process that indicates openness to stimulation and readiness to search for sensory cues within a message. Obviously, attending is very selective—an individual cannot possibly be attentive to each of the hundreds of messages he is exposed to in a single day, so he must constantly be involved in a mental selection process. A stimulus, or some stimuli, must attract an individual's senses more than other environmental stimuli in order to be attended.

Selective attending refers to the choosing of a smaller number of stimuli from a larger array of stimuli in the environment. Two types of variables determine whether the members of an audience will attend to a message. *Message and medium variables* pertain to the actual wording of the message and to the medium through which it is transmitted. And the *variables within the audience* are those dealing with the way audience members receive a message. After the senses of an individual are aroused to attend to a stimulus, further attending depends on how interesting the stimulus is to the individual. This interest depends upon the needs, personality, and past experiences of the audience member.

Variables

A communicator must be aware of the variables of the message he wishes to present and the media available for its transmission. He must determine how he can increase the attending to his message over that of other messages that compete with it. The message's individual design and its relative placement in the media will help determine its attending. The following propositions on attending are designed to facilitate message and media decisions for the marketer.

63

Complexity

II.A1 *A more complex message will not have as high a level of attending as a simple one, unless it is novel or is of high interest to the audience.*

The degree of complexity depends upon the relationship of all the message elements (Berlyne, 1960, p. 38). Complexity increases with the number of distinguishable elements in a message or with the dissimilarity among elements. Thus the degree of complexity varies inversely with the degree to which several elements of a message elicit a single response.

Various investigations provide substantial support for the idea that individuals have a maximum capacity for processing perceptual information—that is, people have a limited span of attention. The more easily the information is organized into distinguishable features, the more successfully and completely it will be attended (G.A. Miller, 1956).

A preference for more complex as opposed to simpler patterns was found in another investigation. A group of children was given an apparatus with six lights and six buttons corresponding to each one of the lights. Five buttons activated a common stimulus for all subjects, while the sixth differed according to complexity and the type of complex stimulus. The investigators found that the children selected the more complex pattern more often than by chance. However, the children did prefer a pattern that was similar to what they had seen before rather than a totally new and complex one. Newness seemed to negate the adverse affect of complexity on preference. To test this hypothesis, complexity was held constant and novelty varied. The children sought designs of relative novelty, or those designs which differed from the standard in one or more aspects, such as color. Completely new stimuli tended to elicit uncertainty or surprise and were generally avoided (Rabinowitz and Robe, 1968).

Marketing Examples of Complexity

The results of these and similar investigations can easily be applied to marketing. If the marketer wants to increase attending with his promotional message, he should keep it simple. For example, beer advertisers have had success using a simple picture of the product with little additional copy. If the nature of the product or communication that the advertiser wishes to present does not allow simplicity, a relatively novel approach will result in attending and tend to offset the disadvantages of complexity.

The Alka Seltzer television commercial that featured an occasional blank screen followed by a picture of a hand or hands throwing tablets into a glass of water drew considerable attending because of its simplicity. The voice-over gave insights into various problems that could be helped by taking the product.

Attending to the product uses was increased because nothing else was apparent to distract from the attending process.

Simple messages can be found on outdoor posters because of the short span of attending, whereas other media lend themselves to more complex messages. Newspapers and magazines provide forums for the communication of more detailed messages, such as those dealing with insurance, automobiles, or business machines.

The stage of product development also affects the complexity of messages. In the initial stage, more attending has to be paid to what the product is, its uses, situations of use, and how to use it. A good example of this is a toaster oven. Product development here involves more complexity than at the product maturity stage, where reminder advertising is more in order; members of the audience already are familiar with the idea that the product can be used *both* as an oven and toaster.

Contrast

II.A2 *A message containing a contrast to the environment in which it appears is more likely to result in attending by members of an audience than a message that is harmonious with the environment.*

What actually creates contrast? Contrast has been attributed to distinctions between, and/or variations of, the following.

1. *Light and dark.* Advertisements with heavy black headlines in large areas of white are examples. They are likely attention-getters, even if the content does not produce continued attending.

2. *Colors.* Colors vary not only in hue but also in intensity, speaking their own psychological language to the attender of the message. Color contrast also can serve to produce attending. Color adds to the mental image of the product, especially products such as foods and textiles. For fabrics, carpeting, and automobiles, color is an important part of the design. Color pictures of food are appetizing, one reason why food manufacturers often choose magazines for their advertising.

3. *Size.* Recognition scores were recorded for half-page and full-page advertisements. Seven issues of three weekly magazines were used. Subjects were selected from ten widely separated urban areas. Results indicated some evidence for the superiority of full-page advertisements to half-page advertisements relative to smaller advertisements placed near them. But evidence on the influence of absolute size shows very little effect within a practical range of sizes (Lucas, 1942, p. 247). See table 10-1.

Although the key to using size to its greatest advantage *is* in the use of contrast, this does not always mean use of the largest possible space. Lucient

Table 10-1
Readership and Size of Advertisements

Magazine	Percent of magazine readers seeing average advertisement	
	Full page	*Half page*
A	31.5	17.0
B	25.6	13.8
C	28.3	16.8

Source: Lucas, *The Controlled Recognition Method for Checking Magazine Readership* (New York: Crowell-Collier, 1942), p. 247.

Picard's Swiss wristwatch illustration was about one-sixteenth of a dark and somber page, with copy a miniscule one-quarter-inch high. Because this small-sized object appeared amidst large advertisements, it was attended to by more readers than otherwise.

4. *Sound level.* In considering contrast of sound, it is assumed that the sound is comfortably audible to start with; beyond this level, the principle of contrast may be applied. In a quiet atmosphere, a loud sound will achieve increased attending; but in the midst of a noisy atmosphere, a sudden quiet will be noticed.

An experiment was conducted to determine the effects of periodic variations in an instructional film's normal loudness level on the learning level of students. The results suggested that more learning resulted from loudness levels above and below normal than from a normal level (Moakley, 1968, p. 4).

In other auditory experiments, subjects have been tested to determine if prior knowledge of frequency, loudness, and so on of the test sounds affected ability to listen and answer accurately. Human performance was raised to within 3 decibels of that predicted for an ideal observer when the subjects had prior knowledge. Moreover, complete uncertainty of the test sounds lowered performance to about 12 to 15 decibels below the ideal observer (Moray, 1969, p. 41).

5. *Movement.* Movement is a form of contrast in two ways. First, movement can be contrasted with a static environment. Human beings are sensitive to anything that moves in their field of vision (Morgan, 1956, p. 164). The human eye involuntarily is attracted to movement in much the same way as the moth is attracted to a flame. A display window that employs some type of animated figures will produce attending. Similarly, a neon sign flashing on a billboard provides a contrast to the static background. As an individual's eyes are attracted to the billboard, he is beginning to attend to the message.

The second type of movement that produces contrast is one that violates basic expectations of regular rhythm or smooth progression. The Salem commercial that pictured a meek-looking girl strolling in the country changed pace when the girl suddenly faced the camera and began to sing in a deep, sexy voice. The sudden movement, combined with the change from the regular rhythm of the commercial, increased attending because of a contrast to basic expectations.

6. *Realistic expectations.* A message that creates a contrast to expectations in real-life situations, even if it seems to fit smoothly into the environment through movement and sound level, also will increase attending. However, it may be at second glance. A white dove flying through the housewife's kitchen window on a television commercial or a Mr. Clean appearing in a woman's home to help her solve her housecleaning problems are examples.

7. *Message clutter.* Most messages are frequently surrounded by competing messages that produce "message clutter." Multiple commercials in end-to-end time slots, combined with announcements about forthcoming programs, plus credits at the end of shows, as well as public-service announcements, have led to viewer complaints about clutter.

Marketing Examples of Contrast

The Volkswagen "Think Small" advertisements were excellent examples of contrast. A stark white background was contrasted with a small black photograph of a Volkswagen. It also carried a contrast to the audience's expectations in the headline, so different from the typical "Think Big" cliché.

An example of movement as a form of contrast to the environment are billboard signs that change messages or characters as the viewer changes his point of vision. If the viewer is in a car and moving, this message change will happen more rapidly, as a contrast to a static environment.

Moving point-of-purchase displays in supermarkets, such as mobiles, are a noticeable contrast with most of the shelf stock displays in the store; thus the novelty of motion can stimulate attending to a product.

Package shape may be used to create contrast. Pepperidge Farms packages its herb stuffing in a bag, whereas other brands appear in a box. The product may be viewed through the see-through cellophane. It also has a much different tactile sensation than the boxes. L'eggs pantyhose packages are egg-shaped, displayed in multilevel circular trays. They contrast with the rest of the store's angular displays and packages through their unorthodox shape, thus calling for increased consumer attending.

Contrast in Type

II.A2.1 *Audience members will more likely notice and find more appealing typography that contains contrasting elements as well as unifying elements, than typography that contains contrasting elements exclusively or unifying elements exclusively.*

Size, weight, letter structure, form, color, texture, and direction of type affect what is perceived. In terms of size, areas occupied by the contrasting elements can be made approximately equal. For example, a single large letter might be followed by a word or words that have about the same general weight as a unit of large type (Dair, 1967, p. 55).

Balanced weight can be achieved through the thickness of lines of a composition or the relation between the printed and the white areas of paper. If the printed area is smaller than the paper through it or around it, the type is considered light. But if the area of ink fills the total area it occupies, the type is considered heavy (Dair, 1967, p. 59). If the weight of lines forming the letters are the same, there is structural similarity. Concord of form results from use of the same typeface, whereas contrast deals with different type families.

Colored areas and black-and-white areas should never be in perfect balance, although colored elements should be massed together. Small areas of warm colors carry substantial impact, whereas the area of cold colors must be larger than the black-and-white areas.

Texture involves the interplay of letter structure and weight, into either a "hard" or "soft" effect. Horizontal movement can be emphasized by heavy leading; and vertical direction can be emphasized by narrow columns of copy. Whereas the design characteristics of a letter determine form, the repetition of individual letters may determine texture. For example, Bank Script is a heavy, slanted stroke that creates a pattern of diagonals throughout the line of type; thus a line can give directional value.

Marketing Examples of Contrast in Type

On the cover of the May 1973 *Better Homes and Gardens,* both unifying and contrasting elements of typography were used. *Better Homes* was presented in larger, more bold letters than *and Gardens*, although the typeface was the same. On the left-hand side of the cover was a list of that month's articles. The main topic was presented in all capitals and in a different color than a short explanation of each, in lower-case printing. But the contrast was unified by making the letters of the main topics the same; and likewise, the explanations were of the same typeface. Further unification was achieved by using the same color in printing in both the magazine name and the listing of main topics.

In a print advertisement, Gorham Sterling employed the principle of contrast. The headline was in a bolder and different typeface than the body, yet it was unified by the use of lower-case letters. At the bottom of the advertisement was *unmistakably Gorham*, with the letters not filled in and in lower case. Next to this larger type were smaller, dark, all-capital print, completing the final sales message: *ORIGINALS IN STERLING, CHINA, CRYSTAL.*

Material Design

II.A2.2 *Audience members will more likely attend to materials that are based on good design characteristics—balance, proportion, sequence, unity, and emphasis—than those of poor design, with the exception that if the materials are very badly designed, then attending will occur.*

From some basic elements of design (Nelson, 1973, p. 103), five principles can be derived.

    1. *Balance.* Formal balance results when every item that goes on one side of an advertisement is repeated in size or shape on the other side. Formal balance is used especially where dignity is the keynote; but such equilibrium may become boring to the eyes because there is nothing unexpected about it. Informal balance creates more excitement. Action is developed through the liveliness of art or photography, the copy, and the headline.

    2. *Proportion.* This principle refers to the relationship of sizes: the depth and width of the advertisement, sizes of elements or areas of the advertisement, the distribution of white space, or the amount of color or dark area compared to noncolor or light area.

    3. *Sequence.* The layout should get the reader to attend to the starting point and lead him through the advertisement in the desired sequence. *Sequence* refers to the correct order in which elements should be "taken in." The eyes move naturally from large to small elements, dark to lighter areas, color to noncolor areas, or unusual shapes to usual shapes. A repeat of shapes and sizes can help the eye recognize related items and move easily. Lines, arrows, or the position of the body may guide eye movements. The line gaze of a person in the illustration is also effective.

    4. *Unit.* This refers to the appearance of relatedness in a layout. Unity can be achieved by elements that are the same basic shape, size, texture, color, or mood. Borders or white space can also unify a layout. A vertical or horizontal base can be created from which all elements of the layout flare out.

    5. *Emphasis.* This can be gained through contrast, a sudden change in direction, size, shape, color, tone, line or texture.

    Although specific elements of a design may be analyzed to produce the best effect, it must be remembered that all elements of the layout (illustration, text, typeface, signature, color) work together to create a total impression. The consumer does not analyze each part of the layout but receives a feeling or image of the whole.

Marketing Examples of Material Design

Good design qualities are not only relevant to television and print advertising but should be taken into consideration throughout all aspects of the marketing mix.

Principles of design are used in merchandise display. And movement is important in a display of related items. One store, using the theme "intimate dining," tied "at-home fashions" together with table settings of fine china, and even made available menu suggestions based on exotic and gourmet foods.

Continuity and unity can be achieved through decor, uniforms worn by salespeople, similar ways of displaying merchandise, and so on. The principle of movement is especially evident during Christmas. Signs or red arrows on floors direct the shopper to the toy or holiday decorations sections.

Balance is also significant. For example, in a department store, the small items—accessories, stationery, and cosmetics—are all located on the same floor level. As a woman shopper proceeds upward in the store, she will find clothing items, and then furniture and appliances. Large or small related items are merchandised together.

Design in Typography

II.A2.3 *Audience members find that certain typefaces facilitate legibility more than others.*

Paterson and Tinker (1932, pp. 605-613) conducted a study of 210 college students, who rated legibility of type. The results are shown in table 10-2 (Tinker, 1963, p. 490; see also Tinker, 1944).

In further studies it was found that print which was judged as pleasing was closely related to judgments of legibility. The typefaces from table 10-2 were used, and visibility measurements were compared with perceptibility data, speed-of-reading data, and readers' judgments. It was found that judged legibility

Table 10-2
Ten Typefaces Ranked According to Reader Opinions of Relative Legibility

Typeface	Average rank	Rank order
Cheltenham	2.3	1
Antique	2.4	2
Bodoni	4.2	3
Old Style	4.6	4
Garamond	5.4	5
American Typewriter	5.5	6
Scotch Roman	6.2	7
Caslon Old Style	6.4	8
Kabel Light	8.2	9
Cloister Black	9.8	10

of typefaces is based upon visibility or perceptibility of the type but has only a slight correlation to speed-of-reading scores. The most pleasing typefaces were judged to be the most legible.

Marketing Examples of Design in Typography

a. *Audience members find that the use of italics retards reading more than normal print, and they prefer normal print over italics.*

Tinker (1955) compared the speed of reading of italics with that of lower-case letters. Ninety-six subjects read each kind of print for three successive 10-minute periods. It was found that italics retarded the speed of reading by 15.5 words per minute.

In an earlier study, Paterson and Tinker (1940, pp. xix-209) found that readers do not like italics: 96 percent of 224 adult subjects judged that lower-case letters could be read more easily and faster than italics.

b. *Audience members find that boldface type does not increase their speed of reading over normal weight type, even though it can be perceived at greater distances.*

Luckiesh and Moss (1940) employed four observers to judge type weight. Memphis type was used: light, medium, bold, and extra bold. Results showed that in terms of visibility and readability, there was an optimum degree of boldness. Boldness showed positive effects as it increased until medium weight was used. Speed of reading, therefore, was not related to boldness of the typeface.

c. *Audience members feel that the use of mixed type is not as legible as type that is uniform in style; but at the same time, they enjoy variation of typefaces.*

College students (Tinker and Paterson, 1946, pp. 631-637) read medley and lower case forms of type and gave opinions of legibility. Speed-of-reading and reader-preference techniques were used. It was found that the medley combinations were read more slowly and judged the least legible. However, in terms of pleasing quality, audience members enjoyed a moderate degree of variation, even though they judged it less legible.

d. *Audience members believe that leading (spacing between lines) facilitates the reading of a message more than if all type of the first line is printed in the same weight.*

Data from Paterson and Tinker (1932, pp. 388-397) suggest that readers believe leading is advantageous for ease and speed of reading. Two hundred and twenty-four readers were asked to rank samples of 10-point type set solid and in 1-, 2-, and 4-point leading in order of legibility. Leading helped make the type appear more legible. In further studies, Paterson and Tinker (1940, pp. xix-209) found that these results hold true only for smaller type. For larger type, it seems that leading should be used solely for esthetic reasons.

e. *Audience members are more likely to prefer double-column printing to single-column printing.*

In the same study (Paterson and Tinker, 1940, pp. xix-209), 241 students were given samples of both single-column and multiple-column printing. Each subject was asked to indicate a preference, and 60.5 percent preferred double-column over single-column printing.

f. *Audience members find that the use of indentation at the beginning of paragraphs will more likely improve the legibility of type than if the paragraphs are not indented.*

Paterson and Tinker (1940, pp. xix-209) tested 180 subjects using the speed-of-reading technique. Printed matter both with and without paragraph indentations was used. It was shown that indenting paragraphs improved the ease and speed of reading.

g. *Audience members find that certain colors of print background can affect print legibility more than others.*

Black print on tinted paper produces no loss in legibility. Stanton and Burtt (1935) employed the speed-of-reading technique using black print on white paper and on ivory paper. No significant differences were found. However, Luckiesh (1923, pp. 246-251) has shown that colored print on colored paper does affect legibility and listed (from best to worst) the order of legibility of 13 combinations of print and background, as follows: black on yellow, green on white, red on white, blue on white, white on blue, black on white, yellow on black, white on red, white on green, white on black, red on yellow, green on red, and red on green.

In an earlier experiment, Griffing and Frang (1896) tested exposure time in relation to colored print and paper. It was found that exposure time necessary for perceiving of printed words was longer for yellow and red paper than for white.

h. *Audience members find that certain positions of type facilitate legibility more than others.*

The closer the type runs to display elements and the greater irregularity of contour, the more reading effort is required. Designs of line or color in and around the area of printed text can serve as counter attractions. They can interfere with reading by drawing attention to themselves and away from the message.

When determining the kinds of typography to be employed, it is important that the choice be within the context of prior tradition, that is, the association and experience of the reader. It is never to be forgotten that the main function of type is to be read. For example, ragged lines give a haphazard impression. "Studies show that experienced readers do not read one line at a time, but two, and sometimes three. Ragged composition makes this kind of reading difficult and thus slows down speed of absorption" (Gottschall, 1964, p. 135).

i. *Audience members do not have great preferences for word spacing, letter spacing, spacing between lines, and spacing between paragraphs as long as the spacing is within the normal range of usage.*

Word spacing, letter spacing, spacing between lines, and spacing between paragraphs is normally left up to the discretion of the typographer. There is no evidence that minute variations within the normal range of spacing affect legibility or speed of reading.

j. *Audience members find lower-case printing more legible than printing in all capitals.*

A great deal of data over the years has indicated that lower-case letters have greater legibility than all capitals (Sanford, 1888). Lower-case letters have more of a contrast than do capital letters between ascenders and descenders. As a result, more characteristic word forms develop that are easier to recognize.

k. *Audience members will more likely attend to a message if the typography facilitates the reading of the message and complements its ideas than if the typography is used only as an attention-getting device, competing with the message content.*

The main function of typography is to put ideas "into the mind" of the reader without making him conscious of the typeface. The type should have three characteristics: (1) It should be legible; that is, it should seem that it can be easily and rapidly read. (2) It should be inviting and attractive to look at. (3) It should be appropriate to the product, layout, or subject of advertising.

Glasker noted the influences that should be taken into consideration when selecting type: (1) the nature of the product advertised, (2) the type of buyer addressed, (3) the benefit promised, (4) the nature of the illustrations, (5) the size of the advertisement, (6) the amount of copy, and (7) the medium (Glasker,

1963, p. 36). The purpose of the particular type form is important. For example, in print advertisements, the goal of display heads is to get people to attend, whereas the goal of the running text is to encourage and facilitate reading.

Type can, by its form, emphasize the quality of the meaning; or the word can, in appearance, approximate its sounds. Some examples are given in figure 10-1.

In another study, the possible relationship between typographic design and the message was investigated. Both university students and a control group of experts (art directors, printers, layout and typographic directors) participated. A series of typographic designs were suggested to solve a typographic representation of the same message. The series included: (1) symmetric layout and Roman type, (2) symmetric layout and sans serif type, (3) asymmetric layout and san serif type, and (4) asymmetric layout and Roman type. The six themes included: (1) invitation card to an art exhibit; (2) invitation to a wedding; (3) advertisement for perfume, intended for a magazine; (4) title page for a book on modern architecture; (5) title page for a book of lyrical verse; and (6) advertisement for an oil stove, intended for a magazine.

The subjects were asked to rank the four typographic solutions in each series according to their "congeniality" value. Results indicated familiar patterns—that is, the subjects chose the traditional style for wedding invitations but the asymmetric style for the architecture book. "The outcome to some extent is the result of learning or habit, and ... it is fashion that governs our attitude toward a particular mode of expression" (Zachrisson, 1965, pp. 156-162).

Additional Marketing Examples of Design in Typography

One manufacturer of women's shoes arranged his copy in a print advertisement in the shape of a side view of a shoe. The arrangement was clever, but the copy was hard to read due to irregular lines and spacing. Readers became so frustrated that they seldom finished reading the copy block. A more effective copy presentation would have been the normal arrangement of block, two- or three-column printing.

The correct use of copy is also important in packaging. The laundry detergent Bold uses simply heavy, bold letters in the printing of the brand name on the box. The typography complements the concept of a powerful detergent as well as exemplifying the name itself. The typography "works" with the message content. However, this same type of lettering would be incongruent with a perfume product. The message content here would be femininity, sex, love, and so on; and the bold letters would add perhaps a brash, cheap look. Flowing script might better represent this selling idea.

In terms of packaging, typography has to create a mood or put across an

Source: Nelson, *The Design of Advertising* (Dubuque, Iowa: William C. Brown, 1973), p. 121. Reprinted with permission.

Figure 10-1. Examples of Different Typefaces that Emphasize the Quality or Meaning of the Words Used.

impression, such as cleanliness, quality, or speed. Glade air freshener combines bold lettering with simplicity, which is coordinated with the overall design of the can.

Intensity

II.A3 *An intense message will be more likely attended to by audience members than a message that lacks intensity, that is, lacks strength and emphasis.*

In a series of tests, one investigator used four light sources of varying intensities and sizes to determine what comprised visual intensity. The idea was to determine which light source appeared the most intense. In one part of the test, pairs of lights were shown alternatively from the same source with single lights. In the second part, two lights were shown from different sources. They were of the same intensity but of differing size. People judged the two lights in part 1 as more intense on the average in 85 percent of the trials; in part 2, the one larger light was chosen as brighter in 85 percent of the trials. It was concluded that more intense stimuli would be attended more rapidly than less intense stimuli; but further, it was noted that size may be regarded as an equivalent to intensity because it is the quantity of light falling on the retina that apparently determines perceived intensity (Berlyne, 1960, p. 38).

A similar relationship of message to its environment appears to apply as well to hearing. It has been proposed that the apparent duration of a brief interval is influenced by the intensity of the stimuli that delimit it.

The more intense the stimuli are, the shorter the interval seems to be. . . . A reverse effect occurs, however, if the interval is defined by a continuous stimulus and the subject is asked to compare two equal intervals made up of stimuli of unequal intensity. The interval with the more intense sound seems to last longer than the interval with the less intense sound. [Cohen, as quoted in Bogart, 1967, p. 118.]

Marketing Examples of Intensity

Visual realism with exceptional clarity applies here, for example, a partially chilled glass with 7-Up, emphasizing the cool, refreshing aspects of the product.

The many bright lights on a movie theater marquee represent an intensity example. The great intensity caused by all these lights illuminating the theater message help to produce attending of passersby to the message.

Preconceptions of the Media

II.A4 *An audience member's preconceived ideas of the purpose, friendliness, timeliness, and credibility of the medium will more likely affect the degree of his positive or negative attending to its message than if he has no preconceived beliefs concerning the medium.*

A housewife may read *Newsweek* by leafing through it quickly, picking out key phrases and major reports that will give her a brief but sufficient idea of what is going on around the world. She may feel that she should keep up with the news; but having dispensed with this "duty" reading, she might then spend an hour or more reading *Vogue,* savoring every page of fashion and cosmetic news. An advertisement in *Vogue* may be more likely to attract her attending than one in *Newsweek.*

Media purpose affects broadcast media also. The radio is most frequently listened to as a supplementary activity. Only occasionally does a person purposely plan to spend time listening to the radio alone. He usually is listening for several specific things—music, news, special programs, or reports, not the commercials.

Marketing Examples of Preconceptions of the Media

Messages appearing on prime-time television or before, during, or after special cultural events result in more attending than do messages presented at 11:30 P.M. Preconceived ideas of purpose, friendliness, and credibility also apply to the types of retail establishments that carry a product. A housewife, for example, may tend to discredit the advice on fashions given by discount store personnel but attend carefully to the same advertising by a popular woman's specialty shop.

The consumer may also have preconceptions about the amount of personnel selling in a store. If it is difficult to find a salesperson, or if the salespeople are too "pushy," the consumer thinks less highly of the store than if the salespeople are attentive and helpful without being constantly on the customer's back.

Message and Media Distractions

II.A4.1 *An audience member who is highly attentive to the medium will more likely decrease his attending to the message than if he pays little attention to the medium.*

Sometimes the fact that advertisements are very obviously trying to sell a product detracts audience-attending from the message. In one experiment, subjects were shown three advertisements—a specific advertisement for watches that showed just the product, an automobile advertisement that showed the product in a certain setting, and an airline advertisement that showed a picturesque village in Europe. The airline advertisement elicited the most desire for the product of the three, with the automobile advertisement second in demand. The audience members could add personal thoughts to the unstructured message of the airline company advertisement, and they did not confine their attending to the product only (Krugman, 1968, pp. 247-248).

As a general rule, attending to the medium aids attending to the message because one leads to the next. However, in some cases the medium itself becomes a distractor. For example, it is not easy to view an entire page of most newspapers at one time; thus trying to glance through a newspaper may become a physically demanding task.

Marketing Examples of Message and Media Distractions

While a scantily clad woman may gain attending from a male audience at a convention booth, chances are that some of her speech on the merits of the industrial equipment upon which she is seated would be lost because of the distraction of her presence. A technical expert in a business suit can better explain such merchandise and gain attending for the product's message.

In certain kinds of modern retail stores, the customer may find himself distracted from the products by the decor of the store. Unfinished wood, animal skins, Indian prints, and a variety of other decorative items may "overpower" a customer's attending to basically simple but useful products.

Position in Print Media

II.A4.2 *No superiority has been definitely established for position in the print media. The value of a specific position depends upon the amount of audience traffic flowing past it.*

Covers, both inside and outside, are sufficiently preferred by magazine advertisers that they will pay more for them than for other pages. Although there has been much discussion of this matter, no position priority has been definitely established. It might be assumed, however, that for some magazines of general interest, advertising in the first part of the issue is attended to more often because of incomplete reading. Despite this possible exception, some media experts have offered this capsulization: "There is no magic superiority about certain page positions in magazines. . . . The value of a specific position to an advertiser depends upon the amount of reader traffic flowing past it" (Brown, Lessler, and Weilbacher, 1957, p. 217).

"The Continuing Study of Newspaper Reading" (sponsored by the Bureau of Advertising of the American Newspaper Publishers Association and the Advertising Research Foundation) does not indicate any position superiority for newspapers. "With the exception of these special newspaper sections with a specific and predictable appeal, the newspapers' power in attracting readers and generating traffic seems to extend generally throughout each issue" (Brown, Lessler, and Weilbacher, 1957, p. 217).

Position in Broadcast Media

II.A4.3 *Vast audience differences occur between different positions—times and adjacent programs—in broadcast media because the sizes of the audiences vary greatly according to the position, as do the demographics of the audience and the cost of the position.*

In broadcast media, position can be controlled. The advertiser can select the position that is the most suitable position for his message within a medium. However, the choice may not be optimal because of the competition for key positions. Moreover, consider the advertiser's lack of control over the program, which may distract or enhance the attending value of his message.

Marketing Examples of Position in Broadcast Media

If an advertisement is conveyed by a member of a program's cast, attending may be increased, for the audience already is attending to that person. For example, Tonight Show's cohost Ed McMahon presented Budweiser commercials and host Johnny Carson advertised his clothes, as well as other companies' products, on his show.

Saturday morning cartoon shows are sponsored by children-oriented products, such as cereals, toys, games, and candy. And daytime serials are sponsored by such woman-oriented products as soaps, perfumes, lotions, and hair coloring.

Length of Message and Attending Span

II.A5 *An audience member's attending decreases as the length of the message increases, other factors, such as interest, being equal.*

In studies of visual perceiving, attending span has been tested by recording the number of times an individual responds to an infrequently presented signal, such as a beep or light flash, within the context of the message. The results of these studies have shown that the rate of response decreases with increased length of the message. For example, a clock test was designed to measure the length of time observers would attend to a pointer advancing around a clock in successive small jumps. Very infrequently the clock would make a double jump, and each person was asked to notice and signal the double jumps. After a half hour, the observers began to miss these jumps more and more often, indicating that their attending wavered (Mackworth, 1963).

What this means in terms of advertising messages is that the longer the message, the greater is the chance that the individual will respond less actively to each message point and the more likely diversions of attending may occur.

Consider also some of the factors in controlling attending span. The favorability of the message environment—favorable extrinsic stimulus conditions and similarity with past experiences, such as with highly valued objects—tends to increase the degree of attending span (Deese, 1955, p. 359).

Although degree of attending span is partly out of the communicator's control, he can either lose or retain attending throughout the time his message is being presented by the way he structures it. In cases in which the message is structured with a few message points widely spaced with either music, other audio or visual activity, or no activity in between, the communicator's task is to assure the individual's attending throughout. The more adequately he can relate one point of his message to another, the better chance he has of retaining the viewer's attending over time. A print advertisement should have a logical pattern of arrangement to facilitate easy attending.

Personal selling has an advantage over simple advertising in increasing attending span because a salesperson can gain attending through personality and can alter techniques to the responses of the audience member with whom he or she is personally dealing. Audience members usually do not like to be discourteous and will not immediately reject the salesperson's message if it is not appealing to them, as they might with an advertisement (Brink and Kelly, 1963, p. 104).

Marketing Examples of Length of Message and Attending Span

Free food samples in a supermarket get a person to participate in the communicative process while munching—attending to the product and the promotion on display.

The intensity of an actual product demonstration can help because it involves real-life action. For example, a demonstration for vacuum cleaners can show the amount of suction, the lightness of the machine, how it can slip easily under furniture, and the uses of each attachment.

Print Message Length

II.A5.1 *Audience members are more likely to attend to a message if sentences are short, to the point, and do not have difficult meanings than if the sentences are long and ambiguous.*

Running text can give dignity to a printed message and lend a rational appearance that can be reassuring to the reader. Plain language and concrete terms are best. Complicated sentences and unusual meanings result in less reader attending.

A good deal of research dealing with attending has been based on the legibility of print. Tinker pointed out that "shapes of letters must be discriminated, characteristic word forms perceived, and continuous text read accurately, rapidly, easily, and with understanding." Legibility deals with those factors which foster the ease and speed of reading (Tinker, 1963, p. 36).

Marketing Examples of Print Message Length

Champion International, in a three-quarter page advertisement, used fairly long sentences in the text. For example, ". . . in the management foresight behind the significant acquisition of the Montana timberlands which enhances the company's potential for long-term growth. This purchase will go a long way toward making us less vulnerable to rising timber prices, and to take full advantage of it, we're building the largest plywood plant in North America right there."

However, Bacardi Rum used shorter sentences that did not lose the reader in its attempt to understand the message: "Here's a basic home tool kit. It's designed especially for do-it-yourself jobs on your taste buds.

"What you see is all you need. A bottle of Bacardi light rum and orange juice for the Screwdriver. Or grapefruit juice for the Monkey Wrench.

". . . So get to work and enjoy yourself."

Number of Thought Units

II.A5.2 *Audience members can remember headlines better if there are few thought units in the headlines than if there are many.*

There is some indication that this refers not just to the number of words in headlines but to the number of thought units as well (Paterson and Tinker, 1940, p. 4). Rudolph (1947, pp. 41-51) found that there is some tendency for headline reading to diminish as the number of words increases. He pointed out that this is not disastrous, since headlines of more than 12 words are read by 80 percent of the people who see advertisements. There is also some evidence that breaking headlines into decks of several lines also depresses readership, although the difference between 2 lines and 4 lines is negligible. Moreover, headline location below the picture is superior to the top of the picture in terms of being noticed.

Marketing Examples of Number of Thought Units

A print advertisement for Py-Co-Pay toothbrushes used the headline "Dentists Want to Save Teeth, Not Pull Them," thus utilizing one related thought unit. This is to the point and memorable.

A similar example is an advertisement for the self-cleaning Whirlpool oven and range. Instead of citing specifics in the headline, such as the advantages of recessed top, removable reflector bowls, and signal lights, the main selling idea is capitalized into one thought unit, "Whirlpool believes a good range should do your dirty work." However, for Pampers diapers, three unrelated thought units were used in a headline: "A newborn spends so little time in his mother's arms. And so much time in diapers. So 1,694 hospitals use Pampers." A great many readers found this headline confusing.

Duration

II.A6 *If a message is presented over a long period of time, it will more likely be attended to than if each aspect of the message is presented all at once.*

It is logical to assume that random encounters increase in rate as time exposure increases. Readership and viewer surveys abundantly support the fact that the number of readers/viewers increases with the number of issues/broadcasts used for advertising delivery. Increases are largely attributable to a "snowball" effect, which was originally a function of message duration, either for the single message or for the repetition of the message at different times and places.

Based on the findings of Zajonc, continued exposure to an advertisement may enhance one's attending to it—a hypothesis based upon word frequencies, stating that words standing for desired reality are more frequently used than words with negative connotations. Nonsense words or unfamiliar words are given more favorable meanings with the passage of time (Zajonc, 1968, pp. 3-13).

Marketing Examples of Duration

When a department store is having a special sale on an item such as sheets, signs throughout the store remind customers of the sale. As they enter the store, shoppers are handed cards with information about the sale; and special notices may be on luncheon tables.

Fuller Brush began its promotions by offering a free gift to each household visited, with the hope of getting into the household to sell Fuller brushes. This small gift is now part of their image, with customers attending to the Fuller Brush man as a man with a gift.

Postdecisional Barriers

II.A7 *When audience members attend to one part of a message, they are more likely to decrease their attending or completely screen out other parts of a message than if they attend to the message as a whole; that is, postdecisional barriers are created.*

Postdecisional barriers can serve either as an advantage or a disadvantage to the communicator. As the message continues in time, the mental barriers are progressively removed, although the basic "mental set" is established at the time the message is first attended. Again, depending upon the way the communicator structures his message, he can control what parts of his message are most readily attended.

Marketing Examples of Postdecisional Barriers

The postdecisional-barrier proposition is properly employed by campaigns that stress one particular product feature in each print advertisement or commercial. Thus an audience member has an opportunity to grasp that one message, and later can relate many features of the coherent campaign to a complete product image. Similarly, for maximum attending, product package and labeling should coincide with the product image.

When automobile manufacturers introduce their new lines, frequently they will do so during one television program. However, each model is advertised in a separate, focused commercial that is separate from the others in time; thus each model is attended to at that time.

11 Variables within the Audience

Background

Regardless of the amount of research and effort that a communicator goes through to get the best message in the most appropriate medium or media, variables within the audience may preclude efficient attending and communication. The following propositions should help to explain why variables within the audience often affect the attending to messages when all message and medium variables seem to be working in the communicator's favor. First, we shall consider external variables, and later, internal variables.

External Variables

Principles concerning external variables deal with circumstances surrounding the audience members that will affect their attending to messages. These variables are external to the audience, factors the audience cannot control; and they also are observable factors. Since a communicator cannot be around all members of his target audience at the time they are exposed to his message, he cannot design his message to accommodate each and every factor. However, he should be aware of these variables and how they affect attending to his messages.

Physical Condition

II.B1 *A message that ordinarily would be attended when an audience member is well rested or relaxed is likely to be passed by when he is physically or mentally fatigued.*

The fatigue element reduces an audience member's ability to attend unless the level of intensity of the message is increased considerably. Fatigue or physical condition also seems to have an overriding effect on the entire process, dampening to some extent the resultant effect of any stimulus or audience variable.

Marketing Examples of Physical Condition

Grocery shopping can be tiring in itself even if one is not fatigued upon entering the store. Crowding, waiting in line, and controlling children all are factors that can contribute to an unpleasant experience and make the consumer less receptive to a message. As a result, progressive stores are brightly decorated to convey a cheery atmosphere, displays are artistically created, and food is presented esthetically. Some stores even have indoor-outdoor carpeting, fresh flowers in vases, and music. To get away from the humdrum atmosphere of a large store, specialty shops are are now appearing with the larger grocery store—delicatessens, special cheese shops, wine shops, and imported food shops. The monotony of going from aisle to aisle is somewhat alleviated by varying the decor, making it appear you are within *another* store at times. The consumer may even experience an old English atmosphere or a Continental one.

The fatigue that may come with shopping is important for point-of-purchase promotion. A large display at the end of an aisle will be more unexpected and noticed. Brightly colored signs to convey a happy experience with the product will alleviate fatigue. The particular design of the package is also helpful.

Special Physical Conditions

II.B1.1 *Poor physical conditions of audience members may reduce their attending capacity; but if these specific physical conditions are related to the subject of the message, the audience's attending capacity will increase.*

Audience members attend to messages that discuss possible solutions to their particular problems, while they may ignore all other messages. For example, members of an audience may be concerned about being overweight and may attend to almost every commercial, billboard, or print layout that has to do with weight reduction to which they are exposed. A young audience member may seek out and attend to messages about products to help his complexion problems, while an elderly individual may attend to messages that tell how he can relieve his arthritis.

Marketing Examples of Special Physical Conditions

If a woman is concerned about complexion or beauty problems, she may not actually be striving for a solution, but she is certainly susceptible to personal selling. Cosmetic demonstrations are good examples. Problems are pointed out, and then the products that can solve these problems are presented. When selling cosmetics, an effective salesperson will run down the list of items the customer might need or want, identifying the problem as well.

Another product developed to meet the physical problems of some consumers is queen size panty hose. Stockings that go by height and weight as opposed to others that fit a variety of body types and as a result never fit correctly are another example.

Chronological Setting

II.B2 *An audience member may increase his attending to messages at certain times of the day, certain days of the week, particular seasons, or certain times within the nation, region, or community.*

Marketing communicators have to be aware of heavy seasonal advertising that may attract attending away from their products. A commercial for a breakfast food, for example, might go unnoticed amidst several commercials for new and exciting Christmas toys.

Marketing Examples of Chronological Setting

Around Christmas time food manufacturers use special promotions to illustrate how their products can be adapted to the holidays. Nut manufacturers offer recipes that show how the product can be used in cookies, cakes, salads, and for snacks for guests.

   Packaging is even adapted to the holidays. L'eggs panty hose, which come in a white, egg-shape package, appear in December in shiny red, green, or gold eggs that can be used for Christmas tree ornaments. Reynolds Wrap also promotes its foil as a material to wrap food gifts or to make ornaments.

Distraction of Environmental Setting

II.B3 *An audience member will more likely attend to a message if he has few distractions in his environment than if his attending is divided.*

An individual will be more likely to attend to a television set if he is sitting in his living room alone than if the room is crowded, noisy, and filled with distractions. Although many distractions are impossible either to measure or to control, the marketer is wise to consider the variety of ways in which the audience may be even minimally distracted by the environment. Messages and media can then be designed to avoid environmental situations of great distraction. Additional discussion of distraction is included in chapters 11 and 26.

Marketing Examples of Distraction of Environmental Setting

An employee of a firm that deals in certain products will be more attentive to displays about equipment his company may need when he is at a trade show or convention than when he is at some other type of program. Thus sales talks, brochures, and displays at the trade program will have a high attending value in that particular environment.

A unique packaging design may be used not only to overcome such distractions as children or crowding but also the distractions of competing products. Once again L'eggs panty hose is a good example—hosiery packaged in an egg instead of a flat package stands out. The package form also calls for a special type of display that also stands out among others.

Internal Variables

The mental state of audience members at the time a message is presented is affected by several immediate, internal variables. These may relate to more than one message or situation and are individual characteristics that are fairly constant over time and have considerable effects upon individuals' ways of attending to messages.

Expectancy

II.B4 *Past experience often determines what is attended to and can prevent attending to messages that are not expected or to which members of the audience are not accustomed.*

Attending is largely controlled by an individual's expectations of probable occurrences. The individual is able to project the past into the future to ready himself for various types of perceiving, and to guide his search behavior, because his expectancies provide him a fairly reliable and valid "map" of a vast number of perceptual possibilities. Thus objective information acts as a cue-triggering device.

An experimental indication of the effect of expectancy on attending has been reported. Two groups of observers—American and Mexican—were asked to view pairs of photographs. One photograph in each pair was an American scene, the other a Mexican scene. When the pairs were presented simultaneously, one to each eye, the Americans tended to see only the American scene, while the Mexicans tended to see only the Mexican scene. This suggests that expectancy, based on habituation and familiarity, made the individuals more ready to attend to the more familiar scene (Vernon, 1960, p. 176).

Another experiment on expectancy was designed to test the manner in which an artifically designed frame of reference would affect the results of attending. The experiment involved informing two different groups of subjects of types of words to look for in a series of 10 words. One group was told to look for words relating to animals or birds, and the other groups was told to look for words relating to transportation. This was to prestructure artifically the interests or expectancies of the individuals in the groups. The actual presentation involved projecting the words tachistoscopically (that is, in a flash box), and exposing each item one-tenth of a second. The purpose was to see if the two groups would perceive the words selectively in accordance with the designed interest pattern. The words used were: horse, baggage, chack, sael, wharl, monkey, passport, berth, dack, and pengion.

The results showed that the groups perceived words that fitted their own interest on the order of five to six times more. For example, the fourth word was perceived to be *sail* by the group told to find words related to transportation and as *seal* by the group told to find words relating to animals. The apparent prestructuring of the interest areas and past experience with the words relating to these areas seemed to encourage attending to information that fit the area of interest and past experiences more than to unfamiliar areas of information (Siipola, 1935).

Marketing Examples of Expectancy

An audience member who leafs through a trade catalogue is expected to find certain promotional messages and will attend to those messages because his past experiences prepare promotional messages and will attend to those messages because his experiences prepare him to find them. Similarly, a product packaged differently may deter attending if the consumer does not expect that particular form of packaging.

Some soft-drink manufacturers introduced soft-drink flavors in plastic bags. This package concept not only was unexpected by the consumer but made the product difficult to recognize—the package was so different from any previous associations of what soft-drink packages look like. Historically, consumers have expected an upright bottle, molded in such a way that it can be grasped and fit comfortably in the hand. Even though the product was displayed in the soft-drink section of supermarkets, it was not recognized immediately as a soft drink.

Attempts to Reduce Dissonance

II.B5 *Attending is selective; and when cognitive dissonance arises, an audience member seeks to reduce dissonance by referring to past actions.*

Dissonance is a measure of contradictory relations among cognitive activities—involving an individual's beliefs and attitudes about the environment and his relationship to it. *Cognitive dissonance,* then, is an antecedent condition in which a person's beliefs and attitudes are in conflict with some other element, such as anticipated behavior or past actions.

Experiments with the effects of a decision to buy a car on attending to automobile advertising were carried out by certain investigators. They found that new car-owners read the advertisements of the make they selected more often than they read other car advertisements. This selective tendency was less marked in car owners who had owned their cars for longer periods of time. The experimenters attributed this tendency to the need for information that supports the purchase decision, that is, to reduce postpurchase cognitive dissonance (Ehrlich, Guttman, Schonbach, and Mills, 1957). A fuller discussion of dissonance can be found in chapter 32 which deals with motivating and persuading.

Marketing Examples of Attempts to Reduce Dissonance

Manufacturers introducing spray hair-grooming products for men encountered a problem of dissonance when dealing with its audience. First was the problem of changing the attitude that men do not use hair grooming products because they are "sissy." Second was the problem of a spray form that was too similar to a woman's hair spray. Third was the belief that men do not "fuss around" with their appearance, that is, that spending a lot of time on appearance of one's hair is only for women. To reduce dissonance, masculine-looking, athletic-type young men were used to demonstrate the product.

A woman's sportswear department, in a department store that stocked merchandise appealing to several age groups, redecorated with psychedelic signs and rock music in the background. Although the same brands of clothing were stocked as before, women 25 years old and older were not attracted to the department because they felt the clothes were perhaps too young for them or that the brands previously featured were no longer located there. Attitudes were not changed—the message was ignored.

Processing Inflow of Information

II.B6 *The higher the priority that an audience member places upon processing inflow of information, the less processing will be available for his outputs.*

Selective attending by audience members to a message involves not only the control of inflow of information but also the distribution of processing of inputs, outputs, transformations, and calculations. Thus selective attending is not only selective because of competition among input-attending stimuli but also because of other phases of the entire stimuli-responses behavior system. A study of the interactions between input and output involves the "ability of a human being to act as a random generator" (Baddeley, 1966, pp. 119-130).

In one experiment, subjects were asked to speak letters of the alphabet at random at a rate paced by a metronome. It was found that redundancy increased as the rate of generation was increased. This same task was then studied when interacted with a secondary distracting task—namely, card sorting. "The effect of adding the secondary task was that the redundancy of the generated sequence increased with the logarithm of the size of the ensemble which the subject was generating" (Moray, 1969, p. 108). The experimenter found also that in the card-sorting tasks, almost no mistakes were made. However, it was later found that when individuals were asked to type while listening for a spoken number they were to add to a consonant, their addition often was in error, although their typing was accurate (Moray, 1969, p. 109). These two studies can be explained if it is assumed that the "information processing capacity of the system is common to both the input and the output aspects of the tasks" (Moray, 1969, p. 109).

Marketing Examples of Processing Flow of Information

The preceding principle on processing inflow of information can be applied to packaging design. Not only must packages appear attractive, of convenient size, and so on in comparison with other packages of similar products, they must also appear to the consumer as easily opened, reusable or conveniently disposable, not easily broken, etc.

This means that at the same time that the consumer is deciding *which* product to buy, he also is calculating whether *any* of the particular products is or can be transformed into something to suit his wants. Here the initial input consists of the different products; and the response is the chosen product, which then becomes the second input. The final response is consequently affected by the initial response as well as by the stimuli.

If an individual thinks he should not buy a particular automobile because he feels it has too "sporty" or "flashy" an image, he might be overlooking some of its superior advantages, such as ease of handling, low cost, or good mileage; that is, his attending to the advertised image of the car can hinder his attending to the actual characteristics of the car that might have stimulated him toward a purchase in the first place.

Relevance and Interest Value

II.B7 *At the time of exposure, the more interested an audience member is in the subject of a message, the more relevant the message becomes and the more attending it receives than if the message content were not relevant or interesting.*

Relevant stimuli are chosen; that is, certain magazines are chosen from a magazine rack and certain food advertisements are read in a newspaper. *Irrelevant* stimuli are those not sought out, as illustrated by newspaper advertisements a reader does not intend to find or read.

Interest in a promotional message does not necessarily have to spring from a strong "drive," however. Casual curiosity or simple search for escape from somewhat monotonous surroundings also can initiate attending if an individual previously had been involved with the subject of the message in some way.

Yet if an individual does have a specific interest in mind when he is exposed to a medium, then messages unrelated to that interest probably will not be attended by him. Various tests have been conducted that attempt to relate the interest value of certain words to the manner in which they are perceived. For example, Dember described a group of experiments based on the hypothesis that an individual in a certain value area, as measured by the Allport-Vernon value questionnaire, will be most sensitive to words in the value areas closest to his own. The threshold of identification when the more familiar words were presented were shown to be *lower* than for less familiar words—a priest identified the word *sacred* more readily than the word *income*; with a businessman, the results were the reverse (Dember, 1960, p. 306).

These experiments were based on an original study by other investigators in which the Allport-Vernon study of values was used to test the relation among recognition, motivation, and interests (Postman, Bruner, and McGinnies, 1948). Although the experimental findings are not free from controversy, it is clear that some relation between the interest patterns of the individual and his perceptual tendencies does exist. Most marketers understand the importance of studying the interests of their consumers as related and unrelated to the product. The marketer's aim must continue to be to appeal to consumers' felt needs and wants.

Marketing Examples of Relevance and Interest Value

Relevance and interest value should be taken into consideration when a promotional campaign is planned. Coca-Cola's campaign of a nostalgic tray as a premium and two free 48-ounce bottles of Coke held high relevance in several respects: trend of nostalgic interest, popularity of old Coca-Cola relics, a useful premium, a good deal (two large bottles of Coke *free*), and high interest in thirst-quenching beverages. On a hot summer afternoon a thirsty consumer will be very interested in an advertisement for a certain cold beer. However, should this same person view the same commercial on a cold winter afternoon, he probably will be less interested in it.

Personal selling is a delicate process for the salesperson, in which he or she has to determine the main interests of the customer. A woman may be more interested in the styling of a dress than in who makes it or the kinds of materials from which it is made. Such information may be ignored if presented, and the customer may become indecisive if the elements that have high interest value for her are not reinforced. Product attributes most important to the audience members should be emphasized, for then the product is obviously "for them."

Ease of Categorization

II.B8 *A message that is highly relevant and familiar to an audience member is more easily categorized than one that is irrelevant and unfamiliar.*

An individual's education, cultural background, and immediate interests, as well as his physical and psychological condition at the time of the message, help to determine the ease with which the individual can categorize a new message.

The importance of expectations and interests in determining the amount of attending to a message was discussed earlier. In the case of a totally unfamiliar, new message, however, the ease with which an individual can categorize that message according to his past experiences determines the degree and style of attending that the message receives.

Although educational and cultural experiences leading to the development of a person's interest categories or lifestyle are relatively easy to understand, an illustration may help to explain the role of "immediate interests" or thought patterns. Certain investigators showed blurred pictures to people who had been deprived of food for varying numbers of hours. When asked to report the associations these blurred pictures called forth, those without food for six hours mentioned food more often than those who had been without food for an hour-and-a-half or for three hours (Levine, Chein, and Murphy, 1942). This study is an example of many studies of psychological deprivation. Although laboratory studies are not situationally comparable to a marketing environment, implications about physical and psychological need states and how they influence categorization of stimuli are applicable in a broad sense.

The subject of categorizing also is discussed in chapter 14.

Marketing Examples of Ease of Categorization

If a new product form is developed, it is necessary to identify the product and associate it with the original form. Otherwise, problems in cue categorization arise. Instant mashed potatoes in a box will be more easily categorized if the package features a picture of the final product and if *mashed potatoes* is emphasized on the box.

Another example is the "slice and bake" cookies. When a consumer thinks of cookies, she or he thinks either of homemade or boxed cookies. At the grocery she or he either buys ingredients to make cookies or goes to the aisle where packaged boxed cookies are displayed. The Pillsbury "slice and bake" cookie product exists in an untypical cookie form and is located not with other cookie products but in the dairy case, disrupting previous ways of categorizing cookies.

Sex Differences

II.B9 *The sex of audience members influences the orientation of their attending to certain messages.*

The masculine attending style differs from the feminine attending style because of dominant traits of each sex. Masculine psychological traits tend to emphasize tough-minded, nonintuitive, assertive, and independent features. Feminine psychological traits in general tend to consist more of emotional, intuitive, and imaginative factors. It might be said that most females appear to exhibit greater sensitivity than most males to social stimuli (Maccoby, 1966). In addition, in a sense an "inner woman" lives in every man. "She" is the creative feminine component of his own being, to which he must become consciously and responsibly related if he would become whole. Moreover, in every woman there lives an "inner man," an embodiment of her own masculine traits.

Marketing Examples of Sex Differences

From a psychological standpoint, an audience member whose orientation is more feminine than masculine would be more likely to attend to a romantic radio monologue about vacation spots than would a more masculine-oriented individual, who might attend to the adventuresomeness of a vacation.

When a woman purchases a dress, her decision initially may be based upon her feelings of "just liking it." The purchase may even be impulsive. But to support and justify her position, she will think of practical reasons why the dress is a good purchase; it may be made to last a long time, styled for wear on many different occasions, and so on.

In the area of cosmetic packaging there are many shapes and varieties in women's products. The shape of a product is an important part of its image. The shapes of perfume bottles, nail polish bottles, lipstick, and mascara are quite feminine. Masculine grooming products do not differentiate themselves as much as women's products in the area of packaging, but they do tend to be more "chunky" and square.

Social Role Differences

II.B10 *The social role of an individual audience member has a significant bearing on the manner in which he will attend to certain information.*

Role is also influenced by opinion leaders and reference groups. Opinion leaders serve as a source of the values an audience member assimilates. Reference groups serve as standards of comparison relative to which the audience member evaluates himself and others. Thus "a person identifying himself with a reference individual seeks to 'approximate the behavior and values of that individual in his several roles' " (Deutsch and Krauss, 1965, p. 194).

Since an individual usually avoids dissonance in his relationships with others, and within himself, it can be assumed that he will attend to messages in harmony with his role and tend to avoid messages that contradict or threaten his position. For example, an adult male might enjoy cartoon shows; but he may not be willing to admit this to his friends because his role dictates that he be serious minded and too mature for such "childish" entertainment.

Marketing Examples of Social Role Differences

Role not only plays a part in the *price* of merchandise purchased but also in the *kind* of products purchased. A career woman would more likely be attracted to "dinner in a box" than would a homemaker. A couple with a high income might purchase imported wines, imported cheeses, and products to be used in gourmet dishes, such as mushrooms, capons, and fresh garlic. A couple with a low income would not even think of having a fine wine for dinner every night but would tend to purchase such products as potatoes and pot roasts.

Where the product is purchased also has a bearing on role. A General Electric hair dryer may be found in a large discount drug store; but because of his status, a high-income individual is more likely to buy it in a department store at a higher price. Similarly, a consumer may attend to an overpriced product because he feels that his role as an executive demands it. In contrast, a less-wealthy consumer who works with others of the same class would attend to the lower-priced product because, even if he could afford it, the higher priced product would contradict his other role behavior.

Pleasant Messages

II.B11 *The more interested an audience member is in pleasant messages, the more likely he will be to ignore and avoid unpleasant messages.*

Zajonc has related correlational evidence, as well as some experimental results, that supports the idea that a perceptual preference exists for pleasant stimuli in words, pictures, and designs. Although the evidence is not conclusive, it is sound for a marketer to heed the general trend of the findings (Zajonc, 1968).

The best way to determine what is pleasant and unpleasant in a message is to reflect on the probable personality characteristics of the audience members. Although this is more difficult for some audiences than for others, at least some estimates can be made of the characteristics of the audience. However, it would be impossible to "pin down" the lifestyles and desires for novelty, pleasure, and relevance within the mind of every audience member; but it would not be impossible to analyze the situation in which the majority of the audience members will be seeing or hearing the message, for example, at home in the evening after work, during the working day, and so on. From this the communicator can attempt to determine the desires and activities of the target audience.

Marketing Examples of Pleasant Messages

Offering consumers samples of a product at point of purchase is an example of a pleasant message. It is a pleasurable experience to consumers to be able to try a product at no cost; and it increases the chances that they will attend to the messages concerning the product.

The "personality" of retail stores may be either pleasurable or unpleasurable. Light, bright colors, airy appearances, and atmospheres of friendliness are pleasurable. Store size may also be pleasurable, or vice versa; some people find large discount stores pleasurable, while others prefer smaller, more personalized stores.

Enjoyment of Novelty

II.B12 *If a member of an audience has personality characteristics that incline him to novelty, or if he has no particular message-type preference at the time of exposing, then novel stimuli, although at the outset irrelevant, may become relevant or pleasant or both.*

Through experimental work, psychologists have attempted to determine whether novel stimuli are effective. Do novel stimuli imply threat and therefore elicit avoidance reactions? Or do novel stimuli lead to desire and curiosity and therefore to an approach reaction. The following quotation will help to explain this problem:

While the bulk of the results . . . supports the hypothesis that repeated exposure is a sufficient condition of attitude enhancement, there are findings and theoretical formulations which appear to be in conflict with the hypothesis. The most pronounced source of ostensibly contradictory results is in the area of exploration and curiosity. There is impressive evidence today that in a free situation the subject (human or animal) will turn toward a novel stimulus in preference to a familiar one. . . .

On the contrary, it is more likely that orienting toward a novel stimulus in preference to a familiar one may indicate that it is less liked rather than it is better liked. Ordinarily, when confronted with a novel stimulus the animal's orienting response enables it to discover if the novel stimulus constitutes a source of danger. It need not explore familiar stimuli in this respect. Novelty is thus commonly associated with uncertainty and with conflict—states that are more likely to produce negative than positive effect. Most recent work indicates quite clearly that exploration and favorable attitudes are in face negatively related. . . .

The balance of the experimental results . . . is in favor of the hypothesis that mere repeated exposure of an individual to a stimulus object enhances his attitude toward it. [Zajonc, 1968, pp. 21-23.]

Other data indicate that "People with a high need for novelty will both explore novel stimuli and like them more intensely than people with a low amount of need. . . ." Direct measures of orientation toward novelty and preference were obtained from the same subjects; and those with the strongest orientation toward novelty (by composing novel stories and devising novel uses for common objects) also described themselves as preferring novel to familiar stimuli (Maddi, 1968, p. 29). Thus novelty may be useful if used to make the message become relevant; but it may be detrimental if carried to an extreme.

Marketing Examples of Enjoyment of Novelty

When packaged cake mixes first were introduced on the market, they were a novel product. Yet after the novelty wore off, the product became a bit of a threat in that the cake practically made itself. With repeated exposure, however, a more positive image was created.

Copy blocks that are shaped like objects or people may be novel, but the difficulty in reading the "choppy" lines may annoy the audience such that the message is never completely read.

"I can't believe I ate the *whole* thing" was a novelty commercial for Alka-Seltzer that became a household phrase.

A Sanforized fabric advertisement that showed an elephant in a pair of Sanforized trousers was an interesting use of the novelty concept. The situation was novel and resulted in attending, as well as represented a favorable aspect of the product—its strength.

12 An Overview of Attending

Implications

The foregoing principles discuss variables that affect the probabilities of attending; and the next part of this book deals with perceiving. It should become evident that significant relationships exist between the variables that affect attending and those which affect perceiving. As with the earlier discussion of exposing, both the attending and the perceiving parts are divided into sections on message and medium variables and variables within the audience.

Model of Attending

Hopefully, the overlapping usage involved in this format will help in the understanding of the overall communication model. The part of the model dealing with attending may now be examined and compared with the one on exposing, before the perceiving part of the communicating process is examined. See figure 12-1.

The attending model is, of course, a subsection of the total communicating model, and other factors than those represented in this model enter into the possibility of exposing, which determines what percentage of the desired audience will reach the attending stage. The factors shown in this model interact to determine whether an individual does or does not attend to a certain message.

Preconceived variables affect the attending aspect of communicating, as they affect exposing and all steps of the process. They include such variables as the audience members' needs and wants, their sociocultural status, their mental set, their personality variables, and other internal and external variables of the communicating environment that cannot be controlled by the communicator.

All the message and medium variables interact in determining the attending value of any message. The complexity, contrast, design, or intensity of the message may either add to or subtract from its attending value. The audience members' preconceptions of the media determine the value they will place upon the messages therein. The distractions of the message and media and the position of the message in print or broadcast media also help to determine the likelihood of that message's gaining more attending than competing messages. The length of the message and attending span, number of thought units, duration, and postdecisional barriers also can be controlled by the communicator as he plans and designs his message.

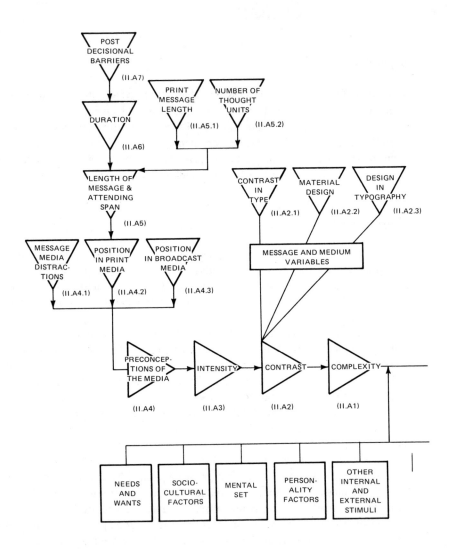

Figure 12-1. The Attending Stage of the Psychological Model of Communicating.

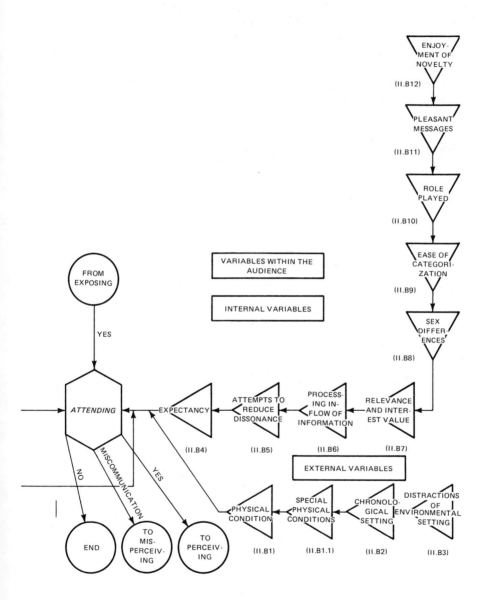

The audience variables help to determine attending in two ways. The external variables include the audience's physical condition, special physical conditions, and factors of the chronological and environmental settings at the time of possible attending. By contrast, the internal variables of the audience members play an equally important role in determining the extent of the attending are expectancy, dissonance, processing inflow information, relevance and interest value, ease of categorization, sex differences, social role differences, pleasant messages, and enjoyment of novelty. As a group, these factors have effects on one another.

If all these factors are considered by a marketer, he will increase the probability that the members of his target audience will attend to his message.

**Part V:
Perceiving**

13 Message and Medium Variables

Background

Once the communicator has assured exposing and attending for his message, his problem becomes one of measuring or determining the kind of interpretation his audience will give to his message. He will want to know if his message is being received in the manner he would most prefer. He will try to control the *perceiving* of his message.

Although the way the audience members perceive a message may not be totally controllable, identifiable, and understandable, parts of the perceiving process can be used to create messages that will be accurately and fully perceived. The relationship between the deliverer of a message and the audience begins after exposing and attending have occurred. The process of communicating has been successful to the point at which the audience members are ready to perceive the message; that is, they are ready to be captured mentally by the communicator.

Perceiving may be defined as a "process of information extraction" (Forgus, 1966, p. 1) "by which people select, organize, and interpret sensory stimulation into a meaningful and coherent picture of the world" (Berelson and Steiner, 1964, p. 88). Perceiving is the process of filtering physical sensations into meaningful thoughts or concepts through the audience members' experiences; it relies heavily on past experience. An individual categorizes new stimuli in terms of his expectations, prejudices, and beliefs. If an appropriate category is not available for a new experience, an old one may be used until a new category is developed.

Parts of the process of perceiving are also a part of the process of attending. Basically, however, attending involves the receiving by the neural and muscular system of certain objects or messages in the process of selecting and deals primarily with the first stages of an elementary classification process in perceiving called *primitive categorization*. Perceiving, however, clearly includes the entire process of attaching meaning of some kind to the object or message. Perceiving always begins if attending has been gained, but the *desired* perceiving may or may not be taking place. The important thing for the communicator to think about is whether or not he is creating a message that will be perceived as he *intends* and will last so that later it can be recognized and recalled.

When an object or message gains attending, the process of perceiving begins. But even with the selecting of one object or one message, the audience member still perceives and uses only a portion of the typical stimulus in constructing an organized meaning, while other stimuli are either completely ignored or play a very minor role. This is the process of *selective perceiving*. Selective perceiving implies that a receiver will accept what he wants to perceive, and this depends on his past experiences and beliefs as well as his present situation or state of mind.

A good example of selective perceiving can be illustrated by observing the different reports newspapers gave, some years ago, of an incident between a famous actor and a young woman on the stage of a New York theater. The following are descriptions of the manner in which the young woman struck the actor (these are eye-witness accounts):

World: Slashed him viciously across the cheek with her gloves.
News: Struck him on the left cheek with a bouquet.
American: Dropped her flowers and slapped him in the face with her gloves.
Times: Slapped his face vigorously with her glove three times.
Herald Tribune: Beat him on the face and head . . . a half dozen blows.
Mirror: Struck him a single time.

Clearly, the variance in the descriptions shows how various interpretations of the same incident can occur through selective perceiving.

Further, the perceiving of a message is often fragmented, and parts of the message fail to take on meaning for the audience member. Without meaning, no permanent impression of the message or message part is likely to be formed, nor will the message be remembered or motivate the audience member to act. An example of this is the television viewer watching a commercial. Any part of the message may go "in one ear and out the other," even if the message has gained his undivided attending. This will occur if, for one of many reasons, he does not attach any meaning to that part of the message.

That a perceiver may consciously or unconsciously see only some of the stimuli present in a message is important. The communicator must try to ensure that those stimuli which are the most important parts of the message are selectively and correctly perceived. In considering this, the communicator must particularly analyze some different forces: the physical stimulus itself; a person's ability to discern it in detail; and the interpretation he puts on it because of his attitudes, values, and interests.

Even sensing itself is a learned skill—an ability to discriminate among similar but slightly different stimuli. A brewmaster can taste differences among individual batches of beer, whereas few beerdrinkers can distinguish among brands in a "blind" test—even their own favorite brand. Usually a beerdrinker has not *learned* how to discriminate among beers.

Upbringing and lifestyle also affect how stimulus discrimination is learned.

Consider the classic experiment of Bruner and Goodman (1947). Working with a group of "rich" and "poor" 10-year-olds, they found that the poor children saw the coins as physically larger than did the rich children. Presumably the greater value of the coins to the poor children influenced their perceptual mechanism, and they amplified the sizes.

Sensory information is also given a specific interpretation based on the context in which it is viewed. The items we choose to perceive are those which are important to our inner needs and wants at the time. We interpret them in relation to the social role we are playing at that moment, and according to the expectations that past experience and the stimuli bring to mind. Personal moods also direct our degree of attending, interests, and interpretations. A young married couple may avidly read furniture and home advertisements but never really note around-the-world travel commercials (of little meaning to them). Based on their learning and past experiences, they perceive furniture and a home as being possessions that will satisfy their *current* needs and wants best.

In fact, as Gestalt psychology has shown, we do not always perceive the individual stimulus at all, but rather the item presented in relation to its surroundings, as we interpret the meaning of those surroundings in terms of past experiences. Thus perceiving is a dynamic process in which associations, meanings, and relations are constantly being built upon, altered, or even dropped; and the process varies from individual to individual.

Looking at it from another (more practical) point of view, the whole area of advertising is a type of communicating (composing a message, someone sending it, it being sent by a particular method, and its reception by someone); thus various aspects of the selective perceiving process mentioned so far can and will come into play and are very applicable in the creation of promotional ideas in marketing. With regard to advertising, the most important point to be made regarding the selective perceiving principle is: no matter how creative or imaginative an advertising campaign is, or how well it is thought of in advertising circles or at the management level, it is of no value if the audience does not perceive the message correctly.

One aspect of selective perceiving that seems contrary to the purpose of advertising has to do with audience members' beliefs and attitudes. Selective perceiving appears to suggest that persuading is an effective tool only when an audience member's mental attitude, based on past experience and the present situation, is compatible with the persuasive activity being used. This implies that persuading is a result of, and not the cause of, the audience's preset attitudes.

However, advertising is a highly persuasive activity in itself. If no audience would ever change its attitudes and beliefs after being contacted through an advertisement, advertising certainly would not be regarded as a persuasive technique for guiding consumer actions. Therefore, even if an audience member has a mental set, advertising still can influence his attitudes to the point of modifying or, more rarely, changing the attitudes of that mental set. An audience member's perceiving is influenced by the message and its context as well as by his personal characteristics. As in all aspects of the communicating process, the propositions dealing with perceiving can be divided into message and medium variables and variables within the audience.

Variables

A message consists of several parts. In printed communications, the illustration, layout, graphic style, and copy, as well as references to the product (or brand), firm, or organization all work together to create an impression the audience members perceive. Perceiving of the message also necessitates an integrating of the media as a total communicating system in perceiving.

The setting of a message can be any physical setting in which a message of any type is displayed. Because different environments can cause different specific topics or ideas to change in importance to an audience, physical surroundings must be taken into consideration. Audience members' presence in various environments can depend upon the time, the day, the week, the month, the season, or the year. Therefore, the variable of time must also be considered as an integral part of the message and media setting.

Related Events

III.A1 *A message is partially defined by the nature of the events to which it relates; the audience member can relate, to some extent, any given communication to current events and situations.*

Certain events can help the communicator to enhance his message. For example, in the year following the first moon landing, advertising for Tang, an orange-juice powder, emphasized the fact that the astronauts had used it during their trip to the moon. The nutritional value of Tang was emphasized by relating it to the astronauts and their need for nutrition on a demanding mission. Of course, this does not imply that *all* competing messages must be related to the moon landing (or an equally prominent event) to be satisfactorily perceived; actually, any really newsworthy event can be used.

Obvious errors in message structuring may occur as a result of the nature of inevitably related events. The most successful communicator will neither completely relate message to event nor completely ignore current events in structuring his messages. The desired combination is one that makes the audience aware that the message is important not only because of its relation to the event or situation at the time but also because of its general non-time-related value.

Marketing Examples of Related Events

It is the daily interaction between the communication and the consumer that is most important. If you have a salesperson selling an article in a sophisticated manner, and in such a way that she or he is building up a positive attitude in the consumer's mind toward herself or himself, it is possible to "transfer" these positive points to the product, the manufacturer, and the retail outlet. One small event in the promotional program can have a lasting effect.

If a manufacturer has a good package, in terms of design and functionality, but if the display technique in the retail outlet is "junky" and "jumbled," positive aspects of the package or product tend not to be perceived.

Physical Environment

III.A2 *The message itself is partly defined by the characteristics of the physical environment in which it is delivered. The audience's perceiving of the message may be sharpened, distorted, obscured, or completely impaired as a result of the physical environment or setting.*

The physical environment may be either a significantly good or significantly bad conductor of a message. A housewife, listening to the radio while her children are shouting in the background, is not as likely to attend or perceive a commercial message as she is if she were driving her car alone and listening to the radio or viewing a passing billboard.

Thus the physical environment can serve as a distractor. Parry (1968, p. 88) lists four types of distractors:

1. The competing stimulus
2. Environmental stress
3. Subjective stress
4. Ignorance of the medium

"Only the first—and just possibly the second—qualify as distractors in the generally accepted sense. The point that links the four in the present context is that all detract from good reception in an undiscriminating way" (Parry, 1968, p. 88). The "competing stimulus" is similar to the noise in artificial systems of communications. "Environmental stress" refers to the conditions for receiving communications, such as noise or temperature. "Subjective stress," or internal stress, includes such states as sensory deprivations, sleepiness, or boredom. "Ignorance of the medium" explains the stress encountered by the absence of a familiar medium.

Although an element such as the physical environment is beyond the limits of the communicator's control, it must be considered in association with the perception of any message. For even if attending has been obtained, certain physical events may cause the audience member to distort his perception of the message considerably. In this connection, see the discussion in chapter 26 regarding motivating and distraction.

Marketing Examples of Physical Environment

Physical environment is important in the area of package display. If a product is not placed in a position of prominent exposure, or if too many products are "cramped" into too small a space, the product (or products) receives less attention than if it (they) were displayed in a section at the end of the aisle or in a special display case "tied in" with the design of the package, signs, and other promotional material. Coca-Cola's display of 48-ounce "crowd pleasers" is a good example.

Also, the type of retail outlet also conveys something about the products displayed. A dress in Saks Fifth Avenue brings to mind expensive, quality, high-fashion, and style, whereas a dress in a mass-merchandise outlet is associated with average quality, mass production, and medium price.

Editorial Environment

III.A3 *The greater the similarity between the message's editorial environment and the message, the greater is the degree and accuracy of perceiving of the message by the audience.*

The *message environment* includes the editorial environment and can be defined as the physical characteristics of the communication medium. Specifically, the editorial environment includes the editorial content, layout, strategy, and so on of the message medium. Editorial environment helps to determine how the audience member will perceive the message. An editorial environment consistent with a message adds to the communication process, whereas inconsistent an editorial environment detracts from the message and hinders its communication. An editorial environment consistent with an audience member's beliefs and attitudes reinforces message perceiving. However, an editorial environment that contradicts or conflicts with the beliefs and attitudes of audience members discourages message perceiving.

Marketing Examples of Editorial Environment

A magazine's editorial approach helps to determine the kinds of people who read the magazine and thus are exposed to its advertisements. The editorial approach influences the reader's receptivity to the advertising. For instance, some magazines concentrate their editorial material in a specific section of the magazine, while others spread the editorial material throughout the issue.

Depending upon editorial strategy, some magazines may be passed along to a relatively large number of different readers. Other magazines are read by a given reader for a longer period of time. In the latter case, with fewer readers per magazine issue, the exposure of the issue's contents to each reader may be more thorough or frequent. For example, in a 1953 national magazine survey it was found that *The Saturday Evening Post* reached 14,050,000 readers per issue, whereas *Life* reached 26,450,000 readers per issue. However, the average time spent reading each magazine was 30 minutes greater for *The Saturday Evening Post*. Thus, although the *Post* had fewer readers per issue than *Life,* each of the *Post* readers was more thorough and spent more time reading the magazine than did each reader of *Life* (Crowell-Collier Company, 1953, p. 9).

In an extensive study involving a national probability sample of female readers aged 15 and over, 12 advertisements were studied. Two equivalent subsamples of female readers were selected for each magazine. Readers in one sample were exposed to a magazine issue containing 6 of the 12 test advertisements to control exposure. In the other sample, readers were exposed to a magazine issue containing the other 6 test advertisements. Readers in both samples were interviewed on their appreciation of all 12 test advertisement brands. The gains in perceiving resulting from one exposure to the advertisements in a particular magazine were established by differences in perceiving level between the exposed and unexposed samples (Politz Research, Inc., 1962, pp. 31-35).

Comparisons were made with different types of consumer magazines to see how they contribute to perceiving of the advertising message among women readers; the women readers of a specialized magazine for women were compared with women readers of a dual-audience weekly magazine. The women's magazine used in the study was *McCall's*, and *Look* and *Life* were the dual-audience weekly magazines. It was found that 28 percent gains in brand perceiving per 100 women exposed to an average advertisement in *McCall's* occurred as compared with 15 percent gains in brand perceiving per 100 women readers exposed to the same advertising in *Look* and *Life*. The advertisements tested were in product categories ranging from food to clothes to automobiles (Politz Research Inc., 1962, p. 23).

Congruity

III.A4 *The greater the congruity or consistency among message elements, the greater are the chances that the entire message will be perceived by the audience as the communicator desires.*

The *congruity* of a stimulus configuration refers to the degree to which stimulus elements appear to be consistent and "seem to fit together." The greater the congruity or consistency among stimulus elements, the greater are the chances that the configuration will be perceived in its entirety or as a whole. In this instance, the whole stimulus pattern is more significant than the sum of its parts.

In the process of perceiving, each configuration of stimuli is, in a sense, categorized by an individual, that is, placed in some category to which certain meanings are attached. "Glamorous female model accustomed to luxurious surroundings" may be one category; "middle-aged, average-looking housewife responsible for household tasks" may be another. "Fun-loving, sociable group of businessmen" and "tender, romantic moments together" are two more categories. The dominant meanings attached to these situations or characterizations are quite distinct and are frequently used in the creation of feelings of favorable motivation toward products or services.

Accordingly, *congruity* may be defined as the perceived impression of belongingness, unity, or harmony within a stimulus configuration that provides sufficient dominant meaning that the communicatee or perceiver can readily think of the stimulus configuration as being in some category of similar configurations.

When a marketing communication is presented, the question is—from the perceiver's standpoint—how do the various parts of the message seem to fit together? If a communicatee perceives incongruous elements within the message rather than a unified whole, it is not likely that the message will create a favorable impression. In other words, congruity is an impression—a mental image or reaction of the communicatee when he has been able to categorize and understand the relationships among the various elements of the message.

The best way to explain the importance of the principle of congruity and incongruity is to analyze the elements of congruity. Many of the ideas underlying the elements of congruity stem from the Gestalt "school" of psychology, focusing around the idea of a wholistic view. Gestalt psychology, arising from the work of Christian von Ehrenfels (1859-1932) and others, made an important contribution to the study of perceiving, with particular attention to *visual* perceiving. The idea most commonly attributed to the Gestalt thinkers is that the whole is greater—more meaningful—than the sum of its parts.

Wertheimer continued experimenting with dots and lines scattered over backgrounds to illustrate organizational factors in aggregation and segregation— "field forces" or "principles of organization" (Wertheimer, 1923). Dots are likely to be seen as falling into groups; and the question is, under what conditions is a group easily segregated from the mass? From Wertheimer's experimental model, Gestalt psychologists have formulated a series of form laws. The Gestalt laws that follow "play an important, if not exclusive, role in producing visual forms" (Katz, 1950, p. 24).

This summary of the "laws of organization," as explained by Wertheimer, follows from his essay entitled "Laws of Organization in Perceptual Forms." Wertheimer uses as illustrations a series of dot groupings in various arrangements.

Although all his illustrations will not be reproduced here, an attempt will be made to exemplify briefly the laws that follow from the original work of Wertheimer and others.

1. The *factor of proximity,* stated simply, is that, other things being equal in a total stimulus situation, those elements which are closest to each other spatially tend to form groups in the mind of the perceiver (Wertheimer, 1938, pp. 72-74). This law does have limits. Proximity is a relative term. One can, if the distances are not too great, see other groupings, but never more than one or two at the same time. The more units there are, the harder it is to see the distant ones as being together. If the distances become too great, then no unification will occur.

The law of proximity may be applied to auditory stimuli as well. Take, for example, a tapping noise. For example, if a person taps the top of a table in short bursts (.. .. .. ..)—the dots representing the taps and the distance between the dots representing time—the taps will be perceived as four sets of two taps instead of eight taps.

2. The *factor of similarity* states that if more than one kind of element is present, the elements that are physically similar tend to form groups. In general, similarity is stronger than proximity, as figure 13-1 illustrates.

In part A, the dark lines appear to form pairs. In part B, the dots and circles tend to form vertical columns. This results from proximity as well as similarity (Wertheimer, 1938, pp. 75-78; and Katz, 1950, pp. 24-25). In part C, the parts that are similar to each other and those which have common differences tend to fall into configurations. Similarity is stronger than proximity when the variables are in opposition. In part D, similarity holds the two types of symbols from yielding to proximal pairing, and the viewer would normally perceive the circles alone or the dots alone as members in a single figure (Vernon, 1954, p. 69). Thus

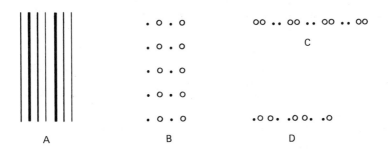

A   B   D

Source: Wertheimer, "Laws of Organization in Perceptual Forms," in W.D. Ellis, ed., *A Source Book of Gestalt Psychology* (New York: Harcourt, Brace and Company, 1938), pp. 95-98 and Katz, *Gestalt Psychology, Its Nature and Significance* (New York: Ronald Press, 1950), pp. 24-25.

Figure 13-1. The Factor of Similarity.

114

messages that are placed together in time or space tend to be perceived as a group, each one losing its individuality. The tendency toward grouping increases proportionally with the similarity of the message content.

3. The *factor of good contour or uniform destiny* states that parts of a figure that have a visual sequence or a common linear destiny tend to form units. Figure 13-2 will exemplify this factor: a row of dots is presented in four separate but identical groups of three.

Let us suppose following the presentation of this visual configuration, that,

then, without the subject's expecting it, but before his eyes, a sudden, slight shift upward is given, say, to d, e, f or to d, e, f and j, k, l together. This shift is 'prostructural,' since it involves an entire group of naturally related dots. A shift upward of, say, c, d, e or of c, d, e and i, j, k would be 'contra-structural' because the common fate (i.e., the shift) to which these dots are subjected does not conform with their natural groupings.

Shifts of the latter kind are far less 'smooth' than those of the former type. The former often call forth from the subject no more than bare recognition that a change has occurred; not so with the latter type. Here it is as if some particular 'opposition' to the change had been encountered. The result is confusing and discomforting. [Wertheimer, 1938, pp. 77-78.]

4. The *factor of objective set* deals with the impressions of the perceiver as a given configuration gradually changes. Consider the configuration in figure 13-3 for example. Suppose that, gradually, the distances between ab and cd, cd and ef, and so on are altered by moving b toward c, c toward d, d toward e, etc. Further, suppose that all five groups of two are shifted a slight bit, with the greatest shift occurring at gh/ij. As one moves down the row from a to j, the original grouping—that is, ab/cd—tends to maintain itself even beyond the middle of the group. Then an upset occurs and the opposite grouping becomes dominant. This means that the row is part of a sequence and the law of its

```
   • • •    • • •    • • •    • • •
   a b c    d e f    g h i    j k l
```

Source: Wertheimer, "Laws of Organization in Perceptual Forms," in W.D. Ellis, ed., *A Source Book of Gestalt Psychology* (New York: Harcourt, Brace and Company, 1938), pp. 95-98 and Katz, *Gestalt Psychology, Its Nature and Significance* (New York: Ronald Press, 1950), pp. 24-25.

Figure 13-2. The Factor of Uniform Destiny or Common Fate. (Wertheimer, 1938, p. 77)

```
   • •    • •    • •    • •    • •
   a b    c d    e f    g h    i j
```

Source: Wertheimer, "Laws of Organization in Perceptual Forms," in W.D. Ellis, ed., *A Source Book of Gestalt Psychology* (New York: Harcourt, Brace and Company, 1938), pp. 95-98 and Katz, *Gestalt Psychology, Its Nature and Significance* (New York: Ronald Press, 1950), pp. 24-25.

Figure 13-3. The Factor of Objective Set. (Wertheimer, 1938, p. 78)

arrangement is such that the constellation resulting from one form of sequence will be different from that given by some *other* sequence. Or, again, a certain objectively ambiguous arrangement will be perfectly definite and unequivocal when given as a part of a sequence (Wertheimer, 1938, pp. 79-80).

5. The *factor of direction* is one that shows how, given the right circumstances, proximity yields in importance to indicated direction. It is this law that prevents parts belonging to different objects from joining. It enables the perceiver to differentiate objects that are in visual contact with each other. For one extremely simple and another more complex illustration, see figure 13-4.

In part A the individual points in segment b are closer, proximally, to the individual points in segment a or c than the points of a and c are to one another. Nevertheless, the perceived configuration is a horizontal line and a vertical line. The same would hold true if b were moved to a 45° angle in either direction. The same would also hold true if the lines were curved rather than straight. In part B the factor of direction becomes particularly clear if the perceiver attempts to see the configuration as abefil and cdghkm rather than acegik and bdfhlm.

6. The *factor of closure* explains that, other conditions being equal, lines that enclose a surface tend to be seen as a unit (Katz, 1950, p. 25). In part A of figure 13-5, lines 1 and 2, 3 and 4, 5 and 6, and 7 and 8 combine to form pairs; but in part B, 2 and 3, 4 and 5, and 6 and 7 combine to form a figure (Katz, 1950, p. 26).

7. The *factor of the good curve or contour* states that parts of a figure that have a "good" curve or contour tend to be perceived as units. *Good* refers here to forms familiar to the observer. Part A of figure 13-6 provides an example of this principle in that the fragments of the diagonals between the upright lines tend to be seen as part of a continuous, partly concealed, transverse line. Observers of part B will normally perceive the figure as a circle and a trapezoid because these are familiar figures (Katz, 1950, pp. 26-27).

8. The *factor of past experience or habit* is best stated by Köhler:

We do not suppose such isolation to be the normal state of affairs. If in all of the examples given we accept direct experience at its face-value, our fundamental

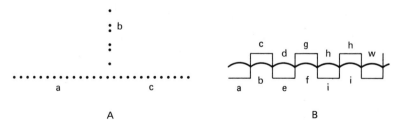

A   B

Source: Wertheimer, "Laws of Organization in Perceptual Forms," in W.D. Ellis, ed., *A Source Book of Gestalt Psychology* (New York: Harcourt, Brace and Company, 1938), pp. 95-98 and Katz, *Gestalt Psychology, Its Nature and Significance* (New York: Ronald Press, 1950), pp. 24-25.

Figure 13-4. The Factor of Direction. (Wertheimer, 1938, pp. 80-82)

116

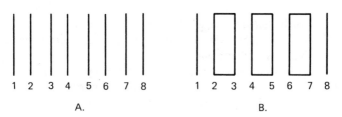

A.   B.

Source: Wertheimer, "Laws of Organization in Perceptual Forms," in W.D. Ellis, ed., *A Source Book of Gestalt Psychology* (New York: Harcourt, Brace and Company, 1938), pp. 95-98 and Katz, *Gestalt Psychology, Its Nature and Significance* (New York: Ronald Press, 1950), pp. 24-25.

Figure 13-5. The Factor of Closure. (Katz, 1950, pp. 25-26)

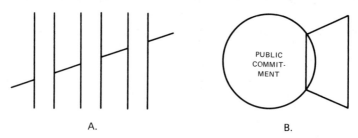

A.   B.

Source: Wertheimer, "Laws of Organization in Perceptual Forms," in W.D. Ellis, ed., *A Source Book of Gestalt Psychology* (New York: Harcourt, Brace and Company, 1938), pp. 95-98 and Katz, *Gestalt Psychology, Its Nature and Significance* (New York: Ronald Press, 1950), pp. 24-25.

Figure 13-6. The Factor of the Good Curve or Contour. (Katz, 1950, pp. 26-27)

assumption about the processes underlying experience and behavior must be opposite to the assumptions of both introspectionists and behaviorists; i.e., instead of reaching to local stimuli by local and mutually independent events, the organism reacts to an actual constellation of stimuli by a total process which, as a functional whole, is its response to the whole situation. [Köhler, 1947, p. 106.]

Experience plays an important role in perceiving—perhaps a more important role than the Gestaltists originally intended to imply. Any impressions of a novel visual configuration should be analyzed with due regard to the possible past experiences and associations of the perceiving.

Marketing Examples of Congruity

One Pall Mall cigarettes advertisement can be used to illustrate the congruity principle. The advertisement consisted of a green, wooded area, a young woman walking through the woods, and the headline, "Pall Mall Menthol 100's. Extra cool . . . extra mild." The illustration was relaxing and cool. It set the atmosphere for the advertisement; the green package for the cigarettes and the green background for the product, the traditional association of menthol and the color green. The copy mentioned the coolness and mildness of the cigarettes. The advertisement displayed blending of the message, copy, product, and art.

Congruity is an important aspect of package design. If a product is advertised as new, then the entire design, structure, and materials used in its package construction must convey this impression. The shape must be different from previous products, or perhaps a size variation. The pictorial or graphic representations also should communicate "new." Typography and the method of transmitting brand name and what the product is should meet the "new" requirements.

Incongruity

III.A4.1 *Incongruous elements in a message are more readily perceived than congruous elements.*

If the communicator chooses to convey a message that does not seem to fit into a pattern with surrounding elements, his message becomes incongruous. This means that stimulus elements that do not seem to fit the pattern tend to create feelings of tension in audience members. To reduce this tension, people will mentally interact with the message, attempting to perceive correctly the meaning of the incongruous elements; in this way only, perceiving and information are achieved. However, too much incongruity in a message can confuse the audience. If this is the case, the message parts may become fragmented, and the process of cue categorizing considerably slowed. This can weaken the effectiveness of the entire message.

One experimenter found that emotional pictures may be misinterpreted unless reinforced by appropriate headlines. The 11 emotional pictures used were taken from advertisements that labeled the emotion in the headline. The pictures were given to subjects separately, and then a list of the labels that matched the poses was supplied. Subjects succeeded in identifying only 5 of the illustrations correctly (Crider, 1936, pp. 748-752).

Deno, Johnson, and Jenkins tested 75 undergraduate students to determine the associative similarity between words and pictures. In free-association test, the responses given by the subjects to word and picture stimuli were compared to determine associative relations. Results showed that words and pictures intended to represent the same concept are often dissimilar (Deno, Johnson, and Jenkins, 1968).

Incongruity is effective if and when it results in attending, which in turn stimulates "curiosity" and thus increases the likelihood of speed and thoroughness in the perceptual process. But incongruity is not likely to be effective when the message has gained *attending* but the audience members are occupied primarily with "cute" and irrelevant parts of the message. While psychological incongruity may gain attending, only psychological congruity can direct the attending of the audience members. Incongruity can also reduce the chance that the message will be experienced as a whole.

Marketing Examples of Incongruity

A classic example of incongruity is the detergent commercial that features Brand X's virtues as being touted by a glamorous model. Her hands are flawless, her makeup impeccable, her dress chic. She smiles at the audience and begins placing a mountain of soiled underwear in a washer. To the audience she may evoke such comments as, "I'll bet she never washed a diaper in her life!" Clearly, congruity is not present in this commercial. As a stimulus configuration, some of the discrete elements lead to perceptions antithetical to, or at best, dissonant with, other elements.

Incongruity also can be seen in the area of public relations. If a retail store has a high reputation of quality, a customer naturally expects courteous responses in cases of returned merchandise, incorrect billing, etc. It is even expected that the phone will be answered in a friendly, concerned manner. Such inconsistencies, if they exist, will reflect negatively on the store image.

Incongruity also can be found in the area of distribution. A customer will expect to find a product in the *type* of store such products are normally found in, or in stores that his experience indicates "carry" such products. For example, a person goes to a reputable camera store to buy a Konica camera photography book because the store is supposed to handle all the needs of a photographer. However, if the customer is told to go to a book store, the incongruity may be unacceptable.

Grouping

III.A4.2 *If audience members perceive a set of stimuli in terms of spatial proximity, configural similarity, or logical continuity—or any combination of these—they will regard these elements as being more related than if the stimuli lacked these kinds of relationships.*

In an article about the psychological aspects of visual communications, Taylor gave a brief analysis of the relative importance of several of the Gestalt principles. He said that three principles—proximity, similarity, and one he called "common movement"—constitute a group of elements that can be called weak

Gestalts, because "although the elements form a group, each element still maintains an internal independence" (Taylor, 1960, p. 126).

Taylor mentioned other aspects of perceiving that he considered relevant. Among these are principles of contrast (that is, color, intensity, etc.), the principle of figure and ground, and the principle of depth perceiving.

Other psychologists have defined principles of perceiving in a manner complementary to these theories. For example, Gibson hypothesized that the manner in which individuals perceive the visual world can be divided into two problems that should be considered separately—the perceiving of the substantial or spatial world and the perceiving of the world of useful and significant things to which individuals ordinarily attend:

The first kind of perception is the "world of colors, textures, surfaces, edges, slopes, shapes, and interspaces." The second is the more familiar world with which we are usually concerned—a world of objects, places, people, signals, and written symbols. The latter shifts from time to time depending on what we are doing at the moment, whereas the former remains a more or less constant background for our experience, and a sort of support for maintaining posture and for moving about. [Gibson, 1950, p. 10.]

Marketing Examples of Grouping

Grouping is a concept that should be used in a well-organized, *total* promotion of a product. Packaging, selling, publicity, public relations, advertising, and sales promotion should all be integrated into a unified image of the product and the manufacturer behind it. Use of the trademark may be carried through each promotional phase, even down to the design of the corporate stationery. Continuity with the message is also an aspect of grouping. If a soap product is advertised as in a big, economical box, then the size of the actual box should convey such an impression on its own merits.

Retailing uses the concept of grouping in varied ways. The trend of "a store within a store" is popular in many department stores. Often imported goods are grouped together; or, as another example, Chinese items may be displayed in a separately designed area that fits the Oriental theme. Special summer recreational equipment will be specially featured in the spring; and in winter, cruise clothes are merchandised in a little area all its own—down-to-the-minute touches of decor. A store also can be integrated by decorative items, such as flower arrangements and repetitive color schemes. Similar items are arranged in spatial proximity, e.g., children's clothes or toys.

Humor

III.A4.3 *It is possible for incongruity in the form of humor to increase perceiving by audience members, as compared with other types of incongruity, or even congruity.*

This proposition is quite different from the previous propositions. Note especially that humor is not to be confused with laughter. In many social situations *laughter* occurs without any humor being connected with it. By contrast, however, *humor* consists of reactions to a perceived inconsistency if all of the following variables are present:

Astonishment
Unexpectedness
Suddenness
Feelings of superiority
Pleasant environmental situation
Appropriate cultural factors
Appropriate subcultural factors.

Humor is likely to be created when the stimulus patterns before the perceiver seem different from the way they seemed previously, or from the way they ought to be, as evaluated through past association. In a sense, humor is a playful use of incongruity. Further, humor involves astonishment coupled with inferred feelings of superiority—a combination usually producing mildly emotive reactions by the communicatee just after the moment at which he has "processed" the message.

In other words, humor is likely to be created by a combination of feelings of superiority about an item, plus the astonished perceiving of a contrast between congruity and incongruity. All of a sudden the stimulus patterns seem different from the way the perceiver thought they would be, or how the perceiver thought they ought to be.

Depending on cultural and individual factors of the individual, humor may or may not be perceived as humor. Note also that when the same type of humor is repeated, accordingly with little or no astonishment, rejection of the intended humor and of the intended message usually results.

Thus humor that is familiar can be a problem. A communication involving subject matter intended to be humorous that is either too familiar to the audience, offensive, or simply not astonishing will fall short of its goals.

A reaction to humor can be carried out through a sense of empathy with the object or thought involved at the time. Humor has value in focusing, suggesting, and reinforcing phases of perceiving because it can renew attending. It also has value to the message's effectiveness because any tension that might be aroused within the perceiver when confronted with a new message may be removed or relieved by including him in the humorous situation. Thus the tension is not carried over into the psychological process of perceiving and dealing with the actual message. The communicator must remember that each time humor is used, it is necessary to bring the audience back to the subject at hand.

Marketing Examples of Humor

The Alka-Seltzer commercials that featured a new bride, her unsuccessful cooking ventures, and her husband who was suffering from severe stomach upset is an example of the effective use of humor. The audience laughs at the bride's new dishes—an overweight dumpling, marshmallowed meatballs, poached oysters—and sympathizes with her husband who is in the bathroom drinking Alka-Seltzer. The advertisement keeps the main focus on the product, however, and reminds the audience at its conclusion, "What love doesn't conquer, Alka-Seltzer will."

Humor can be seen in package design and brand names. General Mills distributes a cereal called "Boo-Berries," a cereal with artificial blueberries and marshmallows in it. A ghost was featured for a sense of identification and image; and children found the ghost "cute" and the name novel and laughable.

Chun King, producer of canned oriental food, used the humor of the unexpected in the award-winning radio advertisement, "The 1966 Chun King." Here the announcer delivered what seemed to be a promotional message for an automobile, until one heard of "bucket bamboo shoots," "power onions," "independent vegetable suspension," and "high performance chicken." The unorthodoxy of the commercial caused special attending and perceiving of the product.

Equivocality

III.A5 *Equivocality is the degree to which a message lends itself to multiple interpretations by the audience members. The greater the equivocality of a message, the greater is the probability that members of an audience will rely upon past experience or expectations in interpreting and organizing their impressions of that message.*

Equivocality may be defined as the degree to which a message lends itself to multiple interpretations by audience members. This differs from ambiguity in that *ambiguity* signifies the lack in distinctness or certainty. In other words, something is equivocal if it can naturally be perceived in one way but is capable of being perceived in another way. Ambiguity, however, is obscure or doubtful. In certain contexts equivocality can imply being intentionally deceptive, but this is not the present case.

Equivocality is best exemplified within messages by analyzing those words and phrases, illustrations, sounds, and so on that can confuse the perceiver (incongruous elements). For instance, many words have several quite distinct dictionary definitions; a facial expression in a picture has a very broad interpretative value; an unidentified sound is equally conducive to multiple impressions (Postman, Bruner, and Mcginnies, 1948).

In a study by Alimaras, 38 female students of psychology at the State University of New York at Stony Brook were asked to write short descriptions of people they knew. One half wrote about a person they liked, the other half about someone they disliked. Then they were asked to rate the described individual using a rating list consisting of 20 bipolar adjective pairs. It was found that more attitudinal ambivalence occurred in situations of negative interpersonal relations than in those of positive interpersonal relations (Alimaras, 1967). In other words, a subject's ability to cope with equivocality was lessened in the negative situation. This also seems true in situations of fatigue, distractions in the environment, or in the case of semantic satiation.

Thus, equivocality may become a problem to the communicator who is trying to put across a message strongly related to but slightly different from a very common idea, situation, or visual configuration. This occurs because audience members most likely will perceive the more common, more usual, or more easily understandable interpretation of the message as a result of previous experience.

Marketing Examples of Equivocality

A promotional campaign illustrating this point was conducted by Sylvania. Advertisements featured a picture of a beautiful hi-fi set with the caption "It sounds a lot better than it looks." On first impression, the reader may become confused about what is being sold—a handsome hi-fi or a hi-fi that delivers top musical qualities. Both these qualities are normally associated with high fidelity sets, yet they are not usually juxtaposed in this manner. Readers accustomed to reading advertisements that emphasize beautiful-sounding music might have misunderstood the general thrust of the advertisement.

Multiple interpretations can occur in brand names, packaging, and advertising. There was a woman's beauty product on the market called "Down-to-Earth, Natural Mineral Mud Wash." The name connoted "dirty," not beauty or cleanliness, normally associated with beauty products; and the packaging was unfeminine and inconsistent with other beauty product packaging (consisting of a brown jar with a brown label and block, masculine typography). The advertising involved a picture of a man, shirt off, in a desert with a shovel and only a small picture of a girl in the copy block. Was this a man's product? The product and promotional campaign had much room for misinterpretation.

Misindexing and Bypassing

III.A5.1 *Equivocality may lead to more misindexing if the intended meaning of the message is not related to the experience of the audience members than if the message applies to an individual's frame of reference. Misindexing, in turn, leads to misperceiving and perhaps to failure of the audience to understand the communicator's message as intended.*

Indexing refers to the placing of new stimuli into mental categories the perceiver feels are appropriate. This is one of the cognitive processes an audience member undergoes in organizing a message. Conversely, misindexing is the improper placement of the new stimuli in categories.

Under certain conditions individuals may be more susceptible to faulty perceiving resulting from the equivocality of the message. The ability to cope accurately with equivocality may be lessened in cases of negative interpersonal situations (Alimaras, 1967), in cases of semantic satiation (Gorfein, 1967), or in cases of fatigue or distractions in the environment.

The practical outcome of misindexing is *bypassing*. When, as a result of equivocality, the message in question is misperceived, the communicator will, or should, soon realize that this may be occurring frequently among the members of his intended audience. It is then his responsibility to take appropriate measures to identify and alter the aspect of the communication that has caused the perceptual tendency to misperceive the configuration and/or the meaning of the message. In connection with misindexing and bypassing, consider also the discussion on leveling and sharpening in chapter 17.

Marketing Examples of Misindexing and Bypassing

In certain instances, bypassing can heighten the effect of a mass communication. A copywriter may use a word with little or no symbolic meaning to describe a product, hoping that the audience members will sharpen the positive meanings for the slogan. For example, the copy line of Schlitz beer, "gusto a real light beer," could mean lightness to beer drinkers who prefer a light brew and strength of flavor to those who like heavier beer.

Packaging and the brand name can lead to misperceiving of the kind of product. In the area of nail care, RRP is a protein-based liquid that is brushed onto the nails. The name itself does not have the glamor typical of most beauty products; it is too scientific and gives no indication of what the product is. More than likely, it sounds like a paint thinner or a type of oil for an automobile. The package is also scientific looking; it contains no elements of feminine beauty or glamor in the design.

14 Variables within the Audience: Cue Categorizing

Background

An audience's perceiving of a message will be influenced both by their physiological disposition and by their psychological disposition, which includes psychological needs and attitudes. These are variables within the audience.

Physiological needs are lowest in the hierarchy of man's needs and usually will not manifest any influence unless they are pointedly denied. To illustrate their influence, consider two men who are seated at a restaurant. One of them is very hungry, and he studies the list of entrees on the menu closely. His friend, however, is very thirsty, and his primary concern is with the menu's beverage portion. Both men are reading from the same menu, but they perceive its contents differently.

At the same time, an individual's psychological needs and personal values or attitudes will influence perceiving. *Attitudes* are enduring, learned predispositions to behave in a consistent way toward a given class of objects (English and English, 1958, p. 50). The internal processing that individuals perform when perceiving messages is governed by their personal attitudes and experiences. These variables of perceiving can be grouped into five sets of factors for study by the communicator. Cue categorizing, symbolic communicating, and associating refer to the steps an individual performs in selective perceiving. Personality correlates and individual differences include further variables that affect all stages in the perceiving process.

Cue Categorizing

Every individual develops a personal set of *categories* that he uses in dealing with the world of both objects and concepts. Categories evolve not only from permanent attitudes but also from temporary dispositions. The prospective car buyer, for example, tends to be a more deliberate and thorough perceiver of a car advertisement than the nonprospect—his reaction toward cars in general is temporarily changed. The visual category of automobiles is more important to him, compared with other objects that confront him visually, than to the audience member who is not shopping for a new car.

125

126

Primitive Categorizing

III.B1 *Each message detected by an audience's senses is given some form of classification on the basis of rudimentary ideas of dimension size, and sound immediately following the moment of contact.*

What the eye perceives through a primitive, rudimentary examination of a certain image, say, of a typewritten word—the fundamental features such as length, height, and the black-white interplay that characterizes print—helps primitively to identify the word according to its image, as well as the perceiver's past experience.

Primitive categorizing can involve various kinds of effort on the part of the receiver. Deciding that a visual configuration is a written word form is a type of primitive categorization. Deciding that an object has the general features or dimensions of, for instance, a book is another. The problem for the composer of the message is to determine what combination of speed and accuracy of perceiving his communicating message and media demands and to limit the basic features that will comprise the primitive categorization accordingly.

The more rapid the viewing or listening, the more likely the primitive categorization must serve as the *sustaining impression*, and that impression is based on a few fundamental characteristics that may or may not be appropriately placed, emphasized, and combined by the creator of the communication. Furthermore, primitive categorizations alone give sufficient information to the perceiver to allow him to reject the stimuli entirely if it does not please him.

Suppose a woman decides to read the day's food advertisements in the newspaper. Once she has found the proper section through selective attending, she continues selectively to attend while she seeks for certain words or images that refer to items about which she may desire information. For example, if she is interested in meats, a picture of the product will allow her a more rapid primitive categorization than printed words would allow while she is in the process of selectively attending. Because of this primitive categorization, then, she may proceed further to analyze the information related to meats by focusing upon the written details. If she is not interested in meats, the picture would have more rapidly repelled her attending from the written matter than would words explaining some special feature of the meat, which might change her mind and hold her attending.

If surrounding stimuli, or the environment, and familiarity are held the same, then the number of distinguishing features is the main deciding factor here. In other words, if two messages are delivered in the same environment and the person's familiarity with the subject is the same for both—for instance, if the subject is identical for both messages—then the number of features easily categorized in the message will be the main factor in deciding which message is more thoroughly perceived. An *optimum* number, *not* a maximum, is desired for each type of message.

Marketing Examples of Primitive Categorizing

When shoppers are scanning newspaper supermarket advertisements to determine what they will buy, they are often looking for sales on particular items that they need. Thus, if an audience member is interested in milk prices, a photograph of a meatloaf made with milk that is advertised will not gain her immediate attending. She will probably primitively categorize this as a meat advertisement and will not realize that it is a combination sale of the products used in the recipe for the meatloaf. Similarly, one of the most used attention-getting instruments for window displays is to exhibit the word *sale* in big, bold letters. For the many consumers interested in thrift, that word triggers a response to stop and investigate.

Both auditory and olfactory cues may be intriguing in an advertising campaign. Rice Krispies has utilized the sound of the product in use: "snap, crackle, and pop." Doritos corn chips emphasized the noise made when eating the product, with the slogan "They taste as good as they crunch."

An olfactory technique—in print advertisements, direct mailings, inside-the-package promotion pieces, stick-on package labels, and point-of-sale handouts—is the "scratch-and-sniff" strip, in which the odor or aroma of the product is produced by scratching the strip. Among the products that have been promoted with these strips are liquor, cosmetics, toiletries, and soaps.

Cue Searching

III.B2 *Before arriving at a final perceiving of a visual or audio stimulus, the audience will search for additional information within that message in order to be able to identify or define it.*

Cue searching is the most *open* of the stages of cue categorizing. The audience member, following initial or primitive categorizing, is the most receptive to additional cues or details within the configuration. A magazine reader turns a page and is confronted with an illustration of a car. By resting his eyes on such features as the general outline and the main internal structural features, he is able to recognize the illustration as a car. Providing he recognizes the image of the car, how does he then specify the type of car? Cues such as the distinctive shape, body design, and special features are sufficient for the reader who is familiar with car brands. Further study of the body trim and finally the manufacturer's emblem and/or signature will render the final cues for categorization that are sufficient even for the person with no previous familiarity with that particular make of car.

The principle of cue searching is supported by experiments by Eriksen. He studied the "perceptual variables that determine the speed with which designated objects can be located from among a large field of objects." He used paper cutouts differing in form, hue, size, and brightness and asked a group of people to differentiate between 49 of them, based on preinstructed cue definitions. The speed with which the viewers could identify the target objects depended on the distinctiveness of the original definition given them concerning the cues of the target object. In the experiment it was shown that cues can be used not only in identification of objects but also in the differentiation of objects. In the first stage Eriksen explained how cutouts that varied in the number of identifiable characteristics could be identified. Then, when presented with slides of these cutouts, his viewers used those cues to differentiate one cutout from another. The better the instructions concerning the cues, the faster the viewers could locate the target objects (Eriksen, 1953, p. 132).

Thus it seems that cue searching is aided by knowledge of or familiarity with the features that are most distinctive in the stimulus. The greater the number of these features, the more rapid the process. Also, the greater the number of these features, the better the chance no confusion with another similar but nonidentical object will occur.

Marketing Examples of Cue Searching

To the communicator the more crucial aspect of the perceiving is related to this idea of similar yet nonidentical objects. As a simple illustration, if two cellophane-wrapped paper packages are shown, each 3 inches long, 2 inches wide, and 1 inch deep, and each one is bright red, there are virtually no cues available to differentiate the objects. Yet if one package has a blue stripe around its base, this one cue may be sufficient evidence for differentiation. If two more packages were shown, also in red paper and wrapped in cellophane but with distinct central designs, another type of differential cue would be available. Thus we arrive at the first of a series of propositions that can be shown to have an overall application.

If a woman is confused as to which of two winter coats to purchase, she will search the labels for cues to help her decide. Such small differentiations as the famous-name label or an insignia that tells that the coat is made of pure wool may be enough to determine which coat she will buy. Tags that designate the manufacturer of the material—for instance, the well-respected name of Burlington Industries—may be a distinguishing feature. On initial examination, the two coats may have seemed of equal quality and style, but the purchaser has learned to trust certain labels.

Guarantees also may be influential, or a voice of authority, such as Arnold Palmer golf shirts. The image of the retail outlet where the product can be purchased may have a positive or negative effect.

Sufficient Number of Cues

III.B2.1 *It is easier for an audience to define a category if enough cues exist at the outset for them to be able to develop a categorization. Enough cues consist of sufficient distinguishing features within the message that the audience member may associate several concepts of size, form, and so on with the configuration.*

The use of distinguishing features is just as necessary in the process of perceiving as the use of emphasis is in attending. The audience member must be able to perceive discrete features—the more, the better. Usually a dominant dimension is used by the audience member for categorizing. For example, advertisements may be distinguished by estimating how many audience members will feel themselves to be in the market for the product or service being described.

One other concept that is related to cue categorizing should be discussed at this point—that is, the idea of stereotyping. *Stereotyping* is one particular and extreme type of cue categorizing; it is an oversimplified and biased perceiving of a group of individuals as having the traits of one restricted social group. Although varying attributes, characteristics, and idiosyncracies differentiate people on the personal level, society classifies "types" of individuals on the basis of certain distinguishable, salient features, such as manner of dress, skin color, facial characteristics, manner of speaking and walking, size, and shape. According to Secord and Backman, "a stereotype is a special form of categorical response; membership in a category is sufficient to evoke the judgment that the person possesses *all* the attributes belonging to that category" (Secord and Backman, 1964, p. 67).

It may be necessary to modify Secord and Backman's extreme position. Perhaps not all attributes are immediately identified with the person; yet the point they make about the way people *generalize* is far from extreme.

Two studies conducted to test this concept (Secord, Bevan, and Katz, 1956; and Secord, 1959) involved presenting people (white) with photographs of individuals whose facial characteristics varied from "markedly Negroid" to "markedly Caucasian." In essence, the test was designed to determine if the stereotype image was reduced for the photographs more characteristically Caucasian. In both studies, a tendency to retain the Negroid classification was found even while the actual stimulus was becoming more Caucasian. Stereotyping, or rapid and often faulty classification, was being utilized in the process of perceptual categorization (Secord and Backman, 1964, p. 67).

The audience member who stereotypes usually distinguishes certain groups as having characteristics different from his and of which he disapproves. Campbell has said, "The greater the real differences between groups on any particular custom, detail of physical appearance, or item of material culture, the more likely it is that that feature will appear in the stereotyped imagery each group has of the other" (Campbell, 1967, p. 821). Hence, stereotyping acts as a filling process, whereby a person infers a whole spectrum of behavior for another, often quite inaccurately.

Marketing Examples of Sufficient Number of Cues

This concept is particularly important in the analysis of product image. In communicating a product personality, easily stereotyped individuals are often utilized to convey an image or feeling about the product. The communicator should keep such categorizations in mind when designing a message for a particular target audience. If he understands their stereotyping categories, he can better design his message to appeal to common beliefs and prejudices and he can avoid appealing to them as an incorrectly stereotyped group, which they might resent.

Rugged Marlboro men symbolize the masculinity associated with Marlboro cigarettes. Stereotyped but sophisticated-looking women are seen in Peck and Peck advertisements: "For a certain kind of woman, there's a certain kind of store—Peck and Peck."

These human stereotypes serve as strong cues that can easily stimulate images in the viewer's or reader's minds. This is intended as an advantage, because the viewer has a tendency to identify positively with the stereotype being depicted. However, it is important to realize that use of a stereotype in an advertisement can be a mistake in terms of limited viewer or reader identification (for a reason as simple as color of hair) and the possibility of evoking images for which the audience members have preconceived negative ideas and attitudes.

Not every man can be rugged and masculine, nor can every woman be sophisticated and attractive. The implication that the products are intended only for those who are or feel they could aspire to the stereotype may be a disadvantage to the advertiser. This will naturally vary for different products.

In personal selling, the types of people in the stores reflect different influences in the store image and the products—compare Kresge's and Marshall Field. Indeed, stores are stereotyped. Bonwit Teller and Brooks Brothers have their individualistic identities.

Accessibility

III.B2.2 *Highly accessible categories are more likely to be successfully used than less accessible ones. Accessibility is determined by the degree of the audience's previous familiarity with stimuli falling into the category in question.*

Accessibility of a category is determined by the ease with which a new set of stimuli can be accepted or included within the category. Although no definite way exists for determining which categories are most accessible for each individual, generally it is safe to assume high accessibility if a perpetual interest exists for the subject to which the category relates, if the image is frequently brought to the public eye, if recently acquired knowledge or news about the category/subject exists, or if the individual or group of individuals that comprise the perceiving audience have special training or interests that makes them particularly familiar with the object or subject.

Highly accessible categories are more likely to be used than less accessible ones—especially if the new stimulus is ambiguous, difficult to discern, and in a somewhat different approach, only tangentially or indirectly related to its correct category. And, as accessibility of a category increases, the greater is the likelihood that incongruous cues will be masked from consciousness.

Marketing Examples of Accessibility

As accessibility increases, less input is necessary for categorization to occur. An example of this lies in the promotion of football games. One does not have to sell the audience on the pleasures of attending, just when, where, and who the competitors are. If a person has reached the stage of brand preference, little personal selling is required, reminder ads are all that is necessary. Marlboro no longer talks about cigarettes, but about "Marlboro Country."

However, problems can arise in the area of new packaging. With the introduction of vegetables boiled right in the plastic bag, people wondered whether they got warm enough to serve. People were familiar with boiling vegetables directly and had to be convinced that this way was more convenient and retained the flavor better.

This concept also applies to product extension or the gateway capacity of new products. Many times new products are entered in anticipation that in the future a complete line will be introduced. The initial product serves to make the future products more accessible in the consumer's eyes—the new stimuli are more easily accepted and included within a current category.

Cue Identity and Transposition

III.B2.3 *The audience's basis for placing a new image or message into a previously established category may be either identity or transpositional similarity. A new message may be the same as a previous one in a number of ways but not in others; and depending upon the number of categories the audience uses, they will or will not make the correct categorization* (Krech and Crutchfield, 1948, pp. 93-94).

The principle of *transposition*, as defined by Reese, states that the ability of an individual to identify correctly a stimulus is not decreased if the stimulus is rearranged in a different pattern (Reese, 1968, p. 9). For example, recognition will not decrease if a melody is transposed from one key to another or if a shape is given another color, size, or spatial orientation. It might, however, be more accurate to refer to a relationship between stimuli, such as the notes of the above-mentioned melody.

Thus a melody used in an advertising campaign could be transposed into another key without loss of the audience's ability to associate the melody with past perceiving. Different individuals can be used to advertise the same product over time. As long as a sufficient number of cues can be associated with previously known categories in both instances, transposition can certainly lead to accurate perceiving, as can identity.

Marketing Examples of Cue Identity and Transposition

Danger for the marketer arises when a nonintended transposition is performed by the audience—that is, two similar advertisements for two separate brands of the same product are seen as the same. The point here is that both distinctiveness *and* transpositional flexibility have their optimums.

The Pepsi-Cola Company made its musical slogan, "You've got a lot to live, and Pepsi's got a lot to give," into such a trademark that just using this line on print advertisements, billboards, car cards, and menus served to remind audience members of the pleasant associations for the fun parts of life with the product as promoted on television commercials. This is an effective use of transposition.

Cover Girl makeup was advertised as the "Clean Make-Up." This was done in every advertisement, although the model and particular Cover Girl product might change. Another example in advertising is "This is the L&M Moment."

Packaging of a product rarely should change entirely. It should remain in some ways like the old, so that people can find and identify it as the product they have purchased before. A sense of congruity is reassuring and aids buyers in saving time during shopping. Too much change might rob the audience member of the familiar cues he needs to make proper categorization and transposition.

Adaptation

III.B2.4 *Audience members adapt with respect to given stimulus magnitudes, depending upon the range of values present in the stimuli being attended at the time.*

One of the original sources of support for the idea of adaptation comes from an idea developed in the nineteenth century known as Weber's law (Underwood, 1966, pp. 164-166). Weber's law is a description of the "just noticeable difference" (j.n.d.) that can be perceived by an individual. In a classic example of this law, the skin is touched at two separate but very close points, and the two touches are perceived as only one touch. The points of contact are then separated; when the subject perceives the touches as two, he has reached the point of j.n.d.

This law was later redefined and quantified by Fechner in the form of a mathematical ratio: $\Delta I/I = K$; where K is a constant ratio, I is the stimulus, and ΔI is the j.n.d. In other words, Weber's law is concerned with the minimal differences that can be detected among stimuli. The j.n.d. varies not only with the sensitivity of the receptor and the type of stimuli but also with the absolute intensity of the stimuli being compared. The size of the least detectable change or increment in intensity is a function of the initial intensity; that is, the stronger the initial stimulus, the greater the difference needs to be before a perceptible difference between stimuli occurs (Britt, 1975b).

Marketing Examples of Adaptation

When only a few brands of a high-turnover product are being advertised, audience members generally will have a lower adaptation level for perceiving those messages than they have when the noise level for that type of product is higher. Thus a laundry soap that rarely advertises may not gain the perceiving of an audience member who is used to hearing many messages for competing products in this highly competitive field.

This concept also becomes important for the small community retailer considering a move into a large mall. He must be aware that the consumer will now judge him in relation to his new surroundings, and their adaptation levels to various sensory modes (for example, promotional displays, prices, colors, etc.) may be quite different than the consumers who frequented his store in the other location.

Many marketers claim that their product is better—milder, sweeter, longer, stronger, cleaner, longer-lasting, and so on—than the leading brand. But *how much* longer or stronger does a product have to be in order to be perceived as such by consumers? Will an increase of 1 millimeter, 2 millimeters, or 3 millimeters in length of a cigarette be noticed by consumers? Experimental procedures using Weber's law can be carried on to determine where the just noticeable difference occurs.

Ambiguity and Misindexing

III.B2.5 *Misindexing is the outcome of erroneous perceiving. It occurs when stimuli are assigned by the audience to a category other than the category the communicator desires. This usually happens when the category the audience chooses is for them more accessible and/or less ambiguous than the one the communicator desires.*

Ambiguity refers to messages that are unusually difficult or new to the viewer or listener. English and English explained that in ambiguous statements or situations "the doubleness of meaning is implicitly attributed to the statement, situation, or object, however much it later may be proved to have been due to the observer" (English and English, 1958, p. 24). Ambiguous figures are those which can be seen in two or more ways, as in the so-called illusions of reversible perspective frequently utilized in psychological experiments in perceiving.

Ambiguity can also mean vague, obscure, difficult to understand. An ambiguous stimulus is "one that can mean more than one thing; a stimulus object that has a double signaling value" (English and English, 1958, p. 25).

The message the audience perceives is not always the message the communicator intends to convey. The meaning of a set of stimuli depends entirely upon the categories to which it is assigned in the audience member's mind. If a cue or entire stimulus fits equally into two categories, the viewer will likely place that cue in the more accessible of the two categories. The operation of two variables in particular will increase the chances of misindexing—high accessibility of a wrong or inappropriate category and high ambiguity in the stimulus itself.

Thus misindexing or misperceiving can occur easily because every individual has a large "storehouse" in his mind. As the individual gains experience in the perceptual world, fewer and fewer things are totally separable from past, stored stimuli, and many overlaps must occur. Hence the communicator must consider other possible stimulus configurations with which his newly planned message might be misindexed and thus misperceived.

Marketing Examples of Ambiguity and Misindexing

Ambiguity can be found in the marketplace in the large discount stores. These stores not only have lower-priced merchandise but carry mass-merchandised items that require little personal selling. These stores also contain high-priced merchandise, such as cameras or stereos, that needs considerable personal selling. The two different types of merchandise call for different promotional strategies. When one enters a discount store to buy a high-priced product, he may have difficulty in finding someone who will "sell it to him."

A product can also be viewed as vague or obscure; that is, it has no real identity. Some of the general household cleaners on the market have been projected as so "general" that when a customer has a particular need, such as washing walls, a product is purchased that is identified with a specific need and how to meet it.

Prior-Entry Effect

III.B2.6 *That stimulus or message which utilizes a certain distinguishing feature first will be considered the original by audience members; all other messages that emphasize the same feature will be compared with the first. The risk always exists that the second message will be considered the imitator and that the audience will be given a negative connotation.*

This concept has significant applications to advertising. Rosser Reeves, a past president of the Ted Bates advertising agency, applied this concept in the formation of theory he terms a "preemptive unique selling proposition" (Reeves, 1961). The Reeves theory of a preemptive unique selling proposition is a practical example of the influence of early information in the formation of cognitive categories. Reeves claims that even though several competitive products possess a common feature, the product that first advertises this characteristic will be perceived as the "original" and its competitors as "me, too" products or imitations. He illustrated, "George Washington Hill, the great tobacco manufacturer, once ran a cigarette campaign with the now famous claim: 'It's toasted!' So, indeed, is every other cigarette, but no other manufacturer had been shrewd enough to see the enormous possibilities in such a simple story" (Reeves, 1961, p. 56).

Although using the idea of the original may well present problems for the advertiser who must announce new or improved product features, he still has the initial advantage of prior entry, which will expedite the consumer's awareness of the product.

Marketing Examples of Prior-Entry Effect

When Gatorade came on the market as a soft drink that entered an individual's system very quickly, it was highly endorsed by sportsmen. Soon, however, other products of a similar nature were introduced, and they too were highly endorsed. But Gatorade remained the first of a completely new type of product and benefited from the prior-entry effect.

McDonald's outlets—with their strategic locations, fast service, and high standards—are an example of the prior-entry effect. Even though Burger King, Big Chef, Burger Delight, and other drive-in restaurants offer quite similar products and services, McDonald's is perceived as the innovator.

The manufacturer who decided to put his soft-serve butter and margarine in reusable refrigerator containers was putting his package to work as a promotional item for months after the product was used. Yet competition also introduced the added benefit so soon afterward that the prior-entry effect tended to be canceled out.

Search Completing

III.B3 *As increased degrees of discrimination are required by the audience in discerning stimuli, cue searching becomes more precise until finally they identify the stimuli. In the early stage of cue searching the audience is most receptive to cues; however, once a tentative categorization has been made, openness is limited to cues that will confirm the categorization. Once confirmation has been completed, incongruent cues are either normalized or gated out, either assimilated or rejected, by the audience.*

Postman, Bruner, and Walk presented groups of viewers with a series of 7-letter nonsense syllables as well as with a series of words. For both types of 7-letter groupings, letters were reversed in the 1st, 4th, and 7th positions. The time required for recognition of the reversed letters of the nonsense type was significantly higher than for the reversed letters in real words (Postman, Bruner, and Walk, 1951). The experimenters believed that the difference in recognition time was a result of the forward letter being a confirmation of the cues expected, that is, confirmation of completion of a search. For the backward letters, the expected stimulus did not occur, and a new hypothesis had to be formed—the search was forced to continue.

Marketing Examples of Search Completing

In personal selling, customers often develop friendships and trusts with certain salespeople in the stores they visit frequently. These salespeople have proved in the past to be honest, reliable, and helpful; so when the customer returns to the store and is faced with a new salesperson, he often underestimates the newcomer's ability in comparison with the familiar salesperson, when actually they both may be equally qualified.

When a person enters a department store, he or she normally knows what kind of store it is—high quality, expensive, low quality, low priced, and so on—and the kind of merchandise sold. This "advance information" will be "solidified" by actually perceiving the kinds of merchandise, the types of shoppers, the types of people in sales positions, the various displays, the decorative aspects of the store, and its general atmosphere. Even if the store begins to age and look shoddy, if it sells high-quality merchandise, customers probably will still perceive it as a high-quality, reputable store.

Step Economizing

III.B3.1 *The audience becomes more capable of economizing the steps of perceiving—primitive categorizing, cue searching, and search completing—with the increased frequency of the occurrence of related events. Each cue may be represented less frequently and the perceptual process will retain its rapidity when this is the case.*

Each time a cue is presented, the individual is faced with the task of attaching meaning to it. The first few times the individual is in the process of attaching meaning to a cue, he will choose between many alternatives before reaching a decision. In other words, if he sees a printed word for the first time, he must read nearly every letter in order to be sure that he has identified the word correctly; but if the same word is presented several times within the same message, he will be capable of spending less time identifying that word because he has eliminated the alternative words that are visually or audially similar to that word on the previous presentation. He economizes the time it takes him to read the entire message because he accumulates prior knowledge and uses it in the process of searching. He will register more readily a previously seen cue when searching for further cues than one he has never seen before.

Bruner, Miller, and Zimmerman showed that the development of discriminative skills in the individual facilitated the matching of cues to categories once the categories had been established and recognized (Bruner, Miller, and Zimmerman, 1955). Using a noise channel as a distractor, the experimenters asked individuals to attempt to recognize a long list of spoken words. The words were presented in lists of 8, 16, 32, and 64. A background noise channel was included, representative of alternative cue meanings the subjects might choose in reporting the words. The point was that to recognize one spoken word in the presence of audial distraction was analogous to perceiving a message cue in the presence of any kind of cognitive distraction.

The results showed that as successive trials were given, the number of words recalled accurately increased. Since the words were presented over and over, the respondents can be said to have economized by rejecting the noise channel as a source leading to correct meaning and concentrating on the tones related to the spoken words only. The emphasis in the findings was that this facility to recall correctly was improved with repetition of the words. Thus step economization, as related to frequency or repetition, is supported.

As to the second part of the statement, it is also true that the "accessibility of categories relates to environmental probabilities." Thus, being able to identify a cue correctly and rapidly is related not only to the number of repetitions of the cue at the time of presentation but also to the number of repetitions of the cue previous to that time—the ratio of the environmental probability that that cue will be present as compared to another cue that is being considered by the individual in the cognitive processing of the initial cue presentations.

Marketing Examples of Step Economizing

Step economizing is seen in dealing with the physical attributes of a product. Quaker had to sell the public first on the concept of instant oatmeal that needed no cooking. Now its advertising can concentrate on the attributes of the Quaker brand without any explanation of the unusual form of preparation involved.

Familiarity and a good brand and corporate image will help to "sell" a product by anyone—including middlemen, retailers, and consumers—by its logo. Coca-Cola is an example.

The familiarity of a package saves time for the consumer and is an asset to the manufacturer. On the display shelf are featured several brands of a product, but if a consumer is familiar with the category and normally buys a certain brand, he is able to pick out the product immediately.

Suppose that a company wanted to promote an instant powdered coffee creamer as just as flavorful and rich as real cream but with half the calories. What one company did was to advertise its brand, Coffee-Mate, as the best creamer, thus segmenting its market in an attempt to appeal only to that section of the audience.

Decreasing Alternatives

III.B3.2 *An audience can define a category much more rapidly if the successively noticed cues are ordered such that they lend a decreasing number of alternative interpretations.*

Considering the evidence for step economizing, it seems to follow that an entire message will be perceived with more efficiency and with more of a systematic and predictable approach if the cues present in the message are identifiable in an order of complexity. In other words, at the initial level of presentation, a word or configuration is large enough so that it may vary in level of complexity and not destroy the pattern of cue searching to follow. The perceiver will most likely pursue to the point of accuracy those words or configurations he initially sees.

It is after this initial exposing that it becomes more important to order cues in wideness of interpretation. Considering the length of a typical message, it is important that the points which follow or fall under the main points be relatively clear of alternative interpretations. If the communicator wants the main points to be remembered concisely, it is important that some less-important subpoint not deter the audience member, requiring him to undergo a complex process of meaning rejection and meaning attaching that may take time and confuse him, possibly reversing the categorization process.

Foley and MacMillan performed an experiment in which they asked five groups of subjects composed of first-year law students, second-year law students, first-year medical students, second-year medical students, and a control group of nonprofessional students to associate words with a list of stimulus words. It was found that the different groups associated the various words with different stimulus words. For example, law students responded to the stimulus word *administer* with such words as *business, estate, govern,* while medical students usually associated *administer* with *dosage, anesthetic,* or *drug.* Thus mental sets through selective sensitization may cause the same objects to have different meanings to different perceivers (Foley and MacMillan, 1943, pp. 293-314).

Clearly, the number of alternative categorizations a person may give to an object is determined by his past experience. His ability to narrow down alternatives is a combination of the limitations of his knowledge—that is, he sees only the configurations in certain numbers of ways—and the breadth of his knowledge—that is, he knows which alternatives he may eliminate, based on experiences of failure of those configurations to fit in similar situations in the past.

One example of this influence of knowledge on the decrease of alternatives is found in much of the classical literature in the psychology of perceiving. A classic illustration is often used in tests of the influence of knowledge on perceiving; see figure 14-1.

Through experience, the perceiver knows that the configuration in the figure is either a vase or two faces—after training with this configuration, he will be able to guide his perceptual patterning along the outlines so that he can alternatingly see both. After training, no further thought is likely given to other intepretations.

Marketing Examples of Decreasing Alternatives

Products in the maturity stage run into various facets of the "alternatives" proposition. In the maturity stage there are a great many competing products that are largely homogeneous. Thus, when a product (for example, toothpaste) is promoted, this product message may have a myriad of alternative interpretations, especially in terms of the other products it competes against. Thus the word *toothpaste* can be interpreted and assessed in a great many different ways based on the variety of promotional efforts by other toothpaste manufacturers. To some it represents "fewer cavities"; to others it means "good breath"; and to

Source: Solley and Murphy, *Development of the Perceptual World* (New York: Basic Books, 1960), p. 263.

Figure 14-1. Rubin Vase/Twins.

still others it means "sex appeal." Thus there are more alternative categorizations than in the product's earlier introductory stage.

Retail stores use this concept in a reverse way by presenting the consumer with many alternatives and thus allowing her or him to use a great many categorizations. A retailer can attract people of both sexes and of all ages to his department store. There are the Easter Bunny, and Santa Claus, or special treats for children. The concept of a department store is that it should meet the wants of many different people. Both bargain basement clothes and the designer clothes are under one roof. There are selections as to the kind of product within the same product specifications and price ranges. For women, fashion shows and beauty consultants are featured. For men, there are special gift consultants and sports promotions where leading sports figures are available to talk about various products.

Cue Eliminating

III.B3.3 *With repetitive practices, the audience may begin to eliminate the perusal of a number of the cues they have come to use in the process of cue searching. The cues used may become limited to those which were used in primitive categorizing.*

Cue eliminating can be either valuable or detrimental to both the communicator and the audience member. It is usually valuable, because without eliminating many of the possible interpretations that any configuration or message presents, perceiving would be an impossibly laborious and time-consuming process. The environment could simply not be dealt with—existence would be quite different from what it is.

Marketing Examples of Cue Eliminating

A Ford Falcon billboard eliminated the use of many cues and made its message evident on the basis of previous advertising. The billboard showed a woman's hand refusing the offer of a man's hand holding a gas nozzle. The word *Falcon* is the sole copy. This advertisement did not even need the primitive cue of the shape of the automobile to remind the audience members that Falcon was being promoted as the small economy car that women could handle easily and that needed little gas per mile.

Packaging illustrates how cue eliminating can be both advantageous and detrimental. On the display shelf, if a customer is used to seeing certain colors on a box arranged in a specific design, he can immediately pick out his purchase on that basis only. But packages can be copied easily. For example, Walgreen's brand of "one-a-day" vitamins and Miles Laboratories One-A-Day vitamins, the original, look quite similar.

Relevant Stimulus Information

III.B3.4 *In considering the composition of the entire message, the communicator will facilitate more perceiving by the audience if he relates main cues to main product features or message points than if he enhances, as cues, points irrelevant to the intent of his message.*

Relevance can only be a meaningful term inasmuch as both the communicator and the audience are in agreement on the overall goal any particular message is attempting to reach. From the outset of the exposing, attending, and perceiving process, it is inherently clear that the communicator is trying to establish a particular point or group of points within the minds of the audience members.

Thus, in the process of examining, accepting, and rejecting cues, the communicator must keep these final goals in mind. The audience member really does not have time to think deeply of the implications involved in each message cue; but if a cue strikes him as particularly unfitting, his conceptualization of the message as a whole very likely will be confused.

Nickerson dealt with relevance in relation to cue searching, and his findings may be useful in understanding the importance of relevant cues (Nickerson, 1967). He asked people to categorize stimuli rapidly according to attributes that satisfied a given criterion. Geometric figures varying in color, shape, and size were presented. The individuals were given a criterion of attributes, and they responded by pressing a pedal appropriate to the attributes they saw. For a cue to contribute to the categorization process, it was necessary that it be relevant to the total object. In other words, the perceiving of cues must be an additive process, and only relevant cues are positive factors. Irrelevant ones largely subtract from the successful impact of the message.

Daniel Starch, in one of the earliest scientific works on advertising, noted the results of experiments that indicated that irrelevant material has less permanent attending value than does relevant copy. In these experiments, subjects were exposed for brief periods to relevant and irrelevant words and illustrations from actual advertisements. The attending values for each type of advertisement ranked, in order:

1. Relevant words
2. Relevant illustrations
3. Irrelevant illustrations
4. Irrelevant words

These ranks were consistent throughout a number of trials. He further noted that the relevant words increased in attending value with successive exposing, whereas all other message parts decreased in value (Starch, 1966, p. 94).

The degree of cue relevance in illustrations can be dependent upon the purpose of the advertisement. If the purpose is to attract many readers with varying degrees of interest in the product, one range of illustrations might be appropriate. If, however, only those readers with an established product or message interest are intended to be addressed, the range of illustrations would likely be much more restricted. Clearly, the use of words should be limited to relevant ones. It is necessary that the perceiver be able to silently rehearse relevant message or cue aspects in order to formulate a completely accurate conception of the message.

The idea of relevant stimulus information applies not only to the content of the message in terms of visual imagery but also to the verbal messages that accompany television commercials, as well as to background music that may be used for radio or television messages.

Marketing Examples of Relevant Stimulus Information

In an advertisement for Kellogg's Corn Flakes several years ago, the illustration pictured a statue of Venus with the quotation "If Venus had arms. . . ." In a test for relevance, people were shown the illustration without the product signature and asked what it suggested to them. Answers ranged from "pencils" to "underwear"; no one mentioned cereal. The same test was performed for a Gold Medal Flour advertisement showing a panoramic picture of a city at night. Responses varied from "insurance" to "men's clothing." No one was reminded of flour by the advertisement.

The Campbell Soup Company for years has stressed the fact that they use only the best of vegetables in their products, and tomato soup is one of their first and most-used products. A simple magazine advertisement that appeared in 1970 emphasized these strong, relevant attributes of the company. A full-page advertisement showed a huge, perfect tomato and a small can of soup. The headline read "We make the best of a good thing." No part of the advertisement was irrelevant to the simple statement.

Likewise, packaging should be relevant to the product, its purpose, and its characteristics, and in no way be irrelevant. Thus gaudy spray-deodorant packaging may be perceived as distracting and irrelevant to the practical purpose of the product itself by male consumers. Also, certain colors may be prohibitive (bad connotations).

In merchandising, the location of goods is important. In a sporting goods store, sports equipment is prominently featured. Such extras as tennis shoes, parkas, and books are secondary because the majority of customers are attracted primarily to the equipment.

Irrelevant Stimulus Information

III.B3.5 *If irrelevant stimuli, such as attending-attracting configurations or sounds, are used in a message, the detriment in perceiving will not be a result of the backtracking jolt that stops the perceiving process but rather the fact that the audience will take longer to examine and to process the entire message. In other words, the audience's rate of perceiving of any message is more dependent upon the amount of information than on the nature of the cues.*

In the early 1960s, Morin, Forrin, and Archer studied the role of irrelevant stimulus information. Dealing with the distinguishing of different configurational stimuli, they found that at advanced levels of performance, the rate of information was not greatly influenced by irrelevant stimulus information. The need for respondents to learn a new or unusual code qualified the test as one at an advanced level of performance. They found the rate of information processing to be related more to the amount of information transmitted than to response uncertainty (Morin, Forrin, and Archer, 1961).

It is now considered valid to assume that the use of irrelevant attracting stimuli is not necessarily always detrimental, but it usually will be when the relevant aspects of the message are substantially complex and exposing time is limited. With a simple message, such as the product-reminder-type message, the use of irrelevant, yet enhancing, configurations or sounds may be quite appropriate. The reaction time required for a longer, information-packed, strictly relevant message may be the same as for a shorter, but more multiaspect, and partially irrelevant message. The number of notable message aspects is one of the most important variables in determining the rate of information processing.

Marketing Examples of Irrelevant Stimulus Information

A communicator must be aware of irrelevant information in point-of-purchase advertising. Given the limited space, as well as the host of competing stimuli (other products, other consumers, etc.), one cannot afford to include irrelevant information (words or pictures) that demands too much from the consumer. If the reaction time associated with having to decipher a message is too long, the consumer may well pass it by, especially if the product is an impulse item or an item with many substitutes.

An advertisement for a seamless aircraft-alloy tubing was guilty of including irrelevant information at the expense of the product message. The advertisement pictured a beautiful, young girl, scantily clad in a bikini, draped across a flat surface. Its headline read "Prime Ribs," and the copy continued with "Regular ribs won't do." A few sentences down, the advertisement began describing the alloy tubing being sold, likening its superiority to the superiority of prime ribs. Elements of the advertisement were too diverse and incongruous to permit ready perceiving.

Cue Normalizing and Cue Resisting

III.B3.6 *For most messages, an audience can be expected to perform a certain amount of cue normalizing and cue resisting. Each individual will not see every aspect of a message. An average audience member will tend to perceive what he wants to perceive in any given message. The product of perceiving is determined not only by the cues available but also by the degree to which the individual tends to eliminate a certain number of cues while arriving at a perceptual product.*

Cue normalizing refers to the absorption by an audience member of a cue into his visual, audio, or verbally logical schema of the majority of the cues in the message. This happens regardless of how well the cue actually fits the rest of the message the audience member is examining. When a cue is *resisted*, it is removed from further consideration by the audience member. It is selectively ignored. This occurs when the cue is too inappropriate to be normalized, i.e., too insignificant to change the overall meaning of the message but too evident to escape an initial glance.

Many perceivers, in responding at a later date to what they saw in any given message will demonstrate a selective pattern of noticed versus ignored cues. A large portion of the things the perceiver fails to notice will make no difference. Some smaller cues simply may be transitional stimuli from one cue to another. Some are necessary adaptations to the nature of the media used. However, occasionally a significant cue may fail to register either accurately or at all with an audience. It is these cases to which this discussion refers.

Thus cue normalizing and cue resisting cover a majority of the reasons for complaints against advertisers and advertising. This is so because the perceptual faculties of individuals are by nature vulnerable to deception. Any public communicator risks the accusation of attempting to smoother over points he fears his audience will reject within a message he is presenting.

In response to these accusations, it is necessary to point out that the nature of communication entails a communicator who submits a concept to scrutiny with the purpose of gaining approval or acceptance of that concept, be it a product, a service, or an idea.

First of all, his most logical approach would be to work from the knowledge that some new information will be slower to gain acceptance than other new information and thus to arrange all information in order of the most easily accepted to the least easily accepted. Second, the main arguments dealing with both sides of this approach must be set forth. Some argue that it is unfair of the communicator to conceal or obscure information or to present it in an unbalanced fashion with regard to product advantages versus disadvantages. Others argue that it is the audience member's responsibility to pursue information, to consider an advertisement for what it is, and to deal with it objectively in relation to other advertisements.

Next, consider what the results would be of altering the structure of advertisements as a result of these arguments. The point here is that it would be no better for advertisers to discontinue the use of subjective appeals that enhance the imaginative tendencies of the audience than it would be for them to go to further extremes to plead their sales cases. *A good advertisement need not reach either extreme.*

Finally, in considering the intentions and positions of the other, it is well to keep in mind both the indisputable intelligence of the consumer and the economic necessity of the advertiser. The interrelation between these two things is the crux of the issue herein. The communicator performs his function best when he considers beforehand with whom he should communicate and whether he has chosen the proper combination of media vehicles to reach that group. Then in creating and delivering his message, he executes his art best when he objectively sets forth the actual advantages to his audience of accepting his message, be it for the sale of a product, service, or idea. He should avoid making nonsupportable intangible claims not only for ethical reasons but because, in perceiving any message, an audience member can learn and react more readily to ideas he can understand and accept as possible. After defining his product, service, or idea as accurately as possible, and by showing the audience member how and where to pursue further information, the communicator should feel free to emphasize his selling points as best he sees fit.

The audience member has a responsibility as well. In the examination of the many messages and advertisements he encounters every day, he develops a rate of buying response that is, optimally, within reasonable limitations for him financially, especially if his resources are used by more than one person. In perceiving any advertising message, he should ask himself what he can learn about the product, service, or idea within this message that can help him decide whether he would want to respond to it.

Marketing Examples of Cue Normalizing and Cue Resisting

A woman examining an advertisement in a fashion magazine may examine every detail of the styling of the garment. Yet she may not notice the details concerning the fabric content, nor the price of the garment; and perhaps she will not even consider that the garment has little or no practical use. Furthermore, she may come to accept the unrealistic background of the photograph or sketch—it may seem almost logical to her to see a model standing in a body of water modeling a formal dress.

In television commercials, often rapid time-sequenced actions come to seem quite logical to viewers. The limitations upon realistic product demonstration resulting from time considerations are accepted with little concern. A 30-second commercial that shows a housewife in the process of baking a cake and also shows the cake as it comes out of the oven seems credible to most viewers.

With this discussion related to the perceiving of the cues within any message as a background, and with this latter entrance into the subject of audience responsibility in perceiving messages, it is now time to discuss some more specific issues related to perceiving.

15 Variables within the Audience: Symbolic Communicating

Background

Stimuli have meanings beyond those directly manifested by the stimuli per se, and audience members may respond to some stimuli in relation to the significances that these stimuli or similar stimuli have acquired for them in their own previous experiences. This is the basis of *symbolic communicating*.

Those stimuli which result in symbolic communicating are *imagery stimuli*, that is, representations that recapture or embody some of the perceptual experiences associated with what the stimuli actually represent. Imagery stimuli may arouse in the audience visual images, auditory images, images of any other sense, or any combination of these. Examples of imagery stimuli are flags, money, and religious articles.

Symbolic communicating can occur either consciously or unconsciously. Therefore, an audience member does not have to think in order to be affected by imagery stimuli and thus to have symbolic communicating occur. Further, symbolic communicating can occur either internally or externally, depending upon the kinds of symbolic representation. For example, *internal* thought about *man* may symbolize something actually being perceived and known as man; and the word *man*, either spoken or printed, is an *external* representation of this inner event.

Because individuals are influenced so much by symbols of objects in addition to or instead of the objects per se, choices of a symbolic stimulus or stimuli are essential for correct communicating. As an example, the choice of a wrong symbolic stimulus or stimuli—a word or a picture—may arouse or suggest images to the audience that are different from and perhaps contrary to the images intended by the communicator.

Symbolic Communicating

Types of Symbols

III.B4 *Each of three types of symbols—conventional, accidental, and universal—specifies a distinct range of communicability to all possible audience members for a message.*

147

A communicator should be aware of these types of symbols if he wishes to create messages that will be perceived correctly by his target audience. Every culture contains a large number of *conventional* symbols—the written word symbolizes concepts, rough sketches represent objects, colors represent characteristics or implications of things or events. In the American culture, for instance, white has been associated with purity, and black with death—this is not the case in all cultures.

A great majority of these conventional symbols are visual. Taylor suggested five basic functions for visual symbols (Taylor, 1960, p. 130):

1. To identify events in time and space
2. To characterize the qualities of objects
3. To evaluate by producing positive or negative feelings
4. To prescribe a form of behavior
5. To provide a general frame of reference for comparison purposes

Taylor further described the visual symbols as having structured qualities that help to determine their ultimate functions. The symbolic form used may be codified (for example, a traffic light) or emphatic (for example, a doodle). Interacting with this is the *content*, which can have spatial (for example, a statue) or temporal (for example, a film) dimensions. Taylor also emphasized that the actual relation of a visual symbol to an object ultimately depends on "the degree of perceptual, intellectual, and emotional closeness" of the visual symbol and the object under consideration. Using such characteristics and relationships in a variety of ways, his position is that visual symbols can be created to communicate any predesired content (Taylor, 1960, p. 124).

Accidental symbols, or personal symbols, relate to an individual's experiences in the past with objects, events, or people. The communicator must remember that most attitudes, beliefs, and opinions develop and maintain themselves through the establishment of these accidental symbolic identifications. Such symbols reinforce themselves every time they recur to the individual, and they are extremely difficult to alter.

Facial expressions of basic reactions, such as happiness, fear, embarrassment, disappointment, disbelief, trust, anger, detachment, anguish, and amusement, are *universal* symbols. Representations of the force and power of the natural elements and the ongoing attempt to preserve life and protect self and others against harm are representable universally. The arts are the best and longest-known example of the successful use of universal symbols.

Marketing Examples of Types of Symbols

A conventional symbol can be used as a positive unifying aspect throughout an entire promotional campaign. Gold Medal flour has used a grandmother figure that conveys the image of old-fashioned goodness to the baked goods made with the flour. The association is that the modern-day woman, can create again the good old-fashioned baked goods that grandmother made. In displays, a small picture of a grandmother can be used to reaffirm the impression.

Accidental symbols can also be used in packaging. For some people twist-off bottle tops are so difficult to get off that the frustrating experience overshadows the package benefit of not having to "dig" in a drawer to find a bottle opener.

Universal symbols, such as facial expressions, are especially effective on billboards. A large, happy face with a big smile plus a food product are enough to imply the simple message that this food is good.

Function of Symbols

III.B5 *The function of symbols is to economize the quantity of referents needed to express a concept and to evoke a group of ideas in the minds of the audience members for the message of the communicator.*

Clearly, the necessity and function of symbols within communication is indisputable for the sheer sake of economy of words, paper, and time. Five other characteristics of symbols make their use less straightforward than a simple matter of economy and imagination. First, symbols often have multiple meanings, that is, any person could attach one of several meanings to a large number of symbolic referents. Second, personal symbols are impossible to identify, isolate, or limit. Third, cultural and subcultural symbols in a mixed-culture environment are difficult to deal with—the danger of offending or evoking misunderstanding is always present. Fourth, the meaning of symbols may vary even within a carefully chosen homogeneous audience. And fifth, it may be necessary to use a symbol in expressing certain concepts, regardless of the danger of ambiguous interpretation.

Some general guidelines can be established to help control the variations in audience response resulting from the use of symbols. The use of visual and auditory symbols may be clarified by clarifying the stimuli themselves. To start with, a clearly identifiable stimulus greatly limits the possibility of misinterpretation. The audience member's environment is also important. By considering what subjects might be in the perceiver's mind at the time he encounters the symbol, the communicator may eliminate other communication failures.

Marketing Examples of Function of Symbols

A point-of-purchase display for cosmetics consisting of a cardboard beautiful girl promoting the product uses the symbol of the beautiful girl to aid the consumer in perceiving the product in a fashionable, beautiful environment.

In department stores, symbols can be incorporated into the decor. In the men's section you find paneled walls, leather chairs, pictures of African animals, and so on, whereas in women's dress departments you see plush carpets, large bouquets of flowers, and velvet-covered loveseats.

Colors

III.B6 *Because of the associations audience members have established regarding different colors, a consistent and significant relationship exists between the colors used in a message and the meanings that may be attached to it. Colors, then, have a psychological effect upon and a symbolic meaning to each audience member.*

Symbolically, color per se is associated with embellishment, with adornment, with possession or attributes above and beyond necessity. In Western culture, additional payment is often required for the use of color. Not only the color television but also the multicolored printed page are associated with a more extravagant way of relating to the public. As color has become more popularly accepted and more commonly used in the everyday indoor and outdoor environment, however, these identifications decrease in their strictness. However, the use of color is still a symbol of a message worthy of some consideration, especially when the color appears in isolation amidst a contrast of less-striking visual space.

Various associations have been established for various colors. Colors can be categorized on many criteria: masculinity versus femininity, natural versus man-made, emotional versus unemotional, expensive versus cheap, warm versus cold, pleasant versus unpleasant, bold versus weak, traditional versus innovative. Desirable colors can be derived through the use of these associations, combined with a knowledge of the item, service, or idea the communicator desires to express.

Individuals within Western culture cannot help but develop several long-established color identifications early in their lifetimes. Among these are the following identifications.

Red with danger, warning, warmth, fire, excitement, anger; psychologically, red is also the most visible color

Blue with calmness, peace, official identifications, especially navy

Green with nature, fertility

Black with death, mourning, evil, formality

Grey with old age, conservatism

White with purity, health and medicine, cleanliness

Yellow with sunshine, daylight

Purple with royalty

Pink with femininity

Brown with masculinity, earth

Gold and *silver* with high value, formal occasions, and currency

In addition, several color combinations have become symbolic—red, white, and blue; red and green; orange and black, representing respectively patriotism, Christmas, and Halloween.

Aside from these traditional symbolic connections, several associations related to personality and emotionality may be identified. *Intense* colors may be preferred by those who have a desire—covert or overt—for self-expression and self-exertion. *Subdued* colors may be preferred by those who deal with people and situations in a less forceful manner. The restraint associated with dignity and upper social class identifications also serves as an attraction to subdued colors.

Dark colors may be identified more closely with seriousness than light colors. Dark and light colors also have differing seasonal associations—fall colors being dark and neutral, spring colors being paler pastels and brighter, often unnatural hues.

In a study using a semantic-differential analysis of the effect of color, the perceiving of various advertised products varied with the use of different colors in the advertisements (Osgood, Suci, and Tannenbaum, 1967, pp. 299-302). With six groups of 20 individuals, 4 color variations of the same advertisements were presented: (1) intense color on the product only; (2) pale color on the product only; (3) product grey with an intensely colored background; and (4) product grey with a pastel background. Differences were found to be significant in regard to the analysis of warmness versus coolness, heaviness versus lightness, and excitingness versus dullness. Reds made the product appear warmer to the individuals, while blues and greens made the products appear to be more cool.

If the color used was one that was not normally associated with that kind of object, the value on the product was diminished. Pastel colors on products were reported to produce somewhat more favorable judgments than intense colors, and color in backgrounds was perceived by the individuals to be somewhat more favorable on the evaluative dimension than color on the product.

The best way for the communicator to deal with the symbolic associations audience members make with colors is to consider the following:

1. The duration of the message—the longer the message, the less the need for colors not related to the product or message.

2. The desired general impression of the product, service, or idea—the urgency of the message, the desire to establish a long-range campaign, and the nature of the copy should be considered.
3. The value of using color per se as compared to the value of emphasizing points within the copy or the illustration as main cues.

Marketing Examples of Color

Because green is normally associated with freshness, nature, and fertility, menthol cigarettes, such as Salems and Kools, are promoted with basic green "nature shots" to imply that the products are natural and healthful.

Product coloring is extremely important. Bread has to look fresh; canned orange juice must look like fresh orange juice; and the color of an expensive dress must connote quality and taste. Coppertone suntan lotion makes use of a bright yellow background in billboards and magazine advertising, conveying the idea of healthful sunshine.

Cosmetics usually are packaged in pastel colors—light green, pink, blue, light yellow, white. A change to red or a darker color would convey harshness, not colors to put on the face. The pastels associated with makeup convey an impression of naturalness, made up but not "too much." This is in addition to the association of pastels as feminine colors.

Value Added

III.B7 *An audience perceives an object or message as different symbolically after having been exposed to a positive presentation, demonstrating, or discussion of that object or message. The audience members perceive the item as more valuable than before, especially if they learn uses for it that coincide with their personal lifestyles.*

Value added usually is discussed in terms of the satisfaction of consumer motivating that extends beyond the primary function of the product. Thus, if a customer wants to attain a feeling of confidence in the product he buys, he may be willing to pay more money.

When perceiving a message, the audience member establishes a significance to the message; and as a result of this association, his perceiving of the entire message, and consequent response to it, comes to be determined in part by his potential response to the significance of the message; that is, the message itself influences the receiver's perceiving of the meaning of the message.

In addition to its information function, advertising adds a new value to the existing values of the product. If *sign* can be used to refer to the advertised product and the word *significate* the thing signified, then the effect of advertising is based on new significates a product can come to signify. Moreover, it is based on the types of significates the product signifies.

Two basic types of significates exist. *Sign-relevant* significates, such as foods, have inherent characteristics because of their physical makeup. *Arbitrary* significates have nothing to do with the sign—such as the masculinity of Marlboros—but are generated by the product image. The arbitrary significate may be located outside the person and signify the approval of a friend—an arbitrary, external significate. If the product reminds the audience member of his own inferiority, then its significate is located inside—arbitrary internal significate (Preston, 1967, p. 213).

The economic concept of value added assumes complete rationality on the part of the purchaser in measuring the worth of items he may choose to buy. In contrast, value added as a psychological principle recognizes that decisions to buy are also based on qualities the purchaser will bring with him in perceiving the product. These qualities are not innately part of the product but are the result of the way the purchaser has perceived the item himself.

On a rational level, the very fact that a product is being advertised gives value, since, without the advertising, very few people would know of it. Moreover, known brands provide a guarantee of uniform quality from one purchase to another and, in most cases, from one product in a line to another. On a less rational level, however, an advertisement generally invests the item with a "personality" as a natural result of the context in which it appears. Hence, the product becomes associated with and changed or modified because of its contexts.

Marketing Examples of Value Added

Several aspects of how a product is displayed and promoted can increase or decrease the value of the product in the minds of audience members. Following are a few examples of variables that affect the perceiving of the value of a product.

1. The product may be shown in action or in use rather than inert.
2. Individuals may be shown using or benefiting from the product rather than isolating it from its users or beneficiaries.
3. The product may be shown in relation to other objects with which it may be used, especially in ways about which the perceiver might not readily think.
4. Discussion, explanation, or dialogue can refer to the advantages and favorable associations the communicator wishes the perceiver to attach to the product, rather than speaking about irrelevant but perhaps attention-

gaining subjects. An exception to this may be humor, but humor is still useful when the relationship of the humorous issue to the product is evident.
5. The environment in which the product is perceived by the audience can contain connecting elements that help to establish the association with the type of enhancement desired by the communicator.
6. The physical appearance and manner of dress the individuals using the product can create and enhance or make improbable an association with the product.

The product image created by the interactions of price, package, promotion, distribution, and the product itself play an important role in how an individual perceives what a product is and how much value is added through positive presentations. The resulting product image is extremely important in marketing, for example, the masculinity of Marlboros, the femininity of Virginia Slims, and the quality and status of a Cadillac.

A retail store can develop value-added characteristics. In addition to the value of the name of the store and the brand names featured, a store may provide services that are perceived as extra benefits for consumers. Examples of gift wrapping of presents, home delivery of purchases, mail-order catalogues, and special sales for charge-account customers. Thus, strengthening the "brand image" for the consumer becomes important in giving added value.

Brand Image

III.B7.1 *An audience member may perceive an item as more valuable than other items because of perceived brand distinctions.*

I.S. White suggested that three factors order the perceiving of a given item: cultural definitions, the brand image, and the physical-sensory product itself (White, 1966). The *cultural factor* initially influences attitudes in such products as filter cigarettes, diet soft drinks, and permanents and is the most general of the factors. The *physical-sensory factor* is the product itself and tends to operate after the product is purchased. Does it really taste better or get clothes whiter? The concern here, however, is with the *brand image*.

Value may be added to an object because of its brand name. The name will assure the consumer of a uniform quality from one purchase to another. The name may become so important that the manufacturer charges a higher price because of the worth of the product in the minds of his customers, for example, Bayer Aspirin.

A distinction must be made between product image and a brand image. *Product image* is the attitude developed by consumers toward a type of product.

Producers of one product type can build an image for their product by working together, and questionable advertising by one producer in the field can hurt the whole industry. *Brand image* is the composite impression of a particular brand as formed by an audience member's perceiving of advertising, packaging, value, and product attributes. Successful brand imagery gives the brand a distinct personality and worth to the consumer (Brink and Kelley, 1963, pp. 155-165).

The brand value also may be added after a purchase has been made. This point is critical for the producer because he wants repeat customers. Here the advertising works as a reinforcement for a consumer's decision. This may lead to the formation of *brand loyalty*, which results from the appreciation of added value. However, added value may be slight, and loyalty is usually fickle. Another brand can often take over a consumer's loyalty through its added value (Mayer, 1958, pp. 311-313).

Marketing Examples of Brand Image

For many product groups, the time eventually comes when the product becomes a household commodity, where formerly it may have been an optional item. At this point, the types of enhancements offered in advertising may be limited to one—the material usefulness of the item. The symbolic security value of the item and the status value attached to certain brands may be diminished to the point that the previous exposing of the item or brand through advertising means very little in terms of purchase potential for the consumer. The housewife, for example, may lose any concern she might have had before the high quality of virtually *all* brands of margarine was established for choosing a highly advertised brand. Margarine may be of no status or security value to her whatsoever.

However, for other items, she still may retain her purchase tendencies for advertised brands beause she has no way of actually checking the quality of the item—dog food may fall in this category for some dog owners. Of course, she may retain her tendencies to buy her clothing, her cosmetic products, and her husband's dress shirts on the basis of brand awareness. The point is, however, that for a certain number of items and brands the quality competition has reached a point of virtual equality, and the consumer is aware of this. He or she will therefore buy merely on the basis of convenience, availability, and other point-of-purchase variables (Epmeier, 1969).

If an object can be enhanced positively by presentation, demonstration, and discussion, it should be noted that the object also can lose its attractiveness to the perceiver through negative enhancement.

Importance of Interests and Values

III.B7.2 *An individual may enhance a message or item (add value) by comparing the message in an item with his own interests and values at a specific point in time.*

Every individual perceives the objects and events he encounters each day in accordance with his own interests, concerns, and values. The ways to enhance a message are all bound by this basic premise. Furthermore, these interests, concerns, and values that each individual has belong in three basic categories. First, some interests deal with the universal need to be supplied with material necessities. Second, some deal with the strivings for security from harm and the prolonging of life. Third, some needs deal with the desire for status, or psychological superiority over other individuals, and escape from the ordinary.

Before giving examples and explanations of each of these types of needs, as expressed through object enhancements, it is necessary to reclarify what was stated in the original proposition. An audience member may find it impossible on subsequent perceiving to separate the product from the enhancing associations brought about by the relating of the object to one of the above types of need. For the audience, then, the product itself may change as a result of the symbolic values or need fulfillments associated with it in the original message.

Psychologist Clark Hull offered an explanation about stimulus generalization that helps to explain the concept of product enhancement. He referred to the positive presentation of any stimulus as a kind of "compound stimulus aggregate." In joining the two stimuli—that is, the product itself and its favorable surroundings—a stimulus compound is created that will evoke a joint reaction (Hull, 1943, pp. 212-213).

A more powerful reaction would result from presenting a product along with a few semirelated aspects of desire, pleasure, or usefulness for the typical audience member. Hull says this holds true although each of the individual components of the message—the object itself, the environment, the individuals involved, the status and security and material associations, and so on—may hold substantial value on their own merit. The combined effect, he implies, is best.

Because of the individual's interest in supplying his material necessities, he must make judgments about various alternative objects he might use in providing the necessities of food, shelter, maintenance, and clothing. The individual must ask himself, "How can this object be useful to me?" and "Is it the best of its kind for the price?" Although the perceiver of the initial message may not have information about the price, quality eventually will be related to cost. It follows, therefore, that a necessary and obvious relationship exists between the actual nature and function of the object and the perceiver's view of it via the message. Such items as food staples, many paper goods, nonobservable clothing items, soaps and cleaners, and tools and utensils fall into this category.

For many messages, the main enhancement of the object involved is through pointing up an individual's needs and wants to assure his security from harm, usually in a rather emotional manner. Examples of objects or services enhanced through this approach are insurance benefits, bank services, home-protection items, seat belts, and so on.

Attachment to an object because of status will occur when the object is associated with its:

1. High price and/or limited privileged access
2. Use by members of the desired or aspired socioeconomic class of the perceiver
3. Novelty in relation to the objects currently known and used by the perceiver and his immediate reference group
4. Appearance of complexity, indicating that the product is used and intended for use by intelligent, aware, progressive people.

When any one or combination of these factors is present in the message-enhancement technique that the communicator uses in presenting the object, the audience member almost inevitably will begin to associate the object with those things which are suggested to him, unless or until he has contradictory information about the object. Even when he obtains such information, it may be difficult for him to change his original ideas about the object.

Marketing Examples of Importance of Interests and Values

By positioning a product in a particular way, certain audience members will identify the product, and naturally, others will not. The same advertisement will be capable of both adding and subtracting value from the item, depending on the individual. If an individual learns uses for an item that conflict with his personal lifestyle, then the item probably will be thought of as less valuable than before.

For example, RC Cola at one time ran the slogan, "Flip with the Zip in RC Cola." In an effort to appeal to a younger market, however, the RC Cola Company changed from this advertising campaign to a new one—that RC Cola has a "Mad, Mad Taste." To individuals who were not "in" and did not wish to be associated with this younger market, the advertisement probably had no appeal. These individuals were outside the target market and probably did not associate themselves with the product—or at least with the product as it was positioned in this particular campaign. Hence, for them, negative enhancement toward RC Cola probably resulted.

Many home demonstrations rely on lists of names from customers in setting up appointments. The demonstrator asks a satisfied customer to recommend the product to a certain number of his friends who will then agree to their own demonstrations. The friends are more likely to perceive the product as valuable if their friend recommended it, and they are more likely to appreciate it if it is demonstrated for them personally.

16 Variables within the Audience: Associating

Background

Each audience member searches each message for a distance relationship he can feel in relation to the product, service, or individual described in the message. He finds this relationship through *associating*, "a functional relationship between psychological phenomena established in the course of individual experience and of such nature that the presence of one tends to evoke the other; or the establishment of such a relationship; or the process whereby the relationship is established" (English and English, 1958, p. 44).

In addition to the ideas about perceiving that were discussed in connection with congruity, another set of ideas relates to the ways in which individuals attempt to group or categorize the things they perceive. Just as each stimulus is searched for a certain amount of congruity in terms of the appearance or sound of the message, audience members seek cues in a message for the establishment of a well-defined distance they can feel in relation to the message. *Distance* refers to the amount of divergence of the attitudes and positions of the message itself and the audience member as judged by him at the time of presentation or shortly thereafter.

Various aspects of perceptual constancy, polarizing, assimilating, and contrasting—some of the principles to be discussed in this chapter—have a wide range of applicability. Although they are discussed here as principles of perceiving, they also operate with other parts of the process of message communicating and reacting. In fact, concepts similar to these principles appear in various places throughout this book. Two specific examples are personality correlates and individual variables, principles that are presented and discussed at the beginning of the next chapter.

Associating

Tendency to Perceptual Constancy

III.B8 *Audience members tend to perceive messages in the way they are accustomed to perceiving them, even though the stimuli change; that is, audience members preserve a relatively stable image of reality in a world where things are constantly changing.*

159

This human tendency is partly a result of people's inner needs. Human beings need to perceive the world in a relatively stable manner so that they can cope with it securely and on their own terms. The point is that a person may tend to perceive a situation in a certain way and continue to perceive it in that way particularly if he feels that his handling of the situation has been successful in the past.

As in the case of congruity (III.A4 in chapter 13) very little empirical research has been done in the area of perceptual constancy that is applicable to this book; and thus, the amount of supporting evidence for this principle is not as great as for most of the other principles. However, this does not negate the validity of this principle as stated here. I believe that such a principle is a valid statement and is evident in marketing behavior. Various marketing examples may serve to reinforce the value of the principle.

Marketing Examples of Tendency to Perceptual Constancy

The principle of perceptual constancy might be illustrated by a woman who has used a certain laundry detergent with satisfaction for many years and, accordingly, is more likely to accept advertising for that product than a woman who has not successfully used the product. The user of the familiar product feels comfortable and safe with her familiar detergent.

Magazine advertisements for Modess in the early 1970s were designed to change the beliefs and attitudes of girls before they developed perceptual constancy about feminine hygiene products. The advertisements stated that mothers rarely tell their daughters why one particular product is the most effective but just start their daughters using their own brand, and the copy asks the audience members to think carefully and to recognize the superiority of Modess products rather than just to buy by habit.

American Motors faced a similar problem in the change of name from Rambler and its change of image for that car. For quite some time, even after a barrage of promotional messages, most people still "saw" American Motors' cars as "Ramblers." To change how people perceived a Rambler meant confronting the relatively stable image constructed over the years—an image that did not correspond to what the car had become: of higher quality, with good service, and a guarantee. Thus, although the product had changed significantly, the image continued to remain fairly constant.

Polarizing

III.B9 *Every message will be polarized to a certain degree by audience members in the process of rapidly comparing their attitudes, positions, and knowledge from previous personal experiences with the content of a message. Because they must establish a definite attitudinal distance from the message, they will tend to interpret the message in such a way that they either definitely will or definitely will not feel a personal relation to the item or message.*

Polarizing is the orientation of the message by the audience members in such a way that it corresponds to their thought processes. A typical example of polarizing is shown by many individuals' reactions to political candidates and elections. Many individuals dislike personal feelings of uncertainty and therefore either dogmatically denounce or support political candidates about whom they really know very little. On the basis of a little exposing and a large amount of generalizing, the would-be objective voter often manages to make decisions more for the sake of having made them rather than for the sake of having contributed a thoughtful vote. This is an example of what is meant by polarizing because of attitude and position on the part of an audience member.

If an audience member recently has read about a message's topic, has been able to recall from his formal education some ideas related to it, and/or has been in familiarized agreement with other facts being presented by the unknown source, the *contrasted*—polarized toward nonacceptance—message will be perceived by him with more objectivity and acceptance than if he could form none of the associations.

Previous use of a product or store similarly will alleviate the tendency of an audience member to make polarized judgments about specific products that are advertised, either as brands or as products to be found in that particular store.

Previous knowledge relates to the use of pictures in "favorably" attempting to polarize a message. In many instances, pictures are the quickest and most dramatic way of expressing ideas. They can arouse feelings and stimulate pleasurable responses that individuals remember from prior experience. They provide a basis for interpretations that are realistic, economical, and connote feelings of intimacy, emotional involvement, meaningfulness, intrinsic beauty, and believability.

To aid in such a polarization Stephen Baker, a noted art director, set forth various conditions pictures should have. They should appeal to such needs as love, food, drink, companionship, and achievement; they should be realistic. If a viewer finds himself discovering things "he knows," he will be more comfortable than others in entering into the situation. Relevance for both the message and what is portrayed is important. If the viewer likes the people in the scene, and if there is someone in the illustration he might like to be, this produces positive responses (Baker, 1961).

Marketing Examples of Polarizing

Various kinds of advertising are directed at getting people publicly to polarize their beliefs and attitudes on certain products. An Ultra Ban 5000 (an underarm deodorant) commercial began by presenting the proposition "Maybe she will— maybe she won't"; and then went on to show how a woman using their product will *not* switch brands when presented with competitive products. This commercial sought to polarize audience members. The decision is either "Yes" or "No"—"Will she?—Won't she?" There is no room for a compromise ("I'll think about it," or "I'm not sure.").

The concept is particularly applicable to store images and can be used either to differentiate a store or make it similar to others. Based on past experience, consumers categorize different stores on appearance, type of personnel, brands carried, prices, and so on. Thus a clear distinction exists between a Saks Fifth Avenue and a Robert Hall store. The consumer also attaches specific meanings and feelings to the different types of stores, and these meanings tend to become polarized. A problem can arise when there are many similar stores; when an individual sees or hears advertising for another new store, he or she may see it in close relation to other stores and images. This mental carry-over process may tend to confuse the audience member. A kind of generalization process can occur, resulting in the positive aspects of the polarizing process being lost to the communicatee because of the similarity.

Model Polarizing

III.B9.1 *If a model (person) is shown or described in a message, the audience members perceive the model or the model's experiences as similar to themselves or their own experiences; that is, the model becomes polarized in their thought processes.*

A *model* is any person in a message whose action or being is characteristic of the function of the message, as perceived by the audience member. Thus association can include the audience member's attempt to view himself as very similar in a particular aspect to a person (model) in a message. This other person may be a movie star, executive, athlete, and so on.

A study by Hornstein on the influence of modeling on behavior may be applied, in this case, to perceiving. Men's wallets were placed in random areas to test any response difference on the part of a finder in his attempt to return the wallet. As a result of his knowledge of some other person's previous attempt to return the same wallet, the new finder associates the earlier finder with himself. The perceiving by the second finder of the similarities in the two finders and their similar experiences influence his actions; that is, it was found that whereas 70 percent of the second finders returned the wallet when the model or earlier finder had similar characteristics and had also returned the wallet, only 33 percent returned the wallet after perceiving that the earlier finder was different from himself. Thus, when the subject and the model are perceived as similar by the subject, he will see the model's experiences as a good indicator of what his own experiences would be if he participated in a similar situation (Hornstein, 1968, p. 222).

Marketing Examples of Model Polarizing

Model polarizing occurs not only with a perceived similarity in physical appearance but also with similarity in lifestyle. Camel cigarette advertising utilized the idea of a young model with whom a young adult audience could identify; and the advertising copy ridiculed the "gimmicks" related to cigarette smoking and countered with a picture of a self-assured, mature young man smoking a Camel Filter cigarette. The closing was "Camel Filters. They're not for everybody. (But then, they don't try to be.)"

The influence of a model in perceiving definitely affects audience members' responses to the messages involving the model. The effects are evident in product advertising; interestingly enough, a woman may be motivated to purchase a particular dishwashing liquid because she perceives herself as similar to the model in the commercial, who begins to lead a more interesting life after washing her dishes with the advertised product.

Modeling is important also in personal selling. If a salesperson can convey similarities of needs and desires between himself or herself and the prospective customer, then the customer will be influenced when the salesperson mentions that he or she owns or uses the product himself or herself.

Previous Knowledge and Polarizing

III.B9.2 *The more the audience knows about the message presented, the less will be the tendency to polarize. The less they know about it, the greater the likelihood that they will polarize, even at the risk of increased inaccuracy.*

In the case in which no previous knowledge is available with which the audience member can compare a new message or stimulus configuration, his memory and creative processes go into action, bringing into visual-mental focus various images that are in some way comparable to the new one being presented. This is seldom the case, but occasionally an individual will be unable to recall pertinent facts or concepts he can use in interpreting a new message. Thus he must treat the message as he would treat a word written in an unknown foreign language, or as he would treat a modern abstract painting.

Auditory-mental imagery may also occur in the message so that both the product and the voice or written words are undergoing a trial-and-error comparison process in the audience member's mind. Within a minute he will have developed a "standard" based on his former attitudes, positions, and knowledge by which he may judge the product regardless of whether or not that standard is really an accurate measure of comparison for the new message or stimulus configuration. If a new stimulus or idea seems to fall very near his "standard," then the actual distance between the two will be *underestimated* by the audience member. If a new stimulus or idea seems to fall rather far away from his "standard," then the actual distance will be *overestimated* by the audience member.

These distortion tendencies must be taken into consideration in the creating of any message format. The communicator should always ask himself, "If someone had never seen this product or heard of this idea or service, what would he likely think about it in viewing this message?" If symbolic references to religious, political, social or ethnic groups are used within the message, the communicator must determine how they are expressed and what attitudes they are likely to evoke in the audience.

Marketing Examples of Previous Knowledge and Polarizing

A woman may view with a great deal of skepticism an advertisement for a hair straightener that shows a model who previously had frizzy hair but now has hair that is perfectly straight and silky. The woman may be skeptical of the claims made, even though she has never used the product, because she has tried other straighteners with no success. She is using as a reference standard her own unhappy experiences.

If a consumer has had unpleasant experiences with a type of container, such as cans that open with a key, then not only may he tend to avoid the particular product he had the experience with but all products in the same kind of container.

Assimilating

III.B10 *If the audience is presented with a message that seems only slightly different from their previously established opinions and attitudes, they often will perceive the message to be closer to their opinions and attitudes than it actually is.*

In order to clarify the sense in which the word *assimilating*—or assimilation—is being used here, it may be helpful to examine a few dictionary definitions that have been used for the term:

1. *Assimilation.* A term usually applied to an immigrant or ethnic minority in the process of being absorbed socially into a receiving society (Mitchell, 1968, p. 9).

2. *Assimilation.* Denotes the process in which one set of cultural traits is relinquished and a new set acquired, through communication and participation (Gould and Kolb, 1964, p. 38).

3. *Assimilation.* The absorption or joining up of a new conscious content to already-prepared subjective material, whereby the similarity of the new content with the waiting subjective material is specially emphasized, even to the prejudice of the independent quality of the new content (Hinsie and Campbell, 1960, p. 71).

4. *Assimilation.* A process by which an unpleasant fact is faced and brought into tolerable relation with the rest of one's experience: a newly crippled person sometimes succeeds in assimilating his new limitations; or, a process of perceiving or apperceiving in which the new content is so similar to a familiar content that the two seem almost identical (English and English, 1958, p. 44).

Clearly, definition 3 and the second part of definition 4 are closest to what is meant by *assimilating* in this book. Although the concept of assimilating has not been widely studied experimentally, a few studies have been made that support the points stated in the proposition.

Kendall and Wolf reported a study in which cartoons intended to ridicule prejudice were misinterpreted in some way by 64 percent of the individuals who saw them. Misinterpretation was most frequent among prejudiced respondents who either saw no satire in the cartoons or interpreted them as supporting their own attitudes (Kendall and Wolf, 1949, pp. 152-178).

As in the case of tendency to perceptual constancy (III.B8), empirical research is not extensive in support of this proposition. Once more, though, the lack of supporting evidence does not nullify the proposition's usefulness or the fact that it is exhibited in marketing behavior. The marketing examples that follow serve to delineate this proposition and to indicate its practicality.

Marketing Examples of Assimilating

The principle of assimilating can be used in long-term promotional campaigns to introduce new ideas slowly to audience members. Once a company has established a feeling of trust among audience members through a long association of truthful advertising and good products, new products introduced by the same company will benefit from the company image and will be assimilated by the audience members into a total product image.

Polaroid, manufacturer of 60-second and 10-second picture cameras, ran a long promotional campaign to win the acceptance of the idea of using Polaroids in place of conventional cameras. Eventually the company offered a full line of almost instant-picture cameras, from quite expensive models to the $25 model. Thus Polaroid could appeal to any pocketbook with a product that produced essentially the same result—a good picture that could be developed and enjoyed a short moment after taking it.

Hallmark, Inc. illustrates this concept in product development in all phases of its promotional program. The company began as a greeting-card business, with cards for special occasions, such as weddings, birthdays, anniversaries, and so on. The company then expanded the kinds of occasions and the people to whom you sent cards. Now there are cards for *bon voyage*, sorry your dog died, congratulations on your promotion, and cards to be sent to second cousins and office coworkers. There are even cards you send to people for no reason except that you are thinking of them—friendship cards.

The thoughtfulness and good taste of the card industry were transferred to wrapping paper, party materials, picture albums, candles, artificial floral arrangements, and special lines of knickknack items such as peanuts. Each new product introduced is tied in with past promotional practices—types of display and the manner of presentation—so that they are immediately accepted.

Contrasting

III.B11 *If the discrepancy between the message viewpoint and the audience member's viewpoint is considered large by them, the message viewpoint will be judged by them as more different than it actually is from their own ideas.*

Conversely to the assimilating experiments, other studies lend validity to the concept of contrasting. For instance, Hovland, Harvey, and Sherif presented communications arguing the desirability of prohibition to three types of people—"drys," "wets," and those "moderately wet." They found that the greater the difference between the attitudes of the recipient and the position advocated by the communicator, the more likely the recipient was to regard the communication as propagandistic and unfair, and even to perceive the stand advocated by the communication as further removed from his own position than it actually was (Hovland, Harvey, and Sherif, 1957). Their findings relate closely to the following definitions.

1. *Contrast.* The juxtaposition of two contrary or opposing sensations or other mental data, which results in intensifying or emphasizing their contrary characteristics.

2. *Contrast.* Heightened awareness of differences resulting from bringing together two items of any sort, either simultaneously or in close succession; to bring out or emphasize differences between two items by putting them close together.

Two further points should be made in discussing assimilating and contrasting. Some of the situational variables mentioned in previous sections on exposing and attending may affect assimilating and contrasting. Some of the conditions that may be affecting the individual's attitudes toward the message may have very little to do with the approach or attitude the message itself conveys but rather deal with other extraneous variables of the environment that may or may not please the individual at the time.

The range of assimilating as well as the limitations and tendencies related to contrasting inaccurately can be extended. It is not known how great an effect a pleasant-surrounding atmosphere per se is in forcing message or item assimilating, whereas the evidence that contrasting will occur in unpleasant or negative situations is more certain.

Marketing Examples of Contrasting

The general implication for advertising is that an advertisement should function either to reinforce existing attitudes and behavior—maintenance of brand loyalty—or to stimulate individuals who are already predisposed to act in the desired manner. For example, a woman who believes that makeup can enhance her looks will be more predisposed to accept an advertisement introducing a new type of foundation than will a woman who disdains such artifices and never wears makeup. Hence the advertisement is created with the first woman in mind.

Yet there are some cases where you can change the product image, to try to "cancel out" any discrepancies. Bonnie Bell makeup appeals to nonmakeup wearers, the outdoor types who are not and do not want to be "city-slickers." Bonnie Bell positions its makeup as protection against wind, cold, and sun instead of as a beautifying agent. By contrasting the "fussy femininity" of makeup with the Bonnie Bell products, the company can combat negative feelings toward its products.

A salesperson may point out a minor discrepancy between two items, such as that one coat is more versatile than another because it has a removable lining. Other discrepancies may then be perceived—such as that the color of the other coat suddenly is not as good as the one with the liner, or not as stylish, or not made as well.

What about the possible advantages or disadvantages of mentioning unfavorable or controversial product aspects that are suspected to be the cause of contrasting on the part of audience members in the past? The best solution for the communicator considering possible changes in promotion is not to begin suddenly pointing up the controversial aspect unless some change favorable to the intended market has accrued and will be readily noticeable to former nonpurchasers—such as price, appearance, or availability. Simply to change the approach to, say, a humorous identification of a product disadvantage or to a logical explanation of it is not likely to be sufficient to induce changes in attitudes that will alleviate contrasting.

Relevance

II.B12 *The more relevant a message is to the past experiences and present state of the members of an audience, and the more that the message seems to be directed to them and applicable to their wants, the more accurately the audience members will perceive and interpret the message.*

Relevance is the degree of perceived relationship, similarity, or correspondence between one configuration of stimuli and another. It may be contrasted with *congruity*, which refers to the degree of unification or intercorrelation within one stimulus configuration or one message part.

Relevance is dependent on the individual's perceiving of whether or not a message may help him to solve a problem, fulfill a need or promise, or provide him with pleasure or excitement. The greater the value of an issue to the audience member, the more thoroughly his interpretation and organization of the message will be in terms of his prior attitudes toward that issue.

An important exception to this principle should be noted. A situation may arise in which an individual is exposed to information on a certain topic that is of high relevance to him but that also contradicts his own beliefs. In these instances, he is likely to misperceive the message.

In an experimental study conducted by Cooper and Jahoda in 1947, it was found that when the distance between a subject's cognitions concerning a topic of communication and the point of view expressed in the communication is great, the communication is often perceived either as propagandistic and unfair or it is distorted so that the individual in a sense reconstructs the message as more compatible with his own views (Cooper and Jahoda, as cited in Festinger, 1957, p. 135). Festinger refers to this phenomenon as "avoidance of dissonance," noting that it often occurs in situations in which the topic is emotionally laden for the individual in addition to being dissonant with his beliefs.

Marketing Examples of Relevance

Successful promotional campaigns should depict a problematic situation that members of the audience can find similar to their own experiences. Certain situations are universally problematic, which is an asset to the marketer. A manufacturer of frozen foods can promote that the foods can always be stocked in the freezer so that if unexpected company comes, the homemaker need not have to rush out to the grocery. Frozen foods can be an insurance against pressures of last-minute food preparation. When the dilemma is pictured, if a woman has had several unpleasant experiences of the sort, or if her lifestyle includes last-minute meals, she can adapt herself easily to the situation and solution.

A package can also be relevant. Large-size boxes of detergents are made for large families where several loads of washing are done per week. In addition, the cereal multipacks are for families where everyone likes a different kind of cereal or desires frequent changes in the kinds they eat.

Relevance is also related to the immediacy of a need or want. This may affect the way a consumer perceives a message and the ones for which he is susceptible. If the consumer has an immediate need for a remedy for a sinus headache, he will be susceptible to messages that speak of curing sinus problems. He will choose perhaps Sin-u-Tab because it identifies his need specifically. If the need is anticipated, the consumer may take more time in determining which product will best fit it. In fact, there may be some question as to whether a sinus medicine is really necessary; and he may conclude that a general aspirin is best (or Anacin or Bufferin) because they meet more than one need.

High Valence

III.B12.1 *The more valent the message, the more accurately and completely it will be perceived, other factors such as potency being equal, than if the message is of low valence.*

A message of *high valence* is one that presents images or words of prevailing or continuing interest to the audience. Needs and wants are closely related to valences. The valence of a certain object or activity depends partly upon the nature of that activity and partly upon the state of the needs and wants of the individual at the time.

An increase in the intensity of needs and wants leads to an increase in the positive valence of certain activities. For example, an increased desire for recreation on the part of an audience member would lead to an increased valence toward messages about recreational activities and an increase in negative valence toward messages about work. Any statement regarding change of needs can be expressed by a statement about certain positive and negative valences (Lewin, 1951, pp. 273-274).

Marketing Examples of High Valence

One IBM magazine advertisement has high valence for many busy executives. The headline "When was the last time you saw the top of your desk?" is illustrated with a familiar view of an overcrowded desktop. Businessmen who are continually bothered with too much paper work will perceive this message as a way to do away with part of their problem through the use of IBM machines.

The promotion of Gerber baby foods is another example of high valence. The pictures of mothers and babies are of such interest to women that even women who do not have children are attracted by the pictures. When a woman does have a child, valence will increase and she will more thoroughly read the copy. The promotion continues to be of high interest value because in addition to promoting baby-food products, the manufacturer also gives helpful hints about raising older children and the health care of children in general.

High Potency

III.B12.2 *The more potent a message is, the more accurately and completely it will be perceived by the audience, other factors such as valence being equal, than if the message is of low potency.*

A message of *high potency* is one that is presented in such a way that it carries high interest value in relation to other stimuli present in the environment of the audience at the time of exposure. *Potency* concerns the transitory interest value of a stimulus. It is the interest value of a particular stimulus, regardless of the valence of its category. Potency is the interest at a specific moment resulting from specific stimulus.

A message that is new or astounding or reinforces an individual's existing attitudes and beliefs will be highly potent. The message will arouse the individual's curiosity and interest. A creative commercial for a very mundane product, for example, would be highly potent. However, potency also could be achieved by making a statement completely opposite to existing attitudes and beliefs. This would stimulate a want for more information about the category, thus arousing interest.

Marketing Examples of High Potency

Amidst a host of business and travel advertisements appearing in a particular issue of *Time*, an educational foundation ran an advertisement headlined "David's IQ is 145. He just flunked out of college." The headline has high potency because it presents two seemingly incongruous statements, hence arousing interest; and its subject matter distinguishes it from other types of advertising in the magazine.

Audience members who were planning a vacation and had become discouraged, believing they could not afford the type of trip they desired, could have found one American Airlines promotion to have particular potency for them. The two-page magazine advertisement included a colorful map of Hawaii that had vacation spots marked at which special savings certificates could be redeemed, and bore the headline "$200 worth of Hawaii free." This message was particularly interesting in relation to other exotic vacation promotions and brochures that offered glorious vacations the audience members could not hope to experience.

Grocery stores featuring samples of a particular food item exemplify high potency. First of all, the consumer is in the store to buy food. There are no distractions from the objective, only competition among various products for attention. Primarily because the shopper normally has the responsibility for preparing meals, she or he will be interested in new food items. A promotion of taste samples—for example, a cheese spread—will be more effective than other packages on the shelf with *new* printed on the outside of the package. The shopper does not have to wonder if the product is good—she or he can taste it.

Another promotional technique is putting paper rings around bottles of soft drinks that announce a special price reduction. Against the rows of soft drinks the product will stand out because of the price promotion.

Mental Set

III.B13 *At the moment of message perceiving, if audience members' thoughts have established a mental set of associations for the message, then the more pertinent it is to the mental set, or the more distinct and potent if different from the mental set, the more likely the message cues will be properly categorized than if the message is not relevant and is not distinct and potent.*

Mental set attunes the individual to a certain category of stimuli and ensures that the pertinent stimuli will be of sufficient strength to be evaluated and categorized within the lower levels of the memory (Haber, 1966, p. 335). For example, if an individual is told that a series of letters will be presented and he is to identify only the letter presented in each group of stimuli, he will identify the number 13 as the capital letter B instead of the number 13, even when shown the stimulus within a series of numerals—1, 5, 10, 3, 17, 13, 20 (Bruner, 1957, p. 137).

The communicator's matching of his message to the audience member's mental set helps to ensure that desired response will be identified in the message and that it will remain in the memory long enough to be evaluated and classified. Mental set, therefore, increases the probability that a stimulus will be initially categorized and evaluated. It also increases the number of stimuli that will be perceived as fitting the set category, because the acceptance limits of the particular category have been artificially expanded (Krech and Crutchfield, 1948, p. 145). The perceived relevance of stimulus inputs thus varies according to the effects of perceptual set.

Marketing Examples of Mental Set

An individual enters a store with a mental set of buying a heavy, durable coat, thinking he will have to pay a high price for it. The salesperson's comments on the coat the consumer seems to like include that it is a nice, light-weight coat, nice for warm weather, nice for those special occasions, and a good buy since it is priced so low. But these comments may "destroy" the mental set of the prospective purchaser. Thinking that he has found just what he needed, he reconsiders, since the salesperson's evaluation of the coat so strikingly differs from his own. The mention of low price makes him think that perhaps he is getting a cheap product because of his expectations to pay a high price and also because of the comparison that the coat chosen was of a lower-price line carried by the store.

A woman may go to the dairy case in a supermarket looking for butter. Her mental set for the package is a box with four "sticks" contained within it. But butter also comes in tubs—soft or whipped. When the new product forms and packaging first were introduced, promotion had to stress that this unrecognizable product *was* butter but now in a soft form for easier spreading. The extra emphasis was on what the product was, and spreading could then be associated with the brand name, Soft _____. This was aided by arranging a brand's tubs next to its stick forms in the dairy case.

Orientation to Act

III.B13.1 *The more likely audience members are to act toward the fulfillment of a particular need or want, the more likely they will be to interpret the messages presented to them in terms of the category to which that need or want corresponds, as compared with leaving some of their needs and wants unfulfilled.*

If the initial category of a stimulus is perceived by an audience member as corresponding to a need or want category, it will have a high relevance value for him. The stimulus must first be properly categorized with a need or want before it can be integrated any further into the perceiving process and still cause immediate action. If the stimulus is not categorized with a need or want, the perceiving process will stop or be changed. If the individual does not have at least a need, the stimulus could be misindexed or perceived differently.

In other words, unless the individual is ready to act, the message will move from the initial categorization differently than if he had a need or want for the item. The message may be perceived and add value to previous attitudes about the item, thus increasing the desire to act, even though presently the individual has a low orientation to act.

Marketing Examples of Orientation to Act

Some types of needs are more immediate than others; for example, the need for food and nourishment is more necessary than the need or want for a yacht. Thus food advertising is more likely to be appropriately categorized than advertising for yachts.

Packaging and price also can exemplify the orientation toward acting. An audience member may be a "thrifty" food shopper and perhaps may need to cut down on her food budget. Thus in shopping for soft drinks she will particularly be susceptible to the larger, more economical sizes.

This concept is especially important in media choice. A consumer reads a certain magazine in anticipation of seeing certain topics, ideas, and products presented. An individual reading *Road & Track* is "tuned in" to an automotive orientation and thus an advertisement for household furniture would be incongruous with his current orientation and tendency to act on automotive matters.

Perceptual Defense

III.B13.2 *When faced with an anxiety-producing or ambiguous situation, members of an audience may tend to distort the message in their perceiving of it; this is known as perceptual defense.*

An individual desires to protect his inner needs and security. As a result, he may be psychologically blind to certain stimuli in his environment. For example, an individual may avoid references to illness, death, or physical injury. Psychological security is also important. A woman may feel threatened by "playboy" images she feels might tend to turn her family-loving husband into a romantic rover.

Most of the research in this area has been conducted with a tachistoscope, flashing "dirty" words onto a screen and measuring recognition thresholds. McGinnies flashed 11 neutral words and 7 socially taboo words, such as *whore*, *rape*, and *bitch*, with exposures below threshold. He increased exposure time by small intervals until the words were correctly perceived. It was found that the neutral words were perceived more quickly than the taboo words. Thus the subjects had exhibited perceptual defense, "blacking out" recognition of undesirable terms (McGinnies, 1949, pp. 244-251).

Another interesting study was conducted by Secord, Bevan, and Katz. Subjects were classified according to their degree of racial prejudice and then had to judge the "Negroidness" of a series of faces varying from mulatto to strongly Negroid in features. More prejudiced subjects perceived the Caucasian faces as having Negroid features. This experiment revealed an interesting function of stereotypes and perceptual defense. The anti-Negroid individual had intensified the stereotypic features of the Negro; prejudice protected the individual's ego from various perceptual stimuli (Secord, Bevan, and Katz, 1956). In this connection, see the discussion in chapter 17 of cultural influences on perceiving.

Marketing Examples of Perceptual Defense

It is difficult for a communicator to overcome perceptual defense; but a concise, unambiguous message will aid in the proper categorization of perceptual stimuli. However, if an audience member is highly prejudiced, relying heavily upon stereotypes, there is little that a communicator can do to reduce perceptual distortion. For example, upper economic income groups may question a mass merchandise outlet's emphasis on price, supposedly at the cost of quality and variety, because such stores also carry high-quality brand name radios, cameras, and small household appliances; thus these people feel that the store is "not for them." They may conclude that the store is for lower economic groups and does not have the standards of quality they desire.

Packaging also may be ambiguous. Even though their package is considerably smaller than other cereal boxes, General Mills Natural Cereal is priced the same as competing breakfast cereals; and the net weight is the same as for other cereal boxes. Yet at the point of purchase the comparison of sizes distorts the message, and the consumer may conclude that the package contents are not equal to those of competitors and therefore is overpriced.

Effect of Expectations

III.B14 *The more heavily that audience members rely upon a past experience in regard to a message, the more likely they are to expect a recurrence of that experience when they are exposed to a message a second time.*

This concept deals to a great extent with built-up attitudes, values, and other cognitive elements that cause an audience member to react at the moment of stimulation. The individual has developed certain attitudes about the stimulus; and if the stimulus is in line with his expectations, then a higher relevance value will result. If it is quite contradictory to his previous attitude, a stimulus could arouse a great interest—incongruity—or be rebuked and cast aside—in other words, not perceived.

One investigator conducted an experiment in which there were significant relationships between the motivational variables and their complementary impression formation variables with respect to the need for affection and academic achievement. "Expectancy motivational variables were significantly more closely related to impression formulation than were those of personal values" (Opochinsky, 1966, p. 6854). Ambiguous situational factors also led to significant relationships between motivational and impression formation variables.

Slides of social situations on the University of Colorado campus that were "relevant" to the subjects were used. The task consisted of three different stimulus situations (affective, academic, and neutral) having different key values. Manuals were written so that a story (impression) was given to each slide to test the salience of both its academic-achievement content and its affective content. The motivational variable measure was obtained from an expectations questionnaire and a personal values questionnaire. These yielded the personal values and expectations for both affective and academic-achievement need areas. The questionnaires were administered separately from the test; and when the task was presented, it was structured as being a test of accuracy in social perception.

An experiment by Jessor dealt with the change in expectancies in related situations after success or failure in the original situation and the degree of generalization between the two situations. Four tasks were based on the subgoals of recognition for academic skill, recognition for physical skill, and love and affection from the opposite sex. The tasks included (1) verbal arithmetic problems (the most goal oriented); (2) measure of vocabulary knowledge; (3) an epicyclic rotor whose speed could be controlled manually; and (4) an interview with a girl who would rate the subjects on warmth, friendliness, and adaptability with the opposite sex (the least goal oriented). It was predicted that reinforcement would result in expectancy changes varying from most to least in the above order.

The tasks were described to 132 male college students, each of whom was asked to rate the score he would get. After completion of a task, he would have another opportunity to make a prediction. Subjects failed on the first test, then were allowed to succeed on the remainder. Test 4 was dropped (Jessor, 1954). Results showed that success or failure in a situation was generalized to similarly constructed tasks or tasks that had similar goals.

Marketing Examples of Effect of Expectations

If an advertiser emphasizes that his product will outperform all competitors—for example, will get your clothes whiter than any other detergent—then the consumer may have high expectancies for the product and be motivated to buy it. A problem arises, however, if initially high expectations are not met. Not only is the consumer disappointed, but his expectations, the next time he sees the product advertised, will be a lot lower.

Because of this expectancy generalization, a manufacturer must promote his product as the *only* product that can meet a particular need. Effort must be made to point out the differences between his product and that of a competitor and why the consumer can meet his wants most successfully with this product. Coca-Cola can point out that the wants of dieters (whose goals are to cut calories and lose weight yet still be able to enjoy a refreshing cola) can best be met by Tab, the only sugar-free cola.

The consumer who expects a detailed and informative "sales pitch" from a salesperson may be disappointed by the salesperson who only hands the potential purchaser a brochure to read and does not offer any further information assistance. This may be particularly true in areas in which there is deep personal interest in the product or service offered, such as life insurance, automobiles, or health care.

Expectations of Reward

III.B14.1 *An audience member more likely will change his beliefs and attitudes if he expects a reward than if he is in a situation where there is no reward. But if the reward is too high, the audience member may become sufficiently suspicious that any belief attitude change will be less favorable.*

Festinger and Carlsmith conducted an experiment in which subjects, after participating in a boring task, received $1 or $20 to lie to another subject by telling him that the test was interesting. The $1 subject found the condition less boring than the $20 subject. "In the $1 condition the subject had less justification for lying than he did in the $20 condition and hence experienced greater dissonance, which he subsequently reduced by justifying his lie. He came to believe that the task was indeed not as boring as he originally thought it was" (Festinger and Carlsmith, 1959).

This interpretation has been criticized; that is, suspicion was aroused in the $20 situation because the payment was considerably beyond the subject's expectations. Thus there was less of a tendency for him to change in the direction of the opinion he was asked to advocate.

Rosenberg conducted a similar experiment; and his explanation for the inverse relationship between the amount of reward and attitude change was that where a subject was offered a large reward, "he may be led to hypothesize that the experimental situation is one in which his autonomy, honesty, and resoluteness in resisting a special kind of bribe are being tested" (Rosenberg, 1965, p. 29). In other words, the test situation the subject was presented with actually was a coverup for the real test of his character.

In an experiment by Gerard, 48 male undergraduates were asked to participate in a survey of public opinion as to whether or not the student government should be able to act or take positions on non-university-related issues. All subjects were told that they would receive $2 for participating. Each person was given either 50 cents, $2, or $5 to write an essay advocating the opposite of his position. The subsequent opinion was measured to determine change from the original stance. In the 50-cent condition, subjects were told that they could be paid only 50 cents because of limited finances, instead of the $2 expected. In the $2 condition, the subjects were paid $2; and in the $4 condition, subjects were told that fewer people had participated and thus the experimenter could pay $4 instead of $2. Subjects were then tested to see if they were in favor of the issue. Results showed partial evidence for both the dissonance explanation of behavior and the incentive explanation (Gerard, 1967, p. 360).

Oftentimes an individual's expectancy is not confirmed. It would be assumed that this would have a negative effect on the individual's attitude toward the issue; but research shows otherwise. Groups of eighth-grade girls were given 5 cents for writing an essay in favor of shortening summer vacation. One group had no expectancy of a possible increase in the financial incentive, whereas the other four groups had either a high (90 percent) or a low (50 percent) expectation of receiving an additional 50 cents (high incentive) or 25 cents (low incentive). Expectations were "disconfirmed" after completing the essay. Attitude discrepant behavior and perceived degree of choice were measured before and after disconfirmation, as well as the degree of satisfaction after disconfirmation. It was found that the disconfirmation of expectancy produced an increase in the positive attitudes toward the issue. But it also was reported that those subjects in the high-incentive condition enjoyed more satisfaction in participating in the study than did the low-incentive group.

From these kinds of experimental results, the communicator must not assume that he can promote attributes that his product does not have. Yet he can develop an image for his product that may promise certain psychological benefits. These satisfactions may come from the prestige of using the product.

Marketing Examples of Expectations of Reward

Elizabeth Arden, an expensive cosmetic line, may promote a face cream in terms of helping to keep women younger looking and more attractive. The product may actually keep the skin moist, but whether one actually becomes more attractive is really a way of feeling. By using the product, the consumer *thinks* she is more attractive; and by using an Elizabeth Arden product, the prestige and expensive image makes the consumer think she is using the best face cream possible. Many women continue to think that more expensive cosmetics are better for their skin. Thus satisfaction may be gained through a product's image as well as its performance.

If a woman receives a coupon worth 10 cents off the regular price of margarine, she will more likely buy the product than if she received a 30-cent coupon. The unusually high offer arouses suspicion that the product could not be that good.

The concept of oversell in personal selling illustrates dissonance in this proposition. In going overboard in selling, a salesperson creates dissonance—the question is, why is he or she selling so hard if the product is good? In many cases a moderate amount of selling is most effective. An example of this proposition is a Coca-Cola premium promotion. Coke was offering the consumer two free 48 ounce bottles of Coke or any of its products with a purchase of one of its old-time trays, for $1.29. Not only was the consumer getting a tray but also a large quantity of free Coke. Because no other soft-drink manufacturer had such a premium offer located in the store, the choice was narrowed down to one. Also, when this particular promotion was over, positive associations remained.

17

Variables within the Audience: Personality Correlates

Personality Correlates

Value Categories and Personality

III.B15 *The more similar a message is to the highest value-orientation category of the intended audience member, the more rapidly the message will be perceived, and the more likely the audience member will be to attach meaning to the message.*

Among the most useful contributions to the marketing communicator is the personality characterization formulated by Spranger and frequently adapted by later investigators. According to Spranger's classification, personalities are generally oriented in six different ways, as shown in table 17-1.

In an experiment by Postman, Bruner, and McGinnies, the recognition thresholds for each of these categories were compared for a number of test volunteers. A time-of-recognition profile was compiled for each person while his Spranger value ratings were noted, by recording the time it took him to recognize words in this category. To obtain an independent measure of personal value orientation, the Allport-Vernon study of values was administered to each subject. These score-profiles were evaluated against population norms (Postman, Bruner, and McGinnies, 1948). The data revealed two main categories of results. First, recognition was the most rapid for theoretical words; second, for economic and aesthetic words; third, for social words; and the longest recognition time was for political and religious words. The fact that the tests were given to Harvard and Radcliffe students may have biased the response to theoretical value-category words.

In addition, the most highly valued category had the lowest recognition threshold across all individual rankings; that is, it took individuals the least time to recognize words within their prominent value class. Each less-important value followed behind the first in the same order for both recognition and previously ranked value.

While personality characteristics differ considerably among individuals, if a communicator is aware of the personality similarities among members of his target audience, he can design his message for maximum perceiving. The personality of the individual always will be a larger determinant of his actions than any other aspect discussed thus far, even though personality never will be

Table 17-1
Spranger's Personality Characterization Classifications

Theoretical	Economic	Aesthetic	Social	Political	Religious
theory	income	beauty	loving	govern	prayer
verify	useful	artist	kindly	famous	sacred
science	wealthy	poetry	devoted	compete	worship
logical	finance	elegant	helpful	citizen	blessed
research	economic	literary	friendly	politics	religion
analysis	commerce	graceful	sociable	dominate	reverent

Source: Postman, Bruner, and McGinnies, "Personal Values as Selective Factors in Perception," *Journal of Abnormal and Social Psychology* 43 (April 1948).
Note: These 36 words were chosen from longer lists that were originally compiled by Spranger.

used as a criterion for planning advertising and promotional strategy. All the general statements that might be made about the average audience member tend to lose their value when individual cases are considered. Basically, this results from the fact that every human has a different personality.

Marketing Examples of Value Categories and Personality

The communicator must be aware of the value categories of his target audience—appearance or good health—when designing his message to sell dishwashing liquids. A dishwashing liquid that bases its messages upon the fact that the product is gentle to women's hands is more likely to be perceived selectively by women who are particularly concerned about their appearance. Women who are more worried about their family's health will selectively perceive messages that accent the sanitizing aspects of the product. Actually, any one product can be designed for either appeal by shaping its product personality.

The same product may be packaged differently to appeal to different consumers. A soap may be packaged in a pretty pink wrapper in order to appeal to women. The same soap may be sold in a dark brown wrapper to male consumers.

Retail stores can convey certain atmospheres and thus reflect the psychological values of a store. For example, the atmosphere of Hallmark Card Shops seems sociable. The decor is bright and cheery; and because the products sold deal with lovingness and thoughtfulness, while in the store customers probably are thinking nice thoughts about their friends or family. And the nature of the store helps to create friendly attitudes of sales personnel toward customers.

Economic connotations are associated with I. Magnin, a high-fashion, high-quality, expensive women's clothing store. Prices are high; the store stocks many specialty items, such as furs and expensive jewelry; the people who shop there dress and behave like upper economic classes; the saleswomen tend to behave the same way; and the decor is elaborate and in excellent taste.

Promotions and demonstrations also carry value orientations. Hellman's mayonnaise promotion on how to make molded salad candles was both sociable and aesthetic, whereas French gourmet cooking demonstrations are aesthetic. During cosmetic demonstrations, a cosmetician speaks of shading, contouring, shaping, accenting, and highlighting—all artistic terms.

Self-Knowledge

III.B16 *The more completely the members of an audience understand and accept themselves, the more capable they will be of understanding and accepting new messages, new individuals, and new events.*

The knowledge that members of an audience have of themselves is directly related to the way they perceive other individuals, their total environment, and the feedback they receive from those individuals in the environment. As a result of extensive research in personality theory and perceiving, one strong conclusion has been evident to researchers: every individual tends to use the self as a referent for the perceiving of others. Investigators have reported a series of research studies that have yielded the following descriptions of the way most people tend to make judgments (Zalkind and Costello, 1962).

1. "Knowing oneself makes it easier to see others accurately" (Zalkind and Costello, September, 1962, p. 227).
2. "One's own characteristics affect the characteristics he is likely to see in others" (Zalkind and Costello, September, 1962, pp. 227-228). "Secure people (compared to insecure) tend to see others as warm rather than cold . . . " (Bossom and Maslow, 1957, pp. 147-148, as cited in Zalkind and Costello, September, 1962, p. 228). "The extent of one's own sociability influences the degree of importance one gives to the sociability of other people when one forms impressions of them" (Benedetti and Hill, 1960, pp. 278-279, as cited in Zalkind and Costello, September, 1962, p. 228). "The person with 'authoritarian' tendencies is more likely to view others in terms of power and is less sensitive to the psychological or personality character-istics of other people than is a nonauthoritarian" (Jones, 1954, pp. 107-127, as cited in Zalkind and Costello, September, 1962, p. 228).
3. "If the perceiver accepts himself as he is, he widens his range of vision in seeing others; he can look at them and be less likely to be very negative or critical. In those areas in which he is more insecure, he sees more problems

in other people" (Weingarten, 1949, pp. 369-400, as cited in Zalkind and Costello, September, 1962, p. 228).

4. "Accuracy in perceiving others is not a single skill. The perceiver tends to interpret the feelings others have about him in terms of his feelings toward them" (Taguiri, Bruner, and Blake, September, 1962, p. 229). "One's ability to perceive others accurately may depend on how sensitive one is to differences between people and also to the norms (outside of oneself) for judging them" (Bronfenbrenner, Harding, and Gollwey, 1958, pp. 29-111, as cited in Zalkind and Costello, September, 1962, p. 228).

· These conclusions may be applied to the perceiving of messages—especially to those messages delivered by people or in print media in which people comprise part of the illustration. The matching of personalities of the perceiver and the deliverer of a message is largely dependent upon a successful application of the preceding principles. It is the responsibility of the communicator to write messages that reach out to the perceiver; this is one situation where "meeting halfway" is not sufficient.

Marketing Examples of Self-Knowledge

In the area of price, if a person perceives himself as thrifty and one who spends wisely, this will limit not only certain price categories of goods but *particular* goods as well. If a person views himself as a reasonable or logical human being, the types of promotion that will be effective for him will not be the catchy, gimmicky sort, but the straightforward, factual type.

The types of media an individual chooses to expose himself to reflect his self-concept. A young on-the-go male will read *Playboy*; his female counterpart, *Cosmopolitan*; an intellectual, *The New Yorker*; a fashion-conscious woman, *Harper's Bazaar*; a socially concerned individual, *Harper's*; a home-oriented woman, *Good Housekeeping*.

Personal selling also must take into consideration the self-concept of an individual. For example, an independent, self-confident person may prefer to be left alone while he is looking over merchandise; he trusts his own judgment and evaluative techniques. A less self-confident shopper may welcome the help of a salesperson; he may be uncertain that on his own he can determine the benefits and disadvantages of competing products, or if any meet his wants and needs. In addition, the more self-confident customers may be more open to considering the purchase of a "new" product concept than those not so self-confident ones.

The type of retail store may reinforce the self-concept or be an affront to it. A mass-merchandise store may be offensive to an upper-class individual who does not operate on as tight a budget as the middle-class consumer, whereas the latter appreciates the store's convenience and low prices.

Self-Image

III.B16.1 *The greater the similarity between the self-images of the members of an audience (that is, the way they perceive themselves) and their images of the message, the greater will be the motivating of the audience members toward the message.*

In a psychological sense, the self does not exist as a single entity. Instead, four components are central to one's self-image, and all are "locked together" like four overlapping circles. The four components—real self, self-image self, looking-glass self, and ideal self—are depicted in figure 17-1.

First, the *real self* is the individual as he really is. The second component is the *self-image self.* The self-image is the way one sees oneself. The real self and the self-image self can differ considerably. Consider the example of the fictitious Don Quixote, whose real self was a highly eccentric imaginative elderly man, gone slightly mad. In contrast, his self-image self was that of a fearless knight in quest of honor, justice, and love. The third component of self is that of the *looking-glass self*, or how one thinks he is perceived by others. Unfortunately, just as the trick mirrors at the carnival can distort one's physical image, so can the looking-glass self appear distorted to the individual. The clarity of how an individual perceives this area of his self depends a good deal upon feedback from others, much of which may be sufficiently distorted or so complex that it is misinterpreted (Leavitt, 1960, pp. 39-40). The fourth part of self is the *ideal*

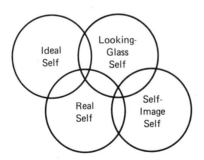

Source: Douglas, Field, and Tarpey, *Human Behavior in Marketing* (Columbus, Ohio: Merrill, 1967), p. 65.

Figure 17-1. Douglas, Field, and Tarpey's Four Interlocking Selves.

self, or how the individual would like to be. Whenever any of the other three components of self does not provide a satisfactory picture to an individual, the ideal self is especially significant.

All four components of the self-concept are important to consider in every promotional undertaking. Most products imply improvement of one's self— whether appearance, physical condition, lifestyle, or ease of doing one's job. However, because these components of the self serve as the fundamental determinants of an individual's behavior, it is important for the communicator to understand not only the concept of the self-image but to recognize the problems encountered in identifying a self-image and determining the factors that will hinder the individual in his attempt to alter his self-image.

Sometimes products are in direct conflict with self-image. In a study by Hamm and Cundiff, housewives ranked 50 products in order of how well each product described the self and ideal self. Products included items that appeared to be a threat to the role of mother and housewife (TV dinners, health foods). They were ranked lowest as items that best described a housewife's self or ideal self. For a product such as TV dinners, an image had to be created to be congruent with the ideal role of the woman, such as "You'll have more time to spend with your children if you use our TV dinners." In this manner, the mother role is brought out and the product is compatible with the self-image. This same study showed that certain products symbolize the self-image of the housewife more than others. Houses, cars, and dresses were most important. Thus self-concept is an important theme in promoting these items (Hamm and Cundiff, 1969).

Marketing Examples of Self-Image

Promotion of a specialty food may be based on the way in which the image of the food fits in with the self-image of the consumer. Expensive or out-of-the-ordinary food may be promoted as especially appealing to the person whose self-image is that of a socially elite, wealthy, and discriminating gourmet.

A woman's real self-image may be that of a harried housewife with three children, with her physical appearance far from neat. Yet her ideal self-image may be that of a woman with perfectly manicured nails, meticulously combed hair, and a slim physique. By appealing to her ideal self-image in promotion, a communicator may find this woman susceptible to beauty products; and so she is portrayed not as the harried housewife but as the well-groomed, attractive woman.

Shalimar perfume ran a print advertisement that communicated with the looking-glass self of women. The message showed a bottle of the perfume; and the headline was "Don't turn around, but the gentleman sitting behind you is wondering who you are."

Application of the self-image principle can be useful in establishing prices and channels of distribution. Placing the product in the wrong type of store or not pricing it correctly will result in a conflict between the image of the product and the self-image of the potential buyer. Such is the case in shampoo. There are low-priced shampoos that are almost identical with the higher-priced, "quality" shampoos; but since a good shampoo is supposed to improve the self-image, many consumers perceive that a good shampoo is priced higher than others.

Number of Categories

III.B17 *Audience members who use fewer categories to describe themselves will also use fewer categories to describe other individuals and objects as compared with people who use more categories to describe themselves and others.*

In discussing the first principle (III.B15) in this chapter, *categories* related to the ways in which a perceiver selects different cues and sorts them to attach meaning to the most important aspects of the message. Here *categories* mean words and descriptions; for example, a person who describes himself with many different words also will describe other people with a variety of descriptions. Audience members differ in both the types of categories they formulate for people and objects in their environment and in the number of categories they utilize.

The number of categories used can be judged by such socioeconomic factors as occupation, education, hobbies, manner of conversing, style of living, and ethnic and subcultural factors. The amount and kinds of descriptions an individual can communicate are dependent upon the types of experiences that person has. It may be assumed that consumers who have a small amount of leisure time as a result of economic necessity are able to give fewer descriptions of relaxation and leisure-time activities and feelings than people who work an 8-hour job. Yet these latter kinds of people may develop more categories in other areas. They may have additional work experiences that expose them to new information and enable them to develop new insights, and this facilitates more descriptions in these areas. Variables such as age affect the amount of description used. It also may be assumed that adult audiences will have more categories than child and youth audiences, simply because of more experience in living. This probably will hold true regardless of educational differences.

Personality factors also have a bearing on the number of categories. The situation can exist in which an individual has a broad background on which to judge new people and objects, yet may have fewer categories than his experience would suggest. His personality may be such that he is narrow-minded, lacks insight, is conservative, tends to be introverted, and has not taken full advantage of the learning experiences his background has offered. As a result, he imposes restrictions upon himself in terms of what categories are relevant.

Marketing Examples of Number of Categories

When dealing with an audience whose level of education is low, it is usually fair to assume that their number of referential categories is limited. Thus an advertisement or promotional message that is simple to understand and that does not refer to obscure or specialized knowledge will best be perceived by these audience members.

One public-service car card appealed to high-school dropouts with the message "I quit school when I were sixteen." The message was simple and blatant enough in its grammatical error to have its message perceived by members of its target audience exposed to it.

A person with a greater number of categories can fit himself into a greater variety of situations and in social contact with a wider range of people than someone with fewer categories; he or she has more experiences to relate to a promotional message. He or she can more easily see himself involved in more situations. If a person restricts the number of categories used to describe himself or herself, he or she limits the number of products that may be perceived as being for him or her. A general approach in promotion will not attract his or her attention—it must identify his or her wants and address them.

This may be illustrated by the type of person who buys Canada Dry as a mixer because it is promoted as a mixer but who would not consider 7-Up or Sprite because they are not specifically defined as mixers but as soft drinks.

Categories can be externally restricted by sexual, socioeconomic, and ethnic factors as well. For example, a man is not likely to perceive messages that deal with female categories, such as babies, cooking, and female cosmetics; and he will tend to avoid any store he believes to be a woman's domain, such as dress shops.

Leveling and Sharpening

III.B18 *A message may be more perceptually distorted if an audience member levels or sharpens it than if the audience member views it objectively.*

Leveling occurs when an individual perceives or recalls something as having greater symmetry, less irregularity, and less incongruity than it objectively has. *Sharpening* occurs when an individual accentuates certain elements of a message, while at the same time submerging other elements. The two processes may occur simultaneously.

The typology of leveling and sharpening was formulated originally to forecast the way different personalities interacted with the ability to remember experiences or past events. Although the use of this type of personality categorization has been replaced by more recent, specific typologies, this categorization was useful as a theory for many years. The communicator may use it to clarify his own understanding of the general process of perceiving.

A message is most likely to be leveled when it contains information with which the audience member is generally in accord but which also includes some information that is unusual. In such cases, the individual probably will feel that he knows what the message is about and ignores the new information contained in it. The marketer who wishes to avoid leveling should decide what portions of his message deviate from what audience members already know about his product or service and then accentuate them sharply in his promotional materials.

Sharpening can work to the advantage of the marketer. If the marketer knows that the majority of his purchasers have favorable attitudes toward his product, he then can employ short, pleasant advertising to reinforce these attitudes. He can rely on audience members to fill in favorable product images after they have seen the reminder advertising and decided why the product is preferred.

Marketing Examples of Leveling and Sharpening

Home-cleaning products often are promoted in television commercials by well-dressed, perfectly-groomed models. If an audience member has been unsuccessful in her use of this product or brand, she will be likely to sharpen the advertisement and ignore the sales message while noticing how out of place the model is in the situation simulated. However, if the audience member has enjoyed using the product, she probably will perceive what the model is saying in favor of the product and ignore the fact that she looks as if she never has used it.

Similarly, a product whose price is lowered for "leader pricing" will not be perceived any differently by the already satisfied customer. However, the dissatisfied customer will be quick to point out this decrease in price is due to inferior quality.

Packaging illustrates the principle of leveling. Manufacturers have so over-used the word *new* that when a product is truly different in physical attributes, it may not be perceived as different. Walking through a supermarket, one can spot dozens of "new" products, whereas in reality perhaps only the package design is different or the product is structurally changed but with minor total improvement.

Sharpening takes place in the situation in which a consumer is trying to justify paying a higher price than he originally intended. He will pay special attention to the "higher quality" he is getting. If a man buys a watch for his wife in this type of situation, he will be susceptible to a series of ideas such as, it really is a better watch; it will keep time more accurately; it is both a luxury and a functional item; it will last for years; my wife really does deserve something extra special. As a result of sharpening other considerations, the original priority of price is lowered on his list of considerations.

Occupation and Status

III.B19 *Certain attitudes are determined and related to occupation and status and affect the ways in which audience members perceive, learn, are motivated, and are persuaded by messages.*

A distinction needs to be made between status and role. *Status* refers to the place in a particular system an individual occupies at a particular time. Statuses will be ascribed to him on the basis of his age, sex, birth, marriage into a particular family, and so on. A *role* is learned on the basis of status. Insofar as it represents overt behavior, role is the dynamic aspect of status. For example, upper economic groups spend a higher percentage of their income on medical and health needs than lower economic groups. This would seem to indicate that they are more concerned with good health and would be more susceptible than others to medical-health products, such as aspirin, cold remedies, vitamins, etc.

Sometimes marketers seek to have a certain product appeal to several different types of consumers rather than to just one type of consumer. But the problem here is that individuals of different status may perceive the same situation, product, or company in different ways. For example, furniture or clothing regarded by one social stratum as attractive may be regarded as vulgar or gaudy by another. A lower-status worker may purchase an expensive car because his immediate boss has one; but whereas the worker may perceive the car as a mechanism to bring him closer to his supervisor, his boss may regard his action as flashy, not suited to his present status.

The point is that a market may be segmented on the basis of consumers' psychological traits. Traditionally, market segmentation has been conceived of mainly in terms of age, sex, occupation, and income. However, personality types also constitute a basis for market segmentation.

Marketing Examples of Occupation and Status

Gottlieb used the following example to illustrate the preceding point. Brominex, a hypothetical product that will serve for illustrative purposes, is a pain-killer sold through drugstores without a prescription. At first one might feel that defining the market for Brominex is simply a matter of determining the traditional demographics of the sufferers and nonsufferers of upset stomachs and headaches. It is true that age and sex are factors that differentiate users from nonusers.

However, the marketing task is more complex. Individual consumer discretion will be involved in deciding at what point pain is severe enough for the use of an analgesic. One individual may put up with any amount of pain or discomfort rather than take anything, while another will take medicine at the slightest suggestion that anything is wrong. Hence, effective advertising for Brominex should consider the health attitudes of ultimate consumers. One would expect to communicate in one way with an individual who did not wish to admit he was ill and was only seeking relief for a localized symptom. Another method of communicating would be used with an individual who complained of various aches and pains but who was seeking to allay nonspecific anxieties (Gottlieb, 1958, p. 152).

One Botany-500 suit advertisement appealed to class-conscious men who want to impress their peers with how they dress. Instead of choosing one particular image to appeal to one particular man, the suit company bought a two-page spread in general-circulation magazines. The headline was, "Botany 500. We can give each man a little more than he expects." This open-ended appeal can be perceived by any audience member according to his particular ideas of his status and role.

The open-ended appeal has been useful in the development of the large discount stores. These stores stock merchandise for both the higher-income and lower-income brackets. For example, the clothing and various household goods carried are in the lower-priced lines; and yet the store also carries high-quality radios, cameras, and hardware-store items. Department stores may operate in this manner also; Marshall Field has lower-priced merchandise in its basement, several different levels of medium-priced lines on the main floors, and designer merchandise as well in special boutiques.

Cultural Influences

III.B20 *A message or communication is more likely to be perceived correctly if the message and media are in agreement with the norms and expectations of the cultural framework in which the audience members reside.*

There are many ways that culture influences an individual's ways of perceiving. Most often these influences go unnoticed because of a lack of exposure to different cultures. An individual is brought up with a given interpretation for stimuli, and he may never realize that his interpretations are biased by his own culture. Something he finds repugnant (eating eels, for example) may be well-accepted for individuals of another culture.

At least three main categories are affected by cultural influences: functional salience, familiarity, and systems of communicating. *Functional salience* refers to nvironmental aspects of a culture that influence perceptual discriminating. Whether or not snails or eels are acceptable or desirable foods is an example. Another is black as a symbol of mourning, or white signifying purity.

Familiarity refers to the frequency of exposure that individuals have to elements that may not be present in another culture. For example, the multitudes of different models of automobiles in the United States might not be recognized by a Zulu tribesman as different models but merely as automobiles. Another aspect of familiarity may involve stereotyping. By creating stereotypes, individuals eliminate the need for constant, close inspection and interpretation of stimuli. A series of *individual* stimuli are reduced to perceived *classes* of stimuli. A given set of characteristics is attributed to each class. An example would be the young man or young woman perceived as a "hippie." By being familiar only with certain characteristics, an individual often eliminates close examination of other relevant stimuli. For instance any girl in blue jeans and a tee-shirt or a boy with long hair became a "hippie" for many people. Simple classification is a result of the creation and reliance upon stereotypes.

Systems of communication refer to language as a technique of classification and labeling. What is of concern is the translation of a communication from one language to another. "It has lost something in the translation" is a familiar phrase—and correct. Because of different influences, what is humorous in one culture may be offensive in another. When reading an article in a foreign language, an individual may not be able to explain concepts fully to someone else. Although the general idea may be translatable, there may not be an equivalent translation for certain nuances of meaning.

Marketing Examples of Cultural Influences

The importance of numbers, because of history, represents distinct opportunities to marketing communicators. An interesting example is the number 76, used by a number of companies in promotions in 1976 to take advantage of the bicentennial celebration of the United States. Buick introduced a special edition of one of its models called "The Spirit of '76" and reinforced the use of the number by painting the cars a "patriotic" (at least in the American culture) red, white, and blue. National Food Stores had a "Lucky '76 Contest" in various stores, where with each purchase a lottery ticket was issued (free) and the customer could enter it in a weekly lottery in which all the cash prizes started with a 76: $7.60, $76.00, $760.00, and $7600.00.

Although the use of stereotypes is prevalent in advertising, note that some of those stereotypes change—something to which marketing communicators must constantly be attuned. The rise of "women's lib," for example, and the increased number and enforcement of antidiscriminatory laws represent attempts to break down cultural stereotypes. Old Milwaukee beer featured several television commercials in which women appeared in what traditionally would have been perceived as men's sports. One in particular shows a group of motorcyclists racing across the countryside and at the end of the race the loser is told to "go get the beer." A little later this individual returns and is praised for getting Old Milwaukee; then the helmet comes off to reveal a woman cyclist. Band-aid brand adhesives featured commercials that show Americans of different ethnic backgrounds using products: Orientals, blacks, Spanish-Americans, and whites. Thus, whereas in earlier years only whites appeared in most advertising, there has been an expansion to include many people other than whites.

18 An Overview of Perceiving

Implications

The foregoing principles involve variables that affect the probabilities of perceiving. These principles represent mediating factors in the process by which people select, organize, and interpret sensory stimulation. If the message has reached the communicatee (through exposing and attending) and has been perceived as the communicator desires, the question of further communicating depends upon whether the message will become part of the audience member's perceiving processes.

In part VI, on learning, we shall discuss ways in which the communicator can try to ensure that his message is learned as he desires. Before proceeding to learning, however, the interrelations of the perceiving variables should be summarized.

Model of Perceiving

Figure 18-1 is a diagrammatic representation of how these principles of perceiving work together. As with models of exposing and attending, preconceived variables (needs and wants, sociocultural status, personality variables, and other internal and external variables) are shown at this stage of the communicating model. They affect *all* stages of the communicating model. And as with the early segments of the total model, the variables affecting this step have been divided into message and medium variables and variables within the audience.

Message and Medium Variables

All the message and medium variables interact in determining the types of perceptual processes that occur after an audience member has been exposed to and attends to a communication. The setting or context in which perceiving takes place partially affects the identification and definition of the message. Thus related events, physical environment, and editorial environment can interact to sharpen, distort, obscure, or completely impair the perceiving of a message. A message consists of many parts that may or may not be perceived as being functionally integrated and/or related meaningfully by audience members.

193

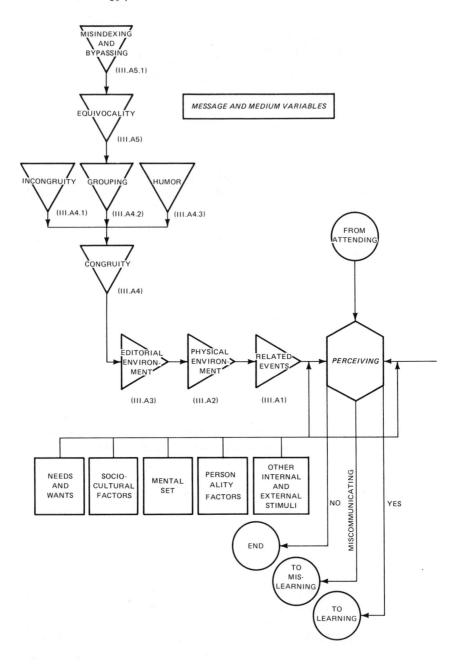

Figure 18-1. The Perceiving Stage of the Psychological Model of Communicating.

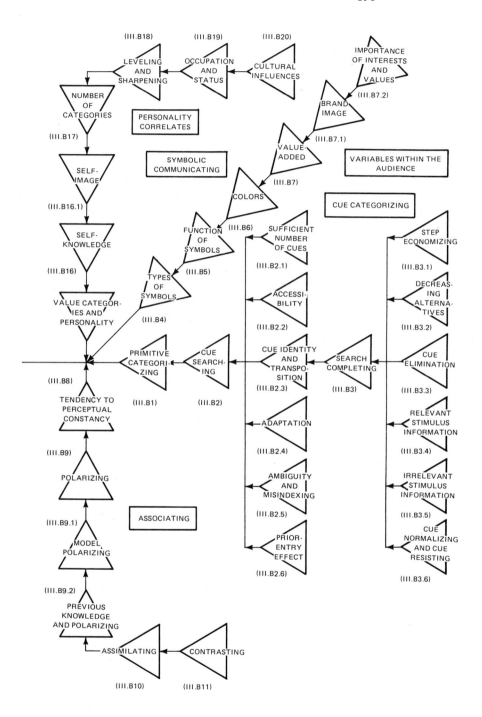

The degrees of congruity, incongruity, grouping, and humor help to determine the extent to which message elements are perceived as consistent and integrated. Equivocality, misindexing, and bypassing become particularly important when the message lends itself to multiple interpretations or is not related to experiences of the audience members.

Audience Variables

The audience variables are divided into four subdivisions: cue categorizing, symbolic communicating, associating, and personality correlates. Cue categorizing involves three basic principles: primitive categorizing, cue searching, and search completing, plus twelve subprinciples. Primitive categorizing serves as the basic form of classification, using rudimentary ideas (dimension, size, sound) directly after the moment of contact. Cue searching and its six subpropositions (sufficient number of cues, accessibility, cue identity and transposition, adaptation, ambiguity and misindexing, and price entry effect) play importance roles as the audience members seek to accumulate additional information within the message before identifying or defining it. The six subpropositions represent various problems and opportunities that pertain to the cues that are drawn up in the searching process. Search completing, however, and its six subpropositions (step economizing, decreasing alternatives, cue eliminating, relevant stimulus information, irrelevant stimulus information, and cue normalizing and cue resisting) take over after a tentative identification has been made in the cue-searching phase.

At this point, the subpropositions serve to identify conditions that can limit cues used to those that confirm the initial categorization. This involves assimilating or rejecting other sets of cues.

Symbolic communicating occurs if stimuli have meanings beyond what is directly manifested by the stimuli per se, and if the audience members respond to the stimuli in relation to the significances that these stimuli or similar stimuli have acquired for them, based on their previous experiences. Thus a communicator must identify carefully the types of symbols that may be applicable because they represent a distinct range of communicability to audience members.

The function of symbols and colors is to evoke a group of ideas in the members of the audience. These represent associations and relationships that have been established between and among symbols and colors and the meanings that the audience members have attached to them. Changes in the "value" of symbols can occur (value added), with importance of interests and values and brand image representing mediating factors in determining the direction and intensity of these changes.

Associating occurs as audience members search each message for relationships they can feel regarding the product, service, or individual described in the message. Associating focuses on the process whereby this relationship is established. Tendency to perceptual constancy and polarizing emphasize the relative stability of the categories used in perceiving, with model polarizing and previous knowledge and polarizing representing factors that can reinforce or upset this stability. Assimilating and contrasting help to determine the different types of perceptual distortion that can occur when messages are slightly different (assimilating occurs) or widely divergent (contrasting occurs).

Relevance, high valence, and high potency, however, influence the degree to which messages are perceived accurately by audience members. A communicator must relate the message to audience members' mental sets and determine current orientations to act (needs and wants) if messages are to be categorized properly. Failure to do this may evoke perceptual defenses that tend to distort the perceiving. This distortion may also occur if the communicator constructs a message that ignores the effect of expectations or expectations of reward that characterize the audience members.

Personality correlates represent still another set of variables that influence the accuracy of perceiving by audience members. Value categories and personality are particularly important to the communicator if messages are to be constructed that are similar to audience members' highly valued categories of orientation. Audience members' self-knowledge and self-image help to determine their ability to understand and accept new messages or events. However, the communicator must be aware that he is affected when leveling and sharpening occur, because of the strong permanence of past knowledge and experiences with products or services. The audience members' understanding and accepting of new messages is influenced further by the number of categories they use to describe themselves.

Finally, it should be kept in mind that the process of perceiving is partially determined by the social milieu in which the audience members reside and interact. Consequently, audience members' occupations and status as well as cultural influences are factors determining the degree to which messages are perceived and understood correctly.

**Part VI:
Learning**

19 Message and Medium Variables: Cognitive Variables

Background

Thus far in this book we have discussed the communicating processes of exposing, attending, and perceiving. All are necessary steps toward the desired result of persuasive mass communications: action or buying. Learning is also a necessary step in that chain. In order for messages to have any effect on consumers, they must first be learned or remembered. The processes of exposing, attending, and perceiving are necessary for learning, but alone are not sufficient. As with the first three steps, learning is a selective, active, complex process.

Learning and its "partner" remembering have been the subject of much research and theorizing in the field of psychology. Each principle outlined in this section does not apply to every message. The importance of each principle to a particular message will vary, depending on the message's approach, the media used, and the audience. The goal is to determine when learning is optimal and to show the communicator why and how to use this knowledge.

Learning is the acquisition by a living organism of a mode of response that is adapted to a motivating problematical situation. *Remembering* is the retention by a living organism of a previously acquired mode of response that is adapted to a motivating problematical situation. Furthermore, the opposite of remembering is *forgetting*, the nonretention of such a mode of response. An elaboration of this definition of learning follows (Britt, 1937, pp. 466-467): (1) the acquisition (2) by a living organism (3) of a mode of response (4) that is adapted (5) to a motivating (6) problematical situation.

1. *The acquisition*: Development, i.e., progressive change in behavior, must occur.

2. *By a living organism*: No learning takes place in inorganic matter. However, the concept of learning is not restricted so as to apply only to those living organisms which are multicellular and which possess a nervous system.

3. *Of a mode of response*: The establishment of change in behavior is necessary, although this change need not necessarily involve overt movement. Some modification of the organismic pattern is what is implied.

4. *Which is adapted*: An adjustment must be made to the situation.

5. *To a motivating*: A stimulus or stimuli must be sufficiently persistent to influence the behavior of the organism to the extent that the behavior is no longer affected in the same way by the same stimulus or stimuli.

201

6. *Problematical situation*: The organism must be confronted by a problem; that is to say, some lack of adjustment must occur between the organism's motivating needs, its immediate equipment, and the sensory situation. Thus, in phenomena such as sensory adaptation and fatigue, there are modifications in the behavior of the organism that are not classified as learning.

Here it is important to note the difference between incidental and intentional learning. The previous definition connotes *intentional learning*, which occurs when an individual is set or "intent" to learn. This is the case when either he is instructed to learn some material or is told that he will be tested on information that will be presented. *Incidental learning* is the complement of intentional learning and includes all other learning that occurs without the intention of the individual. Obviously these two types include all learning. The degree of attending is a most important factor in differentiating intention from incidental learning. And meaningfulness is the key to intentional learning (Britt, 1975).

The learning process means that the organism is potentially capable of continuing to modify its behavior, but not that it will necessarily do so. If the organism continues to modify its behavior to a motivating problematical situation, remembering is involved; that is, the organism has shown a capacity to change its behavior in accordance with past situations or past reactions. If, with repetitions of the same or similar situations, the adjustment between the organism's motivating needs, its reactive equipment, and the sensory situation becomes simpler, more rapid, and more enduring, we have evidence that remembering is occurring.

Finally, learning cannot be considered an entity distinct from remembering. Both occur on the same time continuum; that is to say, remembering is, in certain respects, a continuation of the learning process.

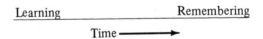

Such an interrelation and integration of the activities of learning and remembering exists that it is accurate to speak of the learning-remembering process. *Forgetting* is really only the activity of remembering described from the opposite point of view. Thus our diagram may be modified:

Learning   Remembering (opposite aspect, Forgetting)
   Time   ⟶

Any attempt to separate learning from remembering is only for the sake of discussion and understanding. Neither is an observable or measurable separate entity in itself, but rather each is part of a continuum during which an organism's behavior changes. For instance, no study can measure learning without also measuring memory, since it is impossible to determine the amount of material originally learned except by asking the subject to remember it. One can measure the amount of material forgotten between time A and time B, but one cannot measure learning in any way except by measuring memory at some point in time.

A further complication is that various stages occur in remembering. The simplest form is *recognition*, which requires that an individual remember that he has seen or learned something previously after being exposed to it the second time. Multiple-choice tests measure recognition: a student may not be able to remember what river Washington crossed, but with the hint that it was either (1) the Potomac, (2) the Delaware, or (3) the Ganges, he may recognize Delaware as the correct answer.

The next simplest form of remembering is *aided recall*, which would involve adding external clues to the preceding example. *Unaided recall* would require the student, with no help, to answer "Delaware" to the question "What river did Washington cross?"

In advertising, the "memory" of the consumer has been divided into these stages, with regard to symbols; and Berelson and Steiner added a fourth stage, *savings*. This refers to facts and ideas that cannot be recalled without some relearning effort, such as mathematics one may have learned many years ago. As it happens, the hardest to accomplish is also the type of symbolic memory that has the shortest life span (Berelson and Steiner, 1964, p. 255);

Shortest-lived "hardest"	1. Unaided recall
	2. Aided recall
Longest-lived "easiest"	3. Recognition
	4. Savings

These categories are not separate entities. They form a continuum along which the degree of material remembered may vary.

As in previous sections of this book, variables of communicating are divided into two groups for investigation: message and medium variables and variables within the audience. The first type of variables can be controlled by the communicator, while the second type are dependent upon characteristics of the particular audience the communicator attempts to reach. This does not mean that the communicator is helpless in the face of audience variables. He can design his message in certain ways to enhance learning and remembering, depending upon the degree to which these variables apply to the target audience.

This chapter and the following chapter relate to the message and medium variables. The present chapter deals with *cognitive variables,* while the next chapter is devoted to *affective variables.*

Cognitive Variables

As indicated, the cognitive variables to be discussed are near to each other in time or sequence and are interrelated.

Passage of Time

IV.A1 *After an item or message has been learned to some extent by an audience member, passage of time is associated with a decrease in the audience member's retention of that item or message.*

Krueger conducted a classic experiment in which he used monosyllabic nouns as the material to be learned. One group of subjects learned the list until they had repeated it perfectly one time. A second group learned the list until they had repeated it perfectly once, then were given additional trials amounting to 50 to 100 percent of the number necessary to reach the first perfect recitation. In other words, if 12 trials were required for the subject to recite the list perfectly once, he was given 6 or 12 additional trials. Following the learning, relearning trials were given either 1, 2, 4, 7, 14, or 28 days later. See table 19-1. While the increased amount of remembering was smaller between 150 and 200 percent, table 19-1 indicates that repetition review significantly aided long-term remembering (Krueger, 1929).

Zielske conducted a study that has been widely discussed—an attempt to measure the rate at which consumers can remember advertising and the rate at which they forget it. Thirteen different advertisements from the same national newspaper campaign were used. The advertised product was a food found in

Table 19-1
Recall Scores as a Function of Degree of Learning

| Interval (Days) | Degree of Learning | | |
| | 100 | 150 | 200 |
	Mean Words Recalled		
1	3.10	4.60	5.83
2	1.80	3.60	4.65
4	.50	2.05	3.30
7	.20	1.30	1.65
14	.15	.65	.90
28	.00	.25	.40

Source: Adapted from Krueger, "The Effect of Overlearning on Retention," *Journal of Experimental Psychology* 12 (February 1929).

almost every home. Reprints of the advertisements were mailed in plain envelopes to women with no other material included. Two groups of women were selected in a systematic random manner from the Chicago phone directory. One group received reprints of the advertisements at weekly intervals every week for the first 13 weeks of the year. The other group received the same 13 reprints but mailed four weeks apart, so that it took a whole year for the women to receive all 13. Recall of the advertisements was measured via telephone interviews throughout the year. The women answered such questions as What did the advertising look like? What did it say about the product? Where did you see it?

Zielske found that exposures at weekly intervals developed remembrance of the advertisements at a faster rate, relative to the number of exposures, than did exposures at 4-week intervals. The rate of forgetting was very rapid. "The intensive burst of thirteen weekly exposures to the advertising made about one-third more different housewives at least temporarily remember the advertisement as the same number of exposures spread out over the year. However, the concentration of exposures during the first thrteen weeks of the year left a large portion of the year with little or no remembrance of the advertising" (Zielske, 1959, p. 241).

A study by Appel related time and retention to the recall of television commercials. He conducted 96 retests, representing 81 different 60-second commercials for 31 brands. The retests were conducted at intervals of one week up to a period of several years. On the day after the commercials were on the air, a random sample of households were phoned. The appropriate member of the household was asked if she saw the commercial. If the answer was yes, she was asked to describe it in detail. For each commercial, a recall score was obtained on the basis of the percentage of respondents who could accurately recall it.

From his results, Appel concluded that there was a slight increase in the recall score with repetition to begin with, which he attributed to learning the information included in the advertisement. Then followed a decline, which was attributed to the advertising "wearing out." His evidence indicated that commercials that initially make a vivid impression upon the consumer benefit more from repeat exposure than do commercials that initially make less of an impression (Appel, 1971).

Several conclusions can be drawn from these studies. First, it seems helpful regularly to remind audience members of a message, to renew their learning and remembering. Second, an intense first impression can be made by a message that is particularly important to an individual, but this should be reinforced over time.

These strong first-impression messages will require less frequency to attain a given level of awareness. Therefore, messages should be designed for initial impact and then must be repeated. A high level of repetition will not overcome the flow of a message that is off target. Audience members may recall the message after a great many repetitions, but they must be able to relate it to their needs and wants to be motivated and persuaded by it. The communicator thus should carefully and clearly express the message as it relates to his audience and continually reinforce their learning through repetition.

Marketing Examples of Passage of Time

Automobile dealers attempt to overcome decreased message retention by sending reminders to those people who have bought a car from them in the past. The dealer reminds the individual of the high-quality automobile he is driving and the special deals he can get from the dealer—any decrease in remembering the original sales message is bolstered by this technique.

To overcome the loss of retention of messages that occurs with the passage of time, advertisers frequently tie in promotional display materials in the store with television messages. Thus a "pick-a-pair" display for Budweiser beer in a grocery outlet would remind the shopper of advertisements that said "Pick a pair of six-packs, buy Bud."

In personal selling, it may be wise to repeat sales points; if a prospective customer has been coming back to a store more than once to consider buying an item, and if the passage of time between these different occasions is significant, then the salesperson should be sure to inform the customer about important ideas mentioned to him before. Just because the ideas have been mentioned does not mean that the customer remembers them.

Repetition and Overexposure

IV.A2 *Repetition aids in the learning of a message, but repetition of identical messages beyond a critical point causes overexposure, with no improvement in learning.*

Repetition of a message aids in learning and in reinforcing what has been learned. Since a message can be repeated either to teach or to reinforce what has been taught, it is useful to understand this distinction when considering the effects of repetition on communicatees. Repetition aids in learning because any single exposure to a message is likely to be too weak a cue, that is, hardly enough to excite an individual's drives above the threshold level. Thus multiple exposures often aid in the learning of a message. However, all learning of a message must finally slow down and then stop, reaching a period of no improvement (Sorenson, 1964, p. 433). Repetition of the learned message at this time can result in *overlearning*.

Although reinforcing a learned message through repetition is not harmful for the learning process, what is harmful is that increasing repetition can cause boredom, which prevents either learning or positive reinforcement. Thus repetition can have two ill effects. It can prevent learning, or it can preclude reinforcement. This means that any message can be repeated too many times; and the message is then said to be overexposed.

A communicator must realize that if a competing message does better than his in a recall test after the competing message has been communicated, the increased recall may be due to increased exposing rather than to a superior content. If recall scores for the competing message are worse, it may be because its effectiveness has begun to decay as a result of overexposure.

The previous principle pointed out that audience members need to be reminded of a message or it will be forgotten over time. A great deal of evidence, both scientific and inferential, implies that repetition enhances learning of a mass communication.

One experiment designed to assess the effects of advertising repetition reinforced the importance of frequency of exposure. Stewart tested brand awareness and sales effects of varying levels of advertising repetition in Fort Wayne, Indiana. He divided the city into four sections and arranged for advertisements for two new products to be presented to each section at different frequency levels. The first section of the city, the control group, received no exposure. The other section of the city received newspapers on four successive Wednesdays with split-run advertisements, that is, with every other copy of the newspaper with advertisement A and the alternate ones with advertisement B. The third group received advertisements on 8 successive Wednesdays. The fourth group was exposed on 20 successive Wednesdays. Stewart was careful to control or account for additional variables, such as competitive advertising, differences between in-store promotions in the various sections of the city, and so on.

His results showed a strong correlation between brand awareness and the amount of advertising in each of the four sections of the city. However, a significantly high degree of awareness existed for the new brands in the sections not exposed to the test advertising. Evidently, the effects of word-of-mouth communication between consumers and the effects of in-store promotions (uniform across all four divisions of the city) created a relatively high degree of brand awareness (Stewart, 1964, pp. 283-288).

Stewart's results also showed that the additional numbers of consumers who tried the new products because of advertising exposure tended to be more marginal consumers. Their interest in the product was, on the average, less than that of the control group. Evidence of this was the fact that in advertising-exposed areas, the number of trial purchasers increased, but the percentage of purchasers preferring the test brands declined with higher levels of advertising. Stewart recognized that a great deal more field research is necessary to validate his results and to provide answers to the many questions raised by the data.

Nevertheless, a tentative conclusion one can draw is that advertising repetition does increase brand awareness and brand trial.

Carrick has provided analysis supporting frequency-building advertising campaigns. Since consumer choices are decisions made under conditions of uncertainty in which consumers have incomplete knowledge, consumers must rely upon "simplified maps . . . simplifications of the real economic world." Carrick noted that brand superiority implied by relatively greater advertising frequency is one such applicable simplification (Carrick, 1959).

However, a great deal of advertiser attention is paid to the significance of advertising, its appeals, its quality of readership, and its design. Carrick suggested that consumers do not respond to significant information for cues suggesting "satisfying" purchase behavior. He held that changes in advertising copy usually do not contribute as much to changes in brand sales and/or brand share as does advertising frequency relative to competitors (Carrick, 1959).

Ray, Sawyer, and Strong conducted their own study, in a format similar to most repetition studies. However, they used more advertisements, different schedules, and a number of testing measures, not just measures of advertising recall. Advertisements were presented in weekly, biweekly, and monthly schedules. The results obtained were quite different, depending on whether the measure used was recall of the specific mail advertisements, brand preference, or mention of the brands advertised.

Advertisement recall had the sharpest curve of the recall measures. It stayed at about 65 percent over the 13-week period. Brand mention had a much more gradual slope. Brand preference showed a slight increase over the first six exposure groups and a negative trend in the following weeks. Underlying the brand preference curve, they felt were a number of different results for individual advertisements and brands. An advertisement for a ballpoint pen produced a negative repetition curve, whereas a different advertisement for the same product caused no repetition effect on brand preference. An advertisement for a particular soap brand showed no repetition effects, while another soap advertisement for a different brand caused a negative repetition curve. All these varied effects on preference occurred for advertisements that produced quite different results on the ad recall and brand mention measures (Ray, Sawyer, and Strong, 1971).

From these studies it becomes clear that while frequency of repetition is important to learning, the content of the message (that is, its significant information) is also a controller of eventual learning. In other words, repetition in and of itself does not foster retention of a message; it can, in fact, reach a detrimental level.

The idea of overexposure has mainly been an academic problem because few advertising budgets have been large enough to allow for the number of exposures required for overexposure to occur. However, with increased budgets, concentrated selling efforts, and increased use of 30-second television commercials, both message repetition and overexposure are becoming significant problems. Certain tests for DuPont showed that additional exposures of advertisements decreased the information level because the respondents had seen enough commercials to reach the saturation point (the point of overexposure) on attention (Barton, 1968). The respondents then exhibited lower learning scores, as decay developed in knowledge previously acquired. In addition, the repetition of identical messages beyond some critical point, in many cases, may actually lead to a negative response (Sturdivant, 1970, p. 177).

The difficult problem, of course, is in determining the critical point after which repetition of a message can cause overexposure and thereby abet forgetting or lead to negative feelings. No absolute answer can be given to this problem; but the following factors, among others, are of paramount importance: the message complexity, the timing of the exposures, the competing messages, the communicatees themselves, and the types of media used.

If the message is simple, it can be learned after only a few repetitions, and thus the chance of overexposure is increased. Overexposure is also likely to be increased if the messages are concentrated in a single period. If the message is not distinctive, it is likely to be sensed not just as repetitive but as annoyingly reptitious.

Marketing Examples of Repetition and Overexposure

One of the more memorable messages for Flair felt-tip marking pens was a television commercial that showed a hand holding the Flair pen and writing the same word over and over again. That word was *Flair*. The announcer added to this by continually saying the word *Flair*. This continuing repetition served the purpose of establishing the brand name in the thinking of the viewer, and associating it with the pen that wrote it.

McDonald's, the national drive-in food chain, uses repetition in location extremely well. By acquiring many choice locations and erecting their symbolic "golden arches" (the letter M in the form of two interlocking arches) above the outlet, people are reminded over and over again of McDonald's outlets.

Continuity of Varied Stimuli

IV.A3 *The audience's learning and remembering of a message is enhanced by repetition with slight variations in the message. This ensures no loss of meaning through overlearning of a single repeated message.*

At the beginning of a series of repeated stimuli, the audience responds to the pleasure of novelty and the gratification of curiosity through increased familiarity with the message. In other words, the audience is receptive during the early stages of repetition. This contrasts with the more traditional view that audience members will perceive and learn the communication only after concentrated repeated stimuli. A message with initially high readership maintains high readership scores with successive repetitions. One study by Starch examined as many as 8 repetitions and found the principle to hold true (Starch, 1966, p. 94). However, readership of messages with low initial scores is not necessarily enhanced by repetition. Readership remains at the same low level.

What happens to a message if it is repeated indefinitely? As pointed out in the earlier discussion of repetition, audience members will eventually become bored with continued exposure; their search for novelty and increased familiarity with the message will be overly satisfied.

A compromise between novelty and the cumulative effects of repetition can be attained by repetition with appropriate amounts of variation in the advertising. The general theme and perceptual structure of the advertisement and/or commercial should be similar. Variation should be achieved by altering the details of the message periodically throughout a campaign. One classic example of this use of varied stimuli is Breck Shampoo's Breck Girl series. The idea throughout the campaign has been that beautiful girls use Breck products. However, through the years many different attractive girls have been used to promote several different Breck products. The original format remained unchanged.

However, similar approaches may not be immediately transferable to other products and services, especially those products having complex sales points. Consumer durables—such as washing machines or vacuum cleaners—are an example. Rather than merely building familiarity with a name and a theme, such products must communicate a sizable amount of information to the audience. How might continuity of stimuli, with appropriate variation, be applied to situations such as this? Basically, the more information a selling message (or any communication) includes, the greater the number of impressions required by the audience to become familiar with the stimuli. Therefore, complex messages require more repetition than simpler messages.

In summary, continuity of stimuli with variation can extend the useful life of a good advertising message. It will, however, only compound the unfortunate effects of weak impressions made by an ill-conceived message. The degree of appropriate variation balanced against appropriate continuity for a good idea depends on the nature and needs of the product or service. A general guide, however, is this: The theme and perceptual structure of the message must remain uniform throughout repetitive exposures. But variation should characterize the attention-getters of the message, the message elements to which the audience is immediately attentive.

Marketing Examples of Continuity of Varied Stimuli

Steinway used varied repetition in promoting their pianos. Their print advertisements all showed a photograph of a portrait of a piano great seated at a Steinway piano. One week they used Liszt; another week they would use Paderewski, Wagner, or Hofmann. But the copy underneath was always the same, "Instrument of the Immortals."

A Crest toothpaste advertising campaign illustrated the concept of varied repetition. Variation was achieved through different casts of characters and situations; continuity was maintained through use of essentially the same copy in every advertisement. In each advertisement a child interrupted one of his parents saying, "Mommy, mommy (daddy, daddy) I have only one cavity!" The parent would then explain to a second adult in the commercial and the audience that she (he) attributed fewer cavities from the last checkup to regular brushing of the teeth with Crest toothpaste.

An advertiser must be careful to present stimuli to consumers in a way that will not lead to overexposure, the state of boredom and satiation created by too much repetition of a message. For example, the television, radio, and print messages of three major soft-drink marketers (Pepsi-Cola, Coca-Cola, and 7-Up) for years have run campaigns that focus on a central theme. Variations were designed uniquely for perception by the youth markets sought by the advertising. 7-Up's "Wet and Wild" theme used radio to particular advantage. The "Wet and Wild" song remained the same throughout each radio spot but varied according to the style of the particular top-name performer singing it. The variations in stylistic presentation were coupled with performers recognized by the target market. Young people found sufficient novelty in each presentation of the "Wet and Wild" theme to continue paying attention to the selling message.

Primacy and Recency

IV.A4 *Audience members experience greater learning of items at the beginning and end of a message than for those items in the middle.*

Based on experiments with remote associations and derived lists (both techniques employing unrelated nonsense material), Ebbinghaus developed the theory that when the human mind is confronted with a list of nonsense terms, the members of the series presented first and last can be recalled with fewer errors than the members of the series learned in the middle. He referred to these effects as *primacy* and *recency*, and in further experiments developed a time-lapse assumption and a theory of reminiscence. The *time-lapse assumption* states that the longer the period of time between two associations, the weaker the first association becomes. The *theory of reminiscence* states that an association made 48 hours prior to an attempt at recall is more accurately remembered than an association only 1 hour old (Ebbinghaus, 1913).

On the basis of Ebbinghaus' work, it is not possible to prove that either primacy or recency is a stronger force in the learning process. Although he did establish theories of primacy and recency, the only thing Ebbinghaus actually demonstrated was that when terms are positioned serially, those terms in the center of the series are recalled to a lesser degree of accuracy than those terms at either end of the series.

Postman and Rau performed an experiment in which subjects memorized series of nonsense words and meaningful words and then repeated them. Their findings showed a primacy effect; that is, fewer errors were made on words at the beginnings of the series than at the ends. A recency effect showed fewer errors in words at the ends of the lists than in the middle (Postman and Rau, 1957, p. 236).

Hovland found that the order of presentation was a more important factor in influencing beliefs, attitudes, and opinions of those subjects with relatively weak desires for understanding than for those with a great desire to learn. The point he makes is that nonsense materials and items of unimportance can be learned without any involvement on the receiver's part (Hovland, 1957, p. 136).

Relating to this proposition, Krugman conducted several tests on television commercials. He set up a trailer in a shopping-center parking lot and tested shoppers' recall of a margarine commercial that was placed in four different positions within a series of commercials. The results of this test revealed the effects of primacy and recency, as shown in table 19-2. This process was repeated for a floor wax, a deodorant, and a hand soap. All product commercials tested for recall showed similar effects for both primacy and recency (Krugman, 1962, p. 631).

In the tests conducted by Krugman, the primary criterion for memory was discovered to be "liked best." He theorized that the effects of the order of

Table 19-2
Recall and Position of Commercials

Numerical Position	Number of Accurate Recalls
1	40 out of 60
2	13 out of 60
3	8 out of 60
4	21 out of 60

Source: Krugman, "An Application of Learning Theory to TV Copy Testing," *Public Opinion Quarterly* 26 (Winter 1962):631.

presentation do not correlate "with copy impact or retention, [but] with awareness and liking." He also stated that his studies resulted in proof that "no correlation existed between order of presentation and an increase in favorable attitude," nor could a correlation be established between an increase in brand rating and the liking for the commercial. Krugman's studies also indicate that commercial copy that produces primacy and recency effects is both durable and wearable, and has the potential to become liked with repetition (Krugman, 1962, p. 632).

Marketing Examples of Primacy and Recency

Oldsmobile made use of this principle in a magazine advertisement that gave seven "down to earth reasons for buying an Olds Ninety Eight." The first and seventh reasons were solid, important, meaningful advantages of the Oldsmobile. However, reasons 2 through 6 were very minor points that could be made about any car. Thus by placing the important material at the beginning and the end, Oldsmobile hoped to get across the two main, important points.

Commonwealth Edison used this principle in a magazine advertisement aimed at bettering the company's image with environmentalists and the pollution-minded public. The advertisements began by stating an important fact—that electricity is used to recycle steel. In the middle of the advertisement, the process was spelled out. At the end, the other important point was made—". . . reducing litter and conserving litter is as important to me as it is to you."

Often salespeople exemplify this proposition in their sales presentations. Exciting, startling, and/or relevant items are used in the opening as an attention getter, while the sales point with the most immediate effect on the specific prospect's situation may be presented in the close. If the prospect takes several days to decide, the sales points of the exciting opening and the immediate closing of the presentation probably will be uppermost in his or her mind.

Relation of Time to Primacy and Recency

IV.A4.1 *As the time interval between learning the first item and the second item of a message increases, the strength of primacy increases over recency.*

Certain of Underwood's experiments have received verification from Hovland, who demonstrated how important it is to consider the length of the "time interval between learning of the second communication and the occasion when remembering is required." Hovland pointed out that when the interval is short, recency is most effective. As the time lapse grows in duration, primacy becomes the stronger (Hovland, Janis, and Kelley, 1953, pp. 112-113).

In an earlier study, Hovland presented the theory that the "steepness of the serial position gradients is a function of the rate of presentation" (Hovland, 1938, p. 351). The order of presentation, then, achieves the highest degree of influence on primacy and recency when it is coupled with a reasonable rate of presentation. When two experiences of equal strength are experienced, the more recent contributes more to the net response tendency of the moment, but this advantage will rapidly dissipate, tending toward equal strengths for the two responses after a long time.

However, of two associations equally strong at the moment, the older will be stronger tomorrow; it will decay less rapidly. (Being equal at the moment implies that the older must once have been stronger.) The longer the time period between the first and second of these two experiences, the greater the recency effects. But the longer the time period after the second experience, the less will be the "weight" of the second in the composite.

In summary, with experiences of equal strengths, the recency effect quickly disappears. However, over time, the primacy effect causes older strong communications to replace communications momentarily strong because they are more recent.

Marketing Examples of Relation of Time to Primacy and Recency

The point mentioned first in an advertisement is the one likely to be best remembered. Therefore, the unique selling proposition usually appears in the headline of a print advertisement, since the headline, to which the reader attends, is perceived first, and will be remembered as he considers the other points in the message.

If a salesperson is going to tell a consumer of the quality and price of a product, he or she will probably use the principles of primacy and recency. First, he or she will mention quality and dwell on it for as long as possible, so that the first item of the message will "sink in" more. Finally, he or she will mention price, hoping by this time that the idea of quality is strong enough to overcome any second thoughts the consumer might have about price.

Since the recency effect is greater when a time interval is involved, marketers of a product that is purchased frequently—such as staples and household items—might be wise to use high frequency; this would tend to increase the probability of a recency effect for shoppers. However, for larger purchases, such as cars, furniture, and appliances, that are usually the result of much fact-seeking and contemplation, primacy effects are most beneficial.

Characteristics of Middle Items

IV.A4.2 *Items in the middle of a message can be learned and recalled best by an audience if these items relate to the items at the beginning and the end of the message.*

The implications of this principle may be disturbing to communicators who use a catchy headline to lead audience members into an advertisement, then deliver the selling message, and then end with a slogan. The members of the audience may learn only the catchy headline and slogan and forget the real heart of the communication. Thus it is vital that headlines and slogans relate directly to the selling message.

A number of studies have shown that items in the middle need not be obscured. Tulving and Patterson had subjects learn one of two lists of words. The first contained 24 unrelated words; the second contained 4 related words scattered throughout 20 other unrelated words. The control list produced both primacy and recency effects. However, the experimental list showed high retention of the 4 related words, illustrating the important concept that points from the middle of a message can be remembered if they are presented properly (Tulving and Patterson, 1968).

Another experiment conducted by Harris and Lown illustrated still another method of raising the retention of items in the middle of a message. Their experiment shows how interitem time distribution affects primacy and recency. Three separate experiments were conducted under three different conditions. Condition I consisted of a presentation of 20 consecutive digits. Condition II consisted of 10 consecutive digits, a 20-second pause, followed by 10 more digits. Condition III consisted of six consecutive digits, a 10-second pause, 7 more digits, a 10-second pause, and 7 more digits. Each subject was provided an answer sheet to correspond with his particular condition. The interitem time distribution of conditions II and III tended to alter the normal effects of primacy and recency, as represented in condition I.

The retention of the items before and after each pause in conditions II and III was increased. Each portion of the lists of conditions II and III showed primacy and recency effects. Condition I had a mean number of 6 digits recalled. Condition II had a mean digit recall of 9; and condition III had a mean digit recall of 10. The experiment shows that as interitem time distribution is inserted into the experiment and increased, the mean level of recall is increased as a result of increased learning of material from the middle of the message. The middle items had become, in effect, beginning and end items of shorter message units (Harris and Lown, 1968).

Marketing Examples of Characteristics of Middle Items

Allstate Insurance Company illustrated this principle in some magazine advertisements. The headline was "Whatever happened to the fun of driving?" Following this was a paragraph of about 250 words telling of reasons for auto accidents, which take the fun out of driving. The ending was "Let's make driving a good thing again." The beginning and end were "tied together" and explained in the middle paragraphs.

Xerox demonstrated the principle in advertising a new computer. The middle items of the full-page advertisement explained the curious headline (see below), and related the end with the beginning.

Headline: "This XEROX machine can't make a copy."
Copy: "It used to be true, if XEROX made the machine, the machine made copies. . . . The XEROX machine above doesn't copy, it computes. . . . So if a machine with our brand name on it doesn't deliver copies to you, don't get upset."
End: "Maybe it's just not supposed to."

Pepperidge Farm food manufacturers ran advertisements before Thanksgiving time on ideas for different types of stuffings for Thanksgiving turkey. The headline was "This Thanksgiving, why settle for one kind of stuffing when it's so easy to serve three?" At the end of the advertisement was a coupon that readers could send in to receive a recipe booklet for stuffing. The middle of the advertisement gave sample recipes incorporating Pepperidge Farm products. The message regarding Pepperidge Farm products was positioned in the middle of the advertisement as a means of facilitating the learning of the message.

Distributed Practice

IV.A5 *Distributed repetitions of a message are more effective in causing audience members to learn the message than massed repetitions of the message, given a certain number of initial exposures.*

Distributed practice refers to repetitions spaced over time so the audience members necessarily will be engaged in other activities between message perceptions. *Massed practice* refers to repetitions of the message one after another (for instance, several television commercials per day for several days).

Studies of the effects of distributed practice generally measure the learning and remembering of lists of words, new textbook material, pictures, and figures. The basic finding has been that when an individual learns something for the first time, he usually learns more by repetition. The most effective way to repeat a communication to produce lasting retention is to spread the repetitions evenly rather than massing them in a short period of time (Berelson and Steiner, 1964, p. 159).

Distributed practice is superior to massed practice in a number of situations. Underwood reviewed much of the research done in this area and noted the qualifications that must be made in assessing the superiority of distributed practice. The superiority of distributed practice for learning new material may result from the advantage of the learner having more time between messages to eliminate errors in perception. Repetition aids learning in perception of errors in interpretation to be presented to the communicatee. He may then think about both the correct and incorrect possibilities, and the next time will learn to eliminate one more possible error. Distributed practice is advantageous because there is more time to eliminate errors. In massed practice the presentations come so rapidly that error tendencies might be merely suppressed rather than actually removed (Underwood, 1961).

Perceptual error is not the only factor that favors distributed practice. Experiments have shown that massed practice acquisition trials lead the subject to perceive the number of trials as fewer than actual. As Underwood stated: "It appears that the 'received' frequency of a massed practice word is appreciably less than its true frequency. . . . a word presented under the massed practice schedule 'behaves' as if it had been presented less frequently than in fact it had" (Underwood, 1967, p. 93). Therefore, given a certain number of repetitions, more repetitions are perceived under distributed-practice conditions than under massed-practice conditions.

The most important qualification to the advantages of distributed practice has to do with interference. For the distributing of messages over a period of time to be advantageous, the activity in between message presentation must not be of an interfering nature. *Interference* refers to similar message points that might confuse the learner or cause him to misperceive the intended message.

It is clear that the experiments reported here differ significantly from the environments in which mass communications are delivered to audience members. In some ways, then, the experiments say very little about which kind of presentations are most effective for learning—massed presentations or distributed presentations.

Some important conclusions can be drawn, however, from experimental research in that (1) every mass audience is, by nature, subject to distractions in between message exposures; and (2) no communicator can control the messages of his competitors. Therefore, the best combination for message presentations is probably a combination of distributed presentations and massed presentations—that is, beginning the campaign with a closely presented group of messages and then continuing to present messages over a less-concentrated but evenly distributed period of time. In this way the communicator has assured maximum initial learning with minimal distractions (the main objection to distributed practice being interference) *and* maximum learning after the campaign has run its course because of the distributed reminders. If the communicator begins to feel that the distributed messages are losing effect, he may justifiably suspect interference from closely related products, from similar-sounding messages, or from other newsworthy events.

It appears that distributed practice, or distributed advertising messages benefit an established product more than a new product. Massed practice or massed advertising messages are more beneficial to the product innovation and are more beneficial than distributed advertising exposures would be for any specific number of advertising exposures. The reasoning is that the product innovation requires the impact of high repetition per unit time in the market-place. The established product requires that the consumer's knowledge of the product and of the brand image be reinforced and kept at a rather stable level. Distributed practice may not be appropriate to the product innovation because knowledge of the new product and its advertised benefits decays more rapidly in the consumer's memory than does knowledge of the older product. This more rapid decay is in part the result of the message's greater vulnerability to retroactive inhibition and proactive inhibition.

However, the established product may show a marginal increase in consumer learning with massed advertising messages, but such massing cannot continue indefinitely. It is most likely that once the media schedule for the established product returns to normal, awareness of the product will return to normal as well. The importance of a rapid increase in product awareness is much greater for the innovative product than for the established product simply because the innovative product must start from an awareness level of nearly zero.

Marketing Examples of Distributed Practice

It has been mentioned that new products often use massed repetitions of their message. This is true because they need to build awareness quickly, by frequent exposure of their product name to the audience members. The initial goal is awareness, rather than an immediately learning of what the product does. After a high awareness level has been obtained, the advertising concentrates more upon consumer understanding. At this point, the campaign often distributes its commercial repetitions more evenly.

For example, when Herbal Essence Shampoo was first introduced, its commercials were massed, presented with high frequency, the goal being to inform consumers of the shampoo's existence. Later on, when the product had been on the market for a few years, its commercials were aired on a less-frequent basis. Consumers had become aware of the product and had had time to learn its attributes. There was not much need to concentrate further on awareness, but rather on learning. By distributing the commercial repetitions, Herbal Essence gave consumers time to think about their product between exposures.

At the opposite end of this problem are products like Coca-Cola—well-known, long-standing products. Consumers know of the existence and of the product attributes. As a result, there is not much new for consumers to *learn* about Coke; most advertising is of the "reminder" type and massed repetition would be inappropriate.

Retroactive Inhibition

IV.A6 *If two sets of associations have been learned one after another by members of an audience, the second tends to impair remembering of the first.*

Retroactive inhibition is defined as the "impairment of the normal effects of a learning activity when it is followed closely by another activity, especially one somewhat similar to the first; or the hypothetical process accountable therefore" (English and English, 1958, p. 263). Retroactive inhibition, to explain it simply, is the forgetting that occurs as a result of interference. Since interference was just discussed in connection with distributed practice, it will not be explained at length here. In the laboratory, retroactive inhibition is produced by experimentally creating interfering activities—this interference, then, becomes the independent variable. With changes in the interfering activity, changes in the amount of forgetting are found to occur.

In his study of retroactive inhibition, Hall summarized a wide situational range of experiments in terms of two general conclusions: (1) as original learning increases, the relative amount of retroactive inhibition decreases when the degree of interpolated learning is constant; and (2) as the degree of interplated learning increases, the amount of retroactive inhibition increases, when the degree of original learning is constant (Hall, 1966, p. 603).

For example, Underwood found that when interfering stimuli were removed in a laboratory situation, forgetting decreased from 75 to 25 percent over a 24-hour period (Underwood, 1957). It is assumed by Underwood and others that the amount of retroactive inhibition and the resulting retention percentages will vary in accordance with the perceived similarity between the activity to be learned and the interfering activity; that is, the more similar the messages are, the more pronounced will be the interfering effects of the second message.

Intervening activities outside the laboratory are inescapable; they are one of the major contributors to the forgetting process. Retroactive inhibition must be considered as an expected effect following the learning of any message conveyed to the typical viewing audience. Therefore, it will be helpful to cite a few of the statements made by theorists who have attempted to determine the circumstances under which the greatest decrease in remembering will occur.

Britt summarized the effect of degrees of similarity on retroactive inhibition as follows:

As the degree of similarity of one of these factors (content, meaning, form, method, operation, environment, etc.) is relatively increased, the degree of retroactive inhibition also tends to increase. A certain point is eventually reached, however, after which increasing the degree of similarity results in more and more actual identity of the various factors ... until at the upper limit, actual identity of all the factors, there may be no inhibition at all but simply repetition. [Britt, 1936, p. 210.]

Given this evidence for the inevitable occurrence of a memory loss resulting from retroactive inhibition, what suggestions can be given to the communicator in constructing messages to resist this effect?

The first thing the communicator can strive for is nonsimilarity between his message and any other message to which the audience may be exposed. He can increase emphasis on the most important parts of his message (such as brand name, the theme music, the product-use illustration, the announcer's voice) in order to increase the degree of original learning. Repetition within a single message presentation will help to consolidate the memory for any given point. It will lessen the chance that interfering material will later be confused with the original facts.

Marketing Examples of Retroactive Inhibition

Retroactive inhibition can occur within a single brand's advertising campaign. Consider the case of a new cookie, for example. Initial advertisements may position this as the best new taste in cookies. If, however, a few months later advertisements illustrate these cookies for use in recipes (for example, as pie crust and topping crumbs), retroactive inhibition may occur. Audience members must first learn of the cookie as a snack food before they are taught that it is a baking ingredient. New products often obtain a confused image through retroactive inhibition by trying to be "all things to all people" too quickly.

7-Up soft-drink advertising illustrates this concept; the "Un-Cola image" campaign effectively inhibited remembering of earlier images. Prior to the Un-Cola advertising appeal, 7-Up had the image of being a mixer for adults to use with alcoholic beverages. Now the original image of 7-Up is difficult to recall; and people think of 7-Up as the Un-Cola, a pleasant youthful alternative to cola beverages.

A General Electric television offering a free corning-ware dish with every "Toast-r-Oven" purchased was an example of this principle. The advertisement began by explaining several unusual uses for the oven, such as making baked croissants; and then all of a sudden switched direction and brought up the fact that "if you buy now, you will receive this beautiful corning-ware dish." After explaining how to get the dish, the advertisement ended, leaving the viewer somewhat confused, wishing that he could remember the process for making baked croissants.

In selling a General Electric toaster and a Procter Silex toaster, if the salesperson illustrates the good points of the G.E. toaster first and those of the Procter Silex second, the positive points of the first toaster may be forgotten by the customer. The information about the Procter Silex serves as an intervening variable, thus inhibiting the remembrance of the G.E. model. Personal selling provides an interesting example of retroactive inhibition. A shopper will go to one salesperson and hear and learn the merits of his or her product, and then go to another to hear a new set of advantages of a different product or brand; and perhaps even a third will be in the picture. The shopper probably will remember the latest message the best, especially if all messages are similar, with no greatly outstanding characteristics.

Marketers also must be concerned about the uniqueness of the physical product. Many products of the same type have the same form. Distinctive external appearances of the product or the package are a must. Retroactive inhibition can effectively eliminate the brand name of a product, even after use, if nothing made that product physically distinguishable among all others of its type.

Proactive Inhibition

IV.A7 *If two sets of associations have been learned one after another by audience members, the former one tends to impair (inhibit) the remembering of the latter one.*

Proactive inhibition is defined as the impairment of the normal effects of a learning activity when preceded by another activity related in time or space (or both). This is especially true for an activity somewhat similar to the new activity. It is, in effect, retroactive inhibition in reverse. Again, similar messages can become confused in an audience member's mind. With proactive inhibition, however, the first message is the better learned and remembered, and it inhibits the correct learning of the second.

Knowledge or attitudes acquired prior to the learning of any new message can be interfering. The presence of a certain amount of information learned in the immediate or distant past can be a negative influence on the degree to which new material may be absorbed. When many possible associations and notable similarities exist between the previously learned information and the new information, the "inhibition" will be greatest.

Keppel and Underwood experimented with 96 students whose task was to recall nonsense syllables. They found the interaction between length of retention interval and the number of potential proactively interfering items to be very evident. In other words, the people involved in the testing learned less new information as more interfering remembrances were brought to their minds. With more time between the message encounter and the required action, a person may remember more interfering material. This may consist of either past events or other messages (Keppel and Underwood, 1962).

An advertising example comes from a study done by Blankenship and Whitely. They asked 85 college students to memorize grocery store advertisements under three conditions: (1) no controlling activity, (2) the study of similar ads prior to their learning task, and (3) learning a nonsense advertisement before learning the test material. It was found that the retention scores of the first and third conditions were not significantly different from one another, while the second group scored poorly (Blankenship and Whitely, 1941).

Consumers are basically unfamiliar with innovative products, and overcoming this marketing barrier is inhibited by proactivity. For example, consumers' knowledge of standard products will decrease their learning about new products until they become aware of the differences of new products. Once again, massed practice effects are desirable for the innovative products because the consumer must be quickly educated to overcome the confusion barrier caused by proactive inhibition.

Similarly, distributed practice is more appropriate to the established product because it is already familiar to consumers. Promotion for the established brand is more meaningful to consumers (a function of prior promotion) and therefore less vulnerable to interference effects.

Marketing Examples of Proactive Inhibition

Proactive inhibition is a theoretical means of understanding that "me-too" advertising is likely to be a waste of marketing dollars. *"Me-too" advertising* is promotion that follows the same sales arguments and similar methods of presentation as the competition does. One example of "me-too" advertising is the rash of menthol cigarette brands in which an attractive, loving, young couple escapes to a sunlit, leafy glade. Once competitor A has established a brand image through advertising, competitors B, C, and D, who follow almost identical copy strategies, will find their efforts diluted by the effects of proactive inhibition. The similarity among the various brands makes learning of the association between the message and the brand B name marginal in comparison to prior learning of the association between the copy strategy and the brand A name.

Restructuring a "bad" image represents a good example of proactive inhibition. Gulf Oil set about staging open meetings with 20,000 dealers to let them air their complaints and help to improve communications. Gulf's public image was "rather lousy" (as stated by a Gulf marketing manager). The task ahead was formidable, since the "bad" image tended to be remembered, thus blocking out the new messages Gulf was trying to get learned.

In personal selling situations, once the consumer has made an association, he tends to think of later associations in terms of the first one; therefore, a salesperson ought to give first emphasis to the most favorable attributes of the product. A Cadillac salesperson may first point out the luxuriousness and the status orientation of the car. Later he or she may tell the customer that the car gets low gas mileage, but this idea may be inhibited by the consumer's earlier association of the car with luxury and status.

Transfer

IV.A8 *Audience members will learn materials that repeat old stimuli and require the same responses more quickly than completely new materials. This is positive transfer. If the repeated stimuli require opposite responses, negative transfer occurs.*

Transfer refers to the effect produced by a new idea or item (an object, individual, situation, or event) on an idea or item already familiar to the subject. By structuring a communication stimulus with such an "associative tie," the process of transfer aids learning and remembering of the communication. For example, if the communicator says "B is like A," an "associative tie" tends to be created for the audience between the familiar idea (item A) and the new and unfamiliar idea (item B).

Transfer will increasingly aid learning and remembering to the extent that the elements of the association are familiar to the individual. The association is effective because reference to the familiar idea or item increases the possibility of recalling previous cognitive activities and remembering experiences. "Transfer of training refers to the fact that the learning or training that has taken place in one task carries over, or transfers, to a second" (Hall, 1966, p. 472).

A transfer is positive if the traces from a previous situation aid in the learning process of a later object or idea. Positive transfer is also called *associative facilitation*. Negative transfer occurs if learning the second task is made more difficult by knowledge of the first. Negative transfer is sometimes called *habit interference*.

In studying transfer, Osgood was confronted with the paradoxical fact that the greatest similarity was responsible for both retroactive interference and positive transfer. Accordingly, "Ordinary learning . . . is at once the theoretical condition for maximal interference but obviously the practical condition for maximal facilitation" (Osgood, 1963, p. 65).

Based upon his experimental evidence, Osgood formulated three propositions:

1. Where stimuli are varied and responses are functionally identical, positive transfer and retroactive facilitation are obtained. The magnitude of both increases as the similarity among the stimulus members increases.
2. Where stimuli are functionally identical and responses are varied, negative transfer and retroactive interference are obtained, the magnitude of both decreasing as similarity between the responses increases.
3. When both stimulus and response members are simultaneously varied, negative transfer and retroactive interference are obtained, the magnitude of both increasing as the stimulus similarity increases.

Many different psychologists studied this subject and tried to determine when similarity of stimuli contribute to positive transfer and when they contribute to negative transfer. Differing theories were set forth. Sartain, North, Strange, and Chapman arrived at a theory of identical components that probably has the best application to mass communications. See table 19-3.

224

Table 19-3

Effects of Various Stimulus-Response Relationships Between First and Second Task on the Amount and Kind of Transfer

Stimulus-Response Relationship	Amount and Kind of Transfer
Case 1: Identical stimuli and identical response	Maximal positive transfer
Case 2: Similar stimuli and identical response	Positive transfer
Case 3: Identical stimuli and similar response	Positive transfer
Case 4: Identical stimuli and different response	Negative transfer if the responses are incompatible; varying results if responses are not incompatible.
Case 5: Different stimuli and identical response	Positive transfer (usually small)
Case 6: Different stimuli and different response	Little or no transfer

Source: Sartain, North, Strange, and Chapman, *Psychology* (New York: McGraw-Hill, 1967), p. 327.

One argument for the adoption of the identical-component theory as applied to marketing communications comes from Anastasi: "Another way of increasing transfer is to provide a variety of tasks as similar as possible to the job task" (Anastasi, 1964, p. 112). In short, the best way to obtain positive transfer is to use identical or nearly identical stimuli.

In the field of marketing communications, transfer can be used to help facilitate the learning of product characteristics. For example, an advertisement may read "The new automatic alarm clock is set in the same way as the old one." In this statement, which is used to teach, the similarity is drawn between the old and the new as to method of operation. Making old responses to new and only slightly different stimuli is relatively easy. The manufacturer was correct in designing his clock this way, and the advertiser correct in mentioning the fact in the copy.

Marketing Examples of Transfer

An example of this principle of transfer can be seen in pricing, where companies introducing new products often gear their prices to the expected prices for a product of that category, especially if the market is heavily competitive and there are no significant differentiations among products. Relating to expected prices is easier than trying to create a new set of expectations for a product category.

Wyler's, a powdered soft-drink manufacturer, used this principle in promotional campaigns using price as the prime discriminant. The advertising showed you what a nickel would buy 20 years ago (a soda for two, a phone call, etc.) and finished with a statement that a glass of Wyler's costs less than a nickel today.

"Sleeping on a Sealy is like sleeping on a cloud." This is a persuasive use of transfer. Although none of us actually has slept on a cloud, we can all imagine what that experience would be like. The softness implied by a cloud has many other associations, such as lightness, freedom, purity. All these are transferred by the individual to the name Sealy. The good feeling of cloud-thought is moved over to Sealy-thought.

Demonstration in messages can use transfer effectively. The "subjective camera angle," in which the camera shoots from over the demonstrator's shoulder, will allow for visual transfer if the skill involved is familiar. If the new way demonstrated is better, emphasis should not be placed on showing a *different* way in which to do a familiar job, but on showing a *better* way to do the job or a *better* manner in which to use the product. An example is the campaign of the Peoples Gas, Light & Coke Company (of Chicago) that emphasized that "Gas Does the Big Jobs Better for Less."

Semantic Generation and Semantic Satiation

IV.A9 *Continued repetition of a meaningless word generates its increased meaningfulness to audience members. However, continued repetition of a meaningful word will render it meaningless to audience members.*

Semantic generation refers to the tendency of continued repetition of a word to increase the word's connotative meaning. *Semantic satiation* is the tendency for a word to lose its connotative meaning through repetition. The phenomena of semantic generation and semantic satiation have consistently been produced in experimental studies designed to measure changes in meaning through repetition of a word stimulus. The data do not conclusively prove existence of certain conditions that definitely will or will not exhibit the phenomena. But such data firmly illustrate the importance of the phenomena to the learning of communications.

A word has meaning when its use as a stimulus evokes an associated response. The greater the meaning of the word, the more definite and precise is the associated response. For example, the word *dog* has a definite cognitive response. The word *grony* has significantly less meaning because it does not evoke a cognitive response or at least does not evoke a uniform cognitive response for an audience member. There is, however, a second dimension to the meaning of a word. Words can have affective meanings that are emotionally rather than cognitively based. *Grony* has little affective meaning, just as it has little cognitive meaning. As a result, *grony* is not considered a word at all. It is undefined—a nonword. The word *love* produces a very definite affective response. A distinctive and uniform emotional response is associated with the word and evoked when it is used as a stimulus. Some words produce strong emotional responses, yet are not consistent in their meaning across a population. Two examples are *communist* and *hippie*. These words tend to evoke different emotional responses in different individuals.

Meaningfulness does not usually refer to consistent associational value across different members of the audience. Rather, a word has meaning to an individual if it evokes a distinct affective and cognitive response for him. Semantic generation and satiation refer to changes in the strength and degree of ambiguity of associations to a word when it is a continuously exposed, repeated stimulus.

Experiments in semantic generation and satiation have relied upon a variety of different scales of meaning by which subjects rate words before and after exposure to the repetition stimulus. The most well-known scales are part of a widely recognized technique in social scientific and marketing research: the semantic differential scales. Osgood, Suci, and Tannenbaum devised their scales through factor analysis of word meanings plotted in a "semantic space." Their three dimensions are the evaluative scale: good versus bad; the potency scale: strong versus weak; and the activity scale: active versus inactive (Osgood, Suci, and Tannenbaum, 1967).

These scales measure the affective meanings of words, rather than the cognitive meanings. For example, we know what a dog is, but a little cognitive shifting will occur with repetition or the word stimulus *dog*. However, emotional associations tied to the word *dog* are capable of shifting under certain conditions. For some people, the word *dog* evokes an emotional response high on the "good" end of the evaluative dimension. To other people, *dog* may evoke an unfavorable response.

Semantic differential scales are bipolar, with seven rating positions on each scale. The words used to describe each scale clearly indicate the subjectivity of the ratings: good versus bad, pretty versus ugly; and clean versus dirty. A word rated in the center of the scale is said to be neutral on the scale. As the word becomes more meaningful, its rating tends toward one of the two extremes. This technique is not new to marketers who have conducted studies of meaning, such as those of brand image.

Many experiments in which subjects have rated words on bipolar scales before and after repetition of the stimulus word have shown that in certain cases a word becomes more meaningful when repeated. The word's meaning was rated closer to one of the poles of the rating scales after the repetition exercise relative to the rating prior to the repetition. These would be cases of semantic generation.

Semantic satiation has been the widely observed tendency of ratings for a word to move toward neutrality on rating scales following repetition. The word tends to lose meaning after repetition.

The question arises, under which conditions do these conflicting observations occur? The process of regression is a useful explanation. According to the regression theory, a word with a neutral initial meaning (the center of the bipolar scale) assumes meaning when repeated. In this generation phase, a word with an originally neutral meaning does not have a defined set of relevant associations. A word with no meaning can evoke almost any type of response with equal validity. Repetition, however, strengthens certain associations with the word, giving it a more distinct meaning.

The regression process works in an opposite manner for words that are initially meaningful. Repetition of a meaningful word tends to extinguish the learned associations with the word, and the word loses meaning. Though regression has not been shown to occur consistently, it has been observed in a great proportion of the studies. It, therefore, seems to be a meaningful explanation of the differences between satiation and generation.

The early phase of semantic generation for a word is likely to be followed by satiation once the word acquires a certain amount of meaning to the individual being tested. This assumption, however, is currently an area of controversy. No researcher has yet been able to define a descriptive relationship between a word's meaning and the point at which satiation sets in during repetition. However, satiation effects tend not to occur when subjects do not consistently engage in cognitive activity concerning the word being repeated. In other words, when subjects must think of the word (and its referrents) while repeating it, satiation is enhanced (Madigan and Paivio, 1967, p. 45). In addition, research has shown that effects of satiation on repeated words can be inhibited when subjects engage in mediating responses during the period of repetition. Miller has shown that effects of satiation on repeated words can be inhibited when subjects engage in mediating responses during the period of satiation. Miller has shown that concurrent motor responses related to the repeated words retard satiation (Miller, 1963, p. 206).

Semantic generation and satiation effects are obviously important considerations in the advertising communication process. Advertising is an essentially verbal communication form. Since advertisers choose words designed to elicit certain responses from consumers, they ought to be aware of the semantic changes possible when such words are repeated. Use of a particular emphasized word, especially one coined for a particular campaign, would be subject to generation as consumers are first exposed to the word. Continued exposure, however, might tend to a threat of satiation.

This effect has been reported, but in the more general sense of satiation of the entire advertisement. A study "which measured variations in attention or interest showed that repeated exposures of a TV commercial do generate a true satiation pattern—that is, attention does increase, pass through a maximum, and decline with increased exposure. This effect caused 'unlearning,' or a 'subsequent decay' of previously acquired product knowledge. Though product knowledge and attention-interest declined with repeated exposure; studies of DuPont advertising showed no significant decline in product attitudes through satiation" (Grose and Birney, 1963, p. 194).

Marketing Examples of Semantic Generation and Semantic Satiation

The clearest implications of the generation and satiation phenomena are for new words created by advertisers. They wish the new and distinctive word to (1) elicit a favorable, learned response from consumers and (2) have that response transferred to the advertised product or service. The word and its favorable meaning are to be uniquely representative of the marketable good.

The Leo Burnett Company (Schlitz's advertising agency) conducted research on the word *gusto* and found it associated with action (energetic, vibrant, breezy, speedy, enthusiasm) and robustness (robust, hearty, strong). When used in the copy phrase, "Real gusto in a great light beer," the word connoted a dominant theme of vigor and masculinity. The word *gusto* was a word that had a wide range of meanings, thus permitting different people to read different intangible qualities into it for the beer. Pontiac Division of General Motors widely advertised the word *widetracking* in an attempt to link the word with the product, the favorable automobile ride and handling characteristics.

These examples illustrate the process of generating meaning for a word initially without specific meaning and creating favorable associations for the word that are then transferred to the product. As was noted, a word can lose its associative and cognitive meaning value through repetition. This is especially true for repetition of a word that initially possesses meaning for the audience members.

What about special phrases used in an advertising campaign, such as cool ones, hot ones, big ones, exciting ones, new ones? It appears that such terms, when repeated, create an effect opposite to that intended by the advertiser. Rather than linking a word to a product through favorable connotations, the words lose their meaning. Consumers then find no meaning in a product that is "new."

It is not clear, however, that the threat of semantic satiation is realized to the extent indicated by experimental research. Certainly advertising campaigns wear out and must be revised, but only over the course of many months or years. This is a time period in which a great many influences besides semantic satiation can lessen the significance of the campaign.

It is only in the experimental laboratory that variables can be sufficiently controlled to isolate generation and satiation causes. Obviously, consumers are not required to make cognitive and verbal responses similar to those in the laboratory (repeating words two to three times per second) which tend to aid satiation. The satiation phenomenon does exist. And although laboratory research cannot suggest the magnitude of satiation that may exist in the mass communication situation, research does imply that satiation might have a role in wearing out an advertising campaign before its time.

As additional marketing examples, *Kleenex* and *Xerox* are excellent examples of words that originally had no meaning and now are almost generic. Whether people are specifically referring to Kleenex brand tissue, or some other brand, they are likely to ask for Kleenex. Almost every copy machine comes to be called a Xerox machine. "I'll get a Xerox of that" is often heard around an office. Yet the copy machine may be some other brand.

Dominant Meaning

IV.A10 *When a statement is made that associates two words, the word with the more dominant meaning will experience less meaning change to audience members than will the other word, which will be changed in meaning because of the association.*

The principle of dominant meaning is built around the assumption that words in our language dominate their associated word groups. This principle implies that strong words, when used in combination with weaker words, help make a statement more explicit, without the dominant word losing any of its significance.

Dominant meaning can be broken down into two areas—the denotative and the connotative. The *denotative meaning* of a word is the dictionary definition, while the *connotative meaning* is the emotional and subjective associations that one builds around a word. *Patriotism* has a specific dictionary meaning, but individuals have connotative reactions to the word. When communicating, one must be aware of the connotative meanings of words.

Dominant meaning may occur when two words are associated. The learned meaning of one word is assumed to be associated with the weaker word with which it is being used. This new combination word would be considered stronger than the two words were separately, but with the originally stronger word still dominating the pair. For example, the word *boy*, standing alone, carries a specific set of referents. But add the word *delinquent*, and one's entire conception of the pair changes. *Delinquent*, the stronger word, makes the pair stronger.

Dominant meaning implies that whenever two words are related by an assertion, the individual perceives the words as combined. Words that are dissimilar in value, such as *kindness* and *killing*, create dissonance by their combination. The dissonance created by the combination can cause misperceiving. Joyce, in a study of attitude change, noted three cases in which advertisements were ineffective for this reason. He found that an advertisement for bottled beer that promoted the idea of "manliness" caused consumers to regard that beer as being stronger than other beers. Apparently, the idea of a beer being "manly" but not "stronger" created dissonance that was easily relieved by understanding the beer *to be* stronger. In another case, a washing powder advertised as "efficient" was thought to be harder on hands. Finally, an advertisement for toilet paper "for men" failed because it was thought to be less comfortable. The strength and connotation of the word in each case proved to be the downfall of the ad. The stronger the intensity of the assertion, the greater is the effect of dominant meaning (Joyce, 1967, p. 90).

Marketing Examples of Dominant Meaning

A car salesman may say "This car is sturdy, because it has unibody construction." In this case *sturdy* has the dominant meaning; it implies to the customer something more definite, whereas *unibody* really says nothing to the average person. As a result of the association, the word *sturdy* will experience little, if any, meaning change, and the customer is likely to see *unibody* as meaning "sturdy" or at least something closer to it than he did before.

United Airlines demonstrated this principle in its 747 advertising campaign in which United's 747 jet liner was called the "Friend Ship." The word *friend* retained the dominant meaning in the advertisement, but United's aircraft and 747 service became the friendly "ship" and the friendly service of the friendly airline.

Chivas Regal, a popular brand of Scotch whiskey, is an example in itself of dominant meaning. *Regal*, a word that is not vague at all is accompanied by *Chivas*, a nebulous word. *Regal* makes the brand sound royal, important, and magnificent; and its meaning does not change. *Chivas* is vague, and each Chivas Regal buyer adds his own personal touch to the meaning of the word to complement his feelings about the product.

Stimulus Complexity

IV.A11 *Messages that consist of several elements or important points will be increased in effectiveness of audience learning when they are shown repeatedly. With increased display, audience members will attend to more cues and thus will learn the messages more completely.*

A variable pertinent to the effects of repetitive communication stimuli is the complexity variable. Messages can be categorized by their complexity, the number of significant points (such as sales points). For example, Leavitt demonstrated that highly structured messages were more easily recalled than those less structured. He defined a *structured message* as one whose parts are organized, coherent, and integrated. His findings were based on results from showing 24 commercials of 4 household products to 30 women, the commercials representing both high and low recall (Leavitt, 1968, pp. 3-6).

Morrison and Darnoff found that a longer time of looking at an advertisement does not necessarily mean better recall of the advertisement. Slides of 30 nationally run magazine advertisements for familiar products were viewed by 120 university students. Of these advertisements, 30 percent were high in complexity and 30 percent low in complexity. Subjects were told that they were participating in either an advertising test or a perceptual test. They reviewed the slides while the looking time was noted; next they were given a memory task, either recognition or recall. They then rated the slides from 1 to 7 on complexity, familiarity, pleasantness, interest, ease of product identification, and novelty. In all conditions, looking time was positively correlated with complexity. There was no relationship between looking time and interestingness (Morrison and Darnoff, 1972).

The effectiveness of messages consisting of more than one main element may be increased by repeated exposure. Greater frequency enables the audience member to attend to cues other than the cue that originally caught his attention. As the elements of the message are learned, an associative interaction increases comprehension of the total message.

Increased repetition allows the audience to attend to the entire range of elements in the complex message. A complex message, such as an advertisement with many selling points, requires repetition if the message is to be learned in its entirety. There exists, however, a point of increasing complexity beyond which people cannot readily categorize all the information and message points simultaneously in each exposure. Such messages are better learned if they are broken into several contiguous messages—see IV.A3, Continuity of Varied Stimuli in this chapter.

Marketing Examples of Stimulus Complexity

Food stores often demonstrate this principle. When trying to convince a housewife to buy a certain food, the store or manufacturer will display pictures of the product, make up recipes, and show the food prepared with the recipes; even samples of the food will be passed out. The product repeatedly displayed like this in varied ways allows the housewife to experience the message in different ways and will be more effective than if she were only shown a picture of the product.

In personal selling, an insurance salesperson attempting to explain the benefits of life insurance in estate planning will repeat certain details of the message at different times during the presentation. Comments like "Only after all your expenses and taxes have been paid does the balance come down to your family," "The family gets only what is left after taxes and expenses, and often it just isn't enough," and "Make sure that your family receives as much as possible of your estate after taxes and expenses" help the client to understand the message and provide for his family's future through life insurance as part of his estate planning.

A study of shoe retailers in Chicago included exposure to their advertising, their clerks, and their windows. Just to touch one phase, their windows communicated quite vocally what economic class they were serving. If a store had many, many shoes in the window, it was a middle- to lower-price store. Conversely, the consumer learned quickly that a high-style, high-price store might have only one shoe in the window, in a setting of abstract art. If a store had good-looking young clerks, this signified a low-price chain store. Older clerks usually meant that the store was for higher-status people.

In a television commercial, American Motors wanted to communicate one basic message—that the consumer could expect reliability from any person or thing associated with its name. The commercial showed four different ways that the American Motors Company was reliable.

1. The car was tested at the factory.
2. Car dealers made special tests.
3. American Motors provided a one-year guarantee to fix or to replace defective parts.
4. Anytime an American Motors car was in the shop for parts, the company would provide a car for use until the other was repaired.

Even if American Motors as a reliable company was not totally communicated by the first cue, all four cues did make the message clear.

Number of Stimulus Cues

VI.A11.1 *Audience members are more likely to remember an illustration if it has a minimum number of cues and separate actions and if it does not have a dual interpretation than if the illustration can be viewed in a number of ways or if it portrays actions competing for attention.*

In conjunction with writing booklets for newly literate adults in Latin America, UNESCO and Pan American Union's Latin American Fundamental Educational

Press evaluated the effectiveness of adding pictures to their booklets. Each person examined a series of illustrations (realistic line drawings; wood cuts, which were not clearcut in terms of items and actions depicted; and stylized drawings, for which no concrete descriptions were possible) with or without captions.

From the results of the research, the following generalizations were made:

(1) Past experience of the viewer largely determines how he will interpret individual objects in the illustration; he will ignore unfamiliar items; (2) past experience affects value judgments even to a greater degree than interpretation of concrete items (for example, smallness and neatness differ); (3) viewers make generalizations on the basis of a limited number of specific details; (4) the use of color in illustrative material adds to the communication value of the illustration if the color adds to the realism; color detracts if it is used unrealistically; (5) captions help viewers to interpret the illustration correctly. [Spaulding, 1956, pp. 37-44.]

Three different levels were constructed by Wesley: (1) minimum structural coherence, that is, no apparent integration of items; (2) subgroup structural coherence, subgroups of about 5 items were cued; and (3) overall structural coherence, the display formed a single unit. There were six displays having identical pictorial and verbal items arranged to form three different levels of structural coherence. The learning task consisted of associating nonsense syllables with each item. A second task for all groups was to learn 20 sentences consisting of nonsense syllables and the name of a profession. The display item associated with the nonsense syllable provided a potential mediator. Learning was higher for groups encountering pictorial displays than for verbal displays. In terms of transfer tasks, pictorial displays were also superior; and transfer of learning was higher for displays with higher structural coherence than minimum or subgrouped structural coherence (Wesley, 1970, pp. 2748-2749).

Spangenberg found further evidence that if detail is *not* placed in a structured pattern, it is soon forgotten. He examined the effects of three different levels of structural coherence on verbal and pictorial displays. The experiment essentially was a duplication of the one just described; and the results reaffirmed the superiority of pictures over verbal groups and the superiority of structural coherence in learning the transfer task (Spangenberg, 1971).

Frost found that visual memory is organized by visual relationships designed into the stimuli. Sixty undergraduate students were presented 32 common objects on cards of both word stimuli and line drawings. Picture 1 set had drawings that belonged to one of 4 shape categories, depending upon whether the drawing was slanted to the left or right or presented in a vertical or horizontal position. Picture 2 set had half the picture 1 drawings, with the rest distributed among the four shape categories. There were three conditions: (1) picture presentation/picture recognition, designed to encourage subjects to encode an image of each stimulus; (2) picture presentation/word recognition, to encourage subject to encode verbally the object's name; and (3) word presentation/word recognition, practice words, a practice-word test, and word stimuli presented.

The cards for each particular set were presented. To minimize the effects of recency and acoustic similarity, subjects worked on syllogism problems for 15 minutes. They then were instructed to give free recall to the names of the 32 objects. Each subject was asked about his methods of retention and retrieval. Subjects in both picture-presentation conditions were asked, as the experimenter read the name, to recall the shape of the stimulus object. Those subjects in word-presentation who formed visualizations of the objects were asked to classify the images according to the 4 shape categories. It was found that the shape of the drawings aided recall; that is, the physical position or location of the stimulus object was a factor in addition to inherent characteristics of the drawing itself during mental categorization. Frost determined that association through verbal labels could not explain the strength of the clustering. That visual memory as assessed during the name recall is not a sufficient explanation. She suggested that spatial organization is the method of organization (Frost, 1971).

Marketing Examples of Number of Stimulus Cues

An effective magazine advertisement should divert a reader from attending to an article or story he is reading, as well as from other advertisements in the same magazine. In other words, brevity of form and appealing pictures increase the chances for both audience attending and learning. Billboard advertising is a special example of the necessity for minimizing the number of cues, making them stand out and guarding against ambiguous interpretations. To get a motorist to attend to a billboard during the few seconds it takes to pass by, the billboard must deliver a bold picture, large lettering, and a brief message. The poster must be distracting enough to get him to attend to it but also must economize as to the number of visual cues presented.

Many successful advertising campaigns have continued with essentially the same theme year after year. If the theme is relevant and closely integrated with the message about the product itself, the continuity enhances brand awareness over time.

In addition to consistency, if the theme can be represented in a recognizable symbol, form, or figure, the memorability of the product increases as the pictorial representative of the theme continues to be attended and perceived. Successful examples of this strategy are the Doughboy for Pillsbury, Tony the Tiger for Kellogg's Frosted Flakes Cereal, and the Campbell Soup Kids. In each case, although separate advertisements run for variations on the theme, the figure(s) representing the product have been a prominent part of the given execution and thus have played a significant role in helping audience members to remember the overall message.

Potency of Pictorial Cues

IV.A12 *If a message is pictorially represented, it is better remembered than if the audience member reads its verbal counterpart.*

Wimer and Lambert found that nonsense syllables, as responses, were learned faster when paired with object stimuli than with stimuli that were names of objects. They constructed 3 lists of 9 paired-associate (PA) words. In the O list the stimuli were 9 common small objects; in the W list the stimuli were the names of the 9 objects; and the M list consisted of 9 mixed stimuli, some from both list O and list W.

Nine nonsense syllables were used as response members for all three lists. The subjects in the experiment first were given a practice list of four pairs of PA, with two word-syllable pairs and two object-syllable pairs. They then were assigned to a list that was learned to a criterion of one errorless trial. It was found that fewer errors were made in the acquisition of the object-syllable list than in the word-syllable or mixed list (Wimer and Lambert, 1959).

Morelli explains the superiority of pictures over words in recall by the fact that pictures arouse concrete images that can easily be controlled. He took 45 university students and tested paired-associate (PA) learning in three conditions by using 20 concrete words combined into 10 PA: (1) picture: pictures depicting the words were drawn above the PA; (2) competing picture: nonsense scribbles were drawn above the words; (3) word alone: the control condition. Results showed that pictures do facilitate PA learning over competing pictures and words (Morelli, 1970).

Paivio, Rogers, and Smythe offered further proof that verbal recall is generally higher for objects or pictures than for their labels. For 80 introductory psychology students, test items consisted of pictures and names of 25 familiar objects: hand, cigar, ladder, bread, horse, soldier, microscope, telephone, kettle, scissors, pencil, fish, lobster, apple, star, leopard, bottle, tree, clock, flag, radio, umbrella, book, stove, and knife. The list was presented a first time with the use of slides. Recall was tested by having students write down those objects they remembered. The slides were presented again, and subjects in the picture condition wrote down the names they had used for the pictures as the slides were shown. It was found that pictures are more effectively stored and retrieved from both long-term memory and from short-term memory, as indicated by higher recall for recent pictures than recent words (Paivio, Rogers, and Smythe, 1968).

To 72 male undergraduates Sampson presented 24 items, half as words and half as line drawings, with or without instructions to try to remember them. The items included arrow, bell, boat, bottle, cat, circle, funnel, lamp, pipe, star, sun, window, bird, book, cane, cup, fish, flower, fork, moon, pencil, square, watch, and wheel. The items were presented on slides; free recall was tested both immediately after the presentation and one day later. Nonstimulus slides contained four differently colored dots, the colors of which were named aloud by the subject; and subjects were told not to respond to the words and pictures, only to the colors. Again, superiority of pictures in recall was demonstrated (Sampson, 1969).

Wicker tested 60 students for stimulus recognition as well as associative recall. There were four test conditions, with the study test procedure employed in all conditions: (1) word-word: subjects presented with 30 PA with concrete noun stimuli; the response was either a number or letter; 30 distractors were presented in the final test only; (2) picture-picture: 3 pairs with simple line drawings corresponding with the 60 words, with the same responses as above; (3) word-picture: word stimuli used in the study trials, combined with the pictures in the test; (4) picture-word: opposite of condition 3. Students were asked to form an association between the two items so as to recall the second item of each pair when presented with the first. The actual test made two requests. First, students were to judge each item on a 5-point scale from absolutely certainty of having not seen the item before to certainty of having seen it. Second, the students were asked to write an associative response. The experimenter explained the superiority of picture finding not as associative learning but rather as the learning differences upon the recognition effect (Wicker, 1970).

Pictures can best realistically show the appearance of physical objects, the setting in which they are used, and the people who use the object. Details can be enlarged. This is important, considering the fact that appearance is a factor, if not the dominating factor, in the sale of nearly every tangible product.

One experimenter (Rudolph, 1947, p. 69) tested different types of illustrations in advertisements to determine which ones were most effective in leading observers into the copy. Negative pictures showing the result of not using the product were outstanding, both in gaining attention and in leading the observer into the test.

The use of color in pictorial cues can also be a determining factor in learning and remembering. Color adds realism. It not only is attention getting but arouses pleasant feelings and produces emotional responses. It can easily emphasize what needs to be emphasized. Of course, the attending value of different colors depends upon their brightness and richness, but color offers a means of contrast, which can be used in a way to relate to the context of the message. Thus clashing colors may increase initial attending but can also annoy the viewer.

Color preferences change according to age, education, income, locality, and seasonality. Although color preferences differ among various audiences, some generalizations can be made. Color carries moods and symbolisms. On the whole, warm colors are inviting to readers, whereas light colors have more lucidity. Colors also have "odor"; for example, pale colors smell like flowers; green smells like a forest. Colors also have appetite appeal; red is reminiscent of apple, cherry, or a rare cut of beef. Colors such as blue, green, violet, and purple have little appetite appeal, whereas peach, orange, buff, and yellow do. Colors also have weight. Black is heavier than white. The use of dark, heavy colors gives a sense of security; and the use of light colors give a feeling of lightness, a flowing feeling.

Marketing Examples of Potency of Pictorial Cues

For pictorial cues in general, several examples can be put forth. Newspaper advertisements run by grocery retailers often display a thick mass of printed words and prices in full-page or two-page spreads. To the casual reader of newspapers, such advertising is not memorable; but the loyal shoppers of a given grocer, as well as those who are extremely price conscious, will remember only certain key bargains as they shop his store or will carry the advertisement with them on their shopping trips. More memorable grocery store advertising will feature small pictures of certain name brands and various produce items. Also, items from those advertisements featuring a smaller-than-average number of items arranged in an ordered manner will be more easily remembered and referred to than others.

The Sears catalogue utilizes the idea of increasing the memorability of listings by displaying photographs of items. Not only are the separate listings more easily remembered in this manner, but also, since the company offers a tremendous number of products in a catalogue hundreds of pages in length, the photographs enable the shopper to make faster references than if he or she had to read carefully printed descriptions of the product.

Hunt's tomato-sauce advertisements use a red background that not only contrasts with the color of the pasta but represents the true color of the product itself. The red color suggests something hot and exciting, which relates to the spicy taste of tomato sauce used in spaghetti.

Color of the product itself is important, of course. Binaca mouthwash is a green liquid, which complements the "frosty mint flavor." The color suggests refreshment and coolness.

Colors also affect packaging. Deep, bright colors are used on laundry-detergent boxes, suggesting a fast-acting, powerful product. But bright colors may have a negative effect if used on cosmetic packaging. It would make the product appear harsh and unnatural.

Color used in the decor of retail stores is important. Pastel colors are used in baby, cosmetic, linen, and lingerie departments, whereas browns and earthy colors are used more in men's sporting goods, gourmet, utensil, and food departments.

20 Message and Medium Variables: Affective Variables

Background

In the previous chapter it was pointed out that the repetition of mass communications is a necessary and important step in furthering the learning process. No single marketing strategy advertisement or promotional message ever changes a consumer's mind. At best, a message may "nudge" an individual's cognitive and attitude structure nearer to actual purchase. Repetition is necessary; but it alone is not sufficient. Messages cannot be "drummed into" peoples' heads. Many other factors affect the learning of a message.

Consumers have natural screening processes, which may cause messages to be selectively perceived and selectively learned. Stimuli that are unpleasant, incongruous, produce anxiety, or are not relevant to people's goals may be perceived but will not be learned because of this screening process.

The preceding discussion of learning variables has dealt with cognitive stimuli, such as word pairs that do not arouse feeling or relate emotionally to the audience members. However, special consideration must be given to affective stimuli, because these stimuli and the responses they evoke are more likely to be learned than factual, cognitive materials.

Affective stimuli are those which arouse feeling tones in an individual. These feelings are less intense than such overwhelming emotions as hate, love, anger, or elation. Corresponding feeling tones would be dislike, liking, frustration, or happiness. Communication stimuli usually are more likely to arouse feeling tones (be affective) than to arouse powerful emotions (be emotional). Mass media therefore require a high level of involvement and intensity not automatically inherent in the various media.

Affective Variables

It must be noted that learning is not automatic, but rather a selective process. According to the principle of *selective retention*, people are more likely than not to retain affective stimuli and associated responses that are congruent with their attitudes and opinions. Affective stimuli and associated responses that are incongruent with a person's attitudes and opinions are less easily retained.

Degree of Affective Value

IV.A12 *The members of an audience will learn and remember messages that have great affective value to them much more than they will learn and remember messages to which they are emotionally neutral.*

One variant to the repetition effect is the question of whether or not pleasant stimuli are better learned and retained than unpleasant stimuli, provided frequency of exposure is constant. A pioneering study by Tait, using connotatively loaded word pairs, showed that pleasant words were better remembered than unpleasant words. But both plesant and unpleasant words were better remembered than words of neutral connotation (Tait, 1913, p. 31).

However, additional studies by other experimenters yield differing views, many of which indicate that unpleasant situations can also be conducive to learning, given an equivalent number of repetitions. Menzies conducted an experiment with 50 university students. Each student wrote a description of some experiences of the preceding day; a week following this he or she wrote a second description of the same experiences, and three weeks after the second recall he or she wrote a third description. In addition, each subject judged the intensities of feeling tones that had prevailed during the original experience and during the recalls. At the second and third recalls, subjects were asked to estimate the frequency of revival of each incident since the previous written reproduction. The results of Menzies' study revealed the following relationships:

1. Frequencies of revival of pleasant, unpleasant, and indifferent experiences showed no important differences. But these frequencies increased as intensities of feeling-tone increased, and this relationship was significantly consistent.
2. There were no significant differences in the percentages of recalled pleasant, unpleasant, and indifferent experiences. These percentages of recall, however, increased as intensities of feeling-tone increased. [Menzies, 1935, p. 278.]

From this study it is evident that frequency and extent of recall for experiences are correlated with the intensity of feeling tone rather than with the quality or nature of the feeling tone or affective stimulus.

A negation of the theory that a single positive correlation exists between the pleasantness and unpleasantness of a stimulus and a subject's retention of that stimulus was also supported by Waters and Leeper. Their study investigated the recall of pleasant and unpleasant experiences by 245 students who had just returned from Christmas vacation. Two recall sessions were held, one immediately following the vacation and the second by different groups at intervals of 2, 4, 7, 14, 28, 49, 70, and 140 days.

During each recall, subjects were asked to give each elaborated experience one of the following degrees of affective value: slightly, moderately, or extremely pleasant or unpleasant. At the second recall the subjects were asked in addition to indicate the frequency in round numbers with which they had reveiwed each experience since its occurrence. Their conclusions were that the degree of affective value was positively related to retention and that no marked relationship existed between retention and the qualitative value of the experience (Waters and Leeper, 1936).

A study by Kanungo and Dutta also supports this theory. They conducted two experiments in which subjects were selected from a linguistic group in India known to have an intense feeling of pride and group identity. In the first experiment, 20 pleasant and 20 unpleasant adjectives, matched for their intensity of affect and usage, were presented to four groups of 20 subjects each. In the second experiment, four groups of 15 subjects were used. In the first experiment, subjects rated and later recalled the adjectives when they were presented as attributes of two different groups, that is, their own group and a fictitious group. In the second experiment, subjects rated and later recalled the adjectives when they were attributed to two different fictitious groups. Thus a greater degree of emotional involvement occurred in experiment 1 than in experiment 2 because of the nature of the group.

The study revealed that the intensity of "affect" of pleasant adjectives was greater than that of unpleasant adjectives when ascribed to one's own group. In essence, the overall results support the hypothesis that under varying degrees of emotional involvement, the perceived intensity of affect of material determines its retention (Kanungo and Dutta, 1966).

Kanungo later conducted a study in which he gave a group a specific set of tasks to perform. Each task was rated as to intensity of affect. After a period of time, the tasks were again performed. In some cases the tasks were recalled, in other cases they were reworked. It was found that those tasks with greater intensity of affect were recalled more frequently (Kanungo, 1968).

Many communicators believe that pleasant stimuli may be more effective at being remembered than unpleasant ones simply because audience members perceive them as having comparatively higher affective intensity. Thus many communicators try to link their messages to pleasant aspects of their audience members' lives.

Marketing Examples of Degree of Effective Value

From the preceding principle it can be concluded that among the most striking and consequently effective advertisements are those which include intensive affective stimuli. A basic example of intensive, unpleasant affective stimuli is the American Cancer Society's 1971 advertisement picturing an ugly woman from whose mouth a cigarette is drooping. The headline reads "Smoking Is Glamorous."

On the opposite end of the continuum, representing those advertisements that are intensely pleasant in their affective stimuli are the varieties of "tasteful" sex appeal. Promotions for U.S. Savings Bonds said "Steal me. Burn me. Throw me away, I'm still yours." Through the use of strong, affective connotations the message brought forth feelings of security as well as patriotism. (The overall theme was "Take stock in America.")

Communicator Credibility

IV.A13 *A message delivered by a communicator perceived to be of high prestige initially will be learned better by audience members than a communication delivered by a communicator perceived to be of low prestige. However, time causes a dissociation of the message content from the communicator.*

No single part of message presentation has been more disputed than the area of communicator credibility. The preponderance of research shows that increased communicator credibility exhibits no greater retention curves, over time, than do communicators with low or neutral credibility communicators.

Hovland and Weiss tested the importance of communicator credibility in message learning. They presented communications to subjects, crediting one to a high-credibility source and the other to a low-credibility source. Their results showed that the individual considered the statements from the high-credibility source more fair and factually justifiable than statements from the low-credibility source. The experiment indicated that high-credibility sources induced greater learning immediately after reception of the communication than low-credibility sources. However, Hovland and Weiss found that one month after exposure the differences between retention of high- and low-credibility source messages had faded. Retention of both sources' communications was equal, with the low-credibility source material exhibiting "latent learning" by actually gaining in retention over the first recall test. Subjects remembered more about the low-credibility source message one month after exposure than they did immediately after exposure because of dissociation of the message from its source (Hovland and Weiss, 1951-1952).

The seeming paradox can be explained by saying that, with the passage of time, subjects may remember and accept what was communicated but not remember who communicated it. In effect, the disassociation of the source from the message results in latent learning, or what is often called the "sleeper effect." When the association between messages and their sources is reestablished, the retention scores return to their original, immediate posttest levels (Kelman and Hovland, 1953, p. 335).

Without reinstatement of the source of the communications, it seems that communicator credibility has little relative effect upon retention of mass communications. The primary effects of communicator credibility lie in the realm of persuading, as discussed later. Communicator credibility actually is a two-dimensional series of variables concerning predictive and evaluative cues related to communicators. But because this relates specifically to ideas of persuading, see part VIII (these considerations will not be discussed here).

Marketing Examples of Communicator Credibility

As noted in the chapters on persuading, communicator credibility applies to advertising primarily in the sense that advertising is often considered a low-credibility source of information. People know that the commercial or advertisement is designed to "sell them something." It is not altruism that motivates a business firm to spend $50,000 on a single advertisement telling consumers the most flavorful cigarette they can choose.

The idea of using celebrities in advertising has been useful for charitable organizations, for instance, the March of Dimes. Such advertisements are aimed at getting immediate action; and celebrities do cause a communication to be learned better than noncelebrities. Later dissociation has no negative effect in this case because the campaigns depend on immediate response.

Noxema and Ayds used Arthur Godfrey, one of the most believable salespeople of all time, to secure believability. His voice of authority added credibility to the products. Certain products, however, lend themselves to the use of a communicator of low prestige. For example, Ivory Liquid used an ordinary, plumpish housewife, being kissed by an equally unimpressive, bespectacled, baldish husband.

Advertising for frequently purchased goods, like detergents, provides a different situation. In this case, learning does not have to take place quickly, so ordinary men and women can be used to promote the product.

Reinforcement

IV.A14 *An audience member is more likely to learn arguments that reinforce his existing beliefs and attitudes than those which dispute these beliefs and attitudes.*

It must be noted that the term *reinforcement* is not used in the classical learning sense of positive or negative rewards. Arguments that reinforce an individual's beliefs, attitudes, or opinions are those which are complementary, that harmonize with his position. Arguments that do not reinforce an individual's existing opinions are those which disagree with his position, that are contrary to his opinion.

Edwards tested the phenomena of reinforcement with a group of college students. The students were divided into three groups: pro-New Deal, neutral, and anti-New Deal. Edwards hypothesized that experiences that harmonized with an existing frame of reference would tend to be learned and remembered better than experiences that conflict with the same frame of reference. *Frame of reference* was defined as the individual's organization of attitudes, wishes, values, and so on. This organization becomes a basis upon which the individual makes decisions and judges behavior. Edwards found that materials that harmonized with an individual's frame of reference was learned better than materials that disagreed (Edwards, 1942).

The relationships of learning and forgetting to reinforcement was studied by Levine and Murphy. Two groups of college students—one pro-Communist and one anti-Communist—were exposed to two paragraphs, one mildly pro-Soviet and the other extremely anti-Soviet. The effects of learning were studied over a four-week period; effects of forgetting were studied over a five-week period. Results showed that each group learned more, and forgot less, of the communications that were harmonious with their own opinions of the Soviets (Levine and Murphy, 1943).

Consumers purchase and consume products and services as a response to particular stimulus situations. They are motivated by particular needs or wants. If a product or service provides the proper reinforcement, consumers learn that purchase of that product or service is an appropriate response. If the product ceases to satisfy the consumer's desires, the product purchase response is no longer rewarded and the purchase response is eventually extinguished.

The greater the number of reinforcements tied to a response, the greater will be learning of the response, assuming equally strong or equally valuable rewards (Deese, 1952), p. 12). However, the conditions of reinforcement can vary greatly. One of the most important determinants of reinforcement effectiveness is the intensity or amount of a particular reward.

Marketing Examples of Reinforcement

The reinforcement theory can be applied to marketing. Learning will be greater if an advertisement agrees with, and reinforces, the audience member's opinions. Advertising will not enable consumers to learn about the product advertised if it refutes their opinions.

Reinforcement is particularly conspicuous in quality-price relationships. The consumer expects to pay more for higher-quality goods. Thus, even if a producer comes out with a superior product at a low price, consumers may believe that the low price connotes lower quality (relatively speaking).

Some of the facts backing up a product story may be entirely true, but too much for the prospect to believe. Ford's LTD was stated to be quieter than a

Rolls-Royce or a Mercedes, and this claim was supported by various reliable testing laboratories. But still it was hard to believe.

Assuming that most Americans were involved in the campaign against pollution, advertisements for phosphate-free or low-phosphate detergents emphasized the antipollution aspects of the detergent. Thus greater attention was directed toward antipollution products advertisements because they reinforced already-existing attitudes toward pollution.

Emphasis

IV.A15 *Stimulus elements perceived by audience members as emphasized are better learned and remembered than those not receiving emphasis. This positive learning effect, however, diminishes as more stimulus elements receive emphasis.*

This principle of emphasis is concerned with exaggeration of congruent elements, to perceived differences in strength of cues within the total stimulus. This causes audience members to become more involved with these elements. Psychologists refer to the "von Restorff phenomenon," which states: "Isolating an item against a crowded or homogenous background facilitates the learning of that isolated item. . . . the ease of learning an isolated item is directly related to the degree which that item is isolated" (Wallace, 1965, p. 410).

Von Restorff presented a series of 10 items to subjects, followed by 10 minutes of memorization of a meaningul text. On the first day, the subjects were presented with a list of 10 different items (geometric figures, words, numbers, etc.). On the second and third days, subjects were shown either a list of 9 numbers and 1 syllable or 9 syllables and 1 number. Compared to the recall of unweighted repeated terms (the average recall of all similar items), the isolated members placed against a homogeneous background showed high recall scores. With this basic knowledge in mind, a detailed analysis can be undertaken (Von Restorff, 1933).

Wallace outlined three ways in which isolation can be achieved (Wallace, 1965).

1. Performing an additional operation to an item within a list, for example, printing an item in red while the remaining items are printed in black. This technique, referred to as *isolation by color*, may be used by the communicator to isolate any item. The isolated term is generally compared with itself in a nonisolated condition.

2. Direct manipulation of items, for example, inserting a different item into a list of similar items. This technique can be called *isolation by material.*

3. Manipulation through the structural organization with a list. The structural technique involves within-subject comparisons, as each subject has both isolated and massed material.

Examples of the first two techniques would be emphasis of a key word or phrase by using larger-sized print. In the first case, the name of the company is emphasized because it is bigger. The second case might use bigger print and a different color to catch the reader's eye.

Television has provided another method in which emphasis can be used—through motion. By either accelerating or slowing motion—by creating illusions through "trick" photography—certain items in a commercial may be emphasized.

A diminishing of the positive effect of emphasis occurs when too many cues are increased in strength. Pillsbury and Rausch conducted an experimental study similar to von Restorff's but used a decreased degree of isolation in order to determine the effect on recall. They found that as items became less and less isolated, a decrease occurred in the remembering of isolated items (Pillsbury and Raush, 1943, p. 298).

Emphasis is a device by which learning can be directed to isolated items or stimuli. Emphasis, in short, is used to convey "prestige" to an element of a message.

Marketing Examples of Emphasis

The highest read advertisement in *Time, Playboy*, and several other magazines in May and June of 1974 was a black-bordered advertisement headlined "FREE." It offered five samples of your choice out of over 100 brand-name products. The one word *FREE* so prominently displayed provided the dramatic emphasis to get the message across simply and quickly.

In a store having a great multiplicity of products to offer, Hanes Hosiery brought out a unique point-of-sale display with its L'eggs panty hose. The stand as well as the panty-hose containers are egg-shaped. This emphasis on shape helped to get people to learn about the product.

Emphasis was overdone by Ronson in promoting its Ronson Comet butane lighter. The one-page advertisement, complete with eight illustrations of the product in use, supplied so many selling facts that nothing less than an actual demonstration could "beat" it. Ronson emphasized all aspects of the Comet lighter. When this was done, the total emphasis of the message was "watered down." The consumer could not possibly learn every facet of a lighter unless he made a concerted effort. And consumers do not have the time or desire to look at each advertisement with the intent to study it.

Rewards

IV.A16 *When the presence of a stimulus has been followed by a reward, this stimulus is more likely to be learned and remembered by audience members than a stimulus that was not followed by a reward.*

Psychological literature is filled with information about rewards, ranking of rewards, reward structure, timing of rewards, and so on. Nearly all psychologists agree that rewards and reinforcements play a large part in human behavior.

Psychologists generally refer to rewards as "reinforcements." Deese defines *reinforcement* as "any stimulus which can increase the strength of a response when it is presented in close temporal conjunction with the occurrence of that response" (Deese, 1952, p. 12). Deese's definition, however, raises a number of questions: What is meant by "increasing the strength of a response?" What kinds of stimuli operate as rewards? How do rewarding stimuli work to strengthen a response? What are the conditions of temporal proximity favoring response reinforcement?

All rewards and reinforcements are not equal. The value of any specific reward can be expressed only in terms of an individual's perception of its value. It has no absolute value. The differences in reward values cut across both demographic and individual lines. For instance, status products such as cars, boats, furniture, and stereo equipment have different reward values for different social classes in general; and specifically, they have different reward values for individuals within the same class.

Reinforcement is of prime importance in mass-communication marketing. Primary reinforcement for marketplace behavior is the benefit derived from the purchase of the product or service (reward). If an individual feels that his appearance is not earning the social approval he desires (the basic motivating want), his behavioral response may be the purhcase of clothing that is more fashionable and suitable to him. Use of the product or service is therefore the primary reward.

Another important reward is produced by belief in the advertising message itself. When the consumer attends to and perceives an advertisement or commercial as truthfully illustrating product benefits wanted or needed by the consumer, he or she anticipates the favorable use of the product. The reassurance gained through such cognitive behavior is itself a reward for perceiving and believing the commercial message.

Delays between response and reinforcement are quite long with regard to most advertising. Certainly, consumers do not and cannot follow enthusiastic requests to "buy it now." But within the chain of marketplace behavior, several response-reinforcement delays take place. Some of these can be reduced through various marketing devices, such as point-of-purchase displays.

The objective of advertising learning is for audience members to learn to purchase and use a specific brand as a response appropriate to the stimulus (triggering perception of the needs and wants). However, the goal of some advertising, and thus the appropriate response to the advertising message, may not be product purchase and repurchase but may be product awareness.

The first reinforcement delay is shortest, and is probably not a delay at all. Secondary reinforcement of anticipation of reward gained through perception and belief of the selling message seems to take place immediately after attending the message. Through this anxiety reduction, the consumer receives the first stage of reinforcement from the product.

The second reinforcement, product purchase, is of a secondary nature because few products, other than services, are used immediately at the point of purchase. There is a delay between the commercial message and the second stage of reinforcement since most advertising takes place in a situation physically removed from actual purchase and selection behavior. The delay time is crucial in the market-behavior chain. It can be reduced through point-of-purchase advertising (thus providing another stimulus at the time and place of the purchase behavior) or through catalogue order by telephone, where consumers can make a purchase decision immediately upon exposure to advertising. And, as noted in the discussion of postpurchase dissonance, the copy on the package label can reduce dissonance as well as further stimulate product use behavior.

Intervening responses between the rewarded response and the actual reinforcement can interfere with the learning situation. This is not true for situations in which there is (1) a clear relationship between the reward and the reinforced response, and (2) there is no clear relationship between the reward and intervening competitive responses. There would appear to be a clear relationship between the response of using a product, attending to its advertising, purchasing it, and the reward (need and want reduction). But there is little relationship between most other competing responses (going to the store, for example). Therefore, the intervening-response theory is not applicable to all possible responses between the advertising and its various rewards.

Marketing Examples of Rewards

This concept of rewards is illustrated in marketing by companies that offer cumulative and noncumulative discounts to their agents. A reward is offered— reduction in price—if the agent orders a quantity or patronizes the dealer over a period of time through total volume. The fact that it "pays to push this product or deal with this company" is learned more readily because of the reward.

An advertisement for Data General, a computer manufacturer, asked: "Do you have the courage to save 50% on your next computer?" Obviously, if the buyer does save that much after purchase, this represents a substantial reward. However, two problems must be faced when presenting such a reward: Is it probable this computer can do this *and* meet the user's needs? Is the statement believable? The potential buyer must learn that the reward is probable and possible.

Gillette offered a $1.00 refund on its two-blade model straight razor as a product introduction. The idea of getting $1.00 back from the purchase provided more incentive to try the product than offering the razor at a cheaper price.

Ranking of Rewards

IV.A16.1 *A reward for reacting to a message will reinforce behavior and cause further learning only if that reward is higher in an audience member's perceived hierarchy of rewards than other possible rewards for reacting to other conflicting messages.*

Just as individuals have hierachies of needs—physiological needs are more basic, for example, than self-fulfillment needs—individuals see rewards in terms of a hierarchy, with some rewards very important and others much less important. It is not enough to claim that a certain product will produce a given reward; after all, other advertisements are doing the same thing. It is important for the mass communicator to find the most attractive reward possible, without going beyond the confines of believability. For instance, advertisers of skin medications use the reward of increased popularity more effectively than less-important rewards (such as the retention of moist skin), provided the audience can believe the claim.

Marketing Examples of Ranking of Rewards

This rewards concept was used for Winston cigarettes when the chance was offered to win a lifetime of bowling by sending in an entry blank. Winston offered a lifetime of bowling *or* $10,000 cash. The company realized that a nonbowler reading the advertisement probably would not be enthused very much if only a lifetime of bowling was offered. The fact that if he won, he could opt to take $10,000 instead probably would mean that the nonbowler could learn the advantages of entering the contest.

Ranking of rewards occurs when a consumer has to choose between several brands of laundry detergents, some of which offer free towels in their boxes, some which include glasses, and some which offer no free gift. The consumer who needs the towels more than the glasses will choose accordingly, providing the towels are also more important than the quality of wash he or she may have been getting from another brand.

Reward Intensity

IV.A16.2 *If a reward is to reinforce members of an audience effectively and cause learning of the message, the reward must have enough value to overcome dissonance aroused by the response that leads to the reward.*

The magnitude of reward is an important consideration. Most individuals will not accept a difficult job without appropriate monetary or personal satisfaction rewards. Nor will risky investments be made unless expected yields on capital can justify the risk. In a sense, the reward must be great enough to justify the behavior required to receive the reward. Nominal rewards cannot justify difficult activities because each behavioral action involves a tradeoff of time, energy, and resources that could have been devoted to another response and reward. Each response has an opportunity cost, the existence of which tends to cause dissonance in the responding organism.

Festinger and Carlsmith demonstrated conditions in which behaviorally induced dissonance affects the relative value of rewards. The experimenters paid two groups of students to participate in an identical and quite dull experiment. One group received $1 per subject; the other group received $20 per subject, with the requirement that all subjects tell other students that the experiment was interesting. Subjects receiving $1 remembered the dull experiment as more interesting better than did the students who received the $20 payment (Festinger and Carlsmith, 1959, p. 205).

Explaining these results, Aronson noted that the requirement of explaining the experiment as interesting created dissonance on the part of subjects. Those subjects receiving the higher reward could justify their "lies." However, the group receiving the nominal dollar had to reduce dissonance through another channel, the channel of remembering the experiment as interesting (Aronson, 1966).

Marketing Examples of Reward Intensity

Thousands of people visited automobile showrooms in southern Michigan when a local dealer association offered a recording of some old Lone Ranger programs for a dollar. The reward was rare and desirable; and people were willing to make the effort to visit the automobile showroom.

It is common practice for banks to promote their establishment and to receive new savers by offering gifts to those who establish new accounts at the bank. In order for the savers to switch accounts, however, they must overcome the dissonance caused by the trouble they must go through to change accounts. The prize given by the bank must be alluring enough to overcome this dissonance and thus make the customer switch his account.

In *Shopper's Voice*, Taste-Freeze instant coffee ran a full-page advertisement. On the adjacent page was a questionnaire about the product, the advertisement, and general marketing information. To fill in the questionnaire would take anywhere from 5 to 15 minutes. Rewarding the reader for his time, Taste-Freeze wisely promised to send 100 green stamps and to give her or him a chance to win 100,000 green stamps in a later drawing.

Timing of Reward

IV.A16.3 *The less time elapsed between the message and the reward it offers, the higher will be the level of the audience members' recall of the message; that is, delaying the reward will hinder learning of the message.*

The notion of close temporal contiguity is essential in nearly every psychological study of operant conditioning. The closer in time the reward is to the act rewarded, the more likely the subject will learn that he is being rewarded for that specific act. Consequently, the more likely he will learn the act itself.

A number of psychologists have carried out studies to show specific effects of delayed reinforcement, or "latency." Champion and McBride found that activities during the reinforcement delay period impaired learning performance. One explanation of this phenomenon is the subject's confusion as to what response is actually being rewarded when several responses intervene between the response to be rewarded and the actual reward (Champion and McBride, 1962).

Some learning situations make the response being rewarded obvious. This is especially true for complex behaviors that, unlike intervening responses in the delay period, are clearly associated with the reward. However, learning word pairs (with proper responses rewarded by knowledge of correctness) does not provide a clear connection between response and reward.

There is some evidence that achievement need and motivation affect the manner in which delayed reinforcement will retard learning. By testing children on reward-delay preferences for both acquisition and free-play behavior, Mendell found:

1. High-achievement children preferred delayed to immediate reward; low-achievement children preferred immediate to delayed reward.
2. Children believing that they have been successful at a task show a significant preference for delayed reward; children who believe that they have failed a task show a significant preference for immediate rewards.
3. Children who are immediately rewarded show significantly higher performance levels at subsequent achievement tasks than children receiving delayed rewards (Mendell, 1967).

An explanation is that low achievers require immediate reinforcement and that when children feel that they have failed in a task, they prefer immediate reinforcement to validate their efforts. The high achievers do not need the immediate reward as much as the low achievers, although it is unclear why they would prefer delayed to immediate reward. Similarly, effort validation is not a salient need when the child believes he has succeeded. Finally, note that the typical delay-of-reinforcement effect was found; immediate reward enhanced learning of the achievement tasks.

Marketing Examples of Timing of Reward

The nature of advertising and buying does not lend itself to a strict adaptation of the timing-of-reward problem. Consumers do not generally run to the store to get their "reward" immediately after the "stimulus" of the advertisement. In this sense, timing of the reward has no bearing on the situation.

However, the literature on timing of reward does have application within the structure of the message itself. Marketers benefit by showing the "reward" that comes from using their product in close contiguity with actual use. Although this may not seem to be an important problem in television commercials of 30 or 60 seconds, perception of the reward for product use could be hindered by interfering dialogue of scenes. In print media especially, the reward needs to be shown to the use of the product to ensure learning of the proper association.

However, providing cents-off on articles at the point of purchase or an in-the-package gift provides an instant reward for choosing a particular brand. Trading stamps given at a supermarket provide incentive for shopping at the store.

In *Reader's Digest*, there may be several serially numbered cards or advertisements headed "You may have already won. . . ." The prizes range from $100 a month for life to 20 Pan American jet trips to Hong Kong. Nearly every one of these affairs requires that the holder of the "lucky number" visit a retail dealer. On the assumption that people will go to great lengths to win a big prize, even when the odds are over a million to one against them, this device may provide an immediately rewarding experience.

Continuity of Rewards

IV.A16.4 *An intermittent schedule of rewards for responses to messages increases the audience members' learning of the messages, whereas continuous reward responses can lead to extinction of the learned responses.*

Intermittent rewards, in contrast to continuous rewards, inoculate audience members against extinction of the learned responses. Although learning is more rapid with continuous rewards (fewer trials to learning), continuous rewards later seem to hasten extinction of the learned responses (fewer unrewarded trials to extinction of the responses).

One explanation of this phenomenon is that during the learning stages of response repetition, individuals find some responses unrewarded and are unable to discriminate between acquisition responses and extinction responses once they are in the extinction phase of the unreinforced responses.

Numerous theories have been developed by a number of psychologists to explain the learning effects created by intermittent reinforcement. Amstel cited frustration as a key element in the partial-reinforcement effect. He proposed that nonrewarded responses created the frustration of nonreward, plus increased behavioral vigor toward the reward. Continuous nonreward, such as during extinction, inhibits the response by creating greater levels of frustration and frustration anticipation. In a partial reinforcement situation, where only some but not all responses are rewarded, increased behavioral vigor is eventually rewarded, and the response is learned better. In effect, the subject is motivated to avoid a nonrewarded situation when the acquisition phase is characterized by partial reinforcement. Continuous reinforcement does not create such an avoidance response, and the learned response is not as strong (Amstel, 1958).

Wilton related similar explanations to dissonance-reduction modes. Nonrewarded acquisition responses create dissonance, which the subject is motivated to reduce. Eventual reward reduces the dissonance; and the vigor of response is aided by the dissonance, reducing behavior of continuous response. In the extinction phase, dissonance-reducing behavior tends to prolong the learned response (Wilton, 1967).

Partial-reinforcement effects are a function of the magnitude of the rewards yielded for correct responses. An experiment by Parker illustrated the interrelationship between partial reinforcement and reward magnitude. He compared the effects of continuous versus intermittent reward in relation to high-value and low-value reward strengths. The typical differences were found between continuous and partial reinforcement for each reward group. As might be expected, the partially reinforced, high-rewarded value group required more trials for extinction to occur than the partially reinforced low-reward value group. However, in the continuous-reinforcement group, the low-reward value group required more trials to extinction than the high-reward value group. A possible explanation is that the high-reward value group experienced a higher degree in inhibitory frustration during extinction than the degree of frustration experienced by the group receiving low-value rewards (Parker, 1967).

Marketing Examples of Continuity of Rewards

Price-off coupons that are "good until . . . " or cosmetics that have annual or semiannual sales illustrate this principle. Polly Bergen's Oil of the Turtle night cream was offered for half price, a saving of $10.00 during an annual sale. Because the sale lasted only one month, it encouraged women to take advantage of the lower price and buy two jars of the cream for the price of one.

Since occasional reinforcement is more efficient than constant reinforcement, marketers should employ special offers or premiums over fairly short periods rather than over extended periods. Short-time offers are perceived as a special bonus, whereas extended offers may come to be expected and actually cause consumers to feel cheated if they are dropped. More brand switching away from a product will occur after an extended offer than after a temporary one. In other words, special reinforcements "work" because they are special or unusual. If they were extended over a long period of time so as to be seen as the normal situation, they tend to lose their positive reinforcement power.

The goal of the marketer using such devices, however, is to lengthen the extinction phase of response to the premium. Note that this discussion considers the response rewarded by the premium and not that part of the response rewarded by product use. If a premium is used continuously as an inducement, its elimination implies more rapid extinction of the premium-oriented response than if the premium were intermittently offered as a reward. Consequently, marketers should offer premiums only over certain periods, interspersed between no-premium periods. The premium should only be a special push to force more than usual amounts of product trial.

However, premiums are not a reliable manner by which to build long-term product loyalty. As noted, part of the favorable product response is actually response to the reward of the premium. Hull's incentive-learning phenomenon showed that response extinction under conditions of incentive learning is more rapid than learning based on application of no incentives in the acquisition phase (Hull, 1952, p. 145). Incentives, such as premiums, are a marginal type of reward good for building spurts of product trial. They do not contribute to long-term product loyalty and are best applied in a partial rather than continuous reinforcement schedule.

As a final example, at Community Discount centers, a Midwest discount department store chain, special sales with drastically reduced prices were announced at various intervals throughout the store and would continue for 5-10 minutes. Since the bargains were announced randomly, the shopper never knew just when he or she might be able to participate in these rewards, thus making trips to Community Discount eagerly anticipated.

Negative Reinforcement and Anxiety Arousal

IV.A16.5 *Audience members learn messages that contain negative information, or that arouse anxiety, in an effort to avoid undesirable consequences; but if the anxiety arousal is too strong, these messages will "backfire" by causing the audience members to tend to ignore them.*

When psychologists refer to *reward* and *reinforcement*, they generally mean "positive reinforcement." But another type of reward is *negative reinforcement*, or punishment in connection with a particular response. Janis and Milholland conducted an experiment relating threat appeals to learning. They asked a group of adults to read similar magazine articles concerning dental hygiene. The articles varied in the degree of threat contained. One contained a strong threat, while the others had a substantially more mild approach. At the conclusion of the experiment, the subjects were given a recall test. Those who had read the strong appeal recalled more of the unfavorable consequences, while the mild-appeal group retained more of the causes and information sources. The experimenters concluded that a selective recall tendency exists in the learning process. They suggested that threat appeals or anxiety arousal can exert an important influence on what is learned and retained from the content of a persuasive communication (Janis and Milholland, 1954).

In some cases, anxieties aroused in the consumer appear to dominate the consideration for motivating behavior. Although generally it is true that positive rewards stimulate learned responses better than negative rewards, some products have particular appeal as avoidance responses to an undesirable condition. Mouthwashes are in this category.

Learning, as well as motivating and persuading, are aided by negative reinforcement, such as the perception of a threat. The punishment of threat occurrence also builds learning ability. A child rapidly acquires the idea that he should not touch hot stoves, *after* he has burned his hand. Use of negative appeals follows the same general rules as those outlined for positive rewards. (The anticipation of punishment as induced by a threat appeal is also a negative reward.) Yet the intended mode of response is opposite from that of positive rewards. Most marketing situations call for positive rather than negative reinforcement. This is due to the general ability of positive reinforcers to influence more effectively acquisition phases of learning.

An important issue to consider when dealing with negative reinforcers, such as perceiving of threat appeals, is the phenomenon of threat-appeal rejection. If the threat is too severe, consumer dissonance levels may be high enough to make the consumer ignore the message rather than change his overt behavior. When using a threat appeal, it is important for the marketer to make overt behavior (purchase and use of the product or service) appear to be the easiest means of reducing the dissonance aroused by the threat appeal and perceived negative reinforcement situation.

*Marketing Examples of Negative Reinforcement
and Anxiety Arousal*

Behavior is not always a response to "get something"; quite often it can be an avoidance response to something the individual considers undesirable. In consumer behavior, it is often unclear whether an individual acts through marketplace devices to avoid something or to gain something. Do audience members

256

purchase new, fashionable clothing to avoid social reprobation or to gain social approbation?

The use of appeals to save the environment have been successful in the introduction of antiphosphate detergents. Their advertising and packaging featured beautiful scenes of clean waterfalls and thus helped to arouse anxiety by implying that only through the use of these products could consumers guarantee clean water forever.

Old American Insurance Company aimed its advertising at those Americans, especially elderly city dwellers, who increasingly fear for their safety. The advertisement opened with a menacing, silhouetted attacker. It warned readers of the dangers of "being mugged, pushed down a flight of stairs by a fleeing thief, or shoved off a curb by a roaming gang of toughs." Furthermore, "You never know what's waiting outside for you, do you? And when you get home, what fears lurk?"

21 Variables within the Audience: Psychological State

Background

The learning of messages has been divided into two areas. Message variables and medium variables, generally within the control of the communicator, already have been discussed. Equally important, however, are those characteristics of audience variables that affect learning. These variables lie beyond the control of the communicator or marketer. They are important because a given audience may exhibit one or more of these characteristics or processes. But it is not the task of the communicator to attempt to control these variables. Rather, he should learn to identify the existence of such variables in situations and understand their implications as to the effectiveness of his presentation. His message should be "tailored" to the audience.

Psychological State

An individual's immediate psychological state affects his learning ability in every situation. The concept of psychological state refers to the total mental state of an individual. In this book the phrase is used with respect to those variables which determine an individual's reactions to a message. In this section we deal with specific variables of the psychological state; for example, the individual's involvement with the message, the perceived relevance of the message, intent to learn, curiosity, the reintegration. It will be shown that the presence or absence of these conditions has either positive or negative effects on learning.

Personality variables influence a person's psychological state. Abelson, for example, has presented evidence that ego-defensive people respond better to factual material than to material that attempts to help them understand their emotional behavior. His explanation is that the attitudes being examined (in this case, anti-Negro feelings) were not so important to the maintenance of these individuals' personalities that they found the examining data threatening and therefore aversive (Abelson, 1959, pp. 62-63). A personality influence this powerful can be an extremely important factor in an examination of psychological state, simply because of its potency.

There are other personality variables that also merit consideration, traits such as introverted-extroverted, masculine-feminine, aggressive-meek, and neurotic-normal. Reactions of introverted and/or meek people might be similar;

257

aggressive and extroverted individuals might behave similarly. But traits such as those mentioned are not precise delineations of an individual's personality. A person who is aggressive in one situation may be meek in another. And, although a person may be regarded as very confident, he may feel a lack of confidence in a specific area. Or an individual who is not considered to be highly confident may have great confidence in one particular field. A neurotic individual may exhibit tendencies toward all the traits mentioned.

The effects these variables can have on learning ability or message reception should be reasonably obvious. Introverted and/or meek individuals may reject a message that uses a threat appeal (even a mild one), while it is doubtful that aggressive and/or extroverted individuals would be greatly influenced by the same appeal. Masculinity or femininity can affect an individual's receptiveness to a particular appeal. While it may be obvious that such variables do affect an individual's psychological state, which in turn affects his behavior and learning abilities, it is not known clearly *how* they affect the individual. Reactions can be projected and hypothesized but not in precise terms.

Open- and Closed-Mindedness

IV.B1 *Closed-minded audience members are less able to learn arguments contrary to their own beliefs and attitudes than are open-minded individuals.*

An individual having a dogmatic cognitive system (closed-mindedness) is resistant to changes in that system. Studies indicate that attempts to modify or change attitudes through learning situations meet with opposition: slowness of learning, difficulty of recall, continued preference for existing beliefs, inaccuracy in learning, and low retention rate. There is some evidence that closed-minded people are highly resistant to change (Rokeach, 1954).

Many studies have been done, linking closed-minded individuals and learning abilities. Ehrlich compared the performance of 57 students in an introductory sociology course. They were given two tests—one before the course began and one after it was completed. From these tests, the open-minded and closed-minded individuals were determined. The results showed that open-minded students entered the course with a higher level of learning and learned more than did closed-minded students (Ehrlich, 1961).

While studying experiments already performed, Ehrlich and Lee found five intervening variables that must be considered. They are belief congruence, novelty, authority, centrality, and syndrome relevance (Ehrlich and Lee, 1969).

Belief Congruence

The degree to which material is belief congruent or incongruent will greatly affect the learning process for both open- and closed-minded people. Adams and

Vidulich (1962) compared the performance of the 18 highest and lowest subjects on dogmatism from a pool of 300 psychology students. Subjects were presented with a paired-associate learning task consisting of two word lists—15 belief-congruent word pairs and 15 belief-incongruent pairs. They found, first, that high-dogmatism subjects made significantly more errors in the incongruent versus congruent associations. Second, high-dogmatism subjects also made significantly more errors than did low-dogmatism subjects in learning the congruent associations.

In a group of 72 high school juniors, Kleck and Wheaton (1967) tested three hypotheses involving preference, recall, and evaluation of belief-congruent and belief-incongruent materials under conditions of public and private commitment to an opinion on teenage driving. They found no difference in preference between open- and closed-minded subjects (all subjects preferred belief-congruent material). There was some difference in evaluation, with high-dogmatism subjects evaluating belief-congruent materials more favorably than low-dogmatism subjects, but no differences were manifest in belief-incongruent materials. Finally, they found high-dogmatism subjects recalled fewer incongruent materials than low-dogmatism subjects.

Lastly, Druckman (1967), after comparing the performance of high- and low-dogmatism subjects in playing management and union roles, found that regardless of role, high-dogmatism subjects resolved fewer issues, were more resistant to compromise, and were more likely to view compromise as defeat.

Novelty

Individuals vary significantly in their ability to accept and incorporate novel or new ideas. "In regard to their conservatism, the dogmatic subjects are confident in what they have been taught to believe, accept the tried and true despite inconsistencies, and are cautious and compromising in regard to new ideas, generally going all with tradition" (Vacchiano, Strauss, and Schiffman, 1968).

Comparing the performance of 24 extremely high with 24 extremely low dogmatism subjects selected from a pool of 614 psychology students, Rokeach, Swanson, and Denny (1960) tested the novelty effect using a chess-play-type problem. The results indicated no difference between open- and close-minded chess players but a significant difference between the open- and close-minded nonchess players in the ability to solve the problem. Close-minded nonplayers performed significantly poorer.

Authority

Authority figures provide an individual with both a source of information and a means of validating that information. "Dependence on authority ranges from rational and tentative, for the open-minded, to arbitrary and absolute, for the closed-minded." The more open a person's belief system, the more his learning and problem-solving behavior should be directed by the requirements of the situation rather than the demands of an authority (Ehrlich and Lee, 1969, p. 254).

Vidulich and Kaiman tested 30 female students from an introductory psychology course—half were high-dogmatism subjects, half were low. Two males were introduced to the subjects, one as a college professor and one as a high-school student. The group was exposed to a light stimulus and asked to write down individually in which direction the light moved. Later they were exposed to the same stimulus; but the males verbally stated answers opposite to the pattern, while the females wrote their responses. It was found that there was a significant interaction between source status and dogmatism; that is, high-dogmatism subjects conformed more with the higher-status male than with the lower-status male (Vidulich and Kaiman, 1961).

Centrality

Basic postulates of centrality are (1) that not all beliefs are equally important; and (2) that the more important a belief to an individual, the more it is resistant to change. An underlying assumption in most research concerning centrality has been that belief-congruent or personally involving materials are more central than incongruent or noninvolving materials.

A test of the centrality hypothesis was conducted by White and Alter. They chose 24 subjects from an introductory psychology class—12 high-dogmatism and 12 low-dogmatism students. Subjects were to sort 140 occupational titles and 149 undesirable social acts into as many piles as they wanted, based on occupational prestige and undesirability. It was found that the high-dogmatism subjects used fewer categories in judging the undesirable acts than did low-dogmatism subjects. High-dogmatism subjects also placed a greater proportion of the acts in the more undesirable categories. Results indicated that for the high-dogmatism subjects the number and width of the categories were responsive to the centrality of the stimuli (White and Alter, 1967).

Syndrome Relevance

Rates of acquisition or change of beliefs are the consequence of the mode in which they are presented. Learning effects derived from the interactions of the characteristics of the mode of presentation with cognitive characteristics of open-minded and closed-minded people may be termed *syndrome relevant*.

Open-mindedness and closed-mindedness can affect the amount of time needed to solve a problem. Rokeach, Oram, Laffey and Denny conducted two experiments on 20 high-dogmatism and 20 low-dogmatism subjects from an introductory psychology course. Subjects were presented with a problem and the new beliefs required for its solution at 5-minute intervals. Open-minded subjects significantly out-performed the closed-minded subjects in the time necessary to solve the problem. In the second experiment the subjects were given all the beliefs required for the solution at the beginning of the problem. Closed-minded individuals took less time to solve this version of the problem than the first version. Open-minded subjects showed no significant differences in performance (Rokeach, Oram, Laffey, and Denny, 1960).

Syndrome relevance also affects attitudes toward the source of a communication. Two classroom groups were exposed to one of two versions—one dogmatic and one undogmatic—of a persuasive speech. Attitudes toward the unidentified speaker were assessed. Subjects low in dogmatism were more favorable to the speaker in the undogmatic speech. Within the high-dogmatic appeal condition, favorable attitudes toward the speaker increased with the subject's dogmatism (McGuckin, 1967). It was found that closed-minded subjects were more favorable to an authoritative speaker regardless of the appeal condition and were much more favorable than open-minded subjects when the appeal was dogmatic. The open-minded subjects were the least favorable to the speaker under the high-dogmatic appeal condition.

In some cases there is conflicting evidence to the closed- and open-mindedness proposition. This means that there is not as high a degree of probability for this principle as there is for others in this book. It can, however, be of use to the communicator. For example, when dealing with a novel item, the more closed-minded individual will not readily accept it. If this is the case, acceptance may be increased by the use of a dogmatic communicator, an authority source.

Rejection by closed-minded individuals may begin with refusal to read articles on subjects not in accord with established ideas. Even if such individuals do read incongruent articles, they are less likely to remember the information. They will also have difficulty determining the relationships among various beliefs or concepts. The source of information and the information itself are not easily separated by closed-minded individuals. For additional information on *Open- and Closed-Mindedness*, see chapters 28 and 33.

Marketing Examples of Open- and Closed-Mindedness

The Travelers Insurance Company took open-mindedness and closed-mindedness into consideration in its magazine advertising about no-fault insurance. The company used this headline: "No-fault auto insurance. If insurance companies are for it, shouldn't you be against it?" The company probably "struck the nerves" of those who were against it no matter what the arguments were on the other side and those who were against it because insurance companies were. The insurance company realized the closed-minded approach of many people on this subject and did a good job of approaching closed-minded people so that they might consider both sides.

This principle is easily applied to personal selling. The salesperson in a store or a door-to-door salesperson has an opportunity to assess the individual with whom he or she is dealing. He or she can then adjust the approach accordingly. Often a closed-minded person will refuse to listen to a door-to-door sales message and may even close the door in the salesperson's face. An open-minded person is much more likely to listen to the salesperson's message before making a decision. It is up to the salesperson to assess the degree of open- or closed-mindedness toward the subject at hand and adjust the presentation accordingly.

Directing a marketing effort at a specific market segment is particularly important in the case of new products. As mentioned earlier, new or novel ideas are not accepted very easily by closed-minded people, so it is important for a marketer to find out if his "proposed" market segment is very close-minded. For example, Mazda's introduction of the rotary engine in its cars would have had a hard time being accepted if the market was dominated by close-minded people; but since the market segment they initially aimed at was relatively open-minded, the new engine was more readily tried. These people relished in trying something new.

Involvement

IV.B2 *If an audience member is highly involved with a message, he or she will more likely learn that message than if he or she is only slightly involved.*

Involvement is more than a simple function of repetition of reinforcement. It requires the individual to perceive learning of the message as a step toward desired goals. Ideally, communication is a two-way flow. It should not be a monologue from the communicator to the receiver. Involvement may be seen as the first step in an individual's response to learning the message.

Krugman noted involvement as one of the basic factors controlling the learning of television commercials. He cited studies showing that long-term remembering was shortened if the material was nonsensical and unimportant to the audience member's frame of reference. However, with ego-involving material, learning comes much slower, but remembering lasts much longer. He stated: "Thus with low involvement one might look for gradual shifts in perceptual structure, aided by repetition, activated by behavioral-choice situations, and followed at some time by attitude change. With high involvement one would look for the classic, more dramatic, and more familiar conflict of ideas at the level of conscious opinion and attitude that precedes changes in overt behavior" (Krugman, 1965, p. 355).

Krugman used this theory to explain why advertisements may not be very successful at selling such ideas as peace or political candidates. "The more common skills of Madison Avenue concern the change processes associated with low involvement, while the very different skills required for high involvement campaigns are usually found elsewhere" (Krugman, 1965, p. 355).

Involvement may be explained as the positive effect of motivation on learning. Three different levels of involvement are: active participating, covert involvement, and vicarious practice.

Marketing Examples of Involvement

In personal selling, the salesperson can "relate" to the customer in an attempt to involve him, for example, by asking questions, trying to draw the customer into a conversation, or demonstrating the product.

Amway (home-care products) utilized this concept effectively in selling its products, which were sold only through salespeople who demonstrate each product in the customer's home. To involve the consumer in the presentation, demonstrations were often done on items found in his home. For example, to demonstrate SA-8 laundry detergent compound, a handkerchief just washed by the customer was rinsed in SA-8, which dissolved the residue remaining in the "clean" handkerchief.

Head and Shoulders dandruff shampoo demonstrated the same point in a very novel print advertisement. The top half of the page was black. The copy underneath instructed the reader to position his head over the top black portion of the page and to shake his head. If little white flakes of the reader's own dandruff appeared before him, he needed the Head and Shoulders product.

Shell Oil Company knew the value of involvement and demonstrated it in its "Safety Series." The newspaper advertisements showed a life-size picture of the accelerator and brake pedals of a car. The reader was asked to sit in a straight chair, lay the newspaper on the floor, put his foot on the gas pedal, hold out his hand, and drop a quarter. He should have been able to move his foot from the gas pedal to the brake before the quarter hit the floor.

Another example of involvement would be the experience of visiting a car dealer. Initially in the showroom, the potential buyer of a new car will view the various models and styles of a given make of automobile. As he carefully looks over each car, he is covertly involved in the product's message, imagining how he would look and feel if he became the car's owner. After choosing a favorite in the showroom, the shopper will be receptive to messages from the salesman or dealer that relate to the product's features and its performance in use. As he sits in the car, feels the upholstery, and looks under its hood, the shopper is demonstrating vicarious use and ownership. At the point where the dealer allows the prospect to drive the car himself, he is actively participating in learning the product's experience.

Active Participating

IV.B2.1 *Audience members learn faster and remember more by active participating than by passive receiving.*

Active participating is overt involvement. *Overt behavior* is observable, external, largely explicit, and involves completed or almost completed responses. By contrast, *covert behavior* is nonobservable, internal, largely implicit, and involves anticipatory responses. The greater the amount of covert involvement an individual has with respect to an item—that is, an object, person, situation, or event—the greater will be the person's learning and remembering of the item and its variables. Active participating results in even more learning and remembering than covert involvement.

A number of studies have shown that active participating can be more effective than passive receiving in changing attitudes, as well as in retaining attitude changes. Probably the most convincing one, which also shows the retention of such attitude changes, was conducted by Watts. He divided his subjects into two groups. One group read a message on a specified topic, and the other was required to write a persuasive argument on the same topic. Watts found that this tactic initially produced equal attitude changes in both groups. However, six weeks later the group that had actively participated by writing still retained a significant attitude change, while the attitudes of the reading group had returned to the same level as the control group. The active participators were also found to have definite drives toward obtaining more information about the topic (Watts, 1967).

Marketing Examples of Active Participating

Advertising messages will be more easily remembered and cause more change of beliefs and attitudes if they elicit some type of active response from the consumer. Assuming that the advertisement does "talk" about the product, the consumer's active response to the advertisement will bring him closer to the final action of buying the product. Involving the consumer is the first step toward that goal; and this can be accomplished in a number of ways. Getting consumers to repeat key phrases or even making puns of the brand name are examples.

Among the methods to obtain "quick action" are price-discount coupons, premium offers, and contests. *Coupons* offer the consumer a price reduction on a particular product and require him to either cut out or send for the coupons and present them at the time of purchase. Advertisers offer in excess of 10 billion coupons a year. The *premium* is a "gift" offered in return for a coupon, usually with a cereal boxtop, wrapper, or some other proof of purchase. The premium itself may be totally unrelated to the product sponsoring it, but it offers "something for nothing" and actively involves the consumer. *Contests* also involve the consumer but require some work on the part of the consumer. At the very least they require that he attend to the advertisement long enough to read the instructions.

Active participating is employed in many aspects of personal selling. A suit salesman should persuade the man looking at suits to try some on and look at himself in the mirror. The customer actively participates rather than just looking at the suit on the hanger. As a result, he is more likely to buy.

Free cheese, pizza, or other prepared food samples offered to customers shopping in supermarkets illustrate this principle. The customer does not have to take anyone else's word for the product's flavor and texture; he can make up his own mind.

Covert Involvement

IV.B2.2 *Covert involvement of audience members is an effective way of learning a message when active involvement cannot be obtained.*

Covert behavior involves internal responses to stimuli. An example would be a hungry person standing in front of a window filled with pastry. One may say that "he isn't doing anything"; but appropriate tests would show that his salivary glands are secreting, his stomach is rhythmically contracting and expanding, marked changes in blood pressure are taking place, and his endocrine glands are pouring substances into the blood (Watson, 1925, p. 15).

Active participating enhances learning but is often very difficult to obtain. No matter how creative a communicator is, some mass communications cannot hope to gain this kind of involvement. In order to be effective, the advertisement must "adapt itself to the perceptual habits of readers" (G.H. Smith, 1954, p. 12). The consumer in selectively attending to certain messages will ignore any advertisement that does not at least secure his covert involvement.

The advertiser must work to involve the consumer mentally, internally, or "create empathy." The consumer may react emotionally to scenes of a beautiful mountain setting, a deserted beach, or of an attractive woman in a sports car. One advantage of this type of involvement over even active participating is that it may imply a promise of reward that the consumer desires but which he may never experience in real life.

It should be pointed out, however, that covert effects can be negative, especially in the case of fear. It was commonly thought that a message showing terrible automobile accidents would sell seat belts by causing great fear. However, it is more probable that consumers will avoid thinking about such fear-evoking things, much less take the time to go out and buy seat belts (which will only remind them of the terrible accidents in the advertisements).

Studies by Janis and Feshbach (1953) on fear appeals, which give specific insight into the tooth-decay and smoking-and-lung-cancer problems, support this possibility. They are presented in the section Anxiety Arousal in chapter 26. See also the discussion in chapter 19.

Marketing Examples of Covert Involvement

The window displays of clothing stores will present clothes that are one or two seasons ahead of the present. The potential shopper will often be attracted to the contrast of the mannequins' clothes against the prevailing weather conditions—for example, heavy coats in summer and beachwear in winter. Thus the window viewer becomes covertly involved with a different and perhaps appealing environment. He can use his imagination and think about warmer weather when it is cold or cooler days when it is hot outdoors.

Eastern Airlines radio commercials employed the listener's covert involvement. The narrator, Orson Welles, described the exotic or especially different aspects of a tourist attraction in one of the cities the airline services. In the background of the narration appropriate sound effects and music were played to lend a feeling of the atmosphere of the vacation spot. The listener could inject himself into the situation through his imagination as he listened to the commercial.

The fizz of opening cans and the crunching of potato chips covertly involve radio listeners in commercials. Similarly, in a bakery, the smell of food lures prospective customers, as does a pine scent sprayed in a store around Christmas time.

Packaging relies very heavily on covert involvement. The products on the shelves must "talk" effectively through their packaging design and shape if they are to attract customers. The beautiful girl with fantastic-looking hair on the Clairol packages gives the customer a view of what her hair could look like (also helps her "see" herself as a blonde or some other hair color).

A Goodyear tire commercial on television showed a woman who was driving alone late at night and had a flat tire in the middle of nowhere, certainly a dangerous predicament. At this point Goodyear entered with its tire-within-a-tire product concept to show effectively how her problem could have been prevented. The audience learned that Goodyear tires keeps going even when punctured.

Vicarious Practice

IV.B2.3 *Learning is strengthened when audience members see an item being demonstrated along with an explanation of its special features, instead of seeing the item not in use.*

The principle of vicarious practice is closely associated with the principle of covert involvement. It means that an individual is sufficiently covertly involved with an item that he vicariously practices its use, as illustrated in the following three examples.

First, learning is strengthened by *seeing* the object in use, with a demonstration or explanation of its special features or benefits. However, the demonstrator should be as similar as possible to the actual consumers who might want the item. If he is not, the consumers' abilities to identify with the demonstration may be hindered.

Second, when teaching motor skills to an individual, it is best to show the performance in the same way that the learner would see the job if he were doing it. Television commercials that employ the "subjective camera angle" (that is, camera shooting over the demonstrator's shoulder) may be very effective, since these shots present products as if the viewers were seeing them themselves.

Finally, specific benefits in the usage of demonstrated items may be learned best through vicarious practice. Perry has observed that imaginary, or vicarious, practice is more effective in various tasks than active practice (Perry, 1939, p. 70). This includes those tasks which consist of learning facts that may be observed without movement. A person may not be able actually to learn how to use a new type of razor by watching and imagining its use; but he may be more likely to learn of its greater efficiency, or some other advantage, through vicarious practice. The key is to involve the consumer in a specific way.

Marketing Examples of Vicarious Practice

Skippy brand peanut butter utilized vicarious practice. In one commercial the moderator explained the advantages of using Skippy brand and then offered the viewer a piece of bread spread with the peanut butter. The bread was passed by the announcer to the foreground of the viewing screen, as if the bread were actually passed through the screen. When the bread was removed from the foreground, a bite had been taken from it.

Vicarious practice is also used by various car dealers in test drives—especially in imports or high-performance cars. The salesman drives the car first, accelerating fast, cornering fairly sharply and braking hard. He tries to show the customer what the car can do. Since many people test-driving a car are fairly conservative in the test drive, this gives the customer a chance to practice vicariously the things he would like to see the car do but can't or wouldn't do in the test drive himself.

In various television commercials the Polaroid Camera Company displayed the ease with which a picture could be taken with its 60-second Polaroid camera. A photograph was taken and revealed during the span of the commercial, thus demonstrating that anyone could develop a beautiful snapshot very easily in one minute by using a Polaroid camera.

Many consumers believe lawnmowers are hard to start. In a series of live television commercials, Sears dramatically demonstrated that its lawnmower is easy to start. The announcer talked about the lawnmower and then bent down and pulled the starter rope; the mower started effortlessly and immediately.

Relevance

IV.B3 *Audience members learn stimuli better if they perceive the stimuli to be relevant to them than if they perceive them as not relevant.*

An individual cannot possibly attend to all the stimuli to which he is exposed. He must screen out many, especially stimuli that seem irrelevant to him. A *relevant stimulus* may be defined as one that is harmonious with the individual's needs and wants. If one lifts a glass of water to his lips and drinks, the cold water going down the throat is felt to be a consequence of the connection that had the act of drinking as an end. Thorndike defined relevance as the degree of connection between an action and the satisfier (Thorndike, 1935, pp. 52-61); that is, if the satisfier (cold water) has a close connection (drinking), it would be considered relevant.

Marketing Examples of Relevance

Advertising of a product or service should be perceived as having a close connection with an individual's goal or reward. For example, Sears, in its campaign for low-phosphate detergent, incorporated the free service of former Secretary of Interior, Stuart Udall. He did a testimonial about fighting pollution by using Sears low-phosphate detergent. Since stoppage of pollution is a relevant topic, employing a top man in the conservation field, such as Stuart Udall, increases the relevancy of the advertisement.

Direct-mail techniques have had to be improved as the average consumer has gradually filtered out most direct mail as being irrelevant. Thus new techniques have included multicolored envelopes, different-shaped envelopes, more-relevant copy on the outside of the envelope, more-personal approaches, and more-enticing offers. One must be aware, though, that even if the consumer does attend to the mail piece (sees it as being relevant), the product offering must also be distinguishably relevant from others offered if some learning is to occur.

In light of the trend toward more full-time employment by women, as well as the increasing popularity of evening shopping, several grocery retail chains have tried staying open until midnight, or even on a continuous, 24-hour basis. Advertising and store-front displays call attention to this convenience, and those shoppers who desire such service will find such messages relevant and remember them.

Manufacturers of cold remedies, vitamins, and pain relievers are quick to utilize the relevance of advertising their products heavily during a major outbreak of bronchial influenza or colds throughout the country.

Meaningfulness

IV.B4 *The more meaningful a message is to an audience member, the more likely it is that the message will be learned than if the message is not meaningful to him.*

The *meaning* of a statement is "what the speaker intends to be understood from it by the listener." Meaningfulness has been defined in terms of a number of variables by psychologists: (1) association value, (2) frequency with which the item is experienced, and (3) pronounceability.

An early study by Glaze involved presenting more than 2000 syllables to 15 subjects. Each syllable was presented separately for 2 seconds. The subjects were asked the meaning of the syllable. If it did not mean anything, they were instructed to say nothing. The association value was measured by the percent of students who made an association (Glaze, 1928).

The second variable of meaningfulness is frequency. Generally, frequency has been determined by the Thorndike-Lorge frequency count. This count was obtained by examining a vast range of reading materials and counting the number of times per million that each particular word appeared. High-frequency words will be more meaningful than low-frequency words (Thorndike and Lorge, 1944).

There have been little or no contradictory experiments reported in the literature for association value and frequency. However, it has been shown in a number of experiments that pronounceability is not correlated with learning. In one experiment, 40 subjects learned homogeneous paired-associate lists consisting of 12 CVCs (consonant-vowel-consonant, such as BOB or WOL) equated for association value and familiarity. Two groups learned lists having low PR (pronounceability rating) (easy to pronounce); and two groups learned high-PR response terms. High- and low-PR groups did not differ significantly either in terms of mean number of trials to reach criterion or mean total number of correct responses.

Paivio and Steeves conducted a study that showed the effect of meaningfulness of value words on remembering. Significant correlations were found between personal values and imagery scores for value-related words in the theoretical, religious, aesthetic, and economic areas, thus suggesting differences in the frequency of relevant word-object associations in prior experience (Paivio and Steeves, 1967). From the data the authors imply that the more a subject can relate to a word, the more likely he is to remember it. The more meaningful the material, the more easily it is learned.

As Kanungo and Dutta (1966) demonstrated, more-meaningful brand names will create greater brand awareness than will less-meaningful names. If a more-meaningful verbal item is learned faster and retained better than a less-meaningful verbal item, then it is worthwhile to demonstrate the usefulness of such measures. High-utility products ensure greater brand awareness than low-utility products. One hundred and forty-three of the MM (more meaningful) and 60 of the LM (low meaningful) brand names were recalled in immediate-recall condition, the recall percentages being 15.88 and 6.66, respectively.

The results support the hypothesis that a brand name having more meaningfulness value is learned and retained better than a brand name having low meaningfulness value. It was observed that in immediate recall, males recalled significantly fewer brand names of female-use products than expected. Females, however, in both immediate and delayed recall, listed significantly more brand names of female-use products and fewer brand names of male-use products. This supports the hypothesis that brand awareness of high-utility products is superior to that of low-utility products. Brand names that have high-scaled meaningfuless value are learned and retained better than those that have low-scaled meaningfulness value (Kanungo and Dutta, 1966).

Marketing Examples of Meaningfulness

Promotional campaign work by Humble Oil and Refining Company was directed in combining their several brand names into one new brand, Exxon. To build a meaningful association of this new name with the company's long-established gasoline products, Humble's mnemonic brand character, the Tiger, of an earlier campaign ("Put a Tiger in your tank") was used in conjunction with the Exxon logo.

A salesperson wants to make what he says meaningful to his customer; he wants the product to be in some way important to this individual. The final outcome of his sale may depend on whether the salesperson has successfully given some meaning to both the product and its relation to the customer. A salesman can make a suit meaningful to a customer by saying earnestly, "This suit really looks good on you" or "In this suit you can go to most any dress-up occasion and rest assured that you're dressed properly." These statements are meaningful to the customer.

The New York Life Insurance Company, in an attempt to reach young fathers, headlined a print advertisement "Babies are funny, wiggly, warm little things who need protection. So do their mothers." Since a new father is apt to be concerned about the protection of his family, this advertisement becomes meaningful to that individual and is therefore more easily learned.

Intent

IV.B5 *If an audience member has been told to learn the contents of a message, he tends to learn more than if the learning is incidental.*

All learning can be divided into intentional and incidental learning. *Intentional learning* occurs when the individual is detetermined to learn materials, usually because of instructions to do so or the knowledge that he is to be tested. *Incidental learning* is simply all other learning that occurs without the intention of the individual.

Two types of experimental design are used to differentiate between these two types of learning. In type I, intentional-learning subjects are given instructions to learn materials. Incidental subjects are exposed to the same materials but given no instructions and are tested unexpectedly. In type II, incidental-learning subjects are given two sets of materials—for instance, a list of names and a list of geometric forms adjacent to the names. Subjects are then tested on the materials or dimensions they were given no instructions to learn.

Incidental and intentional learning are not thought to differ in the process that occurs after favorable responses are aroused to the acquisition of the materials. Therefore, if the message is one that has been sought out by the communicatee or contains materials that are meaningful or relevant to him, the advantages of intentional learning diminish.

However, the intentional-learning situation produces greater recall. Whether the increase is due to some unexplainable brain mechanism or simply because of increased attending or greater meaning is not the important issue. The intentional-learning situation does create higher recall.

Marketing Examples of Intent

Many television commercials make use of this concept, often beginning with someone saying "I'm going to show you something that is of great importance to you." For example, Bayer Aspirin opened some of its television commercials with the words "The Bayer man wants you to know about pain relievers." The advertisement made it obvious that it was teaching something and that the viewer would benefit by paying attention to the message.

A promotional example of intent frequently occurs in department-store shopping. An announcement is made throughout the store calling for shoppers' attention. The announcement then informs the shoppers of a special bargain for a limited period. Such an example might be "Attention, all shoppers! For the next half-hour all phonograph records will be reduced 25 percent from list price." By calling attention to the special sale, the learning process is simplified.

The use of some coupons and premiums also serves to play on this facet of learning. A promotion by a furniture retailer in Chicago featured a huge discount sale: "Read this ad to find out about our *huge* discounts." But to get discounts you had to bring the coupon attached to the newspaper and show it to the salesperson. The promotion was directed to teaching the viewer both about the sale as well as about the fact that you needed the coupon to take advantage of it.

Curiosity

IV.B6 *Novel stimuli that do not create dissonance may arouse curiosity or exploratory behavior and facilitate more learning in an audience member than if the stimuli are not unusual.*

Novelty seems to be the key to curiosity. That incidental learning is caused by the attention-getting ability of novel stimuli has been shown by Baradowski. In an experiment geared to determine the effect of curiosity arousal, subjects were shown illustrations of five strange-looking animals and five familiar animals. Each illustration was paired with a paragraph of verbal information provided as an intentional learning task.

Both intentional and incidental learning were greater for the novel stimuli. Retention of the written material (intentional learning) paired with the unusual animal was found to be much higher than that paired with the common animals, although each paragraph about the strange animals was the same as one of the paragraphs about a familiar animal.

Incidental learning was assessed by a posttest recall of the settings and border colors around each illustration. Five backgrounds were presented, each being used with both a strange and familiar animal. Results indicated that both backgrounds and borders were remembered better for the strange animals (Baradowski, 1967).

Novel stimuli can be effective in increasing learning of an advertising message. The novelty of any message requires that it be surprising, or different, from other messages. In a sense, novelty is a relative term. What is novel today may be commonplace tomorrow, and what is unusual in one context may be commonplace in another. However, novelty can be created by an entirely new stimulus, such as Baradowski's strange animals.

In any case, the main implication for curiosity seems to be that unexpected attributes of messages may elicit information seeking on the part of the consumer. This is based on the assumption that novel stimuli create dissonance and thus produce an exploratory drive to reduce the dissonance.

The dissonance or conflict caused by novel stimuli may be helpful, but it can also be harmful to learning. Advertisements about novel products may cause the consumer to ask himself "Is it that good?" or "What does it do?" or "How does it work?" and thus create an information-seeking drive—involving disbelievable curiosity (see chapter 32). However, if a message produces a degree of conflict that people find unpleasant, they will seek to "screen it out" of their minds, as dissonance theory predicts.

Finally, it has been implicit in this discussion that the novelty of a stimulus depends, in all cases, on the individual. The marketer seeking a novel approach must keep in mind the type of consumer he is attempting to reach and make his idea novel for that type of consumer.

Marketing Examples of Curiosity

To appeal to shopper curiosity, the merchants of a given suburban shopping center will hold special "sidewalk" sales during the warmer months of the year. At this time many sale-priced items are displayed on the sidewalk in front of a store. Salespeople representing a given store will stand outside with the merchandise in much the same way as the street vendors of an earlier era. A shopper whose curiosity has been stimulated by the outdoor display may want to learn more about the store's products by entering its building.

In direct-mail advertising, advertisers also can appeal to the customer's curiosity. "You alone have this lucky number!" entices the reader of direct-mail literature to read further. If the reader feels that someone is trying to trick him, he will toss the mail aside as "junk mail." However, if he is interested in the content, curiosity has served to facilitate learning of the message.

Northwest Orient Airlines, an international passenger-carrying company, presented the news of their routes from Chicago to Florida by using billboards and magazine advertisements showing a map of the United States turned upside down. The caption by the picture read "Fly Northwest to Florida." The curiosity of an upside down map facilitated readers' interest in the message.

L'eggs hosiery made use of a novel package shape to induce product trial. Both the package and the stand that carried the L'eggs products were in the shape of an egg. This novel shape was clearly differentiable from the competing hosiery products and helped contribute to L'eggs early success. It is important to note the continuity between name, package, and product—a lack of continuity could have resulted in consumer dissonance and product rejection.

Redintegration

IV.B7 *A single element of a past configuration of stimuli may elicit the same response in the audience members that was originally elicited by the entire configuration.*

If a communicatee is confronted with a single element of a configuration of stimuli he has learned, he will tend to respond in the same way as he did in the first situation. He redintegrates (or reintegrates) the single element into the original form of the entire element. The response to the original stimulus may become a cue. Feelings and ideas that were elicited by the original stimulus may elicit the original response. For instance, a picture of an orange, which was originally a response to the actual orange, may elicit the same response as a real orange.

Hollingworth tested this hypothesis by giving five individuals a slip of paper bearing secret instructions about a question each was to answer by writing. Each individual received different instructions. The subjects then stood before a tachistoscope that flashed an inscription for a fraction of a second. The inscription had some letters and was shaped like a word, but it was meaningless. Each subject was then told to report "what he had seen."

Each respondent reported that he saw a word that was in line with the question he had received—and each response was different. The inscription, it would appear, served as a cue. It instigated the report that the respondent wrote on the slip. One person had been thinking of baseball, one of shoes, another of food, and so on. What each person reported seems to have been jointly determined by what was presented and by the recent contexts in which words resembling the inscription had appeared (Hollingworth, 1928).

Another instance of redintegration is that people tend to see optical illusions in one particular way, when the illusions might really be seen as something else. Out of the patterns competing for attention, one response or another tends to be redintegrated; that is, with an initial advantage once established, the elements of the response reinforce each other so that competing responses are "elbowed out" (Hollingworth, 1928).

Marketing Examples of Redintegration

This process seems to have implications for advertisers who attempt to "shock" viewers with incongruous situations, such as a surgeon cutting away at a chocolate bar to examine the contents. The stimulus of the surgeon might elicit the viewer's response to hospitals in general whether there is a candy bar on the table or not. This would destroy any attempt to learn about food.

Advertisers could "shape" their advertisements with the editorial or program content surrounding the advertisement in mind, since the content just before the advertisement may cause redintegration of the situations in that context. For instance, the advertisement with the incision into the chocolate bar would be offensive if run between dramatic scenes of an operation portrayed in a television show. The redintegrative process would ruin the effect of the satire. Although it is impossible for the advertiser to know exactly what the context surrounding his commercial will be, he can often estimate accurately.

Trademarks can elicit the redintegrative process. They become a single element that represents an entire company. The Campbell kids or the RCA dog represent a single element that elicits much the same responses as the entire advertisement.

Similarly, figures that are symbolic of a product or message can elicit the redintegrative process. Smokey the Bear is always associated with warnings about forest fires. Tony the Tiger is associated with Sugar Frosted Flakes. When these characters are seen by themselves, the idea or product they represent is immediately recalled.

Prepotency of Cues

IV.B7.1 *In the redintegrative process some details of the previous cues will cause the process more readily than others and thus lead to quicker learning than otherwise by audience members.*

In his discussion of redintegration, Hollingworth pointed out that "some of the details of an antecedent are prepotent. They are more effective than others, are more likely to redintegrate the response formerly made to the total situation. These we may call prepotent details; they have what we may designate 'greater instigative prepotency' " (Hollingworth, 1928, p. 38). Continuing, Hollingworth devised a general scale of prepotency. He maintained that "persons and faces are more easily remembered than objects, objects are more easily remembered than actions, that form is more easily remembered and recognized than color, although colors are more accurately remembered than numbers" (Hollingworth, 1928, p. 38).

Variations of prepotency exist within these categories. Certain shapes are more potent than others, certain colors are more potent than other colors, and certain positions in both time and space are more potent than other positions. Some parts of words are more "determinative" than others. The initial and early letters of a word are often more important than the later ones. Compare *fath* with *ther*, for quick recognition of the word. For this reason, errors in spelling are found in the last half of a word more often than in the first. Also, some letters of a given word are more potent than others. Compare *h_pp_n_ss* to *_a__i_e__* for recognition. The shape of a printed word is often a more effective partial clue than its length. The shape of the words *boy* and *girl* make these words more quickly recognizable than *man* or *woman*. The latter two words are distinguishable by length, not shape, and are not as easily discernible.

Considerations such as these are very often ignored. They can, however, be invaluable in the design of advertising layout and packaging. A name with strong appeal, such as Shakespeare Fly Rods, or a distinctive face, such as Buddy Hackett's, in an advertisement are applications of these prepotencies. However, the distinction must be made between the memory value and the attention value of a cue. The power of a cue to be redintegrated and its power to be redintegrated correctly may not always be the same.

Marketing Examples of Prepotency of Cues

The implications of this type of findings for advertising are important. For example, it is not uncommon for a consumer to repeat a commercial's clever product line and then be unable to recall the product name, or even to use a different product name. This is a result of the prepotency of attention to actions over the potency of accuracy of the product name. If a marketer is more concerned with his advertisement per se than with his product and its attributes, his cues may be misinterpreted by the consumer.

Prepotency of cues can be seen in Campbell's soup commercials. Although a cold-weather scene with the caption "Campbell's soup stops winter cold" elicits a response, the Campbell kids easily accomplish the same purpose. When a person views a cold-winter scene, he does not immediately think of Campbell's soup. But if the Campbell kids are brought into the picture, the association is easily made.

Advertisements for the Jolly Green Giant products usually featured elves as well as the giant. However, the Jolly Green Giant was the dominant character and was the one associated with the vegetable products. But if one saw the elves only, he would not be inclined to associate them with the product.

Distracting

IV.B8 *Learning is less likely to take place under conditions of distraction than under conditions of complete attention. However, this difference is smaller for incidental than for intentional learning.*

Consumers are exposed to many more communications in a day than they can possibly remember. They are exposed to most of these communications while they are responding to other stimuli: participating in other activities and listening or watching other people or other communications. Therefore, in almost every case, less than full attending is given to the communication. In other words, the consumer's attention is distracted from the communication.

Stimuli that do not have anything to do with a message will take part of an audience's attention and act as interference that will cause lower recall. However, for persuasive messages, it seems that more subtle influences exist in a situation with distracting stimuli.

Festinger and Maccoby suggested that when an individual is exposed to a persuasive communication that offers a viewpoint dissimilar to his own, distractive forces will enhance the persuasive impact of the communication. Rather than the distraction acting as "interference to memory," Festinger and Maccoby predicted that distraction will act as "interference to the process of counterargument" (Festinger and Maccoby, 1964). It might be said that the communicatee is thus "caught with his defenses down."

Haaland and Venkatesan (1968) designed an experiment to test the effect of distraction on the presentation of a persuasive communication. They set up both behavioral distractions and visual distractions for two different groups and used a control group with no distractions. The distractions were similar to those used by Festinger and Maccoby: subjects in the behavioral-distraction group filled out a questionnaire as they listened to a tape of the persuasive arguments. Those in the visual-distraction group saw an amusing film as they heard the tape. Results showed that the no-distraction group recalled arguments significantly better than either of the distracted groups and also were influenced the most in terms of resulting attitude change. These results support the learning theory idea of interference, which states that to the extent that persuading requires learning of the opposing viewpoint, distraction will hinder that learning and thus hinder persuading (Haaland and Venkatesan, 1968).

In a different study, Gardner (1966) found no evidence to suggest that exposing a consumer to a persuasive marketing communication under conditions of divided attention would result in increased attitude change. Male college students were tested in situations of differing degrees of commitment and divided attention to the communication. The committed group chose a movie they would like to attend, whereas the uncommitted had no opportunity to do so. Three slot-car racing tasks were used to manipulate attention: undivided attention; low divided attention, where subjects ran the cars slowly; and high divided attention, where they ran the cars at top speed. The communication advocated the movie rated as second most desirable by the subject.

Results showed that those subjects with increased divided attention had low recall of the message, whether they were committed to the message or not. Gardner also noted that previously it was assumed that as attention is increasingly divided, counterargument is also interfered with to a greater extent. In addition, he points out that in a marketing situation consumers do not hold extreme degrees of commitment to products and that dissonance reduction is easy—that is, the consumer does not repurchase the product.

Marketing Examples of Distracting

The competition for shelf facings in retail outlets demonstrates this principle. Competitors want their brand to be the first with which the consumer comes in contact. That is why shelf positioning is so important. Otherwise a product can get "lost" in the midst of 20 other competing products, each distracting the consumer.

Of course, the communicator has no control over the distracting elements that may interfere with his message. However, one can predict what types of distractions are likely at certain hours of the day, for certain types of people, and for different media. For instance, a housewife listening to a radio station in the morning is likely to be distracted by children or housework, whereas in the evening she will be more relaxed and have time for herself. Complicated sales messages will tend to be ignored by consumers who are distracted, incapable of complete attention; thus simple messages are much more effective in such situations.

Displays in supermarkets are good examples of gaining attention in the midst of distraction. Usually the market will place its special items in the middle of the aisle with large signs pointing to them so that the customer can give complete attention to the item while passing by. If the item were placed on the shelf with all the other items, and in small letters the word *special* was written underneath, the shopper probably would not learn about the special because of the other distractions surrounding it.

If a customer is listening to a salesperson explain how an appliance is operated and is distracted, she or he may not have learned what the salesperson was saying. More likely than not, the salesperson will have to begin the explanation all over again. Thus, many times, the salesperson moves the customer to a quieter place to give a demonstration. In the case of a car purchase, he moves the customer to the privacy of his office. The customer's back is to the showroom to avoid distraction.

Predecisional Timing

IV.B9 *Attempts at learning (or persuading) tend to be ignored or discounted if tried immediately after an audience member has committed himself to a judgment based on a previous message.*

Festinger defined every object as having some amount of dissonance in terms of an individual's cognitions. The primary objective of every individual is to reduce the amount of dissonance to nothing, or at least to keep it to a minimum. Physiologically, the body tends toward consistency in itself through homeostasis. Psychologically, the mind tries to maintain a mental balance through the reduction of dissonance (Festinger, 1957, pp. 127-128).

Degrees of commitment to a judgment vary. There are silent agreements, and there are verbal agreements to others. If an individual commits himself to an opinion but does not announce this opinion out loud, his susceptibility to the second side is not diminished. Hovland and Mandell used anonymous statements on a questionnaire, and their conclusion was based on the idea that the person has not taken a public stand that can be viewed by his friends and associates.

The person takes no public risk when committing himself to a private judgment. He does not risk censure by his friends if he should change his opinion. No feeling of social disapproval would result if he changed a private judgment (Hovland and Mandell, 1957).

Lana found that public commitment was not a necessary condition to establish skepticism to a second message. Two groups of subjects were presented with two talks, one in favor of vivisection and one against it. Subjects were skeptical of the communication that was presented second (Lana, 1961).

Predecisional timing is an advantage to the communicator who is able to get his message across first. The priority of message presentation is somewhat dampened by the speed inherent in the mass media and the communicator's ability to change his message quickly to coincide very closely in time to that of his competitors.

Marketing Examples of Predecisional Timing

Effective predecisional timing has been the issue in the criticisms advertising agencies have directed against the television medium. Because of conflicting "spot" scheduling between national networks and local television stations, viewers will often be exposed to commercials from competing brands of the same product within a few minutes of each other. Not only does the second (or even third) message tend to be discounted, but the message of the first brand will also be diminished in effectiveness. After watching three different brands advertise breakfast cereal within 10 minutes on one television channel, the viewer is not likely to retain the distinctive selling feature of any one brand.

Take the example of a woman shopping for a washing machine. If a salesman at store A has convinced her that his model with front-loading is better for her, it is unlikely that a salesman at store B will be able to persuade her that his top-loading model is more suited to her needs. This is especially true if the salesman in store A was able to get her to verbally agree that front-loading is desirable.

Chrysler Imperial illustrated this principle in the advertising campaign: "Before you decide on a LTD, come in and see the Imperial. Test drive it. Fill out a registration form. If in the end you buy a LTD, send us proof-of-purchase and we'll send you $25." In this advertisement, Chrysler was attempting to get people to learn about the Imperial before they made a decision. The company realized that an appeal to a potential customer is not going to be successful if he has already decided on an LTD; the key was to get him before the decision, and this is how they were doing it. This type of appeal is especially effective if it catches a customer before he has actually gone out to look at cars. This stimulus could at least get the customer to look at the Imperial before the LTD.

22 Variables within the Audience: Self-Generated Processes

Background

Some processes of remembering, such as redintegration (which was discussed in the previous chapter), require similar stimuli or cues. However, other remembering processes, such as mental completing, reminiscence, the sleeper effect, and the aha experience, do not. They are accomplished without the aid of outside forces.

However, before these specific principles are delineated, a brief statement of the differences among them will be given, because these five concepts are so similar. *Mental completing* refers to the tendency to remember an incomplete stimulus pattern better than a complete stimulating pattern. *Reminiscence* involves an increment in learning of an incompletely learned task taking place after overt learning behavior has occurred. The *sleeper effect* refers to a disassociation of the content of a message from an untrustworthy or low-credibility source over time. This disassociation results in an increased favorable attitude toward the message content, since the source no longer serves to "block out" the believability of the message. Note that the sleeper effect refers to an increase in favorable-attitude change, whereas reminiscence refers to an increase in amount learned.

In contrast to these two principles is the principle of *perseveration*, which refers to the reemergence of previously communicated messages to the conscious state after a period of absence. Perseveration is *not* perseverence. Also, perseveration does not refer to either an increase in favorable-attitude change nor to an increase in the amount learned—instead, it refers to a spontaneous reappearance of previously learned material.

Finally, the *aha experience*, although quite similar to perseveration, refers to the relatively spontaneous discovery of the solution to a problem. It refers to problem solving where there is only one correct answer, and after trial and error (the duration can vary widely) there is a spontaneous discovery of the answer.

Self-Generated Processes

Mental Completing

IV.B10 *An incomplete stimulus pattern tends to be remembered better than a complete pattern.*

The following incomplete figures tend to be both perceived and remembered as complete patterns.

Recall of these figures as complete is known as *mental completing*. This process is sometimes explained in terms of *closure*. Tiernan explained this phenomenon of closure by saying that there is a tendency ... for nonclosed (geometric) figures to be recalled more easily than closed ones (Tiernan, 1938).

The principle of closure states that behavior (or mental process) tends toward as complete, stable, or "closed" a state as circumstances permit. A related phenomenon is the Zeigarnik effect. In 1927 Zeigarnik conducted an experiment that indicated that incompleted tasks are recalled more frequently than completed tasks. A group of subjects were given 43 tasks consisting of sketching, printing names, and assembling puzzles. Half the tasks were interrupted before completion. After a short time, the subjects were asked to recall the names of the several mixed series of uncompleted and completed tasks. The results indicated that "the uncompleted tasks are remembered 90 percent better than the completed ones." Zeigarnik's explanation of her results involves a person's "tension system" and does not concern the shock effect of the interruption itself. Her theory was that a "tone of tension"—that is, a quasi-need—follows upon the interruption of a task, and that the memory of the task is prolonged by the persistence of this unresolved tension (Zeigarnik, 1927).

Zeigarnik based this explanation on the existence of intention or purpose. A person's state of tension is aroused because his purpose is stymied by the interruption. Therefore, she believed that there is a tendency toward its better retention. In this connection, compare the discussion of Congruity in chapter 13.

In general, most hypotheses concerning the recall differential between completed and noncompleted tasks and stimuli refer to a state of tension aroused in the subject because of incompleteness. Lewin and Hoppe showed that the occurrence of these experiences is not a simple function of the result of the activity but depends on the relation of these results (success or failure) to the momentary level of aspiration (real and ideal goal) of the person and on his ascribing the result of the activity to himself. He showed that these experiences were limited to a rather narrow zone of difficulty, determined essentially by the limits of the ability of the person. In quite too hard and quite too easy tasks, feelings of success and failure do not occur. In analyzing the effects of success and failure on the displacement level of aspirations and the degree of reality of the ideal goal, Hoppe found that these displacements rested on a definite conflict (tension) base. Close relations were found between the level of aspiration and the consciousness of the individual as a social person (Lewin and Hoppe, 1930).

No one has refuted the Zeigarnik effect without considerable qualifications. In general, incompleted tasks do seem to be remembered better than completed ones. The explanation must involve some ideas of closure. The "task" orientation of the Zeigarnik effect concerned completion or noncompletion of motor tasks; yet it seems reasonable to extend the analogy to cognitive tasks, such as perceiving incomplete or complete stimulus patterns.

In addition to enhancing recall of unfinished tasks and incomplete stimuli, anxiety might account for recall of incomplete stimuli as if they were complete. Just as one "waits for the other shoe to drop," a sort of anxiety is produced by incomplete stimulus patterns. In an effort to reduce the anxiety, originally incomplete patterns are remembered as complete. Behavior, such as perceiving a stimulus pattern, is goal oriented. The completed task is rewarded, and completion in itself is a reward.

Heller, hypothesizing that an incomplete advertising slogan will be remembered more readily than a complete slogan, used university undergraduates in an experimental study involving 60 registered advertising slogans. Heller varied the completeness of the slogans and found that in almost every case the slogans that were less complete were remembered better. Another variable, of course, was the degree of familiarity of the slogans.

One of Heller's conditions did not reveal a significant difference, however, and this fact caused him to point up an interesting problem. Simply because a stimulus is incomplete does not mean that it is perceived as incomplete. If it is perceived by the communicatee as complete, it will not exhibit any of the effects attributable to incomplete stimuli.

Heller's incomplete stimuli consisted mostly of words with missing letters; but as he indicated, his study did not mean to imply that advertisements should consist of mutilated or incomplete words. Rather, he suggested the use of such practices as covering a brand name enough so that it requires some concentration to read it, omitting a line or note in a familiar line of verse or song, or mirror images (Heller, 1956, p. 253).

Marketing Examples of Mental Completing

An incomplete message stimulus in an advertisement would seem to be better remembered, other things being equal, than a similar but complete stimulus. Perhaps this is due only to the stark incongruity of an incomplete pattern in a media world characterized by complete advertising stimuli.

In addition, however, the consumer might well undergo some cognitive tension when faced with an incomplete stimulus. Motivated to reduce the tension and thus perceive the stimulus as complete, the consumer must direct attention to the stimulus while attempting to perceive its entirety. In effect, the consumer has concentrated on the selling message or some other facet of the commercial, and one of advertising's central goals is achieved.

Such attention ought to be focused on a part of the advertisement or commercial that actually contributes to selling the product. Appropriate advertising elements would be the brand name, the product "story," the package, or some other element important to perception of the intended selling message. The benefits of closure would be wasted if consumer cognitive processes were directed toward peripheral portions of the advertisement or commercial that do not directly contribute to brand-product-image identification.

Two outstanding examples of advertising constructions capable of benefiting from closure were the campaigns of the R.J. Reynolds Co. (Salem cigarettes) and the Kellogg Company (Kellogg Corn Flakes). In Salem cigarette television commercials built around the jingle "You can take Salem out of the country but you can't take the country out of Salem," the jingle was played only one and one-half times. On the second go-round, the silence following "You can take Salem out of the country but . . . " invited the viewer mentally to complete the audio stimuli. Similarly, a Kellogg Corn Flakes outdoor campaign featured the familiar Kellogg script logotype running off the poster. The audience thus was motivated to attend to the poster by mentally completing the partially written brand name.

Reminiscence

IV.B11 *After a period of an audience member's nonpractice of something learned, without intervening overt practice, an actual gain in recall may occur.*

A person attempts to memorize a poem, then for a few days does not practice it at all. Later, when he tries to recall the poem, he may realize that he can recall more than ever before! This phenomenon or one of a similar nature is part of most peoples' experience. The terms *reminiscence* or *reminiscence effect* might be used to describe the happening; although this psychological term has a much more complicated meaning.

Reminiscence has been called, among other things, an effect, a phenomenon, and a principle. No one theory fully explains it. The definition proposed here is simply an actual gain in recall after a period of nonpractice or nonuse. Inherent in this definition is the meaning of the word *recall* as synonymous with some type of observable performance. *Recall* is not meant to include recognition or identification, which are somewhat less stringent tests of learning. *Recall* is the ability to reproduce either verbally or through motor performance, without cues, the material in question.

Marketing Examples of Reminiscence

In attempting to relate the findings on reminiscence to marketing, there are many problems. Most experimental findings on this subject have been for motor skills. The results of many of these studies have been concluded with statements to the effect that the findings were considered insignificant, largely dependent on the nature of the specific task.

Yes, the idea of reminiscence is controversial in psychology; and we are not yet at the stage where reminiscence theory can be used to help a copywriter write his copy in such a way that "so many units of inhibition today" are sacrificed for a "greater amount of learning tomorrow." A further difficulty is that because the concept of reminiscence involves covert processes, it is difficult to provide precise and observable examples.

However, consider the fact that practically all verbal learning studies involve "incomplete learning," that is, situations in which the material to be learned is not learned perfectly. This is undoubtedly true of messages in the various media to which consumers are exposed. Consumers are bombarded by many messages and seldom make a conscious effort to learn all the facts presented by a single commercial or campaign.

An illustration of the proposition of reminiscence might involve the use of public-service displays and of thoughtful giveaways by retailers. Stores that dedicate window displays to such honored causes as Boy Scouting or charity campaigns leave a favorable impression with present and prospective customers that may persist and grow. In the same way, giving thoughtful rewards for shoppers during a new store's opening may leave lasting favorable impressions with them and later result in an incremented result of the store name.

The principle of reminiscence might be illustrated in personal selling. Whenever a complicated item is presented to a customer, it may take a long time for the facts to "sink in." For example, a camera salesperson explains all the complexities of a camera to a prospect; but too much information is related for the prospect to recall at the moment. But a day or two later he may remember even more of the communication than he could immediately after he left the store— he has had time to organize his thinking about the features of the product.

Sleeper Effect

IV.B11.1 *Covert changes in attitudes under certain circumstances may be greater some time after certain stimuli have been presented than immediately after exposure to the stimuli (the sleeper effect).*

This is a statement of what may be called the *sleeper effect* (Weinberger, 1961). In those instances in which a communication is exposed to an individual only once and he attends to it and perceives it, the one instance of exposing usually results in no measurable effect; or if there is one, the effect is not long-lasting. The sleeper effect (to whatever extent such a phenomenon exists) would be an exception to this pattern. The reason is, as Weinberger points out, that any changes in attitudes resulting from communication are greater after a delay than immediately after exposure (Weinberger, 1961).

Hovland and Weiss conducted a study that involved the presentation of an identical communication to two groups, one in which the communicator was trustworthy, and the other in which the communicator was untrustworthy. Questionnaires were administered before, immediately after, and a month after exposure to the communication. The results from the questionnaire administered directly after the communication revealed no significant differences in the amount of factual information acquired by the subjects when the material was attributed to a high-credibility source, as compared with the amount learned when the same material was attributed to a low-credibility source. However, subjects changed their attitudes in the direction advocated by the communicator in a significantly greater number of cases when the material was attributed to a high-credibility source rather than a low-credibility source.

The results obtained after four weeks revealed what they identified as a sleeper effect. Compared with the changes immediately after the communication, there was a decrease in the extent of agreement with the high-credibility source but an increase in the case of the low-credibility source (Hovland and Weiss, 1951-1952).

Hovland and Weiss also showed that there was a clear difference in the retention of the names of untrustworthy sources for the group initially agreeing with the communicator's position, as compared with those disagreeing. Not only did the sleeper effect occur among the group initially disagreeing with the untrustworthy source, but this group had the poorest retention of the source's name.

From these results Hovland and Weiss posited not only that there is a disassociating of source and content over time but also that the source is forgotten faster than the content. In the situation of the trustworthy source, the forgetting of the content was identified as the main factor accounting for a decrease in opinion change. In the situation of the untrustworthy source, the investigators suggested that the reduction resulting from forgetting probably was more than offset by the removal of the interference associated with initial disbelief ("I heard what he said, but I don't believe it"). Thus the passage of time serves to remove recall of the source as the prime cue to rejection of the message, and thus there is an increase in the extent of agreement with the content of the initial message (Hovland and Weiss, 1951-1952).

The sleeper effect should not be confused with carryover effects. The latter refers to lagged or carryover effects, exemplified by the idea that the effects of advertising on sales are distributed over time or that reactions to advertising are sometimes delayed. For example, during World War II many manufacturers continued to advertise their consumer or industrial products, even though they had converted almost completely to military products (Tull, 1965, p. 46).

Carryover effects frequently are associated with repetitive exposing of a communication, with the belief that favorable impressions established in current time periods will hold over to future time periods and in fact have a cumulative effect. By contrast, the sleeper effect is not concerned with "building up" or getting the audience to "come around" to a point of view as a result of frequent exposing of a communication; but rather it depends on the decline over time of the influence of the environment on the initial reception of a single message. In fact, "it may well be that the frequent repetition common in advertising is likely to create conditions the very opposite of those requisite to the "sleeper effect." Repetition of an advertising message which is initially rejected because of the environment . . . is likely to increase spontaneous association of the message with the unacceptable environment" (Weinberger, 1961, p. 66).

Capon and Hulbert concluded that assembled evidence does not support the existence of the sleeper effect as a generalized phenomenon, although some data do suggest the possibility of a weak effect that operates selectively. Their analysis centered around a wide array of experiments carried out by various researchers concerned with the possibility of the sleeper effect (for example, Hovland; Weiss; Whittaker and Meade; Insko; Greenwald; and Gillig). Capon and Hulbert's main criticisms were of methodological and definitional inconsistencies in the various research studies that indicate that the existence of a general sleeper effect may be highly questionable. In other words, one should be careful in assuming a general sleeper effect for all situations and all people (Capon and Hulbert, 1973).

Related to this discussion, note that Lucas and Britt formed a cumulative theory of advertising based on findings from various experiments:

Repetition of advertising has advantages in memory other than the increased chance of *recency*. Repetition reinforces and strengthens the impression made on the audience. Each time an idea is repeated, the impression becomes stronger. Each time an impression is reestablished, it tends to last longer.
   . . . Each time an impression is repeated, it becomes stronger in two ways. First, it builds to a higher level than the original by combining the influence of the new with the residue of the old. Second, there is a definite tendency for the impression established through space repetitions to fade more slowly in each successive stage. [Lucas and Britt, 1950, p. 80.]

The reminiscence theory may be connected with the problem of the sleeper effect. Learning, in general, requires sorting, reevaluating the associations that have been made, and selective forgetting of segments of events and communications. Thus reminiscence may play a large part in accounting for the sleeper effect.

In this connection, consider also the discussion at the end of chapter 27 of principle V.A19.1 on interaction of credibilities over time.

Marketing Examples of the Sleeper Effect

Obviously we must take into account the question of whether the sleeper effect exists. But if it does, the following examples in marketing would be illustrative.

To convince shoppers of a new brand's durability or performance, a retail store can conduct a live test of the product. For example, two cleansers could be tested competitively for their ability to remove heavy stains; or a new line of nylon hosiery could demonstrate resistance to snags and runs. After delay in additional exposure to the product message, shoppers ultimately may remember and accept the lessons of such dramatic presentations and choose the tested product in preference to customarily purchased brands.

Likewise, samples of new brands of food products in grocery outlets will communicate the brand's message directly. Later, the lesson learned by tasting the sample can affect the purchase decision either to try the brand for the first time or to choose the sampled brand over familiar competitive brands.

Perseveration

IV.B12 *The psychological changes that constitute learning by an audience member continue for a time after the cessation of overt learning activities.*

The psychological principle of perseveration is closely tied to that of reminiscence, discussed in the previous section. To repeat what was said at the beginning of this chapter, perseveration is not the same as perseverance. *Reminiscence* refers to an increment in learning taking place after overt learning behavior on an incompletely learned task. *Perseveration* refers to the reemergence of communicated messages to the conscious state after a period of absence. The crucial difference is that perseveration does not require an increment in learning but is a seemingly spontaneous reappearance of the learned material.

Müller and Pilzecker (1900) apparently were the first to discuss perseveration. They defined the principle as "an idea upon which we have concentrated our attention acquires the capacity to re-enter consciousness immediately thereafter and even to break in upon the course of ideas to which we have meanwhile directed our attention although it seems to derive no association support from the ideas which dominate at the time of re-entrance" (Müller and Plizecker, 1900, p. 23). Müller described perseveration as a spontaneous phenomenon as in the case of a tune coming back to mind as if from nowhere when someone finds himself whistling or humming it over and over again without knowing why (Guilford, 1939, p. 414).

Perseveration is concerned with unintentional recall bringing an idea into consciousness with no apparent stimulus. I have already mentioned the main features of the perseverative process, that is, the persistence of an activity or idea after overt learning processes have stopped and the seemingly automatic way these tendencies occur. There are, however, a few more features that different theorists have attempted to isolate. Despite the lack of empirical data, Woodworth and others posited that the perseverative process is most likely to occur in moments of relaxation. Thus, after one has memorized a list of syllables or a stanza of poetry, snatches of the list or the poem might come back into consciousness without any effort on the learner's part (Woodworth, 1938, pp. 51-52). The process is more likely to occur if the learner rests after the initial learning. This seems consistent with the idea of higher recall when rest follows learning (no proactive inhibition).

Also, the phenomenon of mental completing may be associated with perseveration. If one is prevented from completing an activity in which he was absorbed, this activity may exhibit the effects of perseveration.

Marketing Examples of Perseveration

To attempt to apply the principle of perseveration to marketing and communication requires some calculated guesses. Unlike reminiscence, which may require inhibition initially for its later occurrence, perseveration apparently occurs automatically. Advertising campaigns that attempt to gain greater recall through high frequency would be aided if their message could occasionally come into consciousness without the stimulus of an advertisement.

Since the theory cannot account for the reemergence of the idea into the conscious (no apparent stimulus), it is impossible to suggest what copy or media strategy might cause this to occur. The only possibility seems to stem from the two ideas (1) that perseveration may occur after an activity that interested or excited the learner, and (2) that perseveration is greatest if relaxation follows the learning situation.

Taking the first point, the advertising copywriter can try to generate a message that will "grab" the consumer. For example, the usefulness of a musical brand slogan "running through one's head" is good for creating brand awareness in consumers. This phenomenon may be explained by perseveration and seems to have been advantageous in the musical themes of Coca-Cola, Pepsi, United Airlines, and Salem. Slogans like "I'd walk a mile for a Camel . . . " or "I'd rather fight than switch" for Tareyton may be placed in this category. Exactly what it was about the theme that caused the perseveration is not known. Therefore, it is of use only to realize that perseveration is indicative of a well-learned or interesting message.

A statement by Hepner points up that many readers enjoy the feel of a new word on the tongue. If it develops perseveration in the minds of many readers, the public soon adopts the word for everyday use. Many advertisers have tried to introduce new words but failed to make an expedient choice (Hepner, 1951, p. 430).

The second feature that may help communicators—that perseveration is greater after relaxation—would seem to indicate the perseveration can be very useful to communicators. This is especially true for advertisers, since commercials are often seen or heard while the consumer is relatively relaxed and enjoying television or radio.

For business institutions and retail outlets, the use of night lighting of the company name, logo, or building can draw the attention of passing motorists. For retailers such lighting can promote daily or seasonal sales specials. The learning experience of observing and retaining the lighted message may continue to be remembered by the motoring consumer and influence his purchasing decision at a later time.

Aha Experience

IV.B13 *An aha experience, which is an example of insight learning, usually occurs for audience members only in problem-solving situations, for which only one response is correct.*

An aha experience can occur at almost any time, in any situation. It does not require that the problem to be solved is complex, or even a monumental discovery. It can be something as simple as the discovery of a phone number— "Now, what was Jane's number? 256-0123? No, it was 526-0123!" Or, "What is Sue's husband's name? Ron, Dick? I know, Jerry!" A child's search for Easter eggs could be an aha experience. At some time or another, all of us have had an aha experience.

The discovery of an aha experience is the result of a trial-and-error method in which the person attempting to solve the problem or puzzle continues until he finds the correct solution. When he does, he feels as though he had "hit upon it."

The earliest recorded aha experience may be the discovery by Archimedes of the physical principle that a solid object will displace the same volume of water that the object occupies. There was only one solution to the problem, but it was far from obvious. It was not until Archimedes had discovered the solution that he supposedly cried out, "Eureka! I have found it!"—an aha experience.

Marketing Examples of Aha Experience

An aha experience has happened to many people while shopping. Sometimes a person will go shopping with the intention to buy, but without knowing exactly what he is going to buy. This happens with birthday gifts, at Father's Day, Mother's Day, Christmas, and so on. It can happen to the husband who happens to be walking by the florist shop when he remembers that today is his wedding anniversary. He enters the shop and buys his wife some lovely flowers, proud of himself for having remembered the special day. He never will admit to his wife the actual manner in which he came to remember! For this reason, many florist shops have signs in the window saying: "Flowers for all occasions—wedding, birthday, anniversary."

Point-of-purchase promotional materials utilize the idea of insightful learning on the part of shoppers who may forget the brand associations learned earlier by advertising. For example, a shopper might remember only the favorable impression experienced while watching a television commercial for a product. A display for the particular brand placed in a prominent location in the store, such as the checkout counter, enables the shopper to remember the brand name and purchase it on the way out of the store.

Mail-order catalogues involve their readers in both *reminder* impulse buying and in *suggestion* impulse buying. While an individual is thumbing through the catalogue's many pages, he will be reminded of wants that certain selections could satisfy and also may be stimulated to think of other wants that can be satisfied by purchasing products.

23 Variables within the Audience: Sociocultural Factors

Background

Language, nonverbal communication, culture, and sex differences not only affect every action we make but also influence what and how we learn. Because their influences are felt in virtually every communicating situation, specific propositions regarding the effects of these variables are more difficult to postulate than for other areas of the learning process.

No discussion of learning, however, would be complete without these topics. What follows, then, is a brief discussion of these variables and the manner in which individuals are affected by them in the communication process. Although not supported by as much empirical research as for propositions about learning previously discussed, certain evidence does exist for the propositions given in the present chapter.

Sociocultural Factors

Language

IV.B14 *Language and culture are so interrelated that both communicators and communicatees should infer essentially the same cultural meanings from the language of a message.*

Although no inherent relation exists between language and culture, they are closely intertwined. The most obvious instance is literature, oral and written. Principles of literary style and of pronunciation that are developed in terms of one language cannot always find satisfactory equivalents in a second language. Words designating concepts specific to a given culture are likely to present a serious translation problem. The adoption of a new language is often accompanied by the gradual adoption of a new culture. Even though language and culture are basically independent, they are closely associated in practice.

Language is a learned cultural response, a medium of communication encompassing an individual's total environment. It includes not only national "tongues," but also the various dialects, regional colloquialisms, slang, and even the "jargon" of various trades. The words and phrases that make up any language have meaning only by inference. They are interpreted according to the individual's past experiences. This experience can include language structures, word definitions, feelings about certain words, and their previous usages. Both the communicator and the audience must infer meaning in the same way if a word or message is to be effective.

The effect of language structure on cognitive behavior has applications to persuasive communication. Obviously, a message must "speak the language of the audience." This does not mean the English language. Different segments of the population use different colloquialisms, slang, and jargon. Because of these differences, a message is not learned and understood in the same way by all segments of an audience. Therefore, a message that aims for mental participating in a given action may "lose" communicatees because they do not conceptualize in the same terms. As a result, a communicator may have to "sacrifice" parts of his mass audience in order to communicate clearly with his target audience.

Marketing Examples of Language

Specialty radio stations exist in order to sell to the black listener a line of products that may or may not be specifically tailored to his needs or tasks. The music played is mostly black popular music, and the radio announcer is black. Thus he is able to communicate effectively with his listeners through the use of ethnocentric colloquialisms. This ethnic focus also is reflected in the music and announcing for the commercials.

Basic generic product names may also differ between English-speaking countries. For example, the following are pairs of words referring to the same product in the United States and Canada: *sofa, chesterfield; sneakers, runners; soda, pop;* and *french fries, chips.*

A salesman must be very aware of different slang or colloquialisms as he calls on different types of customers. He may use *right-on* and *nitty-gritty* with some people but dare not use it with others. He must tailor his language to both the product and customer involved.

Nonverbal Communication

IV.B15 *Meaning of a message is conveyed not only by verbal but by nonverbal cues, such as tonal quality, situational context, and physical behavior of the communicator.*

We communicate with words but often convey meanings with the tone of our voice, gestures, facial expressions, and other nonverbal actions. These actions intensify, codify, or even reverse the meaning expressed by the words spoken.

The *tone* of a message is understood by an infant long before he comprehends language. The adolescent soon learns that the phrase "Don't do that again" may or may not need to be heeded depending on the tone of voice used. A dog learns to obey his master's tone of voice. For example, if *good dog* is spoken harshly, in a yelling tone, the dog will react as if he had been scolded. The cues of tonal quality may do any of the following:

1. Reinforce the meaning of the words
2. Distract the listener from the spoken words
3. Contradict what the words seem to mean

If the cues are different from the words, the listener may have difficulty in accepting the spoken message. Specifically, the tonal quality of a message depends upon (Hertzler, 1965, p. 267):

1. Volume (loudness and softness) with which it is delivered
2. Pitch (deep or high tones on the musical scale, monotonous or pitchless)
3. Quality (smooth, rotund, harsh)
4. Tempo (fast, jerky, slow)
5. All these variables in combination

Heinberg conducted an experiment to determine whether or not "spoken language can convey something in addition to the denotation of the sentences. He played six recordings of different dialogues to 366 college freshmen. The listeners were asked to judge emotions common to the speakers and the speakers' motives. There was a high correlation between characteristics perceived by the students and those determined by the California Personality Inventory (Heinberg, 1961, pp. 107-148).

Whether or not these cues can be "giveaways" to personalities is a debatable question. However, some research has shown the existence of "verbal stereotypes," which are used by listeners in judging the speaker. The message communicated by a speaker or announcer may be altered or reinforced by his intonation and by the tendency of views to "stereotype" his vocal quality. Good use of tonal quality can have positive effects on interest, understanding, and learning by the listener. Poor use of tonal quality can interfere with any or all of these three.

Nonverbal cues can take forms other than tonal quality. One of these might be called the *context of situation*. Hall speaks of the "hidden rules" that control people, the cultural norms regarding time and space that affect behavior (Hall, 1969, pp. 107-148). For instance, proximity of the communicator is influenced by culture. The closeness of communicator to listener may imply intimacy, authority, or other things, depending on the cultural norms in action.

The study of body behavior (kinesics) is a particularly interesting form of nonverbal communication. Any person who has "learned how to behave in public" is aware of his response to the awkward or inappropriate behavior of others. Cross-cultural investigation of specific gestural, expressional, or movement complexes quickly reveals that an Arab from Beirut, a Chinese from Taiwan, and a Harlem Negro respond quite differently to apparently identical body behaviors. Structural analysis of even the most discrete facial expression (the smile or the frown), the most explicit gesture (the nod), or the most indicative posture (military uprightness or sag) show such reports to be impressionistic summaries of quite complex and systematically varying particles of activity and, more importantly, always dependent upon other behaviors (Birdwhistell, 1968).

The total image projected by the communicator—his appearance and behavior—is yet another nonverbal cue. For example, clothing can be a nonverbal declaration of the things for which an individual stands.

Marketing Examples of Nonverbal Communication

Door-to-door salesmen communicate an image of their product or service through their use of personal appearance, behavior, and language variables. For many such salesmen, the sales visit is made to a wide variety of prospects whose backgrounds may be dissimilar to their own. Through the skillful use of words understandable to most people, a tone of voice that conveys sincerity and warmth, and an expression recognizable as friendly, the salesman increases the chances that his message will be received and understood.

Physical appearance and situational context are greatly stressed in the use of stereotypes in marketing communications: the haggard mother in housecoat and curlers advocating the need for a "good cup of coffee" and the young, beautiful woman with long, gorgeous hair appearing in the shampoo commercials. The physical and situational stereotypes serve as the nonverbal cues that give the consumer a standard context within which the message is interpreted.

The physical apperance of both the store and its personnel emit nonverbal cues to the customer. The store layout, the merchandise on display, the age of the personnel, how they dress, and other people in the store all create a context within which the salesperson's message will be transmitted and interpreted. How the customer perceives these nonverbal cues (as compatible or not with the verbal cues) will help determine the inferences he or she makes about the product or service involved.

Culture

IV.B16 *A message or communication that is significant to members of an audience because of their cultural background is more likely to be learned and remembered than a message not related to their cultural background.*

An individual's cultural background and experiences—both past and current—affect his learning ability. Every individual is a product of his culture. Culture is shared by members of a society and, in turn, affects their behavior. Consider the following seven aspects of culture (Moore and Lewis, 1952):

1. *Culture is learned.* It is neither instinctive, innate, nor transmitted biologically. It is composed of habits, that is, learned responses to given stimuli.

2. *Culture is inculcated.* Human beings are the only animals developed enough to pass on their acquired habits to their offspring. Anything that an individual learns from another individual or group of indivdiuals may be considered an item of culture.

3. *Culture is social.* It is shared by humans living in organized society, and uniformity is maintained to a considerable extent by societal pressures.

4. *Culture is ideational.* This means that culture is composed of ideas that have been learned.

5. *Culture is gratifying.* It satisfies biological needs as well as wants.

6. *Culture is adaptive.* Human beings must learn appropriate responses in order to survive.

7. *Culture is integrative.* In other words, the norms and institutions of a culture tend to work together to avoid conflicts.

The individual not only is the product of his own culture but is actually influenced and learns from several different environments, which have been called the "concentric rings of culture" by Chase. He gives an example of a fictional character named George Rutherford Adams, who runs a garage, filling station, and milk bar in Middleburg, Connecticut. Basically, five "rings of culture" have influenced George and provide the bases for understanding his behavior. First, he is a product of *civilization.* He understands his geographical location, division of labor, and the use of money. Second, he is part of *Western* civilization. He is a Christian, uses Arabic numerals, and reads from left to right. English is provided by the third ring, the *Anglo-Saxon* culture. The fourth, *North American* civilization, provides him with many of his views of time and manners. Finally, he is influenced by the culture of *New England* (Chase, 1948, pp. 69-74).

Marketing Examples of Culture

Department stores and more recently clothing stores have developed special store areas to appeal to youth, that is, the adolescent culture. Early manifestations of this idea used the "campus shop," which carried the clothes worn by male students in secondary schools and college campuses; and a separate shop area or department was set up for female students.

Later on the trend toward more flamboyant and expressive clothing within the youth culture caused many clothing stores to establish specially decorated "mod" store-within-a-store areas or boutiques. At the extreme, the lines of clothing in some boutiques were promoted to both young men and women, a reflection of the unisex movement in clothing—fashions to be worn by either sex.

Failure to observe cross-cultural differences has resulted in many marketing efforts fizzling. As recently as a few years ago, United States food processors, attempting to sell canned vegetables to Europeans, met with little success. Canned corn in particular had little sales appeal in Europe because it was considered food for animals.

All individuals are products of cultural learning. Because of this, some find it difficult to realize that different people do things in different ways. Hall sums up the problem as follows: "This inherent difficulty to learning to learn differently in a different culture is faced every day by people who go overseas and try to train local personnel. . . . The fact is, however, that once people have learned to learn in a given way, it is extremely hard for them to learn in any other way" (Hall, 1969, p. 5).

In short, messages or communications that are important to consumers because of their cultural training are more likely to be learned and score higher on recall tests than are messages or communications that are less important to them.

Sex Differences

IV.B17 *The learning of a message will be enhanced by certain variables of intelligence, creativity, and environment as determined by one's sex.*

On the basis of much research, it has been found that an individual's learning of a message is enhanced by certain characteristics of his intelligence, creativity, and environment as determined by his sex. For instance, most men have a higher aptitude than women for learning messages concerned with quantitative, technical, and/or scientific material. Women, however, have a higher aptitude for learning messages requiring language skills. These aptitudes are dependent to a great extent on the roles they have learned to assume.

An extensive study by Maccoby dealt with sex differences in intelligence, creativity, achievement, and impulse control. Differences in general intelligence were found to be related to sex, but not by heredity. Rather, environmental differences such as family and role, which also varied in relation to age and life stage, were the crucial factors. Maccoby concluded that women are generally superior in "verbal ability" to men, and that men are superior in matters of "spatial" and "number" ability. Women tend to be more verbally expressive than men. A woman's ability to relate an event, describe a person or object, or verbally discuss a situation tends to surpass a man's ability (Maccoby, 1966, pp. 25-26).

An analysis by Bardwick indicates that for girls there are "personality characteristics of passivity and conformity that tend to preclude success in tasks that basically require an independent, analytic, specific approach." However, there also are "tasks, especially verbal ones, at which girls ought to do extremely well—like vocabulary, spelling, the recalling of names—verbal tasks that require the rather passive acceptance of information and its later recall" (Bardwick, 1971, pp. 99-113).

It is these differences in patterns of abilities that make various test scores misleading estimates of overall intelligence. Aptitudes differ between the sexes so that girls and women score higher than boys and men on verbal tests and coding tests that call for short-term remembering and speed. But arithmetic, block-design, and visuospatial tests are usually most easily solved by males (Hutt and May, 1974).

Learning of concepts is achieved through progressive "memory" associations of logical relations between what is previously known and what is to be learned. This is true for both sexes. Although in this sense no difference has been found between the sexes in concept learning, it is important to remember that women and men have built up somewhat different associations and stores of knowledge from which to infer new relationships. Women and men are not rewarded equally for learning in every situation. The value attached to learning is clearly defined in terms of the relevance of the subject or object in question, as well as in terms of the relevance (to the learner) of treating any subject or object in an analytic or perceptive manner. In other words, "being correct" has differential importance for men and women. "Being correct *about*" topics of importance to each sex specifically contributes much to the explanation of differential funds of information between the sexes.

Most studies agree that females excel in memory. In tests calling for exact repetition of a group of digits or words immediately after presentation, or for reproduction of geometric figures that have been studied for a short time, female superiority has been demonstrated. Where the material to be remembered is more familiar or interesting to males, their superiority is greater than females. Although it has been demonstrated that males are likely to be superior in mathematical abilities, it was found that in the quick learning of specific facts (a basic aptitude for clerical work), women are superior to men (Tyler, 1947, pp. 70-75).

The physiological differences between men and women regarding their ability and mode of visual perceiving are minimal, but socioculturally reinforced variations have been identified. As a general rule, men tend to perceive objects more in terms of their structure, mass, angularity, and spatial interrelations. Women tend to perceive these aspects less because they focus within objects, particularly seeking human or inner characteristics in the visual stimuli.

Evidence by Pishkin and Shurly indicates that women perceive details and subtle cues quicker than men (Pishkin and Shurly, 1965). They are able to grasp a communication quicker. They also remember names and faces better than men and have a greater sensitivity to other people's preferences.

Witkin and colleagues found sex differences in three tests of spatial discrimination: a rod-and-frame test, a tilting-room test, and an embedded-figure test. They concluded that women are less able to break the perceptual set and isolate the figures from the misleading background, whereas men are more able to use an analytic approach to the test and isolate one aspect of the stimuli from misleading cues (Witkin, Lewis, Herzman, Machover, Mussner, and Wapner, 1954, pp. 153-171). From this it would appear that in situations where there are elements in the message that are incongruent with past experiences, women might tend to "cover up" or not notice these incongruent elements—they are likely to come away with one impression instead of conflicting ones.

It is not socially acceptable for a woman to express herself through physical aggression. Her disagreements must be discussed verbally. Her desires must be made known verbally. Her superiority in test scores of English and verbal problem solving throughout school years carries over into her adult life. Her affinity for the verbal may explain greater susceptibility to verbal persuasion.

Summerskill and Darling found that women were more correctly informed than were men about the aspects of domestic occupations, domestic and individual embellishments and adornment, etiquette, fictional literature, and musical technique. Women possessed a greater understanding of social topics related to maternal concern (Summerskill and Darling, 1955, pp. 355-361). Tests given to school girls and boys revealed that girls were more concerned than boys with offensive or rule-breaking behavior; that is, they were more negative about such behavior. Social attitude surveys have shown that these characteristics carry over into adult life.

In a study conducted by Exline it was found that women are more concerned than men with person-oriented information. Women will more often seek person-oriented information rather than achievement orientation. Those high in affiliation relative to achievement are initially less prone to attempt to exert control over group decisions and procedures than are their less-affiliative peers. Also for women more than men, visual presence of others aroused a motive to obtain more personal and less task-oriented information from them. In one experiment, 16 groups of 3 men and 16 groups of 3 women were selected and planned the construction of a design made up of fitted blocks of varying shapes and colors. One half the groups in each sex were categorized into two conditions differentiated as to the visibility or nonvisibility of coworkers. In each subcell there were members of both high need for affiliation and low need. It was found that women discussed the project at hand less than men did and concentrated more on interpersonal relations (Exline, 1962).

Anastasi discussed in detail culturally bound differences between the sexes, such as occupation, play activity, accepted modes of emotional expression. The following were found to be most important to females: personal attractiveness, personal philosophy, planning of the daily schedule of activities, maintenance of mental health, good manners, personal qualities, and home and family relations. To the male the most important items were physical health, safety, money, business affairs, sexual prowess, and sports activities. Anastasi found in a comparison of the two sexes that women were more concerned about other women than men were about one another. Women were more interested in both men's and women's clothing than men were, and women were more interested in men than men were in women (Anastasi, 1958, pp. 62-63).

Bardwick found that while the number of women in the work force is increasing, in general women do not see work as an extension of egocentric interests as much as another means to satisfy traditional motives. The stereotyped, socially acceptable role for women has been to be family-oriented, passive, and dependent. The overwhelming majority of women perceive themselves as working only to benefit the family. The very characteristics that mean success in family roles are antithetical to success in a competitive, egocentric working environment. However, this is an era of changing norms in which the unidimensional stereotype of a woman is no longer accurate. Women are not being forced to accept an either/or proposition in choosing a single role. They find that one can be feminine and still be successful in the working world. The idea of woman as housewife and mother only is no longer clear. As new norms gain clarity and force, roles will become more flexible and less stereotyped (Bardwick, 1973). See also the additional discussion of sex differences in chapter 29.

Marketing Examples of Sex Differences

In the current trend toward equal rights and greater recognition for women, the communicator must be especially careful not to demean the traditional housewife role in his messages. He must learn to appeal to women's intelligence as well as their sense of aesthetics so that he does not offend the members of his audience and does not miss an opportunity to present an informative message to a continually more-informed audience.

With regard to the statement that women are more person-oriented than men, there are several examples: detergent commercials are centered around how a woman's wash looks not only to her family but to her friends; dishwashing detergents also center around how the housewife appears to others based on the cleanliness and shine of her dishes. These types of commercials center around empathy and personal involvement. The success of Avon products door-to-door sales might also be partially the result of a woman's person orientation—they like to talk with other women, especially when related to personal appearance.

Evolution of preferences for the different sexes must also be monitored by the marketer. It wasn't too many years ago that a man wouldn't be "caught dead" in a beauty parlor. The beauty parlor and the barber shop were at opposite ends of the spectrum. But as males became more interested in personal appearance, many barber shops have turned into men's beauty parlors. Only now, to keep a more masculine image, they are called men's hair styling boutiques. Thus the marketer must not assume sexual differences or preferences to be static. He must be aware of possible changes and seize the opportunities.

24 An Overview of Learning

Implications

The principles presented in the book in parts III, IV, and V have pertained to the communicating processes of exposing, attending, and perceiving. All have been identified as necessary steps in moving toward the eventual goals of mass communicating in marketing.

The principles presented in part VI on learning represent the fourth step of the six psychological processes described in this book. Learning and its partner remembering reflect the processes by which people acquire and retain modes of response that have been adapted to motivating problematical situations. A host of variables is blanketed under these two processes; and their interrelations must be considered carefully as to ways in which people acquire and modify their behavior.

Model of Learning

The interrelations of the variables encompassed in the learning process are delineated in figure 24-1. As in the previous models, the preconceived variables (needs and wants, sociocultural status, personality variables, and other internal and external variables) are operating at this stage of the communicating model. Once again, the variables are divided into two groups for investigation: (1) message and medium variables and (2) variables within the audience.

Message and Medium Variables

The message and medium variables are divided into two categories: those of a cognitive nature and those of an affective nature. The cognitive variables apply to characteristics of the message that relate to the thought processes that are intellectual in nature. Many of these variables are also contiguous. This refers to the ways that several messages or several parts of a single communication relate to one another in aiding learning. Although learning and remembering tend to decrease with the passage of time, this can be abated somewhat by repetition, distributed practice, or continuity of varied stimuli; but the communicator must be careful not to overexpose audience members. When using repetition, semantic

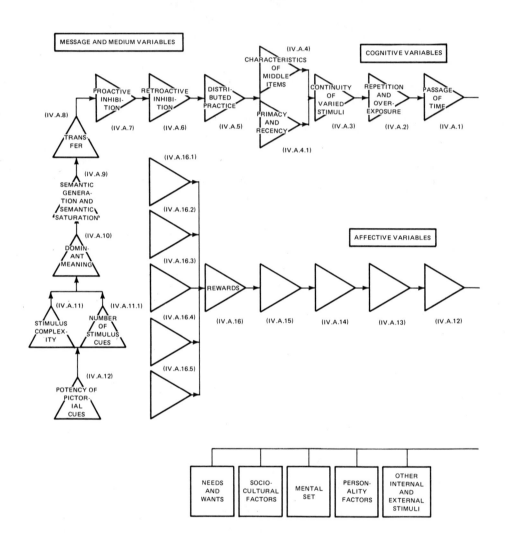

Figure 24-1. The Learning Stage of the Psychological Model of Communicating.

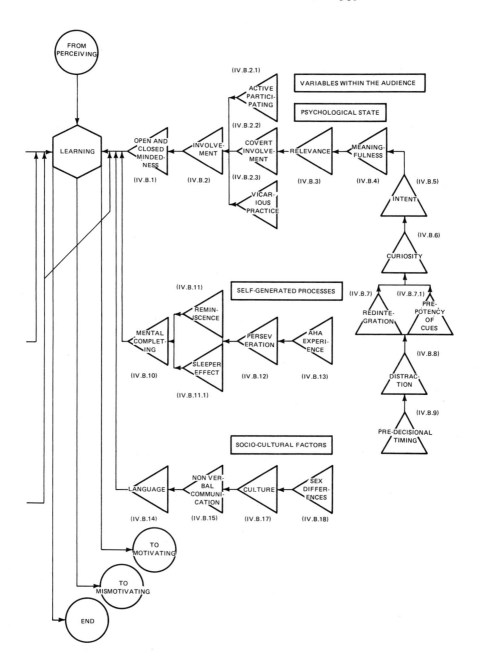

generation and semantic satiation must also be considered. The position of items in a message affect learning, and thus primacy and recency effects become important considerations—with relation of time to primacy and recency and characteristics of middle terms helping to determine the strength of these effects.

Closely related to primacy and recency are the effects of retroactive inhibition and proactive inhibition, which relate to impediments in the learning process when there are certain similarities of two sets of associations in a message. Transfer (positive or negative) becomes particularly relevant when a communicator presents new ideas, items, or responses to audience members; but in associating these with other ideas, etc., he must be aware of the problems associated with dominant meaning. Also, stimulus complexity, number of stimulus cues, and potency of pictorial cues concern the number and type of cues used and their effects on learning and remembering.

Affective variables are those which arouse feeling tones in the individual. These become particularly important in influencing the selective processes that occur in learning, such as selective retention. The degree of affective value of stimulus elements affects learning and remembering, although it is mediated by communicator credibility and other variables. The use of reinforcement and rewards by the communicator when relating to audience members' existing beliefs and attitudes can also increase learning. However, their effect is mediated by the ranking of rewards, reward intensity, timing of rewards, continuity of rewards, and the effects of negative reinforcement and anxiety arousal as perceived by audience members.

Variables Within the Audience

Psychological principles relating to characteristics of the audience are in three categories: psychological state, self-generated processes, and sociocultural factors. As indicated previously, the communicator has substantially less control over these variables than he does with message and medium variables.

An individual's current psychological state (referred to as the total mental state of the individual) affects his learning ability in every situation. An individual's ability to learn new ideas or responses is affected particularly by his open- and closed-mindedness when evaluating his beliefs and attitudes. This also helps to determine the degree of involvement with a message. This involvement, however, is not unidimensional; thus, the communicator must also try to determine the type of involvement elicited—active participating, covert involvement, vicarious practice—since each has distinct problems and opportunities. An audience member's beliefs and attitudes also affect the relevance and meaningfulness of the material to be learned. An individual's actual learning and remembering of this material is enhanced if this learning is intentional (as contrasted with incidental) and also has some curiosity value to it.

Finally, if previous material has been learned and remembered correctly, a communicator can utilize the processes of redintegration and prepotency of cues. To take full advantage of these processes, he also ought to be concerned with environmental conditions (distracting) and time constraints (predecisional timing).

Self-generated processes are primarily remembering processes that do not require current similar stimuli or cues; the effects of outside forces are minimal. To reiterate the distinction made with respect to these psychological principles, incomplete stimulus patterns tend to be remembered better than complete ones when mental completing occurs. Increases in learning of previously incompletely learned material occur after a period of time in reminiscence. An increased favorable attitude change occurs as source and content are disassociated over time if the sleeper effect occurs. Perseveration is the spontaneous reappearance of previously learned material. The aha experience occurs when there is a relatively spontaneous discovery of the solution to a question or problem.

Although the sociocultural principles identified are of a general nature, this does not reduce their importance. The communicator must keep in mind that learning (and remembering)—in fact, the total communicating process—is embedded in a sociocultural milieu that is influenced by the language, nonverbal communication, sex differences, and culture that are characteristic of the audience members with whom he is trying to communicate.

Part VII:
Motivating

25 Beliefs, Attitudes, and Opinions

Motivating and Persuading

Once a message has been perceived and learned and the audience members remember it, the important question is whether the message will affect the audience members as the communicator intends. Therefore, the purpose of a motivational communication is to stimulate the audience to evaluate their own opinions, attitudes, and beliefs in relation to those presented by the communicator. In addition to the perceiving and learning of a message, it must be motivating to the members of the audience.

Before considering factors involved in motivating, it must be emphasized that this is a discussion of motivating—not a discussion of motives, drives, or incentives. Any basic psychology book provides a list of motives, such as thirst, hunger, sleep, social approval, and aggression, or a list of drives, such as maternal drives, fear, or curiosity. And incentives are seen as ways of exploiting existing motives. By contrast, the concept of motivating to be discussed here is a dynamic ongoing process, one that cannot be appropriately described by merely drawing up a list.

The process of motivating involves the creation of a state within an individual or audience that impels or directs his or their behavior to the attainment of a specific goal, that is, a specific attitude or reaction desired by the communicator. To do this, the communicator is concerned with relating a message to the needs and wants of the audience. An audience member will have a greater tendency to be motivated by a message that concerns his own needs and wants than one that does not have such immediacy for him. Since the consumer satisfies his needs and wants by acquiring and using specific objects—such as, products, ideas, or services—the communicator must be acutely aware of audience members' attitudes toward his specific product, service, or idea. Accordingly, the aims of the communicator are threefold—for the audience members to:

1. Know of the existence of the object of communication
2. Know of its uses
3. Relate these to his own wants and needs

The communicator hopes that audience members will perceive the attributes of the object as he intends and evaluate the various attributes of the object in

311

relation to their own value-needs. Specifically, audience members should relate the perceived instrumentality of the object (its attributes) either to satisfy or block their wants and needs.

At this point we need to indicate the differences between *motivating* the audience and *persuading* them. Both processes deal with the beliefs, attitudes, and opinions of the audience members. Both also are concerned with the interactions of audience-message-object characteristics; and both are concerned with influencing behavior in a specific direction or manner. However, the process of *motivating* involves arousing certain responses and making them dominant in the minds of the audience members by relating the message to their needs and wants. In the motivating stage of communicating, the message is related to and is congruent with the audience members' beliefs, attitudes, and opinions. The reinforcing of certain beliefs, attitudes, and opinions has begun.

By contrast, in the process of *persuading,* the communicator tries to change the beliefs, attitudes, and opinions of his audience members. He tries to create dissonance and then to resolve this feeling of unrest by offering his message as the solution. Thus persuading goes beyond relating the message to the audience members' beliefs, attitudes, and opinions and seeks to have them reevaluate their be iefs, attitudes, and opinions. If the message is discrepant with the audience's current beliefs, attitudes, and opinions, it must present reasons for them to change.

Frequently, however, the communicator has to go beyond convincing his audience members that they have a need. He must convince them that his is the best answer to that need. Woods stated that all consumer behavior is motivated, but consumers must often be persuaded as to how to solve their needs. As Woods pointed out, two distinct processes work to determine whether a particular product will be bought or consumed:

1. The process of motivation—someone is hungry and needs food.
2. The process of discrimination—the hunger is satisfied by selecting particular brands of food. [Woods, 1960, p. 123.]

For example, if a particular audience member is in the market for a new tennis racket, it is likely that he will be motivated by advertisements of a tennis racket toward which he has favorable impressions in style, composition, and brand. If he believes that a Wilson T3000 is the finest racket and the racket that he wants, once he has been motivated by a Wilson commercial to buy a racket now, he will be likely to act and purchase the racket. However, if he sees an advertisement for a Head racket, he will be motivated to read it because of his need for a racket. If the advertisement presents ideas that begin to convince him that a Head racket is better than a Wilson for him, he may be *persuaded* by the advertisement to reevaluate his beliefs, attitudes, and opinions; and he may behave by seeking more information about and/or buying a Head racket.

Bayton referred to motivation as a state of need arousal, "a condition exerting 'push' on the individual to engage in those activities which he anticipates will have the highest probability of bringing him gratification of a particular need-pattern" (Bayton, 1958, p. 284).

A communicator is not always sure of whether his message will just have to motivate his target audience members or if it will further have to persuade them. Consumer research studies will not provide him with a true picture of the beliefs, attitudes, and opinions of all audience members. Audience members will not all perceive the message in the same way. Some audience members will be motivated to assess the message as an answer to their needs, and some will have to be persuaded to change their beliefs, attitudes, and opinions so that the message is an acceptable answer for them.

Many of the same principles that apply to motivating also apply to persuading. The communicator usually designs his messages to motivate without being aware if they will further have to persuade his audience. Thus, in this book's discussion of motivating, studies of persuading techniques are also included when a principle deals with both motivating and persuading. The same principles apply whether beliefs, attitudes, and opinions are being reinforced or changed.

However, in part VII on persuading, particular principles are stated for the instances in which the communicator must persuade his audience. These are discussions of variables that apply particularly to the persuading process. These principles would be especially valuable in the circumstances in which a communicator is aware that he has to persuade his audience. Such circumstances might include the introduction of new products or new product concepts.

Motivational Frameworks

Before considering the various principles for motivating, it will be helpful to consider first some motivational frameworks that have been developed to account for the ways in which attitudes are formed, maintained, and altered.

Although no single theory of motivating can account adequately for all the ways in which attitudes are formed, maintained, and altered, it is useful to look at frameworks of attitudes that have been developed in order to explain the motivating process.

In analyzing the attitudes that consumers have toward products in the marketplace, Maloney (1968) posited that attitudes, as well as having motivational functions, must also have cognitive components, that is, expectations of what it would be like to buy, use, or have used a product or brand.

Product-Related Cognitive Experiences

Anticipation of some kind of experience with the product (or service) underlies almost all product purchases. The consumer has an image of how the product is going to satisfy his needs. Accordingly, meanings that the product have for the consumer, in terms of his interactions with it, are what make up his "cognition" of the product. Maloney breaks down this "cognitive element" into three product-related cognitive experiences.

1. *End-product-of-use experience*—this kind of experience is that which sees the product as a means to a specific end—the improvement in appearance one's house will show after a coat of paint.

2. *Product-in-use experience*—this is experience that derives from the feeling one gets while actually using the product—driving a car or eating a meal.

3. *Incidental-to-functional-use experience*—this consists of experience that is not directly related to the functional use of a product but that may nevertheless be crucial in forming the attitudes one has toward it—such as one's impressions of the cost of buying or the convenience of storing a product.

Motivational Appeals

Maloney also listed four minimal classifications of motivational appeals considered important for marketing decision-making.

1. *Rational appeal* (strict presentation of factual information)—based on a problem-solving premise that people must have some facts to go on and that their likes and dislikes grow out of cognitive or factual aspects of attitudes.

2. *Sensory appeal* (promise of good taste, good smell, good feeling)—based on the reward-punishment learning theories of psychology; and stresses the pleasure principle, that most human behavior consciously or unconsciously is directed toward seeking pleasure or avoiding pain.

3. *Social appeal* (promise of prestige, love, acceptance, and related rewards)—recognizes people's needs to be approved, loved, admired, or at least accepted by others.

4. *Ego-attitude support* (bolstering of self-image)—serves to fulfill one's need to define one's own role and recognize one's own worth, without undue concern for the approval of others.

Mode of Evaluation Framework

Maloney brings together the three product-related cognitive experiences and the four motivational appeals into what he calls the "mode of evaluation framework." As indicated in table 25-1, this results in 12 kinds of potential attitudes toward a product that consumers might be expected to use in choosing among products of a given kind.

Examples of appeals that motivate and persuade by utilizing each of the 12 kinds of attitudes indicated in table 25-1 are:

Table 25-1
Mode of Evaluation Framework

| Product-Related Cognitive Experiences | Motivational Appeals | | | |
| | Potential Types of Reward from a Product | | | |
	Rational	Sensory	Social	Ego-attitude support
End-product-of-use	I	II	III	IV
Product-in-use	V	VI	VII	VIII
Incidental-to-functional-use	IX	X	XI	XII

1. Rational rewards from end-product-of-use experience: "Gets clothes cleaner."
2. Sensory rewards from end-product-of-use experience: "Settles upset stomach completely."
3. Social rewards from end-product-of-use experience: "When you care enough to send the very best."
4. Ego-attitude support from end-product-of-use experience: "For the skin you deserve to have."
5. Rational rewards from product-in-use experience: "The flour that needs no sifting."
6. Sensory rewards from product-in-use experience: "Real gusto in a great light beer."
7. Social rewards from product-in-use experience: "A deodorant that keeps you smelling fresh all day."
8. Ego-attitude support from product-in-use experience: "The shoe for the young executive."
9. Rational rewards from incidental-to-functional-use experience: "The plastic pack keeps the cigarettes fresh."
10. Sensory rewards from incidental-to-functional-use experience: "The portable television that's lighter in weight, easier to lift."
11. Social rewards from incidental-to-functional-use experience: "The furniture that identifies the home of modern people."
12. Ego-attitude support from incidental-to-functional-use experience: "Stereo for the man with discriminating taste."

In the promotion of a product or service, one or two of these appeal types should be selected and emphasized, says Maloney. Almost anything might be marketed by focusing upon almost any of these 12 appeal types.

The means of determining which of the 12 to use for a particular product is by selecting which one has the greatest likelihood of probable influence on potential buyers in making the purchase decision, as compared with the other appeals. Exploratory discussions in which consumers are allowed to talk freely about the things that concern them about a product category can help to point out which appeal type should be used for that category. Because it is much easier to reinforce existing attitudes than to change them, the selection of the appropriate appeal or appeals must hinge also upon compatibility with present product image and present attitudes toward the brand.

Beliefs-Attitudes-Opinions

The concepts of belief, attitude, and opinion are basic proponents of psychological literature as well as being central to everyday life. However, because these terms are fundamental for all psychologists, the problem of distinctly defining them is complex. A survey of existing definitions reveals that beliefs, attitudes, and opinions are distinguished from one another by definition, are grouped into one category rather than existing as a three-fold concept, or are arranged in a hierarchical manner with one or two named as the dependent variable(s).

This book presents three fundamental definitions that are original but distilled and reorganized from other similar explanations:

A *belief* is an idea of preference held on a specific point. A grouping of beliefs constitutes an attitude.

An *attitude* is a composite of beliefs that results in a certain behavior pattern toward a given class of objects and situations.

An *opinion* is a view that is the overt manifestation of a belief or an attitude.

Understanding that much of the literature that deals with beliefs, attitudes, and opinions deals with them as a single conviction or uses different definitions than those used here, at many points in this book they will be discussed as *beliefs-attitudes-opinions.* This also indicates the fact that these are interrelated convictions and that which affects one of them is likely to affect them all.

Beliefs

A belief is an idea or preference held on a specific point. A grouping of beliefs constitutes an attitude.

Beliefs are basic. They are the cornerstone of attitude theory. As Rokeach has pointed out, "A belief is any simple proposition, conscious, or unconscious, inferred from what a person says or does, capable of being preceded by the phrase, 'I believe that....'" (Rokeach, 1968, p. 113). Berelson and Steiner classified the terms as follows: "Beliefs are more basic still [than attitudes and opinions], having to do with the central values of life" (Berelson and Steiner, 1964, pp. 557-558).

Rokeach defined five kinds of beliefs. *Primitive beliefs* are supported by 100 percent social consensus and involve the nature of physical reality, social reality, and the self. They are not subject to change. Beliefs of *deep personal experience* are extremely resistant to change and are based upon positive self-images. *Authority beliefs* however, tell individuals whom they can trust for truthful information. These are liable to change if an authority is proven wrong. *Peripheral beliefs* are derived from the authorities one believes in. These beliefs can be changed if the suggestion for change comes from the authority or if the authority belief changes. But the most changeable beliefs are the *inconsequential beliefs*. If they change, the total belief system is not altered significantly (Rokeach, 1963).

No belief or attitude is completely enduring because the individual constantly is being bombarded by new stimuli. If any of these are perceived and attended to by the individual, the chances are that some component of one of his beliefs will be changed or modified, and this will lead to a change of attitudes.

Attitudes

An attitude is a composite of beliefs that results in a certain behavior pattern toward a given class of objects and situations.

G.W. Allport's definition of attitude had five aspects. An attitude is "a mental and neural state of readiness to respond, organized through experience exerting a dynamic and/or directive influence on behavior" (Allport, 1969, pp. 136-148). The five aspects of this definition have been discussed by other psychologists as follows.

1. *"A mental and neural state ..."* An attitude is not a defined entity but rather is a changing concept, an abstraction partially defined in terms of antecedent conditions and consequent behaviors (Allport, 1969, p. 142). After listing criteria for attitudes, Sherif and Sherif (1967) held that attitudes are not temporary states but are more or less enduring.

2. *"... of readiness to respond ..."* An attitude is not a response but is a readiness to respond. Thurstone wrote that an attitude is the potential action toward an object. The eventual response may be (a) positivistic—due to a direct relationship between antecedent and consequent events; (b) paradigmatic—one of the interacting attitudes (or, following my definition, beliefs) is declared the paradigmatic antecedent, while the other is the paradigmatic consequent and the relation between the two is established (any other attitudes and relations

involved are then defined in terms of the original components); (c) mediational-ist—attitude is seen as an intervening variable (a mediating construct) that helps to tie the antecedent and consequent into observable social reality; (d) class-inclusionist—mediating constructs are present in both the antecedent and consequent events; and (e) interactionist—each side works as a function, with attitude as the intervening variable (Thurstone, 1931, pp. 261-262).

3. "... *organized*..." Three components are central to both beliefs and attitudes: (a) cognitive—how the attitude is perceived, its conceptual connota-tion; (b) affective—feeling or emotional component, the liking or disliking of the attitude object; and (c) conative—the gross behavioral tendencies of the person regarding the object (Rosenberg, 1960, pp. 20-22; Insko and Schopler, 1967; and Allport, 1969, pp. 136-148).

4. "... *through experience*..." Kagan identifies five ways of acquiring attitudes (Kagan, 1974, pp. 4-5). The first three are characteristic of childhood; the remaining two are more characteristics of adolescence and adulthood:

a. A child learns attitudes by looking and listening. He hears parents or people whom he respects make statements; and the more he respects them, the more he assumes that their attitudes are more valid than others.

b. Attitudes are learned through reward and punishment.

c. Attitudes are learned through the mechanism of identification. Children and young people would like more power, more status, and more prestige. Since they are lacking these attributes more than adults, they look around to note those people—relatives, friends, fictional heroes—whom they admire and try to detect what attitudes they hold. They then begin to acquire these attitudes in an effort to share vicariously in their power, status, and prestige.

d. The fourth and fifth methods of attitude acquisition are internally gener-ated by the self. Specifically, the fourth method involves a person's definition of his identity. In all cultures a child acquires a way to define himself, although the definition varies from culture to culture, of course. From this definition of self the world takes on a more specific meaning, which in turn results in a specific set of attitudes that correspond with these meanings (for example, "I'm a radical" or "I'm a conservative").

e. The fifth method relates to the human need to have a consistent set of attitudes. Thus, if two attitudes conflict—for example, if I dislike wide lapels, but my tailor, whom I respect, is in favor of them—I may change my attitudes or develop new ones to make the attitudes harmonize with each other.

Thus, not only are attitudes learned, but there are a variety of ways to learn them.

5. "... *exerting a dynamic and/or directive influence on behavior*." If attitudes are merely directive, they will channel action toward one goal or

another; if they are dynamic, they must also affect the amount of energy expanded for that purpose (Allport, 1969, p. 148). Attitude has also been defined as,

an enduring, learned predisposition to behave in a consistent way toward a given class of objects; a persistent mental and/or neural state of readiness to react to a certain class of objects, not as they are, but as they are conceived to be. It is by the consistency of a response to a class of objects that an attitude is identified. The readiness state has a direct effect upon feeling and action related to the object [English and English, 1958, p. 50.]

An attitude, therefore, is not a concrete entity. It cannot be observed nor can it be measured directly. Its existence must be inferred from behavior that is observed.

Some controversy may arise here because of the lack of the word *predisposition* in this book's definition of attitude. Because attitudes can exist both covertly and overtly, the latter coming when the attitude is expressed as an opinion or some type of overt behavior, a covert holding of an attitude is that predisposition to act in a certain manner. It is important to remember, however, that before an overt behavior pattern can be established, the attitude must become overt. Consequently, the words *results in* are the keys to the Allport definition. One holds an attitude that, if expressed, should result in a certain behavior pattern.

Opinions

An opinion is a view that is the overt manifestation of a belief or an attitude.

An attitude or belief can be held covertly or overtly. However, as soon as any overt action is taken where either of the two is involved, an opinion is immediately formed with the relevant attitude or belief as its basis. English and English stated,

An opinion is a belief that one holds to be without emotional commitment or desire, and to be open to reevaluation; since the evidence is not affirmed to be convincing; it is capable of verbal expression under appropriate circumstances. [English and English, 1958, pp. 358-359.]

Although this definition classifies opinion as an overt action, it also holds that an opinion is held without emotional commitment. Since it already has been established that a belief has an affective component, one can abstract from English and English that an opinion is a belief and is capable of verbal expression under appropriate circumstances, at least to oneself. If the belief is expressed only to oneself, it is not an opinion; the belief exists covertly until expressed beyond one's own mind.

At this juncture, it should be emphasized that in no way in this book am I attempting to reify the concepts of belief, attitude, and opinion. Each of these psychological processes is considered to be in a constant state of modification, creation, or change.

Beliefs-Attitudes-Opinions Diagramatically

Beliefs are the primary components of attitudes. They are held on specific points and may exist singly or interact with one or more others to form an attitude. Consider figure 25-1. In this case, B_2, B_3, B_4, and B_5 interact to form attitude A_1. B_1 is held on one point and does not necessarily have to be a part of any belief aggregate.

In figure 25-2, beliefs are shown to be members of more than one attitude system because they are relevant to more than one subject area.

Opinions now must be added to this schematic framework. We have defined them as the "overt manifestations of beliefs and attitudes." An opinion does not exist covertly; it becomes real only when the belief or attitude is expressed in some fashion. At that point, attitude equals opinion, or the set of $(B_1, B_2, B_3, \ldots, B_n)$ equals opinion, as figure 25-3 shows. Further, if $B_{1,2,3,4}$ are each

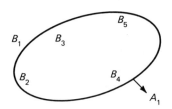

Figure 25-1. Beliefs Forming an Attitude.

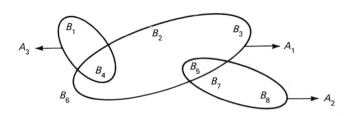

Figure 25-2. Beliefs as Members of More than One Attitude System.

expressed as their composite A_2, then five separate opinions based on the beliefs are expressed as well, as OA_2, as shown in figure 25-4.

Each day we are bombarded by numerous stimuli. Many of them have as their sole purpose a persuasion to change our beliefs and/or attitudes, which will eventually make us follow the pattern desired by the originator of the stimuli. Some stimuli are received and perceived, whereas others are rejected. Because of these stimuli, some of our existing attitudes may be modified. Suppose, for example, an individual has beliefs and an attitude as shown in figure 25-5. As a result of some message, these beliefs and attitudes are bombarded by stimuli (S's). While beliefs B_4 and B_5 reject the stimuli as not being consistent with their present structure, B_1 receives, perceives, and attends to them. This eventually results in a change in this belief (or a modification of it), and it becomes B_1', as shown in figure 25-6. Consequently, A_1 will have to change if the belief composite now has a different valence. Thus the new configuration looks like figure 25-7.

If and when the new beliefs and/or attitudes are expressed, the opinions given will also change. If $B_1 \rightarrow O_{B1}$, then $B_1 \rightarrow B_1'$.

The final step in determining the relationship(s) between beliefs, attitudes, and opinions lies in an analysis of the consistency among them. As indicated

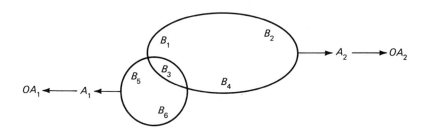

Figure 25-3. Attitudes as a Basis of an Opinion.

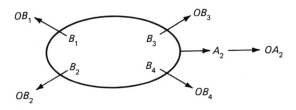

Figure 25-4. Opinions Based on Beliefs.

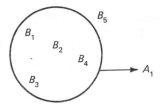

Figure 25-5. Beliefs and an Attitude.

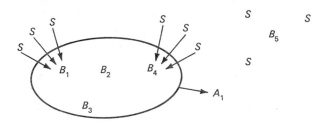

Figure 25-6. Changes in Belief.

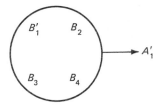

Figure 25-7. Eventual Changes in Belief.

previously, beliefs and attitudes have cognitive, affective, and conative components. Now three different consistencies will be examined: belief-attitude,
belief-opinion, and attitude-opinion.

Belief-Attitude Consistency

The purpose of investigating this type of relationship is to discover whether or
not the valence (positive, neutral, or negative) of an attitude is consistent with

those of the component beliefs. *Valence* is that property of an object by virtue of which the object is sought (positive valence) or avoided (negative valence) or ignored (neutral valence).

Suppose that a man has an attitude that he wants to purchase a television set at a discount store. He has four beliefs relevant to this attitude. They are:

Valence	*Belief*	
Positive	B_1:	Brand name items are priced lower at discount stores than at other outlets.
Negative	B_2:	Customer service is poor in most discount stores.
Negative	B_3:	Displays of merchandise often look manhandled.
Negative	B_4:	Discount stores do not always carry complete product lines.

In this example one can observe a consumer who normally would not shop at a discount store because of beliefs B_2, B_3, and B_4, which he holds. Observe, however, that the price consideration in this case is so important that he will make the purchase regardless of negative beliefs. In other words, one cannot hypothesize that when a series of beliefs is involved, the product or sum of the valences (1 for positive, 0 for neutral, or -1 for negative) will yield the valence of the attitude.

The valence of a belief-composite, that is, the attitude, is dependent upon the strengths of the valences of the component beliefs. Thus one cannot label the relation between beliefs and attitudes, balanced or unbalanced, consistent or inconsistent, because neither the sum nor the product of the component valences will necessarily result in the same valence that the individual assigns to the attitude.

A positive belief may overpower other relevant negative beliefs, to give an attitude a positive valence or vice versa. This idea is quite clear in the preceding example. The price consideration is of such great importance that it overpowered the man's other beliefs about shopping at discount stores.

Belief-Opinion Consistency and Attitude-Opinion Consistency

A person's overt manifestation, that is, his opinions, should be consistent with his corresponding covert beliefs and attitudes. Suppose that a person feels that small foreign cars are unsafe. Later he voices this belief to a friend. His opinion is consistent with his belief. He later attends a cocktail party given by his boss. He does not enjoy alcoholic beverages; but when a high-level executive offers him a martini, he feels that he ought to comment on the good taste of the drink. His expressed opinion is inconsistent with his belief (or attitude depending upon the

circumstances) about liquor. Thus one may say that consistency exists between a
belief and an opinion or between an attitude and an opinion only when there is a
positive-positive, neutral-neutral, or negative-negative relationship between the
elements. See table 25-2.

In conclusion, beliefs, attitudes, and opinions are not the same. *Beliefs* are
the cornerstones of the belief-attitude-opinion hierarchy, *attitudes* are formed
from beliefs, and *opinions* are reliant upon overt manifestations of both these
elements for their existence.

Table 25-2
Comparisons of Belief and Opinion as to Consistency

	Opinion		
Belief	*Positive*	*Neutral*	*Negative*
Positive	Consistent	Inconsistent	Inconsistent
Neutral	Inconsistent	Consistent	Inconsistent
Negative	Inconsistent	Inconsistent	Consistent

26

Message and Medium Variables: Rational and Nonrational Messages

Background

As was indicated in the previous chapter on motivating, although there are differences between motivating and persuading, there also are close relationships between the two processes. And since it is necessary to be motivated before being persuaded, naturally there are variables in the message and medium that are found in both processes. An individual has had to become interested and has had to relate the message to his beliefs-attitudes-opinions. Then, if the message reinforces these, no persuading will be necessary. However, if the message presents conflicting ideas, then persuading will be needed at this point to influence and possibly change beliefs-attitudes-opinions.

Thus the message and medium variables are the same for the two processes, in that the communicator is never sure of whether he will be motivating or persuading. The various principles of the message and medium variables will be discussed in detail in the present section on motivating but will not be duplicated in detail in the part on persuading. However, see chapter 31 for a further discussion of the similarities and differences of motivating and persuading.

Rational Messages

Rational motivating tends to be dominant in some basic decisions, such as deciding whether to rent or buy a house, and emotional motivating tends to play a bigger role in selective decisions in which there is little difference in alternatives, such as brands of cigarettes and other convenience goods. But in any situation both rational and emotional motivating are likely to be working together (Beckman, 1962, p. 77).

A businessman may want to subscribe to a highly regarded and expensive business publication to keep up with the latest ideas and practices and therefore to enhance his business position, and also because it makes him feel important. A woman may want an electric dishwasher to make her household work easier and because most of her friends have one. With so many personalities, products, and situations, countless combinations of buying motives enter into consumer decisions.

Although a variety of buying appeals have been put forth by various marketing authorities, the *rational* appeals might be condensed as follows:

1. *Economy in purchase,* as when trying to purchase a high-cost product, such as an automobile, for the lowest price.
2. *Economy in operation,* as when purchasing a compact car for better gasoline mileage and less expensive maintenance.
3. *Dependability,* as when buying a product that the purchaser must be reasonably sure will always perform as expected when needed, such as an alarm clock.
4. *Durability,* as when a workman purchases outdoor boots for functionality rather than for style.
5. *Convenience,* as when purchasing an electric dishwasher to save time and work.
6. *Money gain,* as when a store owner invests in a new neon sign he hopes will attract more customers and increase his earnings.

Many psychologists have studied the relative persuasive effects of rational and nonrational aspects of communication and have actually come up with little concrete evidence to support the superiority of one form over the other. Some general hypotheses have been developed, however, as to which form of persuading might be best in certain situations.

Bauer suggested that in many situations an appeal that is both highly emotional and highly rational would be the most satisfactory way to produce an attitudinal change. [Bauer, 1967.]

Experimental evidence for this theory was provided by results of a study by Janis and Feshbach in which groups of students heard one of three versions of a prepared talk on dental hygiene. Although the general information and recommendations were the same in all the cases, the talks differed in their anxiety-arousal content. The three talks included strong anxiety appeals with threatening undertones of dire consequences of improper hygiene, moderate anxiety appeals with threats in a mild form, and minimal anxiety appeal with threats replaced by fairly neutral information. It was observed that the most effective appeal was the minimal anxiety one, with conformity to recommend behavior reported by 36 percent of the group. Conformity of 24 percent was reported in the moderate anxiety case, and 8 percent conformity was reported in the strong anxiety case. It was also observed that strong anxiety appeals caused the greatest emotional tensions. From this it was concluded that in certain cases appeals that build up a minimal level of emotional tension are more likely to be effective than those which lead to higher emotional tensions.

Janis and Feshbach attempted to explain these results with the hypothesis that when anxiety is strongly aroused but is not fully relieved by the assurances contained in a mass communication, the audience will become motivated to ignore or to minimize the importance of the threat (Janis and Feshbach, 1953). Cox stated that while the experimental evidence for this hypothesis is slim, at least none of the data contradict the content, and the hypothesis remains consistent with other psychological evidence in the operation of defensive mechanisms (Cox, 1961).

On the basis of these and other studies, it can be assumed, then, that an appeal that is both highly emotional and highly rational will elicit more attitudinal change on the part of the audience members than will an appeal that is primarily emotional or rational. The following propositions will deal with those aspects of a communicator's message which will normally affect the rational aspects of the motivating of his target audience members. These are the quantifiable parts of the physical message and its environment. Nonrational aspects will be discussed in the last half of this chapter.

Order of Presentation

V.A1 *A message is more likely to motivate or change the attitudes of audience members if they are made aware of their needs for a solution before this solution is presented in the message than if the solution is presented before they are made aware of their needs.*

A study by Cohen with college students indicated that when an audience member was not aware of a need, a message had to establish a need before the presentation of a solution would change his attitude. The topic for the study was the giving of course grades on a curve, that is, according to relative class rank. The message that presented information relevant to need satisfaction, after those needs had been aroused, brought more acceptance of the communicator's conclusion by the group who saw it than when a group was presented the information first and the need arousal second. However, subjects that had a great need before they were exposed to either message were persuaded to the same extent no matter what order the presentation of the two parts of the message was given (Cohen, 1964, p. 11).

Levine and Murphy studied learning and forgetting of propaganda and counterpropaganda. Groups that were either pro- or anti-Soviet tended to adhere to their original beliefs, learned quicker, and forgot the opposing argument faster. The strength of the motivation to reject a communication will tend to increase whenever an argument against is presented that the recipient had not spontaneously considered (Levine and Murphy, 1943, p. 515).

Cohen suggested that the effect of the order of presentation was less for those of his subjects who had a high cognitive need (Cohen, 1957). McGuire suggested that other possible motivations might include those which influence the recipient's learning of a communication, and also those which affect his acceptance of the position advocated. [McGuire, 1957.] See also the material on message and medium variables in chapter 19.

Marketing Examples of Order of Presentation

Grocery stores have identified the need of staying open until midnight or all night, especially for the benefit of people who work during the day. Thus they identified and met the needs of this customer group. In this case operating hours are stressed to communicate the message of 18- or 24-hour operation.

In the Colonel Sanders carry-out restaurant operation, the needs of not feeling like cooking or serving large groups of people at dinners or picnics are identified. The solution is to provide high-quality fried chicken to be taken home.

Instant Cream of Wheat identified the need of a hot breakfast that does not have to be cooked, only mixed with hot water. This can be done at the last minute and even fixed by children. Individual proportions are enclosed in simple small packets. These specifics are identified in the promotion, as well as how the product meets the needs of people who are hurried.

Desirable Information

V.A2 *Audience members will be more likely to be motivated by a message if the most desirable information for them is presented first.*

McGuire presented two messages to a group of subjects. In the first message, conclusions consonant with the desires and motives of the subjects were presented first, followed by information that contrasted with their desires and motives. In the other message, the order was reversed. The message that presented the desirable information first elicited more total agreement. He reasoned that when a subject disagreed with the initial subject of the message, his attention waned and consequently so did his learning of the message (McGuire, 1964).

Presentation of undesirable or desirable information or both concerning a subject depends upon the communicator, the subject, and the audience members involved. Since so many variables affect the motivating process, only two generalizations about the presentation of desirable and undesirable information are presented here.

If audience members are likely to doubt the credibility of the communicator, the answer is for the communicator to mention first an item of undesirable information and then answer that objection to help increase his credibility. The use of undesirable information in this situation would be intended to convey to the audience members that no information was being withheld from them and that the communicator was believable. For instance, a couple planning on buying a car might doubt the credibility of the salesman. If he pointed out a dent in the car's bumper but said that it could be fixed if they wanted to buy the car, the couple would probably believe him more readily than if he had delivered a straight selling pitch to them.

If the audience members are not capable of understanding or evaluating both the desirable and undesirable aspects of a subject, only one side should be presented. This idea will be further covered in the discussion of one-sided and two-sided arguments later in this chapter.

Marketing Examples of Desirable Information

Packages often convey the product attributes. The Nabisco Instant Cream of Wheat package—previously mentioned—says, "Mix & Eat" in bold letters. The copy then goes on to mention that the water used must be boiling (thus one has to wait a few minutes), and that if one does not pour all the water in at a time, the cereal is lumpy.

Returnable soft-drink bottles are undesirable to the average consumer. Yet when economy is emphasized, the consumer begins to feel that the manufacturer has the interests of consumers in mind by giving lower prices.

Sales promotions in grocery outlets often only have a large sign emphasizing the price reduction or 2-for-1 sale. To a lot of people, price is the most important factor; and everyone likes a bargain.

Certain retail stores often point out that the customer may have to drive a little out of his way, but that he will be rewarded by excellent buys and unique merchandise. The message is presented in terms of "only 45 minutes from . . . ," which is quite a time commitment in just transportation.

Familiarity

V.A3 When the topic of a message is familiar to the audience members and has high interest value for them, the strongest arguments to motivate them should be placed near the end of the message in climactic order. When the topic is unfamiliar and has low interest value, the strongest argument should be placed first in anticlimactic order.

The climactic presentation of a message is supported in a study, conducted by Cromwell, in which he presented a series of speeches to an audience and measured their relative effect on the audience members. Results indicated that a weak speech seemed to be made weaker by following a strong one. If attending is maintained, the presentation of strong arguments at the outset leads to expectations that are frustrated by the subsequent presentation of weak arguments (Cromwell, 1950).

Some historians believe that the profound effect of Lincoln's Gettysburg

Address was caused, in part, by being the second of two speeches given. The first speech was very long, lasting nearly three hours on a hot afternoon. Lincoln followed with his brief but moving speech. After such a long, dull speech, Lincoln's speech was particularly effective.

The advantage of a climactic versus anticlimactic order is also explained by the learning-theory analysis of the changes in the size of incentives. Hull proposed that a greater tendency to action would be produced if a small incentive is given first, followed by a larger incentive (Hull, 1952, pp. 140-148). When the large incentive is given first, the tendency toward action is reduced, even though the total incentive is the same in both cases.

When a message is unfamiliar or has little interest to the audience members, the strongest arguments should be presented first. This will catch the audience's attention and provide incentive to complete the message. If the weak arguments are presented first, the audience is likely to become bored and disregard the entire message.

Marketing Examples of Familiarity

The level of product development affects whether the strongest argument should be placed toward the beginning or toward the end of a message. When the product is new, the strongest argument is placed at the beginning so as to attract attention and let the audience know that the product exists. When Jiffy Pop was first introduced, promotion emphasized the popping of the corn in a throw-away pan, no messiness. Later the emphasis was on the bulging out of the foil as the corn pops and the excitement of popping corn. The throw-away pan and no mess were presented at the end of the message.

Jello Instant Pudding has a high degree of familiarity. The package is average looking. Yet when Jello Whip & Chill was first introduced, it was in a glamorous package, with the product featured on the front of a tall compote. The package quality and interest value of the latter product was used as part of the promotion, to add to its initial attention-getting ability. From there on, the followup instructions read much the same way as for Jello Instant Pudding.

Primacy and Recency

V.A4 *Audience members will usually be more affected by the first and last parts of a message than by its middle parts. Thus the communicator should place his most motivating or persuading points at the very beginning or end of the message to increase the chances of motivating the audience members as he desires.*

Lund developed his law of primacy in persuasion in answer to the question "When an audience is presented with both sides of an issue, which has the advantage, the side presented first (primacy) or the side presented last (recency)?" Lund's principle was based upon research that consisted of presenting mimeographed, counterbalanced pairs of arguments to groups of college students. The first argument supported one side of a controversial issue, the second supported diametrically the opposite side. His results consistently showed that the first-presented arguments were significantly more effective in influencing opinions concerning the issues involved (Lund, 1925).

The truth of this "law" was questioned after Hovland and Mandell completed their experimentation in 1952. In repeating the Lund experiment, they found a recency effect in three out of four groups (Hovland and Mandell, 1957). The consensus of most psychologists today is that the presence of either a primacy or a recency effect is dependent upon other variables present in the testing situation and the characteristics of the audience.

"When two sides of an issue are presented successively by different communicators, the side presented first does not necessarily have the advantage" (Hovland, 1964, p. 180). As a result of the different variables that enter the primacy and recency effect, most attempts to fit test findings into a theoretical framework have met with little success. Two studies, however, represent the most impressive efforts in this direction.

Anderson and Hovland reported studies with a mathematical model based upon the assumption that the more opinion change for which they asked, the more would be received. Thus, if two successive messages produce the same amount of opinion change, the second would have the advantage. The first would move opinion a given amount and thereby increase the attitude distance between the recipient and the second message. If the second were as effective as the first, it would demand more opinion change and would create a greater change (Anderson and Hovland, 1957).

Yet certain conditions perpetuate a primacy effect. After hearing only one side of a controversial issue, if an individual publicly indicates his position on the issue, the effect on him of a later presentation of the other side of the issue is reduced—an example of a primacy effect (Hovland, Campbell, and Brock, 1957).

In another study, Luchins found that when contradictory information was presented in a single communication by a single communicator, those items presented first tended to dominate the impression received. The test consisted of two paragraphs presented in inverted order to subjects. The paragraphs described a fictional person as either introverted or extroverted. Questionnaires given to the subjects showed the material presented first was more influential than later materials (Luchins, 1957).

In an experiment by Lana, controversial subjects showed a slight tendency toward the primacy effect. The proposition of predecisional timing indicates that if the first argument is accepted, the level of acceptance for the second may be lower. A controversial subject is likely to evoke a stand, so predecisional timing may explain the tendency toward a primacy effect in a controversial subject presentation (Lana, 1963).

Primacy and recency seem to have no effect upon a message that an audience finds too dull to be motivational. However, as level of interest rises, primacy tends to become more effective in motivating an audience than recency.

Marketing Examples of Primacy and Recency

If primacy is most effective in motivating, then the most important product message should be stated first. Headlines should convey the main idea—this is substantiated by the fact the people remember more headlines than body copy. For example, the simple 7-Up promotion of "uncola" said what the product was and was not, in one word.

New package development can be used to differentiate the product from its competition and serve as a primacy effect. Frozen vegetables packaged in 1-pound containers instead of 10 ounces to serve large families better is a main product attribute for the consumer. This attribute should be mentioned first, and it also adds to the uniqueness of the manufacturer who was the first to employ such a package design.

Supermarket managers employ primacy techniques by placing special sales promotion products at the front of the store. For example, canned corn or Triscuits might be on sale during the same week but located in other than their normal display areas. This lures the customer to search for other such bargains; and perhaps feeling that because a few cents were saved on corn, he can now buy a better cut of meat.

The understanding of recency is demonstrated in several promotional fields. Supermarkets advertise toward the end of the week, when most people do most of their shopping for food. Point-of-purchase displays are essential to increase the recency effect. Because of signs and displays of promotional material, manufacturers may have the added advantage of putting in the last claim for the consumer's dollar.

Recency can also affect at the point of purchase. It can convey high quality through distinctness and good design, and also practicality, such as with unbreakable medicine bottles or sprays. It may convey low quality, however, by blending into the environment and not specifying what the product is or how to use it in explicit terms. For example, a higher-quality brand name of canned fruit may have brighter colors and perhaps offer extras, such as salad recipes on the back of the can.

Similarly, new specialty stores—clothing, records, shoes, etc.—will have a grand-opening promotion, which usually includes a contest, gifts, and other devices to attract shoppers away from established stores where they usually do their shopping. Of course the "acid test" of the grand opening's success is whether the new store can win the new loyalty of a significant number of opening's shopper audience and prevent them from reverting to the other stores where they have been buying.

Time

V.A4.1 *In determining the motivational and persuasive influences of a message, the time at which audience members are tested for attitudes influence the effects of primacy and recency. If the individual is tested immediately after the last argument is presented, a strong bias exists toward the recency effect. The argument presented first is more effective if the individual is tested later, however.*

Miller and Campbell studied the effect of time on the primacy-recency theory, using methods that had not been included in any previous research. First, they varied the order in which they presented the arguments—pro-con or con-pro—to a group of subjects who had no prior opinion on the subject of the messages. The investigators varied the time between the first and second messages and the time of testing the effects of the arguments. The results showed that no matter whether the pro or con was presented first, a recency effect was discovered. The longer the time difference between the first and last-heard argument, the greater the effect of recency was. This was only true if the measurement of the second argument followed that argument immediately. When testing was delayed and both arguments were given together, the first was the stronger (Miller and Campbell, 1959).

Insko tested Miller and Campbell's hypothesis and found that the longer the time interval between two opposing persuasive communications, the greater the recency effect on opinions measured immediately after the second communication. By contrast, the longer the time between the second communication and the measurement of opinions, however, the less the recency effect (Insko, 1964).

Miller and Campbell correlated the negatively accelerated forgetting curve of Ebbinghaus to the statement by Hovland, Janis, and Kelly that "in experimental results on simple verbal material, we would predict recency effects when the time interval is short. But the passage of time would tend to decrease this recency effect and permit the other factors making for primacy to become relatively stronger" (Hovland, Janis, and Kelley, 1953, p. 126).

Marketing Examples of Time

Communicators should understand the effects of time on primacy and recency when designing messages because sometimes audience members can be motivated through primacy to go "right out" and buy a product. If a typical purchase is made after a period of reflection rather than on impulse, recency should be used in messages to reach the target audience.

Familiarity through Repetition

V.A4.2 *As audience members become more familiar with the content of a message through repetition, they become very skillful in handling that message; and the effects of primacy and recency become less important.*

The law of frequency states that if individuals do something often enough, in the same situation, then that situation alone will eventually trigger that standard response. Repetition serves as a tie between the situation and the response, increasing the chances of the situation arising and the behavior being performed.

In some cases the connection between the message cue and the desired response can be made very easily. In other cases, the message or the response can be more complex. The latter conditions may require greater repetition before the connection is made. Thyne stated that the important aspects of the message will become known through their reappearance. The effects of primacy and recency thus become less important (Thyne, 1963, p. 82).

Stewart studied the effects of repetitive advertising in newspapers for a new product, Chicken Sara Lee, a frozen, prepared, main dish cooked by the Kitchens of Sara Lee, Inc. He tested consumer awareness of the product in relation to repetitive advertising cycles. One advertisement was run weekly, for 20 consecutive weeks. Tests were made after four advertisements appeared and again after eight advertisements. Results showed that after four exposures, the level of consumer awareness was 25 percent. After eight exposures awareness rose to 29 percent. Stewart found the second set of four exposures increased product knowledge. The number of actual product purchasers also continued to rise as a result of the added exposures. Continued exposure maintained a high level of awareness among consumers and maintained a flow of new prospects trying the product for the first time. When the advertising exposure stopped, the women forgot Chicken Sara Lee. In this case, repetitive advertising served a reminder function (Stewart, 1964, pp. 288-293).

Young pointed out, however, that "emphatic presentation, repetition and development of material to a climax, followed by a review at the cost of the session are well-known means of impressing audiences. Repetition, however, follows the law of diminishing returns. Usually not more than three repetitions may be made effectively, but the number will vary with the intelligence of the audience and the nature of the matter presented" (Young, 1956, p. 306).

Constant repetition may cause the audience members to become bored and weary of the advertisement, or they may overlearn it. While boredom is not desirable, overlearning is not necessarily harmful. Overlearning does not have to lead to boredom. When a child learns to do a figure eight in ice skating, he may repeat the figure again and again. After a great deal of repetition, it can be said that the child has overlearned the figure eight. But the child still enjoys skating it, he is not bored by it.

Marketing Examples of Familiarity through Repetition

In the hotel and motel business, a problem for people is making reservations for travel plans. It is too expensive to call ahead and too tedious to write all those letters. To help combat this problem, various organizations provide their toll-free number to call for reservations anywhere in the country. Message repetition has to be used to get the consumers to remember a relatively long number such as 800-325-3535. In a typical television commercial for Sheraton Motor Inns, the number was continuously put on the screen while the number was also being sung to the viewers. For the magazine portion of the campaign, 800-325-3535 was repeated in 2-inch letters across a double-page spread.

Coca-Cola strives for familiarity through repetition by its use of the phrase "It's the real thing." Yet through different executions, the consumer does not become bored. The Pillsbury doughboy has used this same pattern.

Branch stores of major department stores are designed in such a way as to resemble the main store as well as the other branch stores. Thus the consumer easily can recognize the store wherever he shops and will already be familiar with the layout to help speed his shopping.

One-Sided and Two-Sided Arguments

V.A5 *A presentation of both sides of an argument in a message will more readily motivate audience members if they are well informed, or initially opposed to the communicator's position, or familiar with the issue, or likely to be exposed to opposing views. When the audience members are unfamiliar with the issue, or in favor of the issue, or not informed, a one-sided argument is more effective.*

During World War II, Hovland, Lumsdaine, and Sheffield conducted a study to test the effectiveness of one-sided versus two-sided communications. The investigators presented two communications to two groups of 214 soldiers and a control group of 197. The question asked was "Do you expect a short or long war before Japan surrenders?" The first communication presented a 15-minute talk advocating the strengths of Japan and a long war. The second added material that stressed the U.S. advantages and Japanese weaknesses.

The effectiveness of the communication was related to the initial position of the listener. Those who expected a short war were more motivated by the two-sided approach, whereas the men who believed in a long war were more affected by the one-sided argument. The more-educated men were influenced more by the two-sided argument because they sought both sides of the argument. The less-educated men were more influenced by the one-sided presentation (Hovland, Lumsdaine, and Sheffield, 1949, pp. 201-227).

Chu tested one-sided and two-sided arguments in relation to familiarity and found that one-sided arguments were more effective in persuading subjects when they were unfamiliar with the issue. When subjects were familiar with the issue, the two-sided arguments were most effective (Chu, 1967).

An "inoculation" effect has been found when two-sided presentations are used. In an experiment by Lumsdaine and Janis, groups were exposed to counterarguments before restating their final opinions. Those exposed to the counterpropaganda and the two-sided argument were more resistant to the counterpropaganda than the groups that heard the one-sided argument (Lumsdaine and Janis, 1953).

Janis found that the motivation to accept an argument will tend to increase as the recipient becomes aware of the arguments that support the communicator's conclusion. When opposing arguments are not immediately evident to the audience, it is usually under one of the following conditions (Janis, 1957):

1. The individual is initially unfamiliar with the opposing arguments.
2. The individual is unlikely to recall the opposing arguments because of his weak associative connections.
3. The individual is lacking in motivation to recall pertinent material.

If the affirmative argument is presented first, the negative argument can be tolerated. Yet in most communications a bias in the presentation of pro and con arguments exists. "Although the communication may be characterized as two-sided, it does not give a neutral or completely nonpartisan presentation: the pro arguments (those which support the communicator's conclusions) are more frequently and/or more impressively presented than the con arguments (those which refute any of the pro arguments or which introduce further considerations which foster rejection of the communicator's conclusion)" (Janis, 1957, p. 173).

As far as advertising is concerned, the following basic assumptions can be made concerning the use of one-sided and two-sided arguments. An unintelligent audience, or one that has been exposed to a great deal of advertising favoring a competitor's argument, may inadvertently or selectively perceive only or primarily the argument that it is desirable to refute. For such an audience, the message's comparisons may be dramatic, simple, and quickly made, if they are going to be made at all.

Since comparisons with trivial viewpoints have little meaning, the usefulness of comparisons is greatest when the opposing brands have strong images in the consumer mind and when the present brand's superiorities are not generally accepted. Moreover, comparisons in messages should point to competitors' inadequacies, but without disparaging them. Disparagement of competitors in whom members of an audience believe will not endear the disparager to the audience. The implication would be that people have been stupid to have been believing favorable ideas about a competitive product or service. In short, a comparison should be a factual exposition of whatever information bears on the point of comparison, rather than a disparagement of competitive claims.

The type of approach and repetition also affect the choice of using a one-sided or two-sided argument. Sawyer tested the effects of repetition on the refutational and supportive approaches to advertising communication. He found that the effect of refutational appeal significantly interacts with repetition. The refutational approach "expresses or acknowledges an opposing point-of-view and then proceeds to refute that claim," whereas the supportive appeal is "completely positive, ignoring competitive arguments" (Sawyer, 1973).

Adult females watched a description of a futuristic in-home shopping system in which advertisements were shown. A series of slides were then shown 1, 2, 3, 4, 5, and 6 times, either refuting or supporting the advertisements for five products. Five advertisements for competitive products and 14 buffer advertisements also were included. Competitive advertising employed only the 1-sided appeal. Recall of advertisements were tested, as well as brand attitudes, purchase intentions, and brand usages. Coupons were distributed; and the redemption rate served as a measure of advertising effectiveness.

No support was found for a general hypothesis of greater increases in purchase intentions with repetition of the refutational appeal as compared with the supportive appeal. But for certain segments, repetition of refutational appeals apparently was more effective. These situations include: (1) a new product that must overcome some consumer objections; (2) a brand with a low market share where the objective is to refute a a large competitor's claim of superiority; and (3) a high-selling brand able to isolate a segment that is negatively oriented to that brand (Sawyer, 1973, p. 31).

Subjects did not recall more of the competitive claims in an advertisement than they did of the refutation of the claims. But there is a danger of incomplete or negative recall of the refutational appeal. Thus it is important to emphasize equally both the refuting answer and the "attack" in the advertisement.

It is sometimes advantageous for the communicator to present both sides of the argument, but with seeming or apparent disinterest. In this way, the communicator presents facts without explicit conclusions; but the audience will tend to come to a favorable conclusion concerning the communicator's point of view simply because of the implied superiority of the ideas advanced by the communicator.

Marketing Examples of One-Sided and Two-Sided Arguments

Taster's Choice utilized the two-sided presentation of their message in a 2-page magazine advertisement. One page depicted a steaming cup of coffee placed in front of the company's product. The other page showed an empty cup in front of a percolator. The simple message read: "Taster's Choice makes fresh coffee in seconds. Our competition is still boiling." In other words, both possibilities were considered—preparing instant Taster's Choice coffee and preparing perked coffee. The photographic evidence showed the results and left the conclusion—namely, to buy the more convenient instant coffee—up to the reader to decide.

Bromo Seltzer television advertising used a seemingly disinterested consideration of two possibilities—powdered seltzer or effervescent tablet seltzer. The announcer poured two glasses of water; and in the time necessary to add powdered Bromo and drink it, the tablet seltzer is shown still dissolving. The viewer is led to the conclusion that Bromo Seltzer gives faster relief by such visual evidence.

On a more complex level, *Reader's Digest* promoted foreign advertising in their magazine with a message that compared it with *Time* and *Newsweek* on certain important measures of reader coverage, language flexibility, cost savings, and marketing segmentation flexibilities. Figures and facts were presented for all three magazines, with *Reader's Digest* superior in each category. Readers who were considering advertising overseas were led to a favorable opinion of *Reader's Digest* after reading the advertisement.

A one-sided argument in a message normally takes place when there are no other competitive products in the type of usage category. When electric hair-rollers were first introduced, the argument was that this product curled hair faster and could be used at the last minute. There were no more days or nights having to go around in curlers. When it was discovered that the rollers dried the ends of hair and that steam rollers were preferable, a two-sided argument was used.

Explicit and Implicit Conclusions

V.A6 *Explicit conclusions are effective if the message is complex or difficult to understand, or if a wrong conclusion might be drawn by an audience member. Audiences are more motivated or persuaded to act as the communicator desires through the use of implicit conclusions if the message is simple or easy to understand, or if the audience members are ego-involved with the message's subject matter.*

An *explicit conclusion* is one that is stated, while an *implicit conclusion* is implied or unstated.

Hovland and Mandell designed a study to determine how explicit conclusion making affects beliefs when information is presented in mass media. The study tested the change in attitudes effected by the motives of the communicator as determined by the audience, by the intelligence of the audience, and by the general personality traits of the audience. Tests to find the relevance of these variables were given before and after speeches on the subject of devaluation of currency.

The communicator of a taped radio program was introduced to an audience of college students either as a teacher or as an importer. The former was thought to be impartial and trustworthy to the audience, but the latter was intended to seem partial, since he might have something to gain by convincing the audience of his conclusions. The program material was otherwise the same; but one group heard some conclusions at the end, while the others did not.

A comparison of the results for the two versions of the test revealed that there was a significantly higher degree of opinion change in the desired direction for the group that heard the conclusions than for the group that did not hear them (Hovland and Mandell, 1952).

Thistlethwaite, de Haan, and Kamentsky found that the superiority of explicit conclusions was due to a greater comprehension of the intended conclusion. Their subjects were new recruits to the armed forces. Four types of presentations were made: a clear, well-organized speech with an explicit conclusion; the same speech with an implict conclusion; a poorly organized speech with an explicit conclusion; and the same speech with an implicit conclusion. Among the subjects that understood the conclusion equally well, attitude change was no greater when the speaker did not state the intended conclusion than when he did state the conclusion (Thistlethwaite, de Haan, and Kamentsky, 1955).

Since understanding of the intended conclusion is linked to the superiority of explicit statements, it logically follows that explicitness is increasingly effective in complex communications. When the issue presented in a persuasive message is easily understood, the audience will know the advocated position of the message. Therefore, the type of conclusion drawn is not of primary importance (Karlins and Abelson, 1970, p. 11).

However, when the issue is quite involved and the steps in drawing the conclusions from the premises are difficult, the advantages of having the conclusion drawn explicitly may be quite pronounced. The issue used by Hovland and Mandell in the experiment mentioned previously was above average in complexity, and this may account for the superiority of explicit conclusion drawing in their research (Hovland, Janis, and Kelley, 1953, pp. 100-105).

The degree of intelligence or sophistication of audience members concerning the issue presented has been shown to be an important part in the determining of the effectiveness of explicit versus implicit conclusions. Hovland suggested that in an audience composed of highly intelligent individuals, less need may exist to have the implications spelled out. However, with less-intelligent individuals, it is likely that they will be unable to arrive by themselves at the correct conclusion from the premises alone (Hovland, 1951).

Cooper and Diverman, in a study of reactions to an antiprejudice film, found that the implicit message influenced the more-intelligent members but not the less-intelligent members of the audience. They concluded that "by virtue of their implicit form, such messages may well have been actually inaccessible to the less intelligent group" (Cooper and Diverman, 1951, p. 263).

The results of the Thislethwaite, de Haan, and Kamentsky study (previously described) agree with these findings. Their study concluded that "if a person was intelligent enough to draw the intended conclusions for himself during the course of the speech, it made no difference in his attitude whether the conclusion was actually stated or not." Therefore, the statement of the conclusions was of importance to the less-intelligent subjects, while those of higher intelligence grasped the intended conclusions themselves (Karlins and Abelson, 1970, p. 11).

Marketing Examples of Explicit and Implicit Conclusions

A print advertisement for Volvo utilized the explicit conclusion in comparing the Volvo with a Mercedes Benz. The headline asked, "Can you find the $2300 difference?" After comparing various features and finding no difference between the two brands but the price, the conclusion was "One thing Mercedes gives you that Volvo doesn't is that three-pointed star on the hood. But for $2300 you can buy a lot of stars and the moon too."

Pillsbury's use of the name implies that if the product is made by Pillsbury, it has to be good. Crescent dinner rolls may be promoted with "Pillsbury says it best," implying "another high-quality product."

Through selective distribution a manufacturer may use the type of retail outlet to imply high quality. For example, Pierre Cardin ties might only be found at Bonwit Teller. The high-quality fashion store implicitly suggests that the tie is also of high quality and for a fashion pacesetter.

Immediacy

V.A7 *The greater the immediacy of a message, the more likely the audience will be motivated or persuaded to accept it.*

It should be made clear that immediacy does not refer to a state or quality that impels or constrains. Immediacy is not the same thing as urgency. Instead, *immediacy* refers to the degree of intensity and directness of interaction between a speaker and the object about which he speaks. Most immediate statements are judged as indicating a more positive quality of speaker attitude; that is, the more intense and direct the statement by the communicator, the more the audience will infer that the communicator has a positive attitude toward the object. This analysis is based upon work by Mehrabian in which immediacy was viewed as a measure of the communicator's attitude as shown by his choice of words (Mehrabian, 1967).

While empirical evidence substantiates each step in the argument for the effects of immediacy, apparently no research has been conducted to directly link immediacy to acceptance of the message. This relationship can be inferred from various studies, however, as indicated in the following logical arguments:

1. Experiments have shown that the greater the immediacy shown by the communicator in his statements, the more the audience will infer that the communicator has a more positive quality of speaker attitude toward the object of his message.
2. A more credible source is related to a more positive quality of speaker attitude.
3. In general, the evidence is that a credible source produces a significantly greater attitude change than an incredible counterpart.

The reasoning behind this assertion to support the proposition can be diagrammed:

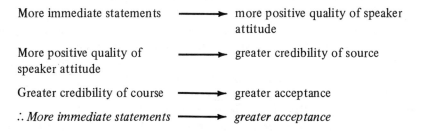

More immediate statements ⟶ more positive quality of speaker attitude

More positive quality of speaker attitude ⟶ greater credibility of source

Greater credibility of course ⟶ greater acceptance

∴ *More immediate statements* ⟶ *greater acceptance*

In his work, Mehrabian presented seven immediacy categories by which an individual's attitude could be analyzed according to the words he employed in his communication. He then conducted an experiment in which identical sentences, with the exception of words that affect the degree of immediacy, were presented to subjects. The subjects were then asked to identify which sentences conveyed a more positive attitude. The experimental results showed that for all immediacy categories considered, the responses on the basis of immediacy criteria could be predicted successfully.

The first step in the argument to support this proposition was substantiated by Mehrabian's initial experiment, conducted to test the extent to which a trained interviewer could infer a communicator's attitudes through his knowledge in immediacy communication. A study in 1968 used the context of the message to clarify the ability of untrained listeners to infer attitudes from the immediacy of statements. Untrained observers consistently interpreted speech immediacy to infer attitudes when provided with information about the degree of speech immediacy appropriate or expected in a given context. Mehrabian concluded that the more immediate the language of the communicator, the more positive quality of speaker attitude will be identifiable (Mehrabian, 1968).

The second step of the argument is that a more-credible source has a more-positive quality of speaker attitude connected with it, and vice versa. This claim can be substantiated by an empirical study conducted to determine the characteristics of communicators that affect a recipient's judgment of the communicator's credibility. A list of characteristics was empirically derived and subjected to a factor analysis in order to assess the adequacy of the model of communicator credibility offered. Although many of the results were not predicted, it was concluded that trustworthiness and expertise were two of the most important characteristics. If an individual is associated with a positive quality of speaker activity—for example, if he is warm and humble—and if his statements have a high degree of intensity and directness through the use of immediacy, he will more likely be believed than if he were thought to have no positive quality because his statements lacked immediacy (Schweitzer and Ginsberg, 1966, pp. 94-101).

The third and final step of the argument to support this proposition relates greater credibility of the source to greater acceptance. Empirical findings suggest that a credible source produces significantly greater attitude change than a noncredible source. In this connection, the theories of Brehm on psychological reactance do not nullify the evidence that supports the credibility-acceptance relationship (Brehm, 1966, pp. 91-119). The discussion of communicator credibility in the following chapter will explain this further.

Thus it can be asserted that the greater the immediacy of the statements by this communicator, the more probable the audience will accept his message. Not only immediacy but also urgency are connected with motivating in accepting a message. If the symbols are so chosen that they convey a sense of immediacy and urgency to an individual of high-need achievement, then he will be more likely to act than if the symbols had not been combined as such.

Marketing Examples of Immediacy

A sale implies the immediacy of a situation. Promotions emphasizing only 15 more days till Christmas also express urgency. Expiration dates on coupons and "limited offer" are other examples of the principle.

In a dress shop it may be mentioned that the shop will not be getting in any more lines of summer clothes; thus, if the customer needs to supplement her wardrobe, she had best do it now.

Itkin Brothers, an office-furniture company, demonstrated the idea of immediacy applied to retailing in their "Sorry Sales." Rather than make up new advertisements to eliminate the listed items that were sold the previous day, the newspaper advertisements that ran on consecutive days, simply crossed the items out to show the reader how the "Sorry Sale" was progressing. This reversed the belief that people can buy what they want when they want it. The last advertisement showed all the items scratched out and the headline "Itkin's Sorry Sale has just ended. Sorry."

Magazines offer price-off coupons in soliciting subscriptions. A limited-offer discount on the subscription price encourages early participation in the offer before it expires.

Prerationalizing

V.A8 A communicator, in proposing a situation about which the audience members are uncertain, can facilitate the motivational and persuasive effect of his message by including reasons to act that audience members will find personally acceptable so that later they may feel their behavior was justified.

Rationalizing refers to justifying an action already taken by providing good or personally acceptable reasons for that action that may differ from the actual reasons. When an individual searches for these reasons before taking a certain action, he is prerationalizing in order to convince himself that he has decided rationally.

Prerationalizing exists and is used only when the consumer already knows and has some ideas about the product. By definition, prerationalizing consists of a personal correlation of data relating to something the individual has already at least a passing acquaintance with. In order for an individual to be stimulated into prerationalization he must first know something about the product or service in question; second, he must be able to understand it; and third, he must be able to relate it to himself or to his unique experience or be able to identify with the product or service.

Implied in this situation is that some conflict exists in any decision for which prerationalizing is needed. If one must prerationalize, he recognizes reasons against taking the future action or his reasons for the action are unacceptable either personally or socially. In a normal decision-making process, the individual usually feels that he can evaluate a situation and rationally make a decision. In a decision where prerationalizing is used, a need or situation starts with a want that already has negative connotations attached to it.

Katona found that certain types of decisions required more than the usual amount of beforehand deliberation. He listed conditions that often call for this "genuine decision making." Among these are expenditures that are considered major and occur fairly rarely, some purchases of new products or first purchases of a product, and awareness of a difference between one's customary behavior and that of the group to which one belongs. It seems like prerationalizing may be occurring in all these situations (Katona, 1964, pp. 289-290).

Sieber and Lanzetta conducted several experiments on subjects placed in decision-making situations. From one study they concluded that decision-making situations typically require that an individual make a selection among alternatives without having sufficient information to make an unequivocal choice. In the face of such uncertainty, the decision maker usually acquired or reorganized information, which was instrumental in reducing uncertainty and response conflict (Seiber and Lanzetta, 1964).

In a later study, Sieber and Lanzetta sought to prove that not only do individuals in uncertain decision-making situations seek further information, but also that the amount of information needed and the amount of forethought that goes into a decision depends on personality traits. They found that those subjects who were able to solve complex problems (seeming to indicate a high level of intelligence) sought more information before making a decision than subjects who were less able to solve complex problems (seeming to indicate a lower level of intelligence). People with simple conceptual structures tended to acquire little prior information to a decision, arrived at a decision rapidly, and gave little or no attention to other choice alternatives (Sieber and Lanzetta, 1966).

Katona and Mueller found that the greatest amount of deliberation and information seeking in connection with a durable-goods purchase occurred among buyers who had a college education, were well under 35 years of age, were white-collar workers, or who liked "shopping around" before making a decision. They also found the conditions surrounding the purchase to be an influence on the need for prerationalizing. The greatest amount of prepurchase information seeking was among people who felt no urgent or immediate need for the product, were considering an expensive or major purchase, were purchasing a type of product for the first time, or had had unsatisfactory experience with a type of product previously (Katona and Mueller, 1955).

It seems a reasonable assumption, then, that consumer buying decisions and actual purchasing can be based on other than truly rational reasons. Because of this, the consumer finds it necessary to create reasons to justify his actions to himself and others, i.e., to rationalize. Thus supplying the consumer with acceptable reasons will encourage him to purchase a product, knowing that he has already created a satisfactory justification for choosing the product, and therefore there is less chance of experiencing undesirable postpurchase anxiety or cognitive dissonance.

Marketing Examples of Prerationalizing

Personal selling can often help a consumer to rationalize a purchase. Brides "to-be" are told that they should choose the very best china and silver because

(1) these are things they will have their entire life and perhaps will even be inherited by future children and grandchildren; (2) they can make those "special occasions" more memorable, such as dinner parties or family Christmas gatherings; (3) quality china and silver add to the "total impression" when doing business entertaining; and (4) although the products are expensive, relatives and friends can buy them for you as wedding presents.

"Cents-off" often provide prerationalizing for buying a product that normally the consumer would consider too expensive. Pantene occasionally has a $2 reduction on its $5 shampoo. In addition, free samples of conditioner and setting lotion are included. The price reduction and free samples are enough incentive to help in overcoming indecisiveness.

Remington Electric Shaver Inc. ran a magazine advertisement that attempted to persuade men that electric shaving was just as personally acceptable as razor shaving. The first picture was a close-up of a frowning man with heavy whiskers. The inside picture showed him smiling, with half of his face cleanly shaved. The copy mentions how the man's son, the "little shaver," had convinced his dad that the electric shaver outshaves the razor. Thus Remington called the "old-fashioned" razor shaving ideas into question without offending, and offered justification for men to try electric shaving.

Loving Care, a hair-coloring product made by Clairol, conducted a long advertising campaign to overcome women's hesitation and doubt over coloring graying hair. One set of print copy asked, "Has your hair aged faster than you have?" It proceeded to point out how Loving Care colored gray hair without changing a woman's natural hair color. The campaign developed from "Hate that gray? Wash it away!" to "You're not getting older, your're getting better." Older women who were unhappy with graying hair could find persuasive reasoning for buying Loving Care in a message that asked, "What would your husband do if suddenly you looked 10 years younger?"

Nonrational Messages

Nonrational communicating is used by a communicator to stimulate emotional more than rational responses from his audience members (Hovland, Janis and Kelley, 1953, p. 58). Varying list of nonrational appeals might be condensed into seven general categories:

1. *Pride and prestige,* as when an individual wishes to command admiration from others because of his purchases.
2. *Emulation,* as when an individual tries to imitate others, especially famous personalities shown in testimonials.
3. *Conformity,* as when individuals try to be in fashion when they buy new clothes.
4. *Individuality,* as when individuals try to gain attention by owning an original or one-of-a-kind.

5. *Comfort,* as when consumers purchase air conditioners.
6. *Pleasure,* as when an individual purchases hobby or sporting equipment or tickets to sporting and amusement events.
7. *Creativeness,* as when an individual seeks to express himself and buys art and craft materials for a do-it-yourself project.

A significant difference between rational and emotional motivating for buying is that emotional motivating is not as likely to be admitted by an individual. If nonrational motivating is not self-approved and socially acceptable, a person probably will not admit buying a product for such reasons. Also, a consumer may not be aware of emotional motivating, and rationalize to himself and others by assigning motives to his behavior that are both rational and socially acceptable (Barksdale, 1964, p. 324).

Hartman compared the relative effects of rational and nonrational appeals in obtaining votes for the Socialist party in Allentown, Pennsylvania in 1935. The Republican and Democratic tickets were fairly evenly divided in the town in terms of support, and the best possible alternative seemed to be the Socialist Party. Five thousand copies of each of two different appeal pamphlets were distributed in two politically "neutral" areas. The rational publication included a number of questions, to be answered "Agree" or "Disagree" by the reader. At the bottom of the list was the statement: "If the number (you have marked) as agreements is larger than the number of disagreements, you are at heart a Socialist."

One such rational question was: "1. We would have much cheaper electric light and power if the industry were owned and operated by various governmental units for the benefit of all the people. Agree—Disagree." The emotional appeal was a hypothetical letter written from a youth to his parents. A portion of the end of the letter read as follows: "We young people are becoming Socialists. We have to be. We can't be honest with ourselves and be anything else."

Following the election, the totals were tabulated and it was found that the highest minority vote was concentrated in the emotional appeal area; the next highest was in the rational area; and the lowest was in the area where no pamphlets were circulated (Hartman, 1936).

It has also been demonstrated that when the audience members have been exposed to prior information on a subject, they are less likely to be affected by nonrational communicating. Lewan and Stotland added this interesting variable to the problem of emotional communicating. Their experiment involved the exposure of 97 twelfth-grade students to certain types of nonrational communicating. The students were first split into two groups. One of the groups received "neutral" information concerning the topic, the other group did not. The two groups were then exposed to the emotional appeals. Using the Likert-type attitude scales (approve, disapprove, strongly approve, strongly disapprove, etc.), it was determined that prior objective information about the topic will tend to make subjects less apt to lower their opinions of the topic after hearing emotional derogatory appeals (Combs and Taylor, 1952).

This is an important aspect of nonrational communicating. It is unlikely that an adult will encounter many subjects during his daily life that will be altogether new to him. More probably, he will have been exposed to some type of prior information. The following principles will further explain different types of nonrational appeals.

Autistic Motivating

V.A9 *A communicator can use autistic motivating in his message to draw the audience members into the communicating process and to motivate them to associate the realities of the message with their own hopes and dreams.*

Autism has been defined as "a tendency in one's thinking or perceiving to be regulated unduly by personal desires or needs at the expense of regulation by objective reality. It entails apprehending the world as closer to one's wishes than it really is" (English and English, 1958, p. 54). When thinking autistically, the individual's thoughts are relatively free of realistic considerations that tend to restrict the mental gratification of unfulfilled wishes and longings.

Autistic thinking is a normal process in everyday life. It serves as an escape from the routine of daily life and from the logical, realistic thinking often demanded by jobs. Undirected daydreaming and other autistic processes of thought serve as relaxation. In addition, autistic thinking often produces creative ideas that can be developed with the use of rational thinking.

Autistic communicating is based on those aspects of imaginative thinking into which an individual can project himself. It establishes an atmosphere of fantasy in which the message's appeals are perceived without the individual applying the constraints of real-world considerations. The communication is fully perceived but not rigidly evaluated by the audience member.

There are no definite rules as to when autistic communicating will be more effective than rational thinking. Its use is not limited to any particular subject matter or audience type.

Marketing Examples of Autistic Motivating

The advertising campaign for Maidenform Bras that was based on the theme "I dreamed I was . . . in my Maidenform Bra" is an example of a successful attempt at autistic communicating. The approach to the product was certainly not logical nor realistic. The woman pictured dreamed that she was in several situations, and audience members were encouraged to accept the situation as a dream rather than as reality.

The Army revised its promotional image to attract young men by emphasizing travel opportunities, job training, and promotion opportunities. Through magazine advertisements, autistic communication was utilized. A photograph of a smiling young man and woman sitting near a fountain in an old-world city invited readers to project themselves into the situation—"Live and work in places tourists only visit."

Whirlpool invited magazine readers to use their imaginations to complete the idea of its message. Underneath a photograph of a window setting and an air conditioner was copy that read: "The temperature in this room is an unbearable 89°. Now watch what happens after we push the Panic Button on the Whirlpool air conditioner in the window." On the following page underneath the same photograph, the advertisement said: "See? A comfortable 74°. Doesn't that feel better!" The reader could imagine the discomfort of a hot room and the relief of a cool room and thus became a participant in the message.

Nondirective Motivating

V.A10 *Nondirective motivating allows the audience members to feel that the views expressed by the communicator are their own. It attempts to eliminate ego-defense mechanisms that can destroy the effectiveness of the communication.*

Directive communicating tells the individual directly what he should believe or do. By contrast, *nondirective communicating* refers to a procedure in which the communicator first establishes an atmosphere of acceptance on the part of the audience and from then on refrains from attempting to direct or influence their behavior. The objective is to have the audience feel that the views being expressed are their own views, and that the views intended by the communicator really were their ideas all along. This is best accomplished when the audience member "carries on" the conversation or discussion, which makes him feel responsible for what is being communicated.

As Hadley wrote of the role of nondirective techniques in advertising: "Instead of telling the person what to buy and giving reasons for it, he can create a friendly, sincere, and understanding atmosphere which shows the benefits of the product to sell. This places the person in a situation where he is able to accept new ideas without threat to his old ideas" (Hadley, 1953, p. 496).

The concept of nondirective motivating and persuading originated from the field of clinical psychology. The therapist was considered to be authoritarian, giving direction to the therapy session and controlling the patient. Rogers discovered the benefits of nondirective psychotherapy. The patient controlled the session, and the therapist would restate or clarify the patient's feelings, not channel these feelings. The patient would come to the therapist to talk out his problems. The therapist stressed the means that would cause the patient to become more conscious of his own attitudes and feelings, with increased insight and self-understanding (Rogers, 1942, p. 123).

The nondirective-communicating approach is patterned after the techniques of psychotherapy. The communicator attempts to build an atmosphere of warmth and friendliness in which audience members will not perceive a direct attack on their opinions. The communicator wants to avoid triggering the audience member's ego-defense mechanisms.

The nondirective method has been proven to be an effective means of fostering behavioral changes. "Evidence suggests that when patients receive high levels of empathy and warmth, there is a significantly more constructive personality and behavioral change than when the patient receives relatively lower levels" (Truax, 1966, p. 1). With audiences that are already familiar with the object of the communication, nondirective messages can function as reminders rather than as initiators of attitude change.

Nondirective techniques have been applied experimentally to classroom teaching with interesting, though often conflicting, results. Experiments in teaching college-level psychology conducted by Faw, Asch, and Cantor generally indicated that learning, as measured by objective tests, was significantly lower for nondirectively taught classes than for conventionally instructed control groups (Faw, 1949; Asch, 1951; and Cantor, 1946).

Two aspects of this research have interesting implications for advertising. First, in all the classroom experiments the majority of nondirectively instructed students reported impressions of the courses that suggested a different type of learning experience from that which resulted from conventional instruction. Students often reported relating course material to their private selves and internalizing psychological concepts—a phenomenon largely absent with conventional instruction.

Second, many of the mature, self-directed individuals achieved much higher levels of learning in nondirectively instructed classes than did individuals with similar personalities and scholastic abilities in the control groups. These results suggest that nondirective techniques of communication have potentially great power, and that their effectiveness could vary radically depending on the personality characteristics of the audience members.

Marketing Examples of Nondirective Motivating

The best example of a communication without the direct intention to sell is that of publicity. Companies or retail outlets participate in community projects or help raise money for charity. For example, the local Pepsi bottling company may sponsor a Little League baseball team in the summer; and a local bank will sell chocolate sundaes for 15 cents during a community garden show.

Retailers may have special open houses with free gifts, refreshments, and entertainment. Here the indirect approach is to get people into the store so they can familiarize themselves with the merchandise as well as enjoy themselves.

Volkswagen ran a promotional campaign that used a nondirective message to promote their cars. Human-interest stories were told about individuals and their satisfied use of VW automobiles. The copy never had to make a direct "sales pitch"–the story alone conveyed the message.

Often promotional advertisements for magazines are directed to potential advertisers but "talk" about the type of people who read the magazine. An advertisement by *Seventeen* magazine pictured a young, attractive woman pensively gazing at the reader; and the message read: "She needs us. She's got all the questions in the world, and all about the world. She has a refreshing sensitivity. A challenging freshness. She's open, positive, and hopeful. She leads the action. We give her confidence. She's America's young woman who needs and reads *Seventeen*."

Anxiety Arousal

V.A11 *Appeals that incite anxiety are motivational and persuasive to the extent that they arouse avoidance responses, but the audience will reject a message in which the appeals are too strong or do not relieve the anxiety aroused.*

English and English (1958) define *anxiety* as "an unpleasant emotional state in which a present and continuously strong desire or drive seems to miss its goal." This state may also be characterized by "a continuous fear of low intensity." A general state of apprehensiveness may occur in an individual without objective justification or cause. Anxiety may be a general drive state, while the anticipation of pain or injury is more indicative of a fear response to a threat.

It is necessary to differentiate threats from anxiety, although many of the psychological experiments cited in this section use the term *threat appeal.* In this connection, see the discussion in the part on learning that deals with negative reinforcement and threat appeals.

A *threat* is a verbal, gestural, or other symbolic expression of intent to injure an individual. In everyday communication, attempts to motivate are not threatening, but they are more likely to merely raise doubts about a subject that is relevant to the audience and thus cause anxiety. The communicator can hardly be considered as a threatening menace. In speaking of appealing to the audience, *appeals* are those communications that arouse emotions or motives in the audience members.

Short-circuit appeals are based upon currently established motives, and long-circuit appeals use reasoning and seek to build up a new motive for action. Strong appeals are intended to challenge the audience's beliefs, to have a high degree of relevance, to arouse interest, to create opinions to be held for a long period of time, to encourage ego involvement, to suggest immediacy, and to suggest that the situation *could* become threatening. Weak appeals may be relevant to the audience, but they do not become so involved or emotionally affected by them.

Hovland, Janis, and Kelley defined *threat appeals,* or what are herein called *anxiety-arousing appeals,* as "those contents of persuasive communication which allude to or describe unfavorable consequences that are alleged to follow from failure to adopt and adhere to the communicator's conclusions" (Hovland, Janis and Kelley, 1953, p. 60). Such an appeal arouses anxiety or concern; but if the emotional intensity reaches a point of fear, the message begins to lose its effectiveness for the audience. The effectiveness of an anxiety-arousing appeal depends upon the intensity of the threat, source credibility, personality factors, prior exposure, and interest value of the message. It is also related to the probability of the dangerous event materializing and to the anticipated magnitude of the damage. The audience takes into consideration the anticipated protection that the communicator's solution will give versus the cost of adopting alternative means of relieving the stressful situation.

In an anxiety-arousing situation the audience is put into a more reactive state than in a situation that is not stressful, and they feel more pressure to restore cognitive balance. It is difficult to define a general stress situation common to all individuals. Differences in memory, for example, yield different responses. Effects depend upon individual cognition and motivational states. Smock has found that individuals placed in stressful situations are quicker to categorize ambiguous stimuli than are more-relaxed subjects. Such a situation includes an increased desire for understanding; for if the audience is informed, it can then react to the stimuli (Smock, 1955).

An anxiety-arousing situation and the individual's responses to it differ when the individual is by himself and when he is in a group. Wrightsman manipulated experimentally the amount of anxiety and fear induced in his subjects while they waited together for an injection. They were told the purpose was to test the immediate effects of change in glucose level. One of the findings of the study was that the subjects tended to change their degree of anxiety in the direction of a closer correspondence with the anxiety felt by other members of their group (Wrightsman, 1960).

Marketing Examples of Anxiety Arousal

A manufacturer may compare the safety of his package to that of a competitor. A producer of canned hams may point out that his cans can be opened by a household can opener instead of by a key device. Thus the sharp edges of the can with a key and lots of cut fingers can be avoided.

Another package concept is the self-injecting razor blade, which is untouched by human hands. The slot on the back of the blade container also relieves the anxiety of having loose used blades around, still able to hurt an unexpecting person.

The Better Vision Institute conducted a campaign that utilized anxiety arousal to motivate readers to have their eyes examined. The reader was invited to imagine the condition of blindness. A print advertisement showed photographs depicting the five senses and asked, "Have you ever thought of which one of your senses would be worst to lose?" The picture of an eye looking straight at the reader was meant to startle and direct him to have an eye examination.

Weak Anxiety Appeals

V.A11.1 *A weak anxiety appeal is more effective than a strong one when the communicator cannot solve the problem presented completely and can rely on the audience to complete the message as they desire, when the situation requires that the audience remember more of the message, or when the appeal challenges the audience's self-esteem.*

When the recommendation in a message cannot solve the anxiety-arousing situation, a weak appeal is more effective than a strong one in reducing the possibility of the audience's rejecting the message. For example, DeWolfe and Governale conducted an experiment in 1964 using nurses who were working with tuberculosis patients. The nurses were divided into three groups and exposed to various levels of anxiety-arousing communication. The experimenters found that maximum persuasive results could be attained by presenting effective moderate fear appeals or by presenting high fear level communications and subsequent alternatives for avoiding the realization of the threat. If the recommendation is not capable of reducing the threat, then the minimal threat is more effective to avoid defensive behavior. In this case, the nurses were told of the chances they were taking and then were told ways to avoid undue exposure to the disease (DeWolfe and Governale, 1964).

Lending support to a weak appeal is the concept of mental completing. This idea suggests that a communication is more likely to be effective if the audience is not given all the information pertaining to the topic but rather is given the opportunity to complete the idea by supplying details. The audience member usually learns and remembers more as he becomes involved in the communication, and the message arouses less cognitive dissonance as the discrepant variables can be omitted or altered. However, the stronger the anxiety-arousing appeal, the more specific the recommendation ought to be. In this connection, consider the discussion on *mental completing* in chapter 22.

Leventhal and Niles conducted a study in which they presented material to smokers and nonsmokers. The weak-fear group watched a sound and color movie depicting certain statistical links with smoking and lung cancer. The moderate-fear group watched the same movie plus a feature film in which a young man hears from his doctor that he has cancer and has to have an operation. This movie ends before the man goes into surgery. The strong-fear group watched everything the moderate group had seen, plus the actual operation on the young man. Following each presentation, all groups were urged to stop smoking. Among the results of the experiment, it was discovered, with the aid of pretesting, that certain subjects were more highly sensitized toward the topic and demonstrated more involvement in the presentations. Further, they found that what was termed the *denial-oriented people* demonstrated little effect. Finally, the experimenters discovered that the strong-fear group began a problem-solving process. Subsequently, they took less chest X-rays than other groups but had a higher quitting rate in smoking habits (Leventhal and Niles, 1964, pp. 459-479).

Jones and Gerard interpreted these results as meaning that the subjects who received strong fear-arousing messages saw X-rays as more tension-producing than smoking. They viewed X-rays almost as a cause of cancer. Thus the arousal of anxiety may be categorically misindexed by the audience when a strong appeal is used (Jones and Gerard, 1967, p. 464).

In situations in which substantial anxiety has been aroused concerning the audience's self-identity, they will attempt to compensate or minimize their feelings of inferiority. This usually results in defensive behavior. The results of a study by Kay and Meyer indicated that a manager's attempts to assist a subordinate by pointing out improvement needs were likely to be perceived by the subordinate as threatening to his self-esteem and to result in defensive behavior. The greater the threat, the less favorable the attitude toward the appraisal system is likely to be, and the less the subsequent constructive improvement in job performance is likely to be realized (Kay and Meyer, 1965). Thus strong anxiety-arousing appeals that question the audience's self-esteem will be rejected. The strength of an anxiety-arousing appeal should be judged by what aspect of the audience members' lives will be affected by the arousal.

The audience member often will be more reactive to anxiety-arousing situations that affect people around him more than himself. The challenge to a belief that is of high significance to him can cause more reaction than a challenge of a belief of little importance. Changing one habit is also not as significant as changing a cluster of habits. An extremely crucial area is the ego or self-image. A very strong appeal could result in immediate rejection or defensive behavior. The basic issues in all these areas are relevance and immediacy. What the individual values most and how closely he sees the anxiety to be will determine his evaluation. As intensity of feeling varies, so must the strength of the appeal according to the situation.

Marketing Examples of Weak Anxiety Appeals

Remington ran a 2-page print advertisement for their instant hair curler that utilized a weak anxiety appeal. The first page showed a photograph of a woman wearing a headful of curlers and a hair net; and the headline read, "Spend less time ugly," in big, bold letters. In its challenge to their self-esteem, the message could get female readers to attend to the advertisement. By reading the copy on the adjoining page, they could find the resolution of this anxiety in the benefits of the Lady Remington Hair Curler.

Certain kinds of businesses develop to handle emergency situations. "One-Hour Martinizing" provides fast cleaning needs that often come up at the last minute and that can be somewhat anxiety arousing.

Food manufacturers have used brand names in such a way as to ensure quality, or at least a consistent level of quality. And at the other end of the scale are off-brands, which national brands imply are not dependable. Thus the anxiety that one might serve unappealing food tends to be relieved.

Strong Anxiety Appeals

V.A11.2 *A strong anxiety appeal is more effective than a weak appeal when the communicator presents a solution to the problem in his message, when the topic is either highly relevant to the audience or one with which they are unfamiliar, or when the communicator is considered to be a highly credible source.*

For the strong appeal to be effective, its recommendation must clearly be able to relieve or avoid anxiety, for increasing the intensity of the emotional arousal also increases the possibility of cognitive imbalance. If the message offers no reassurance that the audience could prevent the anxiety-arousing situation, a defensive-avoidance reaction would develop with a rejection message in order to restore cognitive balance. "These conditions may occur when the recommendation is irrelevant to the threat, impossible to carry out, or can only partially avert the threat with many loopholes" (Lindzey and Aronson, 1969, p. 91). It will result in inattentiveness to the recommendations or defensive behavior.

DeWolfe and Governale found that much anxiety was related to attitude change in their study of TB innoculations. The relevance of the threat was the variable in this case. Presumably, because of the occupation and their hospital environment, the nurses were more aware of the consequences as well as being aware of the urgency of the issue (DeWolfe and Governale, 1964). Thus, if the audience is made aware of the immediacy and relevance of a threat to them, a strong appeal is a more effective communicator.

An anxiety-arousing situation is less motivating when the audience is unfamiliar with or lacks interest in the topic; thus a strong appeal is more effective than a weak appeal in persuading the audience members to act. For example, in a 1960 study of automobile accidents and the safety belt, Berkowitz and Cottingham found that a strong appeal is more convincing than a weak one when the communication is low in interest value. The strong appeal had to be shown to be highly relevant to the audience, and then a higher degree of audience acceptance occurred. Also, because of high audience involvement, they became more disturbed as the issue grew in significance to them (Berkowitz and Cottingham, 1960).

Hewgill and Miller conducted interviews regarding information that their subjects had received concerning fallout shelters. It was shown that a strong appeal can be more effective than a weak one in a situation in which the communicator has high credibility for the audience (Hewgill and Miller, 1965). Credibility will be discussed further in the next chapter.

Marketing Examples of Strong Anxiety Appeals

The use, once again, of a package concept may arouse strong anxiety. An advertiser may show a child who has climbed up to the medicine cabinet and is playing with pills. The advertiser then can show his hard-to-open bottle, which needs both pressure and a twist at the same time to open—something a child would not be able to do. The issue is highly relevant.

Manufacturers of foldup aluminum fire-escape ladders show a burning house with no way of escape. Yet if the ladder is purchased, this threat of death is relieved. Lock companies also capitalize on the threat of burglary. A nighttime picture of a man picking a lock on the front door while a family is sleeping is anxiety arousing. A picture of a family returning from a vacation, only to find their valuable possessions gone, illustrates the principle as well.

Companies may use public-service messages. For example, lock manufacturers may send out promotional pamphlets on what to do if you are planning to take a long vacation—for example, notify the police, have neighbors watch the house, cut off newspapers so that they will not pile up in front of the door, and so on.

Resistance to Anxiety

V.A11.3 *The audience's continuous exposing to an anxiety-arousing situation reduces their emotional reactions to subsequent appeals on the subject.*

Except in the condition of high relevance or immediacy, after several encounters with an anxiety situation, audience members have become bored with the repetition, have built up their defenses to the message, or have resolved the anxiety and have no interest left on the subject.

Through repetition, audiences become accustomed to the anxiety, enabling greater emotional adaptation to the arousal situation. Gladstone hypothesized that such preparatory communications produce some degree of "emotional inoculation" to future threat appeals. Audiences become satiated on the subject. The results of this study indicated that less anxiety was aroused by gradual rather than impulse awareness to the possible discomfort. The audience had time to rehearse their reactions to actual dangers or threats, and some degree of insecurity motivated them to comply with the recommendation before the danger actually materialized (Janis, Lumsdaine, and Gladstone, 1951).

Allyn and Festinger divided high-school students into two groups who heard communications on the issue of the driving age. Half the students were forewarned of the topic. The other group was told only that they would hear a speech but to pay careful attention because they would be questioned about the speaker's personality. The results were that in the forewarned condition the students were relatively uninfluenced by the speaker; they rejected him more than in the "personality conditions," in which instance the speaker did influence their attitudes (Festinger and Maccoby, 1964).

Kirscht and Haefner also concluded that the experience of a series of threatening messages has cumulative effects on the arousal of fear and the appraisal of a threat contained in the messages. They also found that anxiety arousal was facilitated rather than inhibited by a series of messages when vulnerability to a health threat was the subject of the messages. Thus, if the anxiety-arousing situation is highly relevant to the audience and an adequate resolution is presented, a series of messages will make the situation more immediate (Kirscht and Haefner, 1969).

Marketing Examples of Resistance to Anxiety

Vantage cigarettes capitalized on the defenses that smokers had built up against the anticigarette promotions and against the warning label the government had ordered cigarette companies to include on the package. Vantage realized that more than ever people were trying to resist any anxiety created by the antismoking critics. Vantage's cigarette could offer "the lowest 'tar' and nicotine cigarette a smoker will enjoy smoking." To get smokers to attend to Vantage cigarettes, the headline sympathized with people: "Instead of telling us not to smoke, maybe they should tell us what to smoke."

In certain cases a series of messages may increase anxiety rather than reducing it. The American Cancer Society frequently publishes a list of danger signals of cancer. It attempts to relieve high anxiety over the issue by mentioning that if caught in time, a person's life can be saved. Yet the threat has not been reduced because people have been made more aware of the disease and the number of lives lost each year because of it.

Distraction

Unless audience members are highly involved with a message or views it with high credibility, they will more easily be motivated or persuaded in an environment of distractions because they cannot concentrate to formulate strong counterarguments.

The theory of distraction and its relation to the persuasibility of a message was first proposed by Festinger and Maccoby in a study conducted in 1964. The experiment involved implicit persuasion, exemplifying the effectiveness of environmental distraction as a technique of the implicit approach to changing attitudes.

Teenage subjects were divided into two groups. Half the subjects received written instructions that they were to hear a speech against teenage driving and that they would be asked about the speaker's opinions. This was termed the "forewarned condition." The other half received instructions that they would merely hear a speaker and later would be questioned regarding his personality. The results revealed that students who had been forewarned tended to reject the speaker and be less influenced by his arguments than the other group of students in the "personality condition," whose attitudes were significantly influenced by the speaker's communication. Festinger and Maccoby analyze this outcome in the following way:

A good deal of their attention was focused on a task which had little to do with the persuasive communication itself. It may be that, under such circumstances, they still listen to, and hear, the content of the speech that is being delivered but, with a good deal of their attention focused on something irrelevant, they are less able to counterargue while they are listening. [Festinger and Maccoby, 1964, p. 360.]

Lundy, Simonson, and Landers showed the effectiveness of the distraction principle in relation to fear appeals. They proposed that the relevancy of fear, that is, the feelings of fear aroused relative to the content of the persuasive communication, is inversely proportional to the persuasibility of the communication. (Lundy, Simonson, and Landers, 1967).

Distraction alone is not sufficient to increase the effectiveness of a message. The involvement of the audience member and the credibility of the communicator are important variables.

A study by Kiesler and Mathog related these variables to distraction. Two groups of subjects were exposed to four counterattitudinal communications. The amount of interference during the communication and the communicator credibility were altered among the communications. Communicator credibility was altered by information provided prior to the communication—groups were told that the communicator was either a parking lot attendant or a professor with an M.B.A. from Yale. One group of subjects also was told to copy a list of two-digit numbers while listening to two of the speeches. After the communications were heard, the subjects filled out a questionnaire concerning the communicator and were given memory tests concerning the communications.

Kiesler and Mathog found that distraction was most effective when the audience members were very involved with the message and the communicator had high credibility. Distraction served to stop the subjects from forming counterarguments. When the communicator had high credibility, the subjects accepted his arguments. If the communicator was not considered credible and the subjects were not involved with the message, distraction was found to negate the effects of the message and the subjects dismissed both the communicator and the message (Kiesler and Mathog, 1968).

The distraction theory can have either internal or external applications in advertising. *External distractions* are outside activities that affect the audience members at the time they are exposed to an advertisement. The advertiser has no control over this type of distraction. *Internal distraction* can be controlled by the advertiser and can have either positive or negative effects on the audience. Many of the internal distractions have negative effects, which Rosser Reeves has called "vampire claims" and "vampire video." "These vampires, these distraction claims, in other words, feed on the blood of the major claim, weakening it and sapping its strength" (Reeves, 1961, p. 101). Girls in brief bathing suits appearing in a furnace advertisement or an entertainer who draws more attention to himself than to the product he is describing are both forms of vampire video. (See also the discussion of distraction in chapter 21.)

Marketing Examples of Distraction

A person who is concentrating intently on the rush-hour traffic as he drives his car is less likely to attend to a radio commercial or billboard promotion, or be motivated by them, than would a person driving when there is little traffic.

Radio messages often have internal distractions that prevent effective communication. On "rock" stations commercials sometimes are in the background of the rock music, so the listeners become more interested in the music than the message—they sometimes even have a hard time hearing the message.

Perhaps Alka Seltzer had too much distraction in its slice-of-life commercials with the memorable message "I can't believe I ate the whole thing!"—instead of emphasizing the product and its attributes.

27 Message and Medium Variables: Credibility

Credibility

The word *credibility* refers (1) either to the compatibility of a statement with known facts or (2) to the degree of reliance upon the reputation of the individual making a statement or (3) to both. In motivating and persuading, a combination of high-communication credibility and of high-source credibility is of great importance. In other words, the persuasiveness of a communication is a function of both: (1) the credibility of the communication itself—that is, the extent to which the content of the communication agrees with what a hearer or reader knows or believes to be true; and (2) the credibility of the source of the communication—that is, the trustworthiness and expertness of the source as perceived by a hearer or reader. The trustworthiness dimension refers to the degree of confidence in the communicator's intent to communicate the assertions he considers most valid (Hovland, Janis, and Kelley, 1953).

A communication that concurs with an individual's prior beliefs and attitudes is seen as credible despite the credibility of the communicator. However, the degree of credibility of a communication, especially one inconsistent with an individual's beliefs-attitudes-opinions, increases with greater source credibility. For instance, the communication itself may not agree with the prior beliefs-attitudes-opinions of the individual; it may cause cognitive dissonance or "psychological discomfort" for him. Because he is motivated to reduce this discomfort, the individual usually finds it easier to reject this contrary communication. However, if the communicator has considerable credibility, that is, if he is considered highly reputable and trustworthy, it may be easier to accept than to reject the communication and thus reduce dissonance by altering the audience member's beliefs-attitudes-opinions.

The effectiveness of this process may be determined by the extent to which the communication conflicts with an individual's prior beliefs-attitudes-opinions. Beyond a certain point of discrepancy between one's prior views and that of the communication, it becomes easier to reject than to accept the communication, regardless of the source's credibility. This critical point at which it becomes easier to reject the high-source credibility communication depends upon the relative importance to the individual of his own beliefs-attitudes-opinions.

However, the preceding effects actually vary over time. After a length of time during which the individual is not exposed to a communication, even a communication from a high-credibility source loses some of its credibility. But the communication originally presented by a low-credibility source increases in communication credibility over time if the individual originally agreed with the communication.

If members of an audience find a message unbelievable, they will not be motivated or persuaded by it, and the communicating process will cease. It is therefore important for a communicator to know the credibility of his messages for his audience members.

In a 1971 study of the believability of 17 advertising claims, it was found that a minority of a sample of 2629 respondents found any of the slogans to be completely true. The most believable slogan was Alcoa's "Today, Aluminum is something else," which scored completely true with 47 percent of the respondents and partly true with 36 percent. Believability scores fell to a low of 11 percent of the sample who found TWA's "For years the U.S. coach passenger has helped pay our bills. Now we pay you back" to be completely true, while 40 percent rated it as partly true (R.H. Bruskin Associates, 1971). The following are propositions designed to help a communicator improve the believability of his messages.

Fairness of Presentation

V.A13 *The more fair the members of the audience perceive the communicator to be in the presentation of his message, the more they will be motivated to agree with the position advocated by the communication. The less fair the communicator seems, the less agreement he is likely to induce.*

The audience's perceiving of a communication as biased in its presentation has been found to affect its acceptance adversely but has little effect on the learning of the message's content. In this regard, Kelman and Hovland conducted an experiment in which different groups of high school students were asked to listen to a communication advocating extreme leniency in the treatment of juvenile delinquents. The same message was given three times, with the speaker being identified in different roles, ranging from one of low to high credibility. The subjects viewed the high-credibility source as more fair and trustworthy than the low-credibility source every time, even though the messages were identical. On the basis of these results, Hovland and Kelman suggested that attitudes toward fairness and trustworthiness played a greater role in determining credibility than did attributes related to expertness (Kelman and Hovland, 1953). Cohen expanded this proposition by contending that fairness may well be the most important element in a communicator's makeup (Cohen, 1964).

The perceived trustworthiness of the medium also affects the audiences' belief of the messages carried therein. Experiments in media comparisons have demonstrated that the process of persuasion is modified by the channel that delivers the message. A study by Westley and Severin of the degree of trust or credibility placed in each of the mass media revealed the following (Westley and Severin, 1964):

Those who are socially mobile trust newspapers the most.

Those whose party identification is the strongest trust newspapers the least.

Those who consider themselves (and are by objective indices) middle class trust newspapers the most; those who are working class trust television the most.

Those of the highest education trust newspapers the most.

Those who are isolated socially trust newspapers the least.

Marketing Examples of Fairness of Presentation

Certain celebrities have a reputation for endorsing products that perform well. Thus spokesmen such as Arthur Godfrey and Art Linkletter have high trust and high credibility. For years Chet Huntley was known as a trustworthy newsman, and so he had great credibility as a spokesman in commercials, too.

Opinionated Statements

V.A13.1 *If a source initially was perceived as trustworthy by audience members, a message containing opinionated statements will result in a greater favorable-attitude change than a nonopinionated communication. But if a source initially was perceived as untrustworthy, a nonopinionated message will result in a greater favorable-attitude change than an opinionated communication.*

This proposition was originally stated as the findings of studies by Miller and Baseheart (1969). However, studies by Mehrley and McCroskey confirmed Miller and Baseheart's findings. Mehrley and McCroskey determined that opinionated statements convey two kinds of information: the communicator attitude toward an idea or a belief and his attitude toward those who agree or disagree with him. Their study also indicated that when a receiver holds an initially neutral attitude toward a topic, a message containing opinionated-rejection statements (for example, "Only a warmonger would oppose the withdrawal of U.S. troops from Vietnam") results in greater favorable-attitude change than a message containing nonopinionated statements. By contrast, when the receiver initially holds an intense attitude toward the topic, a discrepant message containing nonopinionated statements results in greater favorable-attitude change and higher post-communication credibility ratings than a message containing opinionated-rejection statements (Mehrley and McCroskey, 1970).

Marketing Examples of Opinionated Statements

Most of advertising is fairly well regulated regarding what may and may not be said; wording is limited to nonopinionated statements. However, advertisements do make use of implied opinionated statements. One example of this is, "If it doesn't have 'V-8', it's not a Bloody Merrier."

The most effective examples of the use of opinionated statements are political campaign speeches. In the early 1970s, champions of this kind of rhetoric were Vice President Agnew and Governor George Wallace. However, great caution should be exercised in using opinionated statements. The communicator must be certain to know the initial attitudes of his prospective audience and to use the technique that is most appropriate for the audience. Opinionated statements can also have a very strong negative effect on the credibility of the communicator; and it would be best for most marketers not to offend audiences by using such statements.

Expertness of the Communicator

IV.A14 *The more expert the communicator is perceived to be by the members of the audience, the more likely he will be to motivate and persuade them to agree with his message. However, no amount of "expertise" will suffice if the communicator is not viewed as trustworthy by the audience members.*

The question of expertness is related to trustworthiness in that all the expertness in the world makes no difference if the audience views the speaker as untrustworthy.

Hovland and Weiss presented messages concerning topical issues to their subjects in one experiment. Each message was identical; but in one case the message was attributed to a "high-expert" source and the other was attributed to a source of "low expertness." The audience rated the message from the high source as being more factually justifiable, and it was found to produce more attitude change than the low-expert message (Hovland and Weiss, 1951-1952).

Bauer found that audience members who are exposed to a very complex problem contained in a message from a communicator whom they perceived to be both competent and trustworthy will be likely to accept that source's message without really examining it. However, they might later be very susceptible to counterarguments because they did not really study the problem but merely relied on the source's reputation. But audience members who are exposed to important problems from a source they perceive to be highly competent, but not necessarily trustworthy, will consider their decision on the subject carefully. Such active deciding led to later inoculation against counter-arguments because the audience members were involved in the decision making, had more of a stake in their position on the subject, and had internalized more relevant information (Bauer, 1967).

Thus it becomes clear that competence (expertness) alone will not make a communicator credible. His audience must also trust him; that is, they must believe that he is sharing all the information that he has and is presenting it fairly to them.

Expertness must "take a back seat" to trustworthiness. If the choice is between the communicator who is expert or the communicator who is trustworthy, members of an audience will more likely find the trustworthy communicator more credible. But it is true that the more expert a communicator is perceived to be, the more he will be factually justifiable.

Marketing Examples of Expertness of the Communicator

Frequently marketers refer to their expertness in their particular trade or industry. For instance, some restaurants emphasize the experience of their *maitre d'hotel* in their advertising. They may point out, for example, that he has been selecting menus for more than 20 years in the finest restaurants around the world, thus hoping to enhance the quality image of the restaurant.

Perceived Intent of the Communicator

V.A15 *Regardless of his expertness, a communicator who is perceived as intending to influence his audience in his favor will be perceived as less trustworthy than one who is not perceived as attempting to do so.*

In experiments by Walster and Festinger subjects were exposed to groups discussing topics of relevance to themselves. For one group, subjects were told that those in the discussion were aware that they were being overheard, whereas the other discussion group was unaware that they were being overheard. In subsequent tests involving the subject matter discussed by the groups, subjects were tested for changes in opinions from those expressed prior to the experiment. It was found in both tests that subjects who were told that those in the discussion group were not aware they were being listened to took positions closer to those expressed in the discussion than did subjects for whom those discussing knew they were being overheard. The point is that the person in the aware state is less effective because he is perceived as having an "axe to grind," that is, a point to prove (Walster and Festinger, 1962).

Festinger and Maccoby also concluded that attitude change increases with a reduced ascribing to the communicator of an intent to influence. In an experiment involving a communication against fraternities, they found attitude change to be greater when the communication was accompanied by an irrelevant film on abstract art than when it served as the sound track for an antifraternity film (Festinger and Maccoby, 1964).

In a later experiment the findings of Festinger and Maccoby were replicated. In each of two experiments with college students, Janis, Kaye, and Kirschner found more opinion change from the students if they were given a snack of peanuts and Pepsi while reading a series of persuasive communications than if they were given no food while reading. These opinions cannot be attributed to gratitude to the experimenter since he disassociated himself from the position taken in the message (Janis, Kaye, and Kirschner, 1965).

Weiss and Fine presented evidence that the perceiving of propagandistic intent is not as closely related to the effectiveness of a communication as is perceived fairness of presentation. Congruency between response predispositions of the audience members and the communication appeals was found to be the primary criterion for judgment of fairness and, therefore, for communication effectiveness. Aggression-aroused individuals were found to be more influenced by a punitively oriented communication and less influenced by a leniency-oriented one than were nonaggressive individuals. This was so because aggressive individuals tended to view the communication as more fairly presented, with the opposite being true for the nonaggressive subjects (Weiss and Fine, 1955). Weiss later pointed out that all communications can be considered as coming from a biased source (Weiss, 1956).

Mills and Aronson presented evidence that seems to conflict with the findings of Walster and Festinger. They suggested that an overt, frankly stated desire to influence actually enhances the effectiveness of an *attractive* communicator but that when the communicator is *unattractive,* his stated intention to persuade has no apparent influence on his effectiveness (Mills and Aronson, 1965).

In the Walster and Festinger experiment on the effectiveness of overheard conversations (mentioned previously), it turned out that those who participated in the overheard conversations rated their communicators as more highly credible than those in the regular situation (Walster and Festinger, 1962). Brehm suggested that this finding may be explained by a theory of psychological reactance. According to this theory, an individual has a set of behaviors, any one of which he is free to engage in at any time he wishes. If at some time an individual's free behaviors are threatened or reduced, he will be motivationally aroused to regain any freedom he has lost and to prevent any more freedom from being taken from him. As may be expected, an individual's psychological reactance, or this motivational arousal, will vary directly with the importance of the particular behavior to him, how much freedom is threatened, and how strong the threat is perceived to be (Brehm, 1966). Thus the greater persuasive effect of overhead conversations can be explained by applying this theory. At any time an individual must feel free to behave and think as he pleases. If the audience member perceives that the communicator is trying to influence him in a certain direction, he will feel that his freedom is being threatened and will experience reactance.

Walster, Aronson, and Abrahams reached the conclusion that any communicator, regardless of his prestige, will be seen as more credible when he is arguing for a position opposed to his own best interest. This is so because the communicator is perceived as more expert, more honest, and more influential when doing so. In two separate experiments, junior high school students were divided into two groups. One was presented with booklets containing a news story in which the communicator was advocating a position of benefit to himself. In the other group's booklets, the communicator advocated a position that was obviously directly opposed to his own best interests. Pretests and posttests measured students' attitudes on the subject of the story before and after reading it. Answers to the posttests were scored as they changed in favor of or against the view expressed.

Results indicated that a communicator is more effective when his views on reforms are seen as being opposed to his own best interests. For example, when the topic was whether the court should have more or less power, the criminal was more effective in changing attitudes when he argued for more court power and thus against his best interests than when he was against court power. However, contrary to the Walster et al. findings, the prosecutor, a more prestigious communicator, was almost equally effective whichever way he argued (Walster, Aronson, and Abrahams, 1966).

Thus an indication was found of an interaction between prestige and self-interest, whereby the low-prestige source gained in effectiveness by arguing against his own interests and a high-prestige source could argue in any direction where no difference was found. Walster and her associates did not accept this interaction interpretation in their own studies, claiming that the results with their high school students in this experiment may have been the result of their being more familiar with arguments for strong courts than with arguments against them. And in the second experiment, with a prosecutor and a criminal from the supposedly less-familiar Portuguese court system, the predicted "regardless of his prestige" argument was upheld. However, using this unfamiliar court system, it is uncertain as to whether the students perceived differences in prestige between the criminal and prosecutor.

To remove doubt about the prestige factor, Stone and Eswara tested 168 undergraduate students in a radio-television course. Using the topic of free press-fair trial in courtroom television, they manipulated the variables of self-interest, expertness, and likability of the communication source in a much more carefully regulated study than Walster and her associates. The results of the study replicated the findings that an unlikable source enhanced his own effectiveness in attitude change by arguing against his own best interests, but such was not the case for the likable source (Stone and Eswara, 1969).

As for the variable of expertness and prestige of the communicator, this study did not conclusively demonstrate whether expertness affected ability to persuade. However, one thing was clear: a likeable source is not always more effective in changing attitudes than an unlikable source. If the choice is between likable and unlikable sources who argue against their best interests, the unlikable one is much more effective and does at least bolster the Walster hypothesis that a low-prestige source may be even more effective than a high-prestige communicator.

Marketing Examples of Perceived Intent of the Communicator

Marketers use testimonials to increase the credibility of their messages. It seems that the most effective testimonials are those involving a spokesperson who is perceived as having nothing to gain from his or her testimony.

Perhaps the most credible testimonials of all times were those of Mrs. Eleanor Roosevelt for Good Luck Margarine and past Secretary of the Interior Stuart Udall (highly prestigious regarding the pollution issue) for Sears no-phosphate detergent during the height of the phosphate water pollution issue in 1971. Members of the audience knew that both individuals were sending their fees for doing the commercials to charity, and it was difficult for most people at that time to believe that a President's wife or a former Secretary of the Interior would be personally rewarded for their testimonials.

Personality and Physical Aspects of the Communicator

V.A16 *Certain personality characteristics and physical aspects of the communicator may interact with more objective characteristics to either increase or decrease the chance of the audience members being motivated and persuaded by the message.*

Human beings do not always behave as totally rational beings. Some aspects of the communicator that bear no objective relevance to the topic of the communication can influence communicator credibility as much as relevant aspects of credibility.

Affective or evaluative attitudes often are significant in the interpretation of a communicator's response. Judgments can be based on vocal and nonverbal stimuli. Mehrabian and Wiener sought to discover the ways in which the two variables of tone of voice and actual message content of spoken communication influence the interpretation of the message by its recipient. An inconsistent communication of attitude was expressed in these two components of a message. Positive, neutral, or negative attitudes communicated in single-word contents were each combined with positive, neutral, and negative tones of voice. It was found that variability of inferences by audience members about communicator attitudes was due mainly to variations in tone of voice alone (Mehrabian and Wiener, 1967).

Verbal behavior of the communicator is related to the kinds of inferences observers make about the communicator's feelings. Mehrabian and Wiener, in an earlier experiment, tested immediacy (intensity of interaction between a communicator and the object he communicates about in a verbal message) and showed that this is more significantly associated with the credibility of communications about negative events than otherwise (Mehrabian and Wiener, 1966).

Additional evidence for the personality principle occurs in the work by Schweitzer and Ginsburg, who built a model describing communicator characteristics and their relative effects on communicator credibility. They empirically derived a list of characteristics of people perceived as highly credible by the subjects of the experiment. A set of bipolar rating scales was constructed from this list, and an independent group of subjects rated two hypothetical speakers on the scales. The judgmental responses were factor analyzed in order to assess the dimensions involved in judgment of communicator credibility.

The investigators found the factors that emerged for the highly credible communicator to be much more specific than those for the communicator with low credibility. They concluded that many factors in addition to expertness and trustworthiness play a role in communicator credibility. The authors considered such additional elements as manners, use of the English language, and "inspiration ability" to be important factors of credibility (Schweitzer and Ginsburg, 1966).

In a study investigating the criteria used by receivers in evaluating message sources, Berlo, Lemert, and Mertz isolated three dimensions of the "image" of the source of a persuasive communication as they were perceived by audience members: safety (trustworthiness), qualification (expertness), and dynamism (enthusiasm). They held, like Schweitzer and Ginsburg, that source image should be defined in terms of the perceptions of the receiver, not in terms of objective descriptions of the source (Berlo, Lemert, and Mertz, 1969-1970).

In a study by Fulton, five dimensions of personality—agreeableness, conscientiousness, culture, extroversion, and emotional stability—were varied and measured in order to investigate the dimensions of speaker credibility. Three of the five credibility dimensions were found to be positively and significantly related to personal attraction: agreeableness, conscientiousness, and culture (Fulton, 1970).

The sex of the communicator has been found to have a bearing on communicator credibility. Gudger studied the effects of sex differences upon opinion change and concluded that, at least for our culture, male communicators are more effective in producing opinion change than are females. However, this is subject to several reasonable qualifications. He found also that male superiority is decreased only slightly, if at all, by the feminine character of the topic under discussion. The least amount of opinion change is produced by female communicators to male recipients. Female recipients are more persuasible than males. Furthermore, recipient-communicator similarity was found to affect results, without the similarity being specifically stated (Gudger, 1970).

Marketing Examples of Personality and Physical Aspects of the Communicator

An illustration of the importance of personality factors in communication can be taken from the field of international advertising. The nationalistic flavor attached to various gestures may play an extremely important role in the persuasive message. For example, Italians, more than northern Europeans, tend to use face, arms, and shoulders to illustrate and characterize their speech. Germans, by contrast, are generally much stiffer and more rigid in their gestures. If an Italian speaking in German to a German audience used considerable flowing hand motions as part of his nonverbal communication, most Germans would not "read" this portion of the message in the same ways that many Italians would.

The following two examples demonstrate ways in which personality characteristics and physical aspects of the communicator may interact with more objective characteristics to increase the chance of audience members being motivated by the message. First, Tom Seaver, a baseball player for the New York Mets, and his wife Nancy were in great demand to make commercials, not only because of his record as a baseball player but also because he and his wife portrayed a cleancut, young couple with whom most Americans, especially young married people, could identify. Second, both Orson Welles, famed writer, producer, and actor, and Alexander Scourby, who has been the "voice-over" in numerous commercials, for years were in great demand to be used in the background of broadcast commercials because of their dignified voices.

Communicator-Audience Similarity

V.A17 *Audience members tend to be more easily motivated and persuaded by a communicator they perceive as being similar to themselves than by a communicator who seems dissimilar.*

In a field experiment Brock conducted in the paint department of a large retail store, it was found that a salesman who reported his own magnitude of paint consumption to be similar to that of the purchaser was much more effective in influencing the purchaser to switch to a different price level than one who reported his consumption level to be dissimilar. This confirmed Brock's hypothesis that a recipient's behavior with respect to an object is modifiable by the communicator's appeal to the extent that the recipient perceives that he and the communicator have a similar relationship to the object (Brock, 1965).

Weiss found that a statement by a communicator of opinion congruence with his audience members on an issue of importance to them will facilitate the opinion-changing effectiveness of a following persuasive communication on a different topic. After establishing academic freedom as an area of agreement between communicator and audience, he found subjects more persuaded by an article opposing fluoridation when it was preceded by a statement in favor of academic freedom attributed to the same source than were those for whom a statement on a neutral issue preceded the article (Weiss, 1956).

In studying the process of identification of an individual with a model, the main focus of Burnstein, Stotland, and Zander was on *introjection,* the process by which an individual changes his conception of himself to be more like his concept of the model. An adult model was presented to two separate groups of grade school children as being either highly similar or of little similarity to the children in background and other attributes. To half the groups he described himself as being a very capable deep-sea diver. To the other half he described himself as being deficient in these abilities. He also described some of his preferences related to deep-sea diving. Subjects evaluated themselves on these same abilities both before and after the experiment, as well as indicating their own feelings about deep-sea diving. It was found that the subjects who were told that the diver was highly similar to them in background accepted his preferences more often than subjects who were told that he was not similar to them (Burnstein, Stotland, and Zander, 1961).

A number of investigators have suggested that the greater persuasiveness of a communicator who is seen as being similar to themselves is due to the fact that he is seen as being more attractive. Byrne hypothesized that attraction between individuals is a function of the extent to which reciprocal rewards are present in their interaction. He asserts that any time another individual offers us validation by indicating that his percepts and concepts are congruent with ours, it constitutes a rewarding interaction and one element in forming a positive relationship. Dissimilarity between two individuals' opinions constitutes a punishing interaction and one element in forming a negative relationship. It was hypothesized that:

a. A stranger who is known to have attitudes similar to those of the subject is better liked than a stranger with attitudes dissimilar to those of the subject.

b. A stranger who is known to have attitudes similar to those of the subject is judged to be more intelligent, better informed, more moral, and better adjusted than a stranger with attitudes dissimilar to those of the subject.

c. A stranger who is known to have similar attitudes on issues important to the subject and dissimilar attitudes on unimportant issues is better liked and evaluated more positively than a stranger for whom the reverse is true.

Byrne's results confirmed his first and second hypotheses; the third was only partially proved. Only on some variables did the subjects rate the stranger similar on more-important attitudes more favorably than they did the stranger similar on less-important ones; for others there was no difference (Byrne, 1961, pp. 713-715).

In an investigation by Byrne and Nelson, both the proportion and number of similar attitudes of strangers were investigated for their effects on attraction toward them by subjects. Each of 168 subjects was asked to read an attitude scale purportedly completed by an anonymous stranger and to evaluate him on a number of variables, including attraction toward him. As hypothesized, analysis of variance indicated that attraction was significantly affected by proportion of similar attitudes only. Unimportant was whether the proportion was out of a total of 4, 8, or 16 attitudes measured (Byrne and Nelson, 1965).

A.J. Smith attempted to examine the causal relationship between the perception of similarity in value systems and acceptance of such systems. Subjects were 28 undergraduate students. On the basis of their answers to the revised Allport-Vernon scale of values, each student was presented with two partially completed experimental test booklets. One was designed to be identical with the student's original answers, the other systematically dissimilar.

Subjects were asked to study these, form an impression of each of the other students whose booklets they were said to have received, and then complete the booklet in the same manner as those individuals who had begun it. Ratings were then obtained of the subjects' acceptance of these hypothetical individuals with respect to two criteria: as possible leisure-time friends and as work associates.

Results from the experiment supported the two hypotheses:

1. The extent to which an individual sees another as resembling himself in consequential aspects will determine at least to some degree the extent to which he will accept that individual.

2. The degree to which one individual accepts another is related to the extent to which he projects his own values onto that person (A.J. Smith, 1957).

Mills and Jellison hypothesized that a similar communicator is more persuasive than a dissimilar communicator because similarity affects the perception of a communicator's sincerity and his motivation to communicate honestly. They asked groups of college women to read the same communication, but with varying introductions. Some were informed that the communicator was a musician and those in the audience he addressed were music students; some that the communicator was an engineer and those in the audience he addressed were engineering students; some that the communicator was a musician and those in the audience he addressed were engineering students; and some that the communicator was an engineer and those in the audience he addressed were music students. In confirmation of the hypothesis, agreement with the communicator's position was greater when he was similar to the audience he addressed (Mills and Jellison, 1968).

Mills and Jellison also found that if a communicator sides with his audience on a particular issue but takes an extreme position, he will be perceived as more sincere and competent than if he had adopted a moderate stance on the issue. If a communicator chooses to adopt a position at odds with the views of his audience, the more extreme his position, the more sincere he is perceived to be by the audience. Since the communicator, in supporting an unpopular view, is subjecting himself to criticism, the audience members feel that he is sincerely defending his viewpoint on the matter under consideration (Mills and Jellison, 1968).

Marketing Examples of Communicator-Audience Similarity

It has also been found that a communicator who tells his audience that "everyone's doing it" or that "everybody in your group thinks so" increases the persuasive power of his message. When attributed to the "majority opinion" of a person's reference group, a message appears to have come from a more credible source. The source appears to know the reference group and thus appears similar. In addition, such majority opinion is often more effective than is expert opinion. The influence of majority opinion on the credibility may be a bandwagon effect.

The bandwagon effect inputes a strong value to the message simply because members of the audience perceive that "so many folks can't be wrong." Advertising campaigns such as those for Lark cigarettes ("Show us your pack") and for the former newspaper *Chicago's American* ("We are Number One") used the bandwagon effect in promotion. Another example of the bandwagon effect was the television commercial for Diet Rite Cola in which many different people of both sexes and of various ages and colors took turns singing passages from a jingle whose message was "Everybody Likes It."

Source Credibility and Attitude Discrepancy

V.A18 *Source credibility becomes more important to an audience member in motivating and persuading him as more of his existing attitudes and opinions are challenged by the facts presented in a message, but becomes less important as they concur.*

Hempel conducted a study of the effects of information from two different sources on audience decision making. Information was presented by a salesman and a product-rating publication, with product evaluations taken before and after the presentation of factual information. When the facts presented were contrary to existing opinions, the rating publication had greater influence on the evaluation and commitment of the respondents. When the predispositions were consistent with the communication, more persuading took place (Hempel, 1966).

Berelson and Steiner stated that

the effect on opinion of sources perceived differently as to credibility tends to converge after a period of weeks—the effect of sources with high credibility decreases and the effect of those with low credibility increases in proportion as the audience forgets the sources but retains the content. When the audience has little or no prior knowledge of the communicator's trustworthiness, it tends to decide a question on the basis of the content itself—i.e., the conformity of the content to the predispositions. [Berelson and Steiner, 1964, p. 537.]

Marketing Examples of Source Credibility and Attitude Discrepancies

Audience members who see advertisements telling them to restrict their intake of saturated fats in order to lower their cholesterol level might see these messages as not high in credibility if they were for a certain brand of margarine. However, in 1972 Fleischman's margarine ran an advertisement endorsed by the American College of Cardiology telling audience members to cut down on saturated fats. This organization has enough credibility to many skeptical audience members to cause them to reevaluate their attitudes and change their diets.

Attitude Discrepancy and Decision Importance

V.A18.2 *As the degree of discrepancy between the predisposition of an individual's attitudes, the communicator's attitudes, and the importance of the decision increase, individuals tend to seek information that supports their viewpoint. Audience members thus see sources of such information as highly credible and are likely to be motivated and persuaded by such sources.*

To avoid cognitive dissonance, individuals expose themselves to communications selectively. Studies by Festinger supported this statement. In most cases selective exposure occurs during a postdecisional period. A commitment has been made by the process of decision, which is a necessary condition for dissonance arousal (Festinger, 1964, pp. 41-42).

According to Sears and Freedman, individuals tend to see and hear communications that are favorable or congenial to their predispositions, and they are more likely to see and hear congenial communications than neutral or hostile ones (Sears and Freedman, 1967).

In a study by Brodbeck, attitudes toward wiretapping were measured for a group of students. They were divided into groups according to their attitudes and exposed to a speech that expressed an opposing opinion. Afterwards they were asked to list a member of the class with whom they would like to discuss the issue. After these discussions, the entire group reassembled and filled out an attitude questionnaire. Results indicated that individuals whose confidence in a belief had been shaken by exposure to opposing propaganda preferred and tended to hear arguments from their own side, from people who agreed with them. The consequence of this was that their confidence in their opinion soon returned to its original level (Brodbeck, 1956).

Marketing Examples of Attitude Discrepancy
and Decision Importance

If audience members have invested in a high-cost item, such as an automobile, they often seek reinforcement for their decision to purchase. They will tend to read whatever favorable messages they find about their type of automobile and ignore or discount as unbelievable claims for similar automobiles made by other companies. Below are two examples of how marketing attempts to overcome any discrepancy between consumers' attitudes and the values related to buying a particular product. Promotion can present information designed to reassure consumers by supporting their beliefs about careful shopping and thrift.

For both the people who already had purchased their cars and those who were considering buying cars, American Motors offered a "Buyer Protection Plan" to guarantee repair of any defective parts for one year at no cost. The company's message was designed to assuage anxieties related to car buying—seeking to overcome cognitive dissonance with the statement "We couldn't back them better if we weren't making them better."

Similarly, in marketing less-expensive convenience products, the use of a money-back guarantee for buyers of new brands or new products induces many people to take a chance and buy, with the reassurance that the company actively "stands behind" the product.

Mild Credibility-Discrepancy Interaction

V.A18.2 *If the communicator is perceived as mildly credible, then the greater the amount of change he advocates, the higher the resistance of the recipients of the communication. However, if the communicator is perceived as highly credible, then the greater the discrepancy between a recipient's initial position and the communicator's, the greater the amount of attitude change in the direction advocated.*

Aronson, Turner, and Carlsmith demonstrated that a highly credible communicator is more successful in inducing attitude change than the mildly credible communicator at every point in discrepancy. Furthermore, they found that a mildly credible communicator induces less change with a large discrepancy than with a moderate discrepancy. Under conditions of lower source credibility and large discrepancy, the recipients can disparage the communication and consequently retain their original attitude sets. By contrast, if the source is highly credible, it cannot be easily disparaged; the recipients of the communication can more easily adopt the communicator's position (Aronson, Turner, and Carlsmith, 1963).

A major conceptual framework for this proposition is Festinger's theory of cognitive dissonance. He suggested that an individual who finds that the position advocated by a highly credible communicator differs widely from his own will experience dissonance. In other words, he experiences anxiety because of a perceived incongruity between his prior attitude set and the position advocated by the source. When in a dissonant state, the person is motivated to reduce the dissonance through the easiest means available to him (Festinger, 1957).

This is why Festinger's theory of cognitive dissonance, Tannenbaum's congruity principle (Tannenbaum, 1956), and Rosenberg and Abelson's affective-cognitive consistency model (Rosenberg and Abelson, 1960) are often labeled *homeostatic* theories of attitude change. In physiology, homeostatis is the tendency of the body to remain in a balanced state. In communication theory, *homeostasis* is the tendency of an individual to balance his attitudes by constantly reassessing new communications so that his "belief structures" will not cause dissonance.

In Rosenberg and Abelson's model, cognitive representations of things concrete or abstract serve as the elements, the relations between which are either positive, negative, or null. Cognitive units of "bands" are built out of pairs of elements connected by a relation. The intent is to code all attitudinal cognitions into such bands. If A and B represent concepts of sailing and fun, then a cognitive relationship could be expressed: A p B, indicating a positive relationship between concepts. In representing attitudes, the concepts involved are of affect-arousing significance and as such can usually be represented by their positive or negative character, instead of neutral symbols A or B.

A balanced band is one in which the relationship asserted between two signed concepts is consistent with their signs. Such balanced bands are predicted to be stable and resistent to change. An unbalanced band is one in which the relation between the concepts is inconsistent with their signs. Rosenberg and

Abelson predict that these tend to be unstable and will be likely to undergo change in a balancing direction (Rosenberg and Abelson, 1960).

Dissonance can be reduced in many ways, but experiments in communication that control almost all means of dissonance reduction have reduced recipients' choices either to (1) rejecting the communication content and derogating the communicator or (2) accepting the communicator and thus accepting the content of the message and changing one's attitudes to bring them into line with the attitude expressed in the message. Accordingly, a person will accept a discrepant communication only up to a certain degree of disagreement. At this stage, the easiest means of reducing dissonance is to discredit the communicator and refuse to change existing attitudes.

Marketing Examples of Mild Credibility-Discrepancy Interaction

Duke Snider, famous centerfielder for both the New York and the Los Angeles Dodgers baseball teams, was an example of a mildly credible communicator in terms of product endorsement. Yet by means of a very persuasive visible presentation of hair coloring for men, namely showing only one side of his head at a time, one of which still had gray hair and the other black hair, the message for the hair-coloring product Great Day was convincing and credible.

However, Buzz Aldrin, respected for his courage and skill as a lunar astronaut, could be described as a highly credible communicator in an advertisement for Volkswagen's computer checkup monitor for Volkswagen automobiles. Because people assume that an astronaut must have a considerable degree of competence with technological matters, his word on the technology of a new product tended to be accepted.

Interaction of Source and Message Credibilities

V.A19 *The credibility of a source to audience members is influenced by the message it delivers. Also the credibility of a message can be altered by the source that delivers it. These two degrees of credibility interact to determine if audience members will be motivated and persuaded by the communication.*

Tannenbaum investigated the effects of a communication on the amount of change in the original attitudes of an audience. He demonstrated that the amount of change depends upon the attitudes originally held toward the source of communication and attitudes toward the concept communicated. His hypotheses about the shift in attitude toward both source and concept are the following.

Susceptibility hypothesis: The amount of change of attitude toward an object is inversely proportional to the intensity of original attitude toward it (source or concept).

Relationship hypothesis: (a) The amount of attitude change toward a concept in the direction of that asserted by a communication is directly proportional to the degree of favorableness of the original attitude toward the source. (b) The amount of attitude change toward the source of the communication in a favorable direction is directly proportional to the degree of favorableness of the original attitude toward the concept when the assertion is favorable, but inversely proportional when the assertion is unfavorable.

In his investigations, Tannenbaum used three different topics; three versions of each were written, one favorable, one neutral, and one unfavorable. Semantic differential scales were used for negative or positive judgments by the subjects, undergraduate psychology students, in pretests in which each source and concept was rated on the selected scale. Five weeks later the subjects were exposed again to the material and then were immediately given another rating test. Selection of a favorable, neutral, or unfavorable version for each subject was at random.

The results showed that both favorable and unfavorable versions caused a shift in attitude toward an advocated concept, but not necessarily toward the source. The experiment demonstrated that interaction between attitudes toward the concept and the source of a communication is a factor in attitude change, and that the amount of attitude change is dependent upon the intensity of original attitudes (Tannenbaum, 1956).

Kalman and Eagly investigated the relationship between the attitude toward a communicator and perception of the content of his message in two experiments:

In the first, a marked tendency to misperceive the message of a negative communicator by displacing it away from one's own position (contrast) was found. In the second, this tendency was shown to be a direct function of the strength of the negative feeling toward the communicator. Similarly, the tendency to displace the message of a positive communicator toward one's own position (assimilation) was shown to be a direct function of the strength of positive feeling. [Kelman and Eagly, 1965 p. 78.]

A further investigation of the interaction between source and message credibility was conducted by Atwood. Journalism students at three universities were exposed to one of four conditions in which a high-credibility source delivered a high-credibility message or a low-credibility message and a low-credibility source delivered a high- or low-credibility message. All four conditions were administered at each school. Both high-credibility and low-credibility sources were designed so that they would be perceived as experts by the subjects, but one would be perceived as fair and trustworthy and the other as unfair and untrustworthy.

Following a premessage rating by the students in which these designs were found to be perceived as had been intended, subjects were exposed to one of the four source-message conditions. Afterwards they again rated the sources on a semantic differential scale and answered 10 questions indicating the extent to which they agreed with the message presented. Subjects in the two high-credibility message conditions agreed with the message to a greater extent than did subjects in the two low-message credibility conditions. There were no changes in perceived source credibility in the congruent conditions, in which the high-credibility message or the low-credibility source delivered a low-credibility message. Where the high-credibility source delivered the low-credibility message, the ratings of source expertness, fairness, and trustworthiness were lower on the postmessage rating than on the premessage rating. The low-credibility source that delivered the high-credibility message was rated more trustworthy and more fair on the posttest than on the pretest, while there was no change in ratings of expertness.

From the questions on agreement with the message, it was concluded that subject agreement with the low-credibility message was increased by the high-credibility source; subject agreement with the high-credibility message was not affected by source credibility. The low- and high-credibility sources were believed equally when they presented what was perceived as a high-credibility message (Atwood, 1966).

Marketing Examples of Interaction of Source and Message Credibilities

Over the years *Good Housekeeping* has printed well-researched support for products. The magazine thus has earned high credibility. Now the mere inclusion of a message in *Good Housekeeping* tends to lend credibility to the message.

Crest toothpaste's television commercials focused entirely on a statement of acceptance by the Council on Dental Therapeutics of the American Dental Association, a highly credible source. In every advertisement the quote was read: "Crest has been shown to be effective decay-preventive dentifrice that can be of significant value when used in a conscientiously applied program of oral hygiene and professional care."

But Bayer aspirin commercials on television follow only a mildly credible logic at best, because of its vagueness. The message basically is that "in test after test doctors recommend aspirin for relief of pain . . . and the best aspirin you can buy is Bayer."

Interaction of Credibilities Over Time

V.A19.1 *The probability of attitude change increases over time for the members of an audience exposed to a low-credibility source as the message tends to be dissociated from its source.*

Hovland, Lumsdaine, and Sheffield showed that if one audience group is exposed to a high-credibility source and another to a low-credibility source, the advantage of high over low credibility almost disappears after an interval of several weeks. The increased likelihood of believing a message delivered by a low-credibility source once its source has been dissociated from it is known as the *sleeper effect* (Hovland, Lumsdaine, and Sheffield, 1949, pp. 201-227). This phenomenon was discussed earlier in chapter 22. The point is that despite the initial advantage of high-credibility source, eventually a message from a low-credibility source may produce as much attitude change as that from a high-credibility source.

It is fairly easy to account for decreased attitude change over time in the group initially exposed to the high-credibility source. Perhaps the audience members forgot the message or tended to return to their precommunication dispositions. Although no clearcut explanation exists as to why attitude change sometimes increases over time without a continuing presentation of the persuasive message, Hovland, Lumsdaine, and Sheffield presented the hypothesis that often the audience was predisposed to accept the viewpoint of the communication prior to the communication itself.

A mass communication study also hypothesized that a communication may activate a change of attitude that was nearly ready to take place. It is also possible that the message itself may cause interpersonal communication among members of the audience following exposure to it. Postexperimental interpersonal communication often actually changes attitudes more than the initial message, in what has been referred to as the "two-step flow" of communication (Lazarsfeld, Berelson, and Gaudet, 1948, pp. 106-107). An example of this would be a group exposed to a certain message, the nature of which causes them to discuss it among themselves and consequently change their opinions. Similarly, an individual exposed to a message may be motivated to seek more information about the particular topic, this additional information perhaps causing the actual attitude shift.

Another hypothesis with regard to the sleeper effect is that the message may not at first seem relevant to the audience; but later, new experience makes the particular message appear more relevant than previously to the audience's needs. Hovland and Kelman found that the effect on attitude change between high- and low-credibility-exposed groups tends to coverge after a few weeks; that is, the effect of sources with high credibility decreases and the effect of those with low credibility increases as the audience forgets the sources but retains the content. But when the sources were again identified, the degrees of attitude change diverged as they had initially; attitude change became much greater in the high-credibility group than in the low-credibility group. However, the attitude change in the high credibility group did not return to its original high level but to a somewhat lower level (Hovland and Kelman, 1953).

Marketing Examples of Interaction of Credibilities Over Time

The sleeper effect may be of considerable value to marketers. Recognizing that persuasive effects of low-credibility sources increase over time, Cox hypothesized that an advertiser should schedule his advertising in "bunches" rather than maintaining the same level of exposure throughout the year. If an advertiser schedules almost constant exposure, he is not allowing the sleeper effect to take place. Assuming that credibility of his source is not considered high, attitude change might initially be minimal. However, if enough time is allowed between heavy-exposure periods for the sleeper effect to take place, members of the audience might dissociate the message from the source (Cox, 1961, p. 172).

Instead of constant exposure, then, the marketer might advertise only every third week, using three times the exposure he was using each week before. Hence, the information people learned about the product would be more effective in changing attitudes toward it than if the message had been communicated more frequently. An example of the sleeper effect occurs among shoppers who hear or see advertisements and later on in the store remember the message and associate it with the wrong brand.

28 Variables within the Audience: Individual Variables

Background

Once again the factors affecting communication can be divided into message and medium variables and variables within the audience. In motivating, the factors the communicator should research about his target market are their individual variables and group influences. This chapter and the following one will explain how these variables can alter the ways in which audience members are motivated by a message.

Individual Variables

From a careful examination of the evidence it is possible to extract a few tentative generalizations that are well supported by different investigators using a variety of methods in diverse communication situations. Despite various methodological limitations, the available empirical results throw some light on the relationships between specific personality predispositions and responsiveness to communications. The following propositions will summarize ways communicators can utilize the findings of this research on individual variables.

Self-Confidence

V.B1 *When exposed to motivational messages, audience members of low self-confidence are more readily motivated and persuaded to act as a communicator desires than are individuals of high self-confidence.*

Self-confidence is negatively correlated with susceptibility to motivational messages. Accordingly, the more self-confident an individual is, the less susceptible he is likely to be; and the less self-confident he is, the more susceptible he is likely to be.

After determining whether his subjects were of high or low self-esteem, Cohen conducted a series of tests of self-esteem as related to persuasibility on Air Force personnel and college students. He concluded, "Persons of high self-esteem dealt with their experiences in experimental situations in a way that helped them to maintain their high self-esteem. They tended to respond to

381

failure by evaluating themselves more highly than did individuals with low self-esteem. Furthermore, they became responsive to the group's expectations only when favorable self-evaluation was readily possible. Persons with low self-esteem reacted to their experiences in a way that made it difficult for them to improve their self-regard; they reacted strongly to failure and became responsive to the group's expectations when an unfavorable self-evaluation was most likely" (Cohen, 1959, p. 114).

Cohen's tests also showed indications that individuals having a high degree of self-confidence used ego defenses to help them repress, deny, or ignore challenging and conflicting impulses or ideas. Thus Cohen found that the self-confident individual does not allow his self-esteem to be challenged by new information, new influences, or outside ideas as readily as a low self-confident individual who is not using those ego defenses to protect his self-image.

Nisbett and Gordon tested the level of self-esteem of subjects by first giving them an intelligence test. At a later session they told the subjects whether they had done well or not. They wanted to determine whether subjects who had done badly would be more or less easily motivated, depending on their level of self-esteem. Their results upheld Cohen's conclusions about self-esteem; ego-defense mechanisms used by the high self-esteem individuals were more receptive to the messages than for the low-esteem individuals (Nisbett and Gordon, 1967).

Silverman conducted tests on male Veterans' Administration residents concerning the influence of ego threats on ability to be motivated for high and low self-esteem individuals. Subjects were divided into four groups, and subjects in all groups were given failure treatment or no-failure treatment immediately before a test of ability to be motivated. The conclusions Silverman reached agreed with Cohen's; in other words, defense mechanisms triggered in high self-esteem individuals are more susceptible to motivation (Silverman, 1964).

In studies of personality correlates, Janis concluded that, "persons with low self-esteem tend to be more readily influenced than others. . . . Students who manifested feelings of social inadequacy, inhibition of aggression, and depressive tendencies were found to have the highest persuasibility ratings" (Janis, 1954, p. 518). Moreover, Janis found an additional factor relevant to individuals with low self-evaluation and susceptibility to motivation: group acceptance. He found that people with low self-evaluations need group acceptance to alleviate their feelings of personal inadequacy. These individuals "may be indiscriminately influenced by the anticipation of approval from the communicator or from others who are assumed to share . . . [their] point of view" (Janis, 1954, p. 515).

The discussion of self-confidence has been divided by some psychologists into two parts—general self-confidence and specific self-confidence. *General self-confidence* pertains to personality variables such as the desire to solve problems of social relations or ego-defense mechanisms. This is the type of self-confidence previously discussed. *Specific self-confidence* concerns a particular situation or the solving of a specific task. If an individual feels that he is highly competent to perform a particular task, he is less persuasible concerning his performance of that task than an individual who feels he is incompetent.

The proposition dealing with confidence about a specific activity will be found in chapter 33. As to further discussion of self-confidence, see the section in this chapter on Degree of Perceived Risk.

Marketing Examples of Self-Confidence

In situations where self-confidence is low, personal selling can be especially effective. The salesman's comment that he has one just like the product or that the shoes look good on the consumer will positively affect the attitudes of the shopper with low self-confidence. A high self-confidence individual will not particularly care what the salesman says—he trusts his own judgment of style, practicality, quality, and economy. Thus low self-confidence consumers may prefer a small, more-personalized store where they can get a lot of sales help, whereas their counterparts will prefer a large store where they can shop without interference.

A person of low self-confidence will be more susceptible than a high-level individual to such promotions as new, improved, the best, etc. They are afraid of having inferior products because they reflect on them as poor purchasers. The highly self-confident person will be more skeptical.

Advertising campaigns for various kinds of deodorants and mouthwashes often target their messages to individuals who are low in self-confidence and yearn to be more confident and accepted by others.

Open- and Closed-Mindedness

V.B2 *Closed-minded audience members are less susceptible to motivational messages than are open-minded audience members.*

An open-minded individual is one who is willing to accept new beliefs, who will expose himself to new information and ideas. Closed-mindedness has been referred to as a defense mechanism. Certain individuals are not willing, or able, to accept ideas or opinions contrary to their own; as a result, they become closed-minded, resistant to change. Since motivational messages often deal with attempts to introduce new ideas, or to persuade an individual about someone or something, a closed-minded person offers resistance to such information.

Several studies have been conducted, relating open- and closed-mindedness to susceptibility to motivational messages. They all agree that because of a broader scope, open-minded individuals are more susceptible to persuasion than closed-minded individuals—they are willing to try something new.

Mertz, Miller, and Ballance conducted an experiment with Michigan State University students in an introductory communication course. Their results suggested that closed-minded individuals will be preoccupied with information concerning the source of an incoming message, while an open-minded receiver is more likely to be concerned with the message content (Mertz, Miller, and Ballance, 1966).

Since an open-minded person's opinions presumably are grounded in both source and content beliefs, his response to an imbalancing message should involve reevaluation of both these elements. Special considerations involved in attempting to persuade closed-minded individuals will be discussed in chapter 33; see also the discussion of this subject in chapter 21.

Marketing Examples of Open- and Closed-Mindedness

Several years ago men were closed-minded to the concept of using hair dryers to dry their hair because hair-care items were associated with women. But manufacturers changed the name to a hair blower and, through promotion, changed the product image. Because men would pay attention to the source of the message, the choice of the communicator was important—a masculine athletic figure or an attractive woman. By establishing source credibility, closed-minded consumers finally began to attend to the message.

Open-minded people are more interested in different kinds of products—they like variety; they like to try new things. They will purchase the frozen coq au vin, whereas the closed-minded consumer's attitude that frozen food is not any good will not even allow himself a test. Open-minded people are more likely to buy the latest style or shop at any new store that may open. They are experimentally minded.

Aggressive/Withdrawal Traits

V.B3 *Audience members who possess either extreme aggressive or withdrawal tendencies—within the normal behavior range—are less easily motivated and persuaded than individuals in the range between these two extremes.*

Individuals who openly express hostility and display overt aggression toward others in everyday interpersonal relationships are predisposed to remain relatively uninfluenced by motivational communications. The most cogent evidence for this comes from one of the pioneering investigations of responsiveness to a series of communications—Barry's controlled exposure study of susceptibility to majority opinion. The investigation was carried out with high school students and was replicated with other groups, including inmates in a penal institution.

These groups were given a questionnaire consisting of 40 yes-no items concerning a variety of attitudes and opinions and covering such diverse topics as race relations, government ownership of public utilities, trial marriages, bobbed hair, and card playing. One week later the same questionnaire was repeated but this time along with a series of communications that provided information concerning the answers given by the majority of the group. Changes in positive or negative responses to the questions, as well as certainty ratings, were taken into account in rating each individual's susceptibility to this series of communications.

On the basis of his observations of the subject's overt behavior in various social situations, Barry noted that those with low-susceptibility scores tended to be most irritable or easily annoyed. Pursuing this observation further, he obtained systematic evidence from one or more of the groups covering: (1) average rating by associates of the individual's irritability; (2) the degree to which the individual attributed irritability to his comrades; (3) the expression of critical or hostile attitudes toward others in introspective reports by each individual; and (4) the omission of customary titles of respect in addressing superiors. The first measure was found to be unrelated to susceptibility, but the other three showed a significant inverse relationship. From these findings Barry concluded that low susceptibility is associated with critical, derogatory attitudes toward others. The correlations Barry reports, although subject to other interpretations, seem to be consistent with the hypothesis that there is an inverse relationship between susceptibility to social influence and aggressiveness toward others (Barry, 1931).

Further evidence comes from a number of studies that made use of more indirect indicators of susceptibility to persuading. Newcomb compared students who became more liberal in their attitudes with those who remained conservative during four years of college. He presented a detailed description of the liberal social atmosphere of Bennington—the women's college where the study was carried out—from which it seemed likely that the students with persistent conservative attitudes were, by and large, less susceptible to community influences than those who changed in the liberal direction. An intensive personality study was made of 19 resistant students, and these were compared with 24 others who had shown more than the average amount of attitude change. Newcomb noted that many of the resistant students manifested overt negativism in their classroom behavior, aloofness, and low capacity for social relationships. In some cases negativistic habits were of precollege standing, while in others they apparently represented a reaction to frustrated hopes of social success in college. Fewer of the nonconservatives were considered aggressive, either by the faculty or by the other students (Newcomb, 1943, pp. 146-159).

Roland postulated that low susceptibility to motivational messages was associated with an overtly aggressive orientation, high susceptibility with a defensive need to inhibit strong aggressive motivation, and medium susceptibility with a relative absence of aggressive motivation and inhibition against aggression. In one of his studies, three groups of 15 were selected from an initial sample of 169 first-grade boys enrolled in the public school system of Uniondale, New York. The three groups of high, medium, and low persuasibles were compared on aggressive motivation and conflict ratio. A modified TAT procedure was used to measure aggression and a booklet of incomplete stories was used to measure persuasibility. The results showed that high and low persuasibles had more aggressive motivation than medium persuasibles. High persuasibles had smaller aggression conflict ratios than low persuasibles. Thus the results supported the initial postulates (Roland, 1963).

Most of the studies have found significant correlations of personality attributes with persuasibility for males, but not for females. The research done so far will enable communicators to predict which males will be most influenced, but no parallel attributes enable communicators to pick the females who will be most influenced. More research is needed in this area before the results can be used to construct specific advertising campaigns.

Marketing Examples of Aggressive/Withdrawal Traits

Some automobile manufacturers have constructed their promotion to appeal to aggressive personalities. Advertising that emphasizes speed attracts aggressive people, for a car can serve as a means of aggression. Other promotional campaigns that suggest winning or superiority are also appealing to such people. At times sports equipment is featured in an aggressive manner; and of course, guns and any other kinds of hunting equipment are of themselves aggressive in character. Physical aggression also is indirectly appealed to when health is overemphasized.

Imagination

V.B4 *Audience members of an imaginative nature with strong affinities for symbolism are more easily motivated and persuaded as a communicator desires than are less-imaginative individuals.*

The theoretical basis of this principle is to be found in the assumption that a major mediating mechanism in the process of motivating and attitude change is the anticipation of reward and punishment. A powerful imagination is likely to lead to stronger and more-precise anticipation of the consequences of a change—that is, to enhance persuasibility.

Janis and Field in their study of personality factors influencing susceptibility to motivating messages used the phrase *richness of fantasy* to refer to the relation between imagination and motivation. However, it seems that the basic affinity with symbolism and the faculty of viewing images is the same whether freed or disciplined through a rational process in order to create. Furthermore, the test used by Janis and Field in their experiment measures the capacity of imagining (Janis and Field, 1959). The concept of imagination appears as more operational than *richness of fantasy* and therefore will be used herein.

Osborn recognized the thinking mind as accomplishing a two-fold existence of both a judicial mind and a creative mind. He distinguished rationalization and imagination. Creativity is imagination directed through a rationalization process. Therefore, if a specific place in the audience members' minds can be made for imagination, the close relation with intelligence can be exploited by the communicator (Osborn, 1948, p. 5).

Marketing Examples of Imagination

Imaginative individuals have greater capacities to visualize the product in use and how it will fit into their lifestyle than would less-imaginative people. For the latter group, demonstrations are effective, as well as before-and-after comparisons; and in the area of personal selling, the salesmen will need to go into more detail about product uses, the setting of use, and why the customer needs the product. An imaginative individual will do all this mentally and even may think of new uses for the product.

Certain types of media lend themselves to either one of the two types. Pictorial media may be more effective for the unimaginative individual—for he can then see what the product looks like, the product in use, its different uses, where it is used, and the type of people who use it. Radio advertising may not be as effective because of lack of visuals; and billboards may not be able to show enough characteristics to convey a message. For the imaginative person, the situation would be the reverse.

Degree of Perceived Risk

V.B5 *Audience members who are high-risk perceivers are more willing to seek information and are more motivated by it than are low-risk perceivers.*

Perceived risk is defined by how an individual reacts to a communication or an idea. A *high-risk perceiver* is an individual who feels that a great deal of risk is involved in the acceptance of a communication, idea, or product. This may cause him to reject the concept completely. The risk may be due to the nature of the concept itself or the possible reactions of friends or acquaintances. A *low-risk perceiver* is an individual who feels that, under the same circumstances as above, little or no risk is involved in the situation. He will be more likely than the high-risk perceiver to adopt the concept.

A certain amount of risk is involved in almost every action an individual takes. Each purchase decision a consumer makes carries a degree of risk. "High-ticket" items are regarded as more risky than "small-ticket" items. The perceived risk for a purchase varies with each consumer. Factors that serve to determine risk value are: price; durability; availability; importance of the product; whether it meets the required needs; time—to buy the product or return it if necessary; the self-confidence of the individual; certainty concerning the purchase decision; and so on.

To debate every possible risk factor for every purchase would take more time than the consumer has available. Therefore, patterns of behavior are developed by him to reduce risk: repeated purchase of a particular brand—brand loyalty; channels of information—advertisements, word-of-mouth; and opinion leaders.

The relationship of perceived risk and informal communication was studied by Cunningham. A telephone survey was made of 1200 housewives in a medium-sized city, with questions concerning frequently purchased items usually sold in supermarkets. Three products were selected for study: headache remedies, fabric softeners, and dry spaghetti. Information was collected concerning perceived risk, brand loyalty, and word-of-mouth communication for each product. These products were chosen because it was felt that they represented a range of riskiness, with headache remedies the most risky and dry spathetti the least risky.

Specific results were collected for perceived risk and the existence or word-of-mouth activity, amount of product related discussion, constant of conversation, the nature of the word-of-mouth process, opinion leadership, and generalized self-confidence.

It was found that women perceiving high risk were more likely to have discussed the product in the last six months than were women perceiving low risk. Cunningham suggested that those perceiving high risk were relatively efficient in using informal communications to reduce risk. By contrast, high-risk perceivers were more likely than low-risk perceivers to be involved in a conversation in which (1) negative brand information was recommended, (2) positive brand information was recommended, (3) information was requested rather than volunteered, and (4) new brands were discussed.

Women who perceived high risk were more likely to initiate conversations and were more likely to request information than women who perceived low risk. These findings support the hypothesis of the high-risk perceiver as one who reduces risk through information-seeking. High-risk respondents also were more likely to claim that others came to them for advice, as contrasted with low-risk respondents. Opinion leaders perceiving high risk in a product considered to be of low risk (dry spaghetti) were more involved in the discussion process than opinion leaders on products of high risk (headache remedies).

Women high in generalized self-confidence who were also high in perceived risk were most likely to engage in word-of-mouth discussions. Those low in self-confidence who were also low in perceived risk were least likely to be involved in word-of-mouth discussions. It appears that respondents high in both perceived risk and self-confidence were most likely to use product-related discussion as a method of risk reduction (Cunningham, 1967).

From these results it is easily seen that patterns of behavior develop to reduce the perceived risk of a purchase. Word-of-mouth communications, opinion leaders, and information-seeking are widespread methods of risk reduction.

Arndt tested the relationship of perceived risk, word-of-mouth communication, product acceptance, self-confidence, and information seeking. The subjects of his experiment were 449 wives living in a university housing complex for married students. Each wife was mailed a coupon and a letter from the manufacturer inviting her to buy a new regular coffee. The coupons had to be redeemed within 16 days and were given numbers to identify the buyers; and 16 days after the coffee was introduced, a 30-minute interview was conducted with each respondent. Interviews were completed with 449 out of 495 wives. By the end of the experimental period, 137 of the women had bought at least one can of the coffee.

Results showed that word-of-mouth discussion flowed from early adopters to late adopters and nonadopters. The content of the information received influenced the buying behavior of the receivers. Compared with the nonexposed individuals, those receiving favorable word-of-mouth influences were more likely to buy the coffee, while those exposed to unfavorable word-of-mouth were less likely to buy.

Brand loyalty was associated with perceived risk, which was negatively related to product acceptance. Information appeared to flow from those low in perceived risk to the high-risk perceivers. Compared with low-risk perceivers, those of high risk were more affected by word-of-mouth information.

Respondents low in self-confidence reacted to word-of-mouth in an ego-defensive manner. They were less likely to be exposed to the information. If they were exposed, they seemed to ignore the content of the word-of-mouth discussion. The relationship between self-confidence and exposure to word-of-mouth was positive, whereas the relationship between self-confidence and the impact of word-of-mouth information was curvilinear. Medium self-confidence groups were most responsive to the word-of-mouth comments (Arndt, 1967).

Driscoll, Lanzetta, and McMichael examined the effects of varying the uncertainty of outcome upon subjects preferences for information. They found that preferences for information increased with uncertainty, even though this information was of no apparent instrumental value, i.e., it did not affect outcome in any way. While under all conditions significantly more individuals preferred no information, uncertainty was found to be an important determinant of preference for information. The seemingly universal preference for information just prior to outcome or decision should be noted by the communicator. When a choice of messages is available, it seems to be indicated that the message containing more information—especially relevant information—would more often bias the decision of the audience member, rendering him more persuasible with regard to that message (Driscoll, Lanzetta, and McMichael, 1967).

A new product requires careful consideration. Merely being new is risky. Who manufactures it? How is it different from similar products? How is it similar? If the product is an entirely new concept, it has no point of comparison for the consumer. Information must be provided.

Since word-of-mouth information is an important factor in risk reduction, information must be easily available. If no information is provided, risk will not be greatly reduced, and product acceptance may be retarded. Point-of-purchase material can provide information for both the consumer and the merchandiser. Promotional material aimed specifically at the retail outlets can be helpful, enabling the retailer to answer questions consumers may ask, furthering the flow of word-of-mouth communication.

Marketing Examples of Degree of Perceived Risk

For convenience goods, there are several ways by which promotion can overcome the impression that buying a new product would involve a risk. Price-reduction coupons, free samples sent by mail, and introductory sales often will be enough to induce shoppers to try buying new products instead of their customary brands. Advertising can create an excitement about the product as something new; likewise, informative copy and testimonials from respected sources can enhance a general feeling of dependability related to the product, thus diminishing the apparent riskiness.

The media chosen to convey a message can either reduce or increase risk. If a semiprofessional athlete were to buy a pair of sport shoes, an advertisement placed in *Sports Illustrated* will have more credibility than the same advertisement placed in a financial publication. An advertisement for baby aspirin will have more credibility in *Reader's Digest* than in *MS.*

Packaging also can be used to reduce risk. Medicine bottles and bottles containing poisonous cleaning fluids that are made so as to be difficult to open are risk reducing. Products in nonbreakable containers for use in bathrooms, such as shampoos and mouthwashes, also are risk reducing. The Dixie Cup reduces the chance of glass breakage in bathrooms and kitchens.

The distribution of a product may affect its risk value. A person might buy his color television at a "name" department store, whereas the same product is offered at a lower price at a nearby warehouse establishment; but the purchaser feels more assured, purchasing it from an established store.

A product's stage in its life cycle also affects risk. Risk may be higher at the introduction stage, whereas it is lowest at the maturity stage. If a product has been successful to the point of the maturity stage, it is an indirect comment on the quality that it successfully satisfied the needs of other consumers.

Intelligence

V.B6 *More-intelligent audience members are more responsive to arguments based upon factual evidence (positive correlation) and are more resistant to arguments based upon unsupported generalities and emotional appeals (negative correlation) than are less-intelligent audience members.*

In order to receive a communication or series of communications from a communicator, an audience must possess a certain minimal level of intelligence. This is necessary for them to be able to comprehend a message and to decide whether to accept it or not. However, intelligence, by itself, is not a reliable predictor of an individual's ability to be motivated and persuaded.

Crutchfield, in his study of social influence, hypothesized that high intelligence leads to resistance to the pressure of social influence. He reasoned that an intelligent person can more clearly identify the issues that face him and thus relies more heavily upon his own judgment. A less-intelligent person would view the information as being more ambiguous and thus would rely more upon communication from other sources (Crutchfield, 1955). In addition, DiVesta and Cox also found a negative correlation between intelligence and susceptibility to motivational influence (DiVesta and Cox, 1960).

However, Honkavaara hypothesized that resistance to persuasion is a fundamental personality trait of the feebleminded. He claimed that a biological definition of intelligence would state that the more one is adjustable to the environment, the more intelligent one is (Honkavaara, 1958). Rath and Mirsa substantiated this hypothesis by empirically finding that intelligent people are more likely to conform to the group norm (Rath and Mirsa, 1963).

The two contradictory hypotheses are each substantiated by more than one study. Although these studies were not directly measuring the correlation between susceptibility to motivation and intelligence, they were examining closely related areas. For instance, Murphy, Murphy, and Newcomb, in their summary of the literature of social psychology up to 1937, pointed out that zero or near-zero correlations have consistently been found between intelligence and susceptibility to propaganda (Murphy, Murphy, and Newcomb, 1937, p. 930). More recent investigations, however, have indicated that positive correlations for some communications and negative correlations for others do occur, depending upon the types of arguments and appeals that are used.

Hovland, Janis, and Kelley explained this by stating that two opposing abilities are correlated to intelligence. *Learning ability* enables intelligent individuals to learn and remember a given experience more than less-intelligent individuals. *Critical ability* predisposes the more intelligent to reject interpretations that are unsound or irrational, to be alert to signs of propagandistic intent, and to recognize bias in argumentation. The two abilities would often tend to operate in opposite directions and would therefore mask any positive or negative relationship between intelligence and susceptibility to motivational message (Hovland, Janis, and Kelley, 1953, p. 181).

These two components will interfere according to the types of arguments contained in the communication. This is why an "over-all average relationship between intellectual ability and opinion change is relatively meaningless since it obscures the separate relations—some positive, some negative for separate items" (Hovland, Lumsdaine, and Sheffield, 1949, p. 267).

Hovland, Janis, and Kelley suggested two general hypotheses concerning the conditions under which general intelligence is predictive of responsiveness to motivational communications:

1. Individuals with high intelligence will tend—mainly because of their ability to draw valid inferences—to be more influenced than those with low intellectual ability when exposed to communications that rely primarily on impressive logical arguments.
2. Individuals with high intelligence will tend—mainly because of their superior critical ability—to be less influenced than those with low intelligence when exposed to communications that rely primarily on unsupported generalities or false, illogical, irrelevant argumentation (Hovland, Janis, and Kelley, 1953, p. 183).

Several psychologists have supported these hypotheses with the results of their empirical studies. In addition, several other relationships between intelligence and persuasibility have been tested. Schiller conducted a study with high school boys in an attempt to draw a relationship between intelligence and reaction to advertisements and found several practical rules of thumbs for advertising people.

The more intelligent the audience, the less responsive it was to the factor of color in itself. Also, the more-intelligent audiences preferred advertisements with photos of people to those which contained just photos of objects. Humor was more favorably received in advertisements by individuals with higher rather than low intelligence. For this series of tests, IQ scores were used as a determinant of level of general intelligence (Schiller, 1938).

Kline conducted an experiment with high school sophomores who read one-paragraph messages with varying levels of factual evidence—specific factual evidence, nonspecific factual evidence, no factual evidence. He found that "the effect of type of evidence varies as a positive function of receivers' intelligence.

The existence of factual evidence and the specificity of evidence makes more difference for receivers of high intelligence than for receivers of low intelligence. This difference is sharpest when the effect sought is opinion change or perceived expertness of source" (Kline, 1969, p. 413).

In another experiment, Janis proved that individuals with low intellectual ability and little education tended to be more influenced toward persuasion (thus, highly motivated) than if the communication contained somewhat of a one-sided presentation. This presentation was limited solely to the arguments favoring the communicator's conclusions. Better-educated individuals with high intelligence tended to be more influenced toward persuasion (thus, highly motivated) than if the communication was two-sided, presenting both sides of the argument (Janis, 1963, pp. 57-58).

Marketing Examples of Intelligence

To capture both the high-intelligence and low-intelligence markets, a manufacturer may include two detergents in his line of products. One may emphasize the clean, bright clothes the detergent produces, how your family will love you for it—to the less intelligent audience—while the second product emphasizes that the detergent contains bleach and a fabric softener. The one-step procedure saves the consumer time; and the promotion emphasizes the specific ingredients and what each does to clean one's clothes better—for the more intelligent audience.

The kind of personal selling used also is affected by the educational level of the consumers. When selling furniture to a low-intelligence person, emphasis might be put on economy and the fact that one gets six pieces already matched together. If a salesman were selling Baker furniture to a high-intelligence individual, emphasis would be put on the craftsmanship, individuality, the fact that Baker produces copies of antiques, the effort put into matching veneers, and the time spent finishing the wood.

Postpurchase promotion will be more effective with high-intelligence than with low-intelligence consumers. They have weighed the pros and cons of a product purchase, and are more familiar with the product and issues involved. Dissonance may arise if these cons are not totally resolved. Thus letters sent out after the purchase and specific advertisements aimed at new owners should reinforce their initial decision.

Educational Level

V.B6.1 *Audience members of a relatively low educational level are more motivationally influenced by one-sided messages that express the communicator's views only, while more highly educated individuals are more influenced by messages wherein comparative data are given.*

The need for information on the educational level of an audience becomes even more profound as mass media influences are considered. A strong correlation exists between readership of certain magazines and educational level. Similarly, there are trends in certain types of television programs and the educational level of their audiences. In both magazines and television, the obvious conclusion is that advertisements must be geared to the educational level of the audience to be effective (Lucas and Britt, 1963, pp. 317-319).

The following empirical studies attempted to relate educational level to degree of motivation of audience members. During World War II, the Research Branch of the Army's Information and Education Division investigated to determine if when the weight of evidence supports the main thesis being presented, it is more effective to present only the materials supporting the points being made or to introduce also the arguments of those opposed to the point being made. The experiment was conducted when military experts believed the troops in the European Theater were underestimating the time required to defeat Japan. Two radio commentaries were prepared and presented during the orientation period with no officers attending. One commentary, 15 minutes in length, gave only evidence supporting one side; the other added 4 minutes of opposing arguments. When the results were broken down according to educational level, "it was found that the program which presented both sides was more effective with better educated men and that the program which presented one side was more effective with less educated men" (Hovland, Lumsdaine, and Sheffield, 1949, p. 214).

Rogers presented evidence suggesting that innovators, those who are quick to adopt new ideas, are better educated, more rational, and tend to get information from authoritative sources and the mass media. Later adopters, or laggards, tend to be at a lower educational level and are influenced to adopt mainly by their peers. Rogers' findings seemed to suggest that innovators require more information on both sides of an issue, while laggards are influenced mainly by peers or a one-sided appeal (Rogers, 1962, pp. 174-182).

Marketing Examples of Educational Level

The manufacturers of steam electric rollers point out both the product benefits in terms of hair styling and the fact that electric rollers dry out the ends of one's hair. But the steam rollers are better for hair than the electric rollers, which are simply heated.

In personal selling, a salesman can present two sides of an argument—both the attributes and disadvantages of a product—in such a way as not to lose the sale. The disadvantages can be played down by pointing out that the main requirements of the type of product are this product's advantages, or that all the other competitors have even more disadvantages, or that this manufacturer's product disadvantages do not interfere too much with actual product operation. The attributes can be elaborated upon, while the disadvantages are just mentioned.

Inner- and Other-Directedness

V.B7 Audience members who possess traits of other-directedness and/or who are educated in fields that attract mostly other-directed individuals tend to be more highly susceptible to motivational messages and thus more easily motivated and persuaded by a communicator than are audience members who are more inner-directed.

W.M. Kassarjian developed the "inner-other social preference scale" to consistently determine whether an individual is inner- or other-directed. Individuals' answers to 36 questions presented to them during the test enabled the tester to group the individuals into appropriate inner- or other-directed categories. All the following studies used this test to categorize individuals (W.M. Kassarjian, 1962).

H.H. Kassarjian centered his attention on the preferences of the inner- and other-directed individuals for advertising appeals and types of media. He hypothesized that:

1. Inner- and other-directed individuals would prefer advertisements with an appeal designed to fit their social character types.
2. Other-directed individuals would believe that all people would prefer and be influenced by the same advertisements that motivated themselves.
3. Other-directed individuals would expose themselves more to the mass media than inner-directed individuals (H.H. Kassarjian, 1968).

A panel of psychologists rated 27 pairs of advertisements on the inner- or other-directed scale. These pairs were then presented to 200 business administration students who had been rated according to the same scale. Each pair of advertisements promoted the same product or service but with a different slogan and/or illustration. Kassarjian found that inner-directed students preferred inner-directed appeals and other-directed students chose other-directed advertisements, hence, substantiating the first hypothesis.

The second hypothesis was supported since both inner- and other-directed individuals believed that other individuals would be more influenced by other-directed advertisements than inner-directed ones.

Although the third hypothesis, concerning use of media, was not conclusively supported by empirical data, Kassarjian felt that academic demands, social activities, and living conditions restricted the individuals' potential exposure to the media. However, Kassarjian learned that "other directed students . . . tended to prefer the sports section and local news portions of the newspaper, such as rock and roll and popular music on radio, and the television type of dramatic fare. . . . Inner directed subjects appeared to prefer and be exposed more to classical music on radio, more often read *Time* magazine and the editorials, syndicated columns, and comic sections of the newspaper than their other directed counterparts" (H.H. Kassarjian, 1968, pp. 266-267). Knowledge of these media habits of the inner- and other-directed individuals is as important to the advertiser as knowledge of the themes that have the most influence on them.

Centers and Horowitz tested their hypothesis that other-directed people are more susceptible than inner-directed people to the influences of others. Hence, other-directed people will tend to conform to opinions of others, especially if they are perceived as being socially important. Questionnaires were administered to experimental and control groups of both inner- and other-directed people. The questionnaires given to the experimental groups contained responses of nameless but reportedly important and well-known people. The other-directed individuals were influenced by and conformed to the fictitious important people's responses more than the inner-directed people. Centers and Horowitz suggest that this conformity itself might be a desired goal, since it was apparently self-rewarding (Centers and Horowitz, 1963).

A study conducted by Carment, Miller, and Cervin showed the effects of intelligence and extroversion on susceptibility to motivational messages. Two hundred and forty-eight students took part in an experiment that was based on verbal discussions. It was found that when two extroverted subjects of different intelligence levels were paired against each other, the more-intelligent subject was less persuadable. When two subjects, one introverted and the other extroverted, of high intelligence were paired, it was found that highly intelligent introverts were more likely to be persuaded than highly intelligent extroverts. This last finding was contrary to the general theory that extroverts are more susceptible to social influence than are introverts. The authors felt this could be a specific finding for this experiment and not generally applicable. It can be explained by the possibility that introverts were conditioned to social influence more rapidly than extroverts, because in this experiment a change in opinion occurred as a result of "punishing" or "reinforcing" responses emitted by the other member of the pair. It was found that in most cases the extrovert did not receive the amount of "punishment" or "reinforcement" that the introvert received. It should also be noted that no extrovert publicly changed his opinion to agree with his introverted opponent, although several did so privately (Carment, Miller, and Cervin, 1965).

The fact that the experiment was based on verbal discussions had an effect on the persuasibility. Although these results can be accepted concerning persuasibility in verbal discussion, the general theory put forth by Eysenck is more applicable to advertising where face-to-face discussion is minimal. According to Eysenck, in situations in which the perception or attitudes of the individuals are opposed to group pressure, extroverts will be more likely to be persuaded than introverts (Eysenck, 1957, p. 214).

Marketing Examples of Inner- and Other-Directedness

Advertising campaigns for public causes, such as fire prevention, driver safety, and litter disposal, have tried to convey an impression of social importance and urgency to their audiences. Other-directed individuals probably would need less promotion to motivate their support for a cause that already seems inherently acceptable socially. However, to inspire less other-directed and inner-directed people to adopt certain social behaviors, a more extreme message has to be communicated.

Smokey the Bear preaches that "Only you can prevent forest fires" amid a sadly burned and wasted forest; antilitter television commercials show fields, parks, and roadsides spoiled and "uglied" by trash and paper waste; and automobile safety commercials portray gruesome accidents and injuries that could have been avoided by wearing seat belts. Thus the visual impact of these messages is intended to stir inner-directed individuals out of complacency.

It has been suggested that people in advertisements have positive motivating effects on the audience. Yet if inner-directedness increases with age, this has implications for the kind of people shown in advertising and for other people in personal selling and promotion. Younger ages can be shown pictures of their peer groups. They socialize in large groups, their frame of reference is a group, and frequently they evaluate issues in terms of what the group would think. Yet as the individual grows older, he pairs off with one member of the opposite sex or another couple. An authentic portrayal is man-woman or perhaps two couples. Thus the communicator would not appeal to the latter (as he is growing more inner-directed) in terms of a group, such as a beach scene where 15 people are playing volleyball. This just is not "him."

29 Variables within the Audience: Group Variables

Group Variables

A *group* can be defined as "a number of individuals regarded as having some quality in common" (English and English, 1958, p. 232). An individual is a member of many groups with differing degrees of influence. Some groups are those to which one automatically belongs because of age (teenagers, middle age, old age), sex (male or female), education (high school, college), income ($5000-$10,000, $10,000-$25,000), or marital status (married or single). Groups also can be specific, in which membership is in small face-to-face interaction, such as PTA, sororities, bridge clubs, etc. Some groups may be anticipatory rather than actual. For example, the *nouveau riche* may perceive themselves as having upper-class status, while the established upper class sees the *nouveau riche*'s status as comparatively lower. The following propositions will further explain the effects group membership can have on an audiences' attitudes and behavior.

Family

V.B8 *The degree of cohesiveness of family groups is positively correlated with the degree of family influence upon the members' beliefs, attitudes, and actions. Messages that dispute these family beliefs and attitudes will be likely to have little or no motivational effect upon the audience members with strong family ties because family influences far outweigh the influences of the mass media.*

How does a system of family relationship influence the ideas and value system and thus the behavior of its members? The child's parents are, at least during the early period of infancy, the sole source of gratification, relief from discomfort, protection from danger, and source of reward and recognition. Thus the child's first glimpse of the world and the nature of the adult is provided by the behavior of his parents and other members of the family who may be present. The family provides the youngster with his first and most significant reference group (Hollander, 1967, p. 131).

Various studies have shown positive correlations between parental practices and attitudes and the child's behavior. Peck studied 34 adolescents who were interviewed and diversely tested each year from ages 10 to 18. He correlated four dimensions of family interaction—consistency, democracy, mutual trust, and approval—with six dimensions of personality—ego strength, super ego strength, willing social conformity, spontaneity, friendliness, and hostility-guilt complex. Results indicated that adolescents with high ego strength—that is, those who were mature and rational and who possessed insight into other motives—had parents who were consistent, trusting, and approval giving. Adolescents who felt guilty because of hostile feelings came from autocratic and disapproving families (Peck, 1958).

Following a study of voting behavior, McCloskey and Dahlgren reported that family influence on the stability of a voter's preference increased when the party choice of family members was homogeneous, if political interest and loyalty existed in the family, and if the same family preference had been retained over time. Family influence on the party allegiance became stronger as the degree of communication between family members increased. These same factors undermined party loyalty of family members who had rejected the family (McCloskey and Dahlgren, 1969).

Several other researchers examined the relationship between political party affiliation and family political preferences. Results of a study by Hollander indicated that if both parents had identical political preferences, a two-thirds probability existed that their children would have the same political preferences at maturity (Hollander, 1967, p. 130). The significance of the family in determining political attitudes was also seen in Lazarsfeld's studies in which between two-thirds and three-fourths of the voters voted for the party of their fathers (Krech, Crutchfield, and Ballachey, 1962, p. 195). A study of a group of high school seniors revealed that the opinions of the students in the general area of public policy and public affairs had a higher correlation with the attitudes of their parents than with those of their teachers or peers (Remmers and Weltman, 1947).

These studies substantiate the theory that attitudes of individuals stem in part from their family affiliations. However, to evaluate the significance of correlational studies and to understand the role and limitations of family influences requires a close analysis of the fundamental psychological processes involved. To say that the family is important in shaping attitudes or beliefs is not equivalent to saying that the child will take over attitudes and beliefs ready-made from the parents. The influence is possible, but whether an individual will or will not develop the same beliefs as his parents depends upon the importance and meaning of the belief for the child himself; that is, family influences on attitudes, both their formation and change, must necessarily be viewed in the context of a dynamic pattern of influence that operates mainly indirectly upon the individual family member. Thus the family, because of the influence of outside cultural pressures, can give rise to a negative correlation of attitudes between parents and children as they mature.

Although the complexity of relationships in modern society may mediate direct family influences on motivation of audience members, a large sphere of family influence remains to be considered in the area of communicating. It is within the family influence that initial exposing occurs to beliefs that will later be accepted or rejected by the child later in life.

Marketing Examples of Family

If a family has emphasized thrift and economy, this attitude will affect the purchase behavior of the child as he grows up. Because he has had such an orientation at home, he will be more familiar with and more susceptible to such promotional messages. Such will also be the case where quality has been emphasized. In purchasing furniture, newlyweds may not have a great deal of money to spend; but because quality may have been "ingrained" into them, perhaps they will buy one piece of furniture at a time instead of sacrificing high standards for expediency in furnishing a household.

If authoritarian families produce more passive and dependent children than democratic families, this would suggest that the latter are more open to being motivated toward purchases because of their behavior patterns of making decisions for themselves, not to mention their high degree of open-mindedness. One might find more authoritarian families in certain rural or ethnic areas or in certain religious groups.

There is a tendency for joint decision making to increase as the importance of the product increases. Choice of the type of applesauce purchased may be made by one person; but when such items as a washing machine and furniture are contemplated, both husband and wife will have to make the decision. In terms of choosing a vacation spot, the entire family will usually participate in the decision.

Role

V.B9 *If a message points out discrepancies in a person's role performance, it is more likely to motivate him in the desired direction than if the message simply praises him for certain role behavior.*

A change in role, or the perceiving of it, may change attitudes either directly or indirectly. Changes in role may involve a change in reference group, which leads to a change in attitudes, and then action. However, a change in role may involve a direct change in the actions involved, which will then influence attitudes (Lieberman, 1969, p. 329).

The relative amount of concern for self and one's valued others is a function of numerous personality variables. For family roles, the expectations and prescriptions are known to nearly everyone in society. However, the degree of acceptance of these social commitments will vary with the individual. A free society does not specify too closely the required attitudes or behaviors toward valued others.

Some situations may exist in which threats to self are not psychologically separate from threats to valued others. The sociological and psychological makeup of the individual will determine his perception and reaction toward role dissonance.

Thus messages may be designed so that the referent of the appeal is some other person the audience member values. Human nature is not solely selfish or materialistic, despite frequent preoccupation with selfish needs and gratifications. Happiness and the real meaning of life are truly achieved only through love and involvement with valued others. These roles are important for each individual's own psychological well-being. Messages concerning the importance of this role to others may change attitudes or behavior to their benefit, as well as to one's own.

Marketing Examples of Role

Insurance companies often aim their advertising at the role of the father-husband-provider who is forced to see what would happen to his family were he to die suddenly.

For Band Aid, a sterile-padded plastic bandage, a series of print and television messages are directed at women through their roles as mothers. One advertisement showed a group of young boys playing in the dirt; later, the mother of one of the youngsters removed a Band Aid from a dirty finger revealing to the viewer how clean the bandage had kept the wound. The slogan of the message, "Keep a tiny cut tiny," reemphasized the role of a mother as watchguard of her children's first-aid and hygienic needs.

The same media were used by Goodyear to appeal to the protector role of the husband in advertising for their safety tires. A woman driver was shown stranded with a flat tire, usually in a deserted or dangerous area, or at night. The slogan was, "When there's no man around, Goodyear should be!" The rest of the message explained how the consumer could confidently drive for miles even if the Goodyear tire should go flat, because of a strong inner tire layer.

Sex Differences

V.B10 *Differences in motivating correlated with the sex of an individual result from the roles, needs, and wants that members of each sex have learned from their culture; and these differences must be taken into account in designing messages primarily for one sex.*

Most studies that have tested both males and females have found that in general females are more susceptible to motivational communications than are males. This appears to be more a result of sex roles demanded by society rather than innate biological differences.

During childhood the social norms and training that might possibly influence ability to be motivated are essentially the same for both sexes. Abelson and Lesser found no significant difference in this trait with regard to sex in young children (Abelson and Lesser, 1959). However, as children develop, social pressures impose sex roles on them that strongly shape their personalities. These sex roles are particularly relevant in the areas of intellectual independence and docility.

Janis and Hovland suggested of these acquired cultural roles, "The culture seems to demand of girls greater acquiescence in relation to prestigeful sources of information and a pattern of frictionless social relationships, with the result that girls on the whole are more susceptible to influence.... All the authors who compared males and females suggest that the differences are due to cultural sex roles which require a greater degree of submissiveness on the part of girls" (Janis and Hovland, 1959, pp. 240-246).

This does not mean that males are not capable of being motivated. It simply means that cultural determinants of ability to be motivated tend to be relatively stronger in females. Since cultural sex roles for men are less definitive in prescribing how to react to motivational influence, the personality factors outlined above generally determine a man's level of susceptibility to motivation.

Several studies have shown that adult females generally are more persuadable than adult males. For example, Schneidel gave a group of college students an attitude survey designed to assess opinions on the expansion of federal powers; then the students were shown a film opposing further federal power expansion. Immediately after the film, the students filled out an alternate form of an attitude survey. Schneidel found that women shifted their opinions more than men, as shown by the two surveys. Also women exhibited a greater "generalization of conformity" than men by becoming more negative toward areas of expansion of federal power that were not specifically mentioned in the film (Schneidel, 1963).

McGuire found that in general women are more susceptible to influence, since they demonstrate less confidence in their ability. They have a stronger need for social approval than achievement. The subjects had six different levels of prior group agreement (100, 75, 50, 25, 0 percent and control) and the task was to decide which of three stimulus lights went off first. In the first test, the subjects thought they were responding first; and in the second phase, they thought they were responding last. Women displayed a lower tolerance of group rejection than men. Conformity is also more predominant in mixed-sex groups than in same-sex groups (McGuire, 1964).

Whittaker studied sex differences in susceptibility to interpersonal motivation. Subjects viewed a stationary light point in a dark room and were asked to estimate how much it moved. This illusion is known as the *autokinetic phenomenon.* Subjects were then retested with another subject who had been instructed to disagree with the first subjects to see if their opinions would be influenced. Whitaker found female subjects to be more persuadable than males when confronted with a new opinion. All subjects, regardless of their sex, were motivated to change to a greater degree when paired with male as opposed to female partners (Whitaker, 1965).

In general, psychological studies have found women to be threatened more by loss of social approval than are men. Having a social orientation, a woman's motivation to act will be greater than a man's if it is called to her attention that she may be able to improve the social harmony of her household or alleviate a threat of disapproval by her husband, family, or associates. Also, consider the discussion of sex differences earlier in this book, chapter 23.

Marketing Examples of Sex Differences

Cleaning products have been advertised so as to appeal to both the social-harmony concern in women and to the achievement orientation in men. For women, the emphasis is on not being embarrassed if company should find a smudge of dirt. For men, the promotion includes a bit of competition; it is a matter of speed in waxing the floor or car. Oftentimes the man is portrayed almost as if in competition with the clock and those forces infringing upon his leisure time. One advertisement showed a man and his children frantically cleaning the house before the wife returns from an out-of-town visit.

Diet Pepsi-Cola television and radio commercials were designed to communicate with the roles of the female audience. A musical background called "The Girl Watchers" was played, while the scene showed a shapely but slender young woman being admired by men as she walked by them. The selling point was that men enjoyed looking at women who stayed thin, and that "The girls girl-watchers watch drink Diet Pepsi."

Contac cold pills were promoted in a television commercial that portrayed cartoon characters of a husband and wife, plus a monologue by the wife. A silent, hulking, tired-looking man was shown returning from work, and his wife floated about him on a cushion of air as she pampered him. Her monologue underscored the faithful, attentive nurse role: "Oh, got a cold? Poor baby! . . .How'd you catch that cold anyway? A great big strong man like you, . . . Contac and I will take real good care of you. You'll see."

Status in Group

V.B11 *The higher and more stable the audience members' status within their peer group, the less compulsive they normally will feel to conform to that group's judgments and the more likely they will be to react individually and to influence their reference group to become similarly motivated than if they have a low status within the group.*

Audience members do not function as independent entities in society but interact with other people. They are influenced by this interaction and also influence others through this interaction. This social influence occurs at two levels: the influence of groups on individual members and the personal influence that occurs in face-to-face encounters. Consistent interaction with particular sets of individuals leads an individual to establish himself as a member of this group, and this reference group will thus influence that person's purchasing decisions.

The conspicuousness of a product defines its susceptibility to group influence. The usual consequence of this influence is that it induces individuals to give attention to their status in the eyes of others (Hollander, 1960). Most women, when buying a new dress, will conform to certain standards of style, length, and color that have been established by the reference group to which they belong, but few will want to purchase a dress exactly like one that one or more other members of the group have bought. Thus the question becomes one of discerning the role status plays in effecting the amount of conformity or individuality an individual will display.

In most groups, the ranking of members, implicit or explicit, depends on the extent to which the members represent or realize the norms and values of the group: the more they do, the higher they rank. But it is not just conformity that gets an individual high status in a group. He must also provide services for the others that are in short supply, including not just conformity but a high degree of conformity (Homans, 1961, p. 163).

Hollander investigated the conditions for the acceptance of nonconformity, and based on his findings he postulated the existence of a commodity termed *idiosyncrasy credits.* An individual earns "credits" by conforming to the group norms and by displaying a general competence. As the number of credits increase, the individual is allowed greater degrees of nonconformity without rejection by the group. As this occurs, his status in the group increases with a concomitant increase in what the group expects from him. If he fails to meet this expectation, he may suffer a loss of idiosyncrasy credits and a subsequent loss of status (Hollander, 1960, pp. 365-369). However, the greater accumulation of credits an individual had achieved, the greater his status and the more he can afford to "have a few subtracted" (Hollander, 1958).

Harvey and Consalvi studied the differential conformity of the leader, the second-ranking member, and the lowest-ranking member to pressures in the informal group. They found the second status member, only one step from the top, was significantly more conforming to judgments of the other members than was either the leader or lowest-status man. The leader was least conforming, but not reliably less than the lowest-status member (Harvey and Consalvi, 1960).

Marketing Examples of Status in Group

A most important marketing implication of the principle is the fact that time, energy, and money can be saved by directing advertising and other promotions at the more-stable, higher-status individuals within a given market rather than at the whole segment and orienting appeals in a more personal and individual direction. Instead of promoting group acceptance through the purchase of the product, the break away from the crowd approach can be used in demonstrating that purchase of a product shows independence. By doing this, a communicator can concentrate on a smaller, more-elite group and hopefully through that group reach the entire market.

Both product promotion and packaging of perfume appeals to the individuality of women. Whereas a lot of women wear Chanel No. 5, there are only a certain few who wear Norell; and Norell emphasizes the distinctiveness of the women who wear its product. The shapes of perfume bottles are also used to connote uniqueness.

Certain retail establishments appeal to the needs of distinctiveness by having salespeople bring out clothing from the back of the store to show customers instead of displaying the clothing on long racks. Through familiarity with the salespeople, a customer has the feeling that she is getting something specifically made "for her," instead of something for the masses.

The growing popularity of small specialty stores reflects the "breaking away from the crowd" desire. Many people prefer to buy gift items in stores where they feel that the owner-buyer has picked out each item of merchandise individually in terms of high quality and uniqueness.

Opinion Leaders

V.B12 *A communicator can motivate people effectively by directing his message to certain opinion leaders of theirs who in various ways then transmit the message to less-innovative people.*

Berelson and Steiner defined *opinion leaders* as

those trusted and informed people who exist in virtually all primary groups, who are the models for opinion within their group, who listen and read in the media, and who then pass on information and influence to their circle of relatives, friends and acquaintances. . . . By and large, opinion leaders are like the rank and file of their associates, but of slightly higher educational or social status. They give much greater attention to the mass media on the topics of their opinion leadership. They are better informed, more partisan, and more active than their associates. [Berelson and Steiner, 1964, p. 550.]

For research purposes, Rogers proposed three methods of measuring and locating opinion leaders. The *sociometric* technique consists of asking group members to whom they go for advice and information about ideas and/or products. The *key informant* consists of asking the key individuals in the social system who the opinion leaders are. The *self-designating* technique consists of asking each respondent a series of questions to determine the degree to which he perceives himself to be an opinion leader (Rogers, 1962, pp. 137-161).

One of the problems in trying to rely on opinion leaders to convey information is the problem of locating the opinion leaders and making sure that communications reach them. In trying to do this, the communication may get a great amount of "spillage"–that is, information reaching other members of the group as well as the opinion leaders. However, the advantage if a marketer succeeds in getting his message on personal channels are twofold: the message will get through to the audience more easily and it will become more credible.

Katz and Lazarsfeld isolated what they considered to be the specific characteristics distinguishing leaders from nonleaders. These were position on the social integration and economic ladder, position in the life cycle, and degree of social integration and/or gregariousness. The authors proceeded to throw out the old "trickle-down" theory of influence and eventually arrived at the following profiles of their respective leaders.

1. *Marketing leaders tend to be married women with comparatively large families.* They do not congregate on any particular status level, yet do tend to be quite gregarious. When the flow of influence in this area does cross status boundaries, it can flow upward or downward. Generally speaking, older women have occasion to influence their juniors more than the reverse. Finally, only in the case of a very specific product that falls within the domain of the husband or or child is the immediate family influencing at all.

2. *Fashion leaders are concentrated among young women—these women leaders tend to be very "socially integrated."* Status plays a minor role. It can give a woman a head start for leadership in this area. Some research indicated that fashion influence travels down the status ladder to some extent and can flow upward between age groups.

3. *Public affairs leaders are likely to be older, high status, and male.* There is, in this one case, direct evidence that influence crosses boundaries—traveling down from upper-status individuals to those on the lower levels. Interestingly enough, despite greater political activity on the part of younger people, older people seem to be here a more prominent factor. In any event, males, particularly husbands, make their presence felt here.

4. *Movie-going leaders tend to be concentrated among young girls, as with fashion leaders.* The flow of influence tends to move from younger to older women. Gregariousness was found to be inapplicable here (Katz and Lazarsfeld, 1955, pp. 234-308).

The Revere study, which was conducted in 1948 in New Jersey, sought to determine who the leaders of influence were. The investigators asked the respondents for their opinions as to whom they considered to be influential. Then, of those individuals named as influential, those designated four or more times were subsequently interviewed themselves. Once the leaders had been uncovered, the investigators devoted their whole attention to classifying them into different types. An interesting conclusion of the study was that within the broad sphere of public affairs, one set of individuals was found to be occupied with local affairs and another with cosmopolitan affairs. The study found that the leadership of the local influentials was based upon their central location in the web of interpersonal contacts. That of the cosmopolitan leaders rested on the presumption that they had large amounts of information (Katz and Lazarsfeld, 1955, pp. 73-74).

Whyte's Philadelphia study sought to determine the effect of the "word-of-mouth web," the network of interpersonal communications in influencing air conditioner ownership in a Philadelphia block. Whyte noted that the sheer location of a house on a block could and did play a significant role in opinion leadership, because of sheer influence by neighbors. Whyte acknowledged the power of mass media advertising but concluded that word-of-mouth was then, and will be more so in the future as the consumer becomes even more sophisticated, increasingly critical in determining who buys what and when. He found that word-of-mouth communication had become increasingly important as more and more products were developed and as people knew less and less about the actual manufacture of the products. Whyte also found that word-of-mouth was very important for a person to determine if a certain purchase, say of a dishwasher, would seem acceptable or if that purchase would appear to be "putting on the dog" (Whyte, 1954).

Katz and Menzel studied to determine the manner in which physicians make decisions to adopt new drugs. They found that the factor most strongly associated with the time of adoption of the new drug was the extent of the physician's integration into the medical community; that is, the more frequently a doctor was named by his colleagues as a friend or a discussion partner, the more likely he was to be an innovator with respect to the new drug. Thus the drug study also provided evidence of the strong impact of personal relations, even in the making of scientific decisions (Menzel and Katz, 1955).

Marketing Examples of Opinion Leaders

Various advertising campaigns have made attempts to reach opinion leaders. Often testimonials are used to show target audience members how experts recommend a product. For instance, Lux Soap for many years was advertised as the soap of the stars.

Probably the best way to reach opinion leaders is to advertise to them in the medium from which they are most likely to receive their information. For a woman who considers herself to be a fashion expert, the communicator might choose *Vogue*; the news might "filter" to *McCalls*, which deals with fashion but not high fashion exclusively, as does *Vogue*. Other potential sources of communication are fashion shows or visits by a top designer to a quality store. For example, when Halston appeared at Garfinkel's in Washington, D.C., the store served champagne to all customers who came in to look at the collection.

Certain products can be grouped together under an opinion leader's expertise. If people like modern furniture, it can be assumed that most of them also will like Scandinavian glassware and fabrics, as well as modernistic decorative and entertaining items.

Because opinion leaders actually seek out information, it is best when initially presenting a product to them to do so in a factual manner. The communicator should provide access to any other information that might be wanted and not mentioned in the message.

Opinion leaders are also the people who tend to be innovators. They look for new products, changes, and improvements. Thus any communication that utilizes these areas should attract opinion leaders. Personal selling can play a big part in conveying the message that this product is "the latest thing."

Degree of Conformity

V.B13 *Audience members with a high degree of conformity to group standsrds are less likely than are nonconformists to be motivated by messages in the mass media that conflict with established group norms. However, all audience members are more likely to be motivated by such messages if they offer rewards that outweigh possible group punishment for nonconformity.*

Conformity is a "correspondence to a recognized or required pattern or standard" established by cultural factors (English and English, 1958, p. 111). *Nonconformity* is a movement away from the norm or standard. The tendency to conform is a universal cultural process as a means of communication and social control. It may be thought of in terms of socialization, as well as in terms of a conscious, deliberate response to social pressure. Imitation is a related concept that also may be the unconscious result of developed cultural patterns. Imitation is the acceptance of a model form of behavior. It can be of three types: imitation of conditioned response, imitation after a trial-and-error period, and deliberate imitation (Britt, 1949, pp. 259-260).

The tendency to conform or not to conform is dependent upon social pressure in the form of what might be called a reward or a punishment. *Reward* may be defined as "a satisfaction-yielding stimulus or stimulus object that is obtained upon the successful performance of a task" (English and English, 1958, p. 465), while *punishment* may be thought of as "the infliction of a penalty by one person upon another because the second has done something disapproved by the first or has failed to do something. The penalty may be any kind of dissatisfaction: a painful stimulus (physical or social) or the denial or removal of a satisfaction" (English and English, 1958, p. 431). This reaction to conform may be the result of suggestion.

Deutsch and Gerard differentiated between two types of social influence. *Normative pressure* is "an influence to conform with the positive expectations of another," while *informational pressure* is "an influence to accept information obtained from another as evidence about reality." In a perceptual experiment with some group members deliberately making incorrect and unanimous judgments, Deutsch and Gerard showed that social pressure to conform is stronger than the individual's internalized pressure to conform to his own judgment. If an individual is uncertain about his own judgment, he is more likely to succumb to both normative and informational social influence (Deutsch and Gerard, 1955).

Endler tested the hypothesis that "the more frequent the reinforcement for agreeing, the greater the conformity; and the more frequent the reinforcement for disagreeing, the less the conformity." The subjects of his experiment responded to 36 slides with 8 verbal critical slides and 8 perceptual critical slides by means of a panel of lights. The subjects were tested in situations in which 50 percent of the group disagreed with him, and 100 percent of the group disagreed with him. A control situation also was set up. In two sessions, the subjects were told that they were communicating their judgments to the others. The first session was a social-pressure situation, since half or all the group members disagreed with the subject and conforming behavior was rewarding; that is, the subject received a reinforcement for the continuance of conforming behavior. The second session took place two weeks later, and no pressure to conform and no rewarding reinforcement to act in either direction were given the subject. Results supported the hypothesis that conformity scores were higher for social-pressure situations. Also, as the frequency of reinforcements for agreement increased, the amount of conformity increased (Endler, 1969, p. 155).

Several variables have been found to influence the degree of conformity to group norms. The amount of consensus in the group effects how strongly committed a member will feel toward its norms. The more valuable a group is to an individual, the more likely he will be to conform to its norms. Also, if an individual perceives the group to be more competent than he is, he will be more likely to conform to that group's opinions than if he is familiar with and has personal knowledge of the issues.

Asch conducted an experiment to measure the majority effect on an individual when in the presence of a "true partner" who sided with him against the majority. In the "true partner" situation, the partner announced his estimates before the subject, and results showed a decrease in majority opinion and an increase of independency. When the "true partner" retreated to the side of the majority after beginning the response pattern by siding with the subject, the subject then yielded to majority opinion. When the "true partner" arrived late, the subject did not show signs of complete independence, probably because he had made prior commitments and needed the image of consistency. With a "compromise partner," who sided with the majority on certain tests and with the subject on others, the subject still made moderate errors (Asch, 1952, pp. 189-200).

Hollander, Julian, and Haaland showed that prior conditions of group support influenced later elicitations of conformity behavior in that group. Seventy-six female and 36 male college students were divided into groups of the same sex. They were to judge which stimulus light went off first. In the first test, the subject participated in 20 trials in which he or she was led to believe the group agreed with his or her own response. The levels of group support were 100, 70, and 50 percent, and control. In the last 20 trials, the subject responded last and under the pressure of the group's perceiving the stimulus incorrectly. The 100 percent support condition showed the highest level of conformity, with a corresponding linear decline. In the 70 and 50 percent conditions, subjects were less dependent upon the group and showed lower initial conformity, even though the conformity response was persistent. The control group showed little or no dependence (Hollander, Julian, and Haaland, 1965).

Copp studied the influence of loyalty in a farm cooperative, testing the willingness to remain in the cooperative and to support it in the pursuit of its goals. He interviewed a stratified sample of members and a printed schedule of questions regarding each member's status characteristics, knowledge about the cooperative, participation in the activities of the cooperative, and the attitudes toward the cooperative. He also gathered relevant marketing and price data. He found that those members who defined the situation as compulsory were less loyal than others. Members believed they were getting a better price for their products when no evidence indicated membership affected price scheduling. The amount of influence a member felt he had in the cooperative corresponded to loyalty more so than to the degree to which he participated, and belief in membership benefits were more important than knowledge of actual benefits in determining loyalty (Copp, 1964).

Walker and Heyns conducted an experiment using sorority girls who were members of four different sororities. They were exposed to several sources of norms, which included their general campus group, general sorority group, and own sorority group. They were asked to rate five organizations with differing degrees of familiarity from very good to very poor. The organizations were two fraternities, a campus religious group, the National Association for the Advancement of Colored People, and the Interstate Commerce Commission. The norm and its source were announced. The results showed that the more familiar the organization being judged was, the less likely an individual would conform to his group if it had differing attitudes; but if the subject was unfamiliar with the organization, she would adopt the attitudes of her group (Walker and Heyns, 1962, pp. 24-29).

Marketing Examples of Degree of Conformity

Conformity based on cultural traits may be more rooted and fundamental than that based on group pressure. Several economy-car promotions strike at conformity. Many upper-income people now purchase the compact economy car, although their economic and social status might seem to dictate a luxury car. Volkswagen has imitated the luxury cars that advertise room, with its headline "Think Big" and a 2-page spread of a picture of the interior of a Volkswagen.

A communicator needs to be aware of the conformity tendencies of groups. Adolescents as an age group tend to be more conforming than other age groups. The communicator can capitalize on this by making reference to "what your friends will think."

Couples with small children conform to the behavior of other couples with small children. It is expected that one will take his or her children on picnics, to the beach or circus, and will buy the latest toys for them. One mother will mention a new Fisher-Price toy, and soon most of her friend's children will also own toys made by that company.

Personal Communication

V.B14 *If the view of a message in a mass medium differs greatly from the view of audience members' peers and associates, they will be more likely to be motivated in the direction of their peers than in the direction the message suggests; in other words, personal communication of ideas is more likely to motivate audience members than mass communication.*

Personal communication is direct, person-to-person communication between the sender and the receiver of the message. This interaction is characterized by the presence of direct feedback, a reaction on the part of the receiver that is observed by the communicator (Davis and Webster, 1968, pp. 109-110). The effects of persuasive mass communication are mediated by personal communication, both directly and indirectly. Interaction among members of a given group communicates the group's opinions, attitudes, and beliefs to the individual. Messages are consequently attended to, perceived, and reacted to according to the norms of the group to which the receiver actually belongs, or aspires to belong. Personal communication within the group therefore predisposes the individual to perceive and learn from mass communications.

In a study of factors that influenced voting in Erie County in the elections of 1940, Lazarsfeld, Berelson, and Gaudet found personal relationships to be more influential than the former communications media. The superiority of personal communication was attributed to its greater coverage and certain psychological advantages it had over the formal media. In terms of coverage, they found that "whenever the respondents were asked to report on their recent exposure to campaign communications of all kinds, political discussions were mentioned more frequently than exposure to radio or print." Furthermore, this extra coverage came from just those individuals who were still undecided and therefore open to influence. This led to the intuitive conclusion that personal contact, partly because of its coverage, was more "persuasive" than the mass media (Lazarsfeld, Berelson, and Gaudet, 1948, p. 150).

The psychological advantage of personal communication lies principally in the fact that the individual uses the attitudes and beliefs of others as a standard in evaluating the correctness of his own attitudes and beliefs. The influence of others on the individual involves his need to gain their acceptance or his need to refer to some standard to establish and maintain his own cognitive clarity about his current environment. The following implications may be drawn from the influence of personal communication on the effects of mass media.

1. *Mass communication is generally not a sufficient cause of audience effects*, but rather functions among other factors and conditions external to the communication. Among these mediating factors are personal relationships.

2. *Personal interaction with a group communicates group influence to the individual.* The group's opinions, attitudes, and beliefs thus affect the predisposition of an individual toward incoming communications in general. Depending on their predispositions, individuals select from all the messages they are exposed to, those they will attend to, comprehend, and remember.

3. Besides providing predispositions and norms of behavior for the individual, *groups also serve to pass on communications to their members, thus directly influencing them.*

4. *Persuasive mass communication is better suited to enforce existing attitudes rather than to change them.* The individual's predispositions influence his behavior toward mass communications and its effects on him. Through selective exposure, only favorable messages are generally attended.

Marketing Examples of Personal Communication

One creative way to involve a customer in communicating the news of a retail store to others is through the use of store packaging that is distinctive and recognizable. A shopper walking down the street with one of the store packages in his hand or under his arm is a walking testimonial for the store if the wrappings have a color and design that unmistakably identify it.

A testimonial advertisement can act as strongly as personal communication with one's friends if the individuals "endorsing" the product are credible and if the audience can identify with them as part of their respective peer group. Ivory Soap print advertisements once used pictures and testimonials from families who provided their names and home addresses. One advertisement showed a grandmother, mother, and child who said, "We three generations think it's amazing. Ivory's best for all our complexions and so economical too." The tone of the copy was one of a believable person-to-person communication.

Members of the same group will tend to attend to the same media. They will read the same newspapers and magazines and thus have a point of mutual discussion. An individual buys certain magazines because he may also feel someone in his occupation or economic bracket reads such magazines. For example, a business executive subscribes to *The Wall Street Journal, Business Week, Time*, or *Forbes*, whereas a factory worker has fewer sources to begin with but may read *Reader's Digest*, his union news, and the local newspapers.

Members of a group tend to shop at the same stores. When members see each other in the store or make reference to a particular item in the store, it reinforces the habit of shopping there.

Diffusion of Innovation

V.B15 *The time at which audience members will be motivated or persuaded to accept an innovative idea or product is a function of the process of diffusion of information through social channels. Mass media are important sources of information for initial awareness, but word-of-mouth communicating is the most important source for evaluating information.*

An innovation is any idea, practice, or material artifact perceived to be new by possible adopters (Zaltman and Lin, 1971). In other words, an innovation is anything an audience member perceives to be new to him, and he will seek information about this innovation from those who may know more about it than he does. To whom he goes for the information depends upon how long he has known of the innovation and how close he is to trying it himself.

Personal sources and the mass media share supplemental reinforcement functions in all events. The more important the information, the more likely it is that individuals will learn of it from other individuals. It must be remembered, however, that a greater part of the average person's day is spent in surroundings in which he is exposed to communication from other individuals rather than from the media.

Arndt defined *word-of-mouth advertising* as "oral, person-to-person communication between a perceived non-commercial communicator and a receiver concerning a brand, a product, or a service offered for sale" (Arndt, 1967, p. 190). The persuasive power of word-of-mouth communication has been investigated by a number of researchers. For instance, Eisenstadt concluded, following a study of the absoprtion of new immigrants into Israel, that "the process of communication is therefore conducted within specific channels and through specific persons whose positions within the social system are structured in such a way as to maximize the degree of fulfillment of these functions. Among the channels, two are most important: (a) close, primary, interpersonal relations in which basic mutual identifications are maintained; and (b) persons and agencies in positions of leadership who perform roles of elites within different spheres of the social system" (Eisenstadt, 1952, p. 56). In this group the truly important communicating was thus word-of-mouth.

Word-of-mouth seems to owe some of its potence to the widely shared impression that it provides trustworthy information, especially in the field of evaluative information (as opposed to factual information, where mass media prevail); and hence, it can help people make better buying decisions. This generalization is supported by the studies of Beal and Rogers and Wilkening. In both studies the subjects were asked to report which source of information influenced them most for each stage in the decision process, that is, during awareness, interest, evaluation, trial, and adoption. It was found that use of word-of-mouth increased in the later stages of the adoption process (Beal and Rogers, 1967; and Wilkening, 1956).

A study by Lionberger indicated that the type of information transmitted about farming to farmers was related to characteristics and functions of the transmitting agents. He asked 636 young farm operators in six Wisconsin counties to indicate their major sources of information at three different stages in the acceptance of changes in farming awareness, decision, and action. The investigator found that commercial firms played a less important role in informing the farmer about changes than they played in the other two functions. An explanation may be that the farmers failed to give due credit to commercial sources utilizing farm papers, magazines, and radio programs.

In general, the mass media provided the initial awareness of new techniques, since they could communicate with a wide audience; while friends, neighbors, and other personal contacts were important in evaluating the changes or techniques. These new ideas had to be evaluated with respect to local conditions by family and friends. Finally, agricultural agencies and other farmers had the technical know-how to put new techniques into practice; and thus, information on implementation was sought most often from them (Lionberger, 1960, p. 57).

Word-of-mouth also owes some of its strength to social censorship resulting from interpersonal relationships: "The fact that other people also accept the product gives social support, while the fact that others reject the product may increase the dissonance (following a major purchase decision)" (Arndt, 1967, p. 227).

This generalization was confirmed by Whyte in an observation of neighborhood purchase patterns. The purchase of window air conditioners by residents on a particular block was found to be significantly influenced by the particular network of social influence on that block. The two important components of the network were social traffic, which determined the social contacts that would be made, and the presence of leaders, which determined the influence that would result from the contact (Whyte, 1954).

The implication of these studies is that once a communicator's message has been accepted by some influential members of a group, they will serve as further "advertising" for the message through word-of-mouth communicating.

Marketing Examples of Diffusion of Innovation

An illustration of the way in which marketers can benefit from the reliance of most individuals on their peers in the evaluation stage of the adoption process is provided by the "house-party" technique. This is a form of door-to-door retailing in which the salesman enlists the aid of a present or potential customer, preferably an opinion leader for the commodity being sold. The salesman asks her to invite other potential customers to her home so that a sales presentation may be made to the group as a whole.

Word-of-mouth can be a strong ally of advertisers. Because of their unique method of presentation, certain advertisements will tend to stimulate conversations. If word-of-mouth is favorable, less promotional funds need to be placed in mass media. Word-of-mouth, however, cannot be controlled by marketers and may lead to disparaging rumors. Jacobson told of the rumor that Liggett and Myers employed a leper in its manufacturing facilities for the Chesterfield brand. Company executives felt that it was necessary to finance a public relations campaign aimed at invalidating the rumor (Jacobson, 1948, p. 59).

30 An Overview of Motivating

Implications

Once the message has been perceived and learned (and hopefully the audience members have remembered the intended message), the next step is to assess whether the message will affect the audience members as the communicator intended. The psychological principles on motivating presented in this part of the book were developed to assist the communicator to make this assessment. The sections on motivating versus persuading and beliefs-attitudes are particularly important because they serve as the underlying framework within which the principles operate.

Model of Motivating

Although motivating and persuading "share" various principles, the basic distinctions between the processes must be kept in mind. *Motivating* the message is related to and is congruent with the audience members' beliefs-attitudes. Motivating reinforces these beliefs-attitudes. In contrast, *persuading* goes beyond simply relating the message to current beliefs-attitudes and seeks to have audience members reevaluate them and change them. The interrelations of the variables encompassed in the motivating process are presented in figure 30-1.

The preconceived variables (needs and wants, sociocultural status, personality variables, and other internal and external variables) are still operating at this stage of the communicating process. Similarly, the variables in motivating can be divided into (1) message and medium variables and (2) variables within the audience.

Message and Medium Variables

The message and medium variables in motivating are broken down into three distinct groups: the rational message, the nonrational message, and credibility.

Rational messages are characterized by relatively "calm, orderly, and restrained presentations of either concrete proposals or abstract objectives" (Hartman, 1936, p. 101). Rational messages include objective allusions to audience members' needs and wants. Consequently, the order of presentation of

417

418

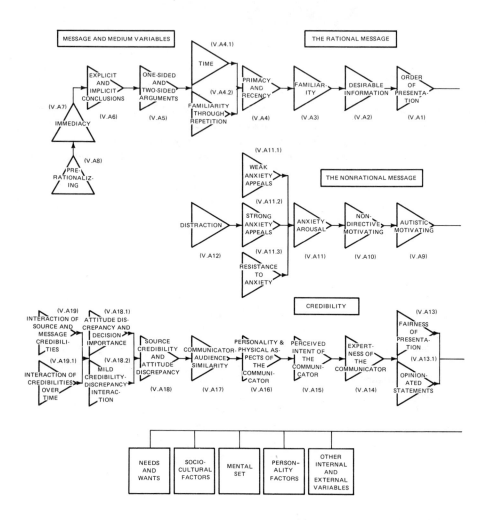

Figure 30-1. The Motivating Stage of the Psychological Model of Communicating. Note that all of the Message and Medium Variables in Figure 30-1 on Motivating Are Identical with the Message and Medium Variables in Figure 34-1 on Persuading.

419

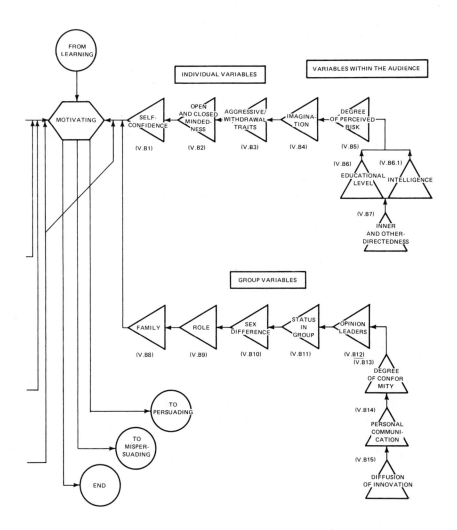

items in a message becomes important, since audience members should be made aware of these needs and wants before solutions are presented.

This can be further enhanced if the message contains desirable information and if the information has a high degree of familiarity to audience members. Spatial and temporal aspects of the elements in a message can, as was also pointed out in part VI on learning, help to determine the effectiveness of a communication. Consequently, the effects of primacy, recency, and time, as well as familiarity through repetition, can serve to stimulate the motivating process. In presenting concrete or abstract arguments or conclusions in a message, the communicator must be aware of the interrelated but differentiated advantages of using one-sided and two-sided arguments and drawing explicit and implicit conclusions. In situations about which the audience members are uncertain, motivating can be facilitated by presenting audience members with reasons that are helpful in prerationalizing but also stress the immediacy of the communication situation at hand.

As mentioned earlier, the nonrational message is used by the communicator to stimulate emotional more than rational responses from audience members. Autistic motivating is particularly effective in this emotional stimulating, when the message presented is associated with audience members' own hopes and dreams.

Nondirective motivating reinforces the process by creating an atmosphere in which audience members feel that the views expressed by the communicator are their own. While the previous two processes are more of a positive reinforcement, the communicator can pursue a less-positive course by presenting messages that are directed toward anxiety arousal. To pursue this effectively, the communication must be identified as to whether the situation is better suited to weak anxiety appeals or strong anxiety appeals. Correspondingly, possible resistance to anxiety appeals by audience members should be anticipated, and if possible, modified. Finally, any gains derived from the utilization of these foregoing principles on both rational and nonrational messages can be rendered useless, or almost so, if there is too much distraction or "noise" in the audience members' environments.

The principles concerning credibility stress the importance of both the compatibility of a statement with known facts and the reliance upon the reputation of the individual making the statement. If audience members feel that there was a fairness of presentation of the message, then acceptance is more likely than otherwise.

Also, if the source was perceived initially as trustworthy, then the presentation of opinionated statements in the communication serves to stimulate acceptance and favorable attitude changes. Correspondingly, message agreement is further enhanced if both the expertness of the communicator and his trustworthiness are accepted by audience members.

However, these positive effects can be negated if the perceived intent of the communicator is seen as being directed toward influencing the audience in his favor. Mediating factors in the preceding processes also include the personality and physical aspects of the communicator as well as the communicator-audience similarity. As in previous sections, the importance and stability of prior beliefs and attitudes serve as basic, determining factors in motivating. When these prior beliefs and attitudes are challenged, problems and opportunities develop that relate to source credibility and attitude discrepancy. When such a situation occurs, the communicator should be aware of various types of interactions, particularly attitude discrepancy and decision importance, as well as mild credibility-discrepancy interaction.

As a final note, when assessing source and message credibilities, the communicator must also keep in mind the various possibilities that can arise through the interactions of source and message credibilities and the interactions of credibilities over time.

Variables within the Audience

In motivating, both individual variables and group variables should be analyzed by the communicator in order to influence his target market effectively.

The psychological principles concerning individual variables were developed to shed some light on the relationships between specific personality predispositions and responsiveness to communications. A communicator needs to be aware that audience members who are high in self-confidence, are closed-minded, or have aggressive withdrawal traits are particularly resistant to attempts to motivate them to act as the communicator desires. However, audience members who possess a high degree of imagination or affinities for symbolism are more easily motivated to act as the communicator desires. In situations of uncertainty, a communicator must be aware of where members of his audience "fall" in terms of degree of perceived risk—high-risk perceivers tend to seek more information than low-risk perceivers. Correspondingly, audience members of high intelligence and educational level are motivated by factual evidence and prefer messages where comparative data are given. A final mediating factor in the motivating process concerns the degree to which audience members are inner- or other-directed—the latter usually being more susceptible to motivational messages.

Social and cultural variables play a major part in the diffusion of new products, and of beliefs and attitudes, because they are important sources for definitions of appropriate behavior and interpretations for group members. The family members and their degree of cohesiveness are particularly important variables because a message that seems in conflict with these beliefs and attitudes will have little motivational effect if family ties are strong. Pointing out discrepancies in audience members' roles and their performance can be an effective motivating strategy; and sex differences and differential status in groups must also be considered.

When confronted with transmitting information about new products or ideas, a communicator must consider the importance of social channels, as in the diffusion of innovations. This process of diffusion can be facilitated greatly if the communicator can identify opinion leaders, as well as obtain some measure of the degree of conformity and personal communication that audience members have with their peers and associates.

We now move to a discussion of persuading of audience members. Keep in mind that all the motivating propositions also apply to persuading. Both steps in the communicating process call for audience members to relate the communicator's messages to their beliefs-attitudes-opinions. In motivating, these convictions are reinforced; and in persuading, the audience is further asked to reevaluate their existing convictions in light of this new information. However, the communicator is often unaware of whether primarily he will be motivating or persuading because he may not know the beliefs and attitudes of his audience. Therefore, these two steps of communicating are closely interrelated.

Part VIII:
Persuading

31 Message and Medium Variables

Background

Persuading is that part of the communicating process which asks audience members to reevaluate their beliefs-attitudes-opinions before they act. Persuading them does not occur in all communicating situations. Only when a communicator tries to change his audience members' beliefs-attitudes-opinions is persuading involved.

If the communicator is trying to relate his message to the needs and wants of his audience, he is trying to motivate them. If they are appropriately motivated, they then probably will behave as he desires. However, if the audience members have been motivated to relate the message to their desires but have found the message to be incongruous with their own beliefs-attitudes-opinions, then the communicator's job becomes one of persuading them. He must try to convince them to change their beliefs-attitudes-opinions in order to be receptive to the contents of his message.

Thus it is the *reinforcing* of beliefs-attitudes-opinions that occurs in motivating, and the *changing* of beliefs-attitudes-opinions that occurs in persuading. For example, if a particular audience member is in the market for a new car, he will be likely to be most motivated by advertisements for cars toward which he has favorable impressions. If he believes that a Cadillac is the finest car and the car that he wants and can afford, once he has been motivated by a Cadillac advertisement to buy a car now, he will be likely to behave and purchase the car. However, if the audience member sees an advertisement for a Lincoln, he will be motivated to read it because of his need for a car. If the advertisement presents convincing arguments that a Lincoln is better than a Cadillac for his wants, he may be persuaded by the advertisement to reevaluate his beliefs-attitudes-opinions, and he may behave to buy or seek more information about Lincolns.

Persuading is that part of communicating for which marketers most often are criticized. This attempt to convince consumers to adopt a new idea or product is often construed by critics as trying to make consumers buy things they do not need. However, consumers are not gullible, passive receivers of all information directed to them in the mass media. Marketers are aware of consumers' abilities to choose from wide varieties of competing products.

The study of persuading, as of all communicating, traditionally has been from the viewpoint of what a communicator *does* to an audience: a phenomenon of one-way influence. Bauer suggested that this model rightfully should be

425

replaced by the view of communicating as a transactional process in which two individuals both give and take in the interaction. He has proposed that the process be seen as a "bargain" between communicator and audience, with the audience being made up of individuals who demand something from the communication to which they are exposed. They must get something from the "manipulator" if he is to get something from them (Bauer, 1964).

Instead of designing products and then trying to convince consumers that the new products are good for them, manufacturers are researching the needs and wants of their target audience members and designing products to fit those qualifications. The marketer's job has moved from one of persuading his audience that they have the need for a new product to one of persuading his audience that this product fills their needs and wants.

Message and Medium Variables

Reinforcement or Change?

VI.A1 *A persuasive communication is more likely to reinforce the existing beliefs-attitudes-opinions of the audience members than to change such predispositions.*

An audience may be regarded as individuals who respond to a promotion or sales idea in a variety of ways, depending on their individual predispositions. Every individual possesses a unique set of beliefs, attitudes, and opinions that determine his behavior. He will accept communications—such as advertisements, promotional ideas, and sales propositions—that are consistent with his own mental set because these communications reinforce his beliefs-attitudes-opinions. Acceptance does not depend solely on logic; after all, individuals often accept as true something they *want* to be true.

Therefore, a great deal of communicating must function either to reinforce existing attitudes and behavior—that is, to maintain brand loyalty—or to stimulate or activate individuals who are already predisposed to act in the desired manner. For example, individuals who enjoy reading murder mysteries are most likely to be on the lookout for, and to be influenced by, advertising of murder mysteries.

The relationship between persuasive communicating and opinion change was studied by Lazarsfeld, Berelson, and Gaudet when they examined the effects of the 1940 presidential campaign upon the residents of Erie County, Ohio. Voter preferences were ascertained in May and later in October, preceding the election. Among 600 respondents, it was found that campaign propaganda reinforced the original, precampaign intentions of 53 percent; 23 percent switched from support for a particular party to "undecided," or vice versa. Only 5 percent had definitely been converted; that is, they changed party lines (Lazarsfeld, Berelson, and Gaudet, 1948). On the basis of this and other studies we can conclude that minor attitude change is more likely to occur than total conversion as a result of a persuasive communicating.

Interpersonal dissemination of information or word-of-mouth communicating is also a significant factor. If one or more of a man's neighbors has had trouble with a certain brand of lawn mower, and consequently disclaimed the product, the individual is not likely to buy that brand. See chapter 27 for discussion of perceived intent of the communicator and chapter 29 regarding diffusion of innovation.

The most important exception to resistance to change is the case of the "inoperative mediating factors." Klapper stated that media are quite effective in forming opinions and attitudes in regard to new issues, particularly when these are unrelated to the "existing attitude cluster." In these cases individuals have not formed attitudes from previous experiences, nor is it likely that any group norms are present; that is, the mediating factors are not present and the communicator may influence his audience directly (Klapper, 1957-1958).

An individual may see an advertisement for a new product, buy the product, and then create his attitude toward that product. The advertisement may only have created a curiosity for the product, while it is the actual experience with it that creates or changes the individual's attitudes. Thus the new attitude was created by reinforcement from the use of the product rather than from suggested change from the message in the mass media.

The point of this discussion is that mass communicating does at some times succeed in changing beliefs-attitudes-opinions, but it is much more likely to be successful in changing these convictions if it operates in conjunction with other forces affecting the particular beliefs-attitudes-opinions in question. In general, mass communicating usually helps to reinforce existing convictions.

Marketing Examples of Reinforcement or Change?

A heavy smoker may try to ignore the advertisements of the American Cancer Society. He may not perceive their commercials as relating to the possibilities of his smoking leading to cancer. He may tend not to retain the information in the advertisements. In fact, by ignoring the Cancer Society commercials, an individual may actually reinforce his own beliefs concerning smoking: that it is not really harmful!

If an individual were to see an advertisement for Datsuns but most of the members of his group have Toyotas, he may tend to disregard the message for Datsuns, or derogate the message. In this manner, groups and their norms are an important variable in the communication process.

Changing Beliefs-Attitudes-Opinions as Related
to Changing Behavior

VI.A2 *Once an individual has committed himself to a specific stance on an issue, a change in his beliefs, attitudes, or opinions will not necessarily result in a change in his external behavior.*

Individuals do not always perceive reality identically. Because of differences in perceiving, a "fact" may not be the same for all individuals. This *selective perceiving* plays a role in persuasive communicating, tending to alter the individual's beliefs and attitudes in order to initiate new responses to the stimuli.

On the basis of their research, DeFleur and Westie concluded that behavior is determined to a considerable degree "by the extent to which the individual is actually or psychologically involved in social systems providing him with norms and beliefs which he can use as guides to behavior" (DeFleur and Westie, 1958, p. 668). They isolated 46 students, half of whom were prejudiced against Negroes and half of whom were not. Each was asked to sign an authorization permitting the use of a photograph of that person sitting with a Negro. The authorizations ranged from limited use in a laboratory experiment to a national publicity campaign. They found that those who were prejudiced were less willing to have the photograph taken and widely used (DeFleur and Westie, 1958).

However, Festinger has called attention to three studies that do not produce such a relationship where attitudes influence behavior (Festinger, 1964). One experiment used mothers with a single child between the ages of 3 and 12 months and measured attitudes and behavior in relation to the timing of toilet training for a period spanning one year. One group of mothers was subjected to a persuasive booklet that advocated beginning training at an age some months later than when training usually begins. The other group was not exposed to any persuasive communication. The two groups were interviewed immediately after the experimental group had read the booklet. The attitude change of the experimental group was considerable in the direction advocated by the persuasive message. The results of the experiment were different than what might have been expected. Although attitudes apparently had been changed by reading the booklet, behavior of the experimental group was less changed than that of the control group. The control group started training their children on the average of 2.0 months later, while the experimental group started their training only 1.2 months later (Maccoby, Romney, Adams, and Maccoby, 1962, pp. 47-52).

In the second study, Fleischman, Harris, and Burtt gave foremen a training course stressing the principles of human relations in dealing with subordinates. Although the results showed that the attitudes of the foremen had changed, no effects were found of differing instructions on actual job performance (Fleischman, Harris, and Burtt, 1955).

In his third example of behavior as unrelated to attitudes, Festinger cited Janis and Feshbach, who had three groups of high school students exposed to three different kinds of persuasive communication on proper care for teeth and gums. A fourth group was a "control" group and received no special communications. The three groups who received the communications differed in the intensity of the threat used in the communication. It was hypothesized that the strong threat appeal would change their behavior most. In reality, however, although they did change behavior, the change did not exceed that of the other groups (Janis and Feshbach, 1953).

Festinger held that these three studies show that one cannot merely assume that a change in attitude necessitates a change in behavior. His explanation for this is that attitudes are changed only temporarily through the momentary impact of a persuasive communication. Such an attitude change is not stable and will disappear unless an environmental change can be brought about to support and maintain it. If after the change the experiences of an individual remain the same, his attitudes will tend to revert (Festinger, 1964).

In considering the conditions under which behavior changes might occur, Pinson and Roberto indicated that the ways that attitude change and behavior change covary can be affected by several intervening variables.

1. *Threats to internal and external validity.* These constitute a set of potential factors that can affect the degree of empirically discernible relationships between attitude and behavior change.

2. The degree to which the consumer perceives *the connection between his attitude change and the possibility of changing his future behavior.*

3. *The "cost" of behavior relative to the "cost" of the act* at an earlier point in time or relative to those other alternative forms of behaving.

4. The degree of *interrelationships among different attitudes* that individually may influence the same behavior.

5. The presence or absence of *opportunities to perform the behavior expected* (for example, Howard and Sheth's (1969) "inhibitory factors").

6. The *time gap* between the attitude change and the expected behavior change (the longer the time gap, the greater are the chances that intervening variables will come into play).

The implication from these points is that we ought to be more concerned with *the conditions under which attitude change precedes behavior change*, as compared with the question of "Does attitude change precede behavior change?" (Pinson and Roberto, 1973).

It is difficult enough for the communicator to change his audience's convictions to fit his message; but even if he can reduce their dissonance by changing their beliefs-attitudes-opinions, he still may not succeed in changing their behavior as he desires. Persuading is thus the most difficult and most uncertain stage of the communicating process.

Marketing Examples of Changing Beliefs-Attitudes-Opinions
as Related to Changing Behavior

In face-to-face interactions, such individuals as clothing-store salesmen, car salesmen, and insurance salesmen can try to persuade prospects to agree with their sales points, since it is awkward to disagree. But a prospect will probably try to delay taking action if this would conflict with the attitudes he held prior to the sales visit.

Promotions for commuting by train in large metropolitan centers may go far to convince people that such transportation could save time and be more comfortable than automobile travel; but car owners do not easily "follow through" by giving up their automobile-commuting habits.

Summary

The differences between motivating and persuading should be clear. *Motivating* is the process of relating a message to the needs and wants of the audience, while *persuading* carries the communicative process one step further by asking audience members to reevaluate and change their beliefs-attitudes-opinions. Persuading takes place in the minds of the audience members, and the only external evidence of a change in attitude or inclination toward a specific behavior occurs when the audience members act. It is possible for a person to be persuaded and not act immediately.

In the stage of motivating, a message is presented that may or may not be incongruous with the individual's belief-attitude-opinion framework. If the message is congruous, it acts as a reinforcement; but if not, dissonance may develop. At this point the individual must make some sort of decision or act to resolve the inconsistencies.

Yet when a communicator creates a message, he rarely knows for sure if he will be reinforcing his audience's beliefs-attitudes-opinions or if he will be trying to change them. Thus he must act on the presumption that he is trying to make an audience feel or believe or act a certain way. His goal is to influence, convince, or satisfy. In other words, he desires the individual to act as he prescribes.

Thus the message and medium variables for persuading are the same as for motivating, because the communicator is never *sure* of whether he will be motivating or persuading. The message and medium variables that apply to motivating and persuading appear in part VI, on motivating.

32

Variables within the Audience: Dissonance Factors

Dissonance Factors

As with all the previous steps in the communicating process, persuading is dependent upon the physical and mental state of the audience members. With persuading, however, the variables within the audience are especially important. If the audience members have attitudes similar to or the same as those of the communicator as expressed in his message, persuading is not involved; his message will reinforce the existing beliefs and motivate the audience members. If, however, the communicator's message causes dissonance in the audience members between or among their existing attitudes and new ones suggested by the communicator, persuading will be necessary.

Whenever audience members must make a choice or a decision that involves alternatives, uncertainty exists. Almost by definition, if a choice is to be made at all, each alternative must have positive attributes. Thus it is likely that an individual may experience uncertainty as to the wisdom of his choice. This uncertainty, or dissonance, results from the inconsistency that exists between one's choice of action and the messages that speak favorably of the rejected alternative.

Cognitive dissonance, a theory developed by Festinger, links attitudes to overt behavior in the individual. It is based upon the served fact that humans as rational beings, normally strive for consistency between what they know and/or believe and what they do. Therefore, human behavior is consistent because humans behave in accordance with their attitudes. The term *cognition* means knowledge or insight—which includes beliefs and opinions—about oneself or one's behavior. *Dissonance* is a term meaning an "inconsistency between two or more cognitive elements" (Secord and Backman, 1964, p. 115). *Consonance* would be two or more cognitive elements that follow from each other and are therefore not inconsistent.

Dissonance or consonance exists only when the cognitive elements are relevant to each other. Moreover, the greater the relevance between cognitive elements, the greater the possible amount of dissonance. To simplify the discussion, the magnitude of dissonance can be looked on as the following ratio but cannot actually be measured in terms of this simplified ratio:

$$\text{Dissonance} = \frac{\text{importance} \times \text{number of dissonant elements}}{\text{importance} \times \text{number of consonant elements}}$$

431

From this it can be seen that "the magnitude of dissonance is a function of the proportion of all relevant cognitive elements that are dissonant. . . . the more nearly equal the relative proportions of consonant and dissonant elements, the greater the dissonance is" (Secord and Backman, 1964, p. 116).

The importance of cognitive dissonance to communication theory is that it is a powerful influence that causes the individual to strive toward dissonance reduction—to reachieve consistency between his attitudes and his actions. According to Festinger, being psychologically uncomfortable will cause an individual to try to reduce the dissonance, which can be done in three ways. He can change his behavior, change the conditions of his environment, or add new cognitive elements to the situation. Festinger has stated that an individual will actively avoid situations and information that would be likely to increase his dissonance (Festinger, 1957, p. 3).

Studies have been made that confirm that recent purchasers of high-importance commodities, such as cars, read advertisements pertaining to their purchase to a greater degree than nonpurchasers. This could possibly be because they are seeking information to confirm their decision. It also could be caused by the perception phenomenon known as "changed figure and ground," which accounts for things that previously escaped attention suddenly entering consciousness because of familiarity with the object (Engel, 1963, p. 58). Whichever the cause, the marketer is presented with an ideal situation to use advertising designed to reduce cognitive dissonance. After selling consumers his product, the communicator then finds them particularly reading his advertisements.

Mills tested the effect of decision making on exposure to positive information and found that new car owners read advertisements for their own car more often than for cars they considered but did not buy. This finding supports the theory that individuals will, in general, seek out supporting information after an important decision in an attempt to reduce dissonance resulting from it. According to this study, the degree of interest that information has for an individual who has recently made an important decision depends on whether or not it supports the choice he has made. Individuals tend to seek out material they expect to favor and they can therefore use to reinforce their choice. This study dealt only with positive information, that is, information presenting good features of an alternative (Ehrlich, Guttman, Schonback, and Mills, 1957). However, Festinger's theory that an individual will seek out dissonance-reducing information is not limited to information that is positive; it applies equally well to negative information about the other alternatives.

While it is erroneous to assume a perfect correspondence between public exposure to a message and the number of messages distributed, it is also false to assume that exposure to messages results in a uniform interpretation and retention of the content of the messages. Individuals not only selectively expose themselves to information to help reduce their dissonance, but they also selectively perceive the information they receive.

Feather tested smokers' sensitivity to information about smoking and lung cancer and their evaluation of the information. The results of the study strongly suggest that states of cognitive dissonance are more likely to influence an individual's evaluation or interpretation of information than his sensitivity to information. One who is engaged in a course of action or who holds a certain belief, attitude, or opinion tends to be more sensitive to information relevant to this course of action, belief, attitude, or opinion. This greater sensitivity occurs irrespective of whether the information supports or does not support the course of action, belief, attitude, or opinion. In many cases, sensitivity to information seems to be governed by this factor of personal relevance, and possible dangers are just as relevant to the cigarette smoker as are possible reinforcements. Thus commitment to a course of action does not necessarily mean that an individual will in future avoid adverse information about his choice.

It appears, then, that the "seeking of relevant information" that Festinger considered typical of a predecision situation also occurs after commitment, and this relevant information may be compatible or incompatible with action or cognition. This is not to say that pressure to reduce cognitive dissonance has no influence on sensitivity, but it is likely that this pressure is often only a minor part of the complex of determinants that influence sensitivity and is frequently overshadowed by other factors. In short, cognitive dissonance appears to have more influence on an individual's evaluation or interpretation of information than on his sensitivity to information in this study (Feather, 1963).

In lieu of an existing dissonance-reducing information source, an individual may deal with cognitive dissonance by selectively recalling previously learned or experienced information in order to restore consonance. For "self-maintenance," individuals tend to retain information supporting attitudes reflected in their past behavior and have difficulty in recalling things that imply those attitudes may have been inappropriate. Selective recall allows the individual to remember those inputs which will be consonant with his existing cognitions, and selective forgetting allows him to discard those inputs which will cause dissonance.

One investigator tried to simulate the effect of a social situation on recall in a study in which he asked subjects to reproduce a 300-word folk story that included a number of unfamiliar notions and obscure connections. Each subject assimilated the story into his own system of culturally determined cognitive categories, which the investigator called "schemata." The story was simplified and elaborated by the subjects to bring the reproduction attempts more in line with expectations. When logical connections were lacking in the original story, the subjects provided them. Elements that seemed inconsistent or irrelevant were omitted. The same tendencies toward condensation and rationalization were even more marked after longer delays (Jones and Gerard, 1967, p. 243).

One of the broader implications of the cognitive-dissonance theory, of particular interest to communicators, is that pressures toward a desired attitude change may be exerted by inducing the individual to commit himself to a behavior in which he would not otherwise have desired to engage. Just as attitudes influence behavior, so behavior if incongruent with attitudes can in turn exert an influence toward change in attitudes.

Brehm tested this theory by inducing junior high school students to eat vegetables they disliked extremely. The theoretical expectations were that commitment to eat disliked food produced dissonance, and that dissonance pressures would be stronger the more of it the individual was committed to eat. He found that the students who became committed to eat the disliked vegetables showed significantly favorable shifts in attitude toward them; their control counterparts, not so committed, did not. Therefore, the results of the study confirmed the theory (Maccoby, Newcomb, and Hartley, 1958, pp. 106-107).

Having built up this background on dissonance theory, the following general conclusions can be proposed.

1. A communicator's messages are far more likely to reinforce present attitudes in audience members (motivate them) than to change them to new attitudes (persuade them).

2. The media are more likely to reinforce attitudes (motivate) than to change them (persuade).

3. The media do not work direct effects upon their audiences but function among and through other factors or forces; and it is these variables that tend to make mass communication a contributing agent of reinforcement as opposed to change.

4. The media can be quite effective in persuading audience members to form attitudes in regard to new issues, particularly when these issues are unrelated to existing attitudes. This implies that new products or new qualities of existing products can be advertised very effectively.

5. Audience predisposition is a controlling influence upon the effects of persuasive mass communication. Such predispositions and their progeny— selective exposure, selective retention, and selective perception—intervene between the supply of available mass communication stimuli and the minds of the audience members.

6. A change in group loyalties or in reference groups may change an individual's predisposition toward consonant opinion changes suggested by mass communication.

7. Group norms or predispositions may become dysfunctional and the individual will therefore become more susceptible to changes suggested by the media (Klapper, 1957-1958).

Attitudinal Homeostasis

VI.B1 *Audience members will more likely strive to reconcile incongruent attitudinal variables when the attitudes they hold are incongruent or inconsistent with either known or communicated facts and ideas than when these attitudes are congruent.*

In other words, when the individual seeks to reconcile discrepant attitudinal elements to reach an equilibrium state, either his original attitudes will be amended to concur with new communications or else the new communication will be rejected and attitude change will not occur. Attitudes tend to remain stable as long as they continue to provide an adequate basis for ordering the individual's world.

The theoretical background for the proposition of attitudinal homeostasis, or the tendency for attitudes to remain stable or fixed, is based upon several related theories: balance theory, pioneered by Heider; Festinger's theory of cognitive dissonance; Osgood and Tannenbaum's congruity theory, which is a special case of balance theory; and Newcomb's strain toward symmetry approach, also similar in many respects to balance theory.

Heider formulated his balance theory in 1946. He was interested in consistencies and congruities with which individuals view their relations with other people and their environment. His fundamental assumption was that an unbalanced state produces tension and generates forces to restore balance (Heider, 1958, p. 201).

Jordan tested Heider's assumptions, which were affirmed. In this study, 288 subjects rated 64 situations involving another individual and an impersonal entity as to the degree of pleasantness or unpleasantness. Jordan found that pleasantness was "a function of balance plus the existence of a gratifying social relationship between two people in the situation." Unpleasantness was "a function of imbalance of the existence of displeasing social relationships between the two people in the situation." Imbalance or unpleasantness resulted in a force to restore balance or pleasantness (Jordan, 1953).

Cartwright and Harary modified Heider's balance to include five elements they felt were lacking: (1) the inclusion of unsymmetric relations; (2) consideration of situations containing any finite number of entities (Heider considered only three); (3) identification of whether a relation existed at all, and delineation if it was an opposite or a complement; (4) delineation of relations of different types (not just Heider's liking and unit formation); (5) widening of the concept of balance for greater empirical applicability. Their modification also included the concept of degree of balance (ranging from 0 to 1), so that problems of balance could be treated statistically and in terms of probability. The result was a general balance definition they believed could be applied to a variety of configurations: communication networks, power systems, sociometric networks, and even neural networks (Cartwright and Harary, 1956).

Osgood and Tannenbaum's congruity theory is a special case of Heider's balance theory. In addition, the study dealt specifically with direction of attitude change. The theory relates attitude change to message source, object or concept, and the nature of the evaluative assertion regarding the source and the object. The congruity theory states that when change in an evaluation or attitude occurs, it will always occur in the "direction of increased congruity with the prevailing frame of reference." Alternatively, "incredulity" will occur: a tendency for the individual not to believe that a statement was either said or meant. The basis for measurement of attitudes in this study was Osgood's semantic differential method (Osgood and Tannenbaum, 1955).

Festinger's cognitive-dissonance theory is perhaps the most widely studied theory of attitudinal consistency. He explained dissonance as "being psychologically uncomfortable, [it] will motivate the person to try to reduce dissonance and achieve consonance. . . . in addition to trying to reduce it, the person will actively avoid situations and information which would likely increase the dissonance" (Festinger, 1957, p. 3). Many studies have been done to test this theory; three will be described here.

One such experiment was performed by Bell, who studied owners of new Chevrolets for postpurchase dissonance and exposure to information patterns. The study was conducted with 289 buyers of new Chevrolets in a large urban area in the western part of the United States during the summer months of 1965. Personal interviews were conducted one to eight days after the purchase. Bell found that the circumstances of the buying situation, the individual's personality, and his persuadability govern the magnitude of dissonance experienced. More specifically, he found that two types of customers were more highly dissonant than other groups: those who were most easily persuaded in the first place and those who had received the poorest service (Bell, 1967).

Another empirical study of dissonance theory dealt with changes of attractiveness of the alternative involved in a decision. Brehm conducted a study in which he asked female subjects to rate eight appliances for desirability; the subjects were then given a choice between two of the eight, given the chosen product, asked to read research reports about four products, and then were asked to rate the products again. Half the subjects were given a choice between products rated similarly, half between products rated differently. The prediction of an increase in the attractiveness of the rejected alternative was confirmed (Brehm, 1956).

A third study dealt with the forced-compliance concept: situations in which the individual is forced (by punishment or reward) to express an opinion publicly that is contrary to his own opinions and beliefs. Festinger and Carlsmith offered experimental subjects either $20 or $1 for telling another person that an experience that had been boring had been enjoyable and interesting. Subjects paid $1 were measured as having higher dissonance scores than those paid $20. They concluded that a large reward is sufficient justification for a small deception, while to mislead an innocent person without significant compensation arouses dissonance. The dissonance is reduced if the liar comes to believe himself, since he then retroactively erases the untruth.

Marketing Examples of Attitudinal Homeostasis

The principle of attitudinal homeostasis is especially applicable to mass communications or advertising principles. Studies have concluded that purchasers tend to reduce any dissonance experienced by exposing themselves to advertisements that act as reinforcements of the positive attributes of the product. Moreover, advertising may function as a means for predecision comparison of products (especially expensive durable goods) to reduce anticipated postdecision dissonance.

Attitudinal homeostasis can be exemplified also in the media selection patterns of individuals. Individuals tend to expose themselves to media that reinforce prevailing attitudes; thus media selection by advertisers would be made with consideration of the attitudes of the target group of consumers.

Market segmentation represents one of the best examples of manufacturers' attempts to achieve attitudinal homeostasis. Market segmentation can relieve dissonance when a product can be used by different age groups or personality types. For example, Bristol-Myers produced Vitalis hair tonic for older men and Score for younger men.

Product names can arouse dissonance. Revlon distributed Revlon Super Natural Hairspray, but ran into difficulties. *Super* meant more holding power, and *natural* meant less; and the consumer was not sure what the product was.

Number and Importance of Positive Attributes

VI.B2 *An audience member will more likely experience less dissonance if a large number of attributes and/or attributes of considerable importance are associated with his chosen alternative than if the number of attributes is small and of less importance.*

If attributes are not additive because of the specific antagonism, the number of positive attributes will not be the only determinant of the decision. Some specific attributes balancing specific opposite ones will have to be found. If attributes can be added, the role of the manufacturer and communicator will be to find as many positive factors as possible to the product so that they will balance the sum of the negative points.

If the second theory is right, the task of the marketing executive will be much more difficult. He will have to find the right attribute balancing the right negative characteristic. He also will have to establish an order of importance of each attribute so that his campaign will bring more emphasis to the positive attributes balancing the larger negative ones. Since the comparisons would be made according to decreasing importance and the procedure would stop as soon as a difference large enough would appear, it is better to state as early in the message as possible the positive elements that will motivate the audience to the proper decision.

Increasing the number and importance of positive attributes is not the only way for the communicator to succeed. He can try to reduce or even eliminate some negative aspects of his product. The consequence of his actions on the attributes of what he has to sell will not only be a decision of purchase made by the prospects, it will also determine a degree of loyalty to his brand. By increasing the value attributed by his audience to the product, he, at the same time, increases their loyalty. The greater the positive difference, the smaller the dissonance and the greater the satisfaction. Since the audience will have a greater satisfaction, they will be more easily persuaded by this communicator in the future.

Marketing Examples of Number and Importance of Positive Attributes

Kelvinator introduced a new line of products that gave the consumer a real product difference—decorator appliances, such as matching sets of dishwashers, refrigerators, stoves, and ovens. The marketing techniques of consumer- and business-publication advertising, sales promotion, sales training, point-of-sale publicity, and product publicity were employed to make consumers aware of this positive and distinctive attribute. Consumers were willing to pay more for appliances coordinated with their kitchen decors; and Kelvinator sales increased dramatically as their new line became a status symbol.

Market segmentation can be based on differing product qualities in the same product category. With several potential selling points a manufacturer can carve out different markets that place priority of certain product attributes over others. Lever Brothers produces Lux with Dermasil for women primarily interested in the care of their hands and Swan for those women more concerned with the cleaning efficiency of a detergent.

Packaging may be used as a positive product attribute. Frozen vegetables that are packaged in plastic bags and immersed in hot water for cooking stress as their selling point "no mess" as compared with the conventional method of preparing vegetables directly in the saucepan. Manufacturers of convenience foods emphasize the time element involved in food preparation; to busy housewives and career women, this is an important attribute.

The stage of product development can affect the kinds of attributes emphasized. IBM first began promoting its computers and copy machines in terms of product performance. For example, the quality of the copies a copy machine made was a main selling point. As the products matured, IBM began to promote itself in terms of a service industry and later emphasized the "weight of decision making," that is, the types of people (businessmen) who depend on their products.

Overlap of Alternatives

VI.B3 *The greater the similarity of the alternatives involved in a decision, the less will be the postdecisional dissonance aroused in audience members; and conversely, the less alike the alternatives are, the greater will be the postdecisional dissonance felt by the audience members.*

To see why greater dissonance results from a decision between dissimilar alternatives, the idea of *cognitive overlap* needs to be made clear. Festinger discusses high and low cognitive overlap as follows: "The degree of overlap is high if many of the elements in the cluster corresponding to one alternative are identical with elements of the cluster corresponding to the other alternative. High cognitive overlap is generally implied when we speak of two things being 'similar.' Low degree of cognitive overlap is generally implied when we speak of two things being 'qualitatively different' " (Festinger, 1957, p. 41).

Brehm and Cohen asked grade school children to rate each of 16 toys on a preference scale. The children then were allowed to choose one of the 16 toys and were asked to rate the toys again. Some were given a choice between qualitatively similar toys (between metal craft sets or between sets of table games), and others were given a choice between quite dissimilar toys (between swimming fins and a model ship). The results confirmed the hypothesis that the toys chosen by each of the children were enhanced in desirability *after* the choices had been made. Furthermore, the study also confirmed that the more dissimilar the objects, the greater the postdecisional dissonance would be (Brehm and Cohen, 1959).

Borck's study of 145 children aged 3 to 12 indicated that dissonance and consequent revaluation of objects were greater for children choosing among dissimilar objects. The children were given a choice between similar objects (two bags of crackers or two toys) or dissimilar objects (a bag of crackers and a toy). Evaluating the objects both before and after their choices showed that the children who chose between dissimilar objects increased their liking for the chosen alternatives and decreased their liking for the rejected alternatives more than in the case of the children who chose between similar objects (Borck, 1963).

This principle can be applied to everyday life in analyzing an individual who has received an unexpected $1000 bonus from his employer. A number of potential alternatives exist for that money. Among those with the highest perceived satisfaction on the part of the consumer might be: saving the money, buying a color television, buying a new wardrobe, or taking a 2-month Caribbean cruise. All these alternatives involve certain cognitive elements. In terms of ways to spend money, these alternatives possess low cognitive overlap; that is, cruising the Caribbean is not very similar to putting the money in the bank. Thus, whatever alternative the individual chooses, he will have had to reject a number of very specific and different alternatives with relatively dissimilar sets of cognitive elements.

Marketing Examples of Overlap of Alternatives

Many implications for the astute marketer are here—action hinging on the product's position in the marketplace and perceived brand image, for example. In order to create a highly desirable brand image and to keep the image clearly defined and superior to potential competitors, the product category must be relatively "empty" and the advertising "noise" level must be relatively low. If a particular brand is perceived by consumers in the marketplace as being distinctly different and superior to those of competitors, dissonance will result when any competing product is bought.

To most motorists, gasolines appear the same. Jersey Standard enhanced Esso brand gasoline by adding the positive attribute of a brand symbol that personified fun—the Tiger in the Tank. Promotional items included tiger tails to hang out of car gas tanks, earmuffs, tee-shirts, and tie clips. The personification of fun with a Tiger made Esso stand out among the brand choices available to car owners.

Honda Motor Company took a product category in which all products were similar in terms of product attributes and created a product image totally unlike anything on the market. To compensate for the American stereotype of motorcycles associated with wild, reckless teenage hoodlums, the company identified its product as a "Honda," never a cycle. The company also was able to differentiate itself from competitors by selling to people who never before had owned a motorcycle. The appeal was to in-groups of educated, sociable young people with the theme, "You Meet the Nicest People on a Honda."

Defects of the Chosen Alternative

VI.B4 *Audience members will experience more dissonance if their preference for the chosen alternative decreases, or if the attractiveness of the rejected alternative increases, than if they are satisfied with their choice.*

If some opinions and/or attitudes that are internally inconsistent coexist within an individual, they are rarely "accepted psychologically as inconsistencies by the person involved. Usually . . . attempts are made to rationalize them. . . . But persons are not always successful in explaining away or in rationalizing inconsistencies to themselves. . . . There is psychological discomfort" (Festinger, 1957, p. 2). One type of this postdecisional dissonance can be brought on through conflict of cultural and personal mores. Human beings as social creatures are expected to conform to many of the norms of society; yet humans as individuals often discover that personal happiness does not always follow the wishes of society.

The various alternatives to a particular decision can become defective in a number of ways. For example, postdecisional dissonance can be brought on through reevaluation of the same factors used in making the decision. A woman may consider both style and color, for example, when choosing between two dresses. On that basis she decides to buy a blue shirtwaist dress instead of a yellow tailored one. After the purchase is made, however, the blue shirtwaist may lose its freshness and the buttons may not seem as attractive as they did in the store. Perhaps the yellow tailored dress may seem very fresh and stylish. Or a combination of both feelings may be present. Any or all of these feelings demonstrate the arousal of postdecisional dissonance based on "another look" at the same factors that contributed to the decision.

Receiving new knowledge that is dissonant with present knowledge or behavior is another common precipitant of postdecisional dissonance. This might be called *cognitive intrusion.* Consider the example of the man who purchases a car that later is discontinued, or the cyclamate user who discovered that cyclamates may be linked to cancer (Straits, 1964).

An important and frequently encountered means of arousing postdecisional dissonance is through nonconfirmation of the expected results from the chosen alternative. When the chosen alternative does not yield the expected result, this disappointment is of course dissonant with the choice. For example, if a person purchases a product with certain expectations of fulfillment, and if the product does not live up to the expectations of the purchaser, anxiety and dissonance will result; and so the other alternative may seem more attractive in retrospect (Hoy and Endler, 1969, p. 208).

Marketing Examples of Defects of the Chosen Alternative

The fashion industry for women cultivates a continuing process of change in the clothes women wear. Mannequins display the "latest style" inside the store and in store windows. The display may cause a dissonant feeling by a shopper for what she presently is wearing; and her displeasure may be further increased by viewing new clothes on the racks. To reduce her anxiety, she will be inclined to buy some new clothes. However, after purchasing a new dress, the shopper may discover that her husband finds it unattractive and overpriced. At this point, dissonance is reinstated and the attractiveness of the chosen alternative diminishes; the rejected alternative, perhaps of using the money for a weekend away, seems more attractive.

Because consumers frequently are confronted with postdecision dissonance, the promise of money-back guarantees may help to combat the problem; that is, knowing that the money will be refunded if he or she is not satisfied with the purchase may create a more positive feeling in the consumer than if he or she feels "stuck" with the purchase.

Sales personnel can be used effectively to prevent postpurchase dissonance arousal. Upon seeing a previous customer, salespeople can inquire how the customer is enjoying the product, or ask if there are any problems or questions he or she might be able to answer.

Postdecisional Reinforcement

VI.B5 *After audience members have responded to a persuasive communication by either covert or overt behavior, or both, they will seek subsequent communications advocating a viewpoint in support of their behavior,/that is, communications that reassure them that they have made the proper decision.*

If an individual has chosen between two makes of automobiles, he is postdecisional. However, the bad features of the car he has chosen and the good features of the car he didn't choose still exist, and this creates dissonance. According to Festinger's analysis, the individual would try to reduce this dissonance. He might read the advertisements for the car he bought and try to find someone who is unhappy with the make of car he didn't buy. In this way he reassures himself that he made the correct choice. Engel conducted a survey to determine the postdecisional readership rate of a Chevrolet advertisement. The study tended to support Festinger's theory by showing a significantly higher readership rate among owners than nonowners of Chevrolet cars (Engel, Wales, and Warsaw, 1967, pp. 546-547).

In seeking to reduce dissonance, an audience member may be motivated to perceive messages in different ways. He may screen out information that either increases dissonance or doesn't contribute to its reduction. He also may enhance a given stimulus with additional information in order that the stimulus become more effective in the reduction of dissonance (Jones and Gerard, 1967, p. 124).

Through selective recall, in a manner similar to selective exposure, an individual tends to remember supportive information that reduces dissonance. For self-maintenance, individuals tend to retain information that supports attitudes reflected in their past behavior and have difficulty recalling things that imply the behavior was inappropriate.

The theory of perceptual distortion says that the greater the dissonance, the greater the tendency of the individual to distort the perceived messages to fit the category of the choice he has made. The difficulty with which one distorts varies directly with the degree of inconsistency that results from the distortion.

The attempt to distort perceived messages in order to reduce dissonance may sometimes produce unexpected results. One interesting example concerned two studies of rumors following disasters. The rumors were recorded immediately after a severe earthquake in India in 1934. The quake was felt over a wide geographical area. The rumors were collected from the area that felt the shock of the earthquake, yet suffered no physical damage. When the earthquake was over, the people had a strong, persistent fear reaction but could see nothing different around them—no destruction, no threatening objects. Thus dissonance existed between cognition corresponding to the fear and the knowledge of what they saw around them. In an attempt to reduce this dissonance, rumors were circulated that produced fear. The rumors mentioned an upcoming severe cyclone, another earthquake, a flood, and certain unforeseeable calamities on a "fatal day" in the future. This, then, is an instance where the reduction of dissonance produced results which looked like anxiety arousal (Festinger, 1957, pp. 72-73).

Marketing Examples of Postdecisional Reinforcement

After buying appliances or clothing, the consumer usually will refer to a wide variety of inserted information that comes with the product. Specifically, the warranty or guarantee, and any promotional pamphlets that are inserted in containers, are important references, as well as "reinforcers," after buying a new toaster or television set. Likewise, after buying a new sweater or suit, the shopper will find that the tags for the manufacturer, the washing instructions, and the statement about garment inspection provide a measure of reinforcement to his decision.

A store's perceived image may create dissonance when it deviates from what the consumer expects from it. But at the same time, the consumer will "smooth over" any discrepancies. For example, the woman's high-fashion clothing store Bergdorf Goodman installed a department for career girls. It is now not just the upper middle class who shop in these stores but the previous customers who still perceive Bergdorf's as a prestigious, elite clothing store.

The media chosen for placement of postdecision reinforcement is important. If a women's shoe manufacturer advertises its product as stylish and of designer quality, a woman would expect to find an advertisement in *Vogue* or *Harper's Bazaar.* If the manufacturer does not advertise there or in an unexpected medium the consumer does not feel meets the proposed product image, say, *Good Housekeeping*, then postdecision dissonance may not be relieved.

Attitude Change to Reduce Dissonance

VI.B6 *In order to satisfy their strong desire to reduce dissonance, audience members are more likely than not to change their attitudes to those presented by the communicator in his message, unless they have strong feelings about that particular attitude.*

A change of attitudes is, of course, the behavior a communicator desires from his audience members when he wants them to change brands, because a commercial shows "facts" that a new brand is superior to the brand being used by the consumer. This example of attitude change is done both to seek a better product and to reinforce the consumers' personal beliefs that they are doing what they should.

In one experiment, Rokeach induced states of dissatisfaction in his subjects concerning the relationships among their values, attitudes, and behavior in particular situations. He studied the long-range effects of such induced states on a group of college freshmen living in residential colleges. They were asked to rank 18 terminal values in order of importance and to state positions in writing toward civil rights demonstrations. One group was then shown a table illustrating the average ranking of previous students, in which freedom ranked first and equality eleventh. The experimenter suggested that students were interested in freedom for themselves but not for other people. To increase their level of dissatisfaction further, the experimental subjects were asked to state the extent of their sympathy with the aims of civil rights demonstrators. They were shown another table that showed the positive relationship between attitudes toward civil rights demonstrations and the value for equality. The control group was not shown the tables. Finally, they all were asked to compare their own rankings of equality and freedom to their positions on civil rights issues. Inconsistencies became apparent.

Measurements of dissatisfaction were obtained by having the subjects rate how satisfied or dissatisfied they were with what they found out about their values and attitudes. The posttest consisted of a letter from the National Association for the Advancement of Colored People sent to the subjects 3 to 5 months later asking them to join. The experimental group who had been shown the two tables exhibited an increase in the ranking of equality over the ranking of the control group. The significant increase in pro-civil-rights attitudes in the experimental group suggested long-range attitude change as well as value change. Attitude change took place following the changes in values. More subjects from the experimental group joined the NAACP and wrote sympathetic letters than those from the control group.

In one of the residential colleges, 5 months later, students were required to register in one of the core areas: (1) ethnic and religious intergroup relations; (2) international relations; (3) justice, morality, and constitutional democracy;

(4) socioeconomic regulatory and welfare policy programs; or (5) urban community policy programs. The results of the registrations suggested long-range behavioral effects of the induced attitude change. The situation had the effect of doubling the experimental students' enrollment in ethnic core programs when compared with the control group's enrollment (Rokeach, 1971).

A communicator can change some attitudes by the creation of dissonance; but two limitations exist on this method of communication. First, the message may be filtered out by the process of selective perception. Second, the message must apply to an attitude in the receiver's area of flexibility or noncommitment. Although the limitations are significant, they do not eliminate the usefulness of this method of communication. If the message deals with something audience members do not have strong feelings about, such as soap or paint, then dissonance can be used to change attitudes.

Marketing Examples of Attitude Change to Reduce Dissonance

One example of this proposition used in advertising was, "Your floors are not as clean as you think they are." A demonstration of Spic and Span cleaning over a spot where the other detergent left dirt behind provides supportive cognitions in favor of the newly proposed attitude. To accept the proposition as true—"Spic and Span is better than the detergent I have been using"—is to create dissonance with an existing attitude—"my detergent cleans as well as I'd like." Thus advertising has prompted, or at least initiated, the reasons for an attitude change in the direction the communicator would like.

Charitable and nonprofit organizations utilize the human tendency to reduce dissonance as their personal solicitors approach people for contributions. When a representative of the March Against Hunger or the March of Dimes asks someone to make a small contribution, the prospect will feel dissonance in trying to ignore the solicitor if he feels that the charity is worthy. To reduce this anxiety, he may oblige the visitor from the charity with a contribution.

The One-A-Day Vitamin promotional theme, "What's a Mother to Do?" also utilized the principle. Dissonance is created when a mother fears that her active family is not getting the proper nutrition because of fast meals and snacking. Advertising may emphasize her concern and problem, but without attributing the possibility of poor nutrition to her neglect of meal preparation.

Effect of Time on Dissonance

VI.B7 *Audience members will take action, over time, to reduce dissonance, with the amount of dissonance reduction being almost directly related to the degree of dissonance initially created.*

The psychological process of dissonance reduction will cause an individual either to change his actions or to change his beliefs-attitudes-opinions. When an action is irrevocable, opinion change is the only available alternative for reducing dissonance. Furthermore, dissonance reduction does not occur spontaneously, but takes place over time as an individual finds additional justification for his opinion—by means of behavioral change—or his action—by means of opinion change.

This theory was supported by the results of an experiment by LoScuito and Perloff. In order to create a dissonance-arousing situation, they had students rank several LP albums according to desirability and then offered them, as a gift, a choice between two closely ranked albums. Reranking after a period of a week showed that indeed, the rejected alternative had significantly decreased in value, while the preferred alternative had improved in ranking (LoScuito and Perloff, 1967).

The rate of dissonance reduction seems to be positively related to the amount of dissonance initially created. In an experiment by Gailon and Watts, two groups of high school students were asked to prepare for an examination. One group was told that they definitely would be required to take the test (1.0 probability), while the other group was told that there was only a 50 percent probability that they would have to take the test (0.5 probability). After the students had been allowed to prepare, it was announced that the examination had been cancelled. The dissonance induced by cancellation of the test was measured immediately for one half of the students, while the other half measured after 20 minutes had elapsed.

Dissonance was measured by means of a questionnaire in which students were asked how much effort they had expended in preparing for an examination, how valuable they thought their preparation had been, how difficult they had expected the test to be, and how willing they would be to persuade others to prepare for such an examination. Answers were indicated on a 15-point scale for each question, with 1 indicating a low score and 15 a high score. High scores were assumed to correlate with greater degree of dissonance.

It was found that time did affect dissonance reduction—students measured 20 minutes after cancellation showed a greater degree of reduction than those measured just after cancellation. The degree of initial dissonance also affected dissonance reduction—students with low initial dissonance (0.5 probability) reduced dissonance to a greater extent than those with high initial dissonance (1.0 probability) (Gailon and Watts, 1967).

In a study by Watts and Holt subjects were asked to rate the probability and desirability of a number of syllogisms. Subjects were then presented with persuasive communications about the major and minor premises of some of the syllogisms. The effects of these communications upon a subsequent rating of the syllogistic conclusions were measured immediately for some subjects and after a 10-minute interval for others. Probability ratings were measured on 100-point scales, ranging from 0 (very improbable) to 100 (very probable). Desirability was measured on 5-point scales, ranging from 0 (very desirable) to 5 (very undesirable). Subjects who were measured after a 10-minute delay showed greater change on the conclusions than those measured immediately after reading the communication. Dissonance created between the communication and the conclusion showed greater reduction after 10 minutes because of greater changes in the subjects' opinion—that is, rating—of the conclusion (Watts and Holt, 1970).

Marketing Examples of Effect of Time on Dissonance

When advertising can persuade the consumer of some additional product benefits of another brand over his presently used brand, then brand switching within a product class may occur over time as a way to reduce dissonance. Likewise, consumers will switch their patronizing of retail establishments when one store is able to convince customers that it is a better place to shop, has more of a selection of products, presents higher-quality products, at lower cost, with friendly sales personnel, and so on.

In terms of price, a great deal of dissonance may be aroused when the consumer is asked to pay a high price. As time goes on, if he is satisfied with the product and becomes convinced that in terms of quality the product is well worth the price, dissonance will be resolved and will no longer be an important issue.

Packaging may also arouse dissonance. If the carton does not allow the consumer to view the product, dissonance may develop because he is unsure of product quality or what he is actually getting. After repeated usage, a quality level will establish itself in the consumer's mind, and no longer will he be concerned that the product is not in a see-through container.

Disbelievable Curiosity

VI.B8 *An audience's disbelievable curiosity increases the likelihood of their being persuaded eventually, provided they actually can find out whether the statement really is true or not.*

Disbelievable curiosity may be defined as the ability of a communication to induce an audience *not* to believe something to the extent that they become so curious that they want to prove they are right that it is not true. If audience members can be made sufficiently curious to go about investigating the truth of the statement, the chances are that greater persuasion will result, provided they can find out whether the statement is true or not.

The questionable statement in the message attracts the perceiver's attention, but he then spends time with the message and tests it through personal observations or by word-of-mouth from others, or both. The degree to which disbelievable curiosity manifests itself is dependent upon the style of the communication, the method in which it is presented, and the personality makeup of the individual himself. The communication must not offend the intended receiver to a degree that it is completely ignored and/or rejected. It must be persuasive enough to compel the individual to prove it wrong.

This proposition reflects a relatively new view of the way in which communicating evokes attitudinal responses in consumers and what these responses mean. The old view judged an advertisement's effectiveness by its ability to lead the consumer through a series of naturally progressive steps, one of which was believing or disbelieving the advertisement (Maloney, 1963). "Most learning theorists' early studies of communicator credibility and communications effectiveness focused upon the simple 'acceptance' or 'rejection' of message content. . . ." (Hovland and Pritzinger, 1957, p. 258). Most recently, however, evidence points to the existence of a middle ground called *curious nonbelief*. Research in recent years has clearly demonstrated that noting, understanding, and believing are not either-or, or go or no-go, occurrences.

One of the early proponents of this theory was Maloney, who stated that, "By its very nature persuasion calls for the communication of messages that will *not* be believed easily" (Maloney, 1963). He added further that if we are to persuade someone to hold a point of view contrary to that which he now holds, we must first get him to *doubt* his present viewpoint and become curious about the viewpoint that we espouse (Maloney, 1962).

In an extensive study, Maloney used six different food advertisements to test what he calls the curious-nonbelief hypothesis. One hundred housewives served as subjects. During in-home interviews, subjects rated food products on several scales and were administered a 10-point readiness-to-serve scale for each rated product. The women were then exposed to test advertisements in a magazine context; they then filled out product ratings a second time and indicated readiness to serve the test products using the same point scale; and finally they were reexposed to the test advertisements and were asked if anything was hard to believe about them. The responses related to belief were classified as reflecting either disbelief or curiosity.

From the results of the experiment, two conclusions were drawn (Maloney, 1962):

1. Two different types of nonbelief response—curiosity and disbelief—are encompassed within a total group of responses made by those who report having found "something hard to believe" in the advertisements studied.
2. Curiosity responses are generally predictive of increased consumer desire to purchase the product. Disbelief responses are generally predictive of relatively little consumer desire to purchase the product.

Maloney added that recent studies strongly suggest that dissonance usually leads to seeking further information relating to the object of the unstable attitude. These studies suggest that persuasive mass media make their greatest contributions to attitude change by making individuals curious enough about the matter at hand to seek further information (Maloney, 1962).

Certain advertising methods may arouse a negative reaction in an individual—"I don't believe it"—which in turn leads to some sort of "cognitive nudge," causing the individual to take a gradually more positive stance—"But I'll try it to see if it's true." Hence, because the individual first doubts his own beliefs, he then becomes curious, seeking more information about the discrepant message he has received. The effort made to gain new information will bring about a final acceptance of the communication and a change in the audience member's viewpoint. Thus effectiveness of a persuasive communication often depends largely upon ability to engender curiosity about that which the persuasive communication is trying to "sell."

Marketing Examples of Disbelievable Curiosity

For the psychological concept of disbelievable curiosity to succeed as a principle to be used in advertising, the individual should think to himself, "Is that possible? No, it can't be. But it just might be. Now let me think. Yes, I believe it just might work, but I'd have to see it to believe it. I must try it." That is the key point in how it relates to advertising—"I must try it." Thus the need for a particular product has been created, which is one of the prime goals of advertising.

A television commercial demonstrating a cake being sliced with a feather induced disbelievable curiosity. This disbelievable curiosity of the cake's actual softness induced viewers to purchase the cake mix to determine the truth for themselves. Thus the message caused disbelievable curiosity and served as a persuasive communication because it generated product purchase.

An advertising campaign for Band-Aid bandages demonstrated the durability of the product by fastening one end of the bandage to an egg and immersing the two in boiling water. While the announcer discussed the product, the egg continued to boil in the presence of the audience and the bandage continued to hold. Such a graphic presentation seemed incredible to many viewers; but in that they could duplicate what was shown, they accepted its validity and were further persuaded to buy Band-Aids.

Curad bandagers ran a "torture" test. In a television commercial a diver with hundreds of Curads over his body dived off a high diving board and swam the length of the pool. The bandages continued to adhere to his body.

Free samples or cents-off coupons offer further incentives for those who hold a disbelievable-curiosity attitude. The product also may be offered at a ridiculously low price for a limited period of time to arouse curiosity.

Incentives

VI.B9 *Audience members more likely will change their beliefs and attitudes in response to strong incentives to change in a particular kind of behavior as well as in response to dissonance than if neither incentives nor dissonance are present.*

Dissonance theory states that an individual will change his beliefs and attitudes in order to bring them into line with behavior that is discrepant with his cognitions. The greater the dissonance, the greater the change will be (Festinger and Carlsmith, 1959). The incentive theory states that greater opinion change will accompany greater incentives (Carlsmith, Collins, and Helmreich, 1966).

By combining these theories, a more applicable theory can be formulated to relate to human behavior. Carlsmith, Collins, and Helmreich found both the dissonance and incentive theories active in their investigation. All subjects were given a dull task; then half were asked to tell another individual the task was interesting, exciting, and fun. The other half of the subjects wrote an anonymous essay to the same effect. All subjects were paid $.50, $1.50, or $5.00 for their participation (Carlsmith, Collins, and Helmreich, 1966).

The results of the first part of the experiment demonstrated the dissonance theory. The subjects with high dissonance—those receiving $.50—had the greatest opinion change. Those with low dissonance—receiving $5.00—showed little opinion change. The results from the essays were consistent with the incentive theory. The subjects with high incentive of $5.00 had the greatest opinion change; the subjects with low incentive of $.50 had little opinion change.

Thus one set of circumstances produced results correlating to the incentive theory, and another, to the dissonance theory. A decision had to be made to determine whether or not both situations created dissonance, which a face-to-face confrontation would be able to determine. Then the subject would be directly responsible for his actions.

The essays, however, were anonymous. The only person who would read them was the experimenter, and he would not know whose essay he read. The subject was not directly responsible for his actions or opinions. He experienced involvement, not dissonance in writing the essay.

When applying this proposition, one must determine whether or not the situation will create dissonance. If the situation will not result in dissonance, then the incentive theory can be applied to the individual's behavior.

Festinger and Carlsmith had a group of subjects perform a dull and tedious task. Their experiment had three conditions: control, $1, and $20. In the control condition the subjects were treated identically in all respects to the subjects in the experimental conditions, except that they never were asked to, and never did, tell a waiting subject that the tasks were enjoyable. The $1 subjects were hired for $1 to tell a waiting subject that tasks, which really were rather dull and boring, were interesting, enjoyable, and lots of fun. The $20 subjects were employed for $20 to do the same thing.

In all comparisons the control condition was regarded as a baseline from which to evaluate the results in the other two conditions. The control condition provided essentially the reactions of subjects to the tasks and opinions about the experiment as falsely explained to them, without the experimental introduction of dissonance. The data from the other conditions were perceived as changes from this baseline.

Festinger and Carlsmith found in postexperimental tests that the subjects who complied for the lower incentive came to believe that the experimental task was actually more enjoyable than did subjects who complied for the $20 incentive. It was concluded that the lower incentive provided little justification for the subject to commit the counterattitudinal act, thus producing dissonance and motivating the subject to change his opinion to quell the dissonance (Festinger and Carlsmith, 1959).

In an attempt to refine the Festinger and Carlsmith findings, Sherman worked with the conditions of counterattitudinal advocacy that create dissonance. He had subjects arrive at an experiment, only to be informed that the experiment would have to be postponed for 15 to 20 minutes because the experimenter was running behind schedule. Using four different groups of subjects in such a condition, the experimenter then suggested to two of the experimental groups (high-choice condition) that if they felt like it, they could help another experimenter on another project while they were waiting for his experiment to begin. One of the two groups was told of a 50 cent payment (low incentive) for participating, while the second was told of a $2.50 payment (high incentive).

The other two groups also were split into high-incentive and low-incentive categories, with the exception that they were *told* to participate in the second experiment (no choice condition) in the 15 to 20 minute interval. At the second experiment, which involved writing counterattitudinal essays on a highly relevant and important issue to the students, the high-choice/no-choice manipulations were maintained. Having completed the task, the subjects returned to their original experiment, where they were given a 10-item questionnaire dealing with different issues, one of which asked for the subject's opinion on the issues about which he had just been asked or upon which he had been told to write a counterattitudinal essay. Sherman found that for dissonance to be aroused as a result of a person's counterattitudinal advocacy, the individual must have felt free to deliver that counterattitudinal statement (Sherman, 1970).

Going one step further, Cooper and Worchel had individual subjects arrive for an experiment, kept them waiting for 5 minutes, and then had them participate in a very dull task of turning a peg one-quarter turn. This was similar to the dull tasks used by Festinger and Carlsmith. The subjects concluded the dull tasks, and then were told the *supposed* objectives of the experiment. Each was informed that prior to the experiment some subjects were met by a confederate who informed them, like himself, how much fun the experiment had been. Others, like himself, were given only enough information to do the task, with no prior introductions to confederates. The experimenter then said that he was comparing the performance of the two groups and explained that he was initially 5 minutes late because his confederate called in and said that he could not work that day, and that the experimenter had been told by an adviser to seek a replacement for the confederate from among his subjects. Each subject then was asked to act as a confederate for the experiment.

One-fourth of the group was told that they would be paid one-half hour experimental credit (low incentive), were led into a room to tell another subject (really a confederate of the experimenter) how much fun the experiment was, and then were led to believe that they had convinced the subject (confederate-convinced condition). Another one-fourth was offered one full hour of credit (high incentive) and also led to believe that they had convinced a subject that the experiment they underwent was fun. The other half of the subjects were split into two groups (low incentives and high incentives); only these subjects were led to believe that they were unsuccessful in convincing confederates of the experimenter that the experiment would be fun (confederate-not-convinced condition).

On the basis of questionnaires filled out afterward, Cooper and Worchel found that those who felt that they were effective in convincing another about something they believed to be untrue and received low incentive for doing so actually came to believe the task was interesting. They then concluded that dissonance was aroused as a result of counterattitudinal advocacy when the subject believed such advocacy was effective or, in other words, produced undesired consequences (Cooper and Worchel, 1970).

Thus by combining a series of studies, a more applicable theory can be formulated to relate to human behavior. For dissonance to be aroused, a person's counterattitudinal advocacy must be public; the person making the statement must be clearly identified as its author; and the person must feel that such a statement was effective in convincing another of its truth. When dissonance arises to affect a person, incentives at a high level will not cause an actual change in beliefs and attitudes. High incentives serve the individual since they give him cause or excuse for doing things he normally would not do. Low incentives do not provide such an excuse for doing things counter to one's beliefs and attitudes. As a result, the only way to terminate the dissonance is to change one's beliefs and attitudes. However, when dissonance is nonexistent, the aforementioned studies indicate that an individual will change his beliefs and attitudes as a direct relationship to the incentive for doing so.

Marketing Examples of Incentives

For marketers, the lesson is clear. When dissonance is existent in the consumer's behavior, a change in beliefs and attitude about the behavior could not be brought about by premiums (incentives). However, in most cases where brand loyalties are not strong or taboos regarding the product or consumer behavior are not existent, dissonance is not created; samples, premiums, coupons, money, and so on could work well in creating attitude change, at least as long as the incentive is still in existence.

Incentives do not necessarily have to be of monetary value or in terms of anything free. Incentives also may be promises of reward for using the product. For example, an advertisement for a certain perfume offers the promise of love and romance for the woman who uses the particular brand. Manufacturers of tennis rackets endorsed by professional tennis players offer the average tennis player the prospect of better playing performance.

Special contests are occasionally conducted to bring added incentive toward the purchase of a particular product or brand. By announcing prizes for its winners, the contest draws special attention to the product; often the rules of the contest limit the prizes to those who have purchased the product. Thus the chance to win a valuable gift or luxury vacation is enough added incentive to motivate prospective purchasers to buy, as long as there is no dissonance in doing so.

33 Variables within the Audience: Individual and Group Variables

Individual Variables

Many psychological studies have raised the question of whether a personality correlate of general susceptibility to persuading exists. Janis conducted two studies with male college students; and the results supported his hypothesis that consistent individual differences in persuasibility were related to such personality factors as feelings of personal inadequacy. In the first study, he used three persuasive messages with logical arguments that had different topics but that all referred to predictions of future events. His second study used five totally heterogeneous topics in the messages, but the arguments were all logical. Both studies showed general persuasability to be associated with personality types (Janis, 1954; and Janis, 1955).

Janis and Field later attempted to determine if a wide range of types of persuasive arguments as well as different types of topics could be used to find a generally persuasible personality variable. They devised a persuasibility test of 10 different appeals ranging from logical arguments used in the mass media about cancer research to hyperbolic, stereotyped journalism in comments about a television comedian. After pretesting the test on 185 individuals, they concluded that the test was reliable for determining which individuals were more persuasible than others. The experimenters found that the predisposition to change one's opinions is not specific to the issue of a persuasive message. The individual differences in persuasibility detected by the test were consistent, such that those individuals most readily persuaded by a message advocating one set of attitudes or opinions were also most likely to be influenced in the opposite direction by a message taking an opposing stand on the same issue (Janis and Field, 1956). Communicators, however, are not able to give such tests to their target audiences, and so they are often interested in how persuading correlates with other, more commonly judged, variables.

Linton and Graham chose college students based on a total socioeconomic demographic scale and measured them by means of (1) opinion-change tests; (2) tests in an autokinetic and tilting-chair situation; (3) embedded figures tests; (4) inner- and other-directedness tests; (5) items from an authoritarian personality questionnaire; (6) human figure drawing tests to study self-image; (7) personality questionnaires; and (8) the Rorschach tests used to investigate personality patterns. The results showed categories of opinion changers and nonchangers. The individual who was easily persuaded was likely to guide his behavior by

455

external standards in other situations as well, to have values that favor conformity, to have an immature and weak concept of himself, to be unimaginative, and to have a limited range of interests. Nonchangers had a mature and strong self-image, valued subjective feelings, were self-assured, and strove to live by their own values regardless of opposition (Linton and Graham, 1959, p. 93).

The following principles are based on further studies to determine how a communicator can best judge the persuasibility of his audience members as related to their individual personality variables.

Confidence About a Specific Activity

VI.B10 *Regardless of their levels of general self-confidence, audience members of low self-confidence about a specific activity are more readily persuaded about the performance of that activity than are audience members of high self-confidence about that activity.*

In their studies of middle- and lower-class women buying nylons with or without a salesperson's advice, Cox and Bauer concluded that, "when specific self-confidence is relatively high, generalized self-confidence will play a reduced role" (Cox and Bauer, 1964, p. 463). In other words, if the subject involved has different levels of general and specific self-confidence, the specific level will be the more influential in determining the degree of susceptibility to persuasive messages once he or she has been motivated.

Gollob and Dittes conducted studies of male Yale University freshmen in which the subjects were made to experience either success or failure on an ego-involving task. Questionnaires given to the subjects after completion of their task were intended to indicate each one's degree of susceptibility to persuasion. It was concluded that individuals with high evaluations of their abilities were not persuaded as readily as individuals with low evaluations of their abilities (Gollob and Dittes, 1965).

Marketing Examples of Confidence About a Specific Activity

Accepting this principle and its linear relationship as having a reasonably high degree of probability, this relationship is applicable to marketing in that persuasive messages are most effective for audiences having low-general or low-specific self-confidence.

Texaco gasoline advertised that "You can trust your car to the man who wears the star. . . ." Individuals who knew little about their cars or how to repair them—low-specific self-confidence—undoubtedly were more easily persuaded that Texaco was a safe place for their cars than would mechanics, who would know how to evaluate the car's repair problems. By aiming at a segment having low-specific self-confidence, the advertiser in this case can persuade a certain audience to use his service.

Certain types of retail establishments may appeal more to either the highly self-confident individual or a person with low self-confidence. If a low self-confident person is in the market for a camera, he will feel more self-assured with the purchase if he buys it from a camera store. Because the store specializes only in photographic equipment, he will conclude that the salesman knows his business. The consumer will feel less secure if he should purchase it in a mass-merchandised store where cameras are only one in thousands of products stocked.

Packaging can aid in helping the person with low self-confidence. A food manufacturer may advertise that his package is 1½ times the size of his competitor's package for the same price. Even though the net weight is printed on the package, it may help for the package to have a dotted line denoting the ½ times increase in size. Produced visually, this may convince the low self-confidence person of the message more than if he has to decide abstractly whether there actually is an increase in size and product quantity.

A person of low self-confidence may be more brand loyal than a high self-confidence person. If he finds a product he can depend upon, he will be reluctant to change—anxious about the risk of poor performance and unknown standards. He also may be more brand-name conscious.

Men generally have low self-confidence when it comes to purchasing women's clothing. At Christmastime, Marshall Field and other large department stores have a special section of women's clothing items and gift consultants to meet specific low self-confidence in this area.

Ego Involvement and Issue Importance

VI.B11 *If audience members are highly ego involved with the issue discussed in a communicator's message, they will be less susceptible to being persuaded by the message than if they were not ego involved with the issue.*

The term *ego involvement* refers to the individual's personal commitment to a given topic. If the individual has strong opinions, is very committed to an issue, he is highly ego involved. If the individual has few personal opinions (or none at all), is not committed to the issue, he is not ego involved.

Sherif has done considerable research concerning ego involvement and attitude change from which he concluded that highly involved individuals have a much broader latitude of rejection for persuasive messages than have individuals who are less involved. According to Sherif, a message that falls into the individual's range of acceptance or noncommitment can be assimilated by the individual. However, a message that falls within the individual's range of nonacceptance will not be assimilated. People who are highly committed or involved have a much narrower range of noncommitment and acceptance. Therefore, they are less susceptible to persuasion (Sherif, 1967, pp. 349-355).

Riland described his experimental work with a group of residents of a small Pennsylvania town. He questioned the group about a certain company in the town and tried to correlate their reactions to the company with their involvement with the company. He concluded that, "There was a very significant, although not extremely high, positive relationship between the intensity of the attitudes expressed and personal involvement in the attitudes toward the company" (Riland, 1959, p. 283). He was not concerned with whether the opinion of the company was good or bad, but rather with the intensity of the attitudes of the group as measured on the basis of Guttman's principle of scalable attitudes. He obtained a U-shaped curve of reactions with both strong positive and strong negative reactions occurring when the person was highly involved (Riland, 1959).

Freedman conducted an experiment with a group of high school students in which he studied the impact of the level of involvement on discrepant (dissonant) communication. His results were basically the same U-shaped curve previously noted. He concluded that the degree of involvement was important because it affected the point along the discrepancy continuum at which the downturn in amount of change occurred. With low involvement, change increased monotonically with discrepancy; while under conditions of high involvement, the relationship was nonmonotonic (Freedman, 1964).

An experiment by Daugherty and Janowitz suggested that if a message's viewpoint is substantially different from his own, an individual may reject it and become even more extreme in his own position. During World War II, propaganda leaflets were prepared in England to try to change opinions about the conditions that prevailed in allied POW camps. The thought was that if the camps were positively portrayed, German soldiers would surrender more easily. An authentic camp in Canada was shown, in which the prisoners played cards and ping pong, and a breakfast meal description was given, consisting of coffee, eggs, and toast. A pretest of current prisoners who knew the conditions showed that even they could not accept the leaflet as truthful because it varied from what they had been lead to expect (Daugherty and Janowitz, 1958, pp. 562-566).

In a situation of low involvement with the issue of a communicator's message, audience members may accept (learn) the message and then "store it away" for possible future use without a conflict taking place. The individual does not realize that the new information is in conflict with his existing attitudes until he is confronted with a situation in which he needs to commit himself on the issue. Such a situation might be the buying of a product. As Krugman wrote, "That is, the purchase situation is the catalyst that resembles or brings out all the potentials for shifts in salience that have accumulated up to that point. The product or package is then seen in a new, somewhat different light although nothing verbalizable may have changed *up to that point"* (Krugman, 1965, p. 354).

In a high-involvement situation, the decision is more likely to be made before the purchaser enters into the buying situation. An example of a high-involvement situation would be political advertising. Rokeach's views of inconsequential beliefs, that is, those beliefs that can be changed without altering the individual's total system of beliefs, reinforce the idea of high-involvement and low-involvement issues. In contrast to other kinds of belief, if these inconsequential beliefs are changed, the total system of beliefs is not altered in any significant way. One might believe, for example, that he can get a better shave from one brand of razor blade than another or that a vacation at the beach is more enjoyable than one in the mountains. If the individual is persuaded to believe the opposite, the change is inconsequential because the rest of his "belief system" will not be affected (Rokeach, 1963).

Marketing Examples of Ego Involvement and Issue Importance

In a market in which brand loyalty is a strong issue affecting purchase, the audience members are likely to be less susceptible to being persuaded by new products' messages. This resistance to being persuaded is a function of the audience members' high ego involvement with their particular brand.

An example of this occurs in the marketing of political candidates. An individual who is strongly affiliated with a party is likely to resist a persuasive message for another party because it interferes with his commitment or ego involvement. Thus in the Kennedy-Nixon debates, declared Republicans thought Nixon was more persuasive, whereas declared Democrats preferred Kennedy's arguments.

Ego involvement may affect store loyalty as well as brand loyalty. A sophisticated woman may purchase her clothes at Saks Fifth Avenue, a high-fashion women's clothing store, and not fathom the possibility of purchasing an article in a mass-merchandise store, which denotes to her average, low quality, unstylish, and unsophisticated. Naturally, Saks is decorated lavishly, and the saleswomen are fashionably dressed and look relatively sophisticated.

The type of media chosen to communicate a message may be ego involved. A man who thinks of himself as an intellectual, a sophisticated man of the world, will buy and read *The New Yorker*. He believes the magazine to be similar to himself, and this image may carry over to all products advertised in the magazine.

Involvement and Advance Awareness

VI.B12 *The high effect on audience members of being forewarned—that is, made aware in advance—about the persuasiveness of a communication is that forewarning reduces or hinders attitude changes of audience members in situations in which they have high involvement but facilitates attitude changes in situations in which they have low involvement.*

Kiesler and Kiesler had subjects read a communication that for two groups contained a warning, stating that the article was designed to make them change their opinions. For one group the warning occurred at the beginning of the article, and for the other group, at the end of the article. Two more groups—one with no warning statement and one with no warning statement nor an article—were included in the study as control groups. When forewarned (the warning at the beginning of the counterattitudinal article), the individual was less influenced by the communication than individuals who read the warning at the end of the article or did not read it at all. In fact, forewarned subjects tended to adopt attitudes even more extreme than held before the forewarning and the following article (Kiesler and Kiesler, 1964).

However, McGuire and Millman found contrary effects. They concluded that when forewarned, the subject will abandon his attitudes and to some extent will support the attitudes advocated in the pending attack. It also was found that to be convinced by a counterargument is very dissonant to one's self-concept. They explained their contradictory findings by the fact that the advance warning implies to the individual reading it that the communication that will follow will be conclusive and that the subject will undoubtedly change his opinion after reading the counterargument. To avoid the dissonance, the reader adopts the counterargument before the attack.

However, McGuire and Millman qualified their belief with some conditions that limit the usefulness of warning a subject of an impending attitudinal attack. The type of issue is a limiting factor. Subjective issues differ from more technical ones in that being persuaded on more technical issues implies close-mindedness and would not enhance one's self-concept. In their experimentation, McGuire and Millman found that warnings of a pending attack on issues of an emotional nature produced more anticipatory attitude changes in subjects than did warnings of an attack on issues of a technical nature. Such an attitude change also depends on whether the person who is being persuaded has low ego involvement with that issue. If ego involvement is high, such distortion of one's own beliefs becomes more difficult (McGuire and Millman, 1965).

It is these two limitations that serve to clear up the seemingly discrepant findings by Kiesler and Kiesler and by McGuire and Millman. The personal involvement of the individual determines whether forewarning of an impending attack on attitudes will be useful in fostering belief change or will only cause a shift to a more extreme position.

Apsler and Sears tested the McGuire and Millman hypothesis and found that forewarning reduced attitude change under conditions of high involvement and facilitated attitude change in low-involvement conditions (Apsler and Sears, 1968).

Kiesler later reported on three experiments with which he showed that forewarning facilitates attitude change in low-involvement situations (noncommitment or low commitment) and hinders change in high-involvement situations (high commitment). In fact, some highly involved subjects adopted even more attitudinally extreme positions after the warning. Each of the experiments consisted of giving students a questionnaire, purportedly a survey regarding a report by a special university committee on one of three different and very current issues among university students. The questionnaire was made up of four proposals, each contrary to the average student's opinion on the issue, and asked for student opinion. The introduction to the questionnaire contained examples of what was proposed inside, and these examples constituted the forewarnings (Kiesler, 1971).

Marketing Examples of Involvement and Advance Awareness

An example of this proposition's application occurs in a new product or service introduction. Since the audience has not been able to make a positive or negative commitment, it is initially a low-involvement situation for them. A forewarning about the persuasiveness of the communication is likely to facilitate attitude change in this situation.

Volkswagen used forewarning when it introduced the VW to the American market. The first visual impression of the car is that it is ugly; thus, the first promotional campaign was "Ugly is only skin deep." A negative aspect of the car was soon transformed into positive product identification.

Forewarning of price often can be turned into a neutral or even a positive identifying factor. Manufacturers often include in their promotion, "Prices slightly higher on the West Coast" (or something similar). Similarly, the American Gas Association forewarned consumers about prices: "More natural gas can give us a cleaner world. But it's going to cost more."

Manufacturers may forewarn about the bulkiness of their package size and inconvenience in getting the product home, yet counteract this negative aspect by emphasizing the positive economics of the purchase. The manufacturers of laundry soap could also emphasize that carrying one huge box home that will last 2 months really is easier than the "hassle" of a medium-size box every two weeks.

Public Commitment

VI.B13 *The beliefs-attitudes-opinions of audience members on specific issues become less subject to change from persuasive communicating once the audience members have committed themselves publicly and feel that their subsequent actions can be checked.*

Public commitment can mean verbalizing to a group or to an individual, or merely writing a statement knowing that its content will be made known to others. Many individuals will not change their original position once they have committed themselves publicly because they are afraid of being challenged with what they had said previously (Hovland, Campbell, and Brock, 1957, p. 23). Usually, the individual who "goes back" on what he has said previously will be negatively socially reinforced for what he has done. When he committed himself the first time, he expected and anticipated a certain desirable social reaction (Rosenberg, Hovland, McGuire, Abelson, and Brehm, 1960, p. 33).

Public commitment was tested in relation to dissonance by Festinger. When an individual stated publicly that he was for candidate X, whether he privately maintained that position or not, he was not likely to change his commitment publicly. Once he had stated his feelings, in order to keep dissonance to a minimum, the individual had to act in a manner complementary with his public statement (Festinger, 1957).

Rosenbaum and Zimmerman discovered another occurrence in the course of their study of public commitment. If a speaker addressed an audience, telling them that he knew their opinion on a given topic but wanted to present opposing information, audience resistance was increased. "The attribution to the audience of an opinion position ... may result in the same kind of resistance to change that a prior public statement made by each member of the audience has been demonstrated to produce" (Rosenbaum and Zimmerman, 1959, p. 248).

Lana divided 100 college students in introductory psychology classes into 8 groups. They were asked two questions: (1) If you know what the word *vivisection* refers to, describe it in one or two sentences, and (2) Also describe, in one or two sentences any recent events that you know of concerning vivisection. The subjects were then separated into "familiar" and "unfamiliar" groups. Prior to pretesting and just before posttesting, the "familiar" group was read a 213-word factual passage describing vivisection. Both groups, after being randomly divided received opinion questionnaires for or against vivisection and, after being divided again, received a pro and con vivisection communication, alternately presented. All groups were then posttested with the same questionnaire used in the pretest. The no-pretest and distinguished-pretest groups changed to a greater degree than the pretested groups. The pretest can act as a commitment the individual has to maintain in the face of opposed—bidirectional—arguments. A single unidirectional communication allows for greater change regardless of pretest. Thus the more complex and multisided a message is, the greater the inhibitory effect of the pretest (Lana, 1966).

Marketing Examples of Public Commitment

The effect of public commitment can be seen in the marketplace. When an individual has a salesperson order a particular item, he has made a commitment regarding that item. If the individual decides later that he does not want that item, he is not very likely to tell the salesperson he no longer wants it. Instead, the chances are that he will purchase the item despite his misgivings. If he does *not* purchase the item, he will give the salesperson several substantial reasons—excuses—for his change of behavior.

Although the psychological principle of public commitment at first glance may not seem to have broad applications to marketing, the goal of the marketer is to change the attitudes of the consumer in a positive manner toward the marketer's product(s). The actual purchase *is* a public commitment—other people in the household may use the product, and friends may notice the brand name of a product. If the consumer is happy with the product and if other people who use it respond in a positive manner—this is both personal and social reinforcement—he or she will be more likley than otherwise to repurchase the product. Continued repurchasing may develop into brand loyalty, which becomes a commitment.

The purchase of a product and the public commitment may commit the consumer to buy other products in the product line. Hoover developed an excellent reputation for quality floor-cleaning equipment. Because the consumer has purchased a Hoover vacuum cleaner and spoken and thought highly of it, she or he may also be committed unconsciously to buying Hoover floor waxes, rug-cleaning detergents, or an electric floor-washer.

Behavioral Commitment

VI.B14 *Once an audience member has agreed to comply with a small request of the communicator, he is more likely to be persuaded to comply with a larger demand from the same source than if he had not made such a previous commitment.*

This principle might be referred to as the *gradation method* or the *foot-in-the-door technique.* In an experiment by Freedman and Fraser, this hypothesis was tested by asking housewives to allow a team of five or six men to come into their homes for two hours to classify the household products they used. This was the "large" request, which was asked after one of two different conditions had been established: after a short interview with one individual (performance condition) or after a condition of contact with the individual, but one in which no request had been made (control condition).

Over 50 percent of the subjects in the performance condition agreed to the larger request, as opposed to less than 25 percent in the control condition. The explanations offered by the experimenters for this increase compliance with increased commitment were twofold. One was a degree of involvement with the experimenter, in which the subject, having agreed to the first request, felt that the experimenter would expect him or her to agree with the second. The subjects, then, felt obligated and did not want to disappoint the experimenter. They also may have felt that they would need a better reason to disagree than to agree.

The second explanation was in terms of the particular issue with which the requests were concerned. Once the individual had taken some action in connection with a particular area of concern, there was probably a tendency to become somewhat more concerned with that topic. This could tend to make the individual more likely to take further action in the same area when asked to do so (Freedman and Fraser, 1966, pp. 195-202).

The terms *involvement* and *commitment* are used almost interchangeably in the literature on attitude change; often, in fact, *involvement* is defined as a degree of *commitment* to a specific response or position. In the preceding experiment, the degree of commitment was explained as being the result of the degree of involvement with a person or issue.

Marketing Examples of Behavioral Commitment

Evidence of this principle in marketing is the fact that a consumer is more likely to try a new product if he or she already uses another product marketed by the same company than if he or she does not. In a sense, the consumer has already made a commitment to that company, which makes it easy for the consumer to commit himself or herself further.

Retailers use such techniques in cosmetic demonstrations. The cosmetician may coax a passing consumer, who perhaps had not even been at the cosmetic counter, to have her face "made over." She grants this small request; and then when the demonstration is completed, she feels obligated to purchase some of the products at the counter.

Certain retailers also offer free gifts, free consultations, or special entertainment if the consumer just enters the store. For example, a professional golfer may be in the recreation section to talk with anyone about golfing equipment or techniques. The consumer is not obligated to buy anything, but because he has taken advantage of the service offered, he feels some kind of a commitment.

Closed-Mindedness and Avoided Situations

VI.B15 *Closed-minded audience members are more susceptible to persuasive messages than are open-minded individuals under conditions of cognitive inconsistency, opinionated language, belief discrepancy, or authority.*

It must be remembered that these conditions are those which closed-minded individuals normally avoid; but upon finding themselves in these positions, they become highly persuadable. In this connection, see the discussion of closed-mindedness above in chapters 21 and 28.

Norris tested cognitive inconsistency situations with open- and closed-minded individuals. Students in an introductory social psychology course were assessed for their open-mindedness using the Rokeach scale. The students then were presented with an attack on a positively evaluated concept, and the relationship between the degree of open-mindedness and the extent of attitude change was measured. The more closed-minded students were more influenced than the open-minded students by a favorable source and experienced significantly greater attitude change. The study also revealed that the manner in which one deals with cognitive inconsistency is related to the significance to him of the topic being discussed, as well as being related to personality (Norris, 1965).

Opinionated language and authority were tested in relation to open- and closed-mindedness by Miller and Lobe. The subjects were 80 students in a basic communication class at Michigan State University. Subjects rated the credibility of six well-known sources and indicated their own attitudes toward six well-known issues in addition to taking a test determining the degree of dogmatism.

Four experimental conditions were used in the study: open-minded, opinionated language; closed-minded, opinionated language; open-minded, non-opinionated language; and closed-minded, nonopinionated language. The basic content was identical for the opinionated and nonopinionated language messages. However, in the opinionated message, two opinionated acceptance statements (for example, "Anyone of any intelligence can plainly see that smoking is related to certain physical ailments") and two opinionated rejection statements (for example, "Some irresponsible citizens seem to feel that tobacco products should be kept on the market") were inserted. The students were asked to rate the communicator's credibility and give their reactions to the communication. Results generally indicated that opinionated language had a greater persuasive impact than nonopinionated language, provided the source was perceived as highly credible (Miller and Lobe, 1967).

In the case of closed-minded subjects, this result is consistent with predictions. Such individuals rely greatly on authority and are greatly concerned with the reward and punishments handed out by authority figures. This should lead closed-minded people to adjust their behavior to conform more closely with what they perceive to be the expectations of the highly credible source. It is felt that the explicit clues to the communicator's opinion provided by the use of opinionated language enhanced the effectiveness of the communication for all subjects.

Marketing Examples of Closed-Mindedness
and Avoided Situations

Although the open- and closed-minded proposition may be difficult for the communicator to apply, it can be useful. A highly credible source increases persuasibility in all cases. Opinionated language seems to increase persuasibility for both types of individuals. When dealing with closed-minded people, the communicator may find it beneficial to link a new product with a more traditional concept. Rather than stressing only a product's newness or novelty, he can link it to an accepted product, then say his product is better, more efficient.

An example might be a new electronic oven. Rather than merely saying that it is all new, entirely different, appeals refer to the old method, too. Baking of potatoes, which used to take 1½ hours, now take just 4 minutes. The concept of electronic ovens is "revolutionary" and could be rejected by a closed-minded individual; but acceptance may be increased by linking it in some ways to traditional methods.

Authoritarian Personality

VI.B16 *Regardless of which side of an issue is taken in a persuasive communication, audience members of authoritarian personality are more persuaded by an appeal utilizing an authority figure than by an informational appeal. By contrast, an informational appeal is more effective for audience members with nonauthoritarian personalities.*

One particular personality pattern, the so-called authoritarian personality, has been the basis for several studies in attitude change because of the particular traits associated with it. One of these traits is a tendency to have almost unquestioned respect for individuals in positions of authority. By using psychological tests that single out individuals with such personality patterns from the general population, experimenters have been able to test them in relation to susceptibility to persuasion.

Rohrer and Sherif found that regardless of which side of an issue was taken, authoritarian people were more persuaded by the remarks of an authority figure than by an informational appeal, which was most effective for nonauthoritarian individuals (Rohrer and Sherif, 1951, pp. 108-110).

In combining authoritarianism, self-confidence, and cognitive complexity (or open-mindedness), an experiment was conducted by Berkowitz and Lundy in which the subjects, college students, were presented with persuasive communications attributed to either a group of army generals or a group of college students. The results showed that while authoritarian personalities tended to be more influenced by authority figures, those low in self-confidence were more easily persuaded by other college students. It was concluded from this that individuals with low self-confidence tend to become more dependent upon others around them and in this manner are more susceptible to influence from individuals who are similar to themselves. One kind of person was found to be susceptible to influence by both colleagues and authorities, namely, the person who was both low in self-confidence and high in cognitive complexity. It was assumed that although they were doubtful as to the correctness of their own opinions, they also were flexible enough to appreciate and accept a different person's position (Berkowitz and Lundy, 1957).

In a well-known experiment by Weiss and Fine, relating aggressiveness to persuasibility, the hypothesis tested was that more-aggressive individuals will be most persuaded by an argument that takes a harsh stance on an issue. It was found that more-aggressive subjects were most persuaded by a communication that advocated harsh treatment of juvenile delinquents, whereas less-aggressive subjects were more persuaded by a communication that took a more sympathetic view (Weiss and Fine, 1955, pp. 246-253).

Marketing Examples of Authoritarian Personality

An example of the use of authority figures in marketing is the common practice of naming franchise businesses, such as fast-food restaurants, after well-known people whose field of accomplishment usually has nothing to do with the business conducted by the franchise. Examples of this are the Arnold Palmer Dry Cleaners franchise and the Roy Rogers Roast Beef Restaurants. In each case, a person's name is used whose field of endeavor has nothing to do with the business; but the "authority" or "expertise" associated with his name transfers to the business that uses his name.

Certain types of media may become authority figures. *Vogue*, a high-fashion beauty magazine, has a monthly column about new beauty products on the market. Thus a woman who is concerned about makeup and skin care will regard *Vogue* as an authoritarian source in this area. Likewise, a man interested in stereo equipment will regard information in specialized stereo magazines as having more authority than stereo information in *Sports Illustrated* or *Time*.

A manufacturer can establish distribution in terms of who his consumers consider authority figures. For example, companies producing hair products, such as conditioners, shampoos, curlers, brushes, or nail care or skin care products may distribute to beauty shops. Women regard their beauticians as experts in these areas and in general feel that anything they would sell in their shops is of high quality.

Through frequent exposure to salespeople, consumers may come to regard them as authorities. Women may ask saleswomen in clothing stores what is stylish this spring or what kind of accessories "go with" a particular suit.

Companies may also establish themselves as authority figures. Johnson & Johnson is viewed as an authority in infant and child care; and Gerber Baby Food is known as an expert in infant nutrition.

Active and Passive Defenses

VI.B17 *Increasing the participation of audience members in the communicator's message—from passive to active defense of beliefs against counterarguments— results in their decreased resistance to persuading through familiar counter- arguments, but increased resistance against new or novel counterarguments.*

McGuire and Papageorgis, investigating the interrelationships among the factors involved in resistance to persuasion, found that differing amounts and timing of participation in the construction of defenses results in varying levels of resistance to persuasion. Thus increasing levels of participation, from passive reading of the arguments to active writing of spontaneous, unguided essays defending the beliefs, resulted in decreasing resistance to persuasion for familiar counterargu- ments, but also resulted in increasing resistance against novel counterarguments. They also found that a double defense, both active and passive, is superior to either one alone in developing resistance to persuading when the same counter- arguments that were refuted earlier are used in the later "attack" or argument (McGuire and Papageorgis, 1961).

Rogers and Thistlethwaite also studied the effects of active and passive defenses in inducing resistance to persuading. Half their subjects read a refutational defense of each of two health truisms, whereas the other half were exposed to active defense treatment of the same truisms and counterarguments. Subjects were asked to write refutations for each of the counterarguments. Half of them in each condition were exposed to attacking messages immediately after exposure to the defenses, whereas the remaining half were exposed to delayed attacks two days later. Results showed that passive defense produced greater resistance to attack than active defense, and also produced greater disparagement of the attack than did active defense. Following active defense, the delayed attack caused greater resistance, while a delay in attack following passive defense caused a decrease in the resistance (Rogers and Thistlethwaite, 1969).

Several experiments have dealt with the effects of active and passive defenses to persuading over time. McGuire demonstrated differing time func- tions for effectiveness of active and passive defenses, as well as for refutational and supportive defenses. According to his findings, active defenses did not follow a consistent trend over time because the threat aroused by the defense could not be coped with until the opportunity arrived for the defense to become effective; and after this, the resistance to attack declined as the threat aroused by the defense decreased over time.

Passive and supportive defenses that provided subjects with belief-bolstering information showed a relatively typical forgetting curve over time. Refutational defenses were subject to both delayed action and simple forgetting, but tended to last longer than the others. In fact, the difference in effect was so striking that no appreciable resistance remained from supportive argument two days afterward, whereas resistance was found one full week after a refutational defense (McGuire, 1962).

Prestige, one of the factors in credibility, can be lowered by situational conditions such as the one just described. The communicator who is perceived to be attempting to persuade to his own advantage, or as having "an axe to grind," loses the credibility that he otherwise might have had in the situation. See the proposition on perceived intent of the communicator in chapter 27.

Defenses against persuasion and their efforts are of particular interest to marketers, particularly as applied to defenses against the persuasive effects of advertising that the individual acquires through what he reads or hears. Much has been written in recent years about the "hidden persuaders" that seek to manipulate the individual against his will. The first inclination of an advertiser to counter such propaganda would probably be to avoid challenging it directly, thus hoping that the individual would forget it. However, in effect this serves to maintain the passive defense the individual has acquired in reading the propaganda.

From the preceding experiments one can see that a passive defense is more persuasive than an active one in countering persuasion of familiar messages such as those presented in advertising. If the advertiser were to challenge those who derogate his messages directly, he would cause the individual audience members to take a more active role in structuring their defenses to persuasion, which would create a more receptive attitude for their message, as well as allowing the advertiser to present his side of the issue.

Marketing Examples of Active and Passive Defenses

Consider the consumer movement in the 1970s against large corporations for their pollution contribution. When audience members began actively participating in consumer movements, they were more likely to resist advertising from large corporations that told how they too were fighting pollution. These new counterarguments that the offending corporations were not contributing to pollution would meet with the active defenses of these audience members.

Avis and Hertz advertising exemplifies this principle. Avis came out with the plea that we are only "number two" in the rent-a-car business, but that "We try harder." Hertz then came out in its promotion saying why Avis is number two, inferior to Hertz's service. Avis ran a promotional campaign with the headline, "The Score: Avis 7, Hertz 0, one tie." It dealt with the speediness offered to a person who wants to rent a car.

Yeasaying and Naysaying

VI.B18 *Audience members who can be characterized as yeasayers tend to be more easily persuaded than audience members who can be called naysayers.*

Couch and Keniston first used the names *yeasayers* and *naysayers* to designate individual response styles that both influence research results and also serve as clues to the personalities of the respondents. The terms *yeasayer* and *naysayer* refer to opposite sides of a continuous distribution and describe tendencies and not iron-clad positions (Couch and Keniston, 1960).

On personality inventories, attitude scales, and survey questionnaires, yeasayers tend to say yes, to agree, to be enthusiastic and uncritical, to give high ratings to objects that impress them favorably. Naysayers are more likely to be controlled in their responses, careful, conservative, and critical. They are more likely to say no, to be moderate rather than enthusiastic, to avoid committing themselves unless they are sure of what they are doing (Wells, 1961; and Wells, 1963).

Becker and Myers put it this way:

"Yeasaying" is characterized as a tendency to take extreme positions—to have attitudes more favorable or less favorable to a social object than might be expected. Thus, a "yeasayer" would be inclined to evaluate a "good" object as very good, and a "bad" object as very bad. "Naysaying," on the other hand, is the tendency to suppress extreme or inflated judgments. [Becker and Myers, 1970, p. 31.]

When a group of respondents to a research project consists of a large number of yeasayers or naysayers, the results of the survey may be biased and invalid. The consequences of such groupings depend in part on the real relationship between the objects being rated. If the objects being rated are in fact of equal value, and one particular responding group contains a large number of yeasayers and another group contains a large number of naysayers, the yeasayers will tend to give higher ratings and will make the object rated appear to be superior—a false conclusion. A similar discrepancy in response also will occur if the objects are different in value.

Communicators are thus obviously interested in the personality differences between yeasayers and naysayers. Couch and Keniston in clinical studies did find these two groups to have different personality characteristics and different beliefs. These differences became evident to the experimenters during their interviews with the subjects:

It was apparent from our clinical reports that yeasayers were much more extroverted in their social orientations. They were usually more voluble, spoke more easily about themselves (though often with little depth), took suggestions readily . . . and made themselves more thoroughly at ease with the interviewer. Naysayers, on the other hand, were characteristically more introverted. They were often shy and always reserved about themselves. Throughout the interview, they required more questioning and prodding; they felt easily criticized, weighed and considered each answer. [Couch and Keniston, 1960, pp. 167-168.]

Marketing Examples of Yeasaying and Naysaying

The problem concerning the biases of respondents to consumer-preference questionnaires is evident. Researchers must be able to devise questions in which the yeasayers' and naysayers' individual biases will be lessened or totally eliminated so that the responses obtained will be valid in determining marketing implications of the data obtained from the study.

However, a marketing implication in itself is the fact that yeasayers tend to be agreeable and more likely to accept persuasive messages than the typical audience members, whereas naysayers tend to be more skeptical of persuasive messages. If a communicator can locate the yeasayers in his particular target audience and appeal to them with his persuasive messages, they can serve as the innovators in the adoption of his new product or new idea.

Group Variables

As stated in part VII, on motivating, mass communucation often does not reach the individual directly but rather reaches him through the groups to which he belongs. New ideas and products are adopted through a process of diffusion. As Katz and Lazarsfeld stated, "an attempt to change an individual's opinion or attitude will not succeed if his opinion is one which he shares with others to whom he is attached, and if the others do not go along with the change" (Katz and Lazarsfeld, 1955, p. 73). The following principles relate the interaction of an audience member and his groups to his persuasibility.

Degree of Conformity

VI.B19 *Individuals who are made aware that one of their opinions differs from a group-supported opinion are more likely to change in the direction of the group opinion than to persist in supporting their original opinion if they value their group membership highly.*

The object of an experiment by Asch was to study the social and personal conditions that induce individuals to resist or give in to group pressures when such pressures are perceived to be contrary to fact. Individuals were placed in a situation where they had to decide whether they would act independently or submit to group pressure. A group of eight individuals was told to match the length of a given line with one of three unequal lines. Each group member announced his judgments publicly. In the midst of the experiment, one individual would suddenly find that his judgments disagreed with those of all the other group members. The other group members had previously met with the experimenter and had been instructed to respond at certain times with unanimous wrong judgments. A total of 50 male college students were tested in this way. The experimenter found that characteristics of the individual were important in the group situations. "Despite the stress of the given conditions, a substantial proportion of individuals retained their independence throughout. At the same time a substantial minority yielded, modifying their judgments in accordance with the majority" (Asch, 1952, p. 10).

Another experiment concerning conformity to group norms was conducted by Goldberg. The subjects were 79 white, male, high school and college students and young businessmen. They were asked to judge the intelligence of 9 male Negroes by looking at their photographs. Some of the pictures were shown to the group more than one time, although all were shown at least once. When pictures were shown more than once, the experimenter told the group what judgment the group as a whole already had made for that picture. The results given to represent the group as a whole was manipulated to test individual reactions to the group influence.

One of the conclusions drawn from the results of the study was: "Knowledge of a group norm by a subject results in the subjects' conforming to (reducing his disagreement with) the group norm . . . " (Goldberg, 1954, p. 329).

Goldberg isolated what he considered to be the determinants of conformity to group norms. The three variables he arrived at were:

1. *Distance*, that is the extent of initial disagreement between an individual's opinion and that of the group.
2. *Exposures*, that is the number of occasions on which the individual is exposed to group norms.
3. The *size* of the group.

In general, he proposed that greater initial distance makes for greater conformity, and that this conformity usually occurs within the first few exposures of the individual to the group (Goldberg, 1954).

Dittes and Kelley conducted an experiment on the value of group membership in determining group conformity in persuasive situations. They divided 103 volunteers from a Yale freshman class into 18 five-man or six-man groups; the subjects had no prior acquaintance with each other. They were told that there would be a cash prize and recognition as a reward for the group that was best in efficiency, smoothness of working together, and soundness of decisions. Unanimous decisions were highly desirable. They also had the opportunity to eliminate anyone who appeared to be detrimental to the group. "Youth gangs" was the subject of discussions for each group. Each group was required to reach a decision concerning particular questions on gangs. After it had reached a decision, each group was given a counternorm communication from someone outside the group. Results showed that the extent to which an individual resisted outside communication depended upon the extent to which he was attracted to or valued his membership in the group and the extent to which he felt the other members were attracted to him. The more highly attracted the individual was to the group, the more he conformed to face-to-face pressure, and the more resistant he became to counternorm communication from outside (Dittes and Kelley, 1956). Thus it becomes clear that in trying to persuade an audience to change their attitudes or opinions, a communicator should find out the convictions of their reference groups and the degree of conformity of these groups.

Marketing Examples of Degree of Conformity

Sporting goods companies often have a professional, such as an Arnold Palmer or Mickey Mantle, autograph or endorse their product line of golf clubs or baseball gloves. The impression desired is that the professional group has a high opinion of the product. Since many audience members want to be professional, the idea is that the average athlete will form an opinion like that of Palmer or Mantle and purchase the products.

Another similar application is in the case of "official" products. Products are often labeled as being used by professional athletic teams, the Olympic team, or astronauts, for instance. It is thus implied that consumers who use such official products are of a class similar to the renowned regular users.

Role

VI.B20 *Audience members who are undergoing a change in their roles will experience attitude changes on issues influenced by the new role.*

The communicator should determine the reference group to which his audience belongs before he constructs his message. The type of language used, such as particular words or phrases or level of sophistication, will vary from group to group. *Cool* and *with it* are typical of a youth group and could not be used when appealing to an older audience. With an upper-class audience the communicator would speak of *distinctions*, while to a lower class he would speak of the *differences.*

Visuals should also authentically represent the type of people the audience associates with or believes to be similar to themselves. If they see people like themselves associated with the product, they are more likely to conform than if they see people who look "strange" to them.

Analysis of situations where investigators have manipulated an individual's role and watched the results prompted Davis (1962) to write, "If . . . a person can act out another role, he is helped to understand both the other role and his own role. Because of this deeper insight, his attitude may change" (Davis, 1962, p. 164).

The fact that role changes in turn result in attitude or opinion changes is well documented. Janis and King conducted a study in which individuals were required to verbalize an opinion contrary to their own in active role playing. The study was prompted by debaters who had reported that they frequently wound up accepting the conclusions they had been arbitrarily assigned to defend. It was suggested that attitude changes may occur even when role playing is artificially induced. The results of Janis and King indicated that the active participants' opinions were more influenced than the passive group, and the active group also showed greater confidence in accepting these new opinions. "The main findings supported the hypothesis that overt verbalization induced by role playing tends to augment the effectiveness of a persuasive communication" (Janis and King, 1954, p. 218).

A second experiment by Janis and King evaluated the importance of the role of improvisation and the satisfaction with one's performance in self-persuasion. Three groups of college students defended the statement that they would be drafted and required to serve a year longer than normal draftees. The control group merely read the prepared persuasive arguments to themselves, while a second group read the same statement aloud. The third group, the test group, improvised their own arguments in defense of the stated position after they had read the prepared communication. The results showed a greater index of satisfaction was produced in the second group than in the test group. However, the test group, the active improvisation group, was the only one in which significant opinion change was induced (Janis and King, 1956).

Leshner tested 215 college students on a 30-item, forced-choice inventory that measured attitude toward supervision. The students then were put into sessions consisting of fictitious industrial problems to which individual roles were added for the role-playing condition. A postquestionnaire was then administered so that information concerning the effect of the experiment could be obtained. The results of the studies showed that when put in these new role situations, more attitude change occurred than simply from group discussion with no role-playing situation (Leshner, 1966).

However, other findings serve as a caution that this resultant attitude change is not a generalized finding but is connected with specific circumstances. Elbing investigated the effect of prior attitudes on role-produced attitude change. He first determined the initial views of 205 students on the issue of right-to-work laws. He then put them through role-playing situations where half took a pro-labor stance (half of these participated and the other half watched the role play), while the other half took a pro-management position (half of them participating and half observing). Finally, the views on this issue for all the students were reassessed. Elbing found that when the initial attitude was compatible with that of the assigned role, there was little change in the individual's attitude as a result of the role experience; and the change that did occur served to make the initial position more extreme. However, when the individual's initial attitude was incompatible with the assigned role, there resulted a change in attitude in the direction of moderation on the issue (Elbing, 1967).

Greenwald gave 66 undergraduate students booklets on the topic of general versus specialized undergraduate education. On page 1, each point of view on this two-sided issue was given and the student had to choose the one with which he agreed. Page 2 of the booklet instructed the student that he was assigned arbitrarily to one side of the issue; he was informed of which side and then told to consider writing an essay on that position and to consider three questions given in the booklet regarding that essay. This portion of the experiment was intended to reinforce the assigned-position manipulation. Pages 3, 4, and 5 of the booklet presented the subjects with 12 statements that concerned the topic discussed; and the subjects were to indicate their reactions to each. Finally, on page 6 the students filled out a 4-item opinion measurement on the general versus specialized education issue.

Greenwald found that students strongly accepted arguments supporting their own position. However, when put in the role of defending a position opposed to their initial one, the students accepted equal amounts of arguments on both sides of the issue. In other words, role playing caused the student to evaluate information opposing their own position in an unbiased fashion (Greenwald, 1969).

Greenwald later conducted another study of attitude change in relation to role. When one group of students was given the opportunity to consider and reject information opposing a view they later were assigned to adopt in a role-playing situation, essay writing on the topic of water fluoridation or Communist China, no attitude change resulted. When such information was withheld prior to role assignment, attitude change did occur. Greenwald concluded, therefore, that "the role-playing effect depends upon the role player's having an opportunity to evaluate counterattitudinal information that has not previously been rejected" (Greenwald, 1970, p. 218).

Marketing Examples of Role

The selling of insurance is a prime example of the application of this principle. As a man's role changes to include the role of husband and father, new, never before considered issues become manifest in his mind. An insurance company aware of such a change can sell the prospective client more insurance by changing his attitude as to how much insurance he needs for his new role.

The marriage of a woman represents a change in role. Regardless of how "liberated" she is, she finds herself responsible for the health and nutrition of her new family of two, and perhaps more in the future. Thus she is more susceptible to food advertising and health promotion. She also finds herself in the "maker" of a home, that is, the person who becomes a semiauthority on interior design and entertainment. As "manager" of the household, she is also responsible for seeing to its maintenance.

Product image may also be built around an individual's group. Bonnie Bell promotes its makeup and beauty products for young women who want to look nice without appearing "too made up" or without taking much time.

Tupper Ware parties demonstrate the usefulness of conformity. Because the party is given by a woman who invites her friends, and because almost everyone there knows everyone else; once a few people buy the products, almost all the others tend to conform by buying also.

Reinforcing through Interacting

VI.B21 *When a communicator persuades an audience member to support a view contrary to his own, positive reinforcement of this new view by a second individual will cause the audience member taking the contrary view to change his attitude on that specific issue and to believe the new argument.*

Evidence is emerging to show that if conversion of attitudes is to be effected, it may be possible to utilize the individual whose attitudes are being changed as an ally in causing this attitude change. For instance, Scott took pairs of students in a general psychology class and asked them to take a stand on any of three issues on which they previously had expressed their opinions. However, the instructions were that each student in the pair defend the side of the issue opposite to his originally expressed view. The vote of those determining the winner of the debate was predetermined, so that the experimenter could determine the effects on attitude change of winning a debate on an issue in which the subject did not initially believe. The subjects in the study initially had extreme attitudes on the issue they debated.

The results of these investigations showed that individuals who "won" tended to change their attitudes in the direction of the positions presented. This effect was found both when the student debated their own side of an issue and when they took the opposite side. A retest of the students 10 days later indicated that some degree of permanency of attitude change may have taken place, even though students had returned to social environments that probably supported their initial attitudes (Scott, 1959).

Kelman conducted a study in which junior high school students were told to write essays either in support of a type of comic book they favored or a type they were against. Rewards were used to induce students to write in support of the book they were against. The students' attitudes toward these books had been measured prior to writing the essay and then again afterwards. The mean attitude-change scores showed that those writing in support of the books they opposed changed more in the direction favoring them than did those who wrote in support of the liked book. Such results are consistent with dissonance theory (Kelman, 1953).

Marketing Examples of Reinforcing through Interacting

As a marketing example, if a consumer is offered a monetary reward for trying a product, the result can be the adoption of the product. If the consumer has favorable attitudes toward the product, this additional reinforcement will strengthen the belief. However, if his attitudes regarding the product are not favorable, the monetary reinforcement can facilitate attitude change.

The "suggestion box" or "complaint or suggestion questionnaire" offers a way in which individuals interact with products or services. In sorting out their ideas, consumers in a sense construct a list of the attributes of the products as well.

Money-back guarantees can facilitate the adoption of a product. If the attitude is already favorable, the guarantee will reinforce the belief that the product must be of good quality, otherwise the manufacturer would not offer a refund. This assumption also enhances previously disfavorable opinions.

Group Decision

VI.B22 *A group setting in which audience members actively participate in making a decision together is more effective in producing attitude and behavior change than is a lecture situation in which participants take a passive role.*

In a pioneering experiment to determine the most effective method of altering food consumption habits, Lewin found that certain methods of group decision were more effective than factual presentations in changing social conduct. When a Red Cross lecturer attempted to influence a group of housewives to serve kidneys, sweetbreads, and other cuts of meat that they might not have considered appropriate for the dinnertable, he was less effective in producing change than was the situation in which smaller groups of women discussed the idea among themselves and arrived at a decision. Lewin explained this finding by pointing out that (Lewin, 1943):

1. The effectiveness of group discussion may be attributed to its being directed toward a favorable decision that reduces forces against change within the individual, rather than applying outside pressure.

2. The directed group discussion and positive decision alters the group standard openly, keeping at a minimum individual variation from this standard.

Sherif found that when an individual was asked to report the extent of movement of a light, he subjectively established a range of extent and a point (a standard or norm) within that range which was peculiar to himself, that is, differing from the range or standard established by other individuals. In addition, when individuals encountered the situation as members of the same group for the first time (not having experienced the effect individually), a range and standard were established by the group, which was peculiar to that group. Of particular importance was the action taken by an individual who had experienced the group situation first. "When a member of the group faces the same situation subsequently *alone*, after once the range and norm of his group have been established, he perceives the situation in terms of the range and norm that he brings from the group situation" (Sherif, 1952, p. 259).

Marketing Examples of Group Decision

In its advertising, Bayer children's aspirin employed the group-decision principle in a general sense. A headline began with the statement "More mothers choose Bayer children's aspirin than any other brand." Other phrases that imply group likeness are: "Enjoyed by the whole family" or "When friends stop by." Products that employ these techniques seem to say "This group likes our product" and so have it on hand when they want or would enjoy it. Thus, because the group of friends or family members likes it, the purchaser should enjoy it as well.

Some retailers in their promotion infer group decision making when they say "Bring the whole family in" or "Bring your husband in to see the new ____." The acknowledgement of a group decision adds credibility to the communicating source.

34 An Overview of Persuading

Implications

Persuading represents the final stage of the communicating model presented in this book. As discussed in part VII, on motivating, both motivating and persuading share the principles created for message and medium variables. However, the two processes are distinct, since *motivating* seeks to reinforce audience members' beliefs and attitudes and *persuading* endeavors to have audience members reevaluate and hopefully change these beliefs and attitudes. Persuading is not an easy task and should not be expected to occur in all communicating situations, although the use of the principles presented in the foregoing sections will serve to increase the probability that persuading will occur.

Model of Persuading

Figure 34-1 diagrammatically represents the persuading process. As in previous sections, the preconceived variables (needs and wants, sociocultural status, personality variables, and other internal and external variables) are operating as mediating factors. Correspondingly, the principles have been divided into message and medium variables and variables within the audience.

Message and Medium Variables

Since the message and medium variables are the same for both motivating and persuading, these are presented only in part VII, on motivating, and not here.

Variables within the Audience

Persuading is dependent upon the physical and mental state of the audience members. Individual variables and group variables are equally important in assessing these states, because if their attitudes are similar to the communicator, persuading is not as necessary as otherwise. If they are *not* similar, they become important factors in aiding the communicator to create messages that might

479

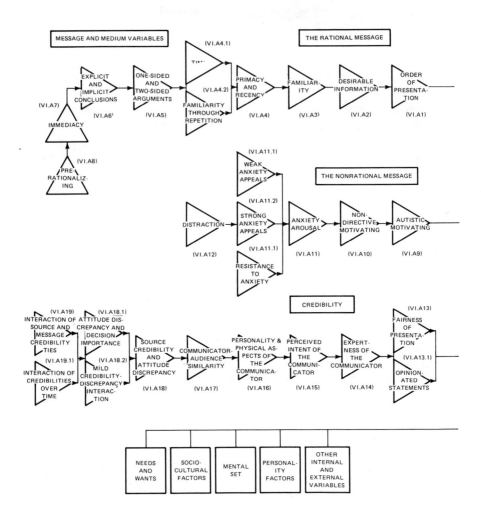

Figure 34-1. The Persuading Stage of the Psychological Model of Communicating. Note that all the Message and Medium Variables in Figure
34-1 on Persuading are Identical with the Message and Medium
Variables in Figure 30-1 on Motivating.

481

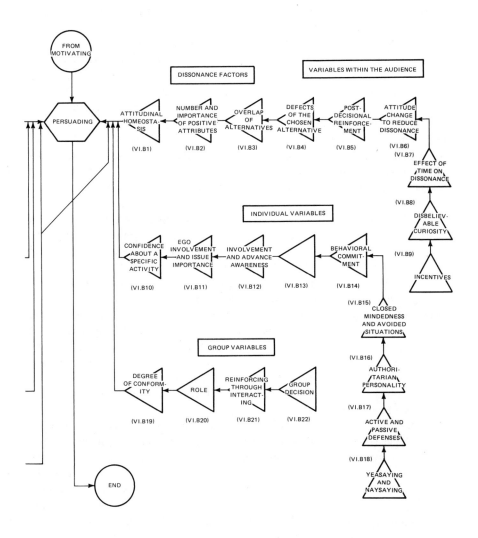

change these beliefs and attitudes. Since the communicator is never entirely sure of the effects his messages will have, he also must be aware of the dissonance factors that might intervene.

Dissonance factors play an important role whenever audience members must make a choice or decision among alternatives where a fairly high degree of uncertainty exists. If audience members' attitudes are incongruent with either known or communicated facts, as after a choice has been made, there is a tendency for these audience members to strive for attitudinal homeostasis. When the choice has been made, dissonance will play only a minor role if there are a large number and/or positive attributes of importance associated with the chosen alternatives, or if there is a high degree of overlap of alternatives (that is, the alternatives are highly similar). However, dissonance tends to be greater if audience members are dissatisfied or find defects with the chosen alternative.

If audience members are experiencing a high degree of dissonance about the chosen alternative, they will seek additional information to aid in postdecisional reinforcement. Correspondingly, if there are not strong feelings associated with those attitudes that relate to the chosen alternative, there is also a high probability that there will be some attitude change to reduce dissonance.

In addition, a communicator wishing to understand dissonance factors must consider the effects of time on dissonance, with the rate of dissonance reduction over time being positively related to the amount of dissonance initially created.

Finally, although disbelievable curiosity can be helpful in initially attempting to persuade audience members to purchase a particular product (especially if they can find out if the statements presented by the communicator are true or not), the use of high incentives should not accompany this strategy if there is a high degree of dissonance associated with the purchase. However, small incentives may prove effective.

The discussion in part VIII, on persuading, also included a series of psychological principles that related to individual variables. Although audience members may have a high level of general self-confidence, a communicator must also determine their confidence about a specific activity—the lower it is, the more easily audience members are persuaded. Involvement and commitment also serve as individual mediating factors in the persuading process. Principles concerning involvement and issue importance and involvement and advance awareness are of particular importance to the communicator, because if audience members are highly ego involved with the issues in a message and have little forewarning about the persuasive content of the message, they will be more susceptible to being persuaded by the message than if low ego involvement and advance warning characterize the communication situation.

Correspondingly, audience members having first agreed to an initially small behavioral commitment requested by the communicator are more likely to be persuaded to comply with a larger demand from their communicator. This will be further stimulated if these audience members have made a public commitment to this behavior as well and feel that their subsequent actions will be checked. A communicator must also endeavor to assess the degree of closed-mindedness of audience members, as well as the degree to which they have authoritarian personalities.

Under conditions of cognitive inconsistency, closed-minded individuals become highly persuadable. If they also have authoritarian personalities, this persuasibility can be enhanced further by appeals utilizing authority figures rather than information. Also, audience members who are yeasayers are more susceptible to persuading than audience members who are naysayers. Finally, a communicator can decrease resistance to persuading through familiar counter-arguments but can increase resistance against new or novel counterarguments if he can stimulate audience members to move from passive to active defenses against counterarguments to the message he is communicating.

Mass communicating often does not reach audience members directly, but rather through the groups to which they belong. Thus group variables can be particularly useful when a communicator seeks to change audience members' beliefs and attitudes through the process of persuading. The higher the degree of conformity individuals have with referent-group opinions, the more likely they are to change their beliefs and attitudes in the direction of the group opinion, if the communicator can make them aware that their beliefs and attitudes and those of the groups differ about an issue. This is further enhanced if the communication pertains to a group decision.

Correspondingly, a communicator can stimulate the persuading process if he can identify audience members who are undergoing changes in their roles and thus more susceptible to attitude changes that relate to these new roles. If the view purported by the communicator is contrary to the views of audience members, then the communicator by positively reinforcing this new view, through interacting with audience members, may persuade audience members to change their views on this specific issue, so that they tend to believe the new argument.

As a final note, it must be stressed that attitude changes are very difficult and cannot be expected to occur in every communicating situation. However, the principles of persuading presented in this section serve to identify ways in which a communicator can increase the probability that persuading will occur in a specific communicating situation.

A Final Word

This book is a pioneering effort. So far as can be determined, it represents the first attempt ever (1) to develop an overall series of psychological principles about human communicating, (2) that are based on and supported by empirical data, (3) that are applicable to various aspects of communication in marketing, and (4) that can be linked together in a logical framework of models of communicating.

Accordingly, at the very beginning of this book two important questions were asked:

1. *What happens psychologically to a person confronted with a marketing communication—such as an advertisement or a sales message?*
2. *How can empirical data from psychological experiments and observations be applied in various areas of marketing communication?*

I have tried to answer both questions by developing a series of almost 200 psychological principles of communication based on experimental and observational findings from the literature of the behavioral sciences. These principles, in turn, have become the basis of a set of descriptive models of the psychological processes of exposing, attending, perceiving, learning, motivating, and persuading.

The psychological principles and the descriptive models set forth in this book should help to "bridge the gap" between certain areas of psychology and certain areas of marketing. But these principles and models are only the beginning.

Please think of this book as the first step in a three-step process dealing with the psychology of marketing communicating.

The second step, then, ought to involve actual testing in marketing situations of the psychological principles set forth in this book. Practically all of these principles ought to become the basis for some type of experimental investigation to determine its degree of validity. The ensuing results should lead to further development of these principles in "operational terms," that is, more precisely and with standards or criteria of measurement.

The third or final step then will be possible. As a followup to the results of these experimental investigations, an important transition can be made from descriptive models to simulation models, to mirror the world of marketing communicating.

References Cited

Aaker, D.A. "On Methods: A Probabalistic Approach to Industrial Media Selection." *Journal of Advertising Research* 8 (September 1968):46-54.

Abelson, H.I. *Persuasion.* New York: Springer, 1959.

Abelson, R.P., and G.S. Lesser, "Measurement of Persuasibility in Children." In I.L. Janis and C.I. Hovland, eds., *Personality and Persuasibility.* New Haven, Conn.: Yale Univ. Press, 1959, pp. 141-166.

Adams, C.F. *Common Sense in Advertising.* New York: McGraw-Hill Book Company, 1965.

Adams, H.E., and R.N. Vidulich. "Dogmatism and Belief Congruence in Paired-Associate Learning." *Psychological Reports* 10 (February 1962):91-94.

Alderson, W. "Needs, Wants, and Creative Marketing." *Cost and Profit Outlook* 8 (September 1955):1-3.

Alimaras, P. "Ambivalence in Situations of Negative Interpersonal Attitudes." *Journal of Psychology* 65, 1 (1967):9-13.

Allport, G.W. "Attitudes." In *Handbook of Social Psychology.* C. Murchinson, ed. Worcester, Mass.: Clark Univ. Press, 1935, pp. 798-884; as quoted in "The Nature of Attitudes and Attitude Change," by W.J. McGuire. In G. Lindzey and E. Aronson, eds., *The Handbook of Social Psychology*, 2d ed. Reading, Mass.: Addison Wesley, 1968, pp. 136-148.

Allyn, J., and L. Festinger. "The Effectiveness of Unanticipated Persuasive Communications." *Journal of Abnormal and Social Psychology* 62 (January 1961):35-40.

Amstel, A. "The Role of Frustrative Nonreward to Noncontinuous Reward Situations." *Psychological Bulletin* 55 (March 1958):102-119.

Anastasi, A. *Differential Psychology.* New York: Macmillan, 1958.

Anastasi, A. *Fields of Applied Psychology.* New York: McGraw-Hill, 1964.

Anderson, N.H., and C.I. Hovland. "The Representation of Ordered Effects in Communication Research." In C.I. Hovland et al., eds., *The Order of Presentation in Persuasion.* New Haven: Yale Univ. Press, 1957, pp. 158-169.

Andreasen, A.R. "Attitudes and Customer Behavior: A Decision Model." In L.E. Preston, ed., *Research Program in Marketing.* Berkeley, California: Institute of Business and Economic Research, Univ. of California, 1965.

Angell, J.R. "The Province of Functional Psychology." *The Psychological Review* 14 (March 1907):61-91.

Appel, V. "On Advertising Wear Out." *Journal of Advertising Research* 11 (February 1971):11-13.

Apsler, R., and D.O. Sears. "Warning, Personal Involvement, and Attitude Change." *Journal of Personality and Social Psychology* 9 (June 1968):162-166.

Arndt, J. "Perceived Risk, Sociometric Integration, and Word of Mouth in the Adoption of a New Food Product." In D.F. Cox, ed., *Risk Taking and Information Handling in Consumer Behavior*. Boston: Division of Research, Graduate School of Business Administration, Harvard University, 1967a, pp. 289-316.

Arndt, J. "Word-of-Mouth Advertising and Informal Communication." In D.F. Cox, ed., *Risk Taking and Information Handling in Consumer Behavior*. Boston: Division of Research, Graduate School of Business Administration, Harvard University, 1967b, pp. 188-239.

Aronson, E. "The Psychology of Insufficient Justification: An Analysis of Some Conflicting Data." In S. Feldman, ed., *Cognitive Consistency*. New York: Academic Press, 1966, pp. 109-133.

Aronson, E., J.A. Turner, and J.M. Carlsmith. "Communicator Credibility and Communication Discrepancy as Determinants of Opinion Change." *Journal of Abnormal and Social Psychology* 67 (July 1963):31-36.

Asch, M.J. "Non-directive Teaching in Psychology: A Study Based on a Controlled Experiment." *Psychological Monographs* 65, 4 (1951):iii-24.

Asch, S.E. "Effects of Group Pressure Upon the Modification and Distortion of Judgments." In G. Swanson, T. Newcomb, and E.I. Hartley, eds., *Readings in Social Psychology*, revised edition, New York: Holt, 1952, pp. 2-11.

Atwood, L.E. "The Effects of Incongruity between Source and Message Credibility." *Journalism Quarterly* 43 (Spring 1966):90-94.

Baddeley, A.D. "The Capacity for Generating Information by Randomization." *Quarterly Journal of Experimental Psychology* 18 (May 1966):119-130.

Baker, S. *Visual Persuasion*. New York: McGraw-Hill, 1961.

Baradowski, W. "Effect of Curiosity on Incidental Learning." *Journal of Educational Psychology* 58 (February 1967):50-55.

Bardwick, J.M. *Psychology of Women*. New York: Harper and Row, 1971.

Bardwick, J.M. "Stimulus/Response: Women's Liberation: Nice Idea, But It Won't Be Easy." *Psychology Today* 6 (May 1973):26-33, and 110-111.

Barksdale, H.C. *Marketing in Progress*. New York: Holt, Rinehart and Winston, 1964.

Barry, H., Jr. "A Test for Negativism and Compliance." *Journal of Abnormal and Social Psychology* 25 (January-March 1931):373-381.

Barton, R. "Advertising Overkill, or How Much Is Enough?" *Media/scope* 12 (December 1968):66.

Bauer, R.A. "The Obstinate Audience: The Influence Process from the Point of View of Social Communication." *The American Psychologist* 19 (May 1964):319-328.

Bauer, R.A. "Perception and the Individual." In L. Bogart, ed., *Psychology in Media Strategy*. Chicago: American Marketing Association, 1966.

Bauer, R.A. "Source Effect and Persuasibility: A New Look." In D.F. Cox, ed., *Risk Taking and Information Handling in Consumer Behavior*, Boston:

Division of Research, Graduate School of Business Administration, Harvard University, 1967, pp. 559-578.

Bayton, J.A. "Motivation, Cognition, Learning—Basic Factors in Consumer Behavior." *Journal of Marketing* 22 (January 1958):282-289.

Beal, G.M., and E.M. Rogers, "Informational Sources in the Adoption Process of New Fabrics." *Journal of Home Economics* 49 (October 1957):630-634.

Becker, R.W., and J.G. Myers. "Yeasaying Response Style." *Journal of Advertising Research* 6 (December 1970):31-37.

Beckman, T.N. *Marketing.* New York: Ronald Press, 1962.

Bell, G.D. "An Automobile Buyer After the Purchase." *Journal of Marketing* 28 (July 1967):12-17.

Berelson, B., and G.A. Steiner. *Human Behavior: An Inventory of Scientific Findings.* New York: Harcourt, Brace & World, 1964.

Berkowitz, L., and D.R. Cottingham. "The Interest Value and Relevance of Fear Arousing Communications." *Journal of Abnormal and Social Psychology* 60 (January 1960):37-43.

Berkowitz, L., and R.M. Lundy. "Personality Characteristics Related to Susceptibility to Influence by Peers or Authority Figures." *Journal of Personality* 25 (March 1957):306-316.

Berlo, D.D., J.B. Lemert, and R.J. Mertz. "Dimensions for Evaluating the Acceptability of Message Sources." *Public Opinion Quarterly* 33 (Winter 1969-1970):563-576.

Berlyne, D.E. *Conflict, Arousal and Curiosity.* New York: McGraw-Hill, 1960.

Biggs, J.B. *Information and Human Learning.* North Melbourne, Australia: Cassell Australia, 1968.

Birdwhistell, R.L. "Kinesics." In D.L. Sills, ed., *International Encyclopedia of the Social Sciences.* New York: Macmillan and Free Press, 1968, pp. 379-384.

Blankenship, A.B., and P.L. Whitely, "Proactive Inhibition in the Recall of Advertising Material." *Journal of Social Psychology* 13 (May 1941):311-322.

Bogart, L. *Strategy in Advertising.* New York: Brace & World, 1967.

Borck, T.C. "Effects of Prior Dishonesty on Postdecision Dissonance." *The Journal of Abnormal and Social Psychology* 66 (April 1963):325-331.

Bråten, S. *Marknads Kommunikation: Analys och Planering dr Extemkommunikation.* Stockholm, Sweden: Beckmans, 1968.

Brehm, J.W. "Post-decision Changes in the Desirability of Alternatives." *Journal of Abnormal and Social Psychology* 52 (May 1956):384-389.

Brehm, J.W. *A Theory of Psychological Reactance.* New York: Academic Press, 1966.

Brehm, J.W., and A.R. Cohen. "Re-evaluation of Choice Alternatives as a Function of Their Number and Qualitative Similarity." *The Journal of Abnormal and Social Psychology* 58 (May 1959):373-378.

Brink, E.L., and W.T. Kelley. *The Management of Promotion: Consumer Behavior and Demand Stimulation.* Englewood Cliffs, New Jersey: Prentice-Hall, 1963.

Britt, S.H. "Theories of Retroactive Inhibition." *The Psychological Review* 43 (May 1936):207-216.

Britt, S.H. "The Learning-Remembering Process (A Reply to Professor Cason)." *Psychological Review* 44 (November 1937):462-469.

Britt, S.H. *Social Psychology of Modern Life*, revised edition. New York: Holt, Rinehart & Winston, 1949, pp. 259-260.

Britt, S.H. "How Weber's Law Can Be Applied to Marketing." *Business Horizons* 18 (February 1975):21-29.

Britt, S.H. "Applying Learning Principles to Marketing." *MSU Business Topics* 23 (Spring 1975a):5-12.

Brock, T.C. "Communicator-Recipient Similarity and Decision Change." *Journal of Personality and Social Psychology* 1 (June 1965):650-654.

Brodbeck, M. "The Role of Small Groups in Mediating the Effects of Propaganda." *Journal of Abnormal and Social Psychology* 52 (March 1956):166-170.

Brown, L.O., R.S. Lessler, and W.M. Weilbacher. *Advertising Media.* New York: Ronald Press, 1957.

Bruner, J.S. "On Perceptual Readiness." *Psychological Review* 64 (March 1957):123-152.

Bruner, J.S., and C.C. Goodman. "Value and Need as Organizing Factors in Perception." *Journal of Abnormal and Social Psychology* 42 (January 1947):33-44.

Bruner, J.S., G.A. Miller, and C. Zimmerman. "Discriminative Skill and Discriminative Matching in Perceptual Recognition." *Journal of Experimental Psychology* 49 (March 1955):187-192.

R.H. Bruskin Associates. "You Say It, But Do They Really Believe It?" *The Bruskin Report* 40 (May 1971):2-3.

Burnstein, E., E. Stotland, and A. Zander. "Similarity to a Model and Self-Evaluation." *Journal of Abnormal and Social Psychology* 62 (March 1961):257-264.

Buzzell, R.D. *Mathematical Models and Marketing Management.* Boston: Division of Research, Graduate School of Business Administration, Harvard University, 1964.

Byrne, D. "Interpersonal Attraction and Attitude Similarity." *Journal of Abnormal and Social Psychology* 62 (May 1961):713-715.

Byrne, D., and D. Nelson. "Attraction as a Linear Function of Proportions of Positive Reinforcements." *Journal of Personality and Social Psychology* 1 (June 1965):659-663.

Campbell, D.T. "Stereotypes and Perception of Group Differences." *American Psychologist* 22 (October 1967):817-829.

Cantor, N. *The Dynamics of Learning.* Buffalo, New York: Foster and Stewert, 1946.

Capon, N., and J. Hulbert. "The Sleeper Effect—An Awakening." *Public Opinion Quarterly* 37 (Fall 1973):333-358.

Carlsmith, J.M., B.E. Collins, and R.K. Helmreich. "Studies in Forced Compliance: I. The Effect of Pressure for Compliance on Attitude Change Produced by Face-to-face Role Playing and Anonymous Essay Writing." *Journal of Personality and Social Psychology* 4 (January 1966):1-13.

Carment, D.W., G.G. Miler, and V.B. Cervin. "Persuasiveness and Persuasibility as Related to Intelligence and Extraversion." *British Journal of Social and Clinical Psychology* 4 (February 1965):1-7.

Carrick, P.M., Jr. "Why Continued Advertising Is Necessary: A New Explanation." *Journal of Marketing* 23 (April 1959):386-398.

Cartwright, D., and F. Harary. "Structural Balance: A Generalization of Heider's Theory." *Psychological Review* 63 (September 1956):277-293.

Centers, R., and M. Horowitz. "Social Character and Conformity: A Differential in Susceptibility to Social Influences." *Journal of Social Psychology* 62 (August 1963):343-349.

Champion, R.A., and D.A. McBride. "Activity During Delay of Reinforcement in Human Learning." *Journal of Experimental Psychology* 63 (June 1962):589-592.

Chase, S. *The Proper Study of Mankind.* New York: Harper and Brothers, 1948.

Chu, G.C. "Prior Familiarity, Perceived Bias and One-Sided Versus Two-Sided Communication." *Journal of Experimental Psychology* 3 (July 1967):243-254.

Cohen, A.R. "Need for Cognition and Order of Communication as Determinants of Opinion Change." In C.I. Hovland and W. Mandell, eds., *The Order of Presentation in Persuasion.* New Haven: Yale Univ. Press, 1957, pp. 79-97.

Cohen, A.R. "Some Implications of Self-Esteem for Social Influence." In I.L. Janis and C.I. Hovland, eds., *Personality and Persuasibility.* New Haven: Yale Univ. Press, 1959.

Cohen, A.R. *Attitude Change and Social Influence.* New York: Basic Books, 1964.

Colley, R.H. *Defining Advertising Goals for Measured Advertising Results.* New York: Association of National Advertisers, 1961.

Combs, A.W., and C. Taylor. "The Effect of the Perception of Mild Degrees of Threat on Performance." *Journal of Abnormal and Social Psychology* 47 (April 1952):420-424.

Cooper, E., and H. Diverman. "Analysis of the Film 'Don't be a Sucker': A Study in Communication." *Public Opinion Quarterly* 15 (Summer 1951):243-264.

Cooper, J., and S. Worchel. "Role of Undesired Consequences in Arousing Cognitive Dissonance." *Journal of Personality and Social Psychology* 16 (October 1970):199-206.

Copp, J.H. "Perceptual Influences on Loyalty in a Farmer Cooperative." *Rural Sociology* 29 (June 1964):168-180.

Couch, A., and K. Keniston. "Yeasayers and Naysayers: Agreeing Response Set as a Personality Variable." *Journal of Abnormal and Social Psychology* 60 (March 1960):151-174.

Cox, D.F. "Clues for Advertising Strategists I." *Harvard Business Review* 39 (September-October 1961*a*):160-176.

Cox, D.F. "Clues for Advertising Strategists II." *Harvard Business Review* 39 (November-December 1961*b*):160-182.

Cox, D.F., and R.A. Bauer. "Self-Confidence and Persuasibility in Women." *Public Opinion Quarterly* 28, 3 (Fall 1964):453-466.

Crider, B. "The Identification of Emotions in Advertising Illustrations." *Journal of Applied Psychology* 20 (December 1936):748-750.

Cromwell, H. "The Relative Effect on Audience Attitude of the First versus the Second Argumentative Speech in a Series." *Speech Monographs* 17 (June 1950):105-122.

Crowell-Collier Company Brochure (1953).

Crutchfield, R.S. "Conformity and Character." *American Psychologist* 10 (May 1955):191-198.

Cunningham, S.M. "Perceived Risk as a Factor in Informal Consumer Communications." In D.F. Cox, ed., *Risk Taking and Information Handling in Consumer Behavior.* Boston: Division of Research, Graduate School of Business Administration, Harvard University, 1967, pp. 265-288.

Dair, C. *Design with Type.* Toronto: Univ. of Toronto Press, 1967.

Daugherty, W., and M. Janowitz, eds. *A Psychological Warfare Casebook.* Baltimore, Maryland: Johns Hopkins Univ. Press, 1958.

Davis, K. *Human Relations at Work.* New York: McGraw-Hill, 1962.

Davis, K.R., and F.E. Webster, Jr. *Sales Force Management.* New York: Ronald Press, 1968.

Deese, J. *The Psychology of Learning.* New York: McGraw-Hill, 1952.

Deese, J. "Some Problems in the Theory of Vigilance." *Psychological Review* 62 (September 1955):359-368.

DeFleur, M.L. *Theories of Mass Communication.* New York: McKay, 1966.

DeFleur, M.L., and F.R. Westie. "Verbal Attitudes and Overt Acts: An Experiment On the Salience of Attitudes." *American Sociological Review* 23 (December 1958):667-673.

Dember, W.N. *The Psychology of Perception.* New York: Holt, 1960.

Deno, S.L., P.E. Johnson, and J.R. Jenkins. "Associative Similarity of Words and Pictures." *Audio Visual Communication Review* 16 (Fall 1968):280-286.

Deutsch, M., and H.B. Gerard. "A Study of Normative and Informational Social Influences upon Individual Judgment." *The Journal of Abnormal and Social Psychology* 51 (November 1955):629-636.

Deutsch, M., and R.M. Kraus. *Theories in Social Psychology*. New York: Basic Books, 1965.

DeWolfe, A.S., and C.N. Governale. "Fear and Attitude Change." *Journal of Abnormal and Social Psychology* 69 (July 1964):119-123.

Dittes, J.E., and H.H. Kelley. "Effects of Different Conditions of Acceptance upon Conformity to Group Norms." *Journal of Abnormal and Social Psychology* 53 (July 1956):100-107.

DiVesta, F.J., and L. Cox. "Some Dispositional Correlates of Conformity Behavior." *Journal of Social Psychology* 52 (November 1960):259-268.

Douglas, J., G.A. Field, and L.X. Tarpey. *Human Behavior in Marketing*. Columbus, Ohio: Merrill, 1967.

Driscoll, J.M., J.T. Lanzetta, and J.S. McMichael. "Preference for Information under Varying Conditions of Outcome Uncertainty, Intensity, and Delay." *Psychological Reports* 21 (October 1967):473-479.

Druckman, D. "Dogmatism, Prenegotiation Experience, and Simulated Group Presentation as Determinants of Diadic Behavior in a Bargaining Situation." *Journal of Personality and Social Psychology* 6 (1967):279-290.

Ebbinghaus, H. *Memory: A Contribution to Experimental Psychology*. Leipzig, 1902. Translated by Ruger and Ressenius, New York, 1913.

Edwards, A.T. "The Retention of Affective Experiences, A Restatement of The Problem." *Psychological Review* 49 (January 1942):43-53.

Ehrlich, D., I. Guttman, P. Schonbach, and J. Mills. "Postdecision Exposure to Relevant Information." *Journal of Abnormal and Social Psychology* 54 (January 1957):98-102.

Ehrlich, H.J. "Dogmatism and Learning." *Journal of Abnormal and Social Psychology* 62 (January 1961):148-149.

Ehrlich, H.J., and D. Lee. "Dogmatism, Learning, and Resistance to Change: A Review and a New Paradigm." *Psychological Bulletin* 71 (April 1969):249-260.

Eisenstadt, S.N. "Communication Processes Among Immigrants in Israel." *Public Opinion Quarterly* 16 (Spring 1952):42-58.

Elbing, A.O., Jr. "The Influence of Prior Attitudes on Role Playing Results." *Personnel Psychology* 20 (Autumn 1967):309-321.

Endler, N.S. "Conformity as a Function of Different Reinforcement Schedules." In H.C. Lindgren, ed., *Contemporary Research in Social Psychology*. New York: Wiley, 1969.

Engel, J.F. "Are Automobile Purchasers Dissonant Consumers?" *The Journal of Marketing* 27 (April 1963):55-58.

Engel, J.F., D.T. Kollat, and R.D. Blackwell. *Consumer Behavior*. New York: Holt, Rinehart and Winston, 2nd edition, Copyright © 1968. Reprinted by permission of Holt, Rinehart and Winston.

Engel, J.F., H.G. Wales, and M.R. Warshaw. *Promotional Strategy*. Homewood, Illinois: Irwin, 1967.

English, H.B., and A.C. English. *A Comprehensive Dictionary of Psychological and Psychoanalytical Terms.* New York: Longmans, Green, and Company, 1958.

Epmeier, W.F. Personal discussion. Public Relations Department, A.C. Nielsen Company, Chicago: November 1969.

Eriksen, C. "Object Location in a Complex Perceptual Field." *Journal of Experimental Psychology* 45 (February 1953):126-132.

Exline, R.W. "Effects of Need for Affiliation, Sex, and the Sight of Others Upon Initial Communications in Problem-Solving Groups." *Journal of Personality* 30 (December 1962):541-546.

Eysenck, H.J. *Dynamics of Anxiety and Hysteria.* London: Routledge and Kegan Paul, 1957.

Faw, V.E. "A Psychotherapeutic Method of Teaching Psychology." *American Psychologist* 4 (April 1949):104-109.

Feather, N.T. "Cognitive Dissonance, Sensitivity, and Evaluation." *Journal of Abnormal and Social Psychology* 66 (February 1963):162-163.

Ferster, C.B., S. Culbertson, and M.C.P. Boren, *Behavior Principles* (Englewood Cliffs, N.J.: Prentice Hall, Inc., 2nd edition, 1975).

Festinger, L. *A Theory of Cognitive Dissonance.* Stanford, California: Stanford Univ. Press, 1957*a*.

Festinger, L. "The Motivating Effect of Cognitive Dissonance." In *Assessment of Human Motives.* New York: Rinehart and Company, 1957*b*.

Festinger, L. "Behavioral Support for Opinion Change." *Public Opinion Quarterly* 28 (Fall 1964a):404-417.

Festinger, L. *Conflict, Decision, and Dissonance.* Palo Alto, California: University of California Press, 1964b.

Festinger, L., and J.M. Carlsmith. "Cognitive Consequences of Forced Compliance." *Journal of Abnormal and Social Psychology.* 58 (March 1959):203-210.

Festinger, L., and N. Maccoby. "On Resistance to Persuasive Communications." *Journal of Abnormal and Social Psychology* 68 (April 1964):359-366.

Fleishman, E.A., E. Harris, and H. Burtt. *Leadership and Supervision in Industry: An Evaluation of a Supervisory Training Program.* Columbus, Ohio: Ohio State University, Bureau of Educational Research, 1955.

Foley, J.P., and Z.L. MacMillan. "Mediated Generalization and the Interpretation of Verbal Behavior." *Journal of Experimental Psychology* 33 (October 1943):229-314.

Forgus, R.H. *Perception.* New York: McGraw-Hill, 1966.

Freedman, J.L. "Involvement, Discrepancy, and Change." *Journal of Abnormal and Social Psychology* 64 (October 1964):290-295.

Freedman, J.L., and S. Fraser. "Compliance Without Pressure: The Foot-in-the-Door Technique." *Journal of Personality and Social Psychology* 4 (August 1966):195-202.

495

Freedman, J.L., and D.O. Sears. "Selective Exposure." *Advances in Experimental Social Psychology* 1 (1965):58-95.

Frost, N. "Clustering by Visual Shape in the Free Recall of Pictorial Stimuli." *Journal of Experimental Psychology* 88 (June 1971):409-413.

Fulton, R.B. "The Measure of Speaker Credibility." *The Journal of Communication* 20 (September 1970):270-279.

Gailon, A.K., and W.A. Watts. "The Time of Measurement Parameter in Studies of Dissonance Reduction." *Journal of Personality* 35 (December 1967):521-534.

Gardner, D. "The Effect of Divided Attention on Attitude Change Induced By a Persuasive Marketing Communication." In R.M. Haas, ed., *Science, Technology, and Marketing*. Chicago: American Marketing Association, 1966, pp. 532-540.

Gerard, H.B. "Compliance, Expectation of Reward, and Opinion Change." *Journal of Personality and Social Psychology* 68 (July 1967):360-364.

Gibson, J.J. "A Critical Review of the Concept of Set in Contemporary Experimental Psychology." *Psychological Bulletin* 38 (November 1941): 781-817.

Gibson, J.J. *The Perception of the Visual World*. Boston: Houghton Mifflin, 1950.

Glasker, H.R. "Checklist for Approving Ads." *Advertising Age* (December 23, 1963):36.

Glaze, J.A. "The Association Value of Nonsense Syllables." *Journal of Genetic Psychology* 35 (June 1928):255-269.

Goldberg, S.C. "Three Situational Determinants of Conformity to Social Norms." *Journal of Abnormal and Social Psychology* 49 (July 1954):325-329.

Gollob, H.F., and J.E. Dittes. "Effects of Manipulated Self-Esteem on Persuasibility Depending on Threat and Complexity of Communication." *Journal of Personality and Social Psychology* 2 (August 1965):195-201.

Gorfein, D.S. "Semantic Satiation and Word Association." *Psychonomic Science* 7 (January 15, 1967):47-48.

Gottlieb, M.J. "Segmentation by Personality Types." in L.H. Stockman, ed., *Advancing Marketing Efficiency*. Chicago: American Marketing Association, 1958, pp. 148-158.

Gottsehall, E.M. *Typographic Directions*. New York: Art Directions, 1964.

Gould, J., and W.L. Kolb. *A Dictionary of the Social Sciences*. New York: The Free Press, 1964.

Greenberg, B. "Voting Intentions, Election Expectations and Exposure to Campaign Information." *Journal of Communication* 15 (September 1965):149-160.

Greenwald, A.G. "The Open-Mindedness of the Counterattitudinal Role Player." *Journal of Experimental Social Psychology* 5 (October 1969):375-388.

Greenwald, A.G. "When Does Role Playing Produce Attitude Change? Toward an Answer." *Journal of Personality and Social Psychology* 16 (October 1970):214-219.

Griffing, H., and S.I. Frang. "On the Condition of Fatigue in Reading." *Psychological Review* 3 (September 1896):513-530.

Grose, R.F., and R.C. Birney, eds., *Transfer of Learning.* New York: Van Nostrand, 1963.

Gudger, C.M. "The Effects of Sex Differences upon Opinion Change." *Dissertation Abstracts International* 31 (December 1970):2549A-2550A.

Guilford, J.P. *General Psychology.* New York: Van Nostrand, 1939.

Haaland, G.A., and M. Venkatesan. "Resistance to Persuasive Communications: An Examination of the Distraction Hypothesis." *Journal of Personality and Social Psychology* 9 (February 1968):167-170.

Haber, R.N. "Nature of the Effect of Set on Perception." *Psychological Review* 73 (August 1966):335-351.

Hadley, H.D. "The Non-directive Approach in Advertising Appeals." *Journal of Applied Psychology* 37 (December 1953):496-498.

Hall, J.F. *The Psychology of Learning.* New York: Lippincott, 1966.

Hall, E.T. *The Silent Language.* New York: Doubleday, 1969.

Hamm, C., and E.W. Cundiff. "Self-Actualization and Product Perception." *Journal of Marketing Research* 6 (November 1969):470-472.

Harris, G.J., and G. Lown. "Interim Time Distribution and Response Compatibility in the Short-Term Serial Retention of Digits." *Psychonomic Science* 10 (March 15, 1968):295-296.

Hartman, G.W. "A Field Experiment on the Comparative Effectiveness of 'Emotional' and 'Rational' Political Leaflets in Determining Election Results." *Journal of Abnormal and Social Psychology* 31 (April-June 1936):99-114.

Harvey, O.J., and C. Consalvi. "Status and Conformity to Pressures in Informal Groups." *Journal of Abnormal and Social Psychology* 60 (March 1960):182-187.

Heider, F. *The Psychology of Interpersonal Relations.* New York: Wiley, 1958.

Heinberg, P. "Factors Related to an Individual's Ability to Perceive the Implications of Dialogues." *Speech Monographs* 28 (November 1961):274-281.

Heller, N. "An Application of Psychological Learning Theory to Advertising." *Journal of Marketing* 20 (January 1956):248-254.

Hempel, D.J. "An Experimental Study of the Effects of Information on Consumer Product Evaluations." In R. Haas, ed., *Science, Technology, and Marketing.* Chicago: American Marketing Association, 1966, pp. 589-597.

Hepner, H.W. *Effective Advertising.* New York: McGraw-Hill, 1941.

Hertzler, J.O. *A Sociology of Language.* New York: Random House, 1965.

Hewgill, M.A., and G.R. Miller. "Source Credibility and Response to Fear Arousing Communications." *Speech Monographs* 32 (June 1965):95-101.

Hinsie, L.E., and R.J. Campbell. *Psychiatric Dictionary*. New York: Oxford Univ. Press, 1960.

Hollander, E.P. "Conformity, Status and Idiosyncrasy Credit." *Psychological Review* 65 (March 1958):117-127.

Hollander, E.P. "Competence and Conformity in the Acceptance of Influence." *Journal of Abnormal and Social Psychology* 61 (November 1960):365-369.

Hollander, E.P. *Principles and Methods of Social Psychology*. New York: Oxford Univ. Press, 1967.

Hollander, E.P., and R.G. Hunt. *Current Perspectives in Social Psychology*. New York: Oxford Univ. Press, 1967.

Hollander, E.P., J.W. Julian, and G.A. Haaland. "Conformity Process and Prior Group Support." *Journal of Personality and Social Psychology* 2 (December 1965):852-858.

Hollingworth, H.L. *Advertising and Selling*. New York: Appleton, 1913.

Hollingworth, H.L. *Psychology: Its Facts and Principles*. New York: Appleton, 1928.

Homans, G.C. *Social Behavior: Its Elementary Forms*. New York: Harcourt, Brace and World, 1961.

Honkavaara, S. "Some Critical Notes Concerning the Concept of Rigidity and Its Measurement." *Journal of Psychology* 45 (January 1958):43-45.

Hornstein, H.A., E. Fisch, and M. Holmes. "Influence of a Model's Feeling about his Behavior and his Relevance as a Comparison Other on Observers Helping Behavior." *Journal of Personality and Social Psychology* 10 (November 1968):222-226.

Hovland, C.I. "Experimental Studies in Rote Learning Theory." *Journal of Experimental Psychology* 22 (April 1938):338-353.

Hovland, C.I. "Changes in Attitude Through Communication." *Journal of Abnormal and Social Psychology* 46 (July 1951):424-437.

Hovland, C.I. "Studies in Persuasion." In H.J. Leavitt and L.R. Pondy, eds., *Managerial Psychology*. Chicago: Univ. of Chicago Press, 1964, pp. 129-190.

Hovland, C.I., and H.C. Kelman. "Reinstatement of the Communicator in Delayed Measurement of Opinion Change." *Journal of Abnormal and Social Psychology* 48 (July 1953):327-335.

Hovland, C.I., and W. Mandell. "An Experimental Comparison of Conclusion-drawing by the Communicator and by the Audience." *Journal of Abnormal and Social Psychology* 47 (July 1952):581-588.

Hovland, C.I., and W. Mandell. "Is There a Law of Primacy in Persuasion?" In C.I. Hovland et al., eds., *The Order of Presentation in Persuasion*. New Haven: Yale Univ. Press, 1957, pp. 13-22.

Hovland, C.I., and H.A. Pritzker. "Extent of Opinion Change as a Function of Amount of Change Advocated." *Journal of Abnormal and Social Psychology* 54 (March 1957):257-261.

Hovland, C.I., and W. Weiss. "The Influence of Source Credibility on Communication Effectiveness." *Public Opinion Quarterly* 15 (Winter 1951-52):635-650.

Hovland, C.I., E.H. Campbell, and T. Brock. "The Effects of 'Commitment' in Opinion Change Following Communication." In C.I. Hovland et al., eds., *Order of Presentation in Persuasion.* New Haven: Yale Univ. Press, 1957.

Hovland, C.I., O.J. Harvey, and M. Sherif. "Assimilation and Contrast Effects in Reactions to Communication and Attitude Change." *Journal of Abnormal and Social Psychology* 55 (September 1957):244-252.

Hovland, C.I., I.L. Janis, and H.H. Kelley. *Communications and Persuasion: Psychological Studies of Opinion Change.* New Haven: Yale Univ. Press, 1953.

Hovland, C.I., A. Lumsdaine, and F.D. Sheffield. *Experiments in Mass Communication* 3. Princeton: Princeton Univ. Press, 1949.

Hovland, C.I., et al. *The Order of Presentation in Persuasion.* New Haven: Yale Univ. Press, 1957.

Howard, J.A., and J.N. Sheth. *The Theory of Buyer Behavior.* New York: Wiley, 1969. Copyright © 1969. Reprinted by permission of John Wiley & Sons, Inc.

Hoy, E., and N. Endler. "Reported Anxiousness and Two Types of Stimulus Incongruity." *Canadian Journal of Behavioural Science* 1 (April 1969):207-214.

Hull, C.L. *Principles of Behavior.* New York: Appleton, 1943.

Hull, C.L. *A Behavior System* New Haven: Yale Univ. Press, 1952.

Hutt, C., and R. May. "Modality and Sex Differences in Recall and Recognition Memory." *Child Development* 45 (March 1974):228-231.

Insko, C.A. "Primacy Versus Recency in Persuasion as a Function of the Timing of Arguments and Measures." *Journal of Abnormal and Social Psychology* 69 (October 1964):381-391.

Insko, C., and J. Schopler. "Triadic Consistency: A Statement of Affective-Cognitive-Conative Tendency." *Psychological Review* 74 (September 1967):361-374.

Jacobson, D.J. *The Affairs of Dame Rumor.* New York: Rinehart, 1948.

Janis, I.L. "Personality Correlates of Susceptibility to Persuasion." *Journal of Personality* 22 (June 1954):504-518.

Janis, I.L. "Anxiety Indices Related to Susceptibility to Persuasion." *Journal of Abnormal and Social Psychology* 51 (November 1955):663-667.

Janis, I.L. "Motivational Effects of Different Sequential Arrangements of Conflicting Arguments." In C.I. Hovland et al., eds., *The Order of Presentation in Persuasion.* New Haven: Yale Univ. Press, 1957, pp. 170-186.

Janis, I.L. "Personality as a Factor in Susceptibility to Persuasion." In W. Schramm, ed., *The Science of Human Communication.* New York: Basic Books, 1963, pp. 54-64.

Janis, I.L., and S. Feshbach. "Effects of Fear-arousing Communications." *Journal of Abnormal and Social Psychology* 48 (January 1953):78-92.

Janis, I.L., and P.B. Field. "A Behavioral Assessment of Persuasibility: Consistency of Individual Differences." *Sociometry* 19 (December 1956):241-259.

Janis, I.L., and P.B. Field. "Sex Differences and Personality Factors Related to Persuasibility." In I.L. Janis and C.I. Hovland, eds., *Personality and Persuasibility*. New Haven: Yale Univ. Press, 1959, pp. 55-64.

Janis, I.L., and C.I. Hovland, eds., *Personality and Persuasibility*. New Haven: Yale Univ. Press, 1959.

Janis, I.L., and B.T. King. "The Influence of Role Playing on Opinion Change." *Journal of Abnormal and Social Psychology* 49 (April 1954):211-218.

Janis, I.L., and B.T. King. "Comparison of the Effectiveness of Improvised Versus Nonimprovised Role Playing in Producing Opinion Changes." *Human Relations* 9 (March 1956):177-186.

Janis, I.L., and C. Milholland. "The Influence of Threat Appeals on Selective Learning of the Content of a Persuasive Communication." *Journal of Psychology* 37 (January 1954):75-80.

Janis, I.L., A.A. Lumsdaine, and A.I. Gladstone. "Effects of Preparatory Communication on Reactions to a Subsequent News Event." *Public Opinion Quarterly* 15 (Fall 1951):487-518.

Jessor, R. "The Generalization of Expectancies." *Journal of Abnormal and Social Psychology* 49 (February 1954):196-200.

Jones, E.E., and H.B. Gerard. *Foundations of Social Psychology*. New York: Wiley, 1967.

Jordan, N. "Behavioral Forces that Are a Function of Attitudes and of Cognitive Organization." *Human Relations* 6 (August 1953):273-287.

Joyce, T. "How Does Advertising Influence Consumer's Buying?" *Advertising Age* 38 (June 5, 1967):90-92.

Kagan, J. "Preschool Enrichment and Learning." In G.J. Williams and S. Gordon, eds., *Clinical Child Psychology and Future Perspectives*. New York: Behavioral Publications, 1974, pp. 4-5.

Kanungo, R.N. "Retention of Affective Material." *Journal of Personality and Social Psychology* 8 (January 1968):63-68.

Kanungo, R.N., and S. Dutta. "Brand Awareness as a Function of Its Meaningfulness, Sequential Position, and Product Utility." *Journal of Applied Psychology* 50 (June 1966):220-224.

Karlins, M., and H.I. Abelson. *Persuasion*. New York: Springer, 1970.

Kassarjian, H.H. "Social Character Differential Preference for Mass Communication." *Journal of Marketing Research* 2 (May 1965):146-163.

Kassarjian, W.M. "A Study of Riesman's Theory of Social Character." *Sociometry* 25 (September 1962):213-230.

Katona, G. *The Mass Consumption Society*. New York: McGraw-Hill, 1964.

Katona, G., and E. Mueller. "A Study of Purchase Decisions." In L.H. Clark, ed., *Consumer Behavior*, Vol. I. Washington Square, N.Y.: New York Univ. Press, 1955, pp. 30-87.

Katz, D. *Gestalt Psychology, Its Nature and Significance.* New York: Ronald Press, 1950.

Katz, E., and P.F. Lazarsfeld. *Personal Influence: The Part Played by People in the Flow of Mass Communication.* New York: Free Press, 1955.

Kay, E., and H.H. Meyer. "Effects of Threat in a Performance Appraisal Interview." *Journal of Applied Psychology* 49 (October 1965):311-317.

Kelman, H.C. "Attitude Change as a Function of Response Restriction." *Human Relations* 6, 3 (1953):185-214.

Kelman, H.C., and A.H. Eagly. "Attitude Toward the Communicator, Perception of Communication Content, and Attitude Change." *Journal of Personality and Social Psychology* 1 (January 1965):63-78.

Kelman, H.C., and C.I. Hovland. " 'Reinstatement' of the Communicator in Delayed Measurement of Opinion Change." *Journal of Abnormal and Social Psychology* 48 (July 1953):327-335.

Kendall, P., and K.M. Wolf. "The Analysis of Deviant Cases in Communications Research." In *Communications Research.* New York: Harper & Brothers, 1949.

Kendler, H.H., and B.J. Underwood. "The Role of Reward in Conditioning Theory." *Psychological Review* 55 (February 1948):209-215.

Keppel, G., and B.J. Underwood. "Proactive Inhibition in Short-term Retention of Single Items." *Journal of Verbal Learning and Verbal Behavior* 1 (October 1962):153-161.

Kiesler, C.A. *The Psychology of Commitment.* New York: Academic Press, 1971.

Kiesler, C.A., and S.B. Kiesler. "Role of Forewarning in Persuasive Communications." *Journal of Abnormal and Social Psychology* 68 (May 1964):547-549.

Kiesler, S.B., and R.B. Mathog. "Distraction Hypothesis in Attitude Change: Effects of Effectiveness." *Psychological Reports* 23 (December 1968):1123-1133.

Kirscht, J.P., and D.P. Haefner. "Reactions to a Sequence of Fear-arousing Messages." *Proceedings, 77th Annual Convention, American Psychological Association.* Washington, D.C.: APA, 1969, pp. 375-376.

Klapper, J.T. "What We Know about the Effects of Mass Communication: The Brink of Hope." *Public Opinion Quarterly* 21 (Winter 1957-58):453-474.

Klapper, J.T. *The Effects of Mass Communication.* Glencoe, Illinois: Free Press, 1960.

Kleck, R.E., and J. Wheaton. "Dogmatism and Responses to Opinion-Consistent and Opinion-Inconsistent Information." *Journal of Personality and Social Psychology* 5 (April 1967):249-252.

Kleppner, O. *Advertising Procedure.* Englewood Cliffs, N.J.: Prentice-Hall, 1966.

Kline, J.A. "Interaction of Evidence and Readers' Intelligence on the Effects of Short Messages." *The Quarterly Journal of Speech* 40 (December 1969):407-413.

Köhler, W. *Gestalt Psychology*. New York: Liveright, 1947.

Kotler, P. *Marketing Management: Analysis, Planning and Control*. Englewood Cliffs, N.J.: Prentice-Hall, 1967.

Krech, D., and R.S. Crutchfield. *Theory and Problems of Social Psychology*. New York: McGraw-Hill, 1948.

Krech, D., R.S. Crutchfield, and E. Ballachey. *Individual in Society: A Textbook of Social Psychology*. New York: McGraw-Hill, 1962.

Krueger, W.C.F. "The Effect of Overlearning on Retention." *Journal of Experimental Psychology* 12 (February 1929):71-78.

Krugman, H.E. "An Application of Learning Theory to TV Copy Testing." *Public Opinion Quarterly* 26 (Winter 1962):626-634.

Krugman, H.E. "The Impact of Television Advertising: Learning Without Involvement." *Public Opinion Quarterly* 29 (Fall 1965):349-356.

Krugman, H.E. "The Measurement of Advertising Involvement." *Public Opinion Quarterly* 30 (Winter 1966-1967):583-596.

Krugman, H.E. "Processes Underlying Exposure to Advertising." *American Psychologist* 23 (April 1968):245-253.

Lana, R.E. "Familiarity and the Order of Presentation of Persuasive Communications." *Journal of Abnormal and Social Psychology* 62 (May 1961):573-577.

Lana, R.E. "Controversy of the Topic and the Order of Presentation in Persuasive Communications." *Psychological Reports* 12 (February 1963):163-170.

Lana, R.E. "Inhibitory Effects of a Pretest on Opinion Change." *Educational and Psychological Measurement* 26 (Spring 1966):139-150.

Lasswell, H.D. "The Structure and Function of Communication in Society." In L. Bryson, ed., *The Communication of Ideas*. New York: Harper and Brothers, 1948.

Lavidge, R.J., and G.A. Steiner. "A Model for Predictive Measurements of Advertising Effectiveness." *Journal of Marketing* 25 (October 1961):59-62. Published by the American Marketing Association.

Lazarsfeld, P.F., B. Berelson, and H. Gaudet. *The People's Choice: How the Voter Makes Up His Mind in the Presidential Campaign*. New York: Columbia Univ. Press, 1948.

Leavitt, C. "Response Structure: A Determinant of Recall." *Journal of Advertising Research* 8 (September 1968):3-6.

Leavitt, H.J. *Managerial Psychology*. Chicago: Univ. of Chicago Press, 1960.

Leshner, M. "Attitude Change: A Comparison Study of Multiple Role-Playing and Group Discussion Under Conditions of Effort, Exposure, and Direction." Unpublished Ph.D. dissertation, Temple University, 1966.

Leventhal, H., and P. Niles. "A Field Experiment on Fear Arousal with Data On the Validity of Questionnaire Measures." *Journal of Personality* 32 (September 1964):459-479.

Levine, R., I. Chein, and G. Murphy. "The Relation of the Intensity of a Need to the Amount of Perceptual Distortion: A Preliminary Report." *Journal of Psychology* 13 (January 1942):283-293.

Levine, J.M., and G. Murphy. "The Learning and Forgetting of Controversial Material." *Journal of Abnormal and Social Psychology* 38 (October 1943):507-517.

Lewin, K. "Forces Behind Food Habits and Methods of Change." In *The Problem of Changing Food Habits: Report of the Committee on Food Habits, 1941-1943*, of *Bulletins of the National Research Council* 108 (October 1943):35-65.

Lewin, K. *Field Theory in Social Science.* New York: Harper and Brothers, 1951.

Lewin, K., and F. Hoppe. "Investigation of the Psychology of Action and Affection." *Psychologische Forschung* 14 (1930):1-68.

Lieberman, S. "The Effects of Changes in Roles on the Attitudes of Role Occupants." In H.C. Lindgren, ed., *Contemporary Research in Social Psychology.* New York: Wiley, 1969, pp. 317-331.

Lindzey, G., and E. Aronson. *The Handbook of Social Psychology.* Reading, Massachusetts: Addison-Wesley, 1969.

Linton, H., and E. Graham. "Personality Correlates of Persuasibility." In C.I. Hovland and I.L. Janis, eds., *Personality and Persuasibility.* New Haven: Yale Univ. Press, 1959, pp. 69-101.

Lionberger, H.F. *Adoption of New Ideas and Practices: A Summary of the Research Dealing with Implications for Action in Facilitating Social Change.* Ames, Iowa: Iowa State Univ. Press, 1960.

LoSciuto, L.A., and R. Perloff. "Influence of Product Preference on Dissonance Reduction." *Journal of Marketing Research* 4 (August 1967):286-289.

Lucas, D.B. *The Controlled Recognition Method for Checking Magazine Readership.* New York: Crowell-Collier, 1942.

Lucas, D.B., and S.H. Britt. *Advertising Psychology and Research.* New York: McGraw-Hill, 1950.

Lucas, D.B., and S.H. Britt. *Measuring Advertising Effectiveness.* New York: McGraw-Hill, 1963.

Luchins, A.S. "Primacy-recency in Impression Formation." In C.I. Hovland, et al., eds., *The Order of Presentation in Persuasion.* New Haven: Yale Univ. Press, 1957, pp. 33-61.

Luckiesh, M. *Light and Color in Advertising and Merchandising.* New York: Van Nostrand, 1923.

Luckiesh, M., and F.K. Moss. "Boldness as a Factor in Type Design and Typography." *Journal of Applied Psychology* 24 (April 1940):170-183.

Lumsdaine, A.A., and I.L. Janis. "Resistance to 'Counterpropaganda' Produced by One-sided and Two-sided Propaganda Presentations." *Public Opinion Quarterly* 17 (Fall 1953):311-318.

Lund, F.H. "The Psychology of Belief: A Study of Its Emotional and Volitional Determinants." *Journal of Abnormal and Social Psychology* 20 (July 1925):174-196.

Lundy, R.M., N.R. Simonson, and A.D. Landers. "Conformity, Persuasibility, and Irrelevant Fear." *The Journal of Communication* 17 (March 1967):39-54.

Maccoby, E. *The Development of Sex Differences.* Stanford, California: Stanford Univ. Press, 1966.

Maccoby, E.E., T.M. Newcomb, and E.L. Hartley, eds. *Readings in Social Psychology.* New York: Holt, 3rd ed., 1958.

Maccoby, N., A.K. Romney, J.S. Adams, and E.E. Maccoby. "Critical Periods in Seeking and Accepting Information." In *Paris-Stanford Studies in Communication.* Stanford, California: Institute for Communication Research, 1962.

MacDonald, C. "Relationships between Advertising Exposure and Purchasing Behavior." *Admap* 5 (April 1969):144-155.

Mackworth, J.F. "The Duration of the Visual Image." *Canadian Journal of Psychology* 17 (March 1963):62-81.

Maddi, S.R. "Meaning, Novelty, and Affect: Comments on Zajonc's Paper." *Journal of Personality and Social Psychology, Monograph Supplement* 9 (June 1968):28-29.

Madison, S.A., and A. Paivia. "Instructional Effects on Semantic Satiation." *Psychonomic Science.* 17 (January 15, 1967):45-46.

Maloney, J.C. "Curiosity Versus Disbelief in Advertising." *Journal of Advertising Research* 2 (June 1962):2-8.

Maloney, J.C. "Is Advertising Believability Really Important?" *Journal of Marketing* 27 (October 1963):1-8.

Maloney, J.C. Lecture presented at Northwestern University Graduate School of Management, 1968.

Mayer, M. *Madison Avenue U.S.A.* New York: Harper and Brothers, 1958.

McCloskey, H., and H. Dahlgren. "Primary Group Influence on Party Loyalty." *American Political Science Review* 53 (September 1969):157-176.

McGinnies, E. "Emotionality and Perceptual Defense." *Psychological Review* 56 (1949):244-251.

McGuckin, H.E., Jr. "The Persuasive Force of Similarity in Cognitive Style between Advocate and Audience." *Speech Monographs* 34 (June 1967):145-151.

McGuire, W.J. "Order of Presentation as a Factor in 'Conditioning' Persuasiveness." In C.I. Hovland et al., eds., *The Order of Presentation in Persuasion.* New Haven: Yale Univ. Press, 1957, pp. 98-114.

McGuire, W.J., "Persistence of the Resistance to Persuasion Induced by Various Types of Prior Belief Defenses." *Journal of Abnormal and Social Psychology* 64 (April 1962):241-248.

McGuire, W.J., and S. Millman. "Antipathy Belief Lowering Following Forewarning of a Persuasive Attack." *Journal of Personality and Social Psychology* 2 (October 1965):471-479.

McGuire, W.J., and D. Papageorgis. "The Relative Efficacy of Various Types of Prior Belief-Defense in Producing Immunity against Persuasion." *Journal of Abnormal and Social Psychology* 62 (March 1961):327-337.

Mehrabian, A. "Attitudes Inferred from Neutral Communications." *Journal of Consulting Psychology* 31 (August 1967):414-417.

Mehrabian, A. "The Effects of Context on Judgments of Speaker's Attitude." *Journal of Personality* 36, 1 (March 1968):21-32.

Mehrabian, A., and M. Wiener. "Non-immediacy Between Communicator and Object of Communication in a Verbal Message." *Journal of Consulting Psychology* 30 (October 1966):420-425.

Mehrabian, A., and M. Wiener. "Decoding of Inconsistent Communications." *Journal of Personality and Social Psychology* 6 (May 1967):109-114.

Mehrley, R.S., and J.C. McCroskey. "Opinionated Statements and Attitude Intensity as Predictors of Attitude Change and Source Credibility." *Speech Monographs* 37 (March 1970):47-52.

Mendell, D.M. "Relating Delay of Gratification to Achievement in Young Children" *Dissertation Abstracts* 28 (September 1967):1169-1170.

Menzel, H., and E. Katz. "Social Relations and Innovation in the Medical Profession—The Epidemology of a New Drug." *Public Opinion Quarterly* 19 (Winter 1955):337-352.

Menzies, R. "Comparative Memory Values of Pleasant, Unpleasant, and Indifferent Experiences." *Journal of Experimental Psychology* 43 (January 1935):267-279. Copyright 1935 by the American Psychological Association. Reprinted by permission.

Mertz, R.J., G.R. Miller, and L. Ballance. "Open and Closed-mindedness and Cognitive Conflict." *Journalism Quarterly* 43 (Autumn 1966):429-433.

Michael, J., and M.D. Adler, "The Trial of an Issue of Fact." *Columbia Law Review I.* Vol. 34 (November 1934):1224-1306; II. Vol. 34 (December 1934):1462-1493.

Miller, A. "Verbal Sensation and the Role of Concurrent Activity." *Journal of Abnormal and Social Psychology* 66 (March 1963):206-212.

Miller, G.A. *Language and Communication.* New York: McGraw-Hill, 1951.

Miller, G.A. "The Magical Number Seven, Plus or Minus Two: Some Limits on Our Capacity for Processing Information." *Psychological Review* 63 (March 1956):81-97.

Miller, N., and D.T. Campbell. "Recency and Primacy in Persuasion as a Function of the Timing of Speeches and Measurements." *Journal of Abnormal and Social Psychology* 59 (July 1959):1-9.

Miller, G.R., and J. Baseheart. "Source Trustworthiness, Opinionated Statements, and Response to Persuasive Communication." *Speech Monographs* 36 (March 1969):1-7.

Miller, G.R., and J. Lobe. "Opinionated Language, Open and Closed-mindedness and Response to Persuasive Communications." *Journal of Communication* 17 (December 1967):333-342.

Mills, J., and E. Aronson. "Opinion Change as a Function of the Communicator's Attractiveness and Desire to Influence." *Journal of Personality and Social Psychology* 1 (February 1965):173-177.

Mills, J., and G.M. Jellison. "Effect on Opinion Change of Similarity Between Communicator and the Audience He Addressed." *Journal of Personality and Social Psychology* 9 (June 1968):153-156.

Mitchell, G.D. *A Dictionary of Sociology* Chicago: Aldine Publishing Company, 1968.

Moakley, F.X. *The Effects of Learning from a Motion Picture Film of Selective Changes in Sound Track Loudness Level.* Washington, D.C.: U.S. Department of Health, Education and Welfare, Office of Education, Bureau of Research, January, 1968.

Moore, O.K., and D.J. Lewis. "Learning Theory and Culture." *Psychological Review* 59 (September 1952):380-388.

Moray, N. *Attention: Selective Processes in Vision and Hearing.* New York: Academic Press, 1969.

Morelli, G. "Pictures and Competing Pictures as Mediators in Paired-associate Learning." *Perceptual and Motor Skills* 30 (June 1970):729-730.

Morgan, C.T. *Introduction to Psychology.* New York: McGraw-Hill, 1956.

Morin, R.E., B. Forrin, and W. Archer. "Information Processing Behavior: The Role of Irrelevant Stimulus Information." *Journal of Experimental Psychology* 61 (January 1961):89-96.

Morrison, B.J., and M.J. Darnoff. "Advertising Complexity and Looking Time." *Journal of Marketing Research* 9 (November 1972):396-400.

Müller, G.E., and A. Pilzecker. "Experimentelle Beiträge zur Lehre von Gedächtris." *Zeitschrift für Psychologie.* Erganzüngsband, I., 1900. Cited in E. Meumann. *The Psychology of Learning.* New York: Appleton, 1913, pp. 166-167.

Murphy, G., L.B. Murphy, and T.M. Newcomb. *Experimental Social Psychology.* New York: Harper and Brothers, revised edition, 1937.

Nelson, R.P. *The Design of Advertising.* Dubuque, Iowa: William C. Brown, 1973.

Newcomb, T.M. *Personality and Social Change.* New York: Dryden, 1943.

Nickerson, R.S. "Categorization Time with Categories Defined by Disjunctions and Conjunctions of Stimulus Attributes." *Journal of Experimental Psychology* 73 (February 1967):211-219.

Nisbett, R.E., and A. Gordon. "Self-esteem and Susceptiblity to Social Influence." *Journal of Personality and Social Psychology* 5 (March 1967):268-276.

Norris, E.L. "Attitude Change as a Function of Open or Closed-mindedness." *Journalism Quarterly* 42 (Autumn 1965):571-575.

Opochinsky, S. "Values, Expectations, and the Formation of Impressions." *Dissertation Abstracts International* 26 (May 1966):6854.

Optner, S.L. *Systems Analysis for Business and Industrial Problem Solving.* Englewood Cliffs, N.J.: Prentice-Hall, 1965.

Osborn, A. *Your Creative Power.* New York: Scribner, 1948.

Osgood, C.E. "The Similarity Paradox in Human Learning: A Resolution." In R.F. Grose and R.C. Birney, eds., *Transfer of Learning.* New York: Van Nostrand, 1963, pp. 64-82.

Osgood, C.E., G.J. Suci, and P.H. Tannenbaum. *The Measurement of Meaning* Urbana, Illinois: Univ. of Illinois Press, 1967.

Osgood, C.E., and P.H. Tannenbaum. "The Principle of Congruity in the Prediction of Attitude Change." *Psychological Review* 62 (January 1955):44-50.

Paivio, A., and R. Steeves. "Relations Between Personal Values and Imagery and Meaningfulness of Value Words." *Perceptual and Motor Skills* 24 (April 1967):357-358.

Paivio, A., T.B. Rogers, and P.C. Smythe. "Why Are Pictures Easier to Recall Than Words?" *Psychonomic Science* 11 (June 5, 1968):137-138.

Parker, R. "Effects of Instructions, Schedules of Reward, and Magnitude of Reward on the Discrimination of Acquisition and Extinction Phases of Learning." *Journal of Experimental Psychology* 75 (February 1967):210-216.

Parry, J. *The Psychology of Human Communication.* New York: American Elsevier, 1968.

Paterson, D.G., and M.A. Tinker. "Studies of Typographical Factors Influencing Speed of Reading: VIII. Space Between Lines or Leading." *Journal of Applied Psychology* 16 (August 1932):388-397 and 605-613.

Paterson, D.G., and M.A. Tinker. *How to Make Type Readable.* New York: Harper and Brothers, 1940.

Peck, R.F. "Family Patterns Correlated with Adolescent Personality Structure." *Journal of Abnormal and Social Psychology* 57 (November 1958):347-350.

Perry, H.M. "The Relative Efficiency of Actual and 'Imaginery Practice' in Five Selected Tasks." *Archives of Psychology* 34, 243 (1939).

Pillsbury, W.B., and H.L. Raush. "An Extension of the Köhler Restorff Inhibition Phenomenon." *American Journal of Psychology* 56 (April 1943):293-298.

Pinson, C., and E.L. Roberto. "Do Attitude Changes Precede Behavior Change?" *Journal of Advertising Research* 13 (August 1973):33-38.

Pishkin, V., and J.T. Shurly. "Auditory Dimensions and Irrelevant Information in Concepts Identification in Males and Females." *Perceptual and Motor Skills* 20 (June 1965):673-683.

Politz, A., Research, Inc. *A 12-months' Study of Better Homes and Gardens.* Des Moines, Iowa: Meredith, 1956.

Politz, A., Research, Inc. *Measurement of Advertising Effectiveness.* Chicago: November 1962.

Postman, L.J., and L. Rau. "Retention as a Function of the Method of Measurement." *University of California Publications in Psychology* 8, 3 (1957).

Postman, L., J.S. Bruner, and E. McGinnies. "Personal Values as Selective Factors in Perception." *Journal of Abnormal and Social Psychology* 43 (April 1948):142-154.

Postman, L, J.S. Bruner, and R.D. Walk. "The Perception of Error." *British Journal of Psychology* 42 (March 1951):1-10.

Preston, I.L. "Theories of Behavior and the Concept of Rationality in Advertising." *Journal of Communication* 17 (September 1967):211-222.

Rabinowitz, F.M., and C.V. Robe. "Children's Choice Behavior as a Function of Stimulus Change, Complexity, Relative Novelty, Surprise and Uncertainty." *Journal of Experimental Psychology* 78 (December 1968):625-633.

Rath, R., and S.K. Mirsa. "Change of Attitudes as a Function of Some Personality Factors." *Journal of Social Psychology* 60 (August 1963):311-317.

Ray, M.L., A.G. Sawyer, and E.C. Strong. "Frequency Effects Revisited." *Journal of Advertising Research* 11 (February 1971):14-20.

Reese, H.W. *The Perception of Stimulus Relations.* New York: Academic Press, 1968.

Reeves, R. *Reality in Advertising.* New York: Knopf, 1961.

Remmers, H.H., and N. Weltman. "Attitude Interrelationships of Youth, Their Parents, and Their Teachers." *Journal of Social Psychology* 26 (August 1947):61-68.

Riland, L.H. "Relationship of the Guttman Components of Attitude Intensity and Personal Involvement." *Journal of Applied Psychology* 43 (August 1959):279-284.

Rogers, C.R. *Counseling and Psychotherapy.* Cambridge, Massachusetts: Riverside Press, 1942.

Rogers, E.M. *Diffusion of Innovations.* New York: Free Press, 1962.

Rogers, E.M. *Modernization Among Peasants: The Impact of Communication.* New York: Holt, Rinehart and Winston, 1969.

Rogers, R., and D. Thistlethwaite. "An Analysis of Active and Passive Defenses in Inducing Resistance to Persuasion." *Journal of Personality and Social Psychology* 11 (April 1969):301-308.

Rohrer, J., and M. Sherif. *Social Psychology at the Crossroads.* New York: Harper & Row, 1951.

Rokeach, M. "The Nature and Meaning of Dogmatism." *Psychological Review* 61 (May 1954):194-204.

Rokeach, M. "Five Kinds of Belief: Images of the Consumer's Changing Mind On and Off Madison Avenue." Paper from the 1963 Eastern Regional Convention, American Association of Advertising Agencies, pp. 4-7.

Rokeach, M. *Beliefs, Attitudes, and Values: A Theory of Organization and Change.* San Francisco: Jossey-Bass, 1968.

Rokeach, M. "Long-range Experimental Modification of Values, Attitudes, and Behavior." *American Psychologist* 26 (May 1971):453-459.

Rokeach, M., A. Oram, J.J. Laffey, and M.R. Denny. "On Party-line Thinking: An Experimental Analogy." In M. Rokeach, *The Open and Closed Mind.* New York: Basic Books, 1960, pp. 225-242.

Rokeach, M., T.S. Swanson, and M.R. Denny. "The Role of Past Experience: A Comparison Between Chess-players and Non-chess Players." In M. Rokeach, *The Open and Closed Mind.* New York: Basic Books, 1960, pp. 215-223.

Roland, A.A. "Persuasibility in Young Children as a Function of Aggressive Motivation and Aggression Conflict." *Journal of Abnormal and Social Psychology* 66 (May 1963):454-461.

Rosenbaum, M.E., and I. Zimmerman. "The Effect of External Commitnent on Response to an Attempt to Change Opinions." *Public Opinion Quarterly* 23 (February 1959):247-254.

Rosenberg, M.J. "Affective-cognitive Consistency." In M.J. Rosenberg, C.I. Hovland, W.J. McGuire, R.P. Abelson, and J.W. Brehm, eds., *Attitude Organization and Change, and Analysis of Consistency among Attitude Components.* New Haven: Yale Univ. Press, 1960.

Rosenberg, M.J. "When Dissonance Fails: On Eliminating Evaluation Apprehension from Attitude Measurement." *Journal of Personality and Social Psychology* 1 (January 1965):28-42.

Rosenberg, M.J., and R.P. Abelson. "An Analysis of Cognitive Balancing." In C.I. Hovland and M.J. Rosenberg, eds., *Attitude Organization and Change.* New Haven: Yale Univ. Press, 1960, pp. 112-163.

Rosenberg, M.J., C.I. Hovland, W.J. McGuire, R.P. Abelson, and J.W. Brehm, eds., *Attitude Organization and Change: An Analysis of Consistency among Attitude Components.* New Haven: Yale Univ. Press, 1960.

Rudolph, H.J. *Attention and Interest Factors in Advertising.* New York: Funk and Wagnalls, in association with Printers' Ink, 1947.

Sampson, J. "Further Study of Encoding and Arousal Factors in Free Recall of Verbal and Visual Material." *Psychonomic Science* 16 (August 1969):221-222.

Sandage, C.H., and V. Fryburger. *Advertising Theory and Practice.* Homewood, Illinois: Irwin, 8th edition, 1971. Reprinted by permission of the publisher.

Sanford, E.C. "The Relative Legibility of the Small Letters." *American Journal of Psychology* 1 (May 1888):402-435.

Sartain, A.Q., A.J. North, J.R. Strange, and H.M. Chapman. *Psychology.* New York: McGraw-Hill, 1967.

Sawyer, A.G. "The Effects of Repetition of Refutational and Supportive Advertising Appeals." *Journal of Marketing Research* 10 (February 1973):23-33.

Schiller, N. "Intelligence Differences in Reaction to Advertisements." *Journal of Applied Psychology* 22 (April 1938):171-173.

Schneidel, T.M. "Sex and Persuasibility." *Speech Monographs* 30 (November 1963):353-358.

Schramm, W.L. *The Process and Effects of Mass Communication.* Urbana, Illinois: Univ. of Illinois Press, revised edition, 1971a.

Schramm, W.L. "The Nature of Communication Between Humans." In W. Schramm and D. F. Roberts, eds., *The Process and Effects of Mass Communication.* Urbana, Ill.: Univ. of Illinois Press, revised edition, 1971b, pp. 1-53. Copyright 1971, University of Illinois Press.

Schramm, W.L., and R. Carter. "Effectiveness of a Political Telethon." *Public Opinion Quarterly* 23 (Spring 1959):121-126.

Schweitzer, D., and G.P. Ginsburg. "Factors of Communicator Credibility." In C.W. Backman and P.F. Secord, eds., *Problems in Social Psychology: Selected Readings.* New York: McGraw-Hill, 1966, pp. 94-101.

Scott, W.A. "Attitude Change by Response Reinforcement: Replication and Extension." *Sociometry* 22 (December 1959):328-335.

Sears, D.O., and J.L. Freedman. "Selective Exposure to Information: A Critical Review." *Public Opinion Quarterly* 31 (Summer 1967):194-213.

Secord, P.F. "Stereotyping add Favorableness in the Perception of Negro Faces." *Journal of Abnormal and Social Psychology.* 59 (November 1959):309-314.

Secord, P.F., and C.W. Backman. *Social Psychology.* New York: McGraw-Hill, 1964.

Secord, P.F., W. Bevan, and D. Katz. "The Negro Stereotype and Perceptual Accentuation." *Journal of Abnormal and Social Psychology* 53 (July 1956):78-83.

Sherif, C.W., and M. Sherif. *Attitude, Ego-involvement and Change.* New York: Wiley, 1967.

Sherif, M. "Group Influences Upon the Formation of Norms and Attitudes." In G.E. Swanson et al., eds., *Readings in Social Psychology.* New York: Holt, Rinehart & Winston, 1952, pp. 249-262.

Sherif, M. *Social Interaction: Process and Products.* Chicago: Aldine, 1967.

Sherman, S.J. "Effects of Choice and Incentive on Attitude Change in a Discrepant Behavior Situation." *Journal of Personality and Social Psychology* 15 (July 1970):245-252.

Sieber, J.E., and J.T. Lanzetta. "Conflict and Conceptual Structure as Determinants of Decision-making Behavior." *Journal of Personality* 32 (December 1964):622-641.

Sieber, J.E., and J.T. Lanzetta. "Some Determinants of Individual Differences in Predecision Information-processing Behavior." *Journal of Personality and Social Psychology* 4 (November 1966):561-571.

Siipola, E.M. "A Group Study of Some Effects of Preparatory Sets." *Psychological Monographs* 46, whole no. 210 (1935).

Silverman, I. "Differential Effects of Ego Threat Upon Persuasibility for High and Low Self-esteem Subjects." *Journal of Abnormal and Social Psychology* 69 (November 1964):567-572.

Smith, A.J. "Similarity of Values and Its Relation to Acceptance and the Projection of Similarity." *Journal of Psychology* 43 (April 1957):251-260.

Smith, G.H. *Motivation Research in Advertising and Marketing.* New York: McGraw-Hill, 1954.

Smock, C.D. "The Influence of Psychological Stress on the Intolerance of Ambiguity." *Journal of Abnormal and Social Psychology* 50 (March 1955):177-182.

Solley, C.M., and G. Murphy. *Development of the Perceptual World.* New York: Basic Books, 1960, p. 25. Copyright 1960 by Basic Books, Inc., New York.

Sorenson, H. *Psychology in Education.* New York: McGraw-Hill, 1964.

Spangenberg, R.W. 'Structural Coherence in Pictorial and Verbal Displays." *Journal of Educational Psychology* 62 (December 1971):514-520.

Spaulding, S. "Communication Potential of Pictorial Illustrations." *Audio Visual Communication Review* 4 (Winter 1956):31-46.

Stanton, F.N., and H.E. Burtt. "The Influence of Surface and Tint of Paper on Speed of Reading." *Journal of Applied Psychology* 19 (December 1935):683-693.

Starch, D. *Measuring Advertising Readership and Results.* New York: McGraw-Hill, 1966.

Stewart, J.B. *Repetitive Advertising in Newspapers: A Study of Two New Products.* Boston, Massachusetts: Boston Univ., 1964.

Stone, V.A., and H.S. Eswara. "The Likability and Self-interest of the Source in Attitude Change." *Journalism Quarterly* 46 (Spring 1969):61-68.

Straits, B.C. "The Pursuit of the Dissonant Consumer." *Journal of Marketing* 28 (July 1964):62-66.

Sturdivant, F.D. *Managerial Analysis in Marketing.* Glenview, Illinois: Scott, Foresman, 1970.

Summerskill, J., and C.D. Darling. "Sex Differences in Adjustment to College." *Journal of Educational Psychology* 46 (October 1955):355-361.

Tait, W. "The Effect of Psycho-physical Attitudes on Memory." *Journal of Abnormal Psychology* 8 (April-May 1913):10-37.

Tannebaum, P.H. "Initial Attitude toward Source and Concept as Factors in Attitude Change through Communication." *Public Opinion Quarterly* 20 (Summer 1956):413-426.

Taylor, I.A. "Symbology." In E. Whitney, ed., *Symbology: The Use of Symbols in Visual Communications.* New York: Hastings House, 1960, pp. 123-138.

Thistlethwaite, D.L., H. de Haan, and J. Kamentsky. "The Effects of Directive and Nondirective Communication Procedures on Attitudes." *Journal of Abnormal and Social Psychology* 51 (July 1955):107-113.

Thorndike, E.L. *The Psychology of Wants, Interests, and Attitudes.* New York: Appleton-Century-Crofts, 1935.

Thorndike, E.L., and I. Lorge. *The Teacher's Word Book of 30,000 Words.* New York: Columbia Univ. Press, 1944.

Thurstone, L.L. "The Measurement of Social Attitudes." *Journal of Abnormal and Social Psychology* 26 (October-December 1931):249-269.

Thyne, J.M. *The Psychology of Learning and Techniques of Teaching.* New York: Philosophical Library, 1963.

Tiernan, J.J. "The Principle of Closure in Terms of Recall and Recognition." *American Journal of Psychology* 51 (January 1938):97-108.

Tinker, M.A. "Criteria for Determining the Readability of Type Faces." *Journal of Educational Psychology* 35 (October 1944):385-396.

Tinker, M.A. "Prolonged Reading Tasks in Visual Research." *Journal of Applied Psychology* 39 (December 1955):444-446.

Tinker, M.A. *Legibility of Print.* Ames, Iowa: Iowa State Univ. Press, 1963.

Tinker, M.A., and D.G. Paterson. "Readability of Mixed Type Forms." *Journal of Applied Psychology* 30 (December 1946):631-637.

Truax, C.B. "Reinforcement and Nonreinforcement in Rogerian Psychotherapy." *Journal of Abnormal Psychology* 71 (February 1966):1-9.

Tull, D.S. "The Carry-over Effect of Advertising." *Journal of Marketing* 29 (April 1965):46-53.

Tulving, E., and R.D. Patterson. "Functional Units and Retrieval Processes in Free Recall." *Journal of Experimental Psychology* 77 (June 1968):239-248.

Tyler, L.E. *The Psychology of Human Differences.* New York: Appleton-Century-Crofts, 1947.

Underwood, B.J. "Interference and Forgetting." *Psychological Review* 64 (January 1957):49-60.

Underwood, B.J. "Ten Years of Massed Practice on Distributed Practice." *Psychological Review* 68 (July 1961):229-247.

Underwood, B.J. *Experimental Psychology.* New York: Appleton-Century-Crofts, 1966.

Underwood, B.J. "Some Correlates of Item Repetition in Free-recall Learning." *Journal of Verbal Learning and Verbal Behavior* 8 (February 1967):83-94.

Vacchiano, R.B., P.S. Strauss, and D.C. Schiffman. "Personality Correlates of Dogmatism." *Journal of Consulting and Clinical Psychology* 32 (May 1968):83-85.

Vernon, M.D. *A Further Study of Visual Perception.* London: Cambridge Univ. Press, 1954.

Vernon, M.D. *The Psychology of Perception.* Baltimore, Maryland: Penguin Books, 1960.

Vidulich, R.M., and J.P. Kaiman. "The Effects of Information Source Status and Dogmatism upon Conformity Behavior." *Journal of Abnormal and Social Psychology* 63 (November 1961):639-642.

Von Restorff, H. "Uber die Virkung von Bereichsbildungen im Spurenfeld." *Psychologie Forschung* 18 (October 1933):299-342.

Walker, E.L., and R.W. Heyns. *An Anatomy for Conformity.* Englewood Cliffs, N.J.: Prentice-Hall, 1962.

Wallace, W.P. "Review of the Historical, Empirical, and Theoretical Status of the Von Restorff Phenomenon." *Psychological Bulletin* 63 (June 1965):410-424.

Walster, E., E. Aronson, and D. Abrahams. "On Increasing the Persuasiveness of a Low Prestige Communicator." *Journal of Experimental Social Psychology* 2 (October 1966):325-342.

Walster, E., and L. Festinger. "The Effectiveness of 'Overhead' Persuasive Communications." *Journal of Abnormal and Social Psychology* 65 (December 1962):395-402.

Wärneryd, K-E., and K. Nowak. *Mass Communication and Advertising.* Stockholm: Economic Research Institute, 1967.

Wasson, C.R., F.D. Sturdivant, and D.H. McConaughy. *Competition and Human Behavior.* New York: Appleton-Century-Crofts, 1968.

Waters, R.H., and R. Leeper. "The Relation of Affective Tone to the Retention of Experiences in Daily Life." *Journal of Experimental Psychology* 19 (April 1936):203-215.

Watson, J.B. *Behaviorism.* New York: Norton, 1925.

Watts, W.A. "Relative Persistence of Opinion Change Induced by Active Compared to Passive Participation." *Journal of Personality and Social Psychology* (January 1967):4-15.

Watts, W.A., and L.E. Holt. "Logical Relationships Among Beliefs and Timing as Factors of Persuasion." *Journal of Personality and Social Psychology* 16 (December 1970):571-582.

Weaver, W., and C.E. Shannon. *The Mathematical Theory of Communication.* Urbana, Illinois: Univ. of Illinois Press, 1949. Copyright 1949 by the University of Illinois Press.

Weinberger, M. "Does the 'Sleeper Effect' Apply to Advertising?" *Journal of Marketing* 25 (October 1961):65-67.

Weiss, W. "Opinion Congruence with a Negative Source on One Issue as a Factor Influencing Agreement on Another Issue." *Journal of Abnormal and Social Psychology* 52 (January 1956):109-114.

Weiss, W., and B. Fine. "Opinion Change as a Function of Some Interpersonal Attributes of the Communicatees." *Journal of Abnormal and Social Psychology* 51 (September 1955):246-253.

Wells, W.D. "The Influence of Yeasaying Response Style." *Journal of Advertising Research* 1 (June 1961):8-17.

Wells, W.D. "How Chronic Overclaimers Distort Survey Findings." *Journal of Advertising Research* 3 (June 1963):8-18.

Wertheimer, M. "Laws of Organization in Perceptual Forms." In W.D. Ellis, ed., *A Source Book of Gestalt Psychology.* New York: Harcourt, Brace and Company, 1938, pp. 71-88. Translated from the original: Wertheimer, M. "Untersuchungen zur Lehre von der Gestalt." II. *Psychologische Forschung* 4 (1923):301-350.

Wesley, R. "Structural Coherence in Verbal and Pictorial Display." *Dissertations Abstracts International* 31, 6-A (December 1970):2748-2749.

Westley, B.H., and W.J. Severin. "Some Correlates of Media Credibility." *Journalism Quarterly* 41 (Summer 1964):325-335.

White, B.J., and R.D. Alter. "Dogmatism and Examination Performance." *Journal of Educational Psychology* 58 (October 1967):285-289.

White, I.S. "The Perception of Value in Products." In J.W. Newman, ed., *On Knowing the Consumer.* New York: Wiley, 1966, pp. 90-106.

Whittaker, J. "Sex Differences and Susceptibility to Interpersonal Persuasion." *Journal of Social Psychology* 66 (June 1965):91-94.

Whyte, W.H., Jr. "The Web of Word of Mouth." *Fortune* 50 (November 1954):140-143 and 204-212.

Wicker, F.W. "On the Locus of Picture-word Differences in Paired-associate Learning." *Journal of Verbal Learning and Verbal Behavior* 9 (February 1970):52-57.

Wiener, N. *Cybernetics.* Cambridge, Massachusetts: M.I.T. Press, 1948. Reprinted by permission of the M.I.T. Press.

Wilkening, E.A. "Roles of Communicating Agents in Technological Changes in Agriculture." *Social Forces* 34 (May 1956):361-367.

Wilton, R. "On Frustration and the PRE." *Psychological Review* 74 (March 1967):149-150.

Wimer, C.C., and W.E. Lambert. "The Differential Effects of Word and Object Stimuli on the Learning of Paired Associates." *Journal of Experimental Psychology* 57 (January 1959):31-36.

Witkin, H.A., H.B. Lewis, M. Herzman, K. Machover, P.B. Mussner, and S. Wapner. *Personality through Perception.* New York: Harper and Row, 1954.

Wolman, B. *Dictionary of Behavioral Science.* New York: Van Nostrand Reinhold, 1973, p. 143.

Woods, W.A. "Psychological Dimensions of Consumer Decision." *Journal of Marketing* 24 (January 1960):15-19.

Woodworth, R.S. *Experimental Psychology.* New York: Holt, 1938.

Wrightsman, L.S. "Effects of Waiting with Others on Changes in Level of Felt Anxiety." *Journal of Abnormal and Social Psychology* 61 (September 1960):216-222.

Young, K. *Social Psychology.* New York: Appleton-Century-Crofts, 3rd ed., 1956.

Young, P.T. *Motivation and Emotion: A Survey of the Determinants of Human and Animal Activity.* New York: Wiley, 1961.

Zachrisson, B. *Studies in the Legibility of Printed Text.* Stockholm: Almqvist and Wiksell, 1965.

Zajonc, R.L. "Attitudinal Effects of Mere Exposure." *Journal of Personality and Social Psychology, Monograph Supplement* 9, 2 (June 1968):1-27.

Zalkind, S.S., and T.W. Costello. "Perception: Some Recent Research and

Implications for Administration." *Administrative Science Quarterly* 7 (September 1962):218-235.

Zaltman, G., and N. Lin. "On the Nature of Innovations." *American Behavioral Scientist* 14 (May-June 1971):651-674.

Zeigarnik, B. "Das Behalten erledigter und unerledigter Handlungen." *Psychological Abstracts* 1 (November 1927):573-574.

Zielske, H.A. "The Remembering and Forgetting of Advertising." *Journal of Marketing* 23 (January 1957):237-243.

Additional References

Adams, J.S. "Reduction of Cognitive Dissonance by Seeking Consonant Information." *Journal of Abnormal and Social Psychology* 62 (January 1961):74-78.

Alcock, W., and C. Noble. "Human Delayed Reward Learning with Different Lengths of Tasks." *Journal of Experimental Psychology* 56 (November 1958):407-412.

Alderson, W. "Needs, Wants, and Creative Marketing." *Cost and Profit Outlook* 8 (September 1955):1-3.

Alexander, M. "The Significance of Ethnic Groups in Marketing New-type Packaged Goods in Greater New York." In L.H. Stockman, ed., *Advancing Marketing Efficiency.* Chicago: American Marketing Association, 1959, pp. 557-561.

Allen, R. "Primacy or Recency: The Order of Presentation." *Journalism Quarterly* 50 (Spring 1973):135-138.

Anderson, B.F. *The Psychology Experiment: An Introduction to the Scientific Method.* Belmont, California: Brooks/Cole, 1968.

Anderson, N.H., and C.I. Hovland. "The Representation of Ordered Effects in Communication Research." In C.I. Hovland et al., eds., *The Order of Presentation in Persuasion.* New Haven: Yale Univ. Press, 1957, pp. 158-169.

Aronson, E., and B.W. Golden. "The Effect of Relevant and Irrelevant Aspects of Communicator Credibility on Opinion Change." *Journal of Personality* 30 (June 1962):135-146.

Atwood, L.E. "The Effects of Incongruity between Source and Message Credibility." *Journalism Quarterly* 43 (Spring 1966):90-94.

Audits and Surveys Company, Inc. *Exposure of Advertising.* New York: Time, 1959, pp. 2-10.

Bakan, P., ed. *Attention.* Princeton, N.J.: Van Nostrand, 1966.

Bales, R.F. "Small Group Theory and Research." In R.K. Merton, ed., *Sociology Today: Problems and Prospects.* New York: Basic Books, 1959, pp. 293-305.

Ballard, P.B. "Oblivescence and Reminiscence." *British Journal of Psychology, Monograph Supplement* 1, 2 (1913):1-47.

Bandura, A., and T.L. Rosenthal. "Vicarious Classical Conditioning as a Function of Arousal Level." *Journal of Personality and Social Psychology* 3 (January 1966):54-62.

Barach, J.A. "Advertising Effectiveness and Risk in the Consumer Decision Process." *Journal of Marketing Research* 6, (August 1969):314-320.

Bauer, R.A. "Limits of Persuasion." *Harvard Business Review* 36 (September-October 1958):105-110.

Bearden, J.H., ed. *Personal Selling: Behavioral Science Readings and Cases.* New York: Wiley, 1967.

Bell, G.D. "Self-Confidence, Persuasibility and Cognitive Dissonance Among Automobile Buyers." In D.F. Cox, ed., *Risk Taking and Information Handling in Consumer Behavior.* Boston: Division of Research, Graduate School of Business Administration, Harvard University, 1967, pp. 442-468.

Benedetti, D.T., and J.G. Hill. "A Determiner of the Centrality of a Trait in Impression Formation." *Journal of Abnormal and Social Psychology* 60 (March 1960):278-279.

Berelson, B. *Content Analysis in Communication Research.* New York: Hafner, 1952.

Berelson, B., P. Lazarsfeld, and W. McPhee. *Voting: A Study of Opinion Formation During a Presidential Campaign.* Chicago: Univ. of Chicago Press, 1954.

Berlyne, D.E. "Curiosity and Exploration." *Science* 153 (July 1, 1966):25-33.

Berscheid, E. "Opinion Change and Communicator-Communicatee Similarity and Dissimilarity." *Journal of Personality and Social Psychology* 4 (December 1966):670-680.

Bettinghaus, E.P., and John R. Baseheart. "Some Specific Factors Affecting Attitude Change." *Journal of Communication* 19 (September 1969):229-235.

Binder, A. "A Statistical Model for the Process of Visual Recognition." *Psychological Review* 62 (March 1955):119-129.

Bolles, R.C. *Theory of Motivation.* New York: Harper and Row, 1967.

Book, A.C. "Recall of Institutional TV Commercials." *Journal of Advertising Research* 5 (June 1965):38-40.

Bossom, J., and A.H. Maslow. "Security of Judges as a Factor in Impressions of Warmth in Others." *Journal of Abnormal and Social Psychology* 55 (July 1957):147-148.

Bourne, F.S. "Group Influence in Marketing and Public Relations." In J.H. Bearden, ed., *Personal Selling: Behavioral Science Readings and Cases.* New York: Wiley, 1967, pp. 151-166.

Boyd, H.W., Jr., and J.W. Newman. *Advertising Management: Selected Readings.* Homewood, Illinois: Irwin, 1968.

Brehm, J.W. "A Dissonance Analysis of Attitude-Discrepant Behavior." In M.J. Rosenberg, C.I. Hovland, W.J. McGuire, R.P. Abelson, and J.W. Brehm, eds., *Attitude Organization and Change: An Analysis of Consistency Among Attitude Components.* New Haven: Yale Univ. Press, 1960, pp. 164-167.

Britt, S.H. "How Advertising Can Use Psychology's Rules of Learning." *Printer's Ink* 252 (September 23, 1955):74, 77, 80.

Britt, S.H. "What About Consumer Behavior and the Behavioral Sciences?" Paper given September 1965, Dublin, Ireland, at Congress of ESOMAR (European Society for Opinion and Market Research).

Bronfenbrenner, U., J. Harding, and M. Gallwey. "The Measurement of Skill in Social Perception." In D.C. McClelland, A.L. Baldwin, U. Bronfenbrenner, and F. Strodtbeck, eds., *Talent and Society*. Princeton, N.J.: Van Nostrand, 1958, pp. 29-111.

Brown, R. *Social Psychology*. New York: Free Press, 1965.

Byrne, D. "Interpersonal Attraction and Attitude Similarity." *Journal of Abnormal and Social Psychology* 62 (May 1961):713-715.

Byrne, D. *An Introduction to Personality*. Englewood Cliffs, N.J.: Prentice-Hall, 1966.

Byrne, D. "Parental Antecedents of Authoritarianism." In H.C. Lindgren, ed., *Contemporary Research in Psychology*. New York: Wiley, 1969, pp. 247-254.

Carey, J.W. "Some Personality Correlates of Persuasibility." In S.A. Greyser, ed., *Toward Scientific Marketing*. Chicago: American Marketing Association, 1964, pp. 30-43.

Carr, H.A. "The Laws of Association." *Psychological Review* 38 (May 1931):212-228.

Centers, R. "An Examination of the Riesman Social Character Typology: A Metropolitan Survey." *Sociometry* 25 (September 1962):231-240.

Cerha, J. *Selective Mass Communication*. Stockholm, Sweden: Kungl. Boktryckeriet P.A. Norstedt & Soner, 1967.

Cherry, C. *On Human Communication*. Published jointly by Technology Press of Massachusetts Institute of Technology and John Wiley & Sons, Inc., Charman & Hall, Ltd., 1957.

Cofer, C.N., and M.H. Appley. *Motivation: Theory and Research*. New York: Wiley, 1964.

Cohen, A.R. "Communication Discrepancy and Attitude Change: A Dissonance Theory Approach." *Journal of Personality* 27 (September 1959):386-396.

Connell, C.F., and J.C. MacDonald. "The Impact of Health News on Attitude and Behavior." *Journalism Quarterly* 33 (Summer 1956):315-323.

Consumer Interest and Advertising Retention. Conducted by Audits & Survey Company, Inc., sponsored by *LOOK Magazine*. Copyright © 1963 by Cowles Magazines and Broadcasting, Inc., pp. 4 and 5.

Cook, V.J. "Group Decision, Social Comparison, and Persuasion in Changing Attitudes." *Journal of Advertising Research* 7 (March 1967):31-37.

Coser, R.L. "Political Involvement and Interpersonal Relations." *Psychiatry* 14 (May 1951):213-222.

Crane, E. *Marketing Communications: A Behavioral Approach to Men, Messages, and Media.* New York: Wiley, 1965.

Dallett, K., and S.G. Wilcox. "Remembering Pictures vs. Remembering Descriptions." *Psychonomic Science* 11 (June 5, 1968):139-140.

Dichter, E. *The Strategy of Desire.* New York: Doubleday, 1960.

Doob, L.W. *Propaganda: Its Psychology and Technique.* New York: Holt, 1935.

Edelstein, A.S. *Perspectives in Mass Communication.* København: Einer Harcks Forlag, 1966.

Eisinger, R., and J. Mills. "Perception of the Sincerity and Competence of a Communicator as a Function of the Extremity of His Position." *Journal of Experimental and Social Psychology* 4 (April 1968):224-232.

Eysenck, H.J. "A Critical and Experimental Study of Color Preferences." *American Journal of Psychology* 54 (November 1941):385-394.

Feigl, H. "Operationalism and Scientific Method." *Psychological Review* 52 (September 1945):250-254.

Festinger, L. "The Theory of Cognitive Dissonance." In W. Schramm, ed., *The Science of Human Communication.* New York: Basic Books, 1963.

Festinger, L., S. Schacter, and K. Back. *Social Pressures in Informal Groups.* New York: Harper and Brothers, 1950.

Fisher, S., and A. Lubin. "Distance as a Determinant of Influence in a Two-Person Social Interaction Situation." *Journal of Abnormal and Social Psychology* 56 (March 1958):230-238.

Gardner, D.M. "The Distraction Hypothesis in Marketing." *Journal of Advertising Research* 10 (December 1970):25-30.

Gerard, H.B., R.A. Wilhelmy, and E.S. Conolley. "Conformity and Group Size." *Journal of Personality and Social Psychology* 8 (January 1968):79-82.

Gibson, J.J. "Useful Dimensions of Sensitivity." *American Psychologist* 18 (January 1963):1-15.

Goldstein, A.G., and J.E. Chance. "Visual Recognition Memory for Complex Configurations." *Perception and Psychophysics* 9 (February 1971): 237-240.

Haber, R.N. *Contemporary Theory and Reserch in Visual Perception.* New York: Holt, Rinehart, & Winston, 1968.

Hattwick, M.S. *How to Use Psychology for Better Advertising.* New York: Prentice-Hall, 1950.

Hayakawa, S.I. *Language in Thought and Action.* New York: Harcourt, Brace and World, 1949.

Heers, D.M. "How the Wife's Working Affects Husband-Wife Interaction." In W.J. Goode, ed., *Readings on the Family and Society.* Englewood Cliffs, N.J.: Prentice-Hall, 1964.

Helson, H. *Adaptation-Level Theory.* New York: Harper & Row, 1964.

Hunt, M.F., and G.R. Miller. "Open and Closed-Mindedness, Belief Discrepant Communication Behavior, and Tolerance for Cognitive Inconsistency." *Journal of Personality and Social Psychology* 8 (January 1968):35-37.

Hyman, H.H. "The Psychology of Status." *Archives of Psychology* 38, whole no. 269, (1942):5-94.

Hyman, H.H., and P.B. Sheatsley. "Some Reasons Why Information Campaigns Fail." *The Public Opinion Quarterly* 11 (Fall 1947):412-423.

Jellison, J.M., and J. Mills. "Effect of Public Commitment upon Opinions." *Journal of Experimental Social Psychology* 5 (May 1969):340-346.

Jersild, A. "Primacy, Recency, Frequency and Vividness." *Journal of Experimental Psychology* 12 (February 1929):58-70.

Jones, E.E. "Authoritarianism as a Determinant of First-impression Formation." *Journal of Personality* 23 (September 1954).

Kassarjian, H.H., and J.B. Cohen. "Cognitive Dissonance and Consumer Behavior." *California Management Review* 7 (Fall 1965):55.

Katona, G., and E. Mueller. "A Study of Purchase Decisions." In L.H. Clark, ed., *Consumer Behavior*, Vol. I. Washington Square, N.Y.: New York Univ. Press, 1955, pp. 30-87.

Katz, D. *Gestalt Psychology, Its Nature and Significance.* New York: Ronald Press, 1950.

Katz, E. "The Two-step Flow of Communication: An Up-to-date Report on an Hypothesis." *Public Opinion Quarterly* 21 (Spring 1957):61-78.

Katz, E. "The Diffusion of New Ideas and Practices." In W. Schramm, ed., *The Science of Human Communication.* New York: Basic Books, 1963.

Kelley, H.H. "Salience of Membership and Resistance to Change of Group-anchored Attitudes." *Human Relations* 8 (August 1955):275-289.

Kelley, H.H., and E.H. Volkart. "The Resistance to Change to Group-anchored Attitudes." *American Sociological Review* 17 (August 1952):453-465.

Key, C. "Recall as a Function of Perceived Relations." *Archives of Psychology* 13 (May 1926):5-106.

Knower, F.H. "Experimental Studies of Changes in Attitudes: I. A Study of the Effect of Oral Argument on Changes of Attitude." *Journal of Social Psychology* 6 (August 1935):315-344.

Korman, A.K. "Relevance of Personal Need Satisfaction for Overall Satisfaction as a Function of Self-esteem." *Journal of Applied Psychology* 51 (December 1967):533-538.

Lana, R.E. "Interest, Media and Order Effects in Persuasive Communications." *Journal of Psychology* 56 (July 1963):9-12.

Lana, R.E., and R.L. Rosnow. "Subject Awareness and Order Effects in Persuasive Communications." *Psychological Reports* 12 (April 1963):523-529.

Lazer, W. "The Role of Models in Marketing." *Journal of Marketing* 26 (April 1962):9-14.

Leibowitz, H. *Visual Perception*. New York: Macmillan, 1965.

Leventhal, H. "Findings and Theory in the Study of Fear Communication." In L. Berkowitz, ed., *Advances in Experimental Social Psychology*, Vol. 5. New York: Academic Press, 1970, pp. 119-186.

MacDonald, C. "Should Attitudes Change Behavior? A Small Exercise in Intuition." *Admap* 5 (December 1969):498-502.

Madigan, S.A., and A. Paivio. "Instructional Effects on Semantic Satiation." *Psychonomic Science* 7 (January 15, 1967):45-46.

Mancuso, J.R. "Why Not Create Opinion Leaders for New Product Introductions?" *Journal of Marketing* 33 (July 1969):20-25.

Mandell, D. "Relating Delay of Gratification to Achievement in Young Children." *Dissertation Abstracts* 28 (September 1967):1169-1170.

Martineau, P. "Non-verbal Communication in Advertising." *Art Direction* (May 1957):74-75.

Mason, R. "An Ordinal Scale for Measuring the Adoption Process." In E. Katz et al., eds., *Studies of Innovation and of Communication to the Public*. Stanford, California: Institute for Communication Research, Stanford University, 1962, pp. 99-116.

Mason, R. "The Use of Information Sources by Influentials in the Adoption Process." *Public Opinion Quarterly* 27 (Fall 1963):455-466.

Mason, R. "The Use of Information Sources in the Process of Adoption." *Rural Sociology* 29 (March 1964):40-52.

McGeoch, J.A. *The Psychology of Human Learning*. New York: Longmans, Green and Co., 1942.

McGeoch, J.A. 'The Influence of Degree of Learning upon Retroactive Inhibition." *American Journal of Psychology* 41 (April 1929):252-262.

Merton, R.K. *Mass Persuasion: The Social Psychology of a War Bond Drive*. New York: Harper, 1946.

Miller, G.R., and M.A. Hewgill. "Some Recent Research on Fear-arousing Message Appeals." *Speech Monographs* 33 (November 1966):377-391.

Miller, N., D. Butler, and J. McMartin. "The Ineffectiveness of Power in Group Interaction." *Sociometry* 32 (March 1969):24-42.

Mills, J., E. Aronson, and H. Robinson. "Selectivity in Exposure to Information." *Journal of Abnormal and Social Psychology* 59 (September 1959):250-253.

Mittelstaedt, R. "A Dissonance Approach to Repeat Purchasing Behavior." *Journal of Marketing Research* 6 (November 1969):444-446.

Myers, J.H., and W.H. Reynolds. *Consumer Behavior and Marketing Management*. Boston: Houghton Mifflin, 1967.

Newcomb, T.M. "The Prediction of Interpersonal Attraction." *American Psychologist* 11 (November 1956):575-586.

Nicosia, F.M. *Consumer Decision Processes: Marketing and Advertising Implications.* Englewood Cliffs, N.J.: Prentice-Hall, 1966, pp. 153-192.

Nixon, H.K. "Two Studies of Attention to Advertisements." *Journal of Applied Psychology* 9 (June 1925):176-187.

Oliver, R.T. *The Psychology of Persuasive Speech.* New York: David McKay, second edition, 1957.

Oshikawa, S. "Can Cognitive Dissonance Theory Explain Consumer Behavior?" *Journal of Marketing* 33 (October 1969):44-49.

Perin, C.T. "A Quantitative Investigation of the Delay of Reinforcement Gradient." *Journal of Experimental Psychology* 32 (January 1943):37-51.

Perkins, F.T. "Symmetry in Visual Recall." *American Journal of Psychology* 44 (July 1932):473-490.

Peterson, J. "Imitation and Mental Adjustment." *Journal of Abnormal and Social Psychology* 17 (April-June 1922):1-15.

Postman, L., J.S. Bruner, and R.D. Walk. "The Perception of Error." *British Journal of Psychology* 42 (March 1951):1-10.

Raynor, J.O. "Future Orientation and Motivation of Immediate Activity." *Psychological Review* 76 (November 1969):606-610.

Rethlingshafer, D. *Motivation as Related to Personality.* New York: McGraw-Hill, 1963.

Riesman, D. *The Lonely Crowd.* New Haven: Yale Univ. Press, 13th printing, 1967.

Robinson, E.S. "Some Factors Determining the Degree of Retroactive Inhibition." *Psychological Monographs* 28 (1920):1-57.

Robinson, E.S., and M. Brown. "Effect of Serial Position upon Memorization." *American Journal of Psychology* 37 (October 1926):538-552.

Rosnov, R.L. "Whatever Happened to the Law of Primacy?" *Journal of Communication* 16 (March 1966):10-31.

Schneider, F.W., and B.L. Kintz. "An Analysis of the Incidental Intentional Learning Dichotomy." *Journal of Experimental Psychology* 73 (January 1967):85-90.

Segall, M., D. Campbell, and M. Herskovits. *The Influence of Culture on Visual Perception.* Indianapolis: Bobbs-Merrill, 1966.

Sherif, C.W., M. Sherif, and R.E. Nebergall. *Attitude and Attitude Change.* Philadelphia: Saunders, 1965.

Sherif, M. "The Formation of a Norm in a Group Situation." In *The Psychology of Social Norms.* New York: Harper & Brothers, 1936, pp. 89-107.

Sherif, M. "The Social Judgment-involvement Approach vs. the Cognitive Dissonance Approach." Paper presented at the meetings of the American Psychological Association, Chicago, 1965.

Sherif, M., and C.I. Hovland. *Social Judgment.* New Haven: Yale Univ. Press, 1961.

Sherrill, P.N. "The Probability of Advertising Exposure." *Journal of Advertising Research* 6 (March 1966):24-25.

Shrable, K., and R.W. Moulton. "Achievement Fantasy as a Function of Expectancies in Picture Cues." Unpublished manuscript, Univ. of California, Berkeley, 1966.

Schuchman, A., and M. Perry. "Self-confidence and Persuasibility in Marketing: A Reappraisal." *Journal of Marketing Research* 6 (May 1969):146-154.

Stafford, J.E. "Effects of Group Influence on Consumer Brand Preferences." *Journal of Marketing Research* 3 (February 1966):68-75.

Stern, H. "The Significance of Impulse Buying Today." *Journal of Marketing* 26 (April 1962):59-62.

Sternthal, B., and C.S. Craig. "Fear Appeals: Revisited and Revised." *Journal of Consumer Research* 1 (December 1974):22-34.

Tannenbaum, P., J. MacCaulay, and E. Norris. "Principles of Congruity and Reduction of Persuasion." *Journal of Personality and Social Psychology* 3 (February 1966):233-238.

Thorndike, E.L. *An Experimental Study of Rewards.* New York: Columbia University Teachers College, 1933.

Thorndike, E.L. *Man and His Works.* Cambridge, Massachusetts: Harvard University Press, 1943.

Tinker, M.A. "The Effect of Color on Visual Apprehension and Perception." *Genetic Psychology Monographs* 11 (February 1932):61-136.

Treisman, A.M. "Selective Attention in Man." *British Medical Bulletin* 20 (Oxford University Press, 1964):12-16.

Venkatesan, M. "Experimental Study of Consumer Behavior Conformity and Independence." *Journal of Marketing Research* 3 (November 1963):384-387.

Warr, P.B., and C. Knapper. *The Perception of People and Events.* London: Wiley, 1968.

Wegrocki, H.J. "The Effect of Prestige Suggestibility on Emotional Attitudes." *Journal of Social Psychology* 5 (August 1934):384-394.

Weingarten, E. "A Study of Selective Perception in Clinical Judgment." *Journal of Personality* 17 (June 1949):369-400.

White, I.S., and S. Ben-Zeev. "Consumer Perception: A Theoretical Guide for New Techniques in Evaluating Advertising Effectiveness." *Proceedings of the American Statistical Association* (1960):29-38.

Whitney, R.A., T. Hubin, and J.D. Murphy. *The New Psychology of Persuasion and Motivation in Selling.* Englewood Cliffs, N.J.: Prentice-Hall, 1965.

523

Wilensky, H.L. "Mass Society and Mass Culture." In B. Berelson and M. Janowitz, eds., *Reader in Public Opinion and Communication.* New York: Free Press, 1966, pp. 293-327.

Worcel, P., and S. Byrne. *Personality Change.* New York: Wiley, 1964.

Zajonc, R. "The Concepts of Balance, Congruity, and Dissonance." *Public Opinion Quarterly* 24 (Summer 1960):280-296.

Zimbardo, P.G. "Involvement and Communications Discrepancy as Determinants of Opinion Conformity." *Journal of Abnormal and Social Psychology* 60 (January 1960):86-94.

Index

Index

Accessibility, 130-131
Action, 29
Active defenses, 468-469
Activities, 48-49
Adaptation, 132-133
Advance awareness, 459-461
Advertising, xvi, 3, 4, 49, 50, 53-56,
    64-70, 71-76, 77-83, 86-87, 89,
    90, 92, 94, 97, 107, 111, 116-
    119, 121-123, 127, 130-133,
    138, 141, 143-146, 148-149,
    152, 155, 157, 160-165, 167-
    171, 173, 175, 184, 186-187,
    189-191, 206, 209, 211, 213-
    216, 218, 220, 222, 225, 228-
    229, 230, 232, 234, 237, 240-
    241, 243, 244-246, 250, 252,
    256, 261, 264, 266-276, 279,
    283, 285, 289-291, 294, 314-
    316, 328-329, 332, 337-338,
    340, 345, 347-348, 350, 352,
    354, 356, 358, 361-362, 366,
    368, 371, 372-373, 375, 377,
    379, 383-384, 386-387, 390,
    393, 397, 402, 404, 408, 409,
    412, 413-414, 416, 427, 432,
    437, 440, 443, 445, 447, 449,
    456-457, 459, 466, 469, 473,
    477-478, 485
Affective stimuli, 239
Affective value, degree of, 240-242
Affective variables, 239-256
Aggressive traits, 384-386
Aha experience, 290-291
Ambiguity, 134-135
Anxiety, resistance to, 355-356
Anxiety appeals, strong, 354-355
Anxiety appeals, weak, 352-354
Anxiety arousal, 254-256, 350-352
Appeals, 167
Assimilating, 164-166
Associating, 159-178
Associative facilitation, 223

Attempts to reduce dissonance, 89-90
Attending, xv, 5, 24, 34, 38, 39, 41,
    61-102, 105
  overview, 99-102
  span, 70-79
Attitude, 37, 125, 311-324, 413, 425,
    426, 428-430, 461-463
Attitude change, 29-30, 37, 107, 444-
    445, 463
Attitude discrepancy, 371-373
Attitude-opinion consistency, 323-324
Attitudinal homeostasis, 434-437
Authoritarian personality, 466-467
Authority, 259-260
Autistic motivating, 347-348
Avoided situations, 464-466
Awareness, 29

Balance, 68, 69, 70, 435
Bandwagon effect, 371
Behavioral commitment, 463-464
Behavioral sciences, 3, 4, 5, 9
Behavioral scientists, xv, xvi
Belief-attitude consistency, 322-323
Belief congruence, 258-259
Belief-opinion consistency, 323-324
Beliefs, 48-49, 311-324, 425-426, 428-
    430, 461-463
Bypassing, 122-123

California-Time Petroleum Company,
    xvii
Categories, 125, 185-186
Categorization, 93-94
Centrality, 260
Change, 425-530
Chronological setting, 87
Closed-mindedness, 383-384, 464-466
Closure, 115
Coca-Cola Company, xvii
Cognitive dissonance, 89, 359, 431-
    434
Cognitive experiences, 313-314

Cognitive overlap, 439
Cognitive variables, 204-238
Color, 65, 72, 150-152, 236-237
Communicating, 3, 4, 5, 9, 15, 26, 38,
    190, 294-296, 311-313, 368,
    412-414, 425, 426, 485
Communicator
    credibility, 242-243
    expertness of, 362-363
    perceived intent of, 363-366
    personality of, 366-368
    physical aspects of, 366-368
Communicator-audience similarity,
    368-371
Compatibility, 48-49, 57
Competing stimulus, 109
Complexity, 64-65
Confidence, 456-457
Conformity, degree of, 409-412, 471-
    473
Congruity, 111-117, 435-436
Consonance, 431-434
Continuity of varied stimuli, 209-211
Contour, 114, 115
Contrast, 65-67, 167
    in type, 67-68
Credibility, 359-379, 465-466
Credibility-discrepancy interaction,
    373-375
Cue categorizing, 125-146
Cue eliminating, 141
Cue identity, 131-132
Cue normalizing, 144-146
Cue resisting, 144-146
Cue searching, 127-128
Cues
    potency of pictorial, 235-237
    prepotency of, 275-276
    sufficient number of, 129-130
Cultural framework, 51, 52-53
Cultural influences, 189-191
Culture, 150-151, 296-298
Curiosity, 272-273
Curious nonbelief, 448-449

Decision importance, 372-373
Decision processes, 30-33

Decreasing alternatives, 138-140
Defects of the chosen alternative, 440-
    442
Desirable information, 328-329
Differential personality, 27
Disbelievable curiosity, 447-449
Discrimination, 312-313
Dissonance, 89-90
Dissonance factor, 431-453
Distance 472
Distracting (distraction), 276-278,
    357-358
    of environmental setting, 49-50
    freedom from, 49-50
Distribution, 55, 57, 118, 185, 340,
    390

Ease of categorization, 93-94
Editorial environment, 110-111
Educational level, 393-395
Ego involvement, 457-459
Emphasis, 69, 245-246
Empirical data, 3, 6, 9, 10
Enjoyment of novelty, 96-97
Environmental setting, 87
Environmental stress, 109
Equivocality, 121-122
Expectancy, 24, 88-89
Expectations, effect of 174-176
Expected benefits of the medium,
    53-54
Explicit conclusions, 338-340
Exposing, xv, 4, 5, 6, 34, 38, 39, 41,
    45-59, 99, 217, 432, 472
    overview, 57-59
External Variables, 85-88

Fairness of presentation, 360-361
Familiarity, 190, 329-330, 334-335
Family, 399-401
Fashion leaders, 407
Feedback, 18-19, 39-41
Flowcharts, 18
Foot-in-the-door technique, 463-464
Forecasting, 17
Forewarning, 460-461
Forced compliance, 436

Gestalt psychology, 107, 112-116
Gradation method, 463-464
Group decision, 478-479
Grouping, 118-119
Group membership effect, 27

Humor, 119-121

Ignorance of the medium, 109
Imagination, 386-387
Immediacy, 340-343
Implicit conclusions, 338-340
Incentives, 450-453
Incongruity, 117-118
Indexing, 123
Individual variables, 381-397, 455-471
Inflow of information, 90-91
Inner-directedness, 395-397
Innovation, diffusion of, 414-416
"Inoculation" effect, 336
Intelligence, 391-393
Intensity, 76
Intent, 271
Interacting, 476-477
    personal, 413
Interests, 155-157
Interest value, 91-93
Interference, 217, 223
Internal and external stimuli, 57
Internal variables, 88-97
Interpretation, 34
Involvement, 262-263, 459-461, 464
    covert, 265-266
Irrelevant stimuli, 92
Irrelevant stimulus information, 143-
    144
Issue importance, 457-459

Language, 293-294
Learning, xv, 5, 6, 38-39, 41, 55, 200-
    307
    overview, 303-307
Length of message, 79-80
Leveling, 186-188
Lifestyle, 51-52, 387

Marsteller Foundation, xvii

Material design, 69-70
Meaning, dominant, 229-230
Meaningfulness, 226, 269-270
Media
    distractions, 281-284
    preconceptions, of, 76-77
Mental completing, 281-284
Mental sets, 15, 42-43, 57, 107, 171-
    172
Marketing, xvi, 1-7, 9, 12, 49, 50, 52,
    55, 64-65, 67-70, 71-76, 77-83,
    85-87, 89, 90-97, 109-110, 116-
    118, 121-123, 127-128, 130-
    137, 139-141, 143-144, 146,
    148, 149-150, 152-155, 157,
    160-165, 167-172, 174-175,
    177-178, 180-184, 186-191,
    206, 209, 211, 213-216, 218,
    220-222, 224-225, 228-230,
    237, 240-241, 243-245, 246,
    249-250, 252-256, 261-279,
    283-285, 288-291, 294, 296-
    297, 301, 312, 328-330, 332-
    334, 335, 337-338, 340-342-
    345, 347-352, 354-356, 358,
    361-363, 366, 368, 371-373,
    375, 377, 379, 383, 384, 386,
    387, 390, 393-395, 397, 401-
    402, 404, 406-409, 412-414,
    416, 427, 430, 437-443, 445,
    447, 449, 452-453, 456-457,
    459, 461, 462-463, 464-467,
    469, 471, 473, 475-478, 485
Message, 47-48, 151
    clutter, 67
    credibility, 375-377
    distractions, 77-78
    length, 80-81
    nonrational, 345-358
    pleasant, 95-96
    rational, 325-345
Middle items, characteristics of, 214-
    216
Misindexing, 122-123, 134-135
Mode of evaluation framework, 314-
    316
Model, models, 9, 13-44, 485

Model, models (cont.)
  advertising, 27-29
  attending, 99-102
  black-box versus behavioral, 16-17
  Colley, 28-29
  of communication, 21-26
  comparisons, 37
  definition and classifications, 15-20
  DeFleur, 25-26
  descriptive versus decision, 16
  Engel, Kollat, and Blackwell, 30-31
  explicit, 16
  Exposing, 57-58
  feedback-control, 23-25
  Freudian, 33
  Howard and Sheth, 30, 32-33
  implicit versus explicit, 15-16
  Klapper, 25
  Lavidge and Steiner, 27-28
  learning, 303-307
  marketing, 27-36
  Marshallian, 33
  mathematical versus verbal, 17-18
  Miller, 22
  motivating, 417-422
  Pavlovian, 33
  perceiving, 193-197
  persuading, 479-483
  promoting, 27-29
  Sandage and Fryburger, 34-35
  Schramm, 22-23, 35-37
  sociocultural, 25-26
  Solley and Murphy, 23-25
  Veblenian, 33
  Wärnerd and Novak, 33-34, 37
  Weaver and Shannon, 22
  Wiener, 23-24
Motivating, xv, 5, 6, 37-38, 41-42, 55,
    309-422, 430-479
  overview, 417-422
Movement, 67-68

Naysaying, 469-471
Needs, 42, 57, 168, 172, 426
"Noise," 34
Nondirective motivating, 348-350
Novelty, 96-97, 259

Objective set, 114
Occupation, 188-189
One-sided arguments, 335-338
Open- and closed-mindedness, 258-
    262, 383-384
Operational terms, 17
Opinionated statements, 361-362
Opinion leaders, 52, 406-409
Opinions, 311-324, 425-426, 428-430,
    461-463
Order of presentation, 327-328
Orientation to act, 172-173
Other-directedness, 395-397
Overexposure, 206-209
Overlap of alternatives, 439-440

Packaging, 67, 74, 87-89, 91, 93-94,
    97, 109-110, 117, 119, 121,
    123, 128, 132, 138, 141, 143,
    149, 152, 168, 172, 174, 187,
    237, 256, 266, 273, 329, 330,
    332, 351-352, 355, 390, 406,
    438, 447, 457
Participation, active, 264-265
Passive defenses, 468-469
Past experience, 115
Perceived risk, degree of, 387-391
Perceiving, xv, 5, 6, 37-39, 41, 103-197,
    360
  overview, 193-197
Perceptual constancy, 159-160
Perceptual defense, 173-174
Perceptual error, 217
Perseveration, 288-290
Personality, 51, 179-181
  correlates, 179-191
  factors, 15, 43, 57
  variables, 257-258
Persuading, xv, 5, 6, 37-38, 41-42, 55,
    311-313, 417-422, 423-483;
  overview, 479-483
Physical condition, 85-86
Physical environment, 109-110
Pleasant messages, 95-96
Polarizing, 160-164
Position in broadcast media, 79
Position in print media, 78-79

Positive attributes, 437-439
Positive behaving, 42
Postdecisional barriers, 83
Postdecisional reinforcement, 442-443
Postdecision dissonance, 442
Postpurchase, 436
Potency, high, 170-171
Practice
    distributed, 266-268
    massed, 266-268
    vicarious, 266-268
Prerationalizing, 343-345
Pressure, informational, 410
Pressure, normative, 410 ·
Price, 95, 172-173, 185, 187, 224,
    248, 252-253, 447, 461
Primacy, 211-214, 330-333, 334
Primitive categorization, 105, 126-127
Principles, 5, 11
Product, 55, 65, 79-80, 86-87, 89, 93,
    94, 95-96, 110, 118-119, 122,
    130-136, 138-140, 143, 152-
    155, 157, 160, 164, 167, 175,
    177, 180, 183, 187, 188-189,
    214, 218, 220-221, 231-232,
    234, 237, 244-245, 249, 288,
    298, 301, 314-316, 330, 335,
    338, 340, 345, 373, 375, 384,
    387, 391, 393, 394-395, 401,
    404, 409, 437-440, 443, 447,
    449, 453, 461, 463-464, 467-
    471, 473, 476, 477
Print message length, 80-81
Prior-entry effect, 135-136
Proactive inhibition, 221-222
Probability, 10-11
Processing inflow of information,
    90-91
Proportion, 69
Proximity, 113
Psychological approach, 1-12
Psychological literature, xvi, 5, 9
Psychological model of marketing,
    36-44
Psychological principles, 1-7, 9-12,
    485
Psychological state, 257-280

Psychology, 4, 5
    of communication, 13-44
Public affairs leaders, 407
Public commitment, 461-463
Public relations, 118-119

Reaction, 34
Realistic expectations, 67
Recency, 211-214, 330-333, 334
Reception, 24
Redintegration, 273-275
References, 487-523
Reinforcement, 243-245, 247, 254,
    256, 425-427
Reinforcing, 476-477
Related events, 108-109
Relevance, 91-93, 143, 167-169, 268-
    269
Relevant information, 433
Relevant stimuli, 92
Relevant stimulus information, 141-
    143
Reminiscence, 284-285, 288
Repeated exposing, 54-56
Repetition, 206-209, 334-335
Retailing, 56, 67, 70, 77-78, 80, 82,
    85-86, 90, 91, 93, 95, 96, 110,
    119, 127-128, 130, 133, 134-
    138, 140, 150, 154, 162, 166,
    170-171, 174, 180-181, 182-
    183, 189, 209, 231-232, 246,
    254, 265, 266, 268, 271-272,
    273, 277-278, 288, 290-291,
    296-297, 328-329, 332-333,
    335, 340, 342-343, 350, 406,
    413-414, 416, 430, 441, 443,
    457, 459, 464, 467, 478
Retroactive inhibition, 218-220
Rewards, 246-252
    continuity of, 252-254
    expectations of, 176-178
    intensity, 249-250
    ranking of, 249
    timing of, 251, 252
Role, 401-402, 473-476

Search completing, 136

Selective appeal, 27
Selective attending, 63, 90
Selective exposure, 27
Selective perceiving, 106
Selective retention, 239
Self-confidence, 381-383, 457
Self-generated processes, 381-391
Self-image, 183-185
Self-knowledge, 181-183
Selling, 52, 77, 87, 92-93, 109, 119,
    130, 136, 163, 167, 172, 175,
    177-178, 182, 206, 213, 214,
    220, 222, 230, 262, 263, 270,
    278, 285, 294, 296, 324, 344,
    345, 383, 393, 394-395, 430,
    442, 462-463, 467, 475, 476
Selves, interlocking, 183-184
Semantic differential scales, 226
Semantic generation, 225-229
Semantic satiation, 225-229
Sequence, 69
Sex differences, 94, 298-302, 402-404
Sharpening, 186-188
Significates, 153
Similarity, 113
Size, 65
Size of the group, 472
Sleeper effect, 285-288, 379
Social psychology, 9
Social role differences, 95
Sociocultural factors, 15, 42, 57, 293-
    302
Sociologists, xvi
S-O-R Models, 2-123
Sound level, 65
Source credibility, 371-372, 375-377
Status, 188-189
    in group, 404-406
Step economizing, 137-138
Stereotypes, 130, 174, 190-191, 296,
    440
Stimuli, internal and external, 43
Stimulus complexity, 230-232
Stimulus cues, number of, 232-234
Subjective stress, 109
Symbolic communicating, 147-157
Symbols, 275
    accidental, 148-149
    function of, 149-150

types of, 147-149
    universal, 148-149
Syndrome relevance, 260-261

Texture, 68
Theoretical framework, 3, 4
Thought units, number of, 81-82
Time, 213-214, 333-334, 377-379,
    445-447
    passage of time, 204-206
Timing, predecisional, 278-279
Transfer, 222-224
Transposition, 131-132
Trial-and-check, 24
Two-sided arguments, 335-338
Two-step flow of communication, 25,
    52
Type, 67-68, 108
Typeface, 68, 70-76
Typography, 70-76

Unawareness, 29
Undesired behaving, 42
Uniform destiny, 113
Unit, 69

Valence, high, 169
Value added, 152-154
Value categories, 179-181
Values, 155-157
Variables, 5
    audience, 38-39, 57, 102, 196-197
    continuing, 57
    group, 399-416, 471-475
    message and medium, 38-39, 47-50,
      57, 63-83, 99, 105-123, 193-
      196, 201-256, 303-306, 325-
      379, 417-421, 425-430, 479
    within the audience, 51-56, 63,
      86-97, 125-191, 257-302, 306,
      307, 381-416, 421-422, 431-
      478, 479-483

Wants, 42, 168, 172, 426
Weber's law, 133
Withdrawal traits, 384-386
Word-of-mouth, 416

Yeasaying, 469-471

About the Author

Steuart Henderson Britt is president of Britt Marketing Ltd. of Evanston, Illinois, devoted to practical problem solving on consumer products, industrial products, and services. Formerly, he was chairman of the Chicago marketing research firm, Britt and Frerichs Inc., which he founded seven years ago.

Previously, he held concurrent positions at Northwestern University as professor of marketing in the Graduate School of Management and professor of advertising in the Medill School of Journalism. During that period he carried out marketing projects and conducted seminars for scores of organizations in the United States, and in 21 major countries of Europe and Asia. Dr. Britt was formerly an executive of the New York advertising agency McCann-Erickson, and the Needham and the Ludgin agencies in Chicago.

His earlier career included faculty appointments in psychology at Columbia University and The George Washington University, followed by concurrent service as expert consultant to the War Manpower Commission, executive secretary of the Emergency Committee in Psychology, and executive director of the Office of Psychological Personnel of the American Psychological Association. His military career in World War II was as a Lieutenant Commander in the top command of the Navy, under Admiral Ernest J. King.

Dr. Britt was one of 10 individuals in the United States and Europe elected to the Hall of Fame in Distribution in 1963, and one of 20 "Leaders in Marketing Thought" selected in 1975.

Author or editor of over 200 articles and 15 books on psychology and marketing, Dr. Britt has served as codeveloper of the Westinghouse Annual Science Talent Search (1942-1960), editor of the McGraw-Hill Series in Marketing and Advertising (1951-1964), editor of the *Journal of Marketing* (1957-1967), marketing consultant for the Leo Burnett Company (1958-1970), producer of the annual "Advertising Age" Creative Workshop (1958-1970), and editorial director of the Marketing Science Institute (1967-1968). He also has been the editor of 52 books for other authors in three different book series.

Dr. Britt's educational background is in both psychology and law. His legal education was at the Washington University School of Law and the Columbia University School of Law; he is a member of the Missouri Bar and the New York Bar. His Ph.D. in psychology is from Yale University.